Philosophy of Sport

Critical Readings, Crucial Issues

Edited by

M. Andrew Holowchak
Ohio University

Prentice
Hall

Upper Saddle River, New Jersey 07458

Library of Congess Cataloging-in-Publication Data

Philosophy of Sport : critical readings, crucial issues / edited by M. Andrew Holowchak.
   p. cm.
  Includes bibliographical references.
  ISBN 0-13-094122-0 (pbk.)
   1. Sports—Philosophy.   I. Holowchak, Mark (date)

GV706 .P483 2002
796'.01—dc21   2001036324

Editorial Director: Charlyce Jones Owen
Acquisitions Editor: Ross Miller
Assistant Editor: Katie Janssen
Editorial Assistant: Carla Worner
Director of Production and Manufacturing: Barbara Kittle
Production Editor: Louise Rothman
Prepress and Manufacturing Manager: Nick Sklitsis
Prepress and Manufacturing Buyer: Sherry Lewis
Marketing Director: Beth Gillett Mejia
Marketing Manager: Chris Ruel
Cover Design: Bruce Kenselaar

Cover Art: Athenian black vase figures. National Archives and Records Administration

This book was set in 10/12 Minion by NK Graphics
and printed and bound by RR Donnelley/Harrisonburg.
The cover was printed by Phoenix Color Corp.

 © 2002 by Pearson Education, Inc.
Upper Saddle River, New Jersey 07458

Printed in the United States of America

10 9 8 7 6 5 4 3

0-13-094122-0

Pearson Education LTD., London
Pearson Education Australia PTY, Limited, Sydney
Pearson Education Singapore, Pte. Ltd
Pearson Education North Asia Ltd, Hong Kong
Pearson Education Canada, Ltd., Toronto
Pearson Educación de Mexico, S.A. de C.V.
Pearson Education—Japan, Tokyo
Pearson Education Malaysia, Pte. Ltd
Pearson Education, Upper Saddle River, New Jersey

To my colleague and friend Albert Mosley,
whose help and encouragement
along the way have been incalculable.

Contents

Chapter Five: Sport and Society

Heroism

Gender

Race

Pedagogy

Sport in Society

Acknowledgments

I would like to thank Robert Thoresen and Dr. Ross Miller of Prentice Hall for their interest in this anthology as well as for their invaluable assistance. Thanks also to production editor Louise Rothman and editorial assistant Carla Worner at Prentice Hall. In addition, I would like to thank my students, who over the years have helped me gain a surer understanding of the right place of sports in our lives. I would also like to thank Professor Arthur Zucker and Kathleen Evans-Romaine of the Institute of Applied Ethics at Ohio University for their assistance in the many sport-related presentations I have given while at Ohio University. In addition, my thanks to reviewers Jeffrey P. Fry, Ball State University, and Thompson M. Faller, University of Portland, for their helpful comments.

Preface

Philosophy of Sport: Critical Readings, Crucial Issues is a collection of readings on topical issues in philosophy of sport that draws principally from philosophy, but contains some writings from sociological and psychological literature with a philosophical slant. In addition to the introduction, the anthology contains forty-three readings on diverse and contemporary philosophical issues in sport from different perspectives. Each article, on its own, invites critical discussion.

The readings are grouped into five chapters. Chapter One is on the nature of sport and contains eight essays with diverse theses. Chapter Two comprises four essays on aesthetics and sport. The third chapter, on ethical issues, discusses sportsmanship, cheating, winning, violence, and performance-enhancing drugs. There are fourteen readings in this section. Chapter Four, dealing with epistemological issues, contains a reading that addresses assessment of moral character in sport and a second that addresses streak playing. Chapter Five, containing fifteen readings, discusses societal issues and sport. The topics are heroism, gender, race, pedagogy, and sport in society.

I have put this anthology together so that it will be serviceable to those inexperienced in philosophy as well as to more advanced students of philosophy. First, to facilitate understanding, I introduce all readings with some prefatory remarks. For difficult readings, these remarks include a helpful summary of the main line of argument. At the end of each reading, I offer a few questions or comments to stimulate critical analysis. In addition, there is a glossary of key terms at the back of the book.

Editor's Introduction

Why Study Philosophy of Sport?

M. Andrew Holowchak
Ohio University

While watching an NFL playoff game on television, I heard one of the broadcasters state that it is important for coaches always to keep players guessing concerning just how well they are performing. This, he elaborated, is what Bill Parcells and Jimmy Johnson practice, and no one doubts their success when it comes to football. The other analyst completely agreed. Each coach, after all, has made it to the Super Bowl on more than one occasion.

Two questions immediately came to mind after I heard this. First, why is it that winning and losing defines successful coaching today? Second, is it not possible to get more out of players by honesty instead of dishonesty? From my own perspective, winning is an important part of sport, but it is certainly not a sufficient indicator of success. Moreover, there are, I am convinced, better and more forthright ways of getting the most out of players than through dishonesty. Other critics, contending that sport is simply patterned after the manner in which we conduct our affairs in everyday life, might disagree. Welcome to the world of philosophy of sport!

What Is Philosophy?

Traditionally and I might even say superficially, *philosophy* has been defined as the "love of wisdom," and *philosophers* as "lovers of wisdom." This at least is what we find when we look into the Greek etymology of the words.[1] These definitions, however, do not help much in telling us just what philosophers do. Many people, I suppose, believe that philosophers are rather disagreeable people, who saunter about and try to show others that they have no grounds for anything they happen to hold true. Others maintain, as I have often heard, that everyone is a philosopher to some degree.

While it is certainly true that philosophers argue much of the time and that all people discuss philosophical issues some of the time, it is not the case that philosophers argue ceaselessly to no fruitful end or that everyone is a philosopher. There is a point to philosophic "contentiousness": Philosophic argument attempts to clarify matters by ridding everyday language of ambiguity and vagueness. What is the payoff? A better understanding of the issues and perhaps even a solution to some stubborn problem.

All of us recognize the vital importance of the various arts and sciences. Art and its various means of expression, of which sport may be one, add fullness, variety, beauty, and flavor to our lives. Science continually makes discoveries that contribute to our health and comfort. We take art and science for granted, yet the thought of what life would be like without either of these is too gruesome for most of us to entertain.

Have you ever stopped to consider what makes art so special to us or why we trust the discoveries of science? If you have, then you have taken at least a rudimentary interest in philosophy. Philosophy takes what seems plainly true, right, or obvious and subjects it to scrutiny in an effort toward deeper understanding. For instance, we take it for granted when a study suggests that vitamin E slows aging and guards against cancer. What after all do we really know about science? Because of ignorance and a measure of security in feeling that others may have the answers that we do not have, we blindly follow when authorities such as scientists speak.

However, study of philosophy gives us the analytical tools to dissect what scientists do and open it to critical examination. Moreover, what it does to science, it does to all other disciplines. Philosophy takes our most fundamental principles and beliefs and asks us for a justification of them. It invites us to ask questions such as, What, if anything, is the best form of political life for humans? How ought we to live our lives? Does God exist? Behind the veneer of things that continually change, is anything eternally unchanging? What is love? What is beauty? Philosophy, then, is the science of sciences.

What Is Sport?

Since many of you reading this introduction are probably athletes or at least avid sports fans, questions like "What is sport?" or "Which team is the best team?" may seem untoward or even absurd. Take some time, however, to reflect seriously on either question, perhaps even enter into a discussion with a willing friend, and you will see that such questions are not easily answered. Let us for instance consider the second question. A typical exchange between you and a friend might go something like this. You begin by saying to your friend, "The best team certainly didn't win the championship this year." Your friend responds, "You're wrong. The team that wins it all in the end is the best team. And Kalamazoo won it all." "But they had a mediocre record going into the playoffs," you state firmly. Your friend counters, "That doesn't matter! They won it all. That's what matters. They *are* the best." "But that's silly," you respond. "Certainly you don't think that the team that ends up on top at the end of the playoffs is *always* the best team, do you?" "I certainly do," says your friend.

"That's why we have playoffs." "Hmm, I'm not sure that I agree at all. . . ." You get the picture.

The question "What is sport?" is even thornier and more challenging, when you open it to philosophic investigation. Some philosophers have argued that sport has a particular nature, and we can grasp that nature through examining its practice over time. Others state that sport evolves over time and the very question of the nature of sport is ill conceived. Sport is roughly what athletes do, they say. Still others, like myself, concede that there is no fixed nature of sport, but argue that we ought to arrive at a rational consensus concerning how sport *ought to be* practiced. What seemed within our gasp has now slipped miserably away.

What Is Philosophy of Sport?

Let us turn our attention to a final question: What is philosophy of sport? Philosophy has historically been divided into five chief subdisciplines: metaphysics (the study of what is real), epistemology (the study of the theory of knowledge), aesthetics (the study of beauty), ethics (the study of how we ought to live), and logic (the study of argument analysis). Yet today philosophers study a diverse field of practical issues, from feminism and race relations to conflict resolution and death. In a sense, philosophers take many of the same questions that arise with respect to the "big five" and apply these to a broad array of today's topics of study. Regarding sport, for instance, we ask questions such as these:

- What is sport?
- Are female athletes of the same rank as men?
- Does sport affect or merely reflect social mores and values?
- Should certain drugs be banned from sport?

- Is sport a species of art?
- Just what place does winning have in sport?

If you are a lover of sport, I'm sure that you'll find each of these questions intriguing.

Because of our tremendous worldwide interest in sportive practice today, there is without question a great need for athletes and mavens of sport, young and old, to be exposed to philosophical thinking pertaining to vital issues in sport.

Epilogue: History of Philosophy of Sport

Philosophy of sport is a discipline that began to flourish first in the 1970s. Since then and with the appearance of the *Journal for the Philosophy of Sport* in 1974, many scholars have begun to make significant contributions to the discipline. Nonetheless, serious critical analysis of sport sufficiently lags behind its burgeoning practice and the omnivorous enthusiasm of its followers today. It is my ardent hope that this modest collection of current and sometimes controversial readings will contribute honestly toward philosophical understanding of the proper place of sport in human society.

Note

1. The Greek word *philein* means "to like" or "to love," and *sophia* means "wisdom."

Chapter One

The Nature of Sport

1   Selections from Homo Ludens

Johan Huizinga

In his book Homo Ludens (Playing Man), *Johan Huizinga analyzes the concept of play as a cultural phenomenon. The objective of his work, he asserts, is to "demonstrate that it is more than a rhetorical comparison to view culture* sub specie ludi *(as a species of play)." Play and culture are tightly interwoven, though play is older than culture itself. Culture "arises in the form of play" and, as culture progresses or regresses, pure play falls ever more into the background.*

Play, Huizinga says, must not be analyzed purely from a scientific point of view. Any attempt to scrutinize play biologically or psychologically loses what is essential to play—fun. Play as fun is a voluntary, free activity that divorces itself from reality and has itself as its end. It is tense and uncertain, and, though it is strictly outside the realm of good or bad, it is perceived to measure certain virtues, such as courage and fairness. Huizinga himself writes of the formal characteristics of play in chapter 1. Play, he says, is a wholly absorbing, free activity that stands outside of life. It proceeds in an orderly way, within fixed rules, and is not done for the sake of material gain. The social groupings that play promotes use disguise to separate themselves from the rest of the world.

This reading comprises selections from two chapters of Homo Ludens: *"Play and Contest as Civilizing Functions" (chapter 3) and "The Play-Element in Contemporary Civilization" (chapter 12).*

In chapter 3, Huizinga states that play has a number of cultural manifestations: art, business, science, and contest. Concerning the last, he asks, Are all contests forms of play? Yes, he responds, for contest is formally identical and functionally very similar to games, which are a form of play. Like games, contests are essentially meaningless. Winning as a part of contest is closely linked with games that feature cooperative or competitive play. Winning is the true end of contest, and its fruits are honor and other rewards of esteem.

Huizinga maintains that the play spirit still predominates in civilization today. Sportive competition, however, resembles play only remotely. With the advent of modern sport in the nineteenth century, sportive games took on a seriousness they have never had before. Pure play nowadays seems to have been buried under sportive systematicity, regimentation, and record keeping. Play is now somber business. Nonetheless, he believes, competitive sport is still play, though a degenerative form.

Huizinga sums by stating that civilization cannot exist without a spirit of play. Reason, faith, and humanity are themselves insufficient for this task. True play is nonpropagandist and encourages a "happy inspiration" without which no society can suitably continue.

From *Homo Ludens* by John Huizinga. Copyright © 1950 by Roy Publishers. Reprinted by permission of Beacon Press, Boston.

Play and Contest as Civilizing Functions

When speaking of the play-element in culture we do not mean that among the various activities of civilized life an important place is reserved for play, nor do we mean that civilization has arisen out of play by some evolutionary process, in the sense that something which was originally play passed into something which was no longer play and could henceforth be called culture. The view we take in the following pages is that culture arises in the form of play, that it is

7

played from the very beginning. Even those activities which aim at the immediate satisfaction of vital needs—hunting, for instance—tend, in archaic society, to take on the play-form. Social life is endued with supra-biological forms, in the shape of play, which enhance its value. It is through this playing that society expresses its interpretation of life and the world. By this we do not mean that play turns into culture, rather that in its earliest phases culture has the play-character, that it proceeds in the shape and the mood of play. In the twin union of play and culture, play is primary. It is an objectively recognizable, a concretely definable thing, whereas culture is only the term which our historical judgement attaches to a particular instance. Such a conception approximates to that of Frobenius who, in his *Kulturgeschichte Afrikas,* speaks of the genesis of culture *"als eines aus dem natür-lichen 'Sein' aufgestiegenen 'Spieles'"* (as a "play" emerging out of natural "being"). In my opinion, however, Frobenius conceives the relationship between play and culture too mystically and describes it altogether too vaguely. He fails to put his finger on the point where culture emerges from play.

As a culture proceeds, either progressing or regressing, the original relationship we have postulated between play and non-play does not remain static. As a rule the play-element gradually recedes into the background, being absorbed for the most part in the sacred sphere. The remainder crystallizes as knowledge: folklore, poetry, philosophy, or in the various forms of judicial and social life. The original play-element is then almost completely hidden behind cultural phenomena. But at any moment, even in a highly developed civilization, the play-"instinct" may reassert itself in full force, drowning the individual and the mass in the intoxication of an immense game.

Naturally enough, the connexion between culture and play is particularly evident in the higher forms of social play where the latter consists in the orderly activity of a group or two opposed groups. Solitary play is productive of culture only in a limited degree. As we have indicated before, all the basic factors of play, both individual and communal, are already present in animal life—to wit, contests, performances, exhibitions, challenges, preenings, struttings and showings-off, pretences, and binding rules. It is doubly remarkable that birds, phylogenetically so far removed from human beings, should have so much in common with them. Woodcocks perform dances, crows hold flying-matches, bower-birds and others decorate their nests, song-birds chant their melodies. Thus competitions and exhibitions as amusements do not proceed from culture, they rather precede it.

"Playing together" has an essentially antithetical character. As a rule it is played between two parties or teams. A dance, a pageant, a performance may, however, be altogether lacking in antithesis. Moreover "antithetical" does not necessarily mean "contending" or "agonistic." A part-song, a chorus, a minuet, the voices in a musical ensemble, the game of cat's cradle—so interesting to the anthropologist because developed into intricate systems of magic with some primitive peoples—are all examples of antithetical play which need not be agonistic although emulation may sometimes be operative in them. Nor infrequently an activity which is self-contained—for instance the performance of a theatrical piece or a piece of music—may incidentally pass into the agonistic category by becoming the occasion of competition for prizes, either in respect of the arrangement or the execution of it, as was the case with Greek drama.

Among the general characteristics of play we reckoned tension and uncertainty. There is always the question: "will it come off?" This condition is fulfilled even when we are playing patience, doing jig-saw puzzles, acrostics, crosswords, diabolo, etc. Tension and uncertainty as to the outcome increase enormously when the antithetical element becomes really agonistic in the play of groups. The passion to win sometimes threatens to obliterate the levity proper to a game. An important distinction emerges here. In games of pure chance the tension felt by the player is only feebly communicated to the on-looker. In themselves, gambling games are very curious subjects for cultural research, but for the development of culture as such we must call them unproductive. They are sterile, adding nothing to life or the mind. The picture changes as soon as play demands application, knowledge, skill, courage, and strength. The more "difficult" the game the greater the tension in the behold-ers. A game of chess may fascinate the onlookers although it still remains unfruitful for culture and devoid of visible charm. But once a game is beautiful to look at its cultural value is obvious; nevertheless its aesthetic value is not indispensa-ble to culture. Physical, intellectual, moral, or spiritual values can equally well raise play to the cultural level. The more apt it is to raise the tone, the intensity of life in the individual or the group, the more readily it will become part of civilization itself. The two ever-recurrent forms in which civilization grows in and as play are the sacred performance and the festal contest.

Here the question broached [earlier] arises once more: are we entitled to include all contests unreservedly in the play-concept? We saw how the Greeks distinguished *agon* from *paidiá*. This could be explained on etymological grounds, since in *paidiá* the childish was evoked so vividly that it could hardly have been applied to the se-rious contests that formed the core of Hellenic social life. The word *agon*, on the other hand, de-fined the contest from quite a different point of view. Its original meaning appears to have been a "gathering" (compare *agora*—"market-place"—to which *agon* is related). Thus, as a term, it had nothing to do with play proper. The essential oneness of play and contest, however, still peeps through when, as we have seen, Plato uses *paignion* for the armed ritual dances of the Kouretes (*ta tohn Kourehtohn enoplia paignia*) and *paidiá* for sacred performances in general. That the majority of Greek contests were fought out in deadly earnest is no reason for separat-ing the agon from play, or for denying the play-character of the former. The contest has all the formal and most of the functional features of a

game. Dutch and German both have a word which expresses this unity very clearly: *wedkamp* and *Wettkampf* respectively. It contains the idea of a play-ground (Latin *campus*) and that of a wager (*Wette*). It is, moreover, the normal word for "contest" in those languages. We would al-lude once more to the remarkable testimony from the Second Book of Samuel, where a fight to the death between two groups was still called "playing," the word used being taken from the sphere of laughter. On numerous Greek vases we can see that a contest of armed men is charac-terized as an agon by the presence of the flute-players who accompany it. At the Olympic games there were duels fought to the death.[1] The mighty *tours de force* accomplished by Thor and his companions in their contest with the Man of Utgardaloki are called *leika*, "play." For all these reasons it would not seem overbold to consider the terminological disparity between contest and play in Greek as the more or less accidental failure to abstract a general concept that would have embraced both. In short, the question as to whether we are entitled to include the contest in the play-category can be answered unhesitat-ingly in the affirmative.

Like all other forms of play, the contest is largely devoid of purpose. That is to say, the ac-tion begins and ends in itself, and the outcome does not contribute to the necessary life-processes of the group. The popular Dutch say-ing to the effect that "it is not the marbles that matter, but the game," expresses this clearly enough. Objectively speaking, the result of the game is unimportant and a matter of indiffer-ence. On a visit to England the Shah of Persia is supposed to have declined the pleasure of at-tending a race meeting, saying that he knew very well that one horse runs faster than another. From his point of view he was perfectly right: he refused to take part in a play-sphere that was alien to him, preferring to remain outside. The outcome of a game or a contest—except, of course, one played for pecuniary profit—is only interesting to those who enter into it as players or spectators, either personally and locally, or else as listeners by radio or viewers by television, etc., and accept its rules. They have become playfellows and choose to be so. For them it is immaterial whether Oxford wins, or Cambridge.

"There is something at stake"—the essence of play is contained in that phrase. But this "something" is not the material result of the play, not the mere fact that the ball is in the hole, but the ideal fact that the game is a success or has been successfully concluded. Success gives that player a satisfaction that lasts a shorter or a longer while as the case may be. The pleasurable feeling of satisfaction mounts with the presence of spectators, though these are not essential to it. A person who gets a game of patience "out" is doubly delighted when somebody is watching him. In all games it is very important that the player should be able to boast of his success to others. . . . The angler is a familiar type in this respect.

Closely connected with play is the idea of winning. Winning, however, presupposes a partner or opponent; solitary play knows no winning, and the attainment of the desired objective here cannot be called by that name.

What is "winning," and what is "won?" Winning means showing oneself superior in the outcome of a game. Nevertheless, the evidence of this superiority tends to confer upon the winner a semblance of superiority in general. In this respect he wins something more than the game as such. He has won esteem, obtained honour; and this honour and esteem at once accrue to the benefit of the group to which the victor belongs. Here we have another very important characteristic of play: success won readily passes from the individual to the group. But the following feature is still more important: the competitive "instinct" is not in the first place a desire for power or a will to dominate. The primary thing is the desire to excel others, to be the first and to be honoured for that. The question whether, in the result, the power of the individual or the group will be increased, takes only a second place. The main thing is to have won. The purest example of a victory which has nothing visible or enjoy-

able about it save the mere fact of winning, is afforded by a game of chess.

We play or compete "for" something. The object for which we play and compete is first and foremost victory, but victory is associated with all the various ways in which it can be enjoyed— for instance, as a triumph celebrated by the group with massed pomp, applause, and ovations. The fruits of victory may be honour, esteem, prestige. As a rule, however, something more than honour is associated with winning. We see this even in the "staking out" of a game: the marking of its limits. Every game has its stake. It can be of material or symbolical value, but also ideal. The stake can be a gold cup or a jewel or a king's daughter or a shilling; the life of the player or the welfare of the whole tribe. It can be a prize or a "gage." This is a most significant word. Etymologically and semantically it is related to the Latin *vadium* (German *Wette*), meaning a "pledge" in the sense of a purely symbolical object thrown down into the "ring" or playground as a token of challenge. It is not quite identical with "prize," which conveys the idea of something intrinsically valuable—for instance, a sum of money—though it may be simply a laurel-wreath. It is very curious how the words "prize," "price," and "praise" all derive more or less directly from the Latin *pretium* but develop in different directions. *Pretium* arose originally in the sphere of exchange and valuation, and presupposed a counter-value. The medieval *pretium justum* or "just price" corresponded approximately to the idea of the modern "market value." Now while *price* remains bound to the sphere of economics, *prize* moves into that of play and competition, and *praise* acquires the exclusive signification of the Latin *laus*. Semantically, it is next to impossible to delimit the field proper to each of the three words. What is equally curious is to see how the word *wage*, originally identical with *gage* in the sense of a symbol of challenge, moves in the reverse direction of *pretium*, i.e. from the play-sphere to the economic sphere and becomes a synonym for "salary" or "earnings." We do not *play* for wages, we *work* for them. Finally, "gains" or "winnings" has nothing to do with any of these words etymologically, though semantically it pertains to both play and economics: the player receives his winnings, the merchant makes them.

We might say that proper to all the derivations of the Latin root *vad* is a sense of passion, of chance, of daring, as regards both economic activity and play-activity. Pure avarice neither trades nor plays; it does not gamble. To dare, to take risks, to bear uncertainty, to endure tension—these are the essence of the play-spirit. Tension adds to the importance of the game and, as it increases, enables the player to forget that he is only playing.

The Greek word for "prize"—*athlon*—is derived by some from the same fruitful root *vad* just discussed. *Athlon* yields *athletes*, the athlete. Here the ideas of contest, struggle, exercise, exertion, endurance, and suffering are united. If we bear in mind that in savage society the majority of agonistic activities really are "agonizing," involving as they do mental and physical hardship; and if we remember also the intimate connexion between *agon* and *agonia* (which latter word originally meant simply "contest," but later "death-struggle" and "fear"), we shall see that in *athletics* we are still moving in that sphere of serious competition which forms our theme.

Competition is not only "for" something, but also "in" and "with" something. People compete to be the first "in" strength or dexterity, in knowledge or riches, in splendour, liberality, noble descent, or in the number of their progeny. They compete "with" bodily strength or force of arms, with their reason or their fists, contending against one another with extravagant displays, big words, boasting, vituperation, and finally with cunning and deceit. To our way of thinking, cheating as a means of winning a game robs the action of its play-character and spoils it altogether, because for us the essence of play is that the rules be kept—that it be fair play. Archaic culture, however, gives the lie to our moral judgement in this respect, as also does the spirit of popular lore. In the fable of the hare and the hedgehog the beau role is reserved for the false player, who wins by fraud. Many of the heroes of mythology win by trickery or by help from without. Pelops bribes the charioteer of Oenomaus to put wax pins into the axles. Jason and Theseus come through their tests successfully, thanks to Medea and Ariadne. Gunther owes his victory to Siegfried. The Kauravas in the *Mahābhārata* win by cheating at dice. Freya double-crosses Wotan into granting the victory to the Langobards. The Ases of Eddic mythology break the oath they have sworn to the Giants. In all these instances the act of fraudulently outwitting somebody else has itself become a subject for competition, a new play-theme, as it were.[2]

The hazy border-line between play and seriousness is illustrated very tellingly by the use of the words "playing" or "gambling" for the machinations on the Stock Exchange. The gambler at the roulette table will readily concede that he is playing; the stock-jobber will not. He will maintain that buying and selling on the off-chance of prices rising or falling is part of the serious business of life, at least of business life, and that it is an economic function of society. In both cases the operative factor is the hope of gain; but whereas in the former the pure fortuitousness of the thing is generally admitted (all "systems" notwithstanding), in the latter the player deludes himself with the fancy that he can calculate the future trends of the market. At any rate the difference of mentality is exceedingly small. . . .

The Play-Element in Contemporary Civilization

. . . The question to which we address ourselves is this: To what extent does the civilization we live in still develop in play-forms? How far does the play-spirit dominate the lives of those who share that civilization? The nineteenth century, we observed, had lost many of the play-elements so characteristic of former ages. Has this leeway been made up or has it increased?

It might seem at first sight that certain phenomena in modern social life have more than compensated for the loss of play-forms. Sport and athletics, as social functions, have steadily increased in scope and conquered ever fresh fields both nationally and internationally.

Contests in skill, strength, and perseverance have, as we have shown, always occupied an important place in every culture either in connexion with ritual or simply for fun and festivity. Feudal society was only really interested in the tournament; the rest was just popular recreation and nothing more. Now the tournament, with its highly dramatic staging and aristocratic embellishments, can hardly be called a sport. It fulfilled one of the functions of the theatre. Only a numerically small upper class took active part in it. This one-sidedness of medieval sporting life was due in large measure to the influence of the Church. The Christian ideal left but little room for the organized practice of sport and the cultivation of bodily exercise, except in so far as the latter contributed to gentle education. Similarly, the Renaissance affords fairly numerous examples of body-training cultivated for the sake of perfection, but only on the part of individuals, never groups or classes. If anything, the emphasis laid by the Humanists on learning and erudition tended to perpetuate the old underestimation of the body, likewise the moral zeal and severe intellectuality of the Reformation and Counter-Reformation. The recognition of games and bodily exercises as important cultural values was withheld right up to the end of the eighteenth century.

The basic forms of sportive competition are, of course, constant through the ages. In some the trial of strength and speed is the whole essence of the contest, as in running and skating matches, chariot and horse races, weight-lifting, swimming, diving, marksmanship, etc.[3] Though human beings have indulged in such activities since the dawn of time, these only take on the character of organized games to a very slight degree. Yet nobody, bearing in mind the agonistic principle which animates them, would hesitate to call them games in the sense of play—which, as we have seen, can be very serious indeed. There are, however, other forms of contest which develop of their own accord into "sports." These are the ball-games.

What we are concerned with here is the transition from occasional amusement to the system of organized clubs and matches. Dutch pictures of the seventeenth century show us burghers and peasants intent upon their game of *kolf;* but, so far as I know, nothing is heard of games being organized in clubs or played as matches. It is obvious that a fixed organization of this kind will most readily occur when two groups play against one another. The great ball-games in particular require the existence of permanent teams, and herein lies the starting-point of modern sport. The process arises quite spontaneously in the meeting of village against village, school against school, one part of a town against the rest, etc. That the process started in nineteenth-century England is understandable up to a point, though how far the specifically Anglo-Saxon bent of mind can be deemed an efficient cause is less certain. But it cannot be doubted that the structure of English life had much to do with it. Local self-government encouraged the spirit of association and solidarity. The absence of obligatory military training favoured the occasion for, and the need of, physical exercise. The peculiar form of education tended to work in the same direction, and finally the geography of the country and the nature of the terrain, on the whole flat and, in the ubiquitous commons, offering the most perfect playing-fields that could be desired, were of the greatest importance. Thus England became the cradle and focus of modern sporting life.

Ever since the last quarter of the nineteenth century, games, in the guise of sport, have been taken more seriously. The rules have become increasingly strict and elaborate. Records are established at a higher, or faster, or longer level than was ever conceivable before. Everybody knows the delightful prints from the first half of the nineteenth century, showing the cricketers in top-hats. This speaks for itself.

Now, with the increasing systematization and regimentation of sport, something of the pure play-quality is inevitably lost. We see this very clearly in the official distinction between amateurs and professionals (or "gentlemen and players" as used pointedly to be said). It means that the play-group marks out those for whom play is no longer play, ranking them inferior to the true players in standing but superior in capacity. The spirit of the professional is no longer the true play-spirit; it is lacking in spontaneity and carelessness. This affects the amateur too, who begins to suffer from an inferiority complex. Between them they push sport further and further away from the play-sphere proper until it becomes a thing *sui-generis:* neither play nor earnest. In modern social life sport occupies a place alongside and apart from the cultural process. The great competitions in archaic cultures had always formed part of the sacred festivals and were indispensable as health- and happiness-bringing activities. This ritual tie has now been completely severed; sport has become profane, "unholy" in every way and has no organic connexion whatever with the structure of society, least of all when prescribed by the government. The ability of modern social techniques to stage mass demonstrations with the maximum of outward show in the field of athletics does not alter the fact that neither the Olympiads nor the organized sports of American Universities nor the loudly trumpeted international contests have, in the smallest degree, raised sport to the level of a culture-creating activity. However important it may be for the players or spectators, it remains sterile. The old play-factor has undergone almost complete atrophy.

This view will probably run counter to the popular feeling of today, according to which sport is the apotheosis of the play-element in our civilization. Nevertheless popular feeling is wrong. By way of emphasizing the fatal shift towards over-seriousness we would point out that it has also infected the non-athletic games where calculation is everything, such as chess and some card-games.

As great many board-games have been known since the earliest times, some even in primitive society, which attached great importance to them largely on account of their chanceful character. Whether they are games of chance or skill they all contain an element of seriousness. The merry play-mood has little scope here, particularly where chance is at a minimum as in chess, draughts, backgammon, halma, etc. Even so all these games remain with the definition of play as given [earlier]. Only recently has publicity seized on them and annexed them to athletics by means of public championships, world tournaments, registered records, and press reportage in a literary style of its own, highly ridiculous to the innocent outsider.

Card-games differ from board-games in that they never succeed in eliminating chance completely. To the extent that chance predominates they fall into the category of gambling and, as such, are little suited to club life and public competition. The more intellectual card-games, on the other hand, leave plenty of room for associate tendencies. It is in this field that the shift towards seriousness and over-seriousness is so striking. From the days of *ombre* and *quadrille* to whist and bridge, card-games have undergone a process of increasing refinement, but only with bridge have the modern social techniques made themselves master of the game. The paraphernalia of handbooks and systems and professional training has made bridge a deadly earnest business. A recent newspaper article estimated the yearly winnings of the Culbertson couple at more than two hundred thousand dollars. An enormous amount of mental energy is expended in this universal craze for bridge with no more tangible result than the exchange of relatively unimportant sums of money. Society as a whole is neither benefited nor damaged by this futile activity. It seems difficult to speak of it as an elevating recreation in the sense of Aristotle's *diagoge*. Proficiency at bridge is a sterile excellence, sharpening the mental faculties very one-sidedly without enriching the soul in any way, fixing and consuming a quantity of intellectual energy that might have been better applied. The most we can say, I think, is that it might have been applied worse. The status of bridge in modern society would indicate, to all appearances, an immense increase in the play-element today. But appearances are deceptive. Really to play, a man must play like a child. Can we assert that this is so in the case of such an ingenious game as bridge? If not, the virtue has gone out of the game. . . .

So that by a devious route we have reached the following conclusion: real civilization cannot exist in the absence of a certain play-element, for civilization presupposes limitation and mastery of the self, the ability not to confuse its own tendencies with the ultimate and highest goal, but to understand that it is enclosed within certain bounds freely accepted. Civilization will, in a sense, always be played according to certain rules, and true civilization will always demand fair play. Fair play is nothing less than good faith expressed in play terms. Hence the cheat or the spoil-sport shatters civilization itself. To be a sound culture-creating force this play-element must be pure. It must not consist in the darkening or debasing of standards set up by reason, faith, or humanity. It must not be a false seeming, masking of political purposes behind the illusion of genuine play-forms. True play knows no propaganda; its aim is in itself, and its familiar spirit is happy inspiration.

In treating of our theme so far we have tried to keep to a play-concept which starts from the positive and generally recognized characteristics of play. We took play in its immediate everyday sense and tried to avoid the philosophical short-circuit that would assert all human action to be

play. Now, at the end of our argument, this point of view awaits us and demands to be taken into account.

"Child's play was what he called all human opinions," says late Greek tradition of Heraclitus. As a pendant to this lapidary saying let us quote at greater length the profound words of Plato which we introduced [earlier]:

> Though human affairs are not worthy of great seriousness it is yet necessary to be serious; happiness is another thing. . . . I say that a man must be serious with the serious, and not the other way about. God alone is worthy of supreme seriousness, but man is made God's play-thing, and that is the best part of him. Therefore every man and woman should live life accordingly, and play the noblest games, and be of another mind from what they are at present. For they deem war a serious thing, though in war there is neither play nor culture worthy the name, which are the things *we* deem most serious. Hence all must live in peace as well as they possibly can. What, then, is the right way of living? Life must be lived as play, playing certain games, making sacrifices, singing and dancing, and then a man will be able to propitiate the gods, and defend himself against his enemies, and win in the contest.

Thus "men will live according to Nature since in most respects they are puppets, yet having a small part in truth." To which Plato's companion rejoins: "You make humanity wholly bad for us, friend, if you say that." And Plato answers: "Forgive me. It was with my eyes on God and moved by Him that I spoke so. If you like, then, humanity is not wholly bad, but worthy of some consideration."[4]

The human mind can only disengage itself from the magic circle of play by turning towards the ultimate. Logical thinking does not go far enough. Surveying all the treasures of the mind and all the splendours of its achievements we shall still find, at the bottom of every serious judgement, something problematical left. In our heart of hearts we know that none of our pronouncements is absolutely conclusive. At that point, where our judgement begins to waver, the feeling that the world is serious after all wavers with it. Instead of the old saw: "All is vanity," the more positive conclusion forces itself upon us that "all is play." A cheap metaphor, no doubt, mere impotence of the mind; yet it is the wisdom Plato arrived at when he called man the plaything of the gods. In singular imagery the thought comes back again in the Book of Proverbs, where Wisdom says: "The Lord possessed me in the beginning of his ways, before he made any thing from the beginning. I was set up from eternity, and of old before the earth was made . . . I was with him forming all things: and was delighted every day, playing before him at all times; playing in the world. And my delights were to be with the children of men.[5]

Whenever we are seized with vertigo at the ceaseless shuttlings and spinnings in our mind of the thought: What is play? What is serious? we shall find the fixed, unmoving point that logic denies us, once more in the sphere of ethics. Play, we began by saying, lies outside morals. In itself it is neither good nor bad. But if we have to decide whether an action to which our will impels us is a serious duty or is licit as play, our moral conscience will at once provide the touchstone. As soon as truth and justice, compassion and forgiveness have part in our resolve to act, our anxious question loses all meaning. One drop of pity is enough to lift our doing beyond intellectual distinctions. Springing as it does from a belief in justice and divine grace, conscience, which

is moral awareness, will always whelm the question that eludes and deludes us to the end, in a lasting silence.

Notes

1. Plutarch deemed this form of contest contrary to the idea of the agon, in which Miss Harrison (*Themis*, pp. 221, 323) agrees with him, wrongly, as it seems to me.

2. I have failed to discover a direct connexion between the hero of the legends who attains his objective by fraud and cunning, and the divine figure who is at once the benefactor and deceiver of man. Cf. W. B. Kristensen, *De goddelijke bedrieger*, Mededeelingen der K. Akad. van Wetenschappen, afd. Lett. No. 3; and J. P. B. Josselin de Jong, *De oorsprong van den goddelijken bedrieger*, ibid. Lett. No. 1.

3. A happy variation of the natatorial contest is found in *Beowulf*, where the aim is to hold your opponent under water until he is drowned.

4. *Laws*, 803–4; cf. also 685. Plato's words echo sombrely in Luther's mouth when he says: "All creatures are God's masks and mummeries" (Erlanger Ausgabe, xi, p. 115).

5. viii, 22–3, 30–1. This is the Douay translation, based on the Vulgate. The text of the English A.V. and R.V. does not bring out the idea of "play."

Questions for Consideration

1. Do you believe that it can rightly be maintained that competitive sport today is fundamentally a form of play, albeit a degenerative form?

2. What does Huizinga mean when he asserts that true civilization requires fair play?

3. Do reason, faith, and humanity debase and darken play as Huizinga suggests they do?

2   The Nature of Sport: A Definitional Effort

John W. Loy, Jr.

This reading of John W. Loy, Jr., is an earlier attempt in philosophy of sport to get a grasp at the nature of the ambiguous term "sport." His focus is definitional and ambitious. He endeavors to take the "loose encompass of sport," given to us by media, and place it on different levels of discourse. In doing so, he borrows critically from important pioneers of philosophy of sport like John Huizinga and Roger Caillois.

Loy's four main distinctions are (1) sport as game occurrence, (2) sport as institutional game, (3) sport as social institution, and (4) sport as social situation. Regarding the first, sport is playful, competitive, a physical skill involving strategy and chance, and a test of physical prowess. Second, as an institutionalized game, sport has an organizational sphere, a technical sphere, a symbolic sphere, and an educational sphere. Third, as a social institution, sport arranges, facilitates, and regulates social value orientations and interests at a primary level (informal, face-to-face relationships in sport), a technical level (larger structures, where everyone still knows everyone else), a managerial level (even larger structures, where not everyone knows everyone else), and a corporate level (where a large, centralized bureaucracy administrates). Last, as social situation, sport involves interaction among persons with an identifiable characteristic focusing involvement through degree and kind. Persons involved in sport comprise producers (primary, secondary, and tertiary) and consumers (primary, secondary, and tertiary).

Reprinted by permission, from John W. Loy, Jr., "The Nature of Sport: A Definitional Effort," *Quest* X (May 1968): 1–15. *Quest* is the journal of the National Association for Physical Education in Higher Education and is published by Human Kinetics, Champaign, IL.

Sport is a highly ambiguous term having different meanings for various people. Its ambiguity is attested to by the range of topics treated in the sport sections of daily newspapers. Here one can find accounts of various sport competitions, advertisements for the latest sport fashions, advice on how to improve one's skills in certain games, and essays on the state of given organized sports, including such matters as recruitment, financial success, and scandal. The broad yet loose encompass of sport reflected in the mass media suggests that sport can and perhaps should be dealt with on different planes of discourse if a better understanding of its nature is to be acquired. As a step in this direction we shall discuss sport as a game occurrence, as an institutional game, as a social institution, and as a social situation or social system.

Sport as a Game Occurrence

Perhaps most often when we think of the meaning of sport, we think of sports. In our perspective sports are considered as a specialized type of game. That is, a sport as one of the many "sports" is viewed as an actual game occurrence or event. Thus in succeeding paragraphs we shall briefly outline what we consider to be the basic characteristics of games in general. In describing these characteristics we shall continually make reference to sports in particular as a special type of game. A game we define as many form of playful competition whose outcome is determined by physical skill, strategy, or chance employed singly or in combination.[1]

Playful

By "playful competition" we mean that any given contest has one or more elements of play. We purposely have not considered game as a subclass of play,[2] for if we had done so, sport would logically become a subset of play and thus preclude the subsumption of professional forms of sport under our definition of the term. However, we wish to recognize that one or more aspects of play constitute basic components of games and that even the most highly organized forms of sport are not completely devoid of play characteristics.

The Dutch historian Johan Huizinga has made probably the most thorough effort to delineate the fundamental qualities of play. He defines play as follows:

> Summing up the formal characteristics of play we might call it a free activity standing quite consciously outside "ordinary" life as being "not serious," but at the same time absorbing the player intensely and utterly. It is an activity connected with no material interest, and no profit can be gained by it. It proceeds within its own proper boundaries of time and space according to fixed rules and in an orderly manner. It promotes the formation of social groupings which tend to surround themselves with secrecy and to stress their differences from the common world by disguise or other means (Huizinga, 1955, p. 13).

Caillois has subjected Huizinga's definition to critical analysis (Caillois, 1961, pp. 3–10) and has redefined play as an activity which is free, separate, uncertain, unproductive, and governed by rules and make-believe (*Ibid.*, pp. 9–10). We shall briefly discuss these qualities ascribed to play by Huizinga and Caillois and suggest how they relate to games in general and to sports in particular.

Free By free is meant that play is a voluntary activity. That is, no one is ever strictly forced to play, playing is done in one's free time, and playing can be initiated and terminated at will.

This characteristic of play is no doubt common to many games, including some forms of amateur sport. It is not, however, a distinguishing feature of all games, especially those classified as professional sport.

Separate By separate Huizinga and Caillois mean that play is spatially and temporally limited. This feature of play is certainly relevant to sports. For many, if not most, forms of sport are conducted in spatially circumscribed environments, examples being the bull-ring, football stadium, golf course, race track, and swimming pool. And with few exceptions every form of sport has rules which precisely determine the duration of a given contest.

Uncertain The course or end result of play cannot be determined beforehand. Similarly, a chief characteristic of all games is that they are marked by an uncertain outcome. Perhaps it is this factor more than any other which lends excitement and tension to any contest. Strikingly uneven competition is routine for the contestants and boring for the spectators; hence efforts to insure a semblance of equality between opposing sides are a notable feature of sport. These efforts typically focus on the matters of size, skill, and experience. Examples of attempts to establish equality based on size are the formation of athletic leagues and conferences composed of social organizations of similar size and the designation of weight classes for boxers and wrestlers. Illustrations of efforts to insure equality among contestants on the basis of skill and experience are the establishment of handicaps for bowlers and golfers, the designation of various levels of competition within a given organization as evidenced by freshmen, junior varsity, and varsity teams in scholastic athletics, and the drafting of players from established teams when adding a new team to a league as done in professional football and basketball.

Unproductive Playing does not in itself result in the creation of new material goods. It is true that in certain games such as poker there may occur an exchange of money or property among players. And it is a truism that in professional sports victory may result in substantial increases of wealth for given individuals. But the case can be made, nevertheless, that a game *per se* is non-utilitarian.[3] For what is produced during any sport competition is a game, and the production of the game is generally carried out in a prescribed setting and conducted according to specific rules.

Governed by Rules   All types of games have agreed-upon rules, be they formal or informal. It is suggested that sports can be distinguished from games in general by the fact that they usually have a greater variety of norms and a larger absolute number of formal norms (i.e., written prescribed and proscribed norms).[4] Similarly, there is a larger number of sanctions and more stringent ones in sports than in games. For example, a basketball player must leave the game after he has committed a fixed number of fouls; a hockey player must spend a certain amount of time in the penalty box after committing a foul; and a football player may be asked to leave the game if he shows unsportsmanlike conduct.

With respect to the normative order of games and sports, one explicit feature is that they usually have definite criteria for determining the winner. Although it is true that some end in a tie, most contests do not permit such an ambivalent termination by providing a means of breaking a deadlock and ascertaining the "final" victor. The various means of determining the winner in sportive endeavors are too numerous to enumerate. But it is relevant to observe that in many sport competitions where "stakes are high," a series of contests is held between opponents in an effort to rule out the element of chance and decide the winner on the basis of merit. A team may be called "lucky" if it beats an opponent once by a narrow margin; but if it does so repeatedly, then the appellations of "better" or "superior" are generally applied.

Make-Believe   By the term make-believe Huizinga and Caillios wish to signify that play

stands outside "ordinary" or "real" life and is distinguished by an "only pretending quality." While some would deny this characteristic of play as being applicable to sport, it is interesting to note that Veblen at the turn of the century stated:

> Sports share this characteristic of make-believe with the games and exploits to which children, especially boys, are habitually inclined. Make-believe does not enter in the same proportion into all sports, but it is present in a very appreciable degree in all (Veblen, 1934, p. 256).

Huizinga observes that the "'only pretending' quality of play betrays a consciousness of the inferiority of play compared with 'seriousness'" (Huizinga, 1955, p. 8). We note here that occasionally one reads of a retiring professional athlete who remarks that he is "giving up the game to take a real job"[5] and that several writers have commented on the essential shallowness of sport.[6] Roger Kahn, for example, has written that:

> The most fascinating and least reported aspect of American sports is the silent and enduring search for a rationale. Stacked against the atomic bomb or even against a patrol in Algeria, the most exciting rally in history may not seem very important, and for the serious and semi-serious people who make their living through sports, triviality is a nagging, damnable thing. Their drive for self-justification has contributed much to the development of sports (Kahn, 1957, p. 10).

On the other hand, Huizinga is careful to point out that "the consciousness of play being 'only pretend' does not by any means prevent it from proceeding with the utmost seriousness" (Huizinga, 1955, p. 8). As examples, need we mention the seriousness with which duffers treat their game of golf, the seriousness which fans accord discussions of their home team, or the seriousness that national governments give to Olympic Games and university alumni to collegiate football?[7,8]

Accepting the fact that the make-believe quality of play has some relevance for sport, it nevertheless remains difficult to empirically ground the "not-ordinary-or-real-life" characteristic of play. However, the "outside-of-real-life" dimension of a game is perhaps best seen in its "as-if" quality, its artificial obstacles, and its potential resources for actualization or production.

In a game the contestants act as if all were equal, and numerous aspects of "external reality" such as race, education, occupation, and financial status are excluded as relevant attributes for the duration of a given contest.[9]

The obstacles individuals encounter in their workaday lives are not usually predetermined by them and are "real" in the sense that they must be adequately coped with if certain inherent and socially conditioned needs are to be met; on the other hand, in games obstacles are artificially created to be overcome. Although these predetermined obstacles set up to be conquered can sometimes attain "life-and-death" significance, as in a difficult Alpine climb, they are not usually essentially related to an individual's daily toil for existence.[10]

Similarly, it is observed that in many "real" life situations the structures and processes needed to cope with a given obstacle are often not at hand; however, in a play or game situation all the structures and processes necessary to deal with any deliberately created obstacle and to realize any possible alternative in course of action are potentially available.[11]

In sum, then, games are playful in that they typically have one or more elements of play: freedom, separateness, uncertainty, unproductiveness, order, and make-believe. In addition to having elements of play, games have components of competition.

Competition

Competition is defined as a struggle for supremacy between two or more opposing sides. We interpret the phrase "between two or more opposing sides" rather broadly to encompass the competitive relationships between man and other objects of nature, both animate and inanimate. Thus competitive relationships include:

1. competition between one individual and another, e.g., a boxing match or a 100-yard dash;
2. competition between one team and another, e.g., a hockey game or a yacht race;
3. competition between an individual or a team and an animate object of nature, e.g., a bullfight or a deer-hunting party;
4. competition between an individual or a team and an inanimate object of nature, e.g., a canoeist running a set of rapids or a mountain climbing expedition; and finally,
5. competition between an individual or team and an "ideal" standard, e.g., an individual - attempting to establish a world land-speed record on the Bonneville salt flats or a basketball team trying to set an all-time scoring record. Competition against an "ideal" standard might also be conceptualized as man against time or space, or as man against himself.[12]

The preceding classification has been set forth to illustrate what we understand by the phrase "two or more opposing sides" and is not intended to be a classification of competition *per se*. While the scheme may have some relevance for such a purpose, its value is limited by the fact that its categories are neither mutually exclusive nor inclusive. For instance, an athlete competing in a cross-country race may be competitively involved in all of the following ways: as an individual against another individual; as a team member against members of an opposing team; and as an individual or team member against an "ideal" standard (e.g., an attempt to set an individual and/or team record for the course).[13]

Physical Skill, Strategy, and Chance

Roberts and Sutton-Smith suggest that the various games of the world can be classified

> . . . on the basis of outcome attributes: (1) games of *physical skill,* in which the outcome is determined by the players' motor activities; (2) games of *strategy,* in which the outcome is determined by rational choices among possible courses of action; and (3) games of *chance,* in which the outcome is determined by guesses or by some uncontrolled artifact such as a die or wheel (Roberts and Sutton-Smith, 1962, p. 166).

Examples of relatively pure forms of competitive activities in each of these categories are weightlifting contests, chess matches, and crap games, respectively. Many, if not most, games are, however, of a mixed nature. Card and board games, for instance, generally illustrate a combination of strategy and chance. Although chance is also associated with sport, its role in determining the outcome of a contest is generally held to a minimum in order that the winning side can attribute its victory to merit rather than to a fluke of nature. Rather interestingly it appears that a major role of chance in sport is to insure equality. For example, the official's flip of a coin before the start of a football game randomly determines what team will receive the kickoff and from what respective side of the field; and similarly the drawing of numbers by competitors in track and swimming is an attempt to assure them equal opportunity of getting assigned a given lane.

Physical Prowess

Having discussed the characteristics which sports share in common with games in general, let us turn to an account of the major attribute which distinguishes sports in particular from games in general. We observe that sports can be distinguished from games by the fact that they demand the demonstration of physical prowess. By the phrase "the demonstration of physical prowess" we mean the employment of developed physical skills and abilities within the context of gross physical activity to conquer an opposing object of nature. Although many games require a minimum of physical skill, they do not usually demand the degree of physical skill required by sports. The idea of "developed physical skills" implies much practice and learning and suggests the attainment of a high level of proficiency in one or more general physical abilities relevant to sport competition, e.g., strength, speed, endurance, or accuracy.

Although the concept of physical prowess permits sports to be generally differentiated from games, numerous borderline areas exist. For example, can a dart game among friends, a horseshoe pitching contest between husband and wife, or a fishing contest between father and son be considered sport? One way to arrive at an answer to these questions is to define a sport as any highly organized game requiring physical prowess. Thus a dart game with friends, a horseshoe pitching contest between spouses, or a fishing contest between a father and son would not be considered sport; but formally sponsored dart, horseshoe, or fishing tournaments would be legitimately labelled sport. An alternative approach to answering the aforementioned questions, however, is to define a sport as an institutionalized game demanding the demonstration of physical prowess. If one accepts the latter approach, then he will arrive at a different set of answers to the above questions. For this approach views a game as a unique event and sport as an institutional pattern. As Weiss has rather nicely put it:

> A game is an occurrence; a sport is a pattern. The one is in the present, the other primarily past, but instantiated in the present. A sport

defines the conditions to which the participants must submit if there is to be a game; a game gives rootage to a set of rules and thereby enables a sport to be exhibited (1967, p. 82).

Sport as an Institutionalized Game

To treat sport as an institutionalized game is to consider sport as an abstract entity. For example, the organization of a football team as described in a rule book can be discussed without reference to the members of any particular team; and the relationships among team members can be characterized without reference to unique personalities or to particular times and places. In treating sport as an institutionalized game we conceive of it as distinctive, enduring patterns of culture and social structure combined into a single complex, the elements of which include values, norms, sanctions, knowledge, and social positions (i.e., roles and statuses).[14] A firm grasp of the meaning of "institutionalization" is necessary for understanding the idea of sport as an institutional pattern, or blueprint if you will, guiding the organization and conduct of given games and sportive endeavors.

The formulation of a set of rules for a game or even their enactment on a particular occasion does not constitute a sport as we have conceptualized it here. The institutionalization of a game implies that it has a tradition of past exemplifications and definite guidelines for future realizations. Moreover, in a concrete game situation the form of a particular sport need not reflect all the characteristics represented in its institutional pattern. The more organized a sport contest in a concrete setting, however, the more likely it will illustrate the institutionalized nature of a given sport. A professional baseball game, for example, is a better illustration of the institutionalized nature of baseball than is a sandlot baseball game; but both games are based on the same institutional pattern and thus may both be considered

forms of sport. In brief, a sport may be treated analytically in terms of its degree of institutionalization and dealt with empirically in terms of its degree of organization. The latter is an empirical instance of the former.

In order to illustrate the institutionalized nature of sport more adequately, we contrast the organizational, technological, symbolic, and educational spheres of sports with those of games. In doing so we consider both games and sports in their most formalized and organized state. We are aware that there are institutionalized games other than sports which possess characteristics similar to the ones we ascribe to sports, as for example chess and bridge; but we contend that such games are in the minority and in any case are excluded as sports because they do not demand the demonstration of physical prowess.

Organizational Sphere

For present purposes we rather arbitrarily discuss the organizational aspects of sports in terms of teams, sponsorship, and government.

Teams Competing sides for most games are usually selected rather spontaneously and typically disband following a given contest. In sports, however, competing groups are generally selected with care and, once membership is established, maintain a stable social organization. Although individual persons may withdraw from such organizations after they are developed, their social positions are taken up by others, and the group endures.[15]

Another differentiating feature is that as a rule sports show a greater degree of role differentiation than games do. Although games often involve several contestants (e.g., poker), the contestants often perform identical activities and thus may be considered to have the same roles and statuses. By contrast, in sports involving a similar number of participants (e.g., basketball), each individual or combination of just a few individuals performs specialized activities within the group and may be said to possess a distinct role. Moreover, to the extent that such specialized and differentiated activities can be ranked in terms of some criteria, they also possess different statuses.

Sponsorship　In addition to there being permanent social groups established for purposes of sport competition, there is usually found in the sport realm social groups which act as sponsoring bodies for sport teams. These sponsoring bodies may be characterized as being direct or indirect. Direct sponsoring groups include municipalities which sponsor Little League baseball teams, universities which support collegiate teams, and business corporations which sponsor AAU teams. Indirect sponsoring groups include sporting goods manufacturers, booster clubs, and sport magazines.

Government　While all types of games have at least a modicum of norms and sanctions associated with them, the various forms of sport are set apart from many games by the fact that they have more—and more formal and more institutionalized—sets of these cultural elements. In games rules are often passed down by oral tradition or spontaneously established for a given contest and forgotten afterwards; or, even where codified, they are often simple and few. In sports rules are usually many, and they are formally codified and typically enforced by a regulatory body. There are international organizations governing most sports, and in America there are relatively large social organizations governing both amateur and professional sports. For example, amateur sports in America are controlled by such groups as the NCAA, AAU, and NAIA; and the major professional sports have national commissioners with enforcing officials to police competition.

Technological Sphere

In a sport, technology denotes the material equipment, physical skills, and body of knowledge which are necessary for the conduct of competition and potentially available for technical improvements in competition. While all types of games require a minimum of knowledge and often a minimum of physical skill and material equipment, the various sports are set apart from many games by the fact that they typically require greater knowledge and involve higher levels of physical skill and necessitate more material equipment. The technological aspects of a sport may be dichotomized into those which are intrinsic and those which are extrinsic. Intrinsic technological aspects of a sport consist of the physical skills, knowledge, and equipment which are required for the conduct of a given contest *per se*. For example, the intrinsic technology of football includes: (a) the equipment necessary for the game—field, ball, uniform, etc.; (b) the repertoire of physical skills necessary for the game—running, passing, kicking, blocking, tackling, etc.; and (c) the knowledge necessary for the game—rules, strategy, etc. Examples of extrinsic technological elements associated with football include: (a) physical equipment such as stadium, press facilities, dressing rooms, etc.; (b) physical skills such as possessed by coaches, cheerleaders, and ground crews; and (c) knowledge such as possessed by coaches, team physicians, and spectators.

Symbolic Sphere

The symbolic dimension of a sport includes elements of secrecy, display, and ritual. Huizinga contends that play "promotes the formation of social groupings which tend to surround themselves with secrecy and to stress their difference from the common world by disguise or other means" (1955, p. 13). Caillois criticizes his contention and states to the contrary that "play tends to remove the very nature of the mysterious." He further observes that "when the secret, the mask or the costume fulfills a sacramental function one can be sure that not play, but an institution is involved" (1961, p. 4).

Somewhat ambivalently we agree with both writers. On the one hand, to the extent that Huizinga means by "secrecy" the act of making distinctions between "play life" and "ordinary life," we accept his proposition that groups engaged in playful competition surround themselves with secrecy. On the other hand, to the extent that he means by "secrecy" something hidden from others, we accept Caillios's edict that an institution and not play is involved.

The latter type of secrecy might well be called "sanctioned secrecy" in sports, for there is associated with many forms of sport competition rather clear norms regarding approved clandestine behavior. For example, football teams are permitted to set up enclosed practice fields, send out scouts to spy on opposing teams, and exchange a limited number of game films revealing the strategies of future opponents. Other kinds of clandestine action such as slush funds established for coaches and gambling on games by players are not always looked upon with such favor.[16]

A thorough reading of Huizinga leads one to conclude that what he means by secrecy is best discussed in terms of display and ritual. He points out, for example, the "the 'differentness' and secrecy of play and most vividly expressed in 'dressing up'" and states that the higher forms of play are "a contest *for* something or a representation *of* something"—adding that "representation means display" (1955, p. 13). The "dressing up" element of play noted by Huizinga is certainly characteristic of most sports. Perhaps it is carried to its greatest height in bullfighting, but it is not absent in some of the less overt forms of sport. Veblen writes:

> It is noticeable, for instance, that even very mild-mannered and matter-of-fact men who go out shooting are apt to carry an excess of arms and accoutrements in order to impress upon their own imagination the seriousness of their undertaking. These huntsmen are also prone to a histrionic, prancing gait and to an elaborate exaggeration of the motions, whether of stealth or of onslaught, involved in their deeds of exploit (1934, p. 256).

A more recent account of "dressing-up" and display in sports has been given by Stone (1955),

who treats display as spectacle and as a counter-force to play. Stone asserts that the tension between the forces of play and display constitute an essential component of sport. The following quotation gives the essence of his account:

> Play and dis-play are precariously balanced in sport, and, once that balance is upset, the whole character of sport in society may be affected. Furthermore, the spectacular element of sport, may, as in the case of American professional wrestling, destroy the game. The rules cease to apply, and the "cheat" and the "spoilsport" replace the players.
>
> The point may be made in another way. The spectacle is predictable and certain; the game, unpredictable and uncertain. Thus spectacular display may be reckoned from the outset of the performance. It is announced by the appearance of the performers—their physiques, costumes, and gestures. On the other hand, the spectacular play is solely a function of the uncertainty of the game (p. 98).

In a somewhat different manner another sociologist, Erving Goffman, has analyzed the factors of the uncertainty of a game and display. Concerning the basis of "fun in games" he states that "mere uncertainty of outcome is not enough to engross the players" (1961, p. 68) and suggests that a successful game must combine "sanctioned display" with problematic outcome. By display Goffman means that "games give the players an opportunity to exhibit attributes valued in the wider social world, such as dexterity, strength, knowledge, intelligence, courage, and self-control" (*Ibid.*). Thus for Goffman display represents spectacular play involving externally relevant attributes, while for Stone display signifies spectacular exhibition involving externally non-relevant attributes with respect to the game situation.

Another concept related to display and spectacle and relevant to sports is that of ritual. According to Leach, "ritual denotes those aspects of prescribed formal behavior which have no direct technological consequences" (1964, p. 607). Ritual may be distinguished from spectacle by the fact that it generally has a greater element of drama and is less ostentatious and more serious. "Ritual actions are 'symbolic' in that they assert something about the state of affairs, but they are not necessarily purposive: i.e., the performer of ritual does not necessarily seek to alter the state of affairs" (*Ibid.*). Empirically ritual can be distinguished from spectacle by the fact that those engaged in ritual express an attitude of solemnity toward it, an attitude which they do not direct toward spectacle.

Examples of rituals in sport are the shaking of hands between team captains before a game, the shaking of hands between team coaches after a game, the singing of the national anthem before a game, and the singing of the school song at the conclusion of a game.[17]

Educational Sphere

The educational sphere focuses on those activities related to the transmission of skills and knowledge to those who lack them. Many if not most people learn to play the majority of socially preferred games in an informal manner. That is, they acquire the required skills and knowledge associated with a given game through the casual instruction of friends or associates. On the other hand, in sports, skills and knowledge are often obtained by means of formal instruction. In short, the educational sphere of sports is institutionalized, whereas in most games it is not. One reason for this situation is the fact that sports require highly developed physical skills as games often do not; to achieve proficiency requires long hours of practice and qualified instruction, i.e., systematized training. Finally, it should be pointed out that associated with the instructional personnel of sport programs are a number of auxiliary personnel such as managers, physicians, and trainers—a situation not commonly found in games.

Sport as a Social Institution

Extending our notion of sport as an institutional pattern still further, we note that in its broadest sense, the term sport supposes a social institution. Schneider writes that the term institution

> ... denotes an aspect of social life in which distinctive value-orientations and interests, centering upon large and important social concern ... generate or are accompanied by distinctive modes of social interaction. Its use emphasizes "important" social phenomena; relationships of "strategic structural significance" (1964, p. 338).

We argue that the magnitude of sport in the Western world justifies its consideration as a social institution. As Boyle succinctly states:

> Sport permeates any number of levels of contemporary society, and it touches upon and deeply influences such disparate elements as status, race relations, business life, automotive design, clothing styles, the concept of the hero, language, and ethical values. For better or worse it gives form and substance to much in American life (1963, pp. 3–4).

When speaking of sport as a social institution, we refer to the sport order. The sport order is composed of all organizations in society which organize, facilitate, and regulate human action in sport situations. Hence, such organizations as sporting goods manufacturers, sport clubs, athletic teams, national governing bodies for amateur and professional sports, publishers of sport magazines, etc., are part of the sport order. For analytical purposes four levels of social organization within the sport order may be distinguished: namely, the primary, technical, managerial, and corporate levels.[18] Organizations at the primary level permit face-to-face relationships among all members and are characterized by the fact that administrative leadership is not formally delegated to one or more persons or positions. An example of a social organization associated with sport at the primary level is an informally organized team in a sandlot baseball game.

Organizations at the technical level are too large to permit simultaneous face-to-face relationships among their members but small enough so that every member knows of every other member. Moreover, unlike organizations at the primary level, organizations at the technical level officially designate administrative leadership positions and allocate individuals to them. Most scholastic and collegiate athletic teams, for example, would be classified as technical organizations with coaches and athletic directors functioning as administrative leaders.

At the managerial level organizations are too large for every member to know every other member but small enough so that all members know one or more of the administrative leaders of the organization. Some of the large professional ball clubs represent social organizations related to sport at the managerial level.

Organizations at the corporate level are characterized by bureaucracy: they have centralized authority, a hierarchy of personnel, and protocol and procedural emphases; and they stress the rationalization of operations and impersonal relationships. A number of the major governing bodies of amateur and professional sport at the national and international levels illustrate sport organizations of the corporate type.

In summary, the sport order is composed of the congeries of primary, technical, managerial, and corporate social organizations which arrange, facilitate, and regulate human action in sport situations. The value of the concept lies in its use in macro-analyses of the social significance of sport. We can make reference to the sport order in a historical and/or comparative perspective. For example, we can speak of the sport order of nineteenth-century America or contrast the sport order of Russia with that of England.

Sport as a Social Situation

As was just noted, the sport order is composed of all social organizations which organize, facilitate, and regulate human action in sport situations. Human "action consists of the structures and processes by which human beings form meaningful intentions and, more or less successfully, implement them in concrete situations" (Parsons, 1966, p. 5). A sport situation consists of any social context wherein individuals are involved with sport. And the term situation denotes "the total set of objects, whether persons, collectivities, culture objects, or himself to which an actor responds" (Friedsam, 1964, p. 667). The set of objects related to a specific sport situation may be quite diverse, ranging from the elements of the social and physical environments of a football game to those associated with two sportniks[19] in a neighborhood bar arguing the pros and cons of the manager of their local baseball team.

Although there are many kinds of sport situations, most if not all may be conceptualized as social systems. A social system may be simply defined as "a set of persons with an identifying characteristic plus a set of relationships established among these persons by interaction" (Caplow, 1964, p. 1). Thus the situation represented by two teams contesting within the confines of a football field, the situation presented by father and son fishing from a boat, and the situation created by a golf pro giving a lesson to a novice each constitutes a social system.

Social systems of prime concern to the sport sociologist are those which directly or indirectly relate to a game occurrence. That is to say, a sport sociologist is often concerned with why man gets involved in sport and what effect his involvement has on other aspects of his social environment. Involvement in a social system related to a game occurrence can be analyzed in terms of degree and kind of involvement.

Degree of involvement can be assessed in terms of frequency, duration, and intensity of involvement. The combination of frequency and duration of involvement may be taken as an index of an individual's "investment" in a sport situation, while intensity of involvement may be considered an index of an individual's "personal commitment" to a given sport situation.[20]

Kind of involvement can be assessed in terms of an individual's relationship to the "means of production" of a game. Those having direct or indirect access to the means of production are considered "actually involved" and are categorized as "producers." Those lacking access to the means of production are considered "vicariously involved" and are categorized as "consumers." We have tentatively identified three categories of producers and three classes of consumers.

Producers may be characterized as being primary, secondary, or tertiary with respect to the production of a game. (1) "Primary producers" are the contestants who play the primary roles in the production of a game, not unlike the roles of actors in the production of a play. (2) "Secondary producers" consist of those individuals, who while not actually competing in a sport contest, perform tasks which have direct technological consequences for the outcome of a game. Secondary producers include club owners, coaches, officials, trainers, and the like. It may be possible to categorize secondary producers as entrepreneurs, managers, and technicians. (3) "Tertiary producers" consist of those who are actively involved in a sport situation but whose activities have no direct technological consequences for the outcome of a game. Examples of tertiary producers are cheerleaders, band members, and concession workers. Tertiary producers may be classified as service personnel.

Consumers, like producers, are designated as being primary, secondary, or tertiary. (1) "Primary consumers" are those individuals who become vicariously involved in a sport through "live" attendance at a sport competition. Primary consumers may be thought of as "active spectators." (2) "Secondary consumers" consist of those who vicariously involve themselves in a sport as spectators via some form of the mass media, such as radio or television. Secondary consumers may be thought of as "passive spectators." (3) "Tertiary consumers" are those who become vicariously involved with sport other than as spectators. Thus an individual who engages in conversation related to sport or a person who reads the sport section of the newspaper would be classified as a tertiary consumer.

In concluding our discussion of the nature of sport we note that a special type of consumer is the *fan*. A fan is defined as an individual who has both a high personal investment in and a high personal commitment to a given sport.

Notes

1. This definition is based largely on the work of Caillois (1961) and Roberts and others (1959). Other definitions and classifications of games having social import are given in Berne (1964) and Piaget (1951).
2. As have done Huizinga (1955), Stone (1955), and Caillois (1961).
3. Cf. Goffman's discussion of "rules of irrelevance" as applied to games and social encounters in general (1961, pp. 19–26).
4. E.g., compare the rules given for games in any edition of Hoyle's *Book of Games* with the NCAA rule book for various collegiate sports.
5. There is, of course, the amateur who gives up the "game" to become a professional.
6. For an early discussion of the problem of legitimation in sport, see Veblen, 1934, pp. 268–270.
7. An excellent philosophical account of play and seriousness is given by Kurt Riezler (1941, pp. 505–517).
8. A sociological treatment of how an individual engaged in an activity can become "caught up" in it is given by Goffman in his analysis of the concept of "spontaneous involvement" (1961, pp. 37–45).
9. For a discussion of how certain aspects of "reality" are excluded from a game situation, see Goffman's treatment of "rules of irrelevance." Contrawise see his treatment of "rules of transformation" for a discussion of how certain aspects of "reality" are permitted to enter a game situation (1961, pp. 29–34).

10. Professional sports provide an exception, of course, especially such a sport as professional bullfighting.

11. Our use of the term "structures and processes" at this point is similar to Goffman's concept of "realized resources" (1961, pp. 16–19).

12. Other possible categories of competition are, of course, animals against animals as seen in horse racing or animals against an artificial animal as seen in dog racing. As noted by Weiss: "When animals or machines race, the speed offers indirect testimony to men's excellence as trainers, coaches, riders, drivers and the like—and thus primarily to an excellence in human leadership, judgment, strategy, and tactics" (1967, p. 22).

13. The interested reader can find examples of sport classifications in Hesseltine (1964), McIntosh (1963), and Sapora and Mitchell (1961).

14. This definition is patterned after one given by Smelser (1963, p. 28).

15. Huizinga states that the existence of permanent teams is, in fact, the starting-point of modern sport (1955, p. 196).

16. Our discussion of "sanctioned secrecy" closely parallels Johnson's discussion of "official secrecy" in bureaucracies (1960, pp. 295–296).

17. For an early sociological treatment of sport, spectacle, exhibition, and drama, see Sumner (1960, pp. 467–501). We note in passing that some writers consider the totality of sport as a ritual; see especially Fromm (1955, p. 132) and Beisser (1967, pp. 148–151 and pp. 214–225).

18. Our discussion of these four levels is similar to Caplow's treatment of small, medium, large, and giant organizations (Caplow, 1964, pp. 26–27).

19. The term *sportnik* refers to an avid fan or sport addict.

20. Cf. McCall and Simmons (1966, pp. 171–172).

Bibliography

Beisser, Arnold R. *The Madness in Sports.* New York: Appleton-Century-Crofts, 1967.

Berne, Eric. *Games People Play.* New York: Grove Press, 1964.

Boyle, Robert H. *Sport—Mirror of American Life.* Boston: Little, Brown, 1963.

Caillois, Roger. *Man Play and Games,* tr. Meyer Barash. New York: Free Press, 1964.

Caplow, Theodore. *Principles of Organization.* New York: Harcourt, Brace and World, 1964.

Fromm, Erich. *The Sane Society.* New York: Fawcett, 1955.

Goffman, Erving. *Encounters.* Indianapolis: Bobbs-Merrills, 1961.

Hesseltine, William B. "Sports," *Collier's Encyclopedia,* 1964.

Huizinga, Johan. *Homo Ludens—A Study of the Play-Element in Culture.* Boston: Beacon Press, 1955.

Johnson, Harry M. *Sociology: A Systematic Introduction.* New York: Harcourt, Brace, 1960.

Kahn, Roger. "Money, Muscles—and Myths," *Nation,* CLXXXV (July 6, 1957), 9–11.

Leach, E. R. "Ritual," in *A Dictionary of the Social Sciences,* ed. Julius Gould and William L. Kolb. New York: Free Press, 1964.

Lüschen, Gunther. "The Interdependence of Sport and Culture." Paper presented at the National Convention of the American Association for Health, Physical Education, and Recreation, Las Vegas, 1967.

McCall, George J., and J. L. Simmons. *Identities and Interactions.* New York: Free Press, 1966.

McIntosh, Peter C. *Sport in Society.* London: C. A. Watts, 1963.

Piaget, Jean. *Play, Dreams, and Imitation in Childhood,* tr. C. Gattegno and F. M. Hodgson. New York: W. W. Norton, 1951.

Riezler, Kurt. "Play and Seriousness," *The Journal of Philosophy,* XXXVIII (1941), 505–517.

Roberts, John M., and others. "Games in Culture," *American Anthropologist,* LXI (1959), 597–605.

———, and Brian Sutton-Smith. "Child Training and Game Involvement," *Ethnology,* I (1962), 166–185.

Sapora, Allen V., and Elmer D. Mitchell. *The Theory of Play and Recreation.* New York: Ronald Press, 1961.

Schneider, Louis. "Institution," in *A Dictionary of the Social Sciences,* ed. Julius Gould and William L. Kolb. New York: Free Press, 1964.

Smelser, Neil J. *The Sociology of Economic Life.* Englewood Cliffs, N.J.: Prentice-Hall, 1963.

Stone, Gregory P. "American Sports: Play and Display," *Chicago Review,* IX (Fall 1955), 83–100.

Sumner, William Graham. *Folkways.* New York: Mentor, 1960.

Torkildsen, George E. "Sport and Culture." M.S. thesis, University of Wisconsin, 1957.

Veblen, Thorstein. *The Theory of the Leisure Class.* New York: Modern Library, 1934.

Weiss, Paul. "Sport: A Philosophic Study." Unpublished manuscript, 1967.

Questions for Consideration

1. Just how successful is Loy's definitional effort in getting at the nature of sport? Is it meant to give us an accurate description of sportive practice, or is his intent merely to rid the term "sport" of some of its ambiguity?

2. Can you suggest any further refinements to his characterization?

3. Has Loy sufficiently shown that sport is essentially a social institution?

3 Tricky Triad: Games, Play, and Sport

Bernard Suits
University of Waterloo

Bernard Suits attempts to distinguish clearly the relationship between games, play, and sport. In a prior writing, Suits had assumed that all athletic competition was a form of game. Here, Suits "recants."

First, he divides play into sophisticated and primitive play. Primitive play is play for its own sake. From primitive play, one can develop certain skills, but such play is not done with these refinements in mind. Sophisticated play in contrast lacks spontaneity and centers on skills developed and used for their own sake. Amateur sport is a type of sophisticated and primitive play.

Next and most critically, he distinguishes between two kinds of competitive sport: performances and rule-governed competitions. Since a game, for Suits, comprises rule-governed skills with artificial constraints, only rule-governed competitions are games. Such competitions, like soccer or volleyball, are governed by internal or constitutive rules. These have as their object the overcoming of certain, specified barriers. A performance, in contrast, is a matter of refining old skills to eliminate constraints. What rules exist are external. Instead of overcoming barriers, performances aim at ideals, such as a perfect dive.

It is because of this last distinction that Suits reformulated his views on the relationship between game, play, and sport.

Since I have already published individual articles on games, play, and sport, one might ask why I am coming around again to peddle commodities that have already been merchandised.[1] There are two reasons: (a) I have changed my views in some important ways about play and sport (though not about games), and (b) I am more interested in this inquiry in relations among the three than I am in distinctions between them.

Let me begin by making a large cut, as it were, between play on the one hand and games and sports on the other. Games and sports are enterprises or institutions, I suggest, in which the exhibition of skill is the paramount consideration, and I am not going to argue that in play the exhibition of skill is not the paramount consideration. Actually I am not going to argue quite that, for an objection immediately arises. Are not games, it will be asked, *play* when they are undertaken as ends in themselves, by amateurs, that is, by those whose gaming is for the love of it, in contrast to professionals, whose gaming is for sometimes astronomical salaries? If so, then the difference between amateur and professional gamespersons would appear to be precisely the difference between play and work. And since in amateur gaming skill *is* the paramount consideration, it would seem false to say of play, or at least to say of all play, that the exhibition of skill is *not* of paramount importance.

This is a serious objection and can be met, if I am to maintain my large cut between play and games/sport by making a distinction between two kinds of activity that are normally called play. It is the distinction between what I shall call primitive and what I shall call sophisticated play. Primitive play is play and only play; sophisticated play is play and something else as well.

Reprinted by permission, from Bernard Suits, "Tricky Triad: Games, Play, and Sport," *Journal of the Philosophy of Sport* XV (1988): 1–9.

Primitive Play

What do I mean by primitive play, such that skill is not its essential ingredient? Well, let us see if we can find a paradigm, or at least an example that will not raise more questions than it answers. How about this one? The baby playing with the water in its bath. Now, I think we can agree that the baby is playing for the following *negative* reason: it is not working, that is, it is not engaged in any instrumental enterprise. More to the point, it is not engaged in bathing itself nor is it assisting its father or mother in being bathed, for the obvious reason that it does not know what it is doing in the water at all. Very well; the baby is not working. But is it doing *anything?* Or is it simply behaving randomly, as a robot whose circuitry is defective might exhibit bits of behavior unrelated to each other and to no purpose? I think not. The baby is not acting randomly or without purpose because it is clear that when the baby plays with the water in its bath there is input on its part—it splashes the water. And there is feedback—it is pleased by its water-splashing; and there is, as a consequence, further input: the baby continues to splash to get further feedback.

Now, it will be pointed out that the more the baby engages in this activity, during this bath and in subsequent baths, the more skillful it will become at splashing, or at least at splashing in ways that pay off. Skills, it will be said, will begin to emerge in the baby's behavior. No doubt. I readily grant that. But, and this is the main point I want to make about play and skill, *the skills learned are not the payoff the baby is seeking.* The baby is not pleased by the fact that it is becoming an accomplished water-splasher; it is pleased by the splashing water.

Primitive play, I suggest, is not concerned primarily with the exercise and enjoyment of skills but with the introduction of new experiences that arise, usually, serendipitously. Still, the repetition of these experiences may very well result in the development of skills directed toward the

recurrence of those experiences, and such skills may, although they need not, come to be valued for their own sake. When that *does* happen we are just beginning to move from primitive play to sophisticated play, that is, to games, and perhaps to something else as well.

Sport

I ask you to keep the foregoing at the back of your mind for the present, for we shall be returning to it. But now I would like to make a head-on attack on sports. This will lead us back, in due course, to the distinction between primitive and sophisticated play, and to an additional, and parallel, distinction.

Although other things are, and are called, sport, I shall confine my remarks this afternoon to sport as the kind of activity exemplified in the Olympic Games. Sports so understood may be defined, or at least described, as competitive events involving a variety of physical (usually in combination with other) human skills, where the superior participant is judged to have exhibited those skills in a superior way. What we are talking about, then, are competitive athletic events. May we say, then, that such sports are the same as athletic *games?* No, we may not. In an article of mine recently reprinted in an anthology on the philosophy of sport, I maintained that sports of the kind we are now considering *were* the same as athletic games.[2] Well, I was wrong. The Olympics (as well as the Commonwealth Games, and so on) contain two distinct types of competitive event, what I have elsewhere called judged as opposed to refereed events. One is a performance and so requires judges. The other is not a performance but a rule-governed interplay of participants, and so requires not judges but law-enforcement officers, that is, referees. Performances require rehearsal, games require practice. To be sure, football teams, in a sense, do rehearse certain moves or plays, but that is simply a part of practice, and victory is not determined by the artistry of such plays or moves but by their effectiveness in winning games. But I submit that diving and gymnastic competitions are no more games than are other judged competitive events such as beauty contests and pie-baking competitions.

Sport and Skills

If you agree with me that the sports of the Olympics are of two quite different kinds, then perhaps you will also agree with me that the skills required by each are also of two quite different kinds. If, as I suggested earlier, play becomes transformed into game when the skills learned in serendipitous play, instead of being instrumental to other payoffs (such as the splashing of bath water) themselves constitute the payoff, then we might consider the possibility that *performances,* in contrast to *games,* arise not out of the increased sophistication of play but out of an increased sophistication of work—or at least of certain serious endeavors.

What possible reason could I have for making this suggestion? Actually I have two reasons. The first is that such a hypothesis presents us with an attractive symmetry in distinguishing games that are sports from performances that are sports. Consider the following example. A boy is walking down the street. He sees a tin can. He idly kicks it and enjoys the sight of it tumbling along the street, and he enjoys the sound of its ear-shattering rattle. Another boy approaches from the opposite direction. As the can reaches him, he kicks it back. We have here the serendipitous origin of Kick-the-Can, field hockey, and a number of other games as well, as goal lines are added, and then perhaps sticks for hitting the can, and then ice and ice skates. This is of course an extremely crude reconstruction of the origin of ice hockey, but then it is not meant to be a historical account. It is, to use Rudyard Kipling's felicitous locution, a "just so" story. You recall, "How the Elephant Got His Trunk" and so on.

Clearly I am not trying to be a sports historian with this crude fable. I am merely suggesting, not terribly imaginatively, how unsophisticated play can become sophisticated play, that is, game.

Now let us consider a "just so" story that explains the origin of sport performances in contrast to sport *games.* A member of an economically primitive culture is engaged in food gathering. He does this by diving into a tropical pool to catch fish. Time passes, the fishing pole and fishing nets are invented, and so it is no longer necessary to employ the skill of diving in order to secure food; indeed, it would be inefficient to do so. Yet the skill of diving into the water has come into existence. Shall our primitive fisherman, then, just quit diving, as a primitive farmer would presumably release his wife from pulling the plow when he got himself a horse? Well it is conceivable, though just barely, that the plow-pulling wife, upon being replaced by a horse, might respond that she was suffering a deprivation. After all, she had spent years acquiring the skill of plow-pulling and now it was all for naught. Perhaps she might be allowed to pull the plow after hours, when the horse wasn't using it. This is what may be called a *not* Just So story.

Let us then return to the now technologically unemployed fish diver, which is, or at least could be, a quite different kettle of . . . ah . . . fish. He, let us say in our plausible Just So fashion, really does want to continue to exercise the skill he has learned but which has become, as the British so delicately put it, redundant. And so he continues to dive, but not for fish because that is no longer the payoff. The payoff has changed from what was formerly instrumental to something else. And so he continues to dive because he enjoys exercising that skill and also, perhaps, because he enjoys displaying that skill to others.

The foregoing suggests that games generate new skills and that performances refine (make more sophisticated) already existing skills. Thus hockey, for example, is not the refinement of an already existing skill. In the first place, getting a hard rubber disc across a line drawn on ice is not an already existing *goal*. And if it were, then putting on skates, learning how to use them, and further burdening oneself with a stick to propel the disc across the line (instead of sensibly using your hand) would not be an already existing skill requiring refinement. No, games generate new skills by erecting artificial constraints just so those constraints can be overcome.

But the case with our diver is very nearly the opposite of that. Since he is no longer diving for fish, he is liberated, as it were, from the constraint of diving at a certain time in a certain way in a certain place. He would not, for example, do back somersaults to catch fish, nor take special care to enter the water in as nearly a vertical posture as possible. We may conclude, therefore, that games generate *new* skills by erecting *artificial* constraints just so those constraints can be overcome, whereas performances eliminate natural constraints in order to refine old skills. There is just one thing wrong with this conclusion. It isn't true. The triad of play, game, and sport is far too tricky to admit of such a tidy resolution.

The falsity of the resolution I have proposed can be established by constructing two more Just So stories. One will show that games can come to be by refining old skills every bit as much as performances can, and the other will show that performances can generate new skills every bit as much as games can.

Once upon a time there was a diver who dived for fish for food. One day the pond into which he dived contained, unbeknown to him, a crocodile who was also fishing for food. Very soon the latter was in hot pursuit of the former. The diver, who was also, not surprisingly, a swimmer, swam away from the crocodile as fast as he could and was soon safely ashore and up a tree, filled not only with immense relief but also with a feeling of intense exhilaration at having outdistanced his aquatic competitor. The crocodile grumbled his way out of the pond to seek fresh waters and he never returned, so the pond was once again safe for unimpeded aquarian for-aging. A happy state of affairs? Not quite. For the diver kept thinking back on the exhilaration he had felt at his swimming victory, and on the satisfaction he had derived from his competitive swimming skills. He pondered. Should he introduce more crocodiles into the pond in order to repeat his earlier victory? But suppose he lost? In that case the game would certainly not be worth it. Then the light dawned, and swimming races were invented. That is to say, a game came into being by refining an old skill.

Can you handle another story? O.K. Once upon a time there was a diver who dived for fish for food. No, this isn't the same story. The diver in this one is a different diver. And the fact that he dived for fish for food is irrelevant anyway. And besides that, there is no crocodile in the story.

No, there is just this person, actually, standing on a bank overhanging a pool of water. On previous occasions our subject had jumped, or sometimes simply flung himself any old way into the water for the fun of it, much as the baby splashed the water in its bath for the fun of it. But one day it came to him that he could also enter the water in a more interesting and demanding way. Why did this idea come to him? Boredom, I should think, which is the mother of play. *Boredom is the mother of play.* I was going to add, "Remember, you heard it here first." And you may have. But I didn't. I stole it from Kierkegaard. But I digress. Boredom prompted him to try entering the water by doing a back somersault. With practice, he became quite adept at this new skill and performed the dive for his own enjoyment and that of a number of onlookers who often gathered to watch the performance. That is to say, a performance came into being by creating a *new* skill.

So. Games can come from work (that is, instrumental activities, like outswimming a crocodile) as well as from play, and so can performances. Does this mean that there is no difference between them? Not at all. It is just that the difference does not lie where it initially appeared to lie. Even so, we have turned up, in our abortive effort to distinguish the two, two other distinctions, namely, the distinction between work-generated and play-generated sport and the distinction between the creation of new skills and the refinement of old skills, and these distinctions may prove useful in illuminating questions other than the one now at issue, namely, the difference between games and performances.

So let us, as Aristotle so frequently used to say, make a new beginning. I have suggested that games are essentially refereed events and that performances are essentially judged events. This, I suggest, is the key to where the difference lies. In games, artificial barriers are erected just so they can be overcome by the use of rule-governed skills. Rules are the crux of games because it is the rules of any particular game that generate the skills appropriate to that game. Blocking in football is a skill required by, and thus generated by, the rules because the rules *rule out*, among other things, the use of machine guns by guards and tackles. That they are refereed calls attention to this fact, because referees see to it that the rules are followed and impose penalties when they are not. But, it might be asked, what about games that have no referees—a pick-up game of football, hockey, or whatever. The answer is that the players of such games, if they are sincere players, referee themselves. The rule-enforcement function is the same in both cases.

Performances, on the other hand, are not rule-governed in that way at all. There are rules, to be sure, but not only are they *not* the crux of performances, they usually take the form of applying to the participants *outside* the arena of contention. I dislike mentioning steroids at this time, but the rule against their use would be the kind of rule typically at issue in the case of performances, what might be called perhaps a pre-event rule. But once a performance is under way, there are no rules, or scarcely any, that need enforcing.

Now it may be objected that, contrary to what I have said, there clearly *are* rules that must be followed while actually engaged in performative sports. For example, the gymnast must not falter or stumble after dismounting from the parallel

bars. It is perfectly permissible to call such a requirement a rule, but it is quite clear, I should think, that such "rules" are entirely different from, say, the offside rules in football and hockey. The offside rule is what has come to be called, by me and many others, a constitutive rule, while the standard of a clean dismount from the parallel bars is a rule of skill, or a tactical rule, or a rule of practice. When I habitually fail to keep my eye on the ball in golf when driving from the tee, for example, I also habitually drive the ball halfway into the ground about two feet beyond the tee. But no one accuses me of cheating, just of incredible incompetence. The case is quite different, however, when I am discovered hand-carrying the ball across the green and dropping it into the cup.

Now, with the exception of what I have called pre-event rules (the steroid example), the rules to which the judges of performances address themselves are, I submit, rules of skill rather than constitutive rules. This suggests a way of distinguishing games from performances more likely to be successful than was my earlier attempt to distinguish them in terms of how their respective skills were *generated*. For it is clear that games and performances both generate their skills, whether out of what I have loosely called work or play. Perhaps, then, the answer lies not in what the skills of games and performances are generated from, but in *how* such skills are generated. And I shall forthwith suggest an answer that I do not believe to be false. Games do so, I suggest, by erecting barriers to be overcome, but performances do so by postulating ideals to be approximated.

In games, *rules*, to repeat the point, are the crux. Just these rules generate just these skills. In performances, ideals are the crux of the matter. Just these ideals generate just these skills. That is why it is possible to speak of a perfect performance, at least in principle, without fear of contradiction, whereas a perfectly played game, as I have tried to show elsewhere, seems to lead to a paradox.

An objection at this point must be stated and

met. In some games referees make what have come to be called "judgment calls." This may initially suggest to some that there is a hybrid sport, neither a game nor a performance but a combination of both, what might be called a gaformance or a pame. I think not. Even though boxing referees and judges can differ in their calls, that is not like gymnastic judges holding up their numbered cards. For boxing officials, even when they differ, are not making their assessments against an ideal of boxing, if there is such a thing, but of one competitor directly against another, even if both are very far indeed from a boxing "ideal" performance. And a pitching umpire is not called upon to assess pitching skill against some standard of excellence: he must simply decide whether each pitch does or does not cross the plate within the strike zone. Such judgment calls not only are *not* the crux of such games in which they are found but, much more important, they are thought of as something very close to being necessary or unavoidable evils. Referees make judgment calls not as to overall performance, and indeed not with respect to performance skills at all, but with respect to *events*. *Did* the tennis ball land within the service court? *Was* the dropped ball a fumble according to the rules? *Did* boxer x strike more blows, and more crucial ones, than his opponent? *Did* and *where did* the saber strike the opponent? That such referential judgments are regarded as less than the best way to decide issues such as these is evidenced by the introduction of technical scoring devices in fencing to *replace* such judgments calls, and of televised playbacks in football. The judgment calls of referees are not judgments about degree of approximation to an ideal but only about what happened under what circumstances.

Sports and Play

Let me begin by making the bald assertion that not all sports are play. That may seem to most of you to be an obvious point, and therefore one

scarcely worth making. Perhaps I can make it more interesting by adding to it an additional claim, to wit, that the events of the recent Olympics and, I believe, of the Olympic Games since their beginning in the mists of Greek history, are not and were not play. Let us return, as I promised we would early in these remarks, to the distinction between what I called primitive and what I called sophisticated play. We have seen, or at least I have seen and hope that you have as well, that primitive play can, though it need not, turn into sophisticated play either in the form of games or of performances, and that these two types of event that figure in the Olympics, and in what are called amateur sports generally, also figure in what are called professional sports. Let us assume, but only for the moment, that the Olympic Games fall within the category of amateur sports. We may then display the relations between play, game, and sport by means of three overlapping circles [Figure 3.1].

The portion of the circle labeled Play which does *not* overlap either Game or Sport, and which I have numbered 1, represents primitive play. The area where only Play and Game overlap is the game instance of sophisticated play, Area 2. Area 3 overlaps neither Play nor Sport, and so although we will find games there, such games are neither athletic events nor instances of sophisticated play. What are they? For the moment we shall call the events in Area 3 professional nonathletic games, such events as professional bridge and poker. Area 4, where only Play and Sport overlap, but not Game, is where amateur performances are located. Area 5 contains amateur games. Area 6 is where professional athletics are found; it is the counterpart of Area 3, where we found professional *non*athletic events. Area 7, the area of Sports that are neither Games nor Play, includes, most significantly for the present analysis, *professional* athletic performances, for the two types of event that appear in our paradigm of Olympic Games have already been assigned to Areas 4 and 5. Whether Area 7 contains other things as well, that is, other sports that are neither play nor games, I leave an open question.

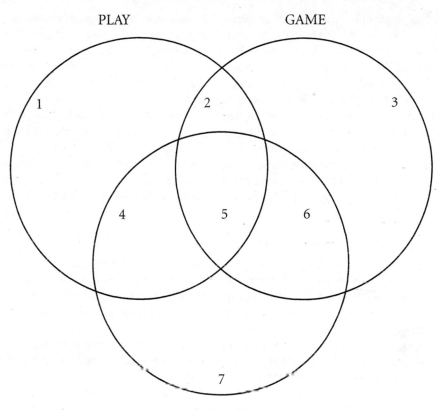

Figure 3.1

At this point a question may arise. If, as I have argued, games and performances are instances of sophisticated play, how is it possible for there to be games and performances that are not play, as in 3, 6, and 7? The answer is that when games become instruments for external purposes (most obviously for acquiring money, as in the form of salaries drawn by players in the NHL, CFL, and so on), then these games, just like their players, lose their amateur standing. And that simply means, consistent with the terminology I have been using throughout, that such games are not played primarily out of love of the game but out of love of what the game can produce, whether playing it is loved or not. Accordingly, I would like to turn now to my concluding section.

Amateur Versus Non-Amateur Standing

In these remarks, I have employed several different terms in referring to a pair of opposites generally acknowledged to be of central importance in a discussion of sports and games. They are, work versus play, serious versus nonserious, instrumental versus noninstrumental, and finally, professional versus amateur. These different verbalizations were intended to refer pretty much to the same pair of opposed conditions. There is a danger of being misled, however, particularly with respect to the distinction between professional and amateur. One is inclined, at least at first, to think of CFL players, for example, as professionals and university players as amateurs—at least in Canada. In the States the division between pro and college football is somewhat less clear, to be sure.

Now with respect to games, and performances as well, the word amateur, it seems to me, is a better word to use for one side of the distinction, for it does convey the notion of play rather than work, of the nonserious rather than the serious, and of the noninstrumental rather than the instrumental. But the word professional is, taken in its usual sense, too narrow to convey what the words work, serious, and instrumental convey. Still, while the word amateur in its literal meaning (one who does x for the love of it) does convey what is wanted, the *connotation* of amateur strongly suggests that it is simply the opposite of professional. I would like therefore to dispense with both words, and substitute for the phrase "amateur event or activity" the phrase "autotelic event or activity," that is, an event or activity valued for itself. And I would like to substitute for "professional" the expression "instrumental activity or event," that is, an event or activity valued not only or even primarily for itself but for some further payoff that the event or activity is expected to provide. And the salary of a professional athlete is, to be sure, a clear example of such an instrumental payoff. But there are other payoffs as well, and those who play or game for them, though not called professionals, are engaged, I shall argue, in instrumental rather than in autotelic activities every bit as much as are professionals.

I should like to put it to you that the games and performances of the Olympics may not be instances of sophisticated play, that is, that they may not be autotelic activities but instrumental activities. The point I want to make is a quite different one from the perennial, or rather quadrennial, point that the Soviet Union, East Germany, and others enter paid professionals into what is supposed to be an amateur undertaking. My point is, rather, that the Olympics, even if all the competitors were amateurs in the

ordinary understanding of that word, would not provide us with good examples of games and performances as play, which is to say that such events would not fall within Areas 4 and 5 of our diagram, as one might suppose, but in Areas 6 and 7.

The reason I say this is because, for participants in Olympic events, playing the game is not the primary payoff the players are seeking. Getting the gold, either for themselves or for their homelands, is the primary payoff—or if not the gold, then the silver or bronze. That is why professionalism has crept into the Olympics, and it is also why steroids have crept in. But paid players and chemicals are not in themselves what render Olympic events instrumental rather than autotelic activities. Even in the absence of paid players or chemicals, I would still want to suggest that they are instrumental rather than autotelic events. For in the Olympics there is *a kind of compulsion* to win that is absent from a friendly game of tennis, or a pick-up game of baseball or hockey. I am suggesting that acting under such a compulsion, rather than the desire to win simply because winning defines the activity one is undertaking, is what turns a game that could be play into something that is not play.

In an old *New Yorker* cartoon, a portly and agitated man dressed in the latest golf toggery is seen speaking angrily to his golfing partner. The caption reads, "Stop saying it's just a game! Godammit, it's *not* just a game!" And he is quite right. For him, golf is not play, and so it is not, therefore, *just* a game.

Notes

1. This paper was presented as the invited Annual Homecoming Lecture of the Faculty of Physical Education of the University of Western Ontario in London, Canada, October 14, 1988.

2. The article in question is "The Elements of Sport," reprinted in *Philosophic Inquiry in Sport*, Edited by William J. Morgan and Klaus V. Meier, Champaign, IL: Human Kinetics, 1988.

Questions for Consideration

1. Has Suits adequately shown by his distinction between performances and rule-governed competitions that not all sports are games?
2. Suits also argues that there is really no coherent notion of "perfection" in practiced sports as there is in performative sports. Do you agree?
3. Why does Suits distinguish between "autotelic" and "instrumental" activities at the end of the reading?
4. Given the available information, fill in each section of Suits's Venn diagram (p. 35) as completely as possible.

4   Triad Trickery: Playing with Sports and Games

Klaus V. Meier
University of Western Ontario

As the title suggests, Klaus V. Meier builds on the work of Bernard Suits, whose views on the nature of sport and its relationship to play and games he regards as seminal. Meier takes on Suits's notion of "game" (specifically its requirement that less efficient means are introduced to bring about some end) with one proviso: that the outcome itself involves a display of skill on behalf of participants. He also agrees with Suits in that not all games are types of play. However, the overall adequacy of Suits's position, summarized as follows, is taken to task.

1. *Some sports are play.*
2. *Some games are play.*
3. *Some sports are games.*
4. *Some sports are not play and some sports are not games.*
5. *Some games are not play and some games are not sports.*
6. *Some sports are not games and some sports are not play.*

Specifically, Meier finds fault with Suits's notion (and a revised one it is) that not all sports are games (i.e., some sports are not games). The reading as a whole is an attempt to show, given Suits's own notion of game, that all sports are indeed games. Additionally, Meier introduces another definition of play, couched in terms of what play is instead of what it is not. In the final section, Meier lists three reasons for taking up the project of defining sport, play, and game.

Reprinted by permission from Klaus V. Meier, "Triad Trickery: Playing with Sport and Games," *Journal of the Philosophy of Sport* XV (1988): 11–30.

At the turn of this century, Graves (2: p. 6) observed that "there are few words in the English language which have such a multiplicity of divergent meanings as the word sport." Almost 100 years later the assertion is most certainly still relevant; that is, contemporary usage of the term demonstrates extensive variability and diversity of both applicability and utilization. Indeed, the specified problem extends beyond "sport" to reflect similar circumstances also encompassing the terms "games" and "play."

Further, even a rudimentary, and certainly a detailed, scrutiny of the literature developed within the last two or three decades in the field of the philosophy of sport and play demonstrates rather clearly that the problems of definition and classification are some of the most basic, contentious, and extensive issues to be found in the entire area. Indeed, it is possible to identify, with only moderate diligence, more than 80 North American, European, and Japanese published articles or chapters that dedicate themselves predominantly or exclusively to this specific task.[1]

The importance of this type of inquiry is readily apparent. To analyze, to clarify, and to understand the diverse nature and structures of games, sport, and play, as well as their significance for an individual or functions within various societies—and to develop substantiated philosophical theories concerned with the interrelationships present among these three forms of human activity—it is necessary, as a prerequisite, to define vigorously and to limit operationally the appropriate range of terminological applicability. Such efforts not only provide illumination but also facilitate legitimate discourse and, thereby, further pertinent philosophical research.

Despite the importance of the problem, however, consensus is conspicuous by its absence and the putative results may be generally characterized as inadequate. Be that as it may, the philosophical labors of Bernard Suits certainly may not be so labeled. In fact, Suits has contributed a remarkably long, successful, and seminal body of writings concerned with pertinent definitional matters. Indeed, his current "Tricky Triad" (21) paper is only the latest effort in, and in one sense perhaps the culmination of, four decades of rigorous reflection about one or more of the relevant three concepts, going back to his own graduate thesis work at the University of Chicago (14). Undoubtedly, his most profound extended work, originally published in 1978 and now generally recognized as one of the most substantive monographs in the field, is *The Grasshopper: Games, Life, and Utopia* (16). In this work, Suits carefully defends a definition of games and game playing from a plethora of possible objections. His current work builds upon that strong foundation.[2]

I

I wish to commence my philosophical critique of Suits' latest position, as well as several components of his previously published writings, by registering, once again, my agreement with his definitions of "game" and "game playing," which I find to be both acceptable and eminently productive. It will surely be remembered that Suits (16: p. 34) provides the following basic description: "to play a game is to engage in an activity directed towards bringing about a specific state of affairs, using only means permitted by rules, where the rules prohibit more efficient in favour of less efficient means, and where such rules are accepted just because they make possible such activity."

The most salient feature of the previous definition, of course, is the deliberate introduction

of less efficient, or more limited means, for the accomplishment of a specified task or the attainment of a goal. In this manner, a game may be distinguished readily from a nongame or "technical" activity. Indeed, "in anything but a game the gratuitous introduction of unnecessary obstacles to the achievement of an end is regarded as a decidedly irrational thing to do, whereas in games it appears to be an absolutely essential thing to do" (17: p. 42).

As previously mentioned, I find this definition to be most acceptable. Since Suits' (15) first formulation, and subsequent refinements and adumbrations (17), several commentators have challenged his positions (e.g., see 1; 5; 13). In my opinion, Suits' (18) own response is sufficient to neutralize most if not all of the pertinent criticisms to be found in these sources. In addition, Morgan's (10) recent thoughtful and detailed reconsideration of a formalistic account of games provides additional, very substantive support. As a consequence, Suits' definition of a game is herein employed as a philosophically defendable starting point.

II

With this important foundation in hand, attention may now be directed to the other two members of the triad, namely, "sport" and "play." I would like to begin with the former. Whereas the concept of "game" now poses no remaining substantial problems of definition, that of "sport," as will become evident shortly, presents more serious difficulties. Prior to an extended critical discussion of Suits' thoughts on this matter, which comprises Section III of this paper, I wish to present a brief contextual note.

The extant philosophy of sport literature presents a manifold and diffuse range of specific activities, descriptions, and purposes claimed to be representative of sport. In addition, a multitude of individual characteristics and factors are often deemed to be essential components of the concept by various writers. A representative, but by no means exhaustive, delineation of selected postulated aspects forwarded as necessary features of sport includes the following: (a) it involves challenge, competition, and conflict; (b) its resolution is dependent upon the adroit utilization of strategy and tactics; (c) rules govern its structure by means of spatial, temporal, and additional restrictions; (d) it is free, unnecessary, and "unreal"; (e) it may be serious or trivial; (f) it entails physical exertion, prowess, or "locatedness," all aimed at the manifestation of physical excellence; (g) participant motives are important to its essence, that is, it is pursued for extrinsic, instrumental reasons or, conversely, solely for intrinsic rewards; (h) it inevitably possesses social as well as moral dimensions; (i) it demands more than one person or, alternatively, it may be performed in solitude; (j) it involves ranking, stratification, organization, and other trappings of institutionalization; and finally (k) it is identical with games or play, it possesses only some of the essential attributes of both, or it is to be located at one end of a "play-game-sport" continuum.

Most assuredly, the postulated attributes and depictions in the previous listing demonstrate the numerous difficulties with which the pertinent philosophy literature is fraught, namely, bland assumptions, spurious distinctions, unsupported generalizations, limited applications and, finally, simple contradictions and logical errors. Despite this regrettable state of affairs, and the continuing presence of diverse if not antinomical views, I wish to contend herein that the task of successfully presenting adequate definitions of sport is by no means precluded. In other words, I think that it is indeed possible to locate the precise boundaries of this activity.

In contrast to the plethora of items previously listed, I wish to claim that all sports possess the same four essential characteristics of games previously delineated and, in addition, one significant, distinguishing feature, namely, sport requires the demonstration of physical skill and, as a consequence, the outcome is dependent, to a

certain degree at least, upon the physical prowess exhibited by the participants. Therefore, whereas physical actions or particular motor movements are insignificant to the resolution of many games, the explicit and varied manifestation of these components is essential to the performance of sport ventures. That is, while the terms and manner of any physical movements conducted in some games are incidental to the position or state moved from or to (12: p. 13), this is certainly not the case in sport. For example, in chess, bridge, and numerous other games, manual dexterity or physical skill has no influence whatsoever on the outcome. Indeed, these games can be played without *any* pertinent motor movements demanded of the participants. Assistants or even machines can move the pieces or display the cards; verbal instructions or commands may suffice and, in fact, chess can be played by mail.

At this point, a qualifying note must be introduced. Although it may be granted readily that increased proficiency of execution is an important differential variable, usually culminating in greater levels of performance and success in the sport occurrence, this does not warrant the conclusion that significant or even moderate skill must be demonstrated by all or even any other participants in a particular sport contest. That is, the sport of racquetball remains a sport even if the participants are novices limited to one hour's previous experience or if they are very unevenly matched against highly skilled opposition. All that may be asserted legitimately is that the required skills demanded of players at an elite level are different from those required for participation at a lower level. Consequently, I wish to assert that the *degree* of physical skill exhibited in a sport is simply *not* a defining characteristic or an essential component of the concept of sport.

III

What is Suits' position on all of this? Unfortunately, despite the auspicious achievement attained in his delineation of the concept of game, when he turns his attention to sport, problems arise rather quickly. For example, in a paper originally published in 1973, Suits (17: p. 43) asserts, "I believe that sports are essentially games. What I mean by this is that the difference between sports and other games is much smaller than the difference between humans and other vertebrates." His employment of the phrase "sports and other games" certainly implies at least some form of substantial identity between the two concepts. This is confirmed only one page later when he states that "all sports appear to be games of skill rather than games of chance" (17: p. 44).[3] However, Suits (17: p. 43) also contends, curiously, that "sport is not a species within the genus *game*. The distinguishing characteristics of sport are more peripheral, more arbitrary, and more contingent than are the differences required to define a species."

The aforementioned minor confusion notwithstanding, it is apparent that, at this stage at least, Suits did in fact wish to support the contention that all sports were forms of games. This may readily be seen to be the case in two later recantations, which by the very act of negation tend to affirm the opinion expressed here. First, in a paper published eight years after his "Elements of Sport" article, Suits (18: p. 61) asserts. "I here repudiate the view I once expressed—though not in *The Grasshopper*—that all sports are simply athletic *games* institutionalized in certain ways." Second, of course, in the current article under discussion, he presents a similar claim: "In an article of mine recently reprinted in an anthology on the philosophy of sport, I maintained that sports of the kind we are now considering [that is, the kinds of activities exemplified in the Olympic Games] *were* the same as athletic games. Well, I was wrong" (21: p. 2).[4]

It is clear that in both of the previously mentioned instances Suits recants the position that he expressed earlier concerning sport as a species of game. However, since it is my intention to repudiate his repudiation, and to contend that his earlier position—albeit abbreviated in a very sig-

nificant manner yet to be specified—is stronger than his current position, it is now necessary for me to scrutinize his former stance, to salvage at least one important characteristic therefrom, and to discard the rest.

Suits presents his earlier reflections on the nature of sport in the following manner:

> I would like to submit for consideration four requirements which, if they are met by any given game, are sufficient to denominate that game a sport. They are: (1) that the game be a game of skill, (2) that the skill be physical, (3) that the game have a wide following, and (4) that the following achieve a certain level of stability. . . . the features are more or less arbitrary, since they are simply facts about sport. (17: p. 43)

I can accept now, as I did for that matter in a paper originally presented in 1978 (6), the first two postulated additional requirements for a game also to be correctly labeled a "sport." It seems to me, however, that economy permits us to collapse the two into one more compact rendition, namely, that the outcome of the game is influenced by, and dependent upon, the demonstration of physical skills, ability, or prowess. This statement still, immediately and correctly, eliminates such activities as chess or bridge from consideration for inclusion.

The third and fourth characteristics, however, are far more problematic; in fact, I wish to argue that they are simply erroneous claims.[5] If taken together, these two components, as Suits (18: p. 61) admits in a passage quoted earlier, mandate that sports be viewed simply as institutionalized games. In forwarding such a claim, of course, Suits is certainly not alone. Despite substantial differences concerning numerous other characteristics, the literature readily attests that many philosophers, and for that matter sociologists and historians, consider sport to be, of necessity, an institutionalized activity. This condition refers to the establishment of norms and codified rules, as well as to the development of formal associations and specific administrative bodies that impose external organizational and regulatory patterns and programs upon previously more informally controlled sports activities. Although it may be readily acknowledged that the current modes of conduct of *certain* sports reflect these components—indeed there are numerous philosophical critiques to be found that stridently criticize the perceived extensive formalization, regulation, rationalization, professionalization, and bureaucratization of many contemporary sports—there is considerable difficulty in claiming that institutionalization is an integral component of the essence of all sport in general.

Is *all* sport institutionalized? I think not. Much has been made—erroneously I wish to contend—of the customs, traditions, regulatory features, external perspectives, and other trappings that surround many sports. However, these components appear to be modes of conducting and regulating the sport occurrence which add color and significance, and enhance particular sports. That is, in a very basic sense these are *peripheral* concerns, ancillary or accidental to the basic nature of the enterprise, not part of the essential constitutive form of sport, and certainly not part of its ontological status. It appears to be more sensible to view sport as extending along an organizational continuum from the relative absence of such aspects to that of extreme regulation.

Another somewhat similar problem concerned with the question of sport as an institutionalized activity arises when matters of degree and duration are considered. Precise identification of *the points of temporal and quantitative sufficiency* becomes a difficult undertaking at best; that is, how long must an activity or a game exist before it becomes eligible for the category of sport, and how many participants, groups, organizing bodies, and nations must engage in the activity? The adjudication of these and similar queries appears largely to be both arbitrary and unsatisfactory.

Perhaps comments on one study available in the philosophical literature will support these admittedly serious allegations. Osterhoudt (12: p. 13), in accepting the alleged necessity of institutional characteristics, lists some physical activities which he asserts fail to meet the full requirements of sport. He claims that such activities as hurling, jai alai, and hula-hooping, among similar others, have an insufficiently wide basis in our historicocultural experience to be included in this category. They have not affected the human circumstances in sufficient measure to have gained anything more than a geographically limited or a historically located practice.

Difficulties arise from this assertion. Osterhoudt suggests that perhaps the best criterion available for determining whether an activity has a sufficiently wide basis is the standard used by the International Olympic Committee (IOC) in its deliberations concerning the inclusion of specific sports in the quadrennial Olympic Games program. However, utilizing such factors as the number of national governing organizations in existence for a particular activity seems to be rather capricious. Also, the IOC must use a different criterion to determine the activities to be placed on the discussion table for consideration for inclusion in the Games. In addition, it would appear to follow that all those activities not included in the Olympics would not be considered sports, an assertion which is, at the very least, highly contentious. For example, any suggestion that rugby, curling, cricket, mountain climbing, and Grand Prix automobile racing are not sports because of failure to meet standards of sufficient measure for inclusion in the Olympics would be greeted with significant debate and incredulity in not a few quarters. Finally, at times, the country hosting the Olympics is permitted to include an activity that is not a component of the permanent program; does this mean that the chosen enterprise is not a sport because it fails to demonstrate sufficient numerical allegiances elsewhere?

At this point it will be instructive to examine the two examples forwarded by Suits to pursue a similar point. He also dismisses the activity of hula-hooping by asserting that, "it would be proper to call Hula-Hoop a craze rather than a sport. . . . Even if Hula-Hoop had lasted for fifty years, it would still be a craze, only a very tiresome craze" (17: p. 45).

I find this comment to be curious indeed, since most dictionary definitions of the term "craze" stipulate that it is "a short-lived popular fashion, a rage, or a limited fad." Thus a craze, by definition, simply cannot extend for half a century. In fact, if hula-hooping had lasted 50 years, would not this longevity in and of itself demonstrate a certain level of stability, if not a wide following? Indeed, very few recreational or sport activities have lasted this long without achieving a modicum of codification or stabilization, if not institutionalization.

The second example Suits (17: p. 45) utilizes in an attempt to buttress his case is the curious enterprise that he terms "Sweat Bead." This activity, although fascinating for Suits, and for that matter the reader, rightly should be dismissed from consideration as a sport. This exclusion, however, is not the direct consequence, as Suits suggests, of the fact that it is a highly idiosyncratic venture lacking a wide following; rather, it should in all probability not even have been forwarded as an appropriate exemplar in the first place, since it is difficult to ascertain, at least from the very sketchy description he provides, what physical skill, if any, is directly involved in sufficiently angering the high-ranking university official to produce the desired results during the pertinent meeting.

Further, to turn in a slightly different direction, it is perhaps worthy of note to state that even if it is accepted that many sports have metamorphized from a folk diversion, or even an elite recreational activity, to a highly visible and institutionalized component of the present social world, this state of affairs is simply a comment on the changing social conditions surrounding

some forms of the enterprise; it is not a reflection of the essential nature of all sport in general, or support for institutionalization as a necessary characteristic. Unfortunately, spatial limitations preclude further discussion of this point and other aspects directly related to it.[6]

Be that as it may, in conclusion, it appears to be legitimate to contend that although many forms of contemporary sport have indeed become highly institutionalized, and further that institutionalized sport is very much a proper and productive area of concern for philosophers and sociologists interested in investigating the social structure, function, and processes of sport, it has not been satisfactorily demonstrated that institutionalization—even to the relatively minor extent indicated by Suits' last two postulated characteristics—is a necessary component of the essence of sport. Thus, I wish to assert that any recourse to institutionalization, as an integral, necessary component of the essential nature of sport, is arbitrary, as well as erroneous and counterproductive; consequently, it should be actively rejected.

IV

Some of the hesitancies that Suits expressed in several of the earlier quoted works are given full voice in the opening paragraphs of the current paper when he states, "I have changed my views in some important ways about play and sport (though not about games)." In the previous section, I have attempted to demonstrate that a change, or at least a partial deletion, is indeed warranted in the early conception of sport that Suits presented. It is now necessary to address specifically the new conceptions of sport and play that are forwarded in "Tricky Triad."

It will be remembered that Suits himself characterizes the first half of his paper as mere prelude. In fact, he labels most of the work undertaken in this portion of the article as an "abortive effort," disavows the tidy resolutions presented therein, and frankly admits that the conclusion arrived at there simply "isn't true" (21: pp. 5, 4). Although I do not intend to discuss most of the contentions or distinctions presented in this preliminary section that Suits eventually discards, it will of course be necessary to analyze the major point championed there and amplified in the second half of the article. I will be forced to conclude that it simply isn't true either.

Utilizing the kinds of activities to be found in the Olympic Games as a guide, Suits (21: p. 2) claims there are two distinct types of sports, namely, "competitive athletic events" and "athletic games." Later he calls these two types of activities "judged performances" and "refereed games." The two are not the same; the latter are asserted to be not performances per se, but rather "a rule-governed interplay of participants" which require "not judges but law-enforcement officers, that is, referees" (21: p. 2).

One of the postulated differences that Suits (21: p. 3) forwards to support his claim is that in football games, for example, "victory is not determined by the artistry" of the called plays or ensuing moves, but rather by "their effectiveness in winning games."[7] In contrast, such enterprises as "diving and gymnastics competitions are no more games than are judged competitive events, such as beauty contests and pie-baking competitions." This is a claim that I am unable to support.

For Suits (21: p. 5) the crux of the distinction is that games are essentially refereed events in which "referees see to it that the rules are followed, and impose penalties when they are not." On the other hand, Suits claims that performances are not rule-governed in that way at all:

There are rules, to be sure, but not only are they *not* the crux of performances, they usually take the form of applying to the participants *outside* the arena of contention. I dislike mentioning steroids at this time, but the rule against their use would be the kind of rule typically at issue in the case of performances,

what might be called perhaps a pre-event rule. But once a performance is under way, there are no rules, or scarcely any, that need enforcing. (21: p. 5)

I find much about the previous statement to be contentious, if not incorrect. However, there are certain aspects with which I am able to concur. The distinction alluded to in the previous quotation is between "constitutive rules" and those that Suits terms "pre-event rules." I wish to address the latter category first. Elsewhere (7: p. 70), I have labeled edicts of this form "auxiliary rules"; these rules specify and regulate "eligibility, admission, training, and other pre-contest requirements." I offer three examples of this particular type of regulation:

first, rules pertaining to the participants' safety or exposure to physical stress, such as "all football players must wear a helmet with a fixed face guard" or "no player may pitch more than three innings in any one age-group baseball game"; second, specific empirical restrictions placed upon participants concerning such attributes as age, sex, or weight; and third, an entire grouping of arbitrary regulations selectively imposed for a variety of social or political reasons. (7: p. 71)

The third category includes such things as the deliberate exclusion of professional athletes, representatives of the Republic of South Africa, or a limitation of no more than three athletes from any one country in a particular sports meet.[8]

Thus, it may be seen that I concur with a part of Suits' assertion in that I have claimed that a rule of this type "is of a different color or nature entirely than constitutive rules and, as such, *has nothing whatsoever to do with the essence of sport*" (7: pp. 70–71). However, I most assuredly *do not concur* with Suits' assertion that these are the only types of rules at work in performative sports, or that "once a performance is under way, there are no rules, or scarcely any, that need enforcing" (21: p. 5).

Let us presume, for the sake of argument, that Suits' assertion is correct—it is *not*, but I shall return to this aspect shortly—and that once a performance is under way, there are indeed no rules, or scarcely any, that need enforcing. Let us even be generous enough to ignore the waffling qualification contained in the phrase "or scarcely any," and agree that a particular event, once started, contains no restraining rules. Would this, on Suits' own definition of a game, disqualify it from being considered a game? No, it would not.

I would like to utilize one of Suits' own noteworthy examples to illustrate the contention forwarded here. Long time devotees of Suits' writings—of which I am most assuredly one—will have little difficulty recalling the story of Ivan and Abdul, so wittily presented in *The Grasshopper* (16). It will be remembered that, after having explored all other opportunities for diversion during their retirement in the backwater capital of Rien-à-faire, the two generals agree to participate in a game without rules, namely, a no-holds-barred fight-to-the-finish. Suits (16: p. 66), in the persona of the Grasshopper, is "quite willing to accept that their fight to the finish *is* a game." Why? Because Ivan did not attempt to destroy Abdul immediately upon committing himself to a fight to the finish with him; that is, he voluntarily accepted the restriction (or rule) that forbade him from making a move in the game before a certain agreed-upon time of commencement. Suits (16: p. 64) acknowledges that a time restriction or limit "is in fact the same as a rule." Thus, the existence of this one rule, obviously one that is applicable to the performance itself, since it specifies the beginning of the event, is sufficient to classify the activity as a competitive *game* even if there are no additional rules in place during the contest or performance itself.

As a result of these deliberations, it would appear as if competitive gymnastics and diving performances—since they are guided, minimally, by rules that dictate such restrictive items as place of competition, starting time, internal diving rotations, each diver's permitted time interval before attempting the next specified dive, and so forth—surely satisfy at least the minimal qualifications for being accurately considered as competitive games. Although this state of affairs is sufficient in and of itself to support the claim being forwarded, there is more to be said.

V

Attention must now be directed toward the specific acts performed within the confines of the competition itself. It will be remembered that Suits asserts that during the types of competitive performances he addresses, there are no rules, or scarcely any, that need enforcing. Suits raises and responds to a potential argument against his own position in the following manner:

> Now, it may be objected which, contrary to what I have said, there clearly *are* rules that must be followed while actually engaged in performative sports. For example, the gymnast must not falter or stumble after dismounting from the parallel bars. It is perfectly permissible to call such a requirement a rule, but is quite clear, I should think, that such "rules" are entirely different from, say, the offside rules in football and hockey. The offside rule is what has to come to be called, by me and by many others, a constitutive rule, while the standard of a clean dismount from the parallel bars is a rule of skill, or a tactical rule, or a rule of practice. (21: pp. 5–6)

This supposed contrast leads Suits (21: p. 6) to contend that "the rules to which the judges of performances address themselves are, I submit, rules of skill rather than constitutive rules."

In my opinion, there are several intriguing aspects to be found in the previous examples forwarded by Suits that warrant at least some comment. First, it is not at all clear that the offside rule in football, for example, is a constitutive rule. In fact, I have suggested elsewhere (7: p. 69) that rules such as these, which specify the penalties to be applied when particular constitutive rules have been violated, may be more appropriately called "regulative." These rules presuppose and regulate antecedently or independently existing forms of behavior, as specified by a set of constitutive rules. However, an absolute dichotomy is by no means championed here; rather, it is suggested that regulative rules are extensions of constitutive rules.

The previous point is of some importance when it is recognized that if the offside rule were solely a constitutive rule, then breaking it would qualify, on Suits' (17: p. 41) conception of a constitutive rule, as an instance of cheating, that is, as a failure to play the game at all, such as being discovered hand-carrying a golf ball across the green and dropping it into the cup. However, the defensive tackle who inadvertently lines up offside is still playing the game, but in a manner that requires, if detected of course, a 5-yard penalty to be assessed against his team.

To return to Suits' "performative sports," it is necessary to note that the gymnast who perceptibly falters or even stumbles after dismounting from the parallel bars is not simply breaking a desirable rule of skill, strategy, or practice. Rather, her failure to "stick the landing," if it is noticed by the judges who are charged with the task of watching for just occurrences, inevitably results in a specific deduction of the points to be awarded. Indeed, in many of the performance sports (e.g., gymnastics, figure skating, diving) a specific predetermined point or percentage thereof is mandatorily deducted from the optimal score for each specified failure. Thus it may be contended that athletic performances have event rules of a regulative variety. This suggests, in turn, given their status as extensions of—and Suits (17: p. 41) also clearly considers them to be such—or perhaps even as subsets of constitutive rules, the presence of other underlying constitutive rules that specifically delineate appropriate and permitted actions.

To summarize partially at this point, it seems as if both the presence of pertinent rules prior to, and specifying the actual point of commencement of, athletic performances, as well as the demands imposed by the regulative if not indeed the constitutive rules necessarily applicable during a performance, cast doubt upon Suits' claim that such activities are not games. Be that as it may, there is a far stronger *third claim* to be made which, in my opinion, undermines his contention entirely, namely, that gymnastics and diving competitions seem to fulfill all of the essential characteristics originally posited by Suits to be integral to the nature of a game. The next section addresses this point in considerable detail.

VI

It will be remembered that Suits (16: p. 41; 21: p. 6) characterizes playing a game as "the voluntary attempt to overcome unnecessary obstacles"; in other words, games erect "barriers to be overcome." The essential component of Suits' definition, of course, is that in games "the rules prohibit use of more efficient in favor of less efficient means" to achieve the specified goal. It seems to me that both gymnastics and diving competitions readily fulfill these requirements.

To begin with, the balance beam competition in gymnastics, for example, it may be asserted that the specified goal of the activity is to perform an interrelated series of stipulated compulsory moves a certain specific number of times, as smoothly and rhythmically as possible. It is readily apparent that achieving the goal of demonstrating the required physical actions would be made considerably easier if the gymnast were to be permitted to perform on the floor, or even if the beam itself were anchored directly to the floor. At the very least, the fear of sustaining potential injury through falling would be greatly minimized, thus facilitating the athlete's greater concentration solely on the execution of the prescribed actions. However, the essential defining characteristic of this particular competitive event is that the requisite actions must be performed while balancing on a wooden beam merely four inches wide, elevated a specific, mandatory vertical distance from the floor mats. Surely this restriction meets the requirements of being an unnecessary obstacle or a deliberate introduction of inefficient means. Further, all other apparatus events, such as the flying rings, the high bar, the uneven bars, also seem to demonstrate this same important limiting characteristic. In fact, even gymnastics events that utilize no piece of apparatus, such as the floor exercise event, have restraints incorporated; the exercise routine must contain a certain mandatory series of maneuvers performed within a rigidly prescribed floor area as well as time limitations and, in the women's events at least, must be coordinated to music.[9]

The previous contention requires further elaboration. The precise limitation of permissible floor space, for example, certainly makes it more difficult for the athlete to generate sufficient momentum or propulsion (that is, to build up enough "steam") to execute successfully an extended and intricate series of flips or somersaults. In addition, stepping beyond the event boundary line elicits mandatory score reductions, which certainly handicaps the pursuit of high scores and may even result, if repeated a sufficient number of times, in disqualification. It is interesting to note that stepping out of bounds while in possession of the ball in such readily acknowledged games as basketball, for example, produces somewhat similar results; that is, the requisite penalty of forfeiture of the ball to the opposing team also handicaps the offending team's efforts to obtain the highest possible score in the contest.

To turn our attention now to the sport of competitive diving, let us presuppose, for the sake of the current argument at least, that Suits (21: p. 4) is correct in contending that a major goal of the activity is to enter the water "in as

nearly a vertical posture as possible" and with as little splash as possible. Be that as it may, there is more to diving competitions than this; otherwise jumping in, or even stepping, from the side of the pool would qualify as admissible acts. This of course is not the case. Instead, unnecessary difficulties or obstacles are deliberately added. For example, the rules of competitive diving dictate that the diver must perform certain prescribed acts from a 1- or 3-meter diving board, a 5-, 7-, or 10-meter platform, and so forth. Thus, the object is not just to enter the water in a vertical position but to do so only after having climbed up stairs to the specified height, walked or run out to the end of the apparatus, and then voluntarily departed to let gravity partially do its work.

However, this is not the only restriction in place. The diver must perform an elongated series of compulsory dives: further, these dives must be distributed over the various mandatory position categories of inward, layout, tuck, and pike. Finally, the number of body twists and/or somersaults required, as well as whether the entry shall be feet or head first, are also clearly specified and regulated (for example, a front dive, tuck position, with 2-1/2 somersaults). These are constitutive rules that define, and thereby make possible, the competition; they are not pre-event rules. If the internal requirements delineating each separate dive are not met (i.e., the diver executes an insufficient number of twists or utilizes the pike rather than the previously declared tuck position), the head diving referee may declare a "no dive," which means that the dive counts as an attempt for that compulsory group but no points are awarded to the diver.

In addition, it is rather apparent that the execution of the specific dive described in the previous paragraph could be facilitated greatly by moving from the 1- or even the 3-meter board to the 5- or 7-meter platform, thereby providing substantial additional time for the successful completion of the requisite intricate moves before hitting the water. Yet the diver accepts the limitation in height above the water as just one of the "barriers to overcome" (21: p. 6). Surely it may be seen that these difficulties or performance obstacles are deliberate artificial constraints, imposed predominantly to increase the inefficiency of attaining the desired prelusory goal. They are, in sum, constitutive rules that are accepted by all concerned "just so the act made possible by such acceptance can occur"; in other words, they are clear examples of what Suits (17: p. 43) terms the "lusory attitude."

Thus it may be asserted that in the sport of diving—even if it is acknowledged, for example, that one of the purposes of the activity is to approximate and display performance ideals, as determined and evaluated by the judgments of the panel of expert judges—this experience is still to be found within, and regulated by, the specific confines of a game. In other words, there is still a deliberate choice of inefficient means to accomplish the task at hand.

To provide support for his postulated distinction between game rules and performance ideals, Suits forwards an example drawn from the sport of boxing. I do not find it to be convincing, however. He contends that boxing judges do not make their assessments against "an ideal of boxing, if there is such a thing, but of one competitor directly against another" (21: p. 6). But surely this also occurs in diving and gymnastics competitions. This state of affairs may be readily ascertained, for example, from the importance of the draw in both of these activities. Thus, judges readily admit that they "leave room" in their scoring to be able to grade the later performers higher in comparison to the earlier performers. That is, the standard of comparison is not only a supposed ideal but also an evaluation that the later competitor, perhaps in spite of a very slight stumble during an apparatus dismount, performed better, in sum, than an earlier competitor who had previously been awarded a score of 9.90 or 9.95 (witness the "imperfect 10s" awarded to athletes late in the gym-

nastics rotation in the 1988 Seoul Olympic Games despite perceptible performance breaks).

At this point, I wish to offer one final observation concerning the major issue under consideration in this section. It may be helpful to state that elsewhere Suits (22: in press) asserts that "it is perfectly obvious that the 100-yard dash, for example, is a game"; in fact, he goes so far as to claim that this activity is a "virtual paradigm of a game." It seems to me that if an event of this type, which is obviously exceedingly simple in terms of applicable performance rules, is to be termed a game, it is very difficult to ascertain how either gymnastics or diving competitions, each comprised of a complex series of imposed rules specifically limiting the means acceptable to attain the required goals, could fail to meet at least the minimal entrance requirements for inclusion in the category of games. The arbitrary restrictions imposed in running straight down a cinder track surely are far less than those exemplified in either gymnastics or diving competitions.

Finally, please note that simply because gymnastics and diving may not generally be called games, or even that they may not at first glance appear to be eligible for inclusion in this genre, is irrelevant by Suits' own admission:

> I submit that when some activity or enterprise not initially included in the hard core group (e.g., because it is not called a game) is seen, upon examination, to conform to the group's definition, then there exists a good *prima facie* reason for granting that the activity or enterprise *is* a game, despite the fact that it is not called one. (22: in press)

In conclusion, I do not think that the arguments Suits presents are either sufficiently grounded or persuasive to establish clearly the proposed distinction between sports that are games and those that are performances. Consequently, I cannot support the distinction; rather, I wish to claim that both forms of activity do indeed satisfy Suits' own definition of games.

VII

In response to some criticism contained within a review of *The Grasshopper* written by Frank McBride, Suits (18: p. 61) offered the following conclusion: "If my definition is accepted, more sports are games than McBride would have thought, and that in general there are more games in heaven and earth than McBride has dreamt of in his philosophy." It would appear justified at this point to extend this criticism to Suits himself, and to assert that, if the previously presented argument is persuasive, there are far

more sports that are games than are dreamt of in Suits' philosophy.

VIII

In the first sentence of the penultimate section of his paper, Suits (21: p. 7) forwards the "bald assertion" that not all sports are play. I have no quarrel with this statement; unfortunately, however, I disagree with much of the remainder of the section. It will be remembered that Suits displays his suggested interrelationships among the concepts of sport, game, and play by means of three overlapping circles, subdivided into seven specific sections (see Figure 4.1).

It is necessary to commence my appraisal of

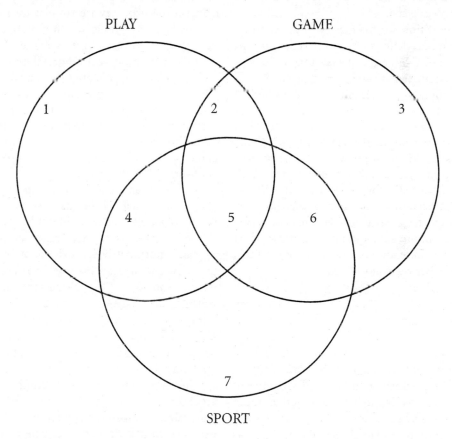

Figure 4.1 *From Suits (21: p. 7).*

this diagram by stating that although I find this specific graphic technique (i.e., the employment of Venn diagrams) to be an effective way of demonstrating the interrelationships among the three activities, I cannot agree with the particular model produced by Suits. More specifically, I find both Sections 4 and 7 to be untenable.

The crux of the matter, of course, is whether there are any sports that are not games. As I have attempted to delineate in the previous sections of this paper, I do not think Suits has demonstrated adequately that sport performances of the type he has chosen to utilize do not fulfill his own requirements for admission to the genus of "game." To reiterate a previously expressed opinion, I find portions of Suits' (17) earlier position on this matter to be more persuasive than his current revised stance.

It is now time for me to present the parameters of a model delineating the interrelationships among sport, games, and play that I think is more accurate than the one forwarded by Suits. I wish to contend that although not all games are sports, all sports are indeed games. That is, a game may also correctly be termed a sport if it possesses the additional characteristic of requiring physical skill or prowess to be demonstrated by the participants in the pursuit of its goal. Thus sport is neither an outgrowth nor an extension of game; rather, it is a game at the same time as it is a sport. Consequently, any form of postulated continuum extending from game to sport is rejected; instead, at least partial conceptual identity is hereby championed.

IX

It is now necessary to turn to the third and last component of the triad, namely "play." There is, within the pertinent philosophical literature of course, considerable debate to be found about the nature and essence of play. Often it is described in terms of what it is not; that is, play is variously perceived as being "not serious, not real, disconnected, non-productive, unneces-

sary, and so forth" (4: p. 116). Despite this situation, I wish to provide a definition based upon the orientation, demeanor, or stance of the participant. It is my opinion that play may be viewed, simply and profitably, as an autotelic activity; in other words, an activity voluntarily pursued for predominantly intrinsic reasons.

If this position is accepted,[10] it is possible to limit the focus appropriately by asserting that depending upon the prevailing circumstances and factors, in other words the context at hand, sports and games may or may not be play. Thus, for present purposes, *context* is more important than *content*. Consequently, if games or sports are pursued voluntarily and for intrinsic reasons, they are also play forms; if they are pursued involuntarily or engaged in predominantly for extrinsic rewards, they are not play forms.

It is helpful to note two things about Suits' (21: pp. 8–9) position on this matter. First, his own distinction between undertakings that are autotelic ("an event or activity valued for itself") and instrumental ("an event or activity valued not only or even primarily for itself but for some further payoff that the event or activity is expected to provide") is very similar to the differentiation I wish to make between "play" and "non-play."

Second, in an earlier paper, Suits (19: p. 19) also assumes that "*all* instances of play *are* instances of autotelic activity." In fact he regards autotelicity as a necessary, if not sufficient, condition of play. Unfortunately, space does not permit me to review and analyze this particular position at length. Nonetheless, for my current purpose— which is *not* to describe play exhaustively but rather is limited in scope to determining *when it is that games and sports are also play phenomena*—I wish to contend that autotelicity is both a necessary and sufficient trait for that aim.

Therefore, to return to the main thrust of the argument here presented, it may be seen that play and sport, for example, are not necessarily exclusive entities. Indeed, it can be maintained that "the competitive fullness of sport and the play gesture are, in a most fundamental sense, wholly compatible but not co-extensive. One can play sport without compromising elements essential to this highly polarized activity" (4: p. 113). Conversely, no trace of play whatsoever need be present in a particular sport venture. In other words, play is not, logically speaking, a necessary of sufficient condition or attribute of either sport or games; however, it may well be an element that enriches either or both endeavors.

The position forwarded here demonstrates the inadequacies of numerous assertions in the applicable literature which claim that play and sport are on opposite ends of a continuum and, thereby, have nothing at all in common. On the contrary, sports and games may be distinguished simply as play or non-play occurrences depending upon the contingencies surrounding or motivating participation. Thus, whereas National League baseball may indeed be viewed most often as a non-play activity, a sandlot game of baseball, incorporating many or even all of the same playing rules, may most definitely be a play occurrence. Despite perhaps radically different orientations in these two events, the sport of baseball is held in common. In other words, particular attitudes or stances manifested by the participants, including motives and inducements for engagement as well as the setting for the action, do not dictate whether a specific activity may legitimately be termed a sport. The

essence of sport is independent of these concerns. However, such factors most certainly determine whether or not the sport activity at hand is also a form of play. These characteristics and relationships are summarized in Figure 4.2.

Several points of information may be emphasized as a means of providing a further explanation of the preceding diagram: (a) all sports are games; (b) not all games are sports; (c) sport and games may or may not be play; (d) sports and games are play if voluntarily pursued for intrinsic rewards; (e) sports and games are non-play if involuntarily pursued or participated in for extrinsic rewards; and finally, (f) play may take forms other than sport or games.

X

How does all of this relate to the scheme outlined by Suits in Figure 4.1? First, it will be remembered that I wholeheartedly accept and adopt his definition of "game," as delineated, virtually unchanged, in many of his works; therefore we are in agreement here. Second, our conceptions of "play" are sufficiently similar—at least for the herein deliberately limited purpose of ascertaining whether particular instances of sports or games are play or non-play occurrences—not to present major difficulties. Third,

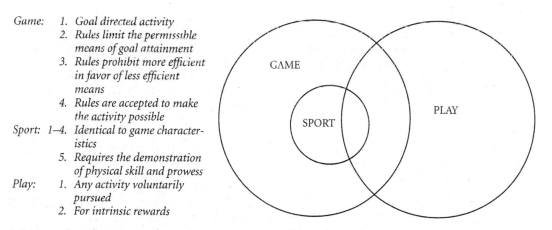

Game: 1. *Goal directed activity*
    2. *Rules limit the permissible means of goal attainment*
    3. *Rules prohibit more efficient in favor of less efficient means*
    4. *Rules are accepted to make the activity possible*

Sport: 1–4. *Identical to game characteristics*
    5. *Requires the demonstration of physical skill and prowess*

Play: 1. *Any activity voluntarily pursued*
    2. *For intrinsic rewards*

Figure 4.2 *The interrelationships among sport, game, and play.*

the concept of "sport," of course, is the source of our greatest differences. I have attempted to demonstrate that Suits' distinction between athletic performances and athletic games is not as unproblematic as he suggests. In my opinion both are, at heart, forms of games. Therefore I wish to champion the claim, in contrast to Suits, that *all sports are indeed games.* Consequently, rather than accepting Suits' depiction of overlapping games and sport circles, as presented in Figure 4.1, I find the structure delineated in Figure 4.2, in which sport is wholly incorporated within the confines of the genus of games, to be more accurate. Be that as it may, I am prepared to accept the claim that there may be two workable species of sport, namely judged and refereed performances. Nonetheless, they both are forms of games.

In summary then, it should be clear that I have herein employed several useful facets of Suits' previous efforts, built upon this strong base, argued against what I perceived to be an erroneous distinction in his current work, and produced a scheme of the interrelationships among sport, game, and play which, in my opinion at least, is more appropriate than the one forwarded by Suits in "Tricky Triad."

XI

It may now be contended that if the definitional characteristics and structure delineated in the preceding analysis are deemed to be worthy of support, the basis and operational limits have thereby been provided to guide further research in the area of the philosophy of sport, play, and games.

Some indication of the direction such analytic endeavor might profitably pursue is given in the following three examples of this scheme's potential applicability: First, it is now possible to determine the proper role of competition in various sport ventures and educational programs by ascertaining what the intended purpose and outcome of the specific contests are. Second, the

results of the inquiry described in the previous sentence contribute toward the determination of the proper place of "winning" and victory in sport, and may indeed provide a substantial defense of a major emphasis on these outcomes. Third, and finally, it is now possible to reflect more rigorously on such cultural comments and critiques, for instance, as those who lament the absence or even the so-termed "death of play" in contemporary sport. Contrary to Huizinga (3), who is perhaps most identified with formulating this particular last perspective, I see no inherent or inexorable play aspect in sport. Regrets may be appropriate, however, for the apparently continuing demise of play in the currently increasing commercialization of much of contemporary sport—as well as of many other facets of our social world, including the areas of art, literature, and architecture—but this state of affairs has nothing necessarily to do with sport and games.

Obviously there is much more to be said on many of the preceding matters that simply cannot be addressed here. However, it is clear that Suits' current work provides a major stimulus for continued reflection and analysis.[11] For this happy occurrence, all those who work in the sphere of the philosophy of sport, games, and play, once again, must be grateful.

Notes

1. It must be acknowledged at the outset that, due to their specific applicability to the task at hand, selection portions of some sections of the current paper are restatements or direct usage of materials contained in two previously published articles (6; 8). When deemed helpful, the reader will be directed to specific additional explanatory or supportive passages contained therein.

2. I am pleased to report that Suits has just recently compiled a new collection of his writings, intended to serve, in part at least, as a sequel to *The Grasshopper.* The new volume, entitled *Grasshopper Soup: Philosophical Essays on Games* (22), is expected to be published within the next year or so.

3. If we were to limit and to read this sentence very charitably to mean "of those sports which are games, they are

games of skill rather than of chance," we would move closer to a position that is not incompatible with the stance Suits later forwards in "Tricky Triad."

4. The article to which Suits here refers is, of course, once again, "The Elements of Sport" (17).

5. Much of the remainder of this particular section, admittedly, is somewhat of a digression from the main thrust of the essay. However, I think that the discussion provided therein is helpful to understand more fully such notions as the postulated transition of certain activities from "primitive" to "sophisticated," or even institutionalized status. This in turn, hopefully, will contribute some useful insight into the essential nature of sport and play.

6. For a much fuller treatment, albeit now somewhat dated, of this particular area of concern from both a philosophical and a sociological perspective, see Meier (6: pp. 85–90).

7. Here Suits appropriates for his own use a distinction more visibly, and certainly more frequently, employed in the aesthetics of sport literature. For a representative selection of papers addressing this particular issue, see Morgan and Meier's anthology (11: pp. 455–540).

8. For a further delineation of the nature and function of auxiliary rules, as well as additional pertinent examples, see Meier (7).

9. These demands and restrictions, by the way, are also elements that provide figure skating with legitimate claims to being considered a game.

10. Clearly it is not possible to present an adequate explanation and supporting structure for the definition here. However, a previously published essay entitled "An Affair of Flutes: An Appreciation of Play" (9) does provide an extended argument dedicated largely to this specific task.

11. There are of course numerous other intriguing items and claims to be found in Suits' paper beyond those treated in the body of the present text: for example, the differentiation between primitive and sophisticated play, the restructuring of the amateur versus nonamateur distinction, and the notion that the compulsion to win somehow turns a game from play to non-play. Unfortunately, spatial limitations preclude a discussion of any of these intriguing issues here.

Bibliography

1. D'Agostino, Fred. "The Ethos of Games." *Journal of the Philosophy of Sport,* VIII (1981), 7–18. Also in *Philosophic Inquiry in Sport.* Edited by William J. Morgan and Klaus V. Meier. Champaign, IL: Human Kinetics, 1988.

2. Graves, H. "A Philosophy of Sport," *Contemporary Review,* 77 (Dec. 1900), 877–893.

3. Huizinga, Johan. *Homo Ludens.* London: Routledge & Kegan Paul, 1950.

4. Kretchmar, R. Scott. "Ontological Possibilities: Sport as Play." *Philosophic Exchange,* 1 (1972), 113–122.

5. McBride, Frank. "A Critique of Mr. Suits' Definition of Game Playing." *Journal of the Philosophy of Sport,* VI (1979), 59–66. Also in *Philosophic Inquiry in Sport.* Edited by William J. Morgan and Klaus V. Meier. Champaign, IL: Human Kinetics, 1988.

6. Meier, Klaus V. "On the Inadequacies of Sociological Definitions of Sport." *International Review of Sport Sociology,* 16(2), (1981), 79–102.

7. Meier, Klaus V. "Restless Sport." *Journal of the Philosophy of Sport,* XII (1985), 64–77.

8. Meier, Klaus V. "Games, Sport, Play." *Proceedings of the PSSS Conference on The Philosophy of Sport Held in Tsukuba, 1986.* Tsukuba, Japan: University of Tsukuba, 1987, 83–89.

9. Meier, Klaus V. "An Affair of Flutes: An Appreciation of Play," *Journal of the Philosophy of Sport,* VII (1980), 24–45. Also in *Philosophic Inquiry in Sport.* Edited by William J. Morgan and Klaus V. Meier. Champaign IL: Human Kinetics, 1988.

10. Morgan, William J. "The Logical Incompatibility Thesis and Rules: A Reconsideration of Formalism as an Account of Games." *Journal of the Philosophy of Sport,* XIV (1987), 1–20.

11. Morgan, William J., and Meier, Klaus V. (Editors). *Philosophic Inquiry in Sport.* Champaign, IL: Human Kinetics, 1988.

12. Osterhoudt, Robert G. "The Term Sport—Some Thoughts on a Proper Name." *International Journal of Physical Education,* 14 (Summer 1977), 11–16.

13. Paddick, Robert J. "Review of Bernard Suits' *The Grasshopper: Games, Life, and Utopia.*" *Journal of the Philosophy of Sport,* VI (1979), 73–78.

14. Suits, Bernard. "Play and Value in the Philosophies of Aristotle, Schiller, and Kierkegaard." Unpublished master's thesis, University of Chicago, 1950.

15. Suits, Bernard. "What Is a Game?" *Philosophy of Science,* 34 (1967), 148–156.

16. Suits, Bernard. *The Grasshopper: Games, Life, and Utopia.* Toronto: University of Toronto Press, 1978.

17. Suits, Bernard. "The Elements of Sport," *Philosophic Inquiry in Sport.* Edited by William J. Morgan and Klaus V. Meier. Champaign, IL: Human Kinetics, 1988.

18. Suits, Bernard. "On McBride on the Definition of Games." *Philosophic Inquiry in Sport.* Edited by William J. Morgan and Klaus V. Meier. Champaign, IL: Human Kinetics, 1988.

19. Suits, Bernard. "Words on Play." *Journal of the Philosophy of Sport,* IV (1977), 117–131. Also in *Philosophic Inquiry in Sport.* Edited by William J. Morgan and Klaus V. Meier. Champaign, IL: Human Kinetics, 1988.

20. Suits, Bernard. "Defending Defining Games." Paper presented at the World Congress of Philosophy conducted in Brighton, England, August 25, 1988. Forthcoming in *Grasshopper Soup.*

21. Suits, Bernard. "Tricky Triad: Games, Play, and Sport." *Journal of the Philosophy of Sport,* XV (1988), 1–9.

22. Suits, Bernard. *Grasshopper Soup: Philosophical Essays on Games.* (in press). University of Toronto.

Questions for Consideration

1. Has Meier effectively debased Suits's view that some sports are not games?

2. Do you find Meier's view of "play" persuasive?

3. Comment on Meier's own reasons for attempting to delineate "sport" from "game" and "play" in section 11 of his paper. Do you agree with his motivation?

5   A Matter of Life and Death: Some Thoughts on the Language of Sport

Jeffrey O. Segrave
Skidmore College

In this reading, Jeffrey Segrave explores the rich and varied language used to describe sporting practices—"sportspeak," as it is sometimes called. In particular, he looks at predominant types of metaphorical conventions: those of violence, those of sex, and those relating to machines. Violence in sport is not a sign of social degradation, but one of social sublimation. Sports allow us to purge pent-up instincts that, if left undischarged, would work toward our own destruction. Sexual metaphors, especially in the more combative sports, seem to suggest homosexual play. But in male-dominated sports, the real combat is heterosexual in nature and the sexual violence here is a violation of space and person, though in a controlled manner. Last, mechanistic metaphors abound. In spite of the de-humanization this suggests, Segrave's view is that mechanistic metaphors are a sign of our attempts to control, even tame, nature. It is an expression of our desire for immortality.

What these metaphoric conventions show is that our use of language in sport reflects a preoccupation with control both over ourselves and over the circumstances surrounding our destiny. Sport stands as a monument that testifies on behalf of our denial of the ultimate triumph of nature over human effort. It is ultimately an expression of human will.

From Jeffrey O. Segrave, *Journal of Sport and Social Issues* Vol. 21 No. 2 (May 1997) pp. 211–220, copyright © 1997 by Sage, Inc. Reprinted by permission of Sage Publications, Inc.

Numerous commentators have noted how the rhetoric of the playing field has infiltrated our national language system (e.g., Hardaway, 1976; Lipsyte, 1975; Palmatier & Ray, 1989). Sociologists in particular have paid considerable attention to the social and political salience of the sports metaphor (Balbus, 1975; Jansen & Sabo, 1994; Lipsky, 1970; Segrave, 1994; Walk, 1995). Moreover, the notion that sport itself is a particularly fitting metaphor for life is so common in America and American literature that it has become a part of our conventional wisdom. But just as the language of sport is used metaphorically in a variety of social discourses, so the language of sport is metaphorically constructed. And it is the language of sport that I am concerned with here—the patois, patter, and banter used daily by sports writers and sportscasters, sports analysts and sports fans, and even sportsmen and sportswomen themselves—a language that has variously been called *sportspeak, sportuguese, sporting lingo,* and *sporting lexicon.*

It is a fascinating, indeed fabulous, language that has historically gained much of its appeal not on the basis of the dull habits of accuracy but largely on the basis of a picturesque, technicolor jargon popularized by the likes of Grantland Rice, Paul Gallico, Ring Lardner, and Damon Runyon during the 1920s, the so-called Golden Age of Sport. There are those who would argue that the sports pages offer some of the best-written, most lively, and most informative prose in the newspaper. There are also those no doubt who would agree with Lewis Gannett of the New York *Herald Tribune* that "most sports writers suffer from hyperthyroid congestion of adjectives and are dope fiends for forced similes and metaphors" (quoted in Smith, 1976, p. 9). In either case, it is clear that sportspeak has developed a distinctive style that leans heavily on hyperbole, or what historian John Rickards Betts (1974) once called "the extremely dramatic, the grossly bombastic, and the spectacularly original" (p. 364). It is also a language laced with metaphor; and to study metaphor, as Lakoff and Turner (1989) argue, is "to be confronted with hidden aspects of one's own mind and one's own culture" (p. 214). To understand the power of metaphor is to understand how we shape our arguments, organize our perceptions, create our ideologies, control our feelings, and, in the end, construct our public and private selves. Our entire language system is, of course, metaphorical in nature. We cannot avoid the use of the metaphor and its consequences; we cannot, as Wittgenstein would say, escape the web of language.

I am concerned here, then, with the web of language woven by the language of sport itself, especially as it relies on metaphor, because every sport has its own distinctive language, based on its own metaphorical preferences. Within this language—both the technical jargon and the informal folk speech, the argot—the mythic dimensions and ontological significance of sport are revealed. I am concerned in particular with the language of sport as it relies on three main metaphorical conventions—namely, the conventions of violence, sex, and the machine. In other words, it seems to me that the language of sport is dominated by the language of violence, the language of sex, and the language of the machine. This is not to say that we do not use other metaphors in the language of sport. We do: Metaphors from the world of finance and art spring to mind. We often hear reference to an athletic move as a thing of beauty or a work of art, or we say that a successful athlete "really put it on the money"; but we talk more often about sport as a battleground (as we did in the tele-

vised production of this year's Super Bowl), about teams as enemies, and about athletes as warriors, or ideological shock troops as Edwards (1980) once characterized them. And we are far more likely to describe an athlete as a well-honed performance machine than as a creative artist. In the end, I wish to argue, these linguistic predilections reveal a particularly striking component of our contemporary ontology, one that attests, I will argue, to our obsessive, if indeed not neurotic, preoccupation with control—control over ourselves and the circumstance in which we find ourselves; control, ultimately, over our lot in life.

By taking this approach, however, let me acknowledge from the very beginning that I tend toward a masculinist analysis of the language of sport, partly no doubt because I cannot escape my own gender construction but mainly because the vast majority of the language of sport is written or mediated by men and hence reflective of a male view of the world. The language of sport, like sport itself, is a male-dominated practice, one that in the end reaffirms male power and privilege.

The Language of Violence

First, and perhaps most strikingly, let me begin by noting that the language of sport relies heavily on the language of violence. As Tannenbaum and Noah (1959) write: "No one wins a game today. Teams rock, sock, roll, stomp, stagger, swamp, rout, decision, down, drop, eke out, topple, top, scalp, and trounce opponents, but no one wins a game" (p. 165). In the vernacular of the 1990s, teams also kill, murder, destroy, slaughter, and bury. The full metaphorical richness of the language of violence is humorously revealed in a delightful spoof published by *The New Yorker* in 1958. The purpose of the editorial was to offer "some advice" to the San Francisco newspapers, ostensibly on the arrival of the newly acquired New York Giants, "about the science and art of baseball-headline verbs," which "we have seen evolve from a simple matter of 'WIN' and 'LOSE' into a structure of periphrasis as complex as heraldry in feudalism's decadence." The general rule therefore was as follows:

> Any three-run margin, *providing the winning team does not exceed ten,* may be described as vanquishing. If, however, the margin is a mere two runs and the losing is five or more, "OUTSLUG" is considered very tasty. You will notice, S. F., the trend called Mounting Polysyllabism, which culminates, at the altitude of double digits, in that trio of Latin-root rhymes, "ANNIHILATE," "OBLITERATE," and "HUMILIATE." E.g., "A'S ANNIHILATE O'S." ("The Talk of the Town," 1958, p. 21)

Nor was the American predilection for mascots lost on *The New Yorker*:

> Each Baltimore journal is restricted by secret covenant to one "BIRDS SOAR" every two weeks. Milwaukee, with a stronger team, is permitted twelve instances of "BRAVES CLAW" before the All-Star game. "TIGERS CLAW" and "CUBS LICK" tend to take care of themselves. As for you, San Francisco, the lack of any synonyms for "giant" briefer than "behemoth" and "Brobdingnagian," together with the long-standing failure of New York's own writers to figure our exactly what giants do (intimidate? stomp?), rather lets you out of the fun. In view of this, and in view of the team's present surprising record, you may therefore write "GIANTS A-MAYS." But don't do it more than once. ("The Talk of the Town," 1958, p. 21)

Mascots and team names are a prime example of how the language of violence has penetrated the language of sport. According to Franks (1982), the 10 most common mascots are Eagles, Tigers, Cougars, Bulldogs, Warriors, Lions, Panthers, Indians, Wildcats, and Bears—images that are typically perceived as savage, powerful, and wild. Mascots, of course, are selected precisely because of their coercive and predatory images: Attributes of violence, dominance, and power are privileged over other attributes such as compassion, cooperation, and individuality. Like sport itself, mascots and team names emphasize male qualities of physicality and aggression at the same time as they reflect a patriarchal and demeaning attitude toward women. To call a women's team Cowboys or Tomcats—that is, to use a male mascot as a false generic—is to contribute to the invisibility and hence inferiority of women's teams (Eitzen & Baca Zinn, 1989). To feminize symbols and mascots—that is, to call the Governors, the Lady Governors, or to feminize the Bears into the Teddy Bears or the Wildcats into the Wild Kittens—is to emphasize gender, not athletic ability (Fuller & Manning, 1987).

But the language of violence is most clearly crystallized in the language of football, a language that reflects the masculinist history of sport, a language, as a result, alive with military metaphor. Sportuguese, in fact, is instrumental in bridging the gap between two institutions that promote masculine hegemony: After all, the language of football is the language of war. There are offensive and defensive lines, and air and ground attacks; we have bombs and blitzes, zones and flags, scouts and platoons; coaches are often referred to as generals and quarterbacks as field commanders. Roger Staubach, the Dallas Cowboys quarterback, for example, was affectionately known as Captain Combat. In particularly grueling contests, commentators often discuss the war going on in the trenches, and there is always the sudden death convention. Not long after the Persian Gulf war, *Sports Illustrated* ran a story revealingly entitled "Big D Day: The Dallas Cowboys Went on the Attack in the NFL Draft and Took All the Right Prisoners" (King, 1991), and Stephen Crane (1944) proclaimed in the *Red Badge of Courage* that he had learned all he knew about war from the football field. So loaded is football with war metaphors that, as Real (1975) notes:

> Super Bowl coaches like Shula and Grant appear on television like field marshals directing troops trained in boot camp, aided by scouts, prepared for complex attack and defense maneuvers with the aid of sophisticated telephone, film, and other modern technology. In an enterprise in which strict disciplinarians like Vince Lombardi and Don Shula have created the powerful empires, the primer for coaches might be military manuals. (p. 37)

In fact, Woody Hayes, the notorious football coach at Ohio State, once explained his quarterback option play as if it had been drawn up by the Pentagon: "You know," he said, "the most effective kind of warfare is siege. You have to attack on broad fronts. And that's all the option is—attacking on a broad front. You know General Sherman ran an option through the south" (quoted in Ross, 1971, p. 35).

Of course, war metaphors are common to many other competitive sports, most of which make little or no effort to hide the frequent allusions to violence, aggression, and confrontation. But neither football in particular nor sport in general is war. The relationship may be intimate. Sport may well have emerged from warrior activities, and it may well have been used—as it currently is under the ideology of character development—for developing moral qualities of body and soul. Certainly, both war and sport contain an element of dire struggle as well as the need for supreme organization, but sport is a sublimation of war, a ritualized form of violence that emerges, like religion and art, from the freedom from necessity. As Santayana (1894) once noted, sport

> is not fought for the sake of any further advantage. There is nothing to conquer or defend except the honor of success. We can become a luxury and flower into artistic

forms, whenever the circumstances of life no longer drain all the energy native to the character. (p. 183)

In other words, sport is controlled violence; or to put it another way, sport is a ritualized form of self-control. As the cultural critic Christopher Lasch (1979) astutely recognized, the crisis in modern sport devolves not from the persistence of a martial ethic, the cult of victory, or our obsession with achievement, but from the collapse of conventions that once restrained rivalry and violence even as they glorified it.

The value of violence in sport, then, lies not in its expression but in its control; it is in fact only by controlling violence that sport sustains our interest and enlivens our attention. Sport detoxifies emotions and instincts that left unchecked would otherwise serve to our destruction, not our edification. Sport in this sense may well be one of our most important civilizing agents.

The Language of Sport

The language of sport is also infused with the language of sex. This has led at least one theorist, anthropologist Alan Dundes (1985), to offer a psychoanalytic explanation of football as "an unconscious homosexual struggle for supremacy" (p. 119):

> The offensive team may try to mount a "drive" in order to "penetrate" the other team's territory. A ball carrier might go "up the middle" or he might "go through the hole." . . . The defense is equally determined to "close the hole." Linesmen may encourage each other to "stick it to 'em." . . . By the end of the game, one of the teams is "on top," namely the one which has "scored" most by getting into the other team's "end zone." The losing team, if the scoring differential is great, may be said to have been "creamed." (Dundes, 1978, pp. 83–85)

Nor is the underlying homosexual paradigm limited to football. Dundes (1985) also notes the homosexual connotations of a number of basketball metaphors, including dribble, shoot, back door, rim shot, swish, slam dunk, spike, stuff, lay-up, and lay-in. Such tropes suggest to Dundes that competitive male team sports, in particular, embody ritualized homosexual combat. If such be the case, then the greatest irony of all for gay men in sport is that being gay and athletic is not a contradiction, and the intricate ways in which gay athletes attempt to manipulate appearances and reality for the purposes of appearing straight are unnecessary (see Pronger, 1990).

But the truth of the matter is that sex metaphors in sport derive from and refer to heterosexual relations, and a patriarchal heterosexuality at that. After all, the default assumption is that virtually everyone in sport is heterosexual: Otherwise, why else segregate locker rooms? But as a result, the language of sport becomes another one of a variety of techniques and cultural practices whereby women are subordinated and inferiorized to men in a complex semiotic that in the end constitutes male power and privilege. The use of sex metaphors in sportspeak linguistically legitimizes the use of physical force and strength. Words like *penetrate, drive,* and *score* have the effect of reducing both the athletic contest and sexual relations to the level of a technical problem, not a problem in human relations and human morality. As Sabo (1994) notes, sexual relations become "games in which women are seen as opponents, his scoring means her defeat" (p. 38).

But like war and sport, sex, too, may be regarded as a stylized form of violent behavior in which one individual physically violates the space and sanctity of the other. But as in sport, and unlike war, the violation of space and person is agreed upon. It is a mutually accepted—indeed, even contrived and desired—violation that serves to morally enlighten and edify the individuals involved. In fact, it is the controlled nature of the violent behavior in sport and sex that

allows both to develop in distinctly aesthetic ways. As Kaelin (1968) argues:

> Not even the bad joke of referring to lovemaking as America's most popular indoor sport could make the comparison profitable. More to the point, however, is the manner in which the creation and release of psychic tension becomes qualitatively one; or, to put the matter in another way, how man's need for violent activity is expressed in a context in which the partner is not destroyed, but edified in and through the experience. (p. 21)

The Language of the Machine

Given the nature and trends of the twentieth century, it is perhaps not unsurprising to also find the language of the machine deeply entrenched in the language of sport. Athletes rev up, burn up the track, work well, produce the goods, and turn out the results. When athletes break down, their machines seize up or they run out of steam or, more in keeping with the current era, they run out of gas. A successful team is like a well-oiled machine, and athletes themselves are sometimes just cogs in a machine. Adorno and Horkheimer (1971) have noted how the "oarsmen, who cannot speak to one another, are each of them yoked in the same rhythm as the modern worker in a factory" (p. 55). Writing in the French newspaper *Le Monde,* Casting offers a particularly striking example of the machine metaphor in her description of the East German handball team:

> Every cog appears to fit in perfectly with the others. Rarely can the comparison of the sports team with a machine have been more accurate: the E. German team is like a steamroller made up of tireless human robots capable of keeping up the same pace for an hour, physically and mentally cast in the same

mold: cast-iron morale, steely nerves and brazen muscles. It would be almost true to speak of a team of steel-workers. (quoted in Brohm, 1978, p. 30)

The language of the machine, like the language of violence and sex, also tends to reflect a male view of the world; impersonal and technical, with a focus on the "other." No wonder at the height of the Cold War we typically and easily characterized the U.S.S.R. Olympic teams as "the Soviet machine" and their athletes as robots, pharmacologically created automatons and decidedly unfeminine. Maybe we need our athletic rivals to be mechanized because machines can be unplugged, and because other more compassionate and humane explanations are more frightening or more demanding. It is particularly easy for men to construct and accept an us-versus-them mentality.

The language of the machine is also, of course, the language of control, not control of the emotions or of the instincts—in short, not control of the self—but control of the environment. Our obsession with machines and technology is after all merely another one of our futile efforts to act upon nature, to tame nature, another one of our efforts to bend an otherwise inert environment to the service of our will. We change nature for our pleasure and satisfaction. Even our arenas and stadiums offer us a tidy microcosm in an otherwise opaque and confused reality, "nature humanized" as Heinegg (1976, p. 154) nicely puts it. So the machine and all that it can master serves as an expression of our efforts to enlarge our human powers of sensation and action.

By likening athletes to machines and the results of the athletic endeavor to productivity, we seek to attain immortality. But in so doing, we depersonalize the athlete, both male and female. No wonder we harbor such ambivalence toward the machine analogy and the technologically created athlete. Even though to treat one's body as if it were a machine is to enter into the spirit of the age, within this model production replaces process, performance supersedes effort, ends replace means, and machine replaces athlete; but nature is controlled and mortality is vanquished.

The Language of Life and Death

To some, the language of the machine in the context of sport is the ultimate language of violence, even the language of death. F. T. Marinetti, the most significant theorist of futurism, worshipped both the athlete and the machine. In Marinetti's masculinist fantasies—fantasies in which "wings are asleep in the flesh of man"—the fully technologized athlete of the future appears in nascent form as a "nonhuman and mechanical being, constructed for an omnipresent velocity, and he will be naturally cruel, omniscient, and combative" (in Flint, 1972, p. 91). This sort of athletic Nietzscheanism also appears in the paintings of Lothar Bechstein (see his *Discus Thrower*) and Albert Janesch (see his *Water Sports*), the sculptures of Joseph Thorak (see his *Comradery*), and in the performance psychologies of East European coaches and sport technocrats, and it crystallizes a tendency toward the utopia of the body-machine, a conservative utopia in which the physique of the athlete is fully mechanized and the psyche is completely eliminated. The language of sport incorporates the athlete-machine synthesis because it is, of course, a modernism; contemporary athletic "training," writes Ellul (1954), "turns men into efficient machines who know no other joy than the grim satisfaction of mastering and exploiting their own bodies" (p. 347). It is also a conception that too easily reminds us of the fantastic ideologies of those Fascists who saw the ultimate glorification of men as mechanized bodies in which both the athlete and the machine were "one of war and of sexuality" (Theweleit, 1989, p. 536). Control in this case becomes repression.

And once again, the thanatological-machinist references in the language of sport are reflective of a male perspective. As Stillion (1985) reminds us, women tend to occupy the middle ground between life and death: In myth, they both give and take life. "Thine it is to give and take life from mortal men," wrote Homer (quoted in Harrison, 1938, p. 4). For men, on the other hand, the issue of death is less complex and sinister: Confrontations with death are violent and impersonal, often linked to issues of courage and patriotism. For men, heroism and death are concurrent themes. Men stoically march off to war, or to "the game"; women weep or cheer.

But the language of sport is not only the language of violence and death. It is also the language of life, and I do not mean simplistically and superficially that sportspeak borrows from all areas of our national language system. I mean that sportspeak at a deeper and certainly more profound level offers us fascinating glimpses of an important ontological sort. Consider, for example, the distinction between playing and being in baseball. Fielders merely play positions, but the batter is at bat and the pitcher pitches or is on the mound. This type of language seems to reaffirm life. It would seem absurd to talk of Kirby Puckett playing the batter for the Minnesota Twins or Roger Clemens playing pitcher for the Red Sox. The more active the role in baseball, the more the players are what they do: "Playing" is reserved for the more passive, defensive roles. The proactive roles instantiate being. The language of being rather than playing also characterizes proximity to home; after all, stranded batters are said to die on base.

Conclusion

So the language of sport, sportspeak, is about life and death; or perhaps I should say, metaphorically, the language of sport is a matter of life and death. As Ross (1971) so eloquently noted, the essence of the life and death issue is crystalized in the sports of baseball and football. Baseball, Ross argues, is a pastoral sport, played in a park, in the spring, the time of birth, renewal, and

promise. Football is more sensational, heroic, and urbane; it is played on a gridiron, in the gloom of winter, the time of death and decay. It is, of course, a well-known portrayal of the mythic significance of sport, a mythic representation that harkens us back to the genesis of sport as a component of various fertility cults whose rituals and ceremonies honored and conventionalized a male-dominated social and political order. Even the Olympic Games emerged in conjunction with the fertility rites of the agrarian god Pelops. But there is more to it than simply a matter of life and death, or a matter of gender.

The language of sport reflects our efforts to control matters of life and death—in short, to control our fate. Sport is a social drama in Turner's (1974) sense, but it is also a cultural

The social drama here is evident as U.S. soccer players Brandi Chastain, Shannon MacMillan, Sara Whalen, and Kate Sobrero celebrate their World Cup victory over China in Pasadena, California, in 1999. Ed.
Mark J. Terrill/AP/Wide World Photos

drama, and it demonstrates how a group draws on rituals and symbols as well as language to face a crisis, the ultimate crisis of its existentiale. Humans have forever been chafed over their powerlessness—powerlessness over themselves and their environment, and particularly over their mortality. We are typically and easily insulted by the final triumph of nature over culture, and seeking to develop concepts that might stay our sentence, we cling to our cultural constructions like sport, a no more or less thinly veiled quest for existential control than any other cultural rite. In the end, however, as Euripides so well understood, questions of control, power, and supremacy are relevant, and the language of sport in all its slangy and facetious style offers us a fascinating window into the very soul of our existence.

Bibliography

Adorno, T. W., & Horkheimer, M. (1971). *Dialectic of enlightenment.* London: Allan Lane.

Balbus, I. (1975). Politics as sport: The political ascendancy of the sports metaphor in America. *Monthly Review, 26,* 26–39.

Betts, J. R. (1974). *America's sporting heritage: 1850–1950.* Reading, MA: Addison-Wesley.

Brohm, J. M. (Ed.). (1978). *Sport: A prison of measured time.* London: Inks Links.

Crane, S. (1944). *Red badge of courage.* New York: Heritage Press.

Dundes, A. (1978). Into the endzone for a touchdown: A psychoanalytic consideration of football. *Western Folklore, 37,* 75–88.

Dundes, A. (1985). The American game of "Smear the Queer" and the homosexual component of male competitive sport and warfare. *Journal of Psychoanalytic Anthropology, 8,* 115–129.

Edwards, H. (1980, February). *Crisis in the Olympic movement.* Paper presented at the Olympic Symposium at Skidmore, Skidmore College, Saratoga Springs, NY.

Eitzen, D. S., & Baca Zinn, M. (1989). The deathletization of women: The naming and gender marking of collegiate sports teams. *Sociology of Sport Journal, 6,* 362–370.

Ellul, J. (1954). *La technique ou l'enjeu du siècle.* Paris: Libràirè A. Colin.

Flint, R. W. (Ed.). (1972). *Marinetti: Selected writings.* New York: Farrar, Straus, & Giroux.

Franks, R. (1982). *What's in a nickname? Exploring the jungle of college athletic mascots.* Amarillo, TX: R. Franks Pub Ranch.

Fuller, J. R., & Manning, E. A. (1987). Violence and sexism in college mascots and symbols: A typology. *Free Inquiry in Creative Sociology, 15,* 61–66.

Hardaway, F. (1976). Foul play: Sports metaphors as public doublespeak. *College English, 38,* 78–82.

Harrison, J. E. (1938). *Myths of Greece and Rome.* London: Harrap.

Heinegg, P. (1976). Philosopher in the playground: Notes on the meaning of sport. *Southern Humanities Review, 10,* 153–156.

Jansen, S., & Sabo, D. (1994). The sport/war metaphor: Hegemonic masculinity, the Persian Gulf War, and the new world order. *Sociology of Sport Journal, 11,* 1–17.

Kaelin, E. F. (1968). The well-played game: Notes toward an aesthetics of sport. *Quest, 10,* 16–28.

King, P. (1991, April 29). Big D Day: The Dallas Cowboys went on the attack in the NFL draft and took all the right prisoners. *Sports Illustrated,* pp. 42–48.

Lakoff, G., & Turner, M. (1989). *More than cool reason.* Chicago: University of Chicago Press.

Lasch, C. (1979). *The culture of narcissism.* London: W. W. Norton.

Lipsky, R. (1970). The athleticization of politics: The political implications of sports symbolism. *Journal of Sport and Social Issues, 3,* 28–37.

Lipsyte, R. (1975). *Sportsworld: An American dreamland.* New York: Quadrangle Books.

Palmatier, R., & Ray, H. (1989). *Sports talk: A dictionary of sports metaphors.* New York: Greenwood.

Pronger, B. (1990). Gay jocks: A phenomenology of gay men in athletics. In M. A. Messner & D. F. Sabo (Eds.), *Sport, men, and the gender order: Critical feminist perspectives* (pp. 141–152). Champaign, IL: Human Kinetics.

Real, M. (1975). Super Bowl: Mythic spectacle. *Journal of Communications, 25,* 31–43.

Ross, M. (1971, January–February). Football red and baseball green. *Chicago Review,* pp. 30–40.

Sabo, D. F. (1994). The myth of the sexual athlete. In M. A. Messner & D. F. Sabo (Eds.), *Sex, violence, & power in sports: Rethinking masculinity* (pp. 36–41). Freedom, CA: Crossing.

Santayana, G. (1894). Philosophy on the bleachers. *Harvard Monthly, 18,* 181–190.

Segrave, J. O. (1994). The perfect 10: "Sportspeak" in the language of sexual relations. *Sociology of Sport Journal, 11,* 95–113.

Smith, R. (1976). *Press box: Red Smith's favorite short stories.* New York: Avon.

Stillion, J. M. (1985). *Death and the sexes: An examination of differential longevity, attitudes, behaviors, and coping skills.* New York: Hemisphere.

The talk of the town. (1958, June 21). *The New Yorker,* p. 21.

Tannenbaum, P., & Noah, J. (1959). Sportuguese: A study of sports page communication. *Journalism Quarterly, 36,* 163–170.

Theweleit, K. (1989). *Male fantasies* (Vol. 2). Minneapolis: University of Minnesota Press.

Turner, V. (1974). *Dramas, fields, and metaphors.* Ithaca, NY. Cornell University Press.

Walk, S. (1995). The footrace metaphor in American presidential rhetoric. *Sociology of Sport Journal, 12,* 36–55.

Questions for Consideration

1. The model Segrave gives here is Freudian. We find, through inspection of metaphors, that what seems most vicious about sport is really a natural reflection of ourselves. Through controlled violence, we curb our naturally aggressive tendencies by offering them some outlet. Do you agree?

2. Does Segrave too easily gloss over *moral* aspects of violence and sexual aggression in sport?

3. The issue of competitive sport providing us with an outlet for pent-up aggression that would otherwise function to destroy us (a drive-reduction or cathartic model of aggression) is an empirical one. A consequence of such a model is that participation (directly or vicariously) in aggressive behavior such as football should reduce the occurrence of such behavior shortly thereafter. Research the current psychological literature on this model. Does exposure to aggressive sport reduce future aggression or enhance the likelihood of such behavior?

6   Practices and Prudence

W. Miller Brown
Trinity College

In this reading, W. Miller Brown argues that philosophical questions about sport—specifically, who ought to participate in them—are really questions about who we are and who we shall be. These questions invite certain "prudential" considerations regarding the practice of sport itself.

Practices, of which sport is one, are complex social activities composed of rules that indicate the aims of such practices and the accepted means of achieving them. These are characterized by internal goods (roughly, rewards from within a sport such as cooperation and courage) and external goods (roughly, rewards from without a sport such as money or fame).

One problem, he notes, is that such a distinction is blurred when it comes to things such as winning, health, or risk taking. Because of this, he concludes that the distinction is perhaps artificial or, at least, unhelpful. This conclusion, he asserts, has prudential implications.

The practice of sport reveals an unequal distribution of external goods because of sex, race, age, and other factors. This is a serious and perhaps insoluble problem. One proposal to even up the distribution of external goods is prudence. Prudence, crudely apprehended, is a demand that participants in sport have an eye not only to the present, but also to the future. Such a demand, Brown believes, is essentially overly cautious and at odds with other values linked to sport: autonomy, courage, and discernment.

Sport is one of many rich and diverse practices that place no demands upon participants except that they share and develop various values in pursuit of the goods attainable through participation.

Reprinted by permission, from W. Miller Brown, "Practices and Prudence," *Journal of the Philosophy of Sport* XVII (1990): 71–84.

A wide variety of means are used to attain these goods: drugs, novel and risky regimens, and biomedical or surgical treatments. Prudence quashes autonomy and suffocates other goods such as creativity, novelty, and pursuit of self-knowledge.

Prudence requires open-endedness and open-mindedness, not caution. For while risk appraisal is statistical, risk taking is personal. This, of course, follows from a view of sport as individual expression, not social practice. Thus, sport will reflect, not solve, social problems. By embracing autonomy and self-determination, we open ourselves up to explore untried pathways of human existence.

Since I first wrote on the topic in 1980, a decade ago, the use of performance-enhancing drugs has remained a subject of much debate, both in the public media and in professional journals.[1] But little, if any, of what has been written has thrown light on the issues I first raised. The reason for this is, I think, clear. And that is that the primary cause of so much concern about drugs in sports is that drug use in general, primarily of euphoria-inducing drugs, remains a topic of national hysteria. The vast treasures we spend, the civil liberties that are threatened, and the propaganda that is distributed, all tend to mask deeper social problems of which drug use is a symptom. It is no wonder we have had such a tough time trying to keep our thoughts straight about our own concerns, sport being so easily enmeshed in our larger social quagmires.

But our deliberations about sport may cast thoughtful light on these broader social concerns. I believe that the curious issue of performance-enhancing drugs is one such case. It is curious because we are so prone to approach the core issue obliquely, as if it were exhausted by comparisons of synthetic compounds and naturally metabolized ones, of the dangers of steroids and those of football, of the naturalness of Mark Spitz's hyperextensive knees or Joan Samuelson's arthroscopically repaired ones. The issue is rather about us: Who are we and what are we to become? We don't know the answers to these questions, though they are as much a matter of what we decide as what we discover. In the meantime we are fighting hard to control the changes that our increasing knowledge may require. The answers will surely affect our decisions about who can play together in our games and sports.

I want to approach this question of participation in two related ways. The first is to reflect on the nature of sport as a type of complex human activity. The second is to speculate about our participation in sports not at any one time, this game or that, this season or another, one sport or two, but rather over a lifetime. My conclusions will be largely negative ones, but they may also suggest an emphasis in our thinking about sports that is different from that usually made. I turn first to consider sports as practices.

I

Although there are many solitary athletic activities, perhaps best thought of as recreational sports (or noncompetitive sports), such as running, sailboarding, hiking, sailing, and so forth, I am mainly interested in those cooperative activities, typically games, that are central to sports as a category. I have in mind games like football and cricket, competitions like foot races and ice skating, and many others. I shall not enter the murky waters of debate on the extent that such activities are governed by rules of various kinds. It seems clear that virtually all of them are. It is similarly clear that efforts at definition here, as in so many cases where philosophers seek exhaustive categories, are threatened by the shoals of several devastating critiques of essentialism.[2] Rather, I want to consider such activities, or

practices, as they are often called, from the point of view of the demands they place on the participants in them.[3]

A recent version of this point of view is that of Alasdair MacIntyre in his book *After Virtue* (6), though my own discussion of the notion will differ somewhat from his. MacIntyre is primarily concerned with the genealogy of virtue that he locates in such practices, including athletic and intellectual games (such as chess). But my concern will be to reflect on how adequate such a conception is as a rough account of many sports and on how it helps us to understand the relation of sports to ourselves as participants.

Let us begin by thinking of practices as complex social activities. We may suppose that they are typically organized in terms of sets of rules that make explicit their purposes and regulate the means acceptable for achieving those purposes.[4] We may think of the purposes, ends, or goals of a practice as its rationale. They are that for which the practice is organized and are typically embodied in the practice's rules, so as to be partially constitutive of the practice. They also tend to determine the goods or benefits to be achieved by the practice. In this sense such goods, such things deemed good to achieve by the practice, are internal to the practice itself. Practices may also be instrumental and seek goods external to their performance, such as entertainment. Different practices are organized to achieve different goods or to achieve similar goods in different ways.

To the extent that different practices have the achievement of similar goods as their purposes, we tend to classify them together as similar kinds of activities. (Our association, for example, has as its purpose the encouraging of philosophical reflections on sport and the exchange of these ideas in an open and critical forum. The good things achieved by such an association are the pleasures of intellectual activities, the pursuit of knowledge, and the fellowship and thoughtful exchanges with others of like mind. In this respect we share similar goods with other philosophical associations.) Of course, the purposes and goods of one practice need not be acceptable to another, and it is an important social inquiry to reflect on the ways in which conflict and support among practices in a society are productive of the achievement of the goods of ever more inclusive practices. A major question, answered largely negatively by western liberal democracies, is whether a society as a whole is a practice in this sense.[5]

A second feature of practices is best reflected in the typical relationship of novice to master, though this is evident in some practices more than in others.[6] The relationship is one of learning through emulation, rehearsal, and sharing in the projects and efforts of those with rich experience in the practice by those who seek also to realize its goods. In the sciences, such apprenticeship is well known as the inducting of young researchers into what Kuhn (5) calls normal science. It is manifested, too, in the use of a practice's history, whether written or oral, as a guide to the central goals of the practice. More importantly, however, is its function in transmitting the standards of excellence that guide and make possible the achievement of the practice's goods. These standards typically govern the attainment of skills needed to repeat past achievements and to extend the range and quality of the goods specified by the practice's rules and traditions. Such skills in the sciences may include facility with mathematics, laboratory techniques, and the solving of typical problems, as well as mastering past solutions to classical problems while learning to give critical play to imagination and invention.

In sport, the relationship is frequently between novice and coach and includes the transmission of skills and values through the careful application of standards of excellence, which are the product of the sport's own history and the coach's prior experience. It is submission to this learning and the standards that govern it that is a prerequisite to mastery, just as it is the ability to extend and enrich the practice's techniques and goals that is the mark of achievement. MacIntyre (6) stresses, in addition, the development of personal qualities or dispositions that are virtues, such as justice, courage, and honesty, which he believes are important to attaining a practice's internal goods. Such dispositions govern the relationships among participants in a practice and make possible the cooperative pursuit of the practice's goals. In sports, we may note the importance of a sense of fairness, a lack of which may seriously jeopardize a participant's ability to achieve some of a sport's goods.

Such virtuous traits facilitate, MacIntyre (6) suggests, the pursuit and achievement of those goods that are characteristic of a practice, and their absence may obstruct the successful pursuit of the practice. Indeed, MacIntyre goes further to claim that such virtues are "necessary components" (6: p. 191) of practices. But this claim is surely dubious.[7] To see this point, however, we must make one more distinction concerning the good things that may be attained by participation in a practice. I have already described practices as having various goods intrinsic to their makeup. We can also distinguish various external goods that may be sought by those who participate in a practice. The latter are easier to illustrate than the former.[8]

External goods are those that are contingent to a practice, ones that have nothing directly to do with the activities of the practice itself. They may be offered as a result of one's excelling in the activities of a practice and thereby become that person's property or possession. Money, fame, power, and privileges are some examples that may enlarge an individual's personal standing. But they are not specific to any one practice or group of practices, and they may sometimes conflict with the continued flourishing or development of the practice itself. Other external goods, such as the entertainment, education, training, or protection of others, may not conflict with a practice's conduct but rather be direct consequences of its most capable performance.

MacIntyre (6) stresses (a) the role of larger social organizations, which he labels institutions, in dealing with such external, and often material, goods and (b) the need for such institutions in providing for and fostering various practices. But if institutions are needed to sustain practices, they are also by their nature liable to affect them by offering external goods and seeking to substitute them for the internal goods intrinsic to the practices they nurture. The importance and centrality of the virtues is thus, MacIntyre holds, to protect those involved in the practices from the potentially corrupting influence of the social institutions that are more likely to lead to the development of vice than of virtue, to dishonesty, injustice, and cowardice. More on this in a moment.

But what more can be said of the goods internal to practices? First, it is important to distinguish the goods of a practice, and the practice itself, from the set of skills that is characteristic of it. A practice is not merely a set of skills, or even a set of skills directed toward some specific end or goal. The laboratory skills of an analytic chemist, however focused on a task of identifying a particular compound, is not a practice, though the pursuit of chemistry is. Similarly, the performance of a slam dunk, however focused on scoring, or even winning a game, is not a practice, though basketball is. But the exercise of relevant skills is intimately connected with the achievement of excellence within a practice and with the goods that are thereby acquired.

MacIntyre (6) is extraordinarily cryptic in his discussion of the goods internal to practices. He claims that the identification of such goods is restricted to those who participate in the practices themselves, though he quickly offers some examples. Two types of goods intrinsic to the practice of portrait painting in western Europe during the 14th to 18th centuries, for example, are, first, the excellence of its products, the skills of the painters, and the portraits themselves; and second, the kind of life exemplified by such painters. What he means by this latter good, I think, is a consequence of my earlier remarks on the transmission of standards and traditions from practitioner to apprentice. One of the good things to be achieved by participating in a practice is the development of human capacities in the manner dictated by a given practice, its goals, skills, styles, and procedures insofar as these promote the flourishing of human powers and potentials. Both of these examples show why internal goods may seem so particular to each practice in which they are sought and achieved.

The distinction between internal and external goods of a practice has a number of clear uses. It can help us to understand the need for institutional support for practices like sports. It also shows just where such a connection carries with it the introduction of new and potentially incompatible goods, of competition among goods, say, money or power or entertainment over fair competition based on skill and merit as defined by the internal standards of play. Unfortunately, however, the distinction is not as clear as I have so far suggested. Only some practices as we know them have products like portraits or theories, and few are easily understood as fostering a way of life. Let me turn more focally to sports and consider the variety of goods with which they may be associated and whether these goods are easily divided into external and internal.

Clearly, a central place will have to be found for the skills and techniques whose acquisition, though a matter of degree, is a sine qua non for full mastery of the sport. I have in mind the rich complex of cognitive and neuromuscular repertoires that are the basics for athletic achievement. Different sports place different demands on participants in this respect, but not uniquely. There are clear carryovers from one sport to another, especially of the psychological skills of concentration, tactical imagination, and physical and intellectual toughness. But neuromuscular skills are transferable as well, even across quite different sports and into other practices. One of the goods of a practice will be the development of these skills and the further achievements that result in the use of these skills in the pursuit of the aims of the practice.

MacIntyre notes (6: p. 197) Aristotle's careful distinction between these accomplishments and the pleasures and satisfactions that accompany them. These, too, are clearly goods of a practice, though ones quite distinct from those satisfactions and pleasures gained from various external rewards such as prizes and bonuses. To play well and to experience the satisfactions of doing so are surely distinguishable from being rewarded for it in various forms by others.[9] The satisfaction of getting a good job as a result of an Olympic gold medal is not the same as the pleasure attendant to the well-performed act in competition. But still, the distinction is not so clear as this neat formulation suggests.

Without the attendant satisfactions of playing well, other rewards would be needed to induce participation, but with such satisfactions, these inducements are often not necessary. Perhaps the point is that satisfactions or pleasures that accompany sports or other practices may be attendant to the activities of the practices in several ways, may motivate and reward participation separately or combined, but in any case are for us, being the creatures we are, psychologically necessary to motivate our activities. The internal/external distinction here does not seem to carry any weight in our understanding of practices. Moreover, some satisfactions, those attendant on winning or on achieving fame or power, inside or outside the practice, are not clearly placed in either type. And this suggests, too, that even within a practice there are competing goods whose joint realization may be unlikely: The winner is not always the best performer.

Winning (or setting records, etc.) is in any case a borderline good. MacIntyre classes winning as an external good (6: p. 274) and as "precisely the same good," whatever the sport or game. But if winning a game, winning a divisional championship, and winning an Olympic gold medal are all the same, and not internal to their respective activities, which I doubt, they still seem internal to sports. We can see winning, along with certain kinds of fame, perhaps with the acquisition of certain kinds of skills and capacities, perhaps even with health or fitness, as goods that cut across various or even all sports, but as internal to sports as a class of activities. Or perhaps we should consider winning as internal to various games, as an end or achievement that is one (but not the only one) of the guiding purposes of sports as practices and a good that, together with the pleasure or satisfaction accompanying it, is an internal good, however common to many sports. Alternatively, we could emphasize the different kinds of winning internal to different sports. Winning at badminton is not the same as winning a marathon, and neither is it like a team win at football.

Health and fitness pose similar problems. Clearly unfit and unhealthy people can participate in sports, even doing so well and achieving sometimes as much as others who are free from injury and disease or other infirmities. Is health, then, a good external to sports, like prizes, salaries, and public adulation?

If we think of health as a goal or motivation, then it is easy to see that it is a good external to sports. Indeed, the skills and activities of sports when directed toward the achievement of health or fitness become exercises, therapies, or remediations. And when someone participates in a sport for reasons of health, we are likely to consider it extraneous to the central goods of the practice of the sport. Health in any case is an elusive quality. It is at least in a negative sense the absence of injury and disease; the notion of positive health as an ideal eludes easy characterization.[10] Perhaps we could say that health or fitness may facilitate and enhance one's participation in a sport. Like fame, health may or may not be attendant on sports participation, but it is not a good of sports themselves as it is of exercise and therapy, which may utilize similar or the same neuromuscular skills and techniques.[11]

This comment requires one complication, however. If lack of health frustrates those pleasures and satisfactions attendant on the mastery of athletic skills and their application in light of a sport's standards of excellence, then, like other extraneous or external factors, it can threaten the practice itself. Excellence in the realization and extension of human powers within a practice can be frustrated and limited by injury, not only for an individual but for all participants.

Health, or at least injury, is closely related in sports to risk, and risk, for many sports, if not all, is a close companion to the very challenge of the practices themselves. Examples are legion: skiing, football, boxing, auto racing, diving. And the injury risked is directly related to the challenges of the sports themselves. Injury is not of itself a good of the practice of the sports themselves. Rather, what we seek is the challenge of doing well something of great difficulty. But some individuals may be motivated by the excitement of the risk of dangerous injury, just as they may be by the prospects of team bonding or the motivation of health or monetary reward.[12]

I conclude, therefore, that, though something can be made of the internal/external distinction of goods of practices like sports, not too much hinges on it, and in many cases the distinction blurs, leaving us with a continuum of goods, some more internal than others, some close and some far from the core features of the practices themselves. This will prove of importance when in the second part of my paper I discuss prudential judgments of sport participation.

What then about the virtues? They are, MacIntyre (6: p. 191), writes, "those goods by reference to which, whether we like it or not, we define our relationships to those other people with whom we share the kind of purposes and standards which inform practices." Are they internal goods? If so, they are internal to all practices alike and not particularly linked to the excellences that are definitive of given practices. If not, then, like winning, in MacIntyre's view, they are external to practices and cannot be appealed to as among the goods that characterize given practices.

It follows, as MacIntyre (6) acknowledges, that there can be "vicious" athletes who play the game but exemplify vice, not virtue. But they are prevented, he believes, from achieving the goods internal to practices. That is, among the internal

goods are "the excellence specific to" a practice, and these "cannot be achieved without the exercise of the virtues" (6: p. 274). What he has in mind are those features of practices, various sports among them, that require various kinds of cooperative activities that depend on honest communication, fair play, and courageous acceptance of risk and mutuality. Where vice is rampant, practices founder; successful cheating occurs only at the price of destroying the trust and cooperation of others. So we may acknowledge that the virtues, such as fair play, courage, and honesty, are required by those practices whose goods include the cooperative, even if competitive, attainment of excellences in the pursuit of common purposes.

But practices may deviate from such standards. Practitioners may themselves be evil; the results of practices may be evil; and it is conceivable that some practice might be itself evil, perhaps the practice of slavery or certain other forms of exploitation or control. Still, the concept of a practice provides a rich context for thinking about many sports, though it is important to see that its teleological structure confers on it a normative character, not simply a descriptive one. No effort at definition is involved in our use of the concept, nor a straight-forward description of various cooperative activities such as sports. Rather, in characterizing sports as practices, I have applied a kind of standard, or paradigm, enabling us to see what fit is possible, what features of sports as practices come to the fore. Because it is a rich and inclusive concept, capable of being applied widely beyond sports to arts, sciences, and political activities, it allows us to see sports as one among several kinds of practices and as sharing in their broad outlines.

For this discussion, what seems evident is that the concept of a practice, and of sports insofar as they are practices, places no limits on the characteristics of participants save that they share and develop various virtues in pursuit of the goods attainable through their participation. The submission to standards of excellence, the mastery of skills, the cooperative pursuit of common goals, the acknowledgment of goods characteristic of a practice and their link to the excellences defined by it: These one can be expected to acquire and pursue. But nothing mentioned here would seem to preclude the use of a wide variety of means to achieve those excellences within the constraints of the practice. That is, the constraints of the practice, including the internalizing of the virtues, are compatible with the use of performance-enhancing drugs, novel and risky training regimes, and biomedical or surgical treatments or modifications of practitioners. Indeed, insofar as these techniques are designed for, and in fact achieve, enhancement of performance, they are fully consonant with the nature of practices. The development of technical skills and extensions of human powers help transform and enrich "the conceptions of the relevant goods and ends" (6: p. 193) that practices embody.

II

I now want to consider a seemingly different approach to our problem, but one that is in fact closely related to the previous discussion. So far we have focused on sports as practices, cooperative forms of human behavior that seek certain kinds of goods and engender the development of certain personal qualities or virtues. These latter bring into focus the interpersonal nature of such practices, their social character, and the need to foster the virtues of fairness and honesty, for example. But because we are interested in conditions that may restrict participation, that is, restrictions on persons, it makes sense to abstract from relations among persons and consider the individual participants themselves. If there are no admission restrictions on participants that are the result of the interpersonal nature of practices, can we justify such restrictions by other means?

I have in mind considering relations not between persons, but those that hold among the different stages of a person's life. Just as theories of justice, say, are often formulated by abstracting

from particular characteristics of individuals that are deemed morally irrelevant, so we may seek to abstract over a lifetime, to see whether we owe ourselves anything from stage to stage in our lives, or better, whether, if we are prudent or rational, we should budget resources over our lifetimes in such a way as to provide appropriately for the different stages of our lives.[13] Athletes are often encouraged to learn, when young, sports that can be available to them when they are old. Similarly, we caution against sports activity at younger ages that may damage one's capacity to enjoy a rich range of sports at later ages. What is the status of such cautionary advice, and can it deal effectively with the issue of performance-enhancing drugs?

We can phrase the problem in this way: What restrictions would rational agents place on participation in sports, or on the sports themselves, in order to allocate prudentially over a lifetime the relevant goods engendered by those practices? Let me recall that the goods in question here are those (internal and external) goods that we found to be characteristic of sports as practices. We should note at the very beginning that some of the relevant (external) goods sometimes made available by the institutions that promote sport practices, money, fame, power, adulation, are not generally available and are allocated on grounds not always directly connected with sports themselves. We could discount this fact about institutionalized sports by assuming that we have solved the problem of the just or fair distribution of these external goods.

Because talents, and success based on talents, are unequally distributed among us and because many other factors, such as sex, race, class, nationality, and resources, that feature in the distribution of external goods are not shared or universal, this is a serious and perhaps insoluble problem. It constitutes the central problem of the threat to practices of institutional control, mentioned earlier. I will return to it shortly, but let us for now abstract from it for the sake of considering how far we can characterize what I shall call the prudential athletic life (PAL).

Projecting the PAL involves two related considerations that are built into the very notion of prudence. One is what Parfit (9: p. 313) calls *"The Requirement of Equal Concern:* A rational person should be *equally* concerned about *all* the parts of his future."[14] That is, we should consider the issue of well-being in our lives to be time neutral: Our well-being when old is equally important as our well-being when young. The second is the prudential strategy of keeping our options open.[15] At any one time when we are relatively young we are inclined to pursue our current projects to the fullest of our ability and resources. But a prudential outlook requires us to keep in mind that at later stages of our lives we may well have different projects, different allegiances, and different priorities and values, and we will then also need to call on our abilities and resources to satisfy the demands of these stages. In our prudential reflections we must be able to abstract from our present concerns and allow for later passions. We cannot, prudentially, commit all now with no thought to what prospects and projects we may then face, ones likely to be quite different from those that entice and fulfill us now and yet every bit as alluring.

This suggests that if we borrow a rhetorical device of Rawls (12), an imaginary "veil of ignorance," selectively informing rational agents in their deliberations about justice, then we can require that our deliberators about a PAL be similarly veiled concerning their ages and other qualities such as talent, sex, wealth, and race. By restricting knowledge in particular about one's age in considering this question, we can hope to avoid age bias. In sports especially, we are likely to bias the young against the old, a bias forbidden by a prudential life-span perspective. In ruling this out, we also disallow information about our life plans at any one time. We impose a kind of tolerance between different stages of our lives. We acknowledge, in effect, that such plans for the good life are frequently incommensurable; we have no independent vantage point from which to assess them all.[16]

But now a more serious problem faces us, one that goes to the heart of both sports and prudence. A prudential viewpoint is inherently a cautious one, one that forgoes extremes with an eye to later enjoyments. In our goal to keep our options open and not to discount the importance of any stages of our lives, we expend our resources warily: Profligacy is prohibited. The difficulty is that this directive is clearly at odds with one important feature of many sports, already mentioned, the element of risk. Many sports involve risk to limb if not life, and some even to life. Can we justify in a prudential account the risk entailed by such activities? The problem is most clear in the contrast between youth and age, the former inclined to risk all, the latter to spend little.

We can try to remove this conflict in a number of ways. One is to discount the possible plans for later stages of our lives as of less value than our current ones, to assume that what is important to us now and worth many risks will be acceptable to us in retrospect at later stages of our lives. But our chronological parochialism here is surely not warranted if my claim about the incommensurability of life plans was persuasive. Any stage of life may devalue the plans of another stage, and it is precisely to avoid this age bias that we need to abstract from age in our general reflections.

Another approach would be to suppose that we are not in fact likely to experience real changes in our life plans at later stages and therefore that allowing for them now is unnecessary. But this is surely just the view of inexperience and ignores both the real likelihood of change in outlook as we grow older and the all too great probability that we will confront genuine contingencies in our lives that we had not expected but will need adequate resources to confront.[17] Still, even with these considerations, a real question remains about risk in sports: Can we afford to rule out too much of it?

We might suppose that risks in sport are eliminable by careful restrictions on physical contact, improvements in equipment, and continuous scrutiny of games by officials to caution against injury. No doubt this is important and effective. But sports carry inherent risks that are ineliminable. Contact sports like boxing and football are easy examples. But gymnastics, yachting, platform diving, and cycling carry their special risks because much of the challenge of these sports and others is a result of the dangerous circumstances of their practice. Many recreational sports, such as mountain climbing and hang gliding, are even more hazardous. And these hazards are directly linked to the (internal) goods and satisfactions of the sports. To seek to eliminate them is to eliminate some of the very features of the sports that draws people to them.

The problem here is that if we seek to limit the risk to participants with an eye to the well-being of later stages of our lives, we may well have to eliminate some sports entirely, or at least so change them that some of their significant goods will be eliminated too: the excellences required to meet and overcome dangerous challenges with high levels of hard-won skill and courage, and the payoffs of adulation, fortune, and self-knowledge. Moreover, if we are to suppose the attainment of these goods is not entirely transient, but that they may be remembered and cherished so as to help fulfill later stages of one's life, their loss will affect more than one's current well-being. It is plausible, too, to suppose that at least some of the virtues we may associate with sport, such as courage, autonomy, and discernment, are not won without the challenges of activities that inherently involve considerable risk.

Even if we prorate risk to age from our age-neutral perspective, allowing greater risk for younger, stronger ages, how can we determine what risk is too much, too threatening to later stages of life to allow to our younger selves? One approach is to reflect on the probabilities of injury associated with various sports. But what probability is too great? What trade-off of risk to injury and benefit of increased (internal) goods now or at a later stage of life is acceptable? And what measure of risk in relation to age is possible?

What a prudential account demands is that we keep our options open, and this requires that we preserve our capacities to engage fully in sports at every stage of our lives so as to be able to realize the goods such practices may offer. We must do this with an eye to the ways our capacities may be expected to change with normal patterns of aging and to the likelihood of changes in our sports-related values during various stages of our lives. This requires that we do not do anything that can prematurely diminish those capacities through injury or misuse. Moreover, it requires that we develop and enhance our capacities and talents as investments for our futures. As a consequence, we must, if we are prudent, carefully select sports (or change them) so as to maximize the probability of our achievement of their goods and minimize the threats to long-term participation by injury or burnout.

Further, a prudential perspective requires that we do enough at any one stage so as not to jeopardize possible activities at later stages. That is, we must not only preserve our capacities and talents but also be required to develop them sufficiently when young so that they are available when we are old. Even if we do not value sports when young, we are obligated by prudence to develop our talents and capacities sufficiently to allow for later changes in our values and life plans. (This conclusion clearly has important implications for political [institutional] policies concerning sports participation by our children, on the assumption that sports participation has some broadly shared value.) This has the further implication that, if we are prudent, we must maintain some minimal level of health and fitness compatible with the possibility of lifetime participation in sports.

Health and talent are veiled in our discussion so far. But we do not need to know our own allotments of these qualities in order to argue that we must preserve them over a prudent athletic life span. Other things are needed in order to ensure the possibility of an athletic life, in particular the goods that I earlier argued are (relatively) external to sports: leisure, wealth, and various social or institutional arrangements, in addition to good health.

We fare no better when we enlarge the payoff to consider these (external) goods as well, which we can hardly avoid doing in light of the dubious nature of the distinction itself. In fact, our prudential account can be limited to sports only when we ignore the external goods attainable by their means. In discussing risk of injury, I have already alluded to the external good of health. Is any risk that threatens health at a later age unacceptable? Or only risks of a certain probability?

So far we have used a thick veil of ignorance for our deliberations, excluding personal information about age, sex, health, talent, wealth, class, and race. The reason is that the goods available in regard to sports, both those relatively internal and those relatively external to the practices, are not in fact distributed independently of these features of our lives. Consequently, were we to be informed how these features have in fact been distributed to us, our reflections on a PAL could be slanted by such information. What may seem prudent to a person of great wealth or superb health may seem quite different to someone of precarious fortunes and health.

We could assume that just that general information is available, as are actuarial data on reasonable expectations for life in our society: the distribution of wealth, talent, and health and their correlations with sex, race, and class. We could clearly ignore such concerns in a just society, one where the goods of life were distributed justly, where one's expected share of those goods could be justified as the outcome of just institutions, including those fostering sports. But in our actual society, this would not be prudent! Until now, our thick veil of ignorance has allowed us to probe what might be called agent-independent goods, such as health, the development of sports-related capacities, and the like. But we ran quickly foul of the problem of risk and the lack of any prudential basis for choice among alternative limits to risky activity.

We must now consider sports in the context of our actual social circumstances, that is, those of an unjust society. When we do so, our perplexities about risk become even greater. Because prudence is in question, we need to acknowledge that sports often offer along with great risk the chance to improve our standing in the lottery of life. We may achieve greater wealth, power, or fame, which can compensate for initial deficiencies in these qualities and thus help provide us with the means for prudential planning in our lives, not just for an athletic lifetime but for other aspects of our lives as well. Because risk must always be balanced with benefit, it seems clear that there may be many cases where risk is justified in light of the prospect of corresponding gain. What is not clear is which goods are to be weighed in the balance and how they are to be compared.

At best, a prudent planner who looks only to internal goods will seek to preserve a range of basic capacities for possible future sports activities. This planning already requires a careful scrutiny of matters of health and development, goods that, though external to sports, may be necessary for athletic activity at any age. When other external goods are considered, prudential planning for an athletic lifetime becomes even more difficult because sports as means to external goods may be in the service of a broader conception of one's life and the prudential considerations made in allowing for a lifetime in which one's well-being goes beyond participation in sports themselves.

We are forced, then, to make our veil of ignorance thinner and thinner. Where it was possible to consider the goods to be achieved by sports practices as agent-independent, little headway seemed possible even in a society where it could be assumed that the basic goods of life were distributed in a just manner. The problem is that although risk appraisal is a statistical matter, risk taking is a personal one. Risk taking is not agent-independent, but, rather, relative to the overall circumstances and goals of individuals.[18] But with a thin veil, our rational and prudential deliberators will opt in more nearly personal terms for opportunities and other goods related to sports. The distinction between external and internal goods, for what it is worth, will scarcely seem useful to someone faced with choices affecting a lifetime that begins with the realities of the lottery of life.[19]

These conclusions have important negative consequences for reflections about performance-enhancing drugs. They suggest that nothing in a conception of sports as practices involving various goods, nor in our efforts to limn the contours of a prudential athletic life span, entails the prohibition of such substances. At most, if one is prudent, one will be wary of anything that may jeopardize one's lifetime sports activity and the goods that may accompany it. But then one will also be wary of many of the sports themselves whose dangers, costs, or low prospects of benefit require them prudently to be avoided. Moreover, these reflections also suggest that a prudent life in sports, or elsewhere, is not necessarily a good one and that if prudence is to have a role in our lives it must be because it serves other values, the realization of which does promote a good life.

It is not difficult to list some of them, the challenge of risk being central: creativity, novelty, freedom and autonomy, and the pursuit of self-knowledge. Sports are not always seen as fostering such values, and the institutions that have supported them have sometimes corrupted them, but not especially by offering so-called external goods to athletes who are lured from the austere pleasures of the practices themselves with the enticements of fame, fortune, and power. Rather, the corruption has stemmed from a denial of these broader virtues in the form of racial and sexual prejudice, national chauvinism, personal exploitation, and greed. Perhaps we must acknowledge the predominantly individual character of sports and their goods and refrain from thinking of them as society writ small. There is a loss for us in this view of sports. They will at most reflect, but not solve, problems of social justice; they will not be social microcosms. But there is a gain as well. We will open sports to explorations of difference, a celebration of the possibilities of change and a recognition of new ways of being human. In that case, society may well come to reflect what happens in sports: the game writ large.[20]

Notes

1. This paper was presented as the Presidential Address at the 18th Annual Meeting of the Philosophic Society for the Study of Sport, conducted at Indiana-Purdue University at Fort Wayne, in Fort Wayne in October 1990. As is customary, it is published [in this journal] in its original form.

2. I have in mind the views of Quine (11), "Two Dogmas of Empiricism," and Morton White (16), "The Analytic and the Synthetic: An Untenable Dualism," and other similar writings.

3. The view of practices as governed by rules was persuasively discussed by Rawls (13) and has spawned many progeny including recent debates in *The Journal of the Philosophy of Sport*. See, for example, Morgan (8) and Meier (7).

4. One of the striking deficiencies of MacIntyre's account (6) of practices is his neglect of this formal aspect of practices that is so evident in games, political associations, scientific disciplines, and other forms of practices.

5. We are inclined to see broad social systems as matrices that allow other practices to flourish with maximum freedom and effectiveness. Hence, the just organization of society becomes a central concern.

6. See Michael Polanyi (10).

7. As Samuel Scheffler (14) has argued. See MacIntyre's reply in the "Postscript to the Second Edition" of *After Virtue* (6).

8. Robert Simon briefly discusses this distinction for different purposes in his book (15: p. 91f).

9. But what of Eric Lidell, as portrayed in Hugh Hudson's 1981 film *Chariots of Fire,* when he remarks, "I believe God made me for a purpose: to go to China. But he also made me fast. And when I run I can feel God's pleasure."? Did Lidell run to please God (an external good) or to experience the pleasure of running fast and well?

10. See Boorse (1); Brown (2).

11. The same may surely be said of dance, which is clearly a practice in the sense developed here. Its frequent link with physical education or sport is an externally imposed association based on superficial similarities that ignore the internal aims and goods of the practices.

12. We can imagine all sports being made safer, much as fencing has been, while maintaining whatever levels of difficulty or challenge were once accompanied by the likelihood of injury or death. Boxing, for example, by the development of protective equipment, as is the case to some extent in football, could be made a sport entirely of

skill, relying not a whit on smashing noses or contusing brains.

13. Rawls's *A Theory of Justice* (12) is a now classical example of abstracting by means of a veil of ignorance over qualities of individuals to arrive at a theory of justice. Normal Daniels, in *Am I My Parents' Keeper?* (3: pp. 40–65), has similarly abstracted over features of individuals to formulate a "Prudential Lifespan Account" of health care.

14. Parfit (9) rejects the Requirement of Equal Concern. See Daniels (3, 4) for a critical discussion of this principle and its role in prudential planning.

15. I rely here on Daniels' (3) excellent discussion of similar issue.

16. This point is made by Daniels (3: p. 59).

17. These points are made by Daniels (3: pp. 59–60).

18. The same is true of institutions and the risk-aversive policies they may be inclined to make. Some advantages clearly will accrue to prudent or cautious policies for institutions like colleges and schools that wish to avoid lawsuits or have reasonable paternalistic goals in regard to children.

19. Nothing I have written should suggest that such injustices will justify the corruptions, feared by MacIntyre (6), from institutional interference in virtuous participation in sports.

20. I am most grateful for the patient, critical comments and discussion of an earlier draft of this paper by my colleagues Howard DeLong and Maurice Wade.

Bibliography

1. Boorse, Christopher. "Health as a Theoretical Concept." *Philosophy of Science,* 44 (1977), 542–573.

2. Brown, W. M. "On Defining 'Disease.'" *The Journal of Medicine and Philosophy,* 10 (1985), 311–328.

3. Daniels, Norman. *Am I My Parents' Keeper? An Essay on Justice Between the Young and the Old.* New York: Oxford, 1988.

4. Daniels, Norman. "Moral Theory and the Plasticity of Persons." *Monist,* 62 (1979), 265–287.

5. Kuhn, Thomas S. *The Structure of Scientific Revolutions. Second Edition.* Chicago: University of Chicago Press, 1970.

6. MacIntyre, Alasdair. *After Virtue. Second Edition.* Notre Dame, IN: University of Notre Dame Press, 1984.

7. Meier, Klaus V. "Performance Prestidigitation." *Journal of the Philosophy of Sport,* XVI (1989), 13–33.

8. Morgan, William J. "The Logical Incompatibility Thesis and Rules: A Reconsideration of Formalism as an Account of Games." *Journal of the Philosophy of Sport,* XIV (1987), 1–20.

9. Parfit, Derek. *Reasons and Persons.* Oxford: Oxford University Press, 1984.

10. Polanyi, Michael. *Personal Knowledge: Towards a Post-Critical Philosophy.* New York: Harper & Row, 1962.

11. Quine, W. V. *From a Logical Point of View. Second Edition.* Cambridge, MA: Harvard University Press, 1980.

12. Rawls, John. *A Theory of Justice.* Cambridge, MA: Harvard University Press, 1971.

13. Rawls, John. "Two Concepts of Rules." *Philosophical Review,* 64 (1955), 3–32.

14. Scheffler, Samuel. "Review of *After Virtue.*" *Philosophical Review,* 92 (1983), 443–447.

15. Simon, Robert L. *Sports and Social Values.* Englewood Cliffs, NJ: Prentice-Hall, 1985.

16. White, Morton G. "The Analytic and the Synthetic: An Untenable Dualism." In *Semantics and the Philosophy of Language.* Edited by Leonard Linsky. Urbana, IL: University of Illinois Press, 1952.

Questions for Consideration

1. Does Brown adequately argue that prudence must take a backseat to other goods? To what extent, then, is prudence itself a good?

2. Though risk is certainly a part of many sports, what is wrong with doing away with those sports that elevate risk above prudential concerns?

3. How much of what Brown has to say hinges on sport's being essentially a matter of individual expression instead of its being social in nature?

4. What limits, if any, do you think Brown would place on the means of achieving the goods of sports?

7 Moral Liberalism and the Atrophy of Sport: Autonomy, Desire, and Social Irresponsibility

M. Andrew Holowchak
Ohio University

Liberalism is the view that humans are independent, autonomous, and self-sufficient, and thus institutional policy is warranted only when it advances these values. As an important element in moral thought today, according to liberalism, a good life consists in the complete freedom of all people to pursue their own desires, provided that little or no harm is done to others along the way.

As moral policy, liberalism also pervades the literature in philosophy of sport. In this reading, I argue that liberalism as moral policy in sport is wrong because liberalism as moral policy is wrong. In addition, correct moral policy cannot merely be the free expression of individuals' desires. Humans are essentially social creatures, thus human autonomy can only be fully realized in social institutions. Human autonomy implies social responsibility—the very thing that liberals decry.

The final section of the reading reconsiders early Greek cosmopolitan and communitarian views as they relate to ancient morality. The overall aim is to blend what is right about liberalism with what is right from antiquity. As essentially social creatures, individuals find autonomy most efficiently within the confines of social institutions. The implications for athletic practice are clear.

Introduction

Liberalism, generally apprehended, is a moral/political philosophy that entails that

An earlier version of this paper appeared in *Contemporary Philosophy*, Vol. XXII, No. 1 & 2. Moultonborough, NH: REALIA, 2000, pp. 30–37.

people are autonomous individuals, whose right to self-determination is paramount. As moral policy, liberalism asserts that as long as my values, based on my desires or wants, do not conflict with yours, then I am both free to do and justified in doing what I want (while all others are free to do the same). My desires individuate me, and freely acting upon them is the purest expression of my autonomy. As political policy, liberalism demands that all institutional interference that does not conduce toward greater liberty is unwarranted and immoral. Moreover, many of today's political liberals assert that government must be indifferent on issues concerning the good life for its citizens.

Liberalism has its roots in the empirical thought of such philosophers as Locke, Hume, and Mill—and has greatly impacted all subsequent moral and political thinking. In political views, its most prominent contemporary spokesperson is the philosopher John Rawls,[1] whose works *A Theory of Justice* (1971) and *Political Liberalism* (1993) have been seminal in reconciling democratic pluralism with liberal justice. The prevailing themes of political liberalism—equal distribution of goods and opportunity, equal rights, governmental noninterference, autonomy, and self-determination—have become prominent themes in moral thinking today. What contemporary moral liberals emphasize, however, is the essentially irrational nature of human behavior: Moral dictates today subserve desires or impulses.

It should come as no surprise then that liberalism pervades the literature in philosophy of sport also. Many of today's philosophers and critics maintain that sport is the culmination of the free, creative efforts of athletes and that impediments to this free play stifle autonomy and, thus, are morally intrusive. Consequently, most attempts at normative analysis or evaluation of sport come at the expense of severe restrictions on the autonomy of athletes and are, thereby, paternalistic.

In this paper, I argue quite simply that liberalism as moral policy in sport is wrong because liberalism as moral policy is wrong. In developing my argument, I first sketch out a brief history of moral thought, then turn to some of the arguments of key proponents of moral liberalism in philosophy of sport today. Next, I argue that philosophic liberals in philosophy of sport can learn something by looking back to the "communitarian" models of early Greek moral thinking or even to the social and political sentiments of the early empiricists who provided the very foundation for liberal morality. Finally, I offer a normative critique of sportive practice today that enumerates the responsibilities that athletes have in competitive sport.

Brief Historical Sketch

Systematic ethical speculation began with the ancient Greeks—most notably Socrates. For the ancient Greeks, the study of ethics was equivalent to the critical analysis of the development of moral character. Aristotle, for example, tells us that the word "ethics" itself comes from two Greek words, each of which was deemed central to development of character: ἔθος, meaning "habit," and ηθος, meaning "character."[2] In short, being a good person is a matter of being rationally habituated to develop a certain unwavering state of character. Having a virtuous character means having a harmonious soul in which the naturally discordant parts behave amicably under the governance of reason.

What is important here is that the Greek ethical ideal focuses on the person doing an action,

instead of the action itself.[3] Though a person's character is thought to be determined (or habituated) by repeated actions over time, once character is formed, it is one's character that principally determines an action's worth. The internal goodness or psychic stability of such moral agents is, according to the Greeks, a better sign of an action's value than the act itself or its consequences. In a word, for the ancient Greeks, an action is judged virtuous because it is performed by a virtuous person.

How, then, is it possible to identify a good person? Aristotle, for example, gives a solution patterned on the medical model of health. The abundantly healthy person, just like one who is dreadfully ill, sticks out in a crowd. In a similar manner, the virtuous person is clearly recognizable by a consistency of behavior that indicates a moral stability of a soul in perfect or, what is more likely, in near-perfect harmony.

Modern accounts of ethics are mostly action, not agent, oriented.[4] We become good men and women by engaging in the right kind of actions. This is certainly consistent with ancient views, where habituation is a critical part of virtuous upbringing, but its emphasis is otherwise. In most modern moral accounts, we are defined by our actions, not by character. Courage today is a matter of engaging in courageous deeds. For the ancient Greeks, courage is a matter of having the right kind of soul—a stable soul that disposes people to act courageously at the appropriate time. With the modern-day emphasis on actions, not agents, questions of ethics (having a good character) are reduced to those of morality (doing good deeds).

Let me now turn to two of the most prominent lines of moral thought today: the views of David Hume and John Stuart Mill's utilitarianism.[5] For both Hume and Mill, right action is determined by obligation or perceived consequences. Character does not enter into the picture.

David Hume, in his *Enquiry Concerning the Principles of Morals*, accepted the existence of moral principles and moral duty,[6] and sought their foundation. The only candidates, he avers, are reason and sentiment. Of his method of investigation, he writes:

> For if we can be so happy, in the course of this enquiry, as to discover the true origin of morals, it will then easily appear how far either sentiment or reason enters into all determinations of this nature. In order to attain this purpose, we shall endeavour to follow a very simple method: We shall analyze that complication of mental qualities, which form what, in common life, we call PERSONAL MERIT: We shall consider every attribute of the mind, which renders a man an object either of esteem and affection, or of hatred and contempt; every habit or sentiment or faculty, which, if ascribed to any person, implies either praise or blame, and may enter into any panegyric or satire of his character and manners.[7]

Yet in the realm of human affairs, which Hume thinks excludes considerations of self-interest, the ultimate appeal to all determinations of duty is utility.[8] What compels us to act on behalf of the communal good of humankind is a psychological bond of sympathy with other humans—a feeling that can only be cultivated in social settings.[9] Though originally and naturally weaker than self-interest, the social sentiment, Hume argues, is in some sense more fundamental than self-interest. Thus, there can be a science of morality, insofar as we apprehend that the grounding principles themselves have their basis in human sentiment, not reason. Reason does, however, function instrumentally in promoting human sentiment and duty.[10] A good person for Hume, acting on a universal feeling, is one whose behavior promotes the common good instead of self-interest.

The second view under consideration, utilitarianism, has affinities with Humean morality. Its most prominent proponent is John Stuart Mill. In his work *Utilitarianism,* Mill puts forth the greatest-happiness principle: "Actions are right in proportion as they tend to promote happiness, wrong as they tend to produce the reverse of happiness."[11] The wording clearly is not categorical, but a comparative notion of right and wrong. No action is right or wrong in and of itself, but only insofar as it has the right or wrong sort of results. The sanction for the greatest-happiness principle is for Mill an inner feeling—a pain "attendant upon violation of duty" that all humans share.[12] Mill's utilitarianism, like Hume's ethics, is thus consequentialist.

Like the empiricists Bacon, Hobbes, and Locke before them,[13] Hume and Mill have each had a marked impact on contemporary moral thought and illustrate nicely the modern emphasis on action, not deed. More importantly, both thinkers have significantly influenced the development of the various manifestations of liberal thought in contemporary morality: especially the notions of self-sufficiency, appetite, and autonomy and the assumption that reason subserves feeling in moral actions. In deriving moral duty from feeling—a universal, social sentiment in humans—not reason, each reduced questions concerning morality to those of human psychology. On such an account, there can be no *philosophically* interesting sense of "ought," as Immanuel Kant maintains,[14] since right action is based upon appetites or natural impulses. Various views of morality today—descriptivism, naturalism, emotivism, and postmodernism—in grounding morality in wanting or desiring of some form, have by fiat reduced morality to one kind or another of hedonism.

What contemporary thinkers have emphasized in this hedonistic legacy is the notion, found especially in Mill, of humans as autonomous, self-determining agents. When adding autonomy to hedonism, the picture of liberal morality we arrive at is the unholy marriage of human autonomy and human irrationality. We flourish when we freely act on our desires and wants, and reason at best functions instrumentally to get us what we want.

Let me turn to what I take to be the most pernicious and vapid account of liberal morality to-day: postmodernism. Postmodernism thrives in certain fashionable philosophical sects, in the sociological literature, and, most importantly for this undertaking, in philosophy of sport. This view is difficult to put into words, for there are as many different formulations as there are adherents, and even adherents often willingly admit to a certain confusion.[15] Whatever their differences, postmodernists to a person all agree that philosophy has come to a turning point where it must be discontinued or, at least, be radically transformed. Strictly speaking, postmodernists reject any substantive or universalized notion of rationality and offer instead a happy antiauthoritarianism that takes as its basis autonomy of desire, embedded within the ever-changing conventions and constructs of society. It rails against any meaningful sense of philosophy as it has been traditionally done and offers nothing substantive in its place. Bob Brecher has this to say concerning postmodernist confusion:

> Postmodernism is the outcome of the destructive dialectic between the twin peaks of empiricism and liberalism: their squeamishness about reason and their misconceivedly atomized—because deracinated—conception of the individual.[16]

A postmodernist morality, if Brecher is right, is liberalism taken to its chaotic extreme. Individuals, as essentially irrational beings, are free to follow the various currents of antagonistic impulses that swirl about helter-skelter within themselves and their vacillating society.[17] With postmodernism, there is absolutely no room for any sensible conception of morality. Thus we are compelled to shun morality and return to the larger notion of ethics—the notion of living a good life—where "good" can only be construed as "going with the flow of one's impulses."

If I am correct in insisting that liberal morality of the sort described is an outstandingly prominent feature of contemporary moral spec-ulation, then today we have moved away from the provinciality of morality and its emphasis on some sense of rightness or wrongness of actions, back to full-fledged ethics. With liberal morality, however, we have not done so from any richer or more complete notion of human agency and culpability. We have done so merely because the notion of a right or wrong action makes no sense when basing morality prominently, if not *exclusively,* upon desires. We have fallen back upon a self-service morality of egoistic hedonism and there is no possibility for reason to intercede.

Moral Liberalism and Sport

Liberalism has also taken root in the philosophy of sport literature with the relatively recent surge of interest in this discipline in the last few decades.[18]

Over the years, W. Miller Brown has been an eloquent spokesperson for political and moral liberalism in philosophy of sport. Since Brown's political views are based upon the kind of moral liberalism I find to be morally inadmissible, I now turn to Brown's arguments on behalf of liberal morality in sport.

In the paper "Paternalism, Drugs, and the Nature of Sports," Brown articulates the most compelling argument on behalf of liberal morality and liberal practice of sport, the paternalist argument, as he defends the use of performance-enhancing drugs in competitions.

> The values, perhaps even a conception of what is good for human life, are associated with sports, not because of their nature, but due to the way we choose to play them. We can indeed forbid the use of drugs in athletics in general, just as we do in the case of children. But ironically, in adopting such a paternalistic stance of insisting that we know better than the athletes themselves how to achieve some more general good which they myopically ignore, we must deny them the very attributes we claim to value:

self-reliance, personal achievement, and autonomy.[19]

In short, on the assumption of autonomy as a great good, to forbid athletes the use of performance-enhancing drugs is to state paternalistically that we know what is best for them as regards their own health and their own values.

Again, in "Practices and Prudence," he takes a liberal approach to risk taking. He writes:

> Where it was possible to consider the goods to be achieved by sports practices as agent-independent, little headway seemed possible even in a society where it could be assumed that the basic goods of life were distributed in a just manner. The problem is that although risk appraisal is a statistical matter, risk taking is a personal one. Risk taking is not agent-independent, but, rather, relative to the overall circumstances and goals of individuals.[20]

In short, the values of one person may not be the values of another. We may know statistically that someone is taking great risk in pursuing a certain sport, a particular manner of practice, or even a special performance-enhancing drug, but this gives us no right to forbid that person the opportunity to take such a risk. Again, the linchpin of his argument is the primacy of autonomy in his axiological system and the subordination of other values, which seem to vary from person to person, to it.

Last, in a 1980 paper—"Ethics, Drugs, and Sport"—Brown argues in effect that normative approaches to philosophy of sport are conservative and ultimately quash autonomy, change, and creativity. He says:

> What is in question here is a powerful moral vision which may be taken to guide our judgments about both the games we play and who may play them together. It is a vision we all share to some extent, but one which I think is increasingly open to doubt. For it embodies, I believe, an essentially conservative attitude toward the human condition which neglects to give sufficient weight to *a primary human value:* freedom. It opts for relative stability, predictability, and control in human affairs, rather than novelty, change, surprise, and creativity. It presupposes a relative fixity in the human condition as opposed to an evolving transformation of what we are. . . . If the question is, as I believe it is, "who or what am I?", the answer can be sought either in a race or on long solitary runs. But the answer will be relative. It will be: in these shoes, on this day, following those workouts and with the aid of whatever substances, given the current state of my knowledge, have become part of my diet, medication, and preparation. Such self-knowledge is as changing as our knowledge in general, whose sources, too, lie in human freedom. Indeed, I suspect that if we survive as a species for another century, our understanding not only of what we are and how we have become what we are, but of what we can make of ourselves, will be so transformed as to render athletics as we know them now obsolete.[21]

In agreement with Brown, Michael Burke has recently argued that our moral condemnation of the use of performance-enhancing drugs in sport is a result of a confusion resulting when an oral culture (and morality) of sport gets fixed into a "written culture of constancy" that is inconsistent with human nature. Sport is dynamic and flowing, and this dynamism and flow are constantly responsible for innovation in and redefinition of sport. He states:

> Drug users test the latitude of the rules in a way that is not as far removed from the change that Dick Fosbury produced with his new technique as we would like to think. New knowledge, technical innovation, training

methods, new materials, and stronger, faster athletes all create redefinitions of games. . . . All testing of the latitude involves egocentric attempts by players to shape the practice. No one attempt is more morally condemnable than any other. All attempts, whether successful or not, involve the production of beneficiaries and victims. The drug user in modern times is a victim, much as the exponents of the scissors method of high jumping were also victims. Both are victims of aesthetic sensibilities of the community.

The definition and redefinition of "sport," he believes, is to be found in the actual practice of sport and not in any written culture, for the latter quashes autonomy in order to preserve constancy of practice.[22]

Against Brown, Burke, and other proponents of moral liberalism like Terrence Roberts, I have elsewhere shown that a normative perspective *most fully* allows autonomy, creativity, and change.[23] It merely mandates social responsibility and accountability for athletic actions. I develop this more thoroughly below.

Individuals and Society

Before addressing the arguments in the previous section, I want to articulate fully just what it is that I do not propose to do in what follows. Throughout, my intent is mostly destructive. I want to show that liberal morality cannot be defended in sport because liberal morality itself cannot be defended. In disavowing liberal morality, I am not thereby championing any specific moral alternative to it that insists upon social responsibility (i.e., deontology, utilitarianism, or virtue theory). I merely want to show that whatever alternative anyone adopts, it cannot be one that embraces a view of autonomy as something independent of social responsibility.

Now I shall respond to the paternalist objection in the manner with which it is often attacked. A common and decisive response to the paternalist objection is that there are no actions that involve only an individual. The reckless driver is an obvious menace to others on the road, but what of the quiet but grotesquely overweight man who sates his hunger each day with burgers and fries at every meal? Unfortunately even these actions in time impact society. Those who live healthily pay the price for those who live without regard for health. This example does not raze liberal morality, but it serves to illustrate a serious objection to it. Individuals' actions take shape within the context of a particular social institution and, thus, have various effects, even if many of these effects often go unnoticed.

Even Mill, perhaps the greatest proponent of liberalism, saw the tension and attempted a rebuff in *On Liberty.* He states, "Each is the proper guardian of his own health, whether bodily or mental and spiritual. *Mankind are greater gainers by suffering each other to live as seems good to themselves than by compelling each to live as seems good to the rest*" (my italics).[24] Clearly, Mill acknowledges that we each must suffer a little "for the sake of the greater good of human freedom."[25] In other words, the man committed to a daily intake of saturated fat may eventually burden society at the age of forty by suffering a debilitating stroke that could have been avoided, or he may merely set a bad example of unhealthy living for those around him—say, his wife, children, and coworkers. Any way you look at it, his actions extend beyond himself. So much for risk taking being a personal matter.

To preserve the freedom to act according to egoistic desires, liberals such as Brown and Burke insist that we are essentially autonomous, wanting individuals first and only incidentally social creatures. Brecher elaborates articulately on the defects of such a position:

Just as the alleged incorrigibility of what we want serves finally to undermine moral justification, so its allegedly value-free conception of harm in the end obscures and even makes paradoxical the liberal insistence that interference with individual autonomy is justified only "to prevent harm to others." For in failing to see individuals as embedded within the society and various sub-groups in which they live, it cannot deal adequately with those harms that are morality-dependent, harms which cannot be recognized from a value-neutral vantage-point.[26]

Contrary to contemporary liberal moralists and liberal social policy, no actions within a society have consequences only for an individual. Repeated, uncriticized actions invite emulation and may become entrenched as social norms and become part of our system of social values. Autonomous individuals, athletes included, have responsibilities to society. Athletes today far too often try to escape from such responsibilities as if their greater visibility and "heroic" status make them worthy of moral praise and immune to moral condemnation. We need only to recall the words of Charles Barkley, "I am not a role model. . . . Just because I can dunk a basketball doesn't mean I should raise your kids."[27] Barkley's point is well taken: He is certainly not responsible for raising anyone else's children. On the other hand, as a professional athlete he ought not thereby to be afforded social and political privileges other contributing citizens of a community are not allowed. We are *all* role models in a sense by virtue of being citizens who are willingly integrated into a political community. Thus, we are all equally responsible for our deeds (on or off whatever "playing field"). One might expect that those in the social spotlight would be better aware of this moral responsibility.

Liberalism as a justification of sportive practice is wrong then, because liberalism as morality is wrong. In addition, adoption of liberal morality is itself harmful, because adoption of false moral views, like liberalism, have insidiously inimical consequences. People are social animals, sport is social practice, and individuals participating in sports have social responsibilities.

The Greek Ethical Ideal

In this section, I return to where I began: Greek ethics. There is, I hope to show, much we can learn today from these ancient thinkers.

In spite of its failings, the Greek view of life was ethically healthier and certainly more robust than is ours. With the stain of liberal thinking in contemporary ethical thinking, there is little sense of rightness or justice today other than that which protects individuals' rights to pursue their own ends through the gratification of their own impulses. Morality and constitutions based on gratification of impulses have no true foundation and cannot endure. Today we delight in disagreement, not for the sake of serving a springboard for consensus or truth in the future, but as an end itself. Our wisdom is equanimity with a touch of buoyant grace in the face of adversity—the ability to tolerate differences of opinion, however absurd and unfounded, with bubbling enthusiasm. Normativism, postmodernists rage, is dead. In its place, anything goes.

Toleration of divergent opinion is, of course, a very good thing—especially in matters unsettled by rational dispute—but it is not and ought not to be an end in itself. As humans, we want answers to the questions we ask. It may be that many of these questions do not presently admit of answers. Others may never admit of answers. Still, levelheaded dispute will serve provisionally, at least, to help us differentiate sensible from senseless questions. This is as Mill emphasizes in *On Liberty* and one of the things that we need to salvage of liberal moral policy.

With a focus on cultivating and maintaining excellence of character and evaluating the justness of an act by the goodness of the person committing that act, Greek ethics placed a premium on responsibility in spite of the fact that they had no sense of "individual" as we do today. "Individual" took meaning only insofar as one took part in one's community or developed a sense of cosmic responsibility. Today, regardless of ethical perspective, we call *actions* just or unjust, not agents performing them. This change of perspective is itself significant for culpability. We do not want to blame ourselves when what we do goes wrong if we can blame the action itself or the appetitive motivating it.

Today's moral liberalism leaves no place for responsibility squarely on the shoulders of an agent. After all, liberal morality is a matter of autonomous agents fulfilling personal desires. Communities are meant only to serve individuals. Cosmopolitanism today, if there can be any meaningful sense, is an individual's freedom to walk the world at large. There is no sense of duty to other, to community, or to anything other than personal desires.

The picture that I draw, many will say, is grossly exaggerated. If we could travel back to ancient Greece, for instance, we would see as much (perhaps even more) lust, greed, indulgence, and selfishness as we do in modern democratic societies. I do not challenge this objection at all, for this is not chiefly what is at issue here. My aim is philosophical and not sociological. The issue here concerns the philosophic visions of Greek times and ours.

The great thinkers of ancient Greece had a broader, grander philosophic vision than our politicians and philosophers, both men and women, have today. Theirs was a rational ideal of binding people together for the common good. The modern liberal ideal is individuation, and reason has the job of securing individuation through fulfilling desires. We would do well to remember what Aristotle has often said: We are, by nature, political animals.[28] Our good is thus to be had principally in political institutions. Autonomy, if it is expressed as an asocial ideal or even if it is just expressed indifferently to institutionalization, is an unhappy ideal. Even the very founders of the empirico-liberal tradition were fully aware of this.

Unlike many of today's moral liberals, the Greek ethicists firmly understood that actions do more than mirror society; they help create society. We need to be reminded that, as communities are founded to serve individuals, they only work well when individuals work together for the good of their communities. Sport itself is social practice, and we, as athletes and fans, are in this for the sake of the common good of all people.

Notes

1. John Rawls, *A Theory of Justice* (Cambridge, Mass.: Belknap, 1971) and *Political Liberalism* (New York: Columbia University Press, 1993).

2. Aristotle, *Nicomachean Ethics* II.1 (Indianapolis: Hackett, 1985).

3. A notable exception is the philosopher Epicurus.

4. With Kant being a prominent exception.

5. There are many types of utilitarian systems, just as there are numerous a priori systems with affinities to that of Kant. Exhaustive elaboration of all such systems is not essential for my argument.

6. David Hume, *An Enquiry Concerning the Principles of Morals* (J. B Schneewind, ed., Indianapolis: Hackett, *Enquiry* 1983): 14–15.

7. Ibid., 15–16.

8. Ibid. 19

9. Ibid., 44, 49.

10. Ibid., 82–85.

11. John Stuart Mill, *Utilitarianism* (George Sher, ed., Indianapolis: Hackett, 1979 [1861]).

12. Ibid., 27–28.

13. Bacon, Hobbes, and Locke each grounded moral assertions upon appetites, desires, or affections, not reason. Locke's account, however, is not so fundamentally irrational. See Francis Bacon, "The Advancement of Learning" in *The Philosophical Works of Francis Bacon* (London: George Routledge & Sons, 1905): 110; Thomas Hobbes, *Leviathan* (Harmondsworth, England: Penguin, 1968); and John Locke, *An Essay Concerning Human Understanding* (P. II. Nidditch, ed., Oxford: Clarendon Press, 1975): 229.

14. Immanuel Kant, *Groundwork of the Metaphysics of Morals* (Cambridge, England: Cambridge University Press, 1998).

15. Kenneth Baynes, James Bohman, and Thomas McCarthy, *After Philosophy: End or Transformation?* (Cambridge, Mass.: MIT Press, 1989): 3.

16. Bob Brecher, *Getting What You Want: A Critique of Liberal Morality* (New York: Routledge, 1998): 4.

17. In philosophy of sport, Terrence Roberts, following Richard Rorty, writes concerning three contenders for a viable postmodernist notion of rationality: "According to

Rorty, there are three uses of the word rationality. First, rationality$_1$ refers to the capacity of human and nonhuman organisms to control and manipulate the environment to get more of what the organism needs and wants. Second, rationality$_2$ is used to refer to a special human capacity in which language as a medium plays a key role that allows humans both to get in touch with nonhuman reality and to describe themselves as different from nonhumans. Third, rationality$_3$ refers to the tolerance of difference and the corresponding willingness to change one's habits either to get yet more of what one wants or to reshape oneself into a different sort of person who wants things other than what was wanted before." Like Rorty, he bars the second from any serious consideration. See Terrence Roberts, "'It's Just Not Cricket': Rorty and Unfamiliar Movements—History of Metaphors in a Sporting Practice," *Journal of the Philosophy of Sport* XXIV (1997): 68. Roberts's view of liberal rationality I have argued elsewhere is incoherent. See M. Andrew Holowchak, "'Aretism' and Pharmacological Ergogenic Aids in Sport: Taking a Shot at Steroids," *Journal of the Philosophy of Sport* XXVII (2000): 35–50.

18. Three of the most outspoken liberals in philosophy of sport are Terrence Roberts, whose views are manifestly Rortian; William J. Morgan, who as I see it champions a neo-Rawlsian sort of political liberalism that is not inconsistent with the type of moral liberalism that I find objectionable; and W. Brown, who is one of the most vocal proponents of moral liberalism today. See William J. Morgan, "Are Sports More So Private or Public Practices? A Critical Look at Some Recent Rortian Interpretations of Sport," *Journal of the Philosophy of Sport* XXVII (2000): 17–34; and W. Miller Brown, "Ethics, Drugs, and Sport," *Journal of the Philosophy of Sport* VII (1980): 15–23; "Paternalism, Drugs, and the Nature of Sports," *Journal of the Philosophy of Sport* XI (1985): 14–22; "Practices and Prudence," *Journal of the Philosophy of Sport* XVII (1990): 71–84; and Roberts "'It's Just Not Cricket.'"

19. W. Miller Brown, "Paternalism, Drugs, and the Nature of Sports," 21.

20. W. Miller Brown, "Practices and Prudence," 246.

21. W. M. Brown, "Ethics, Drugs, and Sport," 22.

22. Michael Burke and Terence J. Roberts, "Drugs in Sport: An Issue of Morality or Sentimentality?" *Journal of the Philosophy of Sport* XXIV (1997): 60.

23. M. Andrew Holowchak, "'Aretism' and Pharmacological Ergogenic Aids in Sport."

24. John Stuart Mill, *On Liberty* (New York: Penguin, 1985): 72.

25. Ibid., 149.

26. Bob Brecher, *Getting What You Want,* 155.

27. Russell W. Gough, *Character Is Everything: Promoting*

Ethical Excellence in Sports (New York: Harcourt Brace College, 1997): 57.

28. Aristotle, *Nicomachean Ethics* I.7.

Bibliography

Aristotle. *Nicomachean Ethics.* Indianapolis: Hackett, 1985.

Bacon, Francis. "The Advancement of Learning," in *The Philosophical Works of Francis Bacon.* London: George Routledge & Sons, 1905.

Baynes, Kenneth, James Bohman, and Thomas McCarthy. *After Philosophy: End or Transformation?* Cambridge, Mass.: MIT Press, 1989.

Brecher, Bob. *Getting What You Want: A Critique of Liberal Morality.* New York: Routledge, 1998.

Brown, W. M. "Ethics, Drugs, and Sport." *Journal of the Philosophy of Sport* VII (1980), 15–23.

———. "Paternalism, Drugs, and the Nature of Sports." *Journal of the Philosophy of Sport* XI (1985), 14–22.

———. "Practices and Prudence." *Journal of the Philosophy of Sport* XVII (1990), 71–84.

Burke, Michael, and Terence J. Roberts. "Drugs in Sport: An Issue of Morality or Sentimentality?" *Journal of the Philosophy of Sport* XXIV (1997), 99–113.

Gough, Russell W. *Character Is Everything: Promoting Ethical Excellence in Sports.* New York: Harcourt Brace College, 1997.

Hobbes, Thomas. *Leviathan.* Harmondsworth, England: Penguin, 1968.

Holowchak, M. Andrew. "'Aretism' and Pharmacological Ergogenic Aids in Sport: Taking a Shot at the Use of Steroids." *Journal of the Philosophy of Sport* XXVII (2000), 35–50.

Hume, David. *An Enquiry Concerning the Principles of Morals.* Ed. J. B Schneewind. Indianapolis: Hackett, 1983.

Kant, Immanuel. *Groundwork of the Metaphysics of Morals.* Trans. Mary Gregor. Cambridge, England: Cambridge University Press, 1998.

Locke, John. *An Essay Concerning Human Understanding.* Ed. P. H. Nidditch. Oxford: Clarendon Press, 1975.

Mill, John Stuart. *Utilitarianism.* 1861. Reprint, ed. George Sher, Indianapolis: Hackett, 1979.

———. *On Liberty.* New York: Penguin, 1985.

Morgan, William J. "Are Sports More So Private or Public Practices? A Critical Look at Some Recent Rortian Interpretations of Sport." *Journal of the Philosophy of Sport* XXVII (2000), 17–34.

Plato. *Five Dialogues.* Trans. G. M. A. Grube. Indianapolis: Hackett, 1981.

———. *Republic.* Trans. G. M. A. Grube. Indianapolis: Hackett, 1992.

Pojman, Louis P. *Ethical Theory: Classical and Contemporary Readings.* New York: Wadsworth, 1995.

Rawls, John. *A Theory of Justice.* Cambridge, Mass.: Belknap, 1971.

———. *Political Liberalism.* New York: Columbia University Press, 1993.

Roberts, Terrence. "'It's Just Not Cricket': Rorty and Unfamiliar Movements—History of Metaphors in a Sporting Practice." *Journal of the Philosophy of Sport* XXIV (1997), 67–78.

Questions for Consideration

1. Can there be a meaningful sense of "morality" based fundamentally on desire (that is, without a meaningful use of reason to tether desire)?

2. To what extent, if any, does the merging of ancient and modern values solve the problem the reading addresses?

3. Contrast the view of sport as it relates to society in this reading with Brown's view. Which view do you think is correct?

8 Is Sport Unique? A Question of Definability

S. K. Wertz
Texas Christian University

A survey of the philosophy-of-sport literature on the nature of sport, S. K. Wertz says, shows two main approaches to the problem of demarcating sport from nonsport. The formalist approach regards sport as closed. As such, it seeks some essence or definition of sport. In contrast, the interpretive approach is open in that it resists any attempt to define sport. Which of these is correct? Wertz attempts to settle this issue once and for all.

If we take the concept of "uniqueness" as regards sport to be some attribute that is exclusive to sport, we do not find anything in sport that answers to this concept. The attributes of sport, we find, are also in other domains, such as art, anthropology, economy, politics, and religion. Sport, we soon discover, has no essence because it is not a closed concept, but rather an open one. The characteristic attributes of sport then are not discrete and singular, but continuous and complex. Although sport has no essence, it is identifiable at any point in time by a nonfixed cluster of attributes.

Since sport fails to be unique in terms of having any fixed nature over time, the philosophical problems of sport are problems other disciplines share.

In this essay I address a variety of issues that pertain to the definability of sport. At the forefront is the demarcation problem, or how sport is distinguished from nonsport activities. Bernard Jeu (21: p. 154) raises these questions in this way:

How do we circumscribe the sphere of what is in essence sport? When is sport no longer properly so called? What is the threshold beyond which the notion of sport becomes something else? In other words, with what should it not be confused?

Answers to these important questions have divided themselves into two main interpretations of the demarcation problem, namely,

- the formalistic/deductive/uniqueness hypothesis, and
- the nonessentialistic/interpretive/satisfiability hypothesis.

The formalistic view insists on formal, exhaustive definitions of sport and regard sport to be a "closed" concept. It is most aptly defended by Hyland, Osterhoudt, and Suits. The interpretive view denies there are such definitions of sport and holds that it is an "open" concept. To defend the interpretive hypothesis leads me in several different directions: the demarcation problem and all its complexities, uniqueness claims, circularity, overinclusiveness, overlapping classes, sport-art relation, and the applied character of sport philosophy. With this conceptual terrain in mind, I want to demonstrate how these questions arose.

I was recently asked by a colleague:[1] Does sport have any unique attributes or are its problems and characteristics all reducible to other areas such as biology, philosophy, psychology, sociology, and so on? The answer, it seems to me, is that sport has no autonomous features, and consequently the features it has are all het-

Reprinted by permission, from S. K. Wertz, "Is Sport Unique? A Question of Definability," *Journal of the Philosophy of Sport*, XXII (1995): 83–93.

eronomous. There is controversy regarding the nature of art[2] but not sport.[3] My argument for this conclusion stems from several considerations.

First, let us consider what is meant by "uniqueness." If by "unique" we mean that a feature F applies *exclusively* to the concept of sport (hereafter called the exclusivity condition or EC for short), then we are committed to the view that F has no interpretation in the domain of nonsport. If this is what is meant by "unique," then I shall argue there are no Fs that apply to sport. Let me explain.

There are many generalizations that attempt to characterize or define sport, but none of these seem to apply just to sport and nothing else. Take for example Richard Galvin's (16) criticism of Drew Hyland and S. K. Wertz's attempts to delineate "sport." Galvin employs EC to demonstrate that arguments fail due to the problem of overinclusiveness (16: p. 90). He queries:

> What if I, having mastered the technical skills, intend to "execute the further moves" of taking out the garbage superbly, even beautifully, or artistically? The problem of overinclusiveness, which plagues Hyland's account, threatens Wertz's position as well. It would not do to claim that taking out the garbage is not an appropriate medium for aesthetic control, since the account would then be viciously circular. Indeed, this is the fundamental problem facing the "sport as art" thesis: how does one argue that sport is an art or has a deep affinity to art whereas taking out the garbage does not? And do so without vicious circularity? I have tried to show why relying on the "shared stance of . . . responsive openness" [which Hyland does] will not suffice. (16: p. 91)

Elsewhere Galvin (15: pp. 523–524) argues:

> We must, however, be able to produce an account of aesthetic control which does not require the attribution of intentions which

involve aesthetic concepts, whether as a necessary or sufficient condition, or make a covert reference to what is to count as an aesthetic medium. Clearly one worry here is fatal overinclusiveness; the other is vicious circularity. We need a principle of aesthetic control which will claim the carpenter's construction of the staircase [in the Loretto Chapel in Santa Fe, New Mexico], the composing of a music piece, and the performance of Peggy Fleming among its instances, but will exclude things like taking out the garbage, changing a flat tire, and the like. But circularity is the Scylla to this Charybdis—the principle of aesthetic control cannot contain the notion of an aesthetic medium as a crucial term in the analysis. Producing such an account is a major project for the view which Wertz proposes.

The logic of Galvin's reasoning works because he assumes that his opponents are trying to isolate an F that has an EC. But if that is the case, then any such F would have to be circular because if it excludes *all* nonsporting activities from the definition of "sport," then all that is left to tap as a viable resource pool is sport itself. So these attempts at defining or characterizing would have to end up in circularity. Let us look at two more cases.

Perhaps the most celebrated case is Bernard Suits's definition of "game-playing":

> To play a game is to attempt to achieve a specific state of affairs [prelusory goal], using only means permitted by rules [lusory means], where the rules prohibit use of more efficient in favour of less efficient means [constitutive rules], and where the rules are accepted just because they make possible such activity [lusory attitude]. (26: p. 41; Suits's brackets)

Galvin would undoubtedly say that this too suffers from overinclusiveness because this definition is satisfied by committee meetings following *Robert's Rules of Order* and by certain Oriental sex practices. If these are excluded, it is perhaps in the description of the lusory attitude (26: pp. 39–48) that then renders the definition circular.

Another case in point is Wertz's characterization of "sport" as a distinctive kind of *samadhi* (the Sanskrit term for concentration or contemplative awareness): "When we are truly absorbed in playing a game, a state of *sport samadhi* is actualized," where the player becomes an extension of the game (30: pp. 124, 216). This characterization begs the question because it presupposes game activities in its description of "sport" just as Suits's definition of "game-playing" does. The charge of circularity seems to hold for all four cases.

I suggest that this is true formally of any definition that seeks Fs that have EC as a requirement and divides the domain of discourse into regions X and non-X. If non-X is ruled out, then X must be appealed to; hence, circularity is unavoidable. But if this is the case, we have required too much of these cases. I claim that there are no Fs that possess EC. Consequently, there are no unique predicates that apply to sport. Sport's Fs are non-EC in character.

This conclusion is not only necessary but desirable. We must look to logical theory for guidance here. Exact definitions and formal characterizations of terms or concepts are equivalence relations (19: p. 186), so of course they would be circular. How could one otherwise substitute the definens (the defining expression) for the definendum (the term being defined) without a change in meaning or truth value? However, this theory of definition is far too stringent for what is required of philosophical definitions or characterizations such as those previously described. An alternative theory can be derived from model theory and the concept of satisfiability in logic.

A particular concept P is satisfiable if and only if objects exist that make the definens or definendum true. In other words, terms such as "game-playing," "aesthetic control over a

medium," "*sport samadhi*," and "responsive openness" apply to objects, and objects exist (in these cases, activities) that make them true because they satisfy the definendum (7: pp. 231, 290). Moves in chess, figure skating and gymnastics floor exercises, a tennis or martial arts episode, and playing basketball, respectively, satisfy the terms and establish their truth. That there are falsifying instances or objects that render the phrases false (such as taking out the garbage) is not decidedly against their truth.

These falsifying instances are contrary but they are not contradictory (i.e., impossible for it to be true in light of the falsifying instance). Or alternatively: "A sentence P is *satisfiable* if it is true in *some* structure" (3: p. 259; second emphasis added), but not in *every* structure (this is what is required of a sentence P to be logically or necessarily true). In other words, "using the notion of satisfaction, we can define what it means for a sentence to be true in a structure" (3: p. 260). Minimally, a definition or characterization is satisfiable if it is true *on at least one interpretation of it* (6: p. 49; emphasis added). If an interpretation exists for the definitions or characterizations previously described then we have a model for them. Arguably, we want these interpretations or models to be paradigms for those activities we describe in the philosophy of sport. And the greater the range of interpretation, the better.

The question is, how fruitful are these interpretations: Do they increase our understanding of the domain in question (i.e., sport)? So the definitions or characterizations should be treated more modestly than Galvin has done so by aligning them with persuasive or revelatory, or even stipulative, definitions rather than synonymous or extensional ones. The former definitions are not falsified by contrary instances, although those kind of instances taken from the domain in question, do lead us to question the worthiness of the definitions. So Galvin's "taking out the garbage or washing the dishes" (15: p. 90) are not interpretations that lead us to reject these definitions as false, but instances such as "a brain surgeon comports himself more responsively and openly than one playing checkers" (15: pp. 88–89) and "sports such as bowling and weightlifting require only a minimum level of responsive openness" (15: p. 89) do raise concern for Hyland's latest phenomenological description (20: pp. 71–80) of the stance of play as responsive openness.

Why? Narrowness seems to be a larger fault than broadness, because those counter instances lie closer to the paradigms. So to prove a theory of sport false, one needs only show that there are admitted examples to which it does not apply. "The conclusion of . . . [an] argument," A. N. Whitehead (33: p. 12) noted, "should then be confronted with circumstances to which it should apply."

The closer we are to the center of the web of belief (to use Quine's famous phrase), the more fundamental our beliefs are. So the aims of criticism are to produce commonly accepted examples that lie near the center of the web and to show that they are excluded from the class in question. Broadness tends to function or dwell on the parameter of the web and, hence, does not appear as decisive. Beliefs such as what today's weather will be, but not what we (or at least Hyland and company) take the stance of play to be, we give up rather easily.

As Daniel Bonevac (7: p. 108) observed, "rarely is a proposed definition directly circular," or what Galvin labelled "viciously circular." "But, in systems of definitions," Bonevac continues in *The Art and Science of Logic*, "indirect [or innocent] circularity is not unusual" (7: p. 108). The four cases I previously stated would belong to the latter kind of circularity rather than to the former. So a pertinent question to ask Wertz is: It is well and good that the definens you propose ("aesthetic control over a medium") are satisfied by figure skating and gymnastics floor exercises, which are sports that allow for individual expression and freedom, but what about competitive dominance sports such as football, which minimizes individual expression and freedom?[4] And Suits needs to be more concerned about

American drag racing and infinite[5] games than Oriental sex practices or committee meetings as possible counterexamples to his definition. *Sport samadhi* does not apply to all instances of game-playing—only those that are successful, highly accomplished, and masterful displays of game-playing. Even some of these may be conceivably done without the kind of awareness I have described (e.g., some highly competitive swimming events). Perhaps Professor Hyland would agree that responsive openness applies more to basketball than bowling or weightlifting. In bowling or weightlifting, a participant usually tries to minimize responsive openness, not enhance or maximize it.

If sport has no unique predicates, then the predicates it has are heteronomous and are found in other human purposive activities. They are borrowed or taken from its surroundings.[6] Because of the abundance of heteronomous predicates, sport has many analogies and analogues with other areas—anthropological, artistic, economic, political, religious, and social. My point about unique predicates is similar, but not identical, to one made by Josef Pieper concerning meaning in play. As a thought experiment, he asked, "How can we visualize something that serves nothing else, that by its very nature has meaning only in its own terms?" (24: p. 214). He evidently thought that it could not be done. "Human acts," Pieper declared, "derive their meaning primarily from their content, from their object, not from the manner in which they are performed. Play, however, seems to be chiefly a mere *modus* of action, a specific way of performing something, at any rate a purely formal determinant" (24: p. 214). If this is the case, play or any other human act like it is not meaningful in itself, but only in relation to other things or activities. Whitehead (33: p. 33) made an analogous point: "You cannot abstract the universe from any entity, actual or non-actual, so as to consider that entity in complete isolation." The point especially applies to the domain of sport. To claim that sport has unique predicates is tantamount to saying that all its actions are meaningless. But sport predicates are meaningful, so their meaning or "satisfaction" is derived from other domains. Hence, interpretations of the previous four cases must find their way into other human purposive activities besides those specified by their authors. How else could it be?

Also, overinclusiveness would be expected of *open* concepts (such as sport) because they are historically evolving as the institutions and participants change. It is those institutions and conventions that decide whether some object or activity (such as taking out the garbage) is an appropriate medium for aesthetic control or not. This, to my mind, is not vicious circularity. Picking out *relevant* features for a concept to satisfy and separating them from *irrelevant* ones is an act of defining that presupposes attributes of the things subsumed under that concept. (Taking out the garbage is not a relevant counterexample because it does not share enough features with sport actions, that is, the conventions that give them meaning.) To this extent, all definitions are circular. But as Bonevac suggested, this is nothing to get overly excited about in that it would bring on wholesale intellectual nihilism. This will not happen. Furthermore, because we can make identifying references to sport while lacking knowledge of its defining essence (if it has one!) an essential definition is unnecessary and indeed undesirable.[7] Essential definitions work for only closed concepts—not open ones such as sport and art.

If "uniqueness" is not understood in terms of EC, then how are we to understand it? There are numerous philosophers of sport who make the uniqueness claim and we need to make sense of that claim. Scott Kretchmar (22: p. 87; emphasis added), for instance, "argue[s] that athletes commonly achieve a *uniquely* human distance from their sport environments by reason of the abstract thinking engaged in by these performers during play." Again he (22: p. 98) adds, the phrase "uniquely human distancing in sport activity."

Hans Lenk (23: p. 443) commented that "the attractiveness and fascination of each unique sport depends also on its specific characteristics as perceived by both the athletes and the spectators." And Lynne Belaief (4: p. 421) foresaw that "sport uniquely addresses the agnostic dimension within life and shows us that we can indeed control and direct it into creative power which can then provide the ground of self-trust and the beginnings of the socialization of trust." "The unique, unchanging feature of baseball," Roger Angell (2: p. 156) wrote, is that "time moves differently, marked by no clock except the events of the game." None of the above have asked themselves what is meant by "unique," and it has remained unanalyzed until now.

Let us return to feature F in our initial definition of uniqueness in the concept of sport. We assumed that F is discrete and singular. What if we entertain the idea that F is continuous and complex. F consists in a set of defining properties that it shares with other purposive activities, and when taken together, they form a unique constellation fairly called sport and nothing else. Robert Osterhoudt (see note 9) has suggested that these "defining properties" are play, competition, and physicality, or the defining property is play of a special competitive and physical type.

This suggestion appears promising initially. Taken separately, these defining properties seem to escape the charge of circularity. Play and competition are shared by all distinctly human activities including religion and art, and physicality is shared by dance as well as sport. Taken together they seem to escape the charge of overinclusiveness and succeed in distinguishing sport from such as taking out the garbage, certain Oriental sex practices, and committee meetings. But what about dance? Dance satisfies these defining properties, in which case the overinclusiveness charge looms overhead. This is a serious charge if individuals such as Osterhoudt want to see these defining properties as essential ones that form a closed concept. Either we do not have the right mix or number of defining properties, or they are nonessential and open (to revision). The latter route I would take following the lead of Wittgenstein and Collingwood.

Long before Wittgenstein (34: Part I), R.G. Collingwood (10: Part II) developed the doctrine of the overlap of classes and foresaw the need for the definition of a concept in philosophy to be coextensive with its entire exposition (10: p. 96). This theory of definition is extreme, but "in a philosophical context," Collingwood argued,

> these species [essence and property] will overlap. And experience of philosophical thought shows that it is so. An essay on a philosophical concept like justice [or here sport] does not ordinarily begin with a definition of the concept and go on by deducing theorems about it [as is done in the exact sciences]; it consists from beginning to end of an attempt to expound the concept in a statement which may properly be described as an extended and reasoned definition. (10: pp. 95–96)

Description and definition come down to the same thing for Collingwood. This is, I think, a useful alternative to the formal theory of definition that is viewed (e.g., 19: p. 196) as equivalence relations.

The constellation idea has some interesting consequences. Is essence distinct from its properties? From the standpoint of Aristotelian metaphysics, only individuals or things have such distinction. Sport is not a thing. "Often we speak of a given sports event as if it were a single event," Robert Boyd (8: p. 97) rightfully observed, "when in fact it is a composition of events." The nature of this composition or constellation is *process* (see Wertz [31]). As Gebauer (17: p. 102) exquisitely expressed:

> One does not engage in sport alone, just as one does not play alone. The individual is only a small part of an extensive network of relations in play. In athletic action a great deal is present that extends beyond the individual gestures, fellow players, competitors, spectators, comparable earlier situations, and out-

comes. The principle of sport is not reduction to an individual but the extension of the human being.

This extension may be appreciated from a methodological point of view as the overlapping of classes. A concept such as sport has a dual significance—philosophical and nonphilosophical. As Collingwood (10: p. 35) described it:

> in its non-philosophical phase it qualifies a limited part of reality, whereas in its philosophical it leaks or escapes out of these limits and invades the neighbouring regions, tending at last to colour our thought of reality as a whole. As a nonphilosophical concept it observes the rules of classification, its instances forming a class separate from other classes; as a philosophical concept it breaks these rules, and the class of its instances overlaps those of its coordinate species.

Sport as a philosophical concept overlaps its coordinate species, principally, religion and art. Dance overlaps sport and art, ritual overlaps sport and religion, and so on. So sport is not distinct from its defining properties; it *is* its properties. And in some cases sport is not distinct from its coordinate species. Here is what Collingwood (10: p. 94) had to say about definitions:

> Definitions here [in exact science] define absolutely. A person possessing a definition knows the essence of the concept perfectly, one who does not possess it does not know that essence at all. In order that this should be possible, two conditions must be fulfilled. First, the essence must be something capable of final and exhaustive statement, and therefore sharply cut off from mere properties. Secondly, an equally sharp line must be drawn between knowing something and not knowing it. Owing to the differences in the structure of their concepts, both these conditions are fulfilled in exact science, neither in

philosophy. A definition in exact science states the essence as distinct from the properties; these, which flow logically from the essence, are stated in theorems.

There is no final and exhaustive statement of the defining properties of sport that would render the concept closed. How could we make such a claim when we are talking about a historical, institutional process? As Jeu (21: p. 159) noticed: "It [sport] could not be made independent of its own existence and its organizational forms." Consequently sport is an open concept, or an overlapping one, in Collingwood's terminology. Essentialists' arguments do not function adequately in the philosophy of sport and the reasons why are admirably brought out in Collingwood's *An Essay on Philosophical Method* (10). Anyone contemplating essentialism should study this masterpiece. "The species of a philosophical genus overlap," he (10: p. 95) reasons, "for essence and property are two species of attribute, and definitions and theorems are two corresponding species of exposition; in a philosophical context, therefore these species will overlap. And experience of philosophical thought shows that it is so." Galvin's overinclusiveness charge stems from thinking of the definitional requirements in philosophy as if it were an exact science, just as René Descartes did. The latter envisioned one method—a mathematical method—for all the sciences and this included philosophy. Galvin may be under the sway of Descartes's grand scheme. And in speaking of the overlapping concept of sport, let us look at this in action with the domain of art.

Another question Galvin raised concerns the appeal to intentions in deciding the question, Can sport be art? The reason why he thinks "it appears strange to maintain that the intentions of third parties can transform an object which is not otherwise a work of art into one which is," is that "the intuition is that the object itself must bear this burden—after all, *it* is the work of art" (15: p. 523). But this sets up an artificial division between intentions and "objects." Works of art

or artistic performances, such as Peggy Fleming's figure skating routines, *embody* intentions, and because they do, an appeal to third party intentions is made. Observers can recognize these *in* those "objects." Indeed, the "objects" have to be *interpreted* in order to classify them one way or another. The question of contemporary art— How does one differentiate an artwork from its ordinary counterpart? (e.g., Andy Warhol's *Campbell Soup Can* [1965] from a regular can of Campbell's soup)—is answered by Arthur Danto (11: p. 172):

Telling artworks from other things is not so simple a matter, even for native speakers, and these days one might not be aware he was on artistic terrain without an artistic theory to tell him so. And part of the reason for this lies in the fact that terrain is constituted artistic in virtue of artistic theories, so that one use of theories, in addition to helping us discriminate art from the rest, consists in making art possible.

These artistic theories *identify* intentions and make interpretations of objects possible. "The intuition," Galvin claims, "is that the object itself must bear this burden [of artistic identification]." It is a neoclassical idea that will not work for contemporary art and the aesthetic sports. In the realm of sport, they have the best possibility of containing artistic expression on the part of performers. It follows that my appeal to the intentions of the audience is not peculiar and it serves to circumvent the main objection to intentionalist criticism (i.e., that the performer could be mistaken or lack the overt intentions).[8] Objects do not inform us of their artistic status, as Galvin's own peculiar ontology suggests, but rather our interpretations (and intentions) make such demarcations. Works of art or art objects are generally the product of intentions. Elsewhere Danto (12: p. 45) put it this way: "The interpretation is not something outside the work: work and interpretation arise together in aesthetic consciousness. As interpretation is inseparable from work, it is inseparable from the artist if it is the artist's work." So the separation of object and intention is a questionable one in the premise of Galvin's argument.

With the constellation or composition idea we can make sense of the uniqueness claim. It is the way that things or events are put together that make sport unique. Perhaps this is all that Kretchmar (22: p. 99) meant when he wrote: "Each performer brings with him a unique set of physical capabilities, a unique history, a distinct set of hopes and desires." And specifically: "The unique fabric of the basketball world is referenced, in part, by this one habit [dribbling]" (22: p. 97). Wertz (30: p. 7) even got into the picture: "There are phenomena uniquely or characteristically associated with the world of sport" (although he does qualify uniqueness by "characteristically," which means that the paradigmatic cases share the features—the Fs—in question). This claim is far weaker than the interpretation I gave of "unique" at the beginning of this essay.

An additional consequence of my initial question (Is sport unique?) is that philosophy of sport has no distinctive problems or issues—they are ones covered by other areas of philosophy. The philosophical problems of human movement are ones found in action theory, metaphysics, and theory of knowledge. There is no autonomous (in the strong sense) philosophy of sport with its own agenda (there is of course in the constellation sense). What this means is that philosophy of sport is truly applied philosophy—no more, no less. What I have demonstrated here that the application of philosophy to the domain of sport is interpretive rather than deductive.

In sum, I have challenged the core arguments of essentialism and hopefully have laid them to rest. It is important that philosophers of sport return to the fundamental questions of methodology from time to time. I have looked to logical theory for guidance in these matters. Galvin's sharp criticism of definitions of sport prompted me to reexamine the issues his discussion raised. Arguments regarding the nature of sport fail, he contended, due to the problems of overinclusiveness, circularity, and uniqueness. I addressed these problems with an eye on the nature and purpose of definition in philosophy and the doctrine of overlapping classes; I was assisted by Collingwood's great work (10) in this area. Building on this structure, I suggested alternative readings of four celebrated definitions of sport along the lines of the nonessentialistic/interpretive/satisfiability hypothesis. This was a much more charitable reading than Galvin's, which evoked the formalistic/deductive/uniqueness hypothesis. Further doubt was cast upon the latter hypothesis by the theoretical isolation required of terms. Context or surroundings became the source of meaning for the interpretive hypothesis; hence, the doctrine of overlapping classes or terms became a major premise in the argument I previously outlined. If criticism in the philosophical literature in sport takes on a new direction, I will feel that my efforts here have been fruitful.[9]

Notes

1. Professor Bill Watson, Department of Chemistry, Texas Christian University, Fort Worth, Spring, 1992. "Reducible" is my chemist friend's choice of words here. It is a technical term that refers to the activity series among chemical elements that are organized in terms of those easily reduced at the top and those reduced with difficulty at the bottom (i.e., molecules of one element are absorbed by another). So it is natural that he would phrase the question this way. I would chose a term closer to Gebauer's "extensions" (17: p. 102), for example, "extensible," in raising the question, Does sport have any unique attributes or are its problems and characteristics all extensible to (or from) other areas in general, such as art, biology, philosophy, psychology, sociology, and so on? Notice that I have added the domain of art to my chemist's list of natural and social sciences, and philosophy. One could add religion as well.

2. See, for example, Blocker (5: ch. 1).

3. Well, maybe not, but I will have more to say about this in the second half of my essay.

4. Consult *Talking a Good Game* (30: ch. 8), for a discussion of this point (especially pp. 197–198).

5. For openers, see (9), (25), (35), and (32) on the notion of infinite games.

6. This is an important philosophical insight. In his presidential address to the Philosophic Society for the Study of Sport at the Greek Oaks Inn, Fort Worth, Texas, October 1993, Gunter Gebauer (17: pp. 102–106) convincingly argued for an analysis of sport actions as mimesis, or interpretations (codifications), of previously interpreted actions such as hand or foot movements. This analysis implies no uniqueness claim; in fact, it could be construed as an argument against it.

7. See Stephen Davies's *Definitions of Art* (13: p. 8), who make a similar point about art.

8. See Wertz (28: especially pp. 511–512) and (29).

9. I wish to thank Robert Osterhoudt and two anonymous reviewers for their lengthy comments on a previous draft of this paper, which was read at the 22nd annual meeting of the Philosophic Society for the Study of Sport held at the University of Western Ontario, London, Ontario, Canada, in October 1994. Professor Osterhoudt gave persistent criticism, which I could not ignore, and this has led to a better essay. Two other anonymous reviewers from the editorial board and the editor, William J. Morgan, of the *Journal of the Philosophy of Sport* recently gave perceptive suggestions and I thank them as well. Errors that remain, of course, are of my own making.

Bibliography

1. Andre, Judith, and James, Davie N. (Eds.) *Rethinking College Athletics*. Philadelphia: Temple University Press, 1991.

2. Angell, Roger. "The Interior Stadium." In *Sport Inside Out: Readings in Literature and Philosophy*. Edited by D.L. Vanderwerken and S.K. Wertz. Fort Worth: Texas Christian University Press, 1985, pp. 147–156.

3. Barwise, Jon, and Etchemendy, John. *The Language of First-Order Logic*. (2nd ed.). Stanford: Center for the Study of Language and Information, 1991.

4. Belaief, Lynne. "Meanings of the Body." In *Sport Inside Out: Readings in Literature and Philosophy*. Edited by D.L. Vanderwerken and S.K. Wertz. Fort Worth: Texas Christian University Press, 1985, pp. 414–434.

5. Blocker, H. Gene. *Philosophy of Art*. New York: Charles Scribner's Sons, 1979.

6. Bonevac, Daniel. *Deduction*. Mountain View, CA: Mayfield Publishing Company, 1987.

7. Bonevac, Daniel. *The Art and Science of Logic*. Mountain View, CA: Mayfield Publishing Company, 1990.

8. Boyd, Robert D. *Critical Reasoning: The Fixation of Belief*. Bessemer, AL: Colonial Press, 1992.

9. Crase, James P. *Finite and Infinite Games: A Vision of Life as Play and Possibility*. New York: The Free Press, 1986.

10. Collingwood, R.G. *An Essay on Philosophical Method*. Oxford: Clarendon Press, 1933.

11. Danto, Arthur C. "The Artistic Enfranchisement of Real Objects: The Art World." In *Aesthetics: A Critical Anthology* (2nd ed.). Edited by George Dickie, Richard Sclafani, and Ronald Roblin. New York: St. Martin's Press, 1989, pp. 171–182.

12. Danto, Arthur C. *The Philosophical Disenfranchisement of Art*. New York: Columbia University Press, 1986.

13. Davies, Stephen. *Definitions of Art*. Ithaca, NY: Cornell University Press, 1991.

14. Dickie, George, Sclafani, Richard, and Roblin, Ronald. (Eds.) *Aesthetics: A Critical Anthology* (2nd ed). New York: St. Martin's Press, 1989.

15. Galvin, Richard F. "Aesthetic Incontinence in Sport." In *Sport Inside Out: Readings in Literature and Philosophy*. Edited by D.L. Vanderwerken and S.K. Wertz. Fort Worth: Texas Christian University Press, 1985, pp. 519–524.

16. Galvin, Richard F. "Nonsense on Stilts: A Skeptical View." In *Rethinking College Athletics*. Edited by Judith Andre and David N. James. Philadelphia: Temple University Press, 1991, pp. 87–99.

17. Gebauer, Gunter. "Sport, Theater, and Ritual: Three Ways of World-Making." *Journal of the Philosophy of Sport*, XX–XXI (1993–1994), 102–106.

18. Gerber, Ellen W. (Ed.). *Sport and the Body: A Philosophical Symposium*. Philadelphia: Lea & Febiger, 1972.

19. Hodges, Wilfrid. *Logic*. New York: Viking Penguin Inc., 1986.

20. Hyland, Drew. "When Power Becomes Gracious: The Affinity of Sport and Art." In *Rethinking Col-*

lege Athletics. Edited by Judith Andre and David N. James. Philadelphia: Temple University Press, 1991, pp. 71–80.

21. Jeu, Bernard. "What Is Sport?" *Diogenes: An International Review of Philosophy and Humanistic Studies,* No. 80 (Winter 1972), 150–163. Translated from the French by R. Blohm.

22. Kretchmar, R. Scott. "'Distancing': An Essay on Abstract Thinking in Sport Performances." In *Sport Inside Out: Readings in Literature and Philosophy*. Edited by D.L. Vanderwerken and S.K. Wertz. Fort Worth: Texas Christian University Press, 1985, pp. 87–103.

23. Lenk, Hans. "Herculean 'Myth' Aspects of Athletics." In *Sport Inside Out: Readings in Literature and Philosophy*. Edited by D.L. Vanderwerken and S.K. Wertz. Fort Worth: Texas Christian University Press, 1985, pp. 435–446.

24. Pieper, Josef. "Play: A Non-Meaningful Act." In *Sport and the Body: A Philosophical Symposium*. Edited by Ellen W. Gerber. Philadelphia: Lea & Febger, 1972, p. 214.

25. Smullyan, Raymond. *5000 B.C. and Other Philosophical Fantasies*. New York: St. Martin's Press, 1983.

26. Suits, Bernard. *The Grasshopper: Games, Life, and Utopia*. Toronto: University of Toronto Press, 1978.

27. Vanderwerken, D.L., and Wertz, S.K. (Eds.) *Sport Inside Out: Readings in Literature and Philosophy*. Fort Worth: Texas Christian University Press, 1985.

28. Wertz, S.K. "Artistic Creativity in Sport." In *Sport Inside Out: Readings in Literature and Philosophy*. Edited by D.L. Vanderwerken and S.K. Wertz. Fort Worth: Texas Christian University Press, 1985, pp. 510–519.

29. Wertz, S.K. "Comments on Galvin." In *Sport Inside Out: Readings in Literature and Philosophy*.

Edited by D.L. Vanderwerken and S.K. Wertz. Fort Worth: Texas Christian University Press, 1985, pp. 525–526.

30. Wertz, S.K. *Talking a Good Game: Inquiries into the Principles of Sport*. Dallas, TX: Southern Methodist University Press, 1991.

31. Wertz, S.K. "The Metaphysics of Sport: The Play as Process." In *The Philosophy of Paul Weiss*, in The Library of Living Philosophers (series), Volume 23. Edited by Lewis E. Hahn, Peru, IL: Open Court Publishing Company, 1995.

32. Wertz, S.K. "Is the Hypergame Paradox a Game or Play?" Forthcoming. An earlier version appeared as "The Hypergame Paradox: Smullyan's Version." *Darshana International,* XVII #3/127 (July 1992), 17–21.

33. Whitehead, Alfred North. *Process and Reality*. New York: The Free Press, 1929/1969.

34. Wittgenstein, Ludwig. *Philosophical Investigations* (3rd ed.). Translated by G.E.M. Anscombe. New York: Macmillan Company, 1953/1958.

35. Zwicker, William S. "Playing Games with Games: The Hypergame Paradox." *American Mathematical Monthly,* XCIV:6 (June–July 1987), 507–514.

Questions for Consideration

1. Sketch out Wertz's argument for the inherent circularity of formalist arguments on behalf of a fixed nature of sport. Is this circularity damning?

2. Overall, has Wertz adequately shown that the formalist approach is untenable?

3. Draw from prior readings and sketch out some of the implications of an open or interpretivist notion of sport.

Chapter Two

Aesthetics and Sport

9 The Well-Played Game: Notes Toward an Aesthetics of Sport

E. F. Kaelin
Florida State University

E. F. Kaelin analyzes competitive sport from the creative perspective of works of art. For Kaelin, what likens sports to art is abstraction. In art as well as sport, this occurs when certain aesthetically insignificant elements become significant within an aesthetic context. Sport is essentially violent activity—a release of psychic tension in a controlled fashion. It becomes aesthetic within a context of edification and, as with art, with the oneness of performance and performer.

There are natural and conventional levels of aesthetic significance. At the natural level, impulses are played out with grace. At the level of convention, artificially set goals allow for the release of psychic tension through sport. Aesthetic sport aims for the highest possible efficiency of motor coordination.

In evaluating works of art, critics work from the "tension" between "surface expressions" and "depth expressions." The former concerns organized sensuous features; the latter deals with recognizable images, ideas, or objects in the surface structure. The interrelatedness of such features is what makes a work aesthetic.

Is a similar pattern manifest in sporting events? Yes, Kaelin answers. In aesthetically evaluating sportive performance, the outcome of the game is irrelevant, though how participants play is not, and this includes desire to win. From the spectator's point of view, the aesthetic element of an event is its dramatic component. Tempo and rhythm of a sporting event determine the buildup and release of tension in spectators. The aesthetic heights of a sportive event occurs when, after sustained dynamic tension, one player or team narrowly defeats the opponent.

When, under the chancellorship of Robert Maynard Hutchins, the University of Chicago "de-emphasized" its commitment to intercollegiate football, reactions to the defection of the Maroons were various. Some critics, recalling the legendary remark of the youthful chancellor—no iron man this—that whenever the desire for physical activity manifested itself, he immediately lay down until it passed off, uttered a resigned "What can you expect?" Others, more rationalistic, if less philosophical, pointed out the poor showing of Chicago's gladiators in recent Big-10 competition as sufficient reason for the radical step: better to save face by quitting than to continue bringing up the rear. Both views tended to ignore the corresponding re-emphasis on intramural sport activities intended to keep those eggheads screwed on to functioning bodies, and not all of them could know of the Manhattan Project developing under the abandoned bleachers of Alonzo Stagg Field. You win some and you lose some; and as all cynics know only too well, if you are the coach and you lose too many, you chance to lose your job as well. Rather than looking for another coach and another site for experimenting on atomic fission, the Chicagoans ended their embarrassment by copping out. The chancellor's tirades against the growing professionalism of the college game were never really heard.

No one was surprised, and only the avid fans of big-time football mourned the passing of an

Reprinted by permission, from E. F. Kaelin, "The Well-Played Game: Notes Toward an Aesthetics of Sport," *Quest* 10 (1968): 16–28.

American institution. The case was different when, about ten years later, the University of Notre Dame made a similar decision. Here was a bigger institution yet. The Fighting Irish with the Polish names were one of the principal reasons for the very existence of South Bend, Indiana. Who were these religious men who decided that a university could be run without the attendant big business of football? Were their souls so hardened that they could no longer respond to the demand of winning one for the Gipper? What else is there to do in the Midwest on a fall Saturday afternoon? No one was naive enough to believe that the lack of distracting spectacles—cultural or otherwise—that is our Midwestern civilization would induce our football-deprived students to pass their time with the books. Thus, not succeeding in their idealism—not even that could make the alumni accept an 8-2 season for the Fighting Irish, where the "8" refers to the number of losses in one season—ND's administration decided to face up to reality: they needed a new coach, someone like Rockne and Layden and Leahy, someone who knew how to win; but they also needed an increased budget to float the necessary football scholarships. The rest of the story is known: they found both, only to have their recent siege on the national championship fended off by the appearance of another national power. Oh, the horror of it: Michigan State University, which fills in the beef on its line with the culturally disadvantaged youth of the Southland and which hires its professors to foment counterrevolution in such places as Vietnam, forced the Irish to play for a tie. They should have done as well in South Vietnam. Who was to console the despondent spirit of the Gipper now? Not Parseghian. He played this one out for his boys who played too hard for too long to accept second place in what turned out to be the only truly national championship competition in college football during recent times. Evidently we build character in our student athletes only by teaching them to win—or at least not to lose—with grace.

Who is to fault such a decision? Shall we repeat it? "It matters not . . . , it's how you play the game. And no one plays for a tie." The desire to win is a necessary part of all competitive sport, as, unfortunately, are the economics and consequently the politics of American universities—always on the make—engaged in big-time football. The question is: does such a mass of interlocking institutions possess a component which is distinctively sporting and distinctively aesthetic? Some of us, spectators and lovers of competitive sports we cannot engage in and participators in those suited to our physical characteristics, claim there is. What we need is a method of inquiry to make clear what we find happening in sport.

I propose to begin my inquiry with some observations on the nature of spectator sports in our American culture. In an affluent society the question of bread is for the most part guaranteed; and where it is not, bread can always be procured if only one is strong enough, agile or skilled enough to perform in the community circus. And there are many circuses in which to perform. Baseball, which lays the oldest and perhaps most fraudulent claim to being America's national pastime, was never played before as great a collective audience as basketball, once it was discovered that an outsized ball could be thrown through a peach basket placed at a suitable height from the floor. Every town in the country has its high school team; every junior college, college, and university that is too small to compete with bigger institutions for the honors of semi-professional football can and does produce basketball teams of acceptable caliber; and some of them rank with the best teams playing anywhere.

But if this were not enough to challenge baseball's claim to supremacy, along came television, which propelled collegiate and professional football into the national consciousness as never before. Where audiences in the stadia, gymnasia, and field houses across the nation were limited to the hundreds of thousands, the new audience for a single performance is currently being measured in the millions. And if the greedy moguls of professional football do not kill the goose that lays this golden egg by overexposing her, the growing trend of football fanship will make it quite plain even to the most rabid of baseball's fans that football is indeed the currently reigning national sport. Are sport appreciators fickle in their affections? Or is there a deeper reason for the rising disaffection with the game played with a bat?

Yes, Virginia, there is. But it is not the greater violence of football, that, appealing to some dark neurotic drive of the spectators, makes it more popular than nine innings of baseball played in the sun or under the lights. Violence it may be which makes the term "gladiator" more applicable to the participant in the contact sport; after all, the original gladiators fought to the death to appease the neuroses of the Roman citizens. But if the greater popularity of football were attributed to this sort of appeal, then ice hockey or lacrosse or boxing should be more popular than football. Violence, even the vicarious experience of violence on the part of the sports fan, is not what makes it a moral equivalent of war, as were the jousts and tournaments of bored knights. The value of violence in sport to both participant and spectator is not in its expression per se, but in its control toward the achievement of a contested end. Where violence may be sufficient to generate interest in an activity, its control is necessary to sustain our continued interest in its expression.

One of the factors which has worked to reduce interest in the game of baseball, moreover, has been precisely the introduction of more violence. When it was discovered that fans were willing to pay to see home runs instead of closely fought ball games, the era of the king of swat was very swiftly changed to that of the rabbit ball, band box ball parks, and the .260 hitter. Violence in this game was thus found to be one of the factors working toward its undoing as an aesthetic phenomenon and hence as a satisfying spectator sport. Pitchers were converted in this unnatural process into throwers, and their opponents in the struggle for survival into bottle bat bombers

whose very cheapness has killed interest in an otherwise intriguing game. Perhaps the game was meant for the Latin Americans and the Japanese after all.

If not the violence of the action, then perhaps the continuity of action, or the lack of it, is the secret of baseball's apparent demise. Consider the experience of introducing a European to the delights of night baseball. Brought up on soccer, in which team, coach, and spectator are all satisfied to win the game by a single goal, 1-0 or 2-1 after a continuous hour's struggle—heaven help the goalie that allows three scores in a single game—our bemused European visitor finds nine innings of walks, hit basemen, home runs, and lengthy rhubarbs an interminable bore. True, it takes some time for him to perceive that the main tension of the game pits the pitcher's power and skill against those of each succeeding batter and that these may be slightly modified by the tension created between the speed of a runner and the "arm" of a defensive fielder; but even when brought to a recognition of these niceties, he can hardly be led to perceive the qualitative character of the game itself. And character discrimination is the essence of aesthetic perception.

In all but a very few instances baseball fails to generate any kind of dramatic unity. Occasionally the loyal fan may wait for the proverbial last inning stand in which the home team overcomes a lead ineptly allowed the visitors in earlier frames, but even this drama is experienced more for itself than as the culmination of many meaningful events leading up to this singular climax of controlled violence. The lack of continuity between the preparation and the climax is all too apparent, and it becomes even more so as viewed on television. Contrast it with a goal line stand in the final seconds of a football game. Who will forget that quarterback sneak of Bart Starr in the last NFL championship game, played on a frozen field, after two prior attempts had failed? Kramer found footing and blocked his man, allowing Starr to penetrate by the distance of half a yard. Twenty-two men were involved in the single action that capped the previous fifty-nine minutes of continuous struggle. The game would have been as beautiful had Dallas's line held; only the irrational support of one team over the other could have changed the character of that game, but then the heroes and the goats would have changed names.

If my observations, though limited, are sufficient to point out one of the differences in appeal between baseball and football (that the action of the one game is diffuse, badly articulated, and rarely climaxing as opposed to the continuous, tightly structured, and usually climaxing action of the other), some ground would have been gained for understanding the greater spectator appeal in the more dramatic game. I propose in what follows to treat my subject from another point of view. I should like to examine the conditions under which the game itself is a vehicle of creative physical activity, akin to that expended in the production and experience of any bona fide work of art.

Such terms as the "superior dramatic action" of the football game over the baseball game may lead one to suspect that the aesthetic properties of athletic contests are to be explained by metaphor or, what amounts to the same thing, by application of a model taken from another context—here, dramatic literature—where the use of the terms is more clearly understood. Such was not my intent. I have referred to the "dramatic action" of competitive sport only to assert for those who have not yet perceived it that the action of organized sports is capable of highly dramatic action. True fans, who are aware of the dramatic content of their sporting events, need no such explanation. What they may lack is a clear understanding of the manner in which those memorable games have achieved the aesthetic character which made them memorable. It is to those fans I now address my efforts.

If I were to use a model of a completely developed aesthetic activity which is understood on its own terms, my choice would not be of a totally dissimilar medium, such as dramatic literature, which works its wonders by the articulation of words and by their meanings, but by the similar medium of dance: human effort expended in kinaesthetic response to the growing needs of a physical situation. In dance, of course, the situation and the responses are mutually determinant and self-contained. My argument will be that competitive sport is capable of the same kind of development, that the sporting event, at its best, is the one which achieves the same sort of mutual determinancy and self-containedness as the most abstract of dance. The "drama" of the sport may indeed produce a more effectively expressive vehicle than what is usually achieved in dance.

The effect of dance, like that of any other art form, is the effect of abstraction. This means only that to make a work of art one needs a medium. Music became an art when sounds were controlled to produce meaningful sequences; painting, when line was used to delineate a form and colored pigments were used to create space tensions. The artwork appears when someone perceives the effects of moving such physical things as sounds, marks, and color pigments out of one context, where they are aesthetically insignificant, into another where they achieve a new interest to perception in a freely created, purely aesthetic context. That the dance itself is rather poorly understood as an art medium is easily grasped, because of the difficulty in our perceiving the abstraction. The dancer moves his body, but so do streetwalkers and ball players; he uses the gestures and movements of his physiological and kinesiological substructure which are already implicit in the acts of walking or swimming or running. If the balletic gesture does nothing more than incorporate our basic bodily movements without an added significance to its occurrence in the aesthetic context, the choreographer or the performing dancer has failed in his task of successful abstraction. For the moment it is sufficient to understand that the medium of the dance and the medium of the sporting event are the same. That is the reason for their comparison.

In another place[1] I have attempted to show the continuous abstraction of human movement from its everyday context, such as walking, stretching, and the like, into the "pure" movements of a creative dance. The abstractive hierarchy runs as follows: at the base is our bodily presence in the natural environment, in which we always move from here to there. The "here" is defined as the center of our own bodily schemata; the "there" may be anything: an object to be grasped or avoided. Under the impulse of our own needs and desires we may wish to kick it, caress it, or merely move it out of the way. Given the necessary sensory-motor coordination we can ordinarily do any of these things. But even at this rather mundane level of human locomotor experience, we may effectuate an abstraction. Having learned to walk to achieve our ends of living, we may begin to play with our motor responses. Here, rather than achieving an end, the activity itself may be changed from means to end. I may walk because I enjoy walking, or I may walk in such a way as to develop a distinctive style of walking.

Whereas walking for the pleasure of walking may develop my muscles or keep them in tone, walking for a distinctive style may develop what traditional aestheticians have always called "grace." It is the abortion of this ideal in the provocative woman's walk which makes her rolling bottom appear obscene, not its invitation to carnal knowledge, which cannot be obscene. When grace is reduced to provocation, the movement is no longer a successful abstraction, being a call to the achievement of another kind of concrete goal. As long as we merely contemplate the move without entering into its enticement, it may retain the discriminable aesthetic quality I have already named; it is merely provocative. But even they who are incapable of the necessary "aesthetic distance" and accept the proffered gambit to engage in the act of love may yet achieve successful aesthetic abstraction. It suffices to separate the act from its normal consequences, an immediate pleasure or pain and the procreation of the race, to find oneself in possession of a "new" artistic medium, the gentle art of coupling, than which no medium is more powerful in the creation and release of psychic tension, climaxing into a moment of peace. It matters little whether we refer to the medium as the art of making love or as the dance of life; the beauty of it is already apparent in the courting gyrations of birds.

The rhythms of sexual gymnastics would be an odd place to look for a model of sporting aesthetics. Not even the bad joke of referring to lovemaking as America's most popular indoor sport could make the comparison profitable. More to the point, however, is the manner in which the creation and release of psychic tension becomes qualitatively one; or, to put the matter in another way, how man's need for violent activity is expressed in a context in which the partner is not destroyed, but edified in and through the experience. The conventionality or the artificiality added to the natural context allows this expression and develops what is distinctively human. I have already referred to the controlled expression of violence as "the moral equivalent of war," and we are constantly being reminded of this fact by all those protest buttons proclaiming that one ought to "Make LOVE not WAR." The slogan makes sense, but how can you get the generals to see that it does? Or the country parsons, for that matter?

Starting with basic human movements engaged in to achieve a natural goal or end, we may come to understand that the order of significance achievable in this way is "natural"; it grows out of the coordination of our bodies to the achievement of natural ends. Developing grace and learning to experience the aesthetics of love are merely two low-order abstractions on this kind of movement, and man possesses this ability in common with all other natural life forms.

A higher order of significance is reached when physical coordination is related to artificially set goals. Here the significance is "conventional." Man has developed a real taste for playing with his motor responses—for distraction, for the maintenance of physical well-being, or for the moral and aesthetic experiences which play, in its most successful forms, affords. We all know the story: terrains are laid out, rules adopted, equipment standardized. The aim is to perform a physical act with the highest possible degree of efficiency. Significance is attained relative to the attainment of the goal.

Unfortunately for many of our aesthetic interests, this significance is often measured in quantitative terms, and thus in terms of winning or losing. So many points conventionally assigned to the prescribed ways of scoring have often led to ignoring the qualitative aspects of the experience itself. But win or lose, the players must perform their allotted tasks in a specific manner; and all the niceties of movement over and above the strict necessity of scoring—and thus of winning or losing—have come to be called "form." Consider the judging of divers or figure skaters; consider also the graceful movements of a powerful batter—Ted Williams was one—who always looks good with a bat in his hands, even while striking out. This same sort of grace can become the object of the physical performance, as it does in synchronized swimming and team calisthenics. In addition to providing the controlled release of violence, such sports as the latter are capable of producing elaborate visual and spatial configurations of no mean attraction.

Dance is merely the last of the hierarchic series of abstractive human movements. The context created is still artificial, yet not conventional (except for the ballet, which never really achieved its independence from music). I prefer to call the meaning of the dance "autosignificance," intending that expression to refer to the fact that any movement of the dance which achieves any kind of significance at all does so by virtue of the relationship it bears to other movements in the context, considered as both means and end of the kinaesthetic expression. All the significance of the dance is internal to the dance. It may englobe many gestures imitative of everyday human locomotive patterns and even subhuman as well; but the significance

of such representational elements is seriously modified for their incorporation into the balletic context. It is not sufficient, for example, for a choreographer to tell his performers to go out and make like a bird or to imitate the actions of a child playing hopscotch; it is the total dance which determines the significance of each of the parts.

Can this model of the self-contained, autosignificant balletic context be applied to our previous understanding of the aesthetic effect of athletic contests? Two considerations are necessary in order to grasp my contention that it can. First, the winning or the losing of the game is irrelevant to its aesthetic evaluation. An honest tie—one which results from an attempt on the part of opposing teams to win—is not therefore an absolute indicator of the failure to achieve aesthetic quality in the performance. Coaches like Parseghian, formerly of Notre Dame, and Peterson, formerly of Florida State, had something else in mind when they decided to play for a tie instead of for victory. Fans with an aesthetic interest can only be disappointed by the calculated decision to accept the tie; even though there is some doubt about the kicker's ability to make the field goal, the decision to go for it instead of for the touchdown which would win the game (as Florida State did against Penn State in the Gator Bowl) is always an anticlimax.

Even when the kicker succeeds, the game itself merely peters out into insignificance. With that decision, the "drama" of the game was lost even if the game itself was not. Thus, although the winning or losing of the game is aesthetically irrelevant, the desire to win is never aesthetically irrelevant.

Besides, the game is made an aesthetic event by the opposition of strength in the wills to win. But desire itself is not sufficient for the highly dramatic sporting event. In any game defined by the opposition of power, skill, and determination in its players, the power and skill cannot be lacking. Expansion teams of professional football and baseball are not aesthetically effective because they can offer no successful competition to the older, more established teams in their respective leagues. They may, of course, succeed in compensating for a lack of power and skill by a superabundance of determination and still participate effectively in the production of an aesthetically meaningful contest of purpose. Worth is still measured in terms of "how you play the game." Playing for a tie is cheating the public.

The second consideration necessary for the understanding of aesthetic quality in sporting events is a point taken from general aesthetic theory. It concerns media and their use to establish significant contexts we call works of art. Someone may have assumed that the previous discussion of abstraction would imply that there are no successful representational art works. This would be a misunderstanding of the process of creation. Some works, and very good ones at that, are highly representational. But no matter how imitative certain of the discriminable elements within the aesthetic context happen to be, the worth of that work is not measurable in terms of the accuracy of representation. If this were the case, the best painting would be the one which most effectively pictured the events of nature and hardly any so-called "serious" music could be considered beautiful at all.

The truth of the matter is that all works of art are abstract in the sense indicated above—that their significance is perceivable only in the context in which they appear, in spite of the fact that the artist must artificially construct this context out of what he already knows and feels about the things he must work with as a medium and, if he chooses to represent objects of nature, about them as well. All his knowledge and skill, all the materials and technological means of expression at his disposal constitute the initial context from which he is to abstract his significance by manipulating the materials of his craft. Whence the term "transformation"[2] to describe the activity of the artist; he creates by transforming existing materials into something uniquely significant.

Dances too may be non-objective, producing no recognizable natural movement or object; or they may be interpretative and include them. We call the first "surface" expressions; the second "depth" expressions. The term "surface" refers to the organized sensuous features of the experience; and "depth" to recognizable images, ideas, or objects represented in the organization of the surface patterns. Since the value of the depth expressions is not to be found in the accuracy of representation, it can be found only in the tense relationship between expressing surface and expressed depth. Call that "tension" or "total expressiveness" of the artwork in question.

Making aesthetic judgments on works of art, then, proceeds from our attempts to perceive the qualitative relatedness of surface or of surface and depth "counters" (anything discriminable within the context). When we feel the expressiveness of the related counters, we are experiencing the expressive quality of the piece in question. Such judgments are made daily on creative dances. Can the same be done for our perception of the qualitative uniqueness of games?

The answer is obvious: yes, if we can isolate the relevant counters of the experience. And this is a matter of perceiving the tensions where they occur. In baseball it is the continuing struggle between pitcher and successive batters which mounts with runners on the bases and is qualified by the intermittent tensions between runners and throwers. But, as pointed out before, these tensions fund into qualitative uniqueness slowly, discontinuously, and hardly ever in a meaningful climax. The game of baseball is at best a summation of innings in which the change of offensive and defensive strategies tends to break the continuity of the action. This is possible in football too. But the rules of the game have been set up to maintain aesthetic quality—and hence spectator interest. A change from defensive to offensive strategy in football is allowed by the interception of passes, in which the defensive player himself assumes the offensive; in the recovery of fumbles; and in effective punting, which may put a whole offensive squad on the defensive if the ball may be downed within the five-yard line. The tempo and rhythm of the game are defined in terms of the building up and the release of dynamic tensions, created ultimately by the opposition of equally capable teams.

Controlled violence in which the opponent is not destroyed, but only defeated, and yet somehow morally edified—such is the essence of competitive sport. It reaches its aesthetic heights when the victor narrowly surpasses a worthy opponent. The game itself considered as an aesthetic object is perceived as a tense experience in which pressure is built up from moment to moment, sustained through continuous opposition, until the climax of victory or defeat. The closer this climax occurs to the end of the game, the stronger is our feeling of its qualitative uniqueness. Sudden death playoffs—and perhaps extra-inning games—are as close as a sport may come to achieving this aesthetic ideal.

We are now in a position to evaluate the possibilities of sport to produce aesthetic experiences. To make the point we may summarize the way in which "significance" is achieved within the levels of abstraction discernible in distinctively human locomotive contexts.

At the most basic level, significance is achieved merely by ordering our bodily existence in accordance with the ends imposed upon it by the natural environment and dominated by biological necessity. We have all learned to walk, run, or swim to increase our control of the conditions of our existence, which is often eked out against a hostile environment. Thus, sometimes with the help of the physical environment and sometimes against its tendency to thwart our growth, we learn to fulfill our vital needs. At this level of experience the possibilities of aesthetic perception are already multiple: we may abstract from the necessity to achieve a particular goal and focus on the movement pattern employed in its achievement, thereby developing "natural" grace. This is recognized as much for its maximum efficiency—the greatest amount of result for the least effort—as for the "beauty" of its execution. The feeling of being at one with nature,

using it to fulfill our own aims with consummate ease, is a direct aesthetic response of the mover to his motion.

But there is another mode of abstraction possible even at this level of human experience. I have used the provocative walk to illustrate the point. He who gives in to the provocation is once again acting to fulfill a basic human and biological need. We may once more abstract from the naturally imposed end—the propagation of our species or the experience of pleasure as the outcome of the act—and concentrate upon the pattern of significance which develops between the dynamic tensions in the sexual drama, which would remain totally devoid of meaning without the building up and release of psychic tension through mutually determinant masculine and feminine movement sequences. Any pleasure which is not just attendant upon the act must be the consciousness of the many kinaesthetic gestures funding to make up the act. Each act of love is qualitatively unique and aesthetically recognizable for the manner in which it creates tensions, releases them, and terminates in ultimate peace. In their intimate dance of life, the partners to the act create a new human entity: the couple, which is still the basis for the continued existence of our species.

Dissatisfaction with their respective roles in the creation of this entity—due in part to inadequate physical and mental preparation, but in part as well to the failure to perceive its aesthetic aspects—has led many a married person to seek its artificial dissolution in divorce. Because of the religious and moral prejudices placed upon the significance of the act of love, we may never as educators be allowed to participate in any form of physical instruction devised to maximize the attainment of this sort of aesthetic value. Older, more primitive societies do, and their members are quite obviously better adapted to the sexual conditions of life.

My aim, in the pursuit of this example, was not to shock or even to astound, but rather, to point out that even at this level of abstraction the process of humanly-directed, conscious bodily movements is capable of a high degree of aesthetic perfection in which the performers and the performance cannot be differentiated.

The same, of course, is true of the dance, which is not less dramatic for being less sexual in explicit expression. Competitive sporting events are somewhat like the dance and somewhat like an act of love. Like the dance, the athletic competition is defined in terms of the artificiality of its goals; like an act of love, the athletic competition represents an expression of human violence undergone under conditions of control in which the partner or opponent is not destroyed, but morally or humanly edified. Unlike the dance, however, the athletic medium is not "pure." The game does not create its own goals as kinaesthetic responses unfold; rather, these are imposed upon the participants by the rules of the game. To be an aesthetic event, therefore, the athletic contests must within the limits of the rules set down for the game become a unique context of dramatically significant tensional wholes. This it does by building up tension, sustaining and complicating it and ultimately releasing the percipient into the state of peace. Well-played, i.e., successfully played, games and they alone succeed in this aesthetic ideal.

To abstract from the conventional goal of the game—to win—means only that the manner of playing the game is aesthetically predominant; and skill, power, and desire to win are the factors determining the manner in which the game is played. Thus it has been truthfully said (at least from the aesthetic point of view) that "It matters not whether you win or lose; it's how you play the game."

Unlike the dance, however, the medium of the sporting event cannot be totally abstracted from a pre-existent aim. The dancer or choreographer creates his end in making the dance, within which the performers (their activities) and the performance are one. The form of the game is always more concrete in that, although winning or losing may be irrelevant to its aes-

thetic significance, the desire to win may never be excluded as one of the determinants of the action. It is for this reason that aesthetic connoisseurs look down their noses at coaches like Notre Dame's Parseghian and Florida State's Peterson. In their calculated decisions to play for ties, they, on one occasion at least, have put the requirement of not losing over the aesthetic ideal of the well-played game.

Lastly, in order to motivate my phenomenological reading of the essence of sporting aesthetics, I have speculated that the declining popularity of baseball in face of the growing interest in football is explicable in aesthetic terms—that the game (or aesthetic product of the one) is inferior in marshalling the aesthetic interest of its viewers.

One point in the foregoing description remains all too sketchy. I refer to the ontological and psychoanalytical commitments in such phrases as "the psychic and moral edification" of the participants in sporting events. For the necessary connections between our existential concept of the body, or consciousness-body, as a "bodily schema" or "bodily image" and the self-creation of the human personality, I can do no better than refer the interested reader to the phenomenological psychoanalytical work of Eugène Minkowski. Two of his central notions, the creative imagination and spontaneity of movement, are contained in articles translated as "Imagination?" and "Spontaneity (. . . spontaneous movement like this!)" found in a recent anthology of readings in existential phenomenology.[3] His point of view on the creation of personality through movement would be necessary for a complete account of aesthetic creation through sensory-motor coordination. We need only keep in mind that any creative artist forms his own personality *qua* artist by transforming his experiences, through significant abstraction, into works of art; and in the arts utilizing human movement as a medium of expression, there is no distinction between the performer and his performance. But a complete account of the communication of aesthetic value through a sporting event was deemed too extravagant a task to be placed upon this author, who chose merely to explain the nature of the aesthetic qualities of a sporting event.

Minkowski's method as well as my own is distinctively phenomenological. His remarks are relevant to an understanding of the way in which the creative locomotor event is performed; mine, to the way in which the sensitive viewer responds to the event as performed. The middle ground, of course, is the event itself. I have only interpreted the rising and falling fortunes of two of our professionalized sports, along with the disgust on the part of some recent football fans at recurring decisions on the part of collegiate coaches to play a game for a tie. Both of these phenomena are meaningful in view of the description given the aesthetic ideal of sporting events, that of the "well-played game."

The beauty of motion referred to as "grace" in the descriptions above is possible at all levels of human motility. For the higher purposes of expressiveness in the dance or of maximal tension in competitive sports it is usually considered of only secondary interest: it represents the exploitation of skill for skill's sake alone. Like the virtuosity of a musical performer, however, that sport technique is the best which is noticed the least.

Give us more coaches who are willing to put their jobs and reputations on the line by going for the well-played game. Let us at least try to go out and win one for the Gipper, who has become in spite of the legend a symbol of the aesthetically dissatisfied sports fan.

Notes

1. See my "Being in the Body" in the NAPCEW Report *Aesthetics and Human Movement* (Washington, D.C., 1964), pp. 84–103.

2. Cf. its use by Roger Fry in *Transformations* (Garden City, N.Y.: Doubleday Anchor Books, 1956).

3. See Lawrence and O'Connor, eds., *Readings in Existential Phenomenology* (Englewood Cliffs, N.J.: Prentice-Hall, 1967), pp. 75–92, 168–177.

Questions for Consideration

1. Is the aesthetic efficiency to which Kaelin refers an efficiency of psychic release or one of physical performance, or both?

2. Toward the very end of the reading, Kaelin writes, "That sport technique is best which is noticed the least." What does he mean by this?

3. Do you agree with Kaelin that there is no aesthetic place for the aim of playing for a tie in a well-played game?

10   The Aesthetic in Sport

David Best

David Best argues that sport is sometimes mistakenly referred to as a form of art. Such a mistake occurs, he says, because of failure to distinguish properly between the aesthetic and the artistic.

Best begins by a lengthy analysis of the aesthetic. The aesthetic is more a way of perceiving an object or action than it is an objective feature of it. Still, aesthetic judgments are not inescapably subjective, for they happen only against a backdrop of objective features and can be evaluated only by reference to them.

The aesthetic, as a concept, is nonpurposive and any object can admit of aesthetic evaluation, though some objects more readily admit of this than others. Evaluating the aesthetic element of some thing or action, however, cannot be a matter of perceiving it as a means toward some end. For example, to view a painting exclusively as a potential investment is to cease to see it as aesthetic. Looked at in this way, the overwhelming majority of sports are not aesthetic, for in sports the aim is identifiable independently of its means, or nearly so. In other words, there are many different means, delimited by rules, toward the same end. For the aesthetic, there can be no such separation of means and end. When art is evaluated, every feature of it is relevant to its aesthetic assessment. There is, in terms of the aesthetic, only one means to the end.

Best then makes a distinction between aesthetic and purposive sports. A purposive sport is one in which the aesthetic is relatively unimportant and where the means to the end are many and varied. Ice hockey and American football are examples. In contrast, an aesthetic sport, like synchronized swimming, is one in which the aim essentially involves the aesthetic. Are aesthetic sports, he asks, art?

No, he answers flatly. Even in aesthetic sports, the means never reaches identification with the end. The means may be sufficient for the end, but it is seldom necessary as well. Moreover, sport achieves its ends via a variety of means delimited by certain canons of right play. In art, means is equivalent to end and there are no canons to limit expression.

Finally, just how does the aesthetic differ from the artistic? Best says that the artistic is a much narrower concept. The artistic is limited to intentionally created objects or actions. Additionally, art fundamentally allows for the expression of some conception of life's issues; the aesthetic does not. If this is correct, Best states, then it is plain to see why art may be about sport, and why sport may not be about art.

There appears to be a considerable and increasing interest in looking at various sporting activities from the aesthetic point of view. In this paper I shall examine a central characteristic of paradigm cases of objects of the aesthetic attitude, namely works of art, in order to see to what extent it is applicable to sport. Finally, I shall consider the question of whether sports in general, or at least those sports in which the aesthetic is ineliminable, can be legitimately be regarded as forms of art. It will be shown that discussion of this topic is confused by a failure to recognise the significance of the distinction between the aesthetic and the artistic.

The Aesthetic Point of View

It might be asked whether all sports can be considered from the aesthetic point of view, when

Reprinted from David Best, *Philosophy and Human Movement* (London: Allen & Unwin, 1978), 99–122. Copyright 1978 by Allen & Unwin Ltd. Reprinted by permission.

one takes account of the great and increasingly varied range of such activities. That question at least can be answered clearly in the affirmative, for any object or activity can be considered aesthetically—cars, mountains, even mathematical proofs and philosophical arguments.

This raises a point discussed earlier, that it is less conducive to error to regard the aesthetic as a way of perceiving an object or activity than as a constituent feature of it. I mention this because the term "aesthetic content" is often used, and it carries the misleading implication that the aesthetic is some sort of element which can be added or subtracted. In order to clarify the point it may be worth considering a way in which the notion of aesthetic content was once defended. It was argued that the aesthetic cannot be merely a point of view since this fails to account for the fact that some objects and activities are more interesting aesthetically than others. Thus, it was said, there must be aesthetic content since, for instance, the appearance of a car could be affected by altering physical features of it, and in a similar way gracefulness could be added to or subtracted from a movement.

A factor which may well contribute to confusion on this issue is a failure to distinguish two ways in which "aesthetic" is used. These can be broadly characterised as (1) evaluative, and (2) conceptual. An example of the former is: "Borzov is an aesthetic athlete." This is to use the term in a positive evaluative way, and is roughly equivalent to "graceful," or "aesthetically pleasing." But it is clearly the latter usage which is our concern, and this includes both the beautiful and the ugly; the graceful and the clumsy; the aesthetically interesting and the aesthetically uninteresting. Thus whatever one's opinion of the appearance of the car, it has to be considered from the aesthetic point of view in order for any relevant judgement to be offered.

Now certainly it does not necessarily indicate a misapprehension to use the term "aesthetic content." It depends what is meant by it, and there are two possibilities:

(1) To assert that A is part of the content of B would normally imply that A is a constituent feature or component of B, and that therefore a close examination of B will reveal it. This naturally leads to the kind of error discussed earlier. For, since statements about aesthetic content cannot be supported by empirical investigation, there will be a strong temptation to assume either that the aesthetic content is non-physical and somehow lying behind the physical object or activity, or that the aesthetic is a purely subjective content, not in the object itself but solely in the mind of the perceiver. And since in neither case can any sense be given to the notion of justification of aesthetic judgements, this is to reduce them to vacuity.

(2) However, if the term "aesthetic content" is used to make the point that it is only by reference to objective features that aesthetic judgements can be justified, then the notion is unexceptionable. There is a complex issue here, which involves the distinction between physical movements and actions . . . To make the point briefly, precisely the same physical movements may be aesthetically pleasing in one context yet displeasing in another. For example, one may regard a series of movements in a dance as poor aesthetically until it is pointed out that one has misinterpreted the performance. Under the different interpretation they can now be seen as superb. Although there is no physical difference in movements, the revised judgement is based upon the way in which the new interpretation has determined a different context. Nevertheless, the new interpretation and aesthetic judgement depend solely upon *objective* aspects of the movements. (I consider the nature of the objective reasons given in support of aesthetic judgements in another book, 1974.)

Thus, aesthetic judgements are certainly answerable in this way to observable physical features, and if the point of using the term "aesthetic content" is to emphasise the fact no confusion need arise. However, since it is so frequently used in, or with the misleading implications of, the former sense, it is, in my view, wiser to eschew the term.

The Aesthetic Concept

Although anything can be considered from the aesthetic aspect, some activities and objects are more centrally of aesthetic interest than others. Works of art, to take a paradigm case, are primarily of aesthetic interest, although even they can be considered from other points of view. For instance, paintings are commonly considered as an investment. Hence we need to ask what distinguishes the aesthetic from other ways of looking at objects. One important characteristic is that the aesthetic is a non-functional or non-purposive concept. To take a central example again, when we are considering a work of art from the aesthetic point of view we are not considering it in relation to some external function or purpose it serves. It cannot be evaluated aesthetically according to its degree of success in achieving some such extrinsic end. By contrast, when a painting is considered as an investment, then it is assessed in relation to an extrinsic end, namely that of maximum appreciation in financial value.

This characteristic of the aesthetic immediately raises an insuperable objection to theories which propose an oversimple relation between sport and the aesthetic by identifying them too closely. For example, it is sometimes claimed that sport just *is* an art form (for example, see Anthony, 1968), and it has been suggested that the aesthetic is the concept which unifies all the activities subsumed under the heading of physical education (see Carlisle, 1969). But there are many sports, indeed the great majority, which are like the painting considered as an investment in that there is an aim or purpose which can be identified independently of the way it is accomplished. That is, the *manner* of achievement of the primary purpose is of little or no significance as long as it comes within the rules. For example, it is normally far more important for a football or hockey team *that* a goal is scored than *how* it is scored. In very many sports of this kind the over-riding factor is the achievement of some

such independently specifiable end, since that is the mark of success.

This non-purposive character of the aesthetic is often misunderstood. Such a misunderstanding is manifested in the commonly supposed consequence that therefore there can be no point in art. The presupposition underlying this misunderstanding is that an activity can intelligibly be said to be of point or value only in relation to some external purpose towards which it is directed. Now in cases where such an extrinsic end is the primary consideration, evaluation does depend on it. As we have seen, a painting considered solely as an investment would be evaluated entirely according to its degree of success in achieving maximum capital appreciation. Where the attainment of the end is the over-riding consideration, the means of attaining it obviously becomes relatively unimportant. It would not matter, for instance, what sort of painting it was as long as the end was realised. Similarly, if someone should wish to improve the petrol consumption of his car by changing the carburettor, the design of the new one and the materials from which it is made would be unimportant as long as it succeeded in giving maximum mileage per gallon.

However, the purpose of art cannot be specified in this way, although the misapprehension we are now considering stems from the mistaken assumption that the point of an activity *must* somehow be identifiable as an end or purpose distinct from the activity itself. Yet where art, or more generally the aesthetic, is concerned, the distinction between means and end is inapplicable. For instance, the question "What is the purpose of that novel?" can be answered comprehensively only in terms of the novel itself. It might be objected that this is not entirely true, since the purpose of some novels could be given as, for example, exposing certain deleterious social conditions. But this objection misses the point I am trying to make, for if the purpose is the external one of exposing those social conditions then in principle it could equally well, or perhaps better, be realised in other ways, such as the publication of a social survey or a political speech. The report of the social survey is evaluated solely by reference to its purpose of effectively conveying the information, whereas this would be quite inappropriate as a standard for the aesthetic evaluation of a novel. To put the same point another way, from the point of view of efficient conveying of information, the precise form and style of writing of the report is unimportant except in so far as it affects the achievement of that purpose. One report could be as good as another, although the style of writing or compilation was different from or even inferior to the other. There could not be a parallel situation in art in which, for example, one poem might be said to be as good as another although not so well written. This is an aspect of the complex problem of form and content in the arts. To put it briefly, there is a peculiarly intimate connection between the form of an object of aesthetic appreciation, i.e. the particular medium of expression, and its content, i.e. what is expressed in it. So that in art there cannot be a change of form of expression without a corresponding change in what is expressed. It is important to recognise that this is a logical point. For even if one way of writing the report were the clearest and most efficient, this is a mere contingent matter since it is always possible that a better method may be devised. But it is not a contingent matter that the best way of expressing the content of Solzhenitsyn's *One Day in the Life of Ivan Denisovich* is in the particular form of that novel, i.e. it would make no sense to suggest that its content could be more effectively conveyed in another way. So that the question becomes "What is the purpose of this particular way of exposing the social conditions?" The end cannot be specified as "exposing such and such social conditions," but only as "exposing such and such social conditions in this particular way and no other." And to give a comprehensive account of what is meant by "in this particular way and no other" one would have to produce nothing less than the whole novel. The end cannot be identified apart from the manner of achieving it, and that is another way of

saying that the presupposition encapsulated in the question, of explanation in terms of purposive action directed onto an external end, is unintelligible in the sphere of aesthetics. In short, in an important sense the answer to "What is the purpose of that novel?" will amount to a rejection of the question.

A further objection, which has important implications for the aesthetic in sport, might be that in that case how can we criticise a work of art if it can be justified only in terms of itself and there is nothing else with which it can be compared? There is a great deal to be said about the common misapprehension that to engage in critical reasoning is necessarily to generalise (see Bambrough, 1973). It is sufficient for my argument to recognise that critical appreciation of art consists largely in giving reasons why particular features contribute so effectively to or detract from *this particular* work of art. The important point for our purposes is to see again that the end is inseparable from the means of achieving it, for any suggested improvement is given in terms of the particular work of art in question. Another way of putting this point is to say that every feature of a work of art is relevant to the aesthetic assessment of it, whereas when we are judging something as a means to an end, there are irrelevant features of the means, or equally effective alternative means, of achieving the required end. To say that X is an irrelevant feature is always a criticism of a work of art, whereas this is not true of a functional object.

It is true that the aim in a sport cannot be considered in isolation from the rules or norms of that particular sport. Scoring a goal in hockey is not just a matter of getting the ball between the opponents' posts, but requires conformity to the laws of the game. Such requirements are implicit in the meaning of the term "scoring a goal." Nevertheless, in contrast to a work of art, within those limits there are many ways of achieving the end, i.e., of scoring a goal, in hockey.

The Gap: Purposive and Aesthetic Sports

At this point we need to direct our attention to the difference between types of sporting activities with respect to the relative importance of the aesthetic. On the one hand, there are those sports, which I shall call "purposive" and which form the great majority, where the aesthetic is normally relatively unimportant. This category would include football, climbing, track and field events, orienteering, and squash. In each of these sports the purpose can be specified independently of the manner of achieving it as long as it conforms to the limits set by the rules or norms—for example, scoring a goal and climbing the Eiger. Even in such sports as these, of course, certain moves or movements, indeed whole games or performances, can be considered from the aesthetic point of view, but it is not central to the activity. It should be recognised that this is a logical point. For example, an activity could obviously still count as football even if there were never a concern for the aesthetic. By contrast, it could not count as football if no one ever tried to score a goal. That is, in these sports it is the independently specifiable purpose which at least largely defines the character of the activity, and the aesthetic is incidental.

On the other hand, there is a category of sports in which the aim cannot be specified in isolation from the aesthetic, for example, synchronised swimming, trampolining, gymnastics, figure-skating, and diving. I shall call these "aesthetic" sports since they are similar to the arts in that their purpose cannot be considered apart from the manner of achieving it. There is an intrinsic end which cannot be identified apart from the means. Consider, for example, the notion of a vault in formal gymnastics. The end is not simply to get over the box somehow or other, even if one were to do so in a clumsy way and collapse afterwards in an uncontrolled manner. The way in which the appropriate movements are performed is not incidental but central to such a sport. That is, the aim cannot be specified simply as "getting over the box," but only in terms of the manner of achievement required. Indeed, aesthetic norms are implicit in the meaning of terms like "vault" and "dive," in that to vault over a box is not the same as to jump over it, or to get over it somehow or other. Although such terms as "vault" are not employed in Modern Educational Gymnastics, the same issue of principle applies. There may be greater flexibility in the possibilities of answering a particular task in Educational as compared with more formal gymnastics, yet it is still important to consider how, aesthetically, the task is answered. Clumsy, uncontrolled movements would not be regarded as contributing to an adequate way of answering the task, whichever of the indefinite number of ways may be chosen. Similarly, not any way of dropping into the water would count as a dive. One would have to satisfy

Russians Ekatarina Gordeeva and Sergei Grinkov demonstrate the artistry and grace that characterize aesthetic sports like figure skating. Ed.
Richard Martin/Allsport Photography

at least to a minimal extent the aesthetic requirement built into the meaning of the term for a performance to count as even a bad dive.

The distinction, then, is clear. A purposive sport is one in which within the rules or conventions, there is an indefinite variety of ways of achieving the end which at least largely defines the game. By contrast, an aesthetic sport is one in which the purpose cannot be specified independently of the manner of achieving it. For instance, it would make no sense to suggest to a figure-skater that it did not matter *how* he performed his movements, as long as he achieved the purpose of the sport, since that purpose inevitably *concerns* the manner of performance. It would make perfectly good sense to urge a football team to score goals without caring how they scored them. Perhaps the point can be made most clearly by reference to the example given above, of the aesthetic norms built into terms such as "vault" and "dive," for whereas not *any* way of dropping into the water could count as even a bad dive, *any* way of getting the ball between the opponents' posts, as long as it is within the rules, would count as a goal, albeit a very clumsy or lucky one.

There is a common tendency to distinguish between these two types of sports in terms of competition. For example, in an interesting article on this topic, Reid (1970) distinguishes between what I have called purposive and aesthetic sports in the following way:

> Games come at the end of a kind of spectrum. In most games, competition against an opponent (individual or team) is assumed . . . At the other end of the spectrum there are gymnastics, diving, skating . . . in which grace, the manner in which the activity is carried out, seems to be of central importance.

Against this, I would point out that competition in Olympic gymnastics, skating and diving can be every bit as keen as it can be in Rugby football. Reid is adopting the prevalent but mistaken practice of contrasting the competitive with the aesthetic. Yet, for instance, it is quite apparent that, on occasion, competition between dance companies, and between rival dancers within the same company, can be as intense and as nasty as it can in ice-hockey. Moreover, to take a paradigm case, there are competitive music festivals, in which a similar spirit may be engendered. The great Korean violinist, Kyung-Wha Chung, after winning first prize in one competition, remarked: "It was one of the worst experiences of my life, because competitions bring out the worst in people."

Closing the Gap

We can now return to the original question concerning the characterisation of the aesthetic way of looking at sport. By examining the paradigm cases of sports in which the aesthetic is logically inseparable from what the performer is trying to achieve, we might hope to discover aspects of this way of considering them which can be found to apply even to purposive sports, when they are looked at aesthetically.

In figure-skating, diving, synchronised swimming, trampolining and Olympic gymnastics it is of the first importance that there should be no wasted energy and no superfluous movements. Champion gymnasts, like Nadia Comaneçi and Ludmilla Tourischeva, not only perform striking physical feats, but do so with such remarkable economy and efficiency of effort that it often looks effortless. There is an intensive concentration of the gymnast's effort so that it is all directed precisely and concisely onto that specific task. Any irrelevant movement or excessive expenditure of energy would detract from the quality of the performance as a whole, just as superfluous or exaggerated words, words which fail to contribute with maximum compression of meaning to the total effect, detract from the quality of a poem as a whole.

However, even in the case of the aesthetic sports there is still, although no doubt to a very limited extent, an externally identifiable aim; for example the requirements set by each particular movement, and by the particular group of movements, in gymnastics. Now it might be thought that it would be justifiable to regard such stringencies as analogous to, say, the form of a sonnet. That is, it may be thought more appropriate to regard them as setting a framework within which the performer has the opportunity to reveal his expertise in moving gracefully than as an externally identifiable aim. There is certainly something in this notion, but it is significant that there is no analogy in aesthetic sports with poetic license. The poet may take liberties with the sonnet form without necessarily detracting from the quality of the sonnet, but if the gymnast deviates from the requirements of, for instance, a vault, however gracefully, then that inevitably does detract from the standard of the performance. Nevertheless, the main point for our purposes is that even if, in the aesthetic sports, the means never quite reaches the ultimate or complete identification with the end which is such an important distinguishing feature of the concept of art, it at least closely approximates to such an identification. The gap between means and end is almost, if not quite, completely closed.

Now I want to suggest that the same consideration applies to our aesthetic appreciation of sports of the purposive kind. However successful a sportsman may be in achieving the principal aim of his particular activity, our *aesthetic* acclaim is reserved for him who achieves it with maximum economy and efficiency of effort. We may admire the remarkable stamina and consistent success of an athlete such as Zatopek, but he was not an aesthetically attractive runner because so much of his movement seemed irrelevant to the ideal of most direct accomplishment of the task. The ungainliness of his style was constituted by the extraneous rolls or jerks which seemed wasteful in that they were not concisely aimed at achieving the most efficient use of his energy.

So to consider the purposive sports from the aesthetic point of view is to reduce the gap between means and end. It is, as nearly as possible, to telescope them into the ideal of unity. From a purely purposive point of view any way of winning, within the rules, will do, whereas not *any* way of winning will do as far as aesthetic considerations are concerned. There is a narrower range of possibilities available for the achievement of an end in an aesthetically pleasing way, since the end is no longer simply to win, but to win with the greatest economy and efficiency of effort. Nevertheless, the highest aesthetic satisfaction is experienced and given by the sportsman who not only performs with graceful economy, but who also *achieves* his purpose. The tennis player who serves a clean ace with impeccable style has, and gives to the spectator, far more aesthetic satisfaction than when he fractionally faults with an equally impeccable style. In the case of the purposive sports there is an independently specifiable framework, i.e., one which does not require the sort of judgement to assess achievement which is necessary in the aesthetic sports. Maximum aesthetic success still requires the attainment of the end, and the aesthetic in any degree requires direction onto that end, but the number of ways of achieving such success is reduced in comparison with the purely purposive interest of simply accomplishing the end in an independently specifiable sense.

This characteristic of the aesthetic in activities which are primarily functional also applies to the examples cited earlier of mathematical proofs and philosophical arguments. The proof of a theorem in Euclidean geometry or a philosophical argument is aesthetically pleasing to the extent that there is a clean and concisely directed focus of effort. Any over-elaborate, irrelevant, or repetitious section, in either case, would detract from the maximum economy in achieving the conclusion which gives greatest aesthetic satisfaction. Rhetorical flourishes, however aesthetically effective in other contexts, such as a political speech, detract aesthetically from a philosophical argument by fussily blurring the ideal of a straight, direct line to the conclusion. The aesthetic satisfaction given by rhetoric in a political speech is related to the latter's different purpose of producing a convincing or winning argument rather than a valid one.

The aesthetic pleasure which we derive from sporting events of the purposive kind, such as hurdling and putting the shot, is, then, derived from looking at, or performing, actions which we take to be approaching the ideal of totally concise direction towards the required end of the particular activity. Skiing provides a good example. The stylish skier seems superbly economical, his body automatically accommodating itself, apparently without conscious effort on his part, to the most appropriate and efficient positions for the various types and conditions of terrain. By contrast, the skiing in a slalom race often appears ungainly because it looks forced and less concisely directed. The skier in such an event may achieve greater speed, but only by the expenditure of a disproportionate amount of additional effort. Similarly, athletes at the end of a distance race often abandon the smooth, graceful style with which they have run the greater part of the race. They achieve greater speed but at a disproportionate cost, since ungainly, irrelevant movements appear—the head rolls, the body lurches, and so on. In rowing, too, some oarsmen can produce a faster speed with poor style but more, if less effectively produced, power. Even though it is wasteful, the net effective power may still be greater than that of the oarsman who directs his more limited gross power with far more efficiency and therefore with more pleasing aesthetic effect. It is often said that a good big 'un will beat a good little 'un. It is also true in many sports, unfortunately, that a poor big 'un may well beat a far better little 'un.

Perhaps these considerations do something to explain the heightened aesthetic awareness which is achieved by watching slow-motion films and television replays, since (1) we have more time to appreciate the manner of the performance, and (2) the object of the action, the purpose, in an extrinsic sense, becomes less important. That is, our attention is directed more to the character of the action than to its result. We can see whether and how every detail of every movement in the action as a whole contributes to making it the most efficient and economical way of accomplishing that particular purpose. A smooth, flowing style is more highly regarded aesthetically because it appears to require less effort for the same result than a jerky one. Nevertheless, as was mentioned above, achievement of the purpose is still important. However graceful and superbly directed the movements of a pole-vaulter, our aesthetic pleasure in his performance is marred if he knocks the bar off.

One additional and related factor is that some people naturally move gracefully whatever they may be doing, and this may contribute to the aesthetic effect of their actions in sport. If I may be pardoned for the outrageous pun, Muhammad Ali provides a striking example.

Several questions remain. For example, why are some sporting events regarded as less aesthetically pleasing than others, i.e., where we are not comparing actions within the same context of direction onto a common end, but comparing actions in different contexts? For instance, in my view the butterfly stroke in swimming, however well performed, seems less aesthetically pleasing than the crawl. Perhaps this is because it looks less efficient as a way of moving through the water, since there appears to be a disproportionate expenditure of effort in relation to the achievement. A similar example is race walking which, even at its best, never seems to me to be an aesthetically pleasing event. Perhaps, again, this is because one feels that the same effort would be more efficiently employed if the walker broke into a run. In each of these cases one is implicitly setting a wider context, seeing the action in terms of a wider purpose, of movement through water and movement over the ground respectively. But what of a sport such as weight-lifting, which many regard as providing little or no aesthetic pleasure, although it is hard to discover a wider context, a more economical direction on to a wider or similar end in another activity, with which we are implicitly comparing it? Perhaps the explanation lies simply in a general tendency to prefer, from an aesthetic point of view, sports which allow for smooth, flowing movements in the achievement of the primary purpose. Nevertheless, for the devotee, there are no doubt, "beautiful" lifts, so called because they accomplish maximum direction of effort.

Now the objection has been made against my account that it fails to differentiate the aesthetic from the skillful. I think two points are sufficient to overcome this objection. First, as a careful reading of the chapter will reveal, my argument, if valid, shows that in sport the two concepts are certainly intimately related, but it also shows that they are not entirely co-extensive. I have marked some ways in which they diverge.

The second and more important point is this. Even if it were true that my argument had not revealed a distinction between the two concepts, that would not constitute an objection to it. For why should not those features of an action in virtue of which it is called skilful also be those in virtue of which it is called aesthetically pleasing? Wittgenstein once wrote. "Ethics and aesthetics are one." Whether or not one would want to accept that statement will depend on Wittgenstein's argument for it. One cannot simply dismiss it on the grounds that it *must* be self-defeating to offer a characterisation of the aesthetic which also characterises the ethical.

The supposed objection seems to incorporate the preconception that to have characterised the aesthetic is to have specified those essential features which can be shared by no other concept. This would be like denying that ginger can be an essential ingredient in ginger cakes on the ground that it is *also* an ingredient in ginger ale. The objector produced no argument, but simply assumed that an account which also fitted the skilful could not be adequate as an account of the aesthetic. So, in response to this supposed objection, I could simply reply: "You are right, I concede that my argument does not entirely distinguish the aesthetic from the skilful. But so far from constituting an objection to my argument, what you have provided amounts to a rough summary of it."

Context and Aesthetic Feeling

The foregoing argument raises two related considerations which have an important bearing upon the notion of aesthetic *experience* in sport. First, a movement cannot be considered aesthetically in isolation, but only in the context of a particular action in a particular sport. A graceful sweep of the left arm may be very effective in a dance, but the same movement may look ugly and absurd as part of a service action in tennis, or of a pitcher's action in baseball, since it detracts from the ideal of total concentration of effort to achieve the specific task. A specific movement is aesthetically satisfying only if, in the context of the action as a whole, it is seen as forming a unified structure which is regarded as the most economical and efficient method of achieving the required end.

Secondly, there is a danger of serious misconception arising from a mistaken dependence upon feelings as criteria of aesthetic quality, whether in sport or in any other activity, including dance and the other arts. This is part of the misconception to which we alluded earlier, and consists of taking the feeling of the performer or spectator as the ultimate arbiter. Yet, as we have seen, any feeling is intelligible only if it can be identified by its typical manifestation in behaviour. This is what Wittgenstein (1953) meant by saying that an inner process stands in need of outward criteria. Thus, in the present case, it is the observable physical movement which identifies the feeling and not, as is often believed, the inner feeling which suffuses the physical movement with aesthetic quality or meaning. The feeling could not even be identified if it were not normally experienced in certain objectively recognisable circumstances. One should resist the temptation, commonly encountered in discussion of dance and other forms of movement, to believe that it is how a movement feels which determines its character or effectiveness, whether aesthetic or purposive. That it feels right is no guarantee that it is right. Inexperienced oarsmen in an "eight" are often tempted to heave their bodies round violently in an attempt to propel the boat more quickly, because such an action gives a feeling of much greater power. Yet in fact it will upset the balance of the boat and thus reduce the effectiveness of the rowing of the crew as a whole. The most effective stroke action can best be judged by the coach who is watching the whole perform- ance from the bank, not by the feeling of the indi- vidual oarsmen or even of all the crew. Similarly, in tennis and skiing, to take just two examples, the feeling of an action is often misleading as to its maximum efficiency. A common error in skiing is to lean into the slope and at a certain stage in his progress a learner starts to make turns for the first time which feel very good. Yet, however exhilarat- ing the feeling, if he is leaning the wrong way he will be considerably hampered from making fur- ther progress, because in fact he is not directing his efforts in the most effective manner. There are in- numerable other such examples one could cite, and this, of course, has important implications for education. If the arbiter of success in physical ac- tivities is what the students feel, rather than what they can be observed to do, it is hard to see how such activities can be learned and taught.

However, to refer to an objection which we considered earlier, it is important not to misun- derstand this point by going to the opposite ex- treme, for I am not saying that we cannot be guided by such feelings, or that they are of no value. My point is that they are useful and reli- able only to the extent that they are answerable to patterns of behaviour which can be *observed* to be most efficiently directed onto the particu- lar task. This reveals the connection between this and the preceding point, for it is clear that the character and efficiency of a particular move- ment cannot be considered in isolation from the whole set of related movements of which it forms a part, and from the purpose towards which they are, as a whole, directed. Thus the context in which the movement occurs is a fac- tor of an importance which it is impossible to exaggerate, since the feeling could not even be identified, let alone evaluated, if it were not nor-

mally experienced as part of an objectively recognisable action.

In this respect I should like to question what is often said about the aesthetic attitude, namely that it is essentially or predominantly contempla- tive. Reid (1970), for instance, says: "In an aes- thetic situation we attend to what we perceive in what is sometimes called a 'contemplative' way." Now it may be that a concern with the arts and the aesthetic is largely contemplative, but I see no reason to deny, indeed I see good reason to insist, that one can have what are most appropriately called aesthetic *feelings* while actually performing an activity. There are numerous examples, such as a well-executed dive, a finely timed stroke in squash, a smoothly accomplished series of move- ments in gymnastics, an outing in an "eight" when the whole crew is pulling in unison, with unwavering balance, and a training run when one's body seems to be completely under one's control. For many, the feelings derived from such performances are part of the enjoyment of par- ticipation, and "aesthetic" seems the most appro- priate way to characterise them. Reid says that "a dancer or actor in the full activity of dancing or acting is often, perhaps always, in some degree contemplating the product of his activity." Later, he says of games players: "There is no time while the operation is going on to dwell upon aesthetic qualities . . . Afterwards, the participant may look back upon his experience contemplatively with perhaps some aesthetic satisfaction." Again, of the aesthetic in cricket, he remarks: "The bats- man may enjoy it too, although at the moment of play he has no time to dwell upon it. But to pro- duce exquisite strokes for contemplation is not part of his dominating motive as he is actually engaged in the game . . ." Yet the batsman's aes- thetic experience is not necessarily dependent upon his having time at the moment of playing the stroke to "dwell upon it," nor is it limited to a retrospective contemplation of his performance. If he plays a perfectly timed cover drive with the ball flashing smoothly and apparently effortlessly from the face of his bat to the boundary, the aes- thetic satisfaction of the batsman is intrinsic to what he is doing. The aesthetic is not a distinct but perhaps concurrent activity, and it need not depend upon detached or retrospective contemplation. His experience is logically inseparable from the stroke he is playing, in that it is identifiable only by his particular action in that context. And it is quite natural, unexceptionable, and perhaps unavoidable to call such an experience "aesthetic." "Kinaesthetic or "tactile" would not tell the whole story by any means, since producing the same physical movement in a quite different context, for instance in a laboratory, could not count as producing the same feeling. Indeed, it is significant that we tend naturally to employ aesthetic terms to describe the feelings involved in such actions. We say that a stroke felt "beautiful," and it was so to the extent that it was efficiently executed in relation to the specific purpose of the action in the sport concerned. Many participants in physical activities have experienced the exquisite feeling, for instance, of performing a dance or gymnastic sequence, of sailing over the bar in a pole vault, or of accomplishing a fluent series of Christis with skis immaculately parallel. It is difficult to know how to describe these feelings other than as "aesthetic." It is certainly the way in which those of us who have taken part in such activities tend spontaneously to refer to them. So, although I do not wish to deny that contemplation is an important part of the aesthetic, I would contend that it is not exhaustive. It is by no means unusual to experience aesthetic feelings, properly so called, while actually engaged and fully involved in physical activities. Moreover, many of us who have derived considerable pleasure from a wide variety of sporting activities would want to insist that such aesthetic experience constitutes a large part of the enjoyment of participation.

The Aesthetic
and the Artistic

In the case of the purposive sports, then, as the actions become more and more directly aimed, with maximum economy and efficiency, at the required end, they become more and more specific, and the gap between means and end is to that extent reduced. That is, increasingly it is less possible to specify the means apart from the end. In these sports the gap will, nevertheless, never be entirely closed in that there cannot be the complete identification of means and end, or more accurately perhaps, the inappropriateness of the distinction between means and end, which obtains in the case of art. For even if in fact there is a single most efficient and economical way of achieving a particular end, this is a contingent matter. The evolution of improved high-jumping methods is a good example. The scissor jump was once regarded as the most efficient method, but it has been overtaken by the straddle, the Western roll and the Fosbury flop.

There remains an interesting question. The aesthetic sports have been shown to be similar to the arts with respect to the impossibility of distinguishing means and ends. Does this mean that such sports can legitimately be regarded as art forms? I should want to insist that they cannot, for two reasons. First, as we have seen, there is good reason to doubt whether the means/end distinction ever quite becomes inappropriate, although it almost reaches that point, even in the aesthetic sports. That is, unlike dance, in these sports there is still an externally specifiable aim even though, for instance, it is impossible entirely to specify what the gymnast is trying to achieve apart from the way in which he is trying to achieve it. Perhaps this is what some physical educationists are getting at when they say, rather vaguely, that a distinction between gymnastics and dance is that the former is objective while the latter is subjective.

However, it is the second reason which is the more important one, and this concerns the distinction which is almost universally overlooked or oversimplified, and therefore misconceived, between the aesthetic and the artistic. The aesthetic applies, for instance, to sunsets, birdsong and mountain ranges, whereas the artistic tends to be limited, at least in its central uses, to artifacts or performances intentionally created by man—*objets trouvés*, if regarded as art, would be so in an extended sense. Throughout this paper I have so far followed the common practice of taking "aesthetic" to refer to the genus of which the artistic is a species. My reason for doing so is that any other difference between the two concepts is of no consequence to my main argument, since their logical character with respect to the possibility of distinguishing between means and end is the same. However, in order to consider the question of whether any sport can justifiably be regarded as an art form a more adequate distinction between the aesthetic and the artistic is required, and on examination it becomes clear that there is a much more important issue here than is commonly supposed. I can begin to bring out the issue to which I refer by considering Reid's answer to the question. He is prepared to allow that what I call the aesthetic sports may justifiably be called art, but in my view his conclusion is invalidated because his own formulation of the distinction overlooks a crucial characteristic of art. He writes (1970):

> When we are talking about the category of art, as distinct from the category of the aesthetic, we must be firm, I think, in insisting that in art there is someone who has made (or is making) purposefully an artifact, and that in his purpose there is contained as an essential part the idea of producing an object (not necessarily a "thing": it could be a movement or a piece of music) in some medium for aesthetic contemplation . . . the movement (of a gymnast, skater, diver), carried out in accordance with the general formula, has aesthetic quality fused into it, transforming it into an art quality . . . The question is whether the production of aesthetic value is intrinsically part of the purpose of these sports. (If so, on my assumptions, they will be in part, at least, art.)

This certainly has the merit of excluding natural phenomena such as sunsets and roses, but some people might regard his exclusion of *objets*

trouvés as somewhat difficult to justify. What, in my view, is worse, this conception would include much which we should be strongly disinclined to call "art." For example, a wallpaper pattern is normally designed to give aesthetic pleasure, but it would not on that account, at least in the great majority of cases, be regarded as art. Many such counter-examples spring to mind; for instance the paint on the walls of my office, the shape of radiators and spectacles, and coloured toilet paper. In each case the intention is to give aesthetic pleasure, but none is art (which is not necessarily to deny that, in certain unusual circumstances, any of them could be considered as art, or as part of a work of art).

Reid has done sufficient in my view to show clearly that the great majority of sports cannot legitimately be regarded as art. For the *principal* aim in most sports is certainly not to produce performances for aesthetic pleasure. The aesthetic is incidental. And if it should be argued against me that nevertheless such purposive sports *could* be considered from the aesthetic point of view, my reply would be that so could everything else. Hence, if that were to be regarded as the distinguishing feature of art then *everything* would be art, and thus the term "art" would no longer have any application.

Nevertheless, Reid's formulation fails, I think, because he overlooks the central aspect of the concept of art which underlies the fact that these are cases where one may appreciate a work of art aesthetically but not artistically. To understand the significance of this point, consider the following example. Some years ago I went to watch a performance by Ram Gopal, the great Indian classical dancer, and I was enthralled by the exhilarating quality of his movements. Yet I did not appreciate, because I could not have understood, his dance artistically, for there is an enormous number of precise meanings given to hand gestures in Indian classical dance, of which I knew none. So it seems clear that my appreciation was of the aesthetic not the artistic.

This example brings out the important characteristic of the concept of art which I particularly want to emphasise, since it is generally overlooked by those who conflate "aesthetic" and "artistic." Moreover, the failure to recognise it is probably the main source of misconceived distinctions between the two terms. I shall first outline the point roughly, and go on to elucidate it more fully in relation to other claims made for sport as art.

It is distinctive of any art form that its conventions allow for the possibility of the expression of a conception of life situations. Thus the arts are characteristically concerned with contemporary moral, social, political, and emotional issues. Yet this is not true of the aesthetic. I think it is because he does not recognise the significance of this point that Reid is prepared to allow that the aesthetic sports may legitimately be regarded as art forms. But it is this characteristic of art which is my reason for insisting that even those sports in which the aesthetic is intrinsic, and which are therefore performed to give aesthetic satisfaction, cannot justifiably be considered as art. For in synchronised swimming, figure-skating, diving, trampolining, and gymnastics, the performer does not, as part of the convention of the activity, have the possibility of expressing through his particular medium his view of life situations. It is difficult to imagine a gymnast who included in his sequence movements which expressed his view of war, or of love in a competitive society, or of any other such issue. Certainly if he did so it would, unlike art, *detract* to that extent from his performance.

Of course there are cases, even in the accredited arts, such as abstract paintings and dances, where we are urged not to look for a meaning but simply to enjoy the line, colour, movement, etc., without trying to read anything into them. But it is intrinsic to the notion of an art form that it can at least *allow for* the possibility of considering issues of social concern, and this is not possible in the aesthetic sports. Incidentally, if I am right that the activities of art and sport are quite distinct, this poses problems for those who suggest that the aesthetic sports may provide one method of, perhaps an introduction to, educa-

tion in the arts, although of course this is not in the least to cast doubt on their aesthetic value. At their best these sports are undoubtedly superb aesthetically, but they are not, in my view, art.

Sport and Art

Partly in order to bring out more fully the important characteristic of the concept of art which I have just outlined, and partly because of the widespread misconception on the issue, I should like further to elucidate my reasons for denying the common supposition that sport can legitimately be considered as art.

As we have seen, it is clear that there is a distinction between the aesthetic and the artistic, even though it may be difficult precisely to delineate it. Yet, in the literature on sport, one still very frequently encounters an illicit slide from such terms as "beautiful" and "graceful" to "art." An author will refer to a general interest in the beauty of the movement in various sporting activities, and will assume implicitly or explicitly that this entitles such activities to be considered as art. Anthony (1968) and Reid (1970) give several examples, and the same confusion runs through Carlisle (1969) who writes, for instance, that "various forms of dance are accepted as art forms and aesthetic criteria are also applied in other activities, e.g., ice-skating, diving, Olympic gymnastics, and synchronised swimming." A more recent example is Lowe (1976) who writes: "By analysing dance, as one of the performing arts, with the object of deducing the aesthetic components . . . a step will be taken closer to the clarification of the beauty of sport as a performing art." So far as I can understand this, Lowe seems to be guilty of the confusion to which I refer, since clearly "beauty" and its cognates do not necessarily imply "art." To say that a young lady is beautiful is not to say that she is a work of art.

For the reasons already given, I submit that, despite the amount of literature on the topic, we should finally abandon this persistent but misguided attempt to characterise sport *in general* as art. Quite apart from what seems to me the obvious misconception involved, I just do not see why it should be thought that sport would somehow be endowed with greater respectability if it could be shown to be art.

There is, of course, a much more convincing case to be made for the credentials of the aesthetic sports as art, although even here I do not think it succeeds. My rejection of the case hinges on the way I have characterised the distinction between the aesthetic and the artistic. It would seem that any attempt to draw this distinction in terms of definition, or by reference to particular kinds of objects or performances, is almost certainly doomed to failure. Hence I distinguish the two concepts by drawing attention to a characteristic which is central to any legitimate art *form*, rather than to a work of art within that medium. Thus, to repeat the point, my own formulation is that any art form, properly so-called, must at least *allow for* the possibility of the expression of a conception of life issues, such as contemporary moral, social, and political problems. Such a possibility is an *intrinsic* part of the concept of art, by which I mean that without it an activity could not count as a legitimate art form. It is certainly a crucial factor in the ways in which the arts have influenced society. Examples abound. For instance, it is reported that during the occupation of France in the war a German officer, indicating the painting *Guernica,* asked Picasso, "Did you do that? " To which Picasso replied, "No, you did."

By contrast, such a possibility is not intrinsic to any sport. However, this point has been misunderstood, as a result of which it has been argued against me that in sport, too, there can be comment on life issues. The commonest example cited was that of black American athletes on the rostrum at the Olympic Games, who gave the clenched-fist salute for Black Power during the playing of the national anthem. But this does not constitute a counter-example, since such a gesture is clearly *extrinsic* to, not made from within, the conventions of sport as such. The conventions of art are in this respect significantly differ-

ent from those in sport, since it is certainly intrinsic to art that a view could be expressed, for instance on colour discrimination, as in Athol Fugard's plays about the issue in South Africa.

We have seen that since aesthetic terms such as "beauty" are often applied to sport, it is sometimes erroneously supposed that therefore sport is art. A similar misconception occurs with respect to the terms "dramatic," "tragic," and their cognates. These terms are used in a notoriously slippery way, hence it certainly cannot be assumed that they are used in other contexts as they are in art. For instance, if I were to leap up during a meeting, shout abusive terms, and hurl a cup through a window, that would certainly be dramatic, but I am modest enough to assume that no one would regard it as artistic.

It is an understood part of the convention that tragedy in a play happens to the *fictional characters* being portrayed, and not to the actors, i.e., the living people taking part. By contrast, and ignoring for a moment the issue of whether it would be legitimately employed in such a context, "tragedy" in sport *does* happen to the participants, i.e. to the living people taking part. For example, let us imagine that I am playing the part of Gloucester, in the play *King Lear*. In the scene where his eyes are put out it is agonising for the character in the play, Gloucester; not for me, the actor. There is no comparable convention in sport such that it would make sense to say of a serious injury in Rugby that it occurred to the full-back, and not to the man who was playing full-back. While in Canada recently, I was given an interesting illustration of the point. A party of Eskimos, attending a performance of *Othello*, were appalled to see what they took to be the killing of people on the stage. They had to be reassured by being taken backstage after the performance to see the actors still alive. The Eskimos had assumed that different actors would be required for each performance.

To put the point roughly, it is a central convention of art, in contrast to sport, that the object of one's attention is an *imagined* object. Thus a term such as "tragic," used of art, has to be understood as deriving its meaning from that convention. Yet, although this is a central convention of art, it is overlooked or misconstrued by most of those who argue that sport is art, or drama. This omission vitiates a good deal of the literature on the topic. Reid (1970) gives several examples, including that of Maheu, who claims that "spectator sports are the true theatre of our day"; Carlisle (1969) who supports the contention that cricket is "an art form both dramatic and visual"; Kitchin, who in an article on "Sport as drama" writes of international soccer: "This is the authentic theatre in the round, from which Hungary's Manager made a thirty-yard running exit with both hands clenched over his eyes . . . Soccer is drama without a script." Similarly, Keenan (1973) in an article entitled "The athletic contest as a 'tragic' form of art," writes: "There is no doubt that athletic contests, like other human endeavours, provide drama. No one would question whether Bannister's effort which produced the first sub-four-minute mile was dramatic." But I would seriously question whether, indeed I would deny that, "dramatic" is being used here in the same sense as when it occurs in the context of discussion of a play, since the relevant convention is lacking. That there is no comparable convention in sport can be brought out most clearly by the lack of any analogue with a fictional character. What happens to Gloucester does not happen to the person playing the part of Gloucester. The analogue in sport would have to be something like: "What happened to Hungary's Manager did not happen to the man who held the position as manager," and "What happened to the athlete who completed the first sub-four-minute mile did not happen to Bannister, who took part in the race," both of which are palpably absurd.

There are two common uses of the term "tragic" which are outside, and which therefore should not be confused with its use within, the conventions of drama:

(1) Where the term is used, for instance, of serious injury to a sportsman, the analogue in a play would be serious injury to an actor, for example in an accident during a duelling scene.

"Tragic" in this sense does not depend on conventions at all, whether sporting or artistic, but is used to refer to a poignantly sad and distressing event in real life, such as a seriously crippling or fatal accident or illness.

(2) On the other hand, in the irritatingly prevalent but barbarously debased sense of the term where "tragic" is used, for instance, of the failure of a sportsman to achieve a success on which he had set his heart, the analogue in drama would be not some tragic event in a play but, for instance, the failure of an actor in a crucial role, or his failure to obtain a role which he earnestly wanted. It is still quite different from the use of the term within the conventions of drama. Strangely enough, Keenan (1973) recognises this point to some extent, yet fails to realise that it undermines his whole case. He writes: "We can truly sympathise with classic efforts of athletic excellence that end in tragedy. They parallel the difficult episodes in life." As one example, he cites an Olympic marathon race:

> The amazing Pietri entered the stadium with an enormous lead on the field, needing only to negotiate the last 385 yards to win. His effort had left him in an obvious state of extreme physical fatigue . . . The crowd cheered lustily for him to continue, to fight off the fatigue, to win. His final collapse came near the finish line as the eventual winner . . . was just entering the stadium.

This example, so far from supporting Kennan's case reveals the fatal flaw in it, for "tragedy" here is used in the latter sense adumbrated above, and is totally different from the way the term is used within and as part of the conventions of drama. The point can be brought sharply into focus by recognising that a poignantly tragic moment in drama is a *triumph*, a mark of *success*, for an actor, whereas, by contrast a "tragic" moment in sport is a *failure*, even if a noble and courageous failure, for the competitor.

The importance of the conventions of art can be brought out in another way, by reference to the use of the term "illusion." In the context of the arts "illusion" is not employed as it would be of, for instance, a mirage. One actually, if mistakenly, believes that an oasis is there, whereas one does not actually believe that someone is being murdered on a stage. Or at least, if one should actually believe that someone is being murdered this significantly reveals a failure to grasp one of the most important conventions of drama. The term "illusion" is used in a different, if related, sense in the context of art. I say that the sense is related because, for instance, the actors, threatre management and producer, by means of lighting, stage effects and a high standard of acting, try to induce the audience to suspend their disbelief, as it were. Nevertheless, as Scruton (1974) puts it, our experience of representation and expression in art "derives from imagination, not belief."

Of course this is not in the least to deny that it is possible to be imaginative in sport, although I have been rather surprisingly misunderstood in this respect. What it does deny is that there are analogous conventions in sport such that the participants have to be imagined, as one has to imagine the characters in a play or novel.

In short, the misconception of those writers who persist in what I firmly believe are misguided attempts to argue that sport is an art form, stems from their ignoring or misconstruing the crucial importance of the *art* aspect of a work of art. For instance, one commonly experiences emotional responses to both artistic and sporting performances, and as both spectator and performer. Now, emotional feelings can be identified only by criteria, of which the most important is what is called the "intensional object," i.e. the kind of object towards which the emotion is directed. In the case of art, the intensional object cannot be characterised in isolation from the relevant conventions. The point becomes particularly clear, perhaps, when we think how we can be moved by completely non-naturalistic works of art, such as surrealism, abstract expressionism, and an allegory such as *Le Petit Prince* by St-Exupéry.

Now of course with respect to sport, too, the intensional object cannot be characterised independently of the conventions of that particular kind of activity. The point was brought home vividly to me when for the first time I watched an American Football match, which was a keenly contested local derby between two rival high schools. There was considerable partisan excitement, but I was unable to share in it because I did not understand the game. As an even clearer example, a friend in Jasper told me of his experience, while working in the Northwest Territories, of trying to teach the local Eskimos how to play soccer. He was frustrated, apparently, by their inability to understand, or at least refusal to accept, that the purpose of the game was to defeat the opposing team. The Eskimos were much too genial to adopt such an uncivilised, competitive ethos, hence if a team were winning, members of it would promptly score in their own goal in order to be generous to their opponents.

So one certainly needs to understand the conventions of sport, too, in order to become emotionally involved in the appropriate way. But the conventions of sport are in important respects very different from those of art, even in the case of aesthetic sports such as figure-skating. The champion skater John Curry has strongly expressed his conviction that figure-skating *should* be regarded as an art form, and the superb Canadian skater, Toller Cranston, is frequently quoted as a counter-example by Canadians. He, too, apparently, has often insisted that figure-skating is an art. However, this contention is based on a confusion, and in my opinion it would be clearer to conceive of them as two quite distinct kinds of activity. Then we should have on one hand the *sport* of figure-skating, and on the other hand, the *art* of modern dance on ice, which these skaters want to create as a new art form. It is interesting that Toller Cranston is said to have expressed annoyance at the limitations imposed by the conventions and rules of the *sport,* and has made his point forcefully by *deliberately* performing his figure-skating in several competitions *as* an art form. For instance, in response to the music he had flouted the canons of the sport by performing movements which *did* express his view of life situations. But it is significant that, much to his further chagrin, he *lost* marks for doing so. In my view the judges were quite right. The context of sport, even an aesthetic sport, is not appropriate for art. It is significant, perhaps, and tacitly concedes my point, that John Curry has put his convictions into practice by creating "The John Curry Theatre of Skating."

Now it might be objected that in denying in this way that sport can legitimately be regarded as art I was simply being stipulative. That is, it might be said that this is arbitrarily to lay down how the term "art" should be used. This objection is of the same kind as that which was discussed earlier with respect to the use of "intellectual," and it can be met in a similar way. Certainly philosophers cannot legislate how words should be used, and what is to count as correct usage. "Artistic" could be used as synonymous with "aesthetic," and there could be no *philosophical* objection to what I regard as barbarously degenerate uses such as "the art of cooking." The philosophical point is that, however the term may be used, this will not *remove*, even although it may blur, the relevant distinction. That is, if "art" were to be used as broadly as this, there would still be a distinction between those forms of activity which have, and those which do not have, intrinsic to their conventions, the possibility of comment on life issues in the way described. And in such a case, it would be necessary to employ some other term to mark those which have this kind of convention. Hence it seems to me much less conducive to confusion to restrict "art" to such activities.

To repeat the point, then, in my opinion it is high time we buried once for all the prolix attempts to show that sport is art. It may be of interest to point up illuminating similarities, but only confusion can accrue from the attempt to equate the two kinds of activity. In the case of an aesthetic sport such as figure-skating the suggestion is at least initially plausible because of the widespread failure to recognise the important distinction between the aesthetic and the artistic, and because figure-skating, unlike, for instance, football, can so easily become an art form. But in the case of the purposive sports, which constitute the great majority, there is not even a *prima facie* case, even though there may be many movements in such sports which are superb aesthetically.

Rather ironically, the fact that sporting activities and the movements of athletes have been the subject for art, for instance in painting and sculpture, is sometimes adduced, at least by implication, in support of the contention that sport is art. For example, Lowe (1976) writes:

> Among sculptors, R. Tait McKenzie has brought a fine sense of movement to his athletic studies cast in bronze. There is no question about the aesthetic qualities of these art works: hence they provide intrinsic clues to or grasp of the elusive nature of beauty in sport.

I say that it is ironic because examination reveals that this kind of argument achieves the very opposite of what its authors intend, since it makes the point which could also be regarded as a summary of my distinction between the aesthetic and the artistic. For whereas sport can be the subject of art, art could not be the subject of sport. Indeed, the very notion of a *subject* of sport makes no sense.

Bibliography

Anthony, W. J., "Sport and physical education as a means of aesthetic education," *British Journal of Physical Education,* vol. 60, no. 179 (March 1968).

Bambrough, J. R., "To reason is to generalise," *The Listener,* vol. 89, no. 2285 (11 January 1973).

Best, D., *Expression in Movement and the Arts* (London: Lepus Books, Henry Kimpton Publishers, 1974).

Carlisle, R., "The concept of physical education," *Proceedings of the Philosophy of Education Society of Great Britain,* vol. 3 (January 1969).

Keenan, F., "The athletic contest as a 'tragic' form of art," in *The Philosophy of Sport,* ed. R. G. Oster-houdt (Springfield, Illinois: C. C. Thomas, 1973).

Lowe, B., "Toward scientific analysis of the beauty of sport," *British Journal of Physical Education,* vol. 7, no. 4 (July 1976).

Reid, L. A., "Sport, the aesthetic and art," *British Journal of Educational Studies,* vol. 18, no. 3 (1970).

Scruton, R., *Art and Imagination* (London: Methuen, 1974).

Wittgenstein, L., *Philosophical Investigations* (Oxford: Basil Blackwell, 1953).

Questions for Consideration

1. Since Best considers the aesthetic in sport as an economy or efficiency of action, it has been objected that the aesthetic comes to look much like the skillful. How does he deal with this objection?

2. How might Best deal with nonsportive examples of the aesthetic, such as an aesthetic sunset?

3. How is it possible for us to narrow the distance between aesthetic appreciation of aesthetic sports and that of purposive sports?

4. If Best is correct in his assessment of sport not being art, do you think this is a fatal flaw of sport?

11   Beauty, Sport, and Gender

J. M. Boxill
University of Tampa

J. M. Boxill takes another look at arguments intended to show that sport is not a form of art. Responding to critics such as Paul Ziff, Louis Reid, and especially David Best, she examines four elements that are said to differentiate sport and art: (1) skill as technical efficiency in sport overshadows skill in art as style, grace, and form; (2) desire for victory in sport has no counterpart in art; (3) beauty is not the sole aim of sport, as it is with art; and (4) there is no intentional statement about the human condition, as there is with art, when athletes behave aesthetically.

Each of the four claims, she asserts, is false. First, style, grace, and form are an important part of sport. One has only to consider an athlete who is dissatisfied after having played badly and won. Next, she says, there is something similar to desire for victory in art. Would some, if not most, musicians be satisfied with awkwardly hitting the right notes rather than gracefully hitting the wrong ones? Third, she states that beauty may not be the sole aim of sport, but it is not the sole aim of art either. An artist may want to express something in a work through beauty. He may also want to sell his work. Last, athletes make statements about life situations. Every game—with rules, relationships, and penalties—is life in microcosm.

Boxill concludes by stating that since sport is compatible with art in each of these aspects, "sport is a form of art."

With a head fake to the right, Dr. J takes a long stride left toward the basket, glides upward from his left foot, is airborne with the basketball high over his head, and in one fluid motion slams the ball through the hoop. It is the human body at its best, operating against obstacles set by nature and obstacles artificially created. It is the ultimate one-on-one move at its most beautiful.

Kareem Abdul-Jabbar receives a pass at the low post and is quickly double-teamed. With a pass fake, he takes a drop step toward the basket, holds the ball high over his head, and in one flowing movement lets go a "sky hook." This is Kareem's "patented" shot; it is the hook shot as only Kareem can do it. There is no question that these movements have great aesthetic value. But can we thereby conclude that they are art? A bird in flight, a beautiful sunset, a beautiful waterfall— these have aesthetic value, but we do not thereby conclude they are art. Louis Reid (3: p. 249) maintains that "many movements in games or athletics or gymnastics have great positive aesthetic value; but it is wrong to jump to the conclusion that they are *art*, any more than the flight of a bird is art."

In a similar vein, David Best (1: p. 211) maintains that, "The aesthetic applies, for instance . . . to sunsets, bird song and mountain ranges, whereas the artistic is limited, at least in its central uses, to artifacts and performances intentionally created by man." And Paul Ziff (4: p. 45) maintains that "mechanical efficiency may or may not be aesthetic but such efficiency is not intended by the athlete to be beautiful. A lack of intention to be beautiful thereby disqualifies sport as potentially aesthetic."

These positions resist the idea that sport can be an art form. However, there are those of us who wish to place sport in the realm of art. Perhaps one of the boldest positions is set out by C. L. R. James in *Beyond a Boundary* (2). The book

Reprinted by permission, from J. M. Boxill, "Beauty, Sport, and Gender," *Journal of the Philosophy of Sport* XI (1985): 36–47.

deals specifically with cricket, but can be extended to all sports. "The aestheticians," he says, "have scorned to take notice of popular sports and games—to their own detriment. The aridity and confusion . . . will continue until they include organized games and the people who watch them as an integral part of their data" (2: p. 192).

Thus, that sport is an art form is not a new idea. So why another paper? Because I think my position differs from the others—it answers the critics and goes beyond. To establish my position, I must answer those critics. Ziff, Best, and Reid maintain that certain features that are essential to sport preclude its consideration as an art form or an aesthetic experience. They grant that there may be aesthetic qualities to sports and games, but these are only by-products. As Reid (3: p. 252) puts it, "The aesthetic qualities of games and sports are by-products. . . . They can be important and precious by-products, but by-products they are none the less."

The main features which are claimed to keep sport outside the realm of art are these:

1. The concern for skill in the form of technical efficiency overshadows the essential art ingredients of style, grace, and form.
2. The strong desire for victory in competitive sports overshadows the aim of beauty.
3. Even if one of the aims of sport is beauty, it is not the sole aim.
4. Finally, even when athletes aim at beauty, they are not consciously making any statement about the human condition.

So, given these features that appear to be undeniable, why try to elevate sport beyond its simple importance as a source of pleasure and meaning to its millions of participants and spectators? Why indeed? Because it is precisely these aesthetic qualities that account for the pleasure and meaning of sports to its participants and spectators. If "elevating" it is what I am doing, then so be it; I simply aim to place sport in its proper position.

I will contest each of the reasons for claiming that sport is not art. I will argue that the concern for efficiency in sport is paralleled by a concern for efficiency in the acknowledged art form, and in neither case does it overshadow the concern for beauty; that similarly the desire for victory in competitive sport does not necessarily overshadow the concern for beauty; that even if beauty is not the sole aim of sport, neither is it the sole aim in the acknowledged art forms; and finally, that it is a false assumption that sport makes no statement about the human condition. More positively I will argue that just as art is self-expression, so too is sport; that in both art and sport, self-expression is hampered by a lack of skill; and finally, that sport is as valid a means of self-expression for women as it is for men.

For various, mostly false, reasons, women have been denied access to the single most available means of self-expression. In referring to beauty in relationship to women, it is usually referred to in terms of women as objects of beauty, not as creators of beauty. Women's bodies were deemed aesthetic in themselves, and to be viewed in the same way as any other object of natural beauty. To go beyond this "natural beauty," and to create beauty is to destroy the female-feminine object of beauty.

"Feminine" beauty can be retained only in such art forms as dance or in the "form" sports such as gymnastics, swimming, and diving. The other so-called "masculine" sports destroy feminine bodies; they present dangers to the female body. But many of these form sports are not available or suitable to all women and, as a result, a great many women have had no vehicle for self-expression. Hence, in establishing that sport is an art form, I further maintain that just as sport provides a vehicle for self-expression in men, it too provides a vehicle for women. Indeed, sport is the single most available means of self-expression for both men and women.

I

Let me now examine the interrelationships among skill, technical efficiency, and beauty in sport and in art. Nobody denies that skill and technical efficiency are necessary to sport. In order to play any game well, one must develop to a certain skill level. Fledgling athletes look clumsy and perform clumsily because their bodies are developing, and they are just beginning to learn the skills. Basketball is a sport that exhibits clearly the athlete's developmental process from its beginnings to the level attained by Dr. J or Abdul-Jabbar. It also illustrates the position I hold regarding women in sports.

Basketball played at the junior high level—boys or girls—is painful to watch. Most of the players are not in tune with their bodies, and their coordination level is low. As a result, their skill level is low. They are playing an "adult" game with a regulation-size ball at a regulation height, and getting the ball down court and making a basket are major accomplishments. There is little strategy, pattern, or style in the game at this level. At the high-school level, the coordination and technique are beginning to commensurate with the skill necessary for aesthetic appeal. Of course, some players are significantly better than others, and this is true for both boys and girls. But because of size differential, the boys develop more of the skills necessary for aesthetic appeal. Further, the boys' training at this level is much more intensified than the girls', whose lack of training also contributes to a lower skill level. It has certainly improved over the years, but a deficit still remains.

At the college level the skills are more finely tuned and a high efficiency level is reached. Athletes at this level of skill begin to improvise and add personal style to the game, which then becomes their "signature." These additions are impossible without the requisite mastery of basic techniques. For only when the basics are mastered as the skill is performed efficiently, with the least expenditure of resources, can a performer aim at beauty or make an aesthetic response. At this level of efficiency the acquisition and improvement of technical skill are no longer ends in themselves: Here the performer as athlete aims at beauty.

As basketball is played today, at least, the skill, accuracy, and grace displayed by males are superior to those displayed by women. This is why spectators usually prefer to watch men play rather than women. Even though women can be graceful, add a basketball and a different kind of grace is required. To see what the human body can do with a round ball and hoop is often awe-inspiring. What Dr. J, Kareem Abdul-Jabbar, and James Worthy can do with a basketball is breathtaking.

The women are only beginning to display this type of bodily excellence. It is interesting to note that beginning with the 1984–85 season the collegiate women will be using a smaller ball—although the same height hoop. This, in my opinion, will enhance the skill level, because hand size is very important in basketball. Players with small hands have difficulty handling the ball; the larger the hands, the better the control. Obviously, women have smaller hands, so their ball control is less proficient than men's. For most women dunking is impossible even if they can jump high enough; they need to be able to "palm" the ball with ease. Only a few women can do this. Most men can, however, and this is a significant factor in developing a high skill level.

In gymnastics there is little difference between skill levels for men and women. However, there are significant differences in their performances. The women perform on uneven parallel bars and a balance beam, whereas the men perform on even parallels, rings, and a high bar. The skills required are different, and men and women both display bodily excellence at high skill levels. The women's events generally emphasize the qualities of flexibility, coordination, and grace. The men's events emphasize other qualities such as strength and agility. While both men and women do floor exercises, the performances differ. Nevertheless, a high level of skill and efficiency is still required for a performer to aim at beauty or make an aesthetic response in the audience. And, the aesthetic response is greater in those who understand and appreciate the intricacies of this sport as well as others. Gymnastics is also a sport in which efficiency and beauty are inseparable. There is a streamlining which is itself beautiful. Other examples of this are ski-jumping, high-jumping, and pole-vaulting. Of these, it is hard to say that efficiency is the sole aim, since to be efficient is to be beautiful. In other cases such as basketball, once efficiency is attained, style is added where the aim is beauty.

All of what I have said about the relation between efficiency and beauty in sport may be applied to the relation between the two in art. Just as in sport, it is undeniable that skill and technical expertise are important in the acknowledged arts, for example, music, painting, and dance. Does this preclude their being art? Clearly, skill and technical expertise are as necessary to art as they are to sport.

It can scarcely be said that a musician's performance which lacks technical efficiency or skill has aesthetic appeal. We suffer through our children's piano recitals, dance recitals, art shows, and beginning orchestra concerts. Some display a certain potential. We see a *potential* for aesthetic appeal, but the lack of skill or techniques renders any aesthetic appeal slim. (This is not to say, of course, that the "young artists" themselves do not have an aesthetic experience.) We attend these event out of loyalty or parental pride, not for any aesthetic appeal. Only when a certain skill level is attained can there be an aesthetically beautiful performance. At first the concern is mastering basics and achieving a skill level; in playing an instrument, for example, hitting the right note is the primary concern, then hitting the right notes in a certain pattern and speed. Only when this is achieved can style be considered and only then can there be any aesthetic appeal. There is no wasted energy, no superfluous movement.

In literature, the writer's end is to express a certain thought. The resultant writing is efficient if the thought is expressed with no waste of words; every word counts in that each says something. The end result is beautiful precisely because it is efficient. Verbosity is not efficient, nor is it beautiful. In music the connection be-

tween beauty and efficiency may not be quite as strong. When playing a composition efficiently, you waste no energy; now you can begin to add style and grace in trying to produce the aesthetically pleasing rendition. Efficiency and beauty may not be identical, but efficiency is necessary for the beautiful. Thus, in art there is a definite and important relation between efficiency and beauty. In some cases they too are inseparable, and in others efficiency is as necessary a condition as beauty.

Thus the development of technique, skill, and efficiency is as important to acknowledged art forms as it is in sports. This development in sport parallels that of art, and I conclude that, contrary to Ziff (4), it cannot be the case that concern for technical efficiency overshadows the essential art ingredients. Indeed, skill and technical efficiency are necessary to these ingredients. Thus this first feature does not preclude sport from being an art form.

II

The argument in Section I establishes a parallel between sport and art with respect to efficiency and beauty, but it is not enough to show that sport is an art form. There are still many respects in which sport fails to parallel the acknowledged art forms. One of these is the strong desire for victory in sports. This has no parallel in other art forms, and this, it is argued, excludes sport from the realm of art. It is allowed that there may be some aesthetic appeal to these sports whose main concerns is victory, but if there is any it is a by-product, or is incidental to the sport and is subordinate to the main purpose of victory. As "proof" of this claim, Best (1: p. 201) poses this question to a player: "Which would you prefer, to score three goals in a clumsy manner, or to miss them all with graceful movements?" The answer, he feels, is obvious.

Let's pose a similar question to a musician performing Beethoven's Fifth at a recital: Which would you prefer—to hit right notes awkwardly or hit the wrong notes smoothly? Let's ask the gymnast at a competition a similar question: Which would you prefer—to perform a double flip with a half-twist clumsily, or a simple walk-over with graceful movements? Are the answers obvious? No, the answers aren't obvious in any of these cases including Best's. In posing the question to begin with, he is assuming the peculiar psychology of winning at all costs, and that is a bold assumption for this is not always the case. Most assuredly the desire for victory is strong in every competitive event, yet that is not the only object. Some athletes would prefer to lose with a well played performance than win in a lousy performance. Some coaches would rather that their teams lose through a well played game than win by a fluke or with a lousy game. Where the well played game is stressed, victory takes a back seat. Where winning at all costs is stressed, the well played game is secondary. This is especially true where victory is tied to money or some other external aim.

But, let's take some examples: In basketball, except for the pros, men's basketball allows for a stall game. This maneuver allows weaker teams to compete with stronger teams at a more even level. Now some coaches use it to win and some shun it in favor of a well played game which attempts to display bodily excellence. This same holds true for athletes. Some want to play the stall-game to go for the win, and some would prefer to display their skills with style with the possibility of losing. Of course, a stall game can demonstrate its own elements of style! Often, however, the stall is justified because of the diverse skill levels of teams, so that a lesser skilled team is not made to look bad by a more highly skilled team. In the pros, where the level of skill is the highest, a 24-second clock precludes any stall. Interestingly, in college women's basketball, there is a 30-second clock to prevent the "boring," usually unaesthetic, stall-game.

In basketball someone must win; that is a feature of the rules. However, not every player or coach aims solely at winning. What about cases in which, say, Larry Bird puts up an awkward shot at mid-court to win and it goes in? Would he not prefer that to losing with a "beautiful" attempt? First of all, this is only one shot out of an entire game, a game which requires great efficiency. For the entire game to come down to this one shot, both teams must have performed well and displayed a great amount of bodily excellence. And second, to be able to make that shot, a player must have prior skill. It is a one-in-a-million shot! Yet is this any different from, say, a painter who tries some new technique or medium that might fail or might achieve just the expression he wanted in the painting? But it shows great skill.

Let me illustrate another example that the answer to Best's question is not so obvious. Let us say that USC is playing UCLA in football, the score is 21-18 in favor of UCLA, and USC has the ball on UCLA's 35-yard-line with 30 seconds to go in the game. The options are to go for the tie with a field goal or to go for a win with a touchdown. Now some coaches and players would go for the win and perhaps lose, and others would prefer not to lose and go for the tie. The point is, a well played game that is aesthetically pleasing is often the primary aim and is preferred to winning "at all costs." Thus, I do not believe Best's question has the obvious answer that he believes it does.

There are further confusions in the question and the conclusion he draws from it. Granted, many differences exist in sport and acknowledged art forms. But there are also a great many differences among acknowledged art forms themselves. What accounts for many of these differences is the medium through which the art is displayed. The medium provides the vehicle for self-expression. The abilities and skills required are also very different for each. Dance requires tremendous bodily strength, coordination, and grace. Instrumental music requires a good ear and finger dexterity. Sculpture demands artistic hands, good visual perception, and a steady hand. Poetry requires a tremendous facility with words. And as I said earlier, a definite skill level is necessary if the works are to produce an aesthetic response. In fact, if there is an aesthetic response, we assume a high level of skill.

The more we understand, the more we appreciate the difficulties and intricacies involved that enhance the aesthetic response. Further, certain restrictions within the chosen media provide a specific discipline without the various art forms. These serve to enhance the art itself. For example, a sonnet puts limits on the number of lines; there is great flexibility within this form, but to be able to express oneself effectively within the framework of the sonnet the poet must possess great skill to produce a work of art that is aesthetically pleasing.

Now, the medium for sports is competition—competition involving people against people, as in games, competition involving people against nature, as in mountain climbing, and competition involving people and animals against other people and animals, as in equestrian events or horse racing. But critical to the competition is victory: In most cases someone must win and someone must lose. A significant feature of the competitive games is the set of rules that define the game and the process of victory. These rules can be very strict, as in basketball, football, soccer, or baseball, yet they allow for much creativity and provide a vehicle for self-expression. The rules are so designed as to require bodily excellence, to provide a vehicle to display beauty. The rules provide a discipline in which skill and efficiency are required, not simply brute strength and size.

In sports requiring only brute strength or size, there is limited spectator appeal, which is part of the reason why rules are made or revised—to reward spectator appeal, (i.e., aesthetic appeal). Some rules may be added or revised for safety reasons, but most are revised to ensure technical skill or bodily excellence over mere strength and size, which I argue increases aesthetic appeal and thus spectator appeal. This is done in various ways. The aesthetic response is best when two teams are somewhat evenly matched, where each team is challenged and the

outcome is not a foregone conclusion; so rules are revised to try to bring about this situation. But in every one of these revisions the concern is always for bodily excellence. For example, the 3-second lane in basketball was widened to prevent a 7-footer from just standing next to the basket waiting for a lob pass inside. We still have the lob pass inside, but either it has to be one move around a defender, which requires timing, coordination, and accuracy, or it requires a move or shot away from the basket. The rule designers are well aware of this; they are deliberately establishing a challenge, and it is this challenge which forces bodily excellence that produces an aesthetic response and an aesthetic experience.

As stated in Section I, the player's first concern is getting the basics mastered and/or figuring out a shot selection. However, once this is done, he or she is concerned with style, with aesthetics. Dr. J doesn't simply score—he does it with style, with a fluid, graceful style and often with a flourish to enhance the beauty of the movement. Abdul-Jabbar adds style to a normal hook shot; he is challenged, and these challenges provide opportunities for his patented sky-hook.

One may object that the player's concern is still for efficiency; that is, what is the most efficient way of scoring, dribbling, catching, or batting? This is true enough. But the most efficient method is usually one that displays bodily excellence and exhibits the body in harmony with the equipment and/or the factors of nature. When the body is moving efficiently, it displays a fluidity and grace that is its beauty. The running of Emil Zapotek was not aesthetically pleasing even though he won; but this doesn't undermine the aesthetics of sport. At the time of his victories little was known about bodily efficiency; as more technical knowledge was gained, runners were trained to get the body moving efficiently. The greater the efficiency, the more it approaches the aesthetics of the body, to a point at which efficiency and beauty fuse into one. This is demonstrated by the grace, beauty, and efficiency of athletes like Mary Decker, Wilma Rudolph,

Francie LaRue, Sebastian Coe, Evelyn Ashford, and Greg Scott. It is repeated in swimming, where efficiency and beauty fuse into one. Mark Spitz displayed this beautifully; Mary T. Meager displays it now in her record-breaking butterfly events. As swum by Tracy Caulkins, the breast-stroke achieves a high level of aesthetic appeal.

Now there is a further confusion by Best. He says that in sport the aim is victory. We have seen that this is not necessarily true for the player. But it is necessarily false for the designer of the game, who aims at designing the rules so that skill becomes a necessary condition for beauty. Continual changes in the game are made to rule out victory of the unskilled, that is, the unbeautiful. Thus, even if the player is concerned with efficiency, this must be within the discipline of the rules designed to bring out the beautiful. The designers of the rules have little concern for efficiency and can have no concern with victory; the designers' main concern is spectator appeal (i.e., aesthetic appeal), an appeal that requires and enhances bodily excellence.

There is also an intermediary the coach (the choreographer). The coach's job is to harmonize the players in accordance with the game design. Players must be coached to play their parts, much as the director of a play must coach the actors to play their parts. He or she does this by "walking through" and by breaking the pattern into segments and drilling these separately, much as a music conductor breaks a composition into bars. Then the coach puts all the parts together in harmony. Each player must attain a complementary level of skill, and when it looks good it leads to success. The coach sets the tone and plays a significant part in determining the style of play. Only when there is harmony can there be beauty.

Without a doubt, some coaches aim at winning at all costs; others aim at a well played game. Generally, a well played game achieves victory but this is not always the case. One thing is sure though: A well played game that is aesthetically pleasing can only take place in competition that involves a desire to win. Without the desire to win, there is a lack of concentration and of artistic performance. A mediocre performance seldom portrays beauty in any art form. The desire to be good, and in the context of competitive games the desire for victory, does not subordinate aesthetics; it often enhances it. And in some cases this is necessary for beauty to emerge. The desire for victory is not necessarily a desire to win at any cost. The desire for a well played, aesthetically pleasing game need not be subordinate to the desire for victory.

III

The third feature claimed to exclude sport from art allows that beauty can be an aim of an athlete, but not the sole aim. But is beauty the *sole* aim of the artists in the acknowledged art forms? Does not the poet or novelist aim at getting a point across? May not the composer of musical compositions want to reflect a social situation? May not the artist in his or her painting aim at expressing an idea, however commonplace or trite? Best (1: p. 200) does not deny this, but maintains that these ends cannot be identified apart from the manner of achieving them. The end is inseparable from the means of achieving it. In sport, in particular competitive sports, the end can be specified independently of the manner of achieving it *as long as it conforms to the rules of the game* (1: p. 201, emphasis mine). In other words, there are very many ways of achieving the desired end, and the various means do not affect or change the end.

In art, however, "there cannot be a change of form of expression without a corresponding change in what is expressed" (1: p. 200). Does Best mean by this that a work of art cannot be improved, that any attempt to rework a piece is itself a different piece altogether? There are different versions of *The Rubiyat;* when A. E. Housman's notes were examined, different versions of the same poem were found, indicating an attempt to rework and improve the one poem. Yet are they different versions or are they different works altogether? According to Best, they would be different works, with each expressing something different. However, I doubt if that was Housman's feeling. He was trying to improve the original; the message was the same. He was merely trying to convey it in the most beautiful, most effective manner. Now it may be that all the early versions conveyed the same message, but the final version did so in the most vivid and most beautiful way.

To illustrate his point, Best (1: p. 200) showed a disanalogy between a social survey report and a work of art. The report is evaluated by how effectively it conveys the information, whereas this would be irrelevant to the *aesthetic* judgment of a novel. In a report, however, the aim is to convey the information most effectively where the appeal is intellectual, where the information is set out logically, and where logical conclusions may be drawn. Style may be important if it makes a stronger appeal to the intellect, that is, if it makes the information more understandable. Thus, the sole aim is conveying the information. In a work of art there is more. The artist wishes to convey a message not by an appeal to our intellect but by an appeal to our emotions or our sense of beauty. And this is the aim of the aesthetic. The artist uses beauty to get his or her message across. This is why it takes less time to write a report on social conditions than to write a novel expressing the social conditions. The artist is not simply concerned with beauty; if he or she were, then while he/she may reflect aspects of life situations, he/she would not consciously be making any statement about the human condition.

Thus, the sole aim of the artist is not beauty; he or she wants to express something as well—not just in *any* way—only in a beautiful way. But he/she wants to express it nonetheless. The artist may in addition want to sell his/her works. Does this make it any less art?

Now, I agree that when the athlete's aim is beauty it is not the sole aim. The athlete wants to win, not necessarily in *any* way, but in a way that displays his or her skill and bodily excellence. The athlete in this sense uses beauty to achieve his or

her goals, much as the artist does. The rules of the game play a significant part here as they are designed to bring out bodily excellence, that is, the aesthetic performance. Obviously, sometimes victory is achieved in a nonaesthetic way, and sometimes this is not satisfying to either the athletes or the spectators. After a successful defense of his title, former boxing champion Johnny Bumphus was quoted as saying that although he won, he was not at all satisfied with his performance because it was not artistic.

Thus, I believe I have shown that while athletes may aim at beauty, it is not the sole aim, nor is it the sole aim of the artist. In both cases, beauty is not only an aim in itself but also a means to achieve some other aim; for the artist it is a means of self-expression; for the athlete it is a means to victory and in this may also be a means to self-expression.

IV

The feature that Best feels clearly excludes sport from art is that art forms are limited to artifacts or performances intentionally created by humans in which there is at least the possibility of a close involvement with life situations.

The novels of Charles Dickens express the social conditions of the England of his time. Beethoven's Fifth Symphony expresses the awesomeness of death. Dylan Thomas in "Poem to this Father" expresses a defiance of death. These are all creations by men which definitely involve life situations. Then there are dramatic plays. For example, in *Cyrano de Bergerac*, Rostand is clearly making a statement about love; it is also the old theme of beauty and the beast. Just as Cyrano uses Christian in the play to express his love for Roxanne, Rostand uses the characters to express his theme. The actors who play the various roles are not themselves consciously making the statement, but through their self-expressions put together as a whole, the statement is conveyed to the audience.

The play is the vehicle for the theme of love; it

is also the vehicle for self-expression by the actors. To successfully portray Cyrano, the actor must put a lot of himself into the role. It must be played with style; it cannot simply be a speaking of words. It can be played successfully in many personal styles, but it cannot be played by everyone. This style is the actor's self-expression—his way of achieving an aesthetic experience. He wants to make the part of Cyrano believable, and he wants it to be beautiful. The combined contributions of the playwright and the actor account for the aesthetic experience. It is especially so when his performance has evoked an aesthetic response from his viewers. In this, let it be remembered that the performer is not consciously making a statement about love, although through his self expression he portrays or reflects the statement of the playwright.

I maintain there is a parallel situation in sports. In Section II I made a distinction between the designer and the performer, and there is this same distinction in plays, as already shown. In competitive sports there is no question that the games themselves are intentional creations of the human being. Like art in general, they are spawned from leisure. But they are not simply play activities; they are artificially created, rule-governed activities set apart from the work-a-day world, and they have their own boundaries in time, and space. The rules and boundaries vary in restrictiveness. Basketball is played in a limited space (96 ft × 50 ft), has specific time periods, and has a set of restrictive rules that are explicit about what can and cannot be done in an attempt to score. The rules are fewer and less restrictive in cross-country skiing. They are nonetheless performances intentionally created and not *"objets trouvés."*

For the parallel to work, at least the designers must consciously be making a statement about the human condition. To a certain degree there must be the possibility of a close involvement with life situations. I maintain there is much that is being said intentionally. In every competitive sport, several things are taking place. Each game displays relationships that are or ought to be found in society. There is competition, yet cooperation—cooperation among players as well as cooperation of each according to the promulgated rules. If a rule is broken, there are immediate consequences. The impartial referees and umpires determine when a rule is broken, and the designers of course determine the rules. The designers are definitely concerned with establishing rules that stress achievement through effort, with the rules designed to reduce achievement through raw talent alone. Rules are designed to require that discipline, self-sacrifice, and technical efficiency be exhibited to achieve success. When done at its best—with style—athletes achieve aesthetic experiences for themselves and evoke aesthetic responses from the audience.

The aesthetic appeal is minimal when the skill level is low, as when lack of skill hampers self-expression, or when success is achieved through mere strength or innate, undisciplined talent. This may account for the high spectator interest in women's tennis and in men's basketball as opposed to women's basketball. In tennis, strength is the determining factor of success for men; in the women's game, a high level of skill, efficiency, and strategy combines for a beautiful performance. In women's basketball, the skill level is still somewhat low and thus there is a correspondingly low aesthetic appeal. In the men's game, however, the skill level is significantly higher and reaches its peak in the National Basketball Association. Because the skill level is so high, players have the qualifications to add style and aim for beauty. This evokes aesthetic responses in viewers and achieves the aesthetic experience for the athlete.

The definers of the rules that characterize and sustain a game intend both that there be a concern with life situations and that the performances exhibit this aesthetically. James (2) maintains that certain features ought to be included in cricket to express the social history of the time. In basketball the 3-second lane was widened to prevent success without hard work. This expresses the idea of success through effort and is a concept constantly stressed by coaches—usually by referring to parallel real-life involvements. It is interesting to note that the New Games evolved because their creators did not like the social conditions expressed or taught in the usual competitive games. They generally feel that competition is stressed to the detriment of cooperation; besides, at the end of competition there is always a loser. But in New Games cooperation is stressed because it is felt that cooperation is what sustains a society. Rules are deliberately created for this purpose, and the performers learn this very important lesson in playing these games.

The expressions of life situations are manifested differently in sports than in the traditional art forms, but there are deviations among the other art forms as well. Thus, it is wrong to say that sport has no involvement with life situations or that it makes no statement about the human condition.

V

The previous sections have answered the main criticisms used in excluding sport from art. Given that the essential features of sport and of art are compatible, I maintain that sport is an art form. Not only are they compatible, but in some cases they enhance one another. The essential feature of efficiency is necessary for both sport and art; the feature of sport that concerns the desire to win is required for beauty; the aim of beauty is not the sole aim of either sport or art; and sport, like other art forms, maintains a close involvement with life situations. In this concluding section, I will discuss one other feature which is as essential to sport as it is to art—self-expression. Since much has been said already, I will only put together what has gone before.

First of all, self-expression literally means to express oneself. There are different ways of doing this in one's work or one's play; through words, body movements, music, pictures. Art certainly provides a vehicle for self-expression. The individual's desire is to create beauty. It is the desire for an aesthetic experience, and the experience is accomplished when the expression of oneself is achieved. Poets use words; artists use visual media. We allow actors to use scripts to express themselves and achieve an aesthetic experience. This is paralleled by the athletes. Athletes must perform at their best, and then they may add style to their performance. Their style and success are their self-expressions. In both art and sport, self-expression is hampered by a lack of skill. The actor playing Cyrano must know the words, expressions, and movements before he can add his own flair. The athlete must do the same.

Dr. J, Abdul-Jabbar, James Worthy, Walter Payton—they must have control of the basics before they can perform with style. This is true for all athletes and artists, be they men or women. A performance or work cannot be beautiful unless the basics are mastered. Women are just beginning to achieve the skill level necessary for self-expression and for an aesthetic performance. Until recently, this means of self-expression was not available to them. That is, certain "form" sports were available and considered feminine, but these were not suited for all. In fact, we are finding that the so-called masculine competitive sports can be played just as skillfully and efficiently by the women as they are by men. This does not mean women have to compete with men. I believe there is an aesthetic reason for women generally not to compete with men, and this follows from my position that aesthetic experiences and aesthetic responses are found in evenly matched, well-played games. This is why boxing, for example, has different weight classes. There is no contest between a heavyweight and a flyweight.

In other sports the men's game and the women's game emphasize different qualities, as in gymnastics; or different styles of games, as in basketball. In some sports it may be aesthetically pleasing for men and women to compete together, as in diving or in equestrian events. And some woman may have the ability to compete against a man in a masculine sport. But generally women need not compete with men to achieve an aesthetic experience or evoke an aesthetic response.

However, opening up sports equally to women shows that developing one's skills is as aesthetically pleasing for women as for men. It illustrates that for women, as for men, there is a potential for success through discipline and hard work; and it indicates a level of equality that was previously denied. This helps make sense of Marx's notion that we are all artists; we are all capable of having aesthetic experience. This is not possible for all of us when art is restricted to the acknowledged art forms. But, by accepting sports as an art form, we have provided a vehicle for self-expression and aesthetic experience to a large group of people who previously had no such vehicle.

Bibliography

1. Best, David (1974). "The Aesthetic in Sport." *British Journal of Aesthetics,* 14, 197–213.
2. James, C. L. R. (1983). *Beyond a Boundary.* New York: Pantheon.
3. Reid, Louis A. (1970). "Sport, the Aesthetic, and Art." *British Journal of Educational Studies,* 18, 245–258.
4. Ziff, Paul (1974). "A Fine Forehand." *Journal of the Philosophy of Sport,* 1, 92–109.

Questions for Consideration

1. Does Boxill adequately demonstrate that all the perceived differences between sport and art are untenable?
2. If so, is this enough to show that sport is a species of art? In other words, Boxill seems to work on the assumption that the four characteristic features of art outlined in the reading are its defining features. Are they?
3. Can you think of any other relevant dissimilarities between sport and art that Boxill hasn't considered?

12 Differences between Sport and Art

Christopher Cordner
University of Melbourne

Like Best's position that "sport is not art," Christopher Cordner's stand strives to distinguish between sport and art. Beginning with an enumeration of ways in which sport and art resemble each other, Cordner then differentiates them in a way that he feels allows for a more accurate and less intellectualist depiction of art than Best's.

Best's position is that art necessarily admits of the possibility for expression of life issues while sport does not (and even seems to disallow it). Cordner agrees that expression of life issues is not a defining feature of sport, but he does not think that this is a part of art. Is a portrait of a face a comment on it, or even a social or moral statement? No, it is a realization of certain qualities or values in the face, such as delicacy or weakness. Instead of life issues, art depicts "life values."

If this is so, then Best's demarcation between sport and art is now less pronounced. In Cordner's view, sport can have meaning in precisely the same way that art does.

Best also distinguishes sport from art in that the object of the latter is "imaginatively constituted," while the former, whose objects are actual, is not. The obvious difficulty with this is abstract art, which does not seem to have any such objects, though it still has meaning in that it realizes life values. As such, the division between sport and art is artificial in that sport, which itself realizes life values, would still be assimilable under nonrepresentational art. Thus, imaginative structuring of an object cannot differentiate art from sport.

How art differs from sport, Cordner states, is that art effects a "temporary self-enclosing" of the

imagination in a spectatorial aspect. Works of art are for looking at, listening to, and reading. Works of art are "objects of contemplation," while sport may be contemplated but this need not be the case. In other words, works of art are created exclusively as ends in themselves.

Recently, a number of writers have discussed whether sports are, or can be, arts (see for example Reid [8], Wertz [11], and Ziff [12]). David Best (1, 2, 3, 4) has argued that they cannot. While I agree with much of what Best says, I do not find his ways of distinguishing sports from arts fully convincing. In this paper I have two aims. My main aim is to show how I think the relation between sports and arts is best conceived. I shall approach this task via a critical discussion of Best's ways of distinguishing the two kinds of activity. My hope is that a critical discussion of the relation between sports and arts will illuminate the place of both in our lives. My secondary aim in the paper is to survey some of the resemblances that can be found between sports and arts. While many writers have discussed such resemblances, I know of no concise recapitulation of them. It will help our appreciation of the relation between sports and arts to begin by setting out some of the resemblances between the two fields of activity.

Some may think this enterprise doomed from the start. Sport and art, it may be thought, are obviously fundamentally different kinds of activity. It is not hard to draw up a commonly agreed catalogue of their differences: art expresses ideas, feelings, states of mind (has a meaning), while sport expresses nothing (has no

Reprinted by permission, from Christopher Cordner, "Differences between Sport and Art," *Journal of the Philosophy of Sport*, XV (1988): 31–47.

"meaning"); artists create, while athletes only exert themselves; the arts are somehow mental while sports are somehow physical; the artist aims to create beauty, the athlete aims to do well in a competition. And the catalogue could be extended. My view is that this catalogue is a collection of half-truths. We need a way of thinking about the relation between sports and arts that will enable us to evaluate it.

As Nelson Goodman has reminded us, anything resembles anything else in an infinite number of ways. We must restrict our search to those resemblances between sports and arts that are salient and important. So, what such resemblances are there between the activities of sport and art in the modern western world?[1]

There is no need for us to begin by defining sports and arts. Examples of the two kinds of activity are readily enough agreed upon, and they are all we need to get the discussion afloat. We can begin by noticing that the domains of sport and art each have both a participatory and a spectatorial aspect. There are practicing artists and athletes on the one hand, and there are spectators of sport and art on the other. (These two classes of people of course overlap.) In this respect the activities of sport and art differ from, for example, dinner parties, conversations, religious ceremonies, political rallies, and scientific research. None of these activities either is, or issues in something that is, institutionalized as for-being-looked-at.

But I may be said to be missing an important distinction here. It may be held that arts are essentially made for looking at or listening to, whereas sports are not. So, music is to-be-listened-to, painting to-be-looked-at, even in some cases there is in fact no audience. Sports, by contrast, are essentially to-be-played, and the spectatorial interest in them is an additional nonessential feature that just happens to be very prominent in our culture. I think there is something in this distinction, though perhaps less than there once would have been. Before the 19th century I suppose the idea that one might go to see a football match as one goes to see a

play would have been ludicrous. But this is now commonly accepted, as is the idea that the game itself (like many other games) can be evaluated in terms of what it has to offer spectators. More than this, even changes in the rules are now often made on the basis of spectatorial considerations. Changes presently being considered to the play-on rule in Australian Rules football, and pass interference rules in American football, are aimed at improving the game as a spectacle, while in cricket the introduction of a 90 over minimum per day's test play, the proposed limiting of a bowler's length of run-up, and various changes over the years to the lbw rule, all owe to consideration of the game's spectator appeal. That is to say, it is arguable that our concept of sport, perhaps unlike that of our ancestors, is in part a concept of that which is to be seen and evaluated from a spectator's point of view.

Even if sport shares this feature with art, it does not follow that the spectatorial aspect enters the practice of sport in the same way it enters the practice of art. There remains a general difference in the focus of attention of sports players and artists in the practice of their respective activities. Every move the artist makes has to be submitted to the question, "What does/will this sound/look like?" and the move will be incorporated or not into the work of art on the basis of the answer to this question. That is to say, the spectator's point of view provides key constraints on an artist's moves in creating or performing. It does not characteristically do so for the sports player. The sports player does not aim at excellence in his or her activity by seeking to make what he/she does look as good as possible. The sports player seeks to kick the goal, or to sidestep his/her opponent, or to play the passing shot. In the practice of sport there is not the same conception of and responsiveness to the demands of the spectator's viewpoint that there is in the practice of art.

This distinction between the artist and the athlete is blurred at one important point. In the so-called "aesthetic sports" the practitioner does indeed guide his or her practice by reference to how it will look. Examples of such sports are ice-skating, gymnastics, diving, and ski-jumping. The demand that it look good is not brought to these sports only by the spectators; for that demand also constrains every step taken by the performers. The spectator's point of view seems to be as closely integrated with the practice of these sports as it is with the practice of art. It does not follow of course that these sports are performing arts, although a number of writers have drawn this conclusion. I shall return to this issue toward the end of the paper.

Let us turn to some common preconceptions about the differences between sports and arts. It is sometimes said that sports are physical while arts are mental. But for any content I can give to this opposition it seems plain false. Golf and lawn bowls are both much less physically taxing than the dance, while any serious athlete can spend as much time thinking about how to improve his or her performance as any artist can, and as much time experimenting with new strategies, techniques, and lines of attack. (American football generates endless playbooks and treatises on tactics.) Perhaps the mental/physical opposition is getting at something else—that art "has a meaning" while sport does not. This important question we shall postpone until we come to consider David Best's proposed criterion of distinction between sports and arts.

The claim that arts are creative while sports are not is also difficult to defend. Indeed, we can probably define the greats in both the arts and sports fields as those who have extended the possibilities of excellence within their domains. Great musicians and dancers enable us to see more in the works they perform than we could before, while the creators of those works themselves have given us music and dance of undreamed richness and power. So it is across the arts, but also in the field of sports. Arnold Palmer is said to have invented attacking golf; the serve and volley game of the 1940s changed the way tennis was played, and Borg changed it again with his introduction of vicious top-spin into the game. Not only individual players of

course but combinations of them, and coaches as well, continually discover new possibilities within their fields of activity.

Still, there may remain some general difference between the possible extent of creativity in sport and in art. David Best notes that any deviation from the currently given is potentially valuable in a work of art, while this is not so in sport. Potentially valuable deviations in sport must be within the rules of the sport and must aim to contribute to what already counts as success in that sport. (This is true even of the "aesthetic" sports.) This still leaves enormous room for flair, imagination, and striking and unforeseen departures from the way things have until now been done in that sport. But the rules of sports, and the guiding aim of scoring more than the opposition, or of getting to the tape first, are constraints on deviations from the given for which there is no analogue in the case of art. There may be a deep distinction between sport and art here; but my present point is that it should not blind us to the fact, indeed the great importance, of creativity in sport.

We might note too that the best athletes and the best artists attract us because of the distinctiveness of their genius. Barenboem and Brendel play Beethoven's sonatas very differently, each in a way that highlights different strengths of theirs in bringing out different qualities in the music. As a performing artist, of course, each remains under the constraint of having to play this piece of music. Likewise, Eric Dickerson and Walter Payton, both great running backs, each has his own distinctive style, his own footballing genius, exploiting different possibilities in backfield play. The present point applies to the nonperforming arts also. Joyce's remark in *Portrait of the Artist as a Young Man* that the artist ideally disappears behind his work, and is not visible in it, expresses a false ideal. The Mozartian stamp of all of Mozart's wonderfully varied music is not some improperly dissolved residue that the music would be better off without. It is the distinctively Mozartian musical genius that so compels us. The distinctively weighty, balanced yet passionate Johnsonian presence in the prose of that great writer—in ways typically Augustan yet also uniquely Johnsonian—is not a failure of his writing to achieve an impersonality in which it would be indistinguishable from any other great writing, but is of the essence of Johnson's genius. Each work of an artist can of course also have its own distinctive genius, just as each performance of an athlete can have its own stamp of genius. And each work or performance can modify, as it is infused by, our broader sense of the Mozartian or the Dickersonian.

There is frequently thought to be a difference of motive underlying the activity of the artist and the sports player. Three common candidates for an artist's motivation are these: to create beauty, or more generally to create objects of aesthetic value; and/or to express his or her feelings; and/or to "tell it like it is." Sports players, on the other hand, are often thought to be motivated by quite different sorts of things: the desire for money, fame or prestige, physical exercise, victory, being the best in their field. But this romantic view of art and pejorative view of sport courts confusion of motive for doing X with focus of attention in doing X. We have already seen that there is commonly a difference of focus of attention of artist and athlete in the practice of their respective activities. But the focus of attention an activity requires does not determine people's motives for engaging in it. In playing bridge I shall have to attend to the bidding and the cards, but I may play the game in order to keep my wits sharp, to be socially acceptable, to win fame as a player, or for the company. The general difference in the artist's and the athlete's focus of attention in the practice of their respective activities should not lead us to assume general differences in their motives for engaging in those activities. In both spheres an indefinitely wide range of motives is operative. An artist, like a sports player, may be moved by the desire to be the best in a given field, to make something perfect, to earn fame and fortune, to please an audience, or *épater le bourgeois*. Or he/she may just love painting or writing or running or baseball.[2]

One obvious resemblance between sports and arts lies in the domains of their occurrence. Where sport has its courts, its fields, and its stadia, art has its stages, its canvasses, and its concert halls. Within those boundaries, a body of conventions and rules operate that do not operate in everyday life. When Othello smothers Desdemona, no one is really killed, and the yokel who rushed on stage to stop the Moor would simply fail to grasp the conventions of the theatre. Equally, the actor who carried on like Othello after leaving the stage would be arrested for murder. So with the linebacker who hurls his weight into bruising tackles on the football field: These take place within the governing rules of the sport, and there is no simple carry-over of them into everyday life. Art, like sport, takes place within an arena separated from the everyday world, whether by the frame around the canvas, or the touchline, the edge of the hockey rink, or the stage in the theatre.[3]

The activities that take place within these artificially demarcated domains are self-enclosed. We are characteristically interested in them for their own sake, as we say, and not for the sake of some further end which they serve. But there is an ambiguity in this formulation. I may go to the theatre because I want to have something to talk about at the cocktail party next week, or to please my wife. In one sense, I do not want to see the play for its own sake. But the point of the play can be appreciated fully, and only, by close attention to the drama, whatever my motive for going to see it. In this sense, if I am interested in the play I am interested in it for its own sake. A legal trial, by contrast, has its point in relation to a system of justice: It seeks to determine the guilt or innocence of the party on trial (or to resolve some other conflict). Crucial to the point of the trial is its social effect—what it determines about the lives of those subject to it and how it alters their relation to the community to which they belong. Similarly, the effecting of a change in the marital status and the subsequent life of the man and woman at its center, and of a change in their relations with others, is crucial to a wedding ceremony. Trials and weddings are not self-enclosed activities whose purpose or point could be fully grasped by one who takes an interest in them for their own sake. Indeed I can grasp a good part of that point quite without attending to the activity of the trial or wedding as it progressively unfolds, if I know what trials and weddings are for.

But there is nothing analogous that art and sport are for. What they are "for" is captured only by the various predicates we need to use to express our experience of each occasion of them. It is of course possible for us to "bracket" any social activity, so to speak, and to treat it as if it were just the kind of self-enclosed bodying-forth that works of art and sporting events are. So one could regard a trial as just a drama, a wedding as a kind of dance. But this bracketing is dangerous because in succumbing to it we are denying, or at least ignoring, part of what is crucial to the social function of these events. By contrast, the bracketing of the actual social world is built into the spectator aspect of both sports and arts, which aspect belongs to their institutional character.

In saying this I am not denying the obvious fact that in the modern world the institutions of art and of sport have enormous social impact. The art market and professional sports are big business. Actors and sports performers can make a livelihood from their performances, and entrepreneurs, promoters, advertisers, publishers, record companies, movie houses, and so on all have flourishing involvements in sports and arts. My point is only that in both sports and arts a full interest in the sport performance or the work of art is adequately realized in one's attention to the performance or work itself. One need not identify or refer to any further purpose or function fulfilled by it.

About art this claim is of course the conventional wisdom of one tradition of thought. But surely there is an obvious objection to extending the claim to sport. For a certain outcome is crucial to at least many sporting activities—winning and losing. Even if Lombardi was wrong to say of sport that "winning is the only thing," surely the centrality of winning and losing to the playing of sport makes sports very different from the arts, where these concepts have no place. For the interest of both spectator and performer is referred to something beyond the present unfolding of the activity, namely the outcome of the contest. (The earlier claim about difference of performer motive seeks another hearing here also; for surely the sports player can and often does have winning as his or her motive, and this motive can have no place in the practice of art.)

Let us accept that winning and losing do have a place in sport and no place in art. What follows from this? To begin with, it is certain that winning is not by itself the aim of sport-playing. A sports coach once began a book by saying that he had a surefire formula that would enable anyone to win every time he or she competed in a sporting contest: "Never compete against anyone who is nearly as good as you are." That nobody who is genuinely interested in sports, either as player or spectator, could want to follow, or could want his/her team to follow, that formula makes the point. Players aim to win, certainly, but they want to win as the outcome of having achieved a level of excellence—at least excellence for them—in play. It could even be argued that a player genuinely interested in sports is not in fact concerned with winning at all but only with the excellence of the game in which he or she takes part. That concern of course requires him/her to try hard to win, but arguably does not require a concern with the actual outcome.[4]

If this point is questionable as far as some players are concerned, I think that the fully absorbed spectator is not concerned with who wins. If it be replied that many fans are more interested in the outcome of a game than in the excellence of play, this shows only that those fans are less fans of the sport than they are supporters of a team. This makes them analogous to the person who is more interested in the price the painting sells for than in the picture itself, or more interested in whether the film "Out of Africa" increased tourism to that continent than in the film itself. I do not say there is anything wrong with such interests, only that in both cases they are interests in something other than the sport or the work of art in question.

I am not saying, either, that spectators with a genuine interest in the sport have no interest in the contest—the competitive struggle between the players or the teams. Of course they do, and must do so if attending to what is before them, because in competitive sports the contest is a chief vehicle for realizing excellence of play. Perhaps one kind of excellence may be realized in the masterful domination of an event by one player or team that is outstanding—McEnroe in the 1984 Wimbledon final for example—but this is less satisfying than an event in which two players or teams both play wonderfully well, and do so only by answering the challenges posed by the other's good play. Ideal sports watchers, then, if we can so dub them, are indeed absorbed by the competitive struggle, but not because they are concerned who wins. Their interest is in what unfolds before them and only in that. A concern with who wins, by contrast, is engaged not by what unfolds before them but only by the score at the final bell.

I have been trying to suggest some salient resemblances between sports and arts, mainly through criticism of some misconceptions on which supposed differences have been based. I have argued that both domains of activity have a spectatorial aspect; that there is no generally interesting distinction in the kinds of motive for which artists and athletes follow their pursuits; that creativity is to be found in both domains; and that even given the goal of winning in sports, the ideal spectator's interest is as wholly engaged by what unfolds before him or her as is the interest of the lover of the arts.

None of this means, of course, that there are no important differences between sports and arts; and we have already noted some differences while outlining misconceptions. In the rest of the paper I shall try to dig a bit deeper in specifying the relation between these fields of human activity. David Best provides what he takes to be a crucial criterion of demarcation of sport from art. As his criterion recapitulates a plausible and commonly held view, I shall approach my own sketch through comment on Best's line of thought. He writes,

> any art form, properly so-called, must at least allow for the possibility of the expression of a conception of life-issues such as contemporary moral, social and political problems. Such a possibility is an intrinsic part of the concept of art, by which I mean that without it an activity could not count as a legitimate art form. (1: p. 117)

Best draws a contrast with sports. He says (2: p. 353) that if a gymnast, for example, were to include in his routine movements that did express a view of war or love, say, this would not add to but detract from the sporting performance. It would be an intrusion into the gymnastic performance of something which had nothing to do with gymnastics. I agree with Best that the possibility of a sports performer's setting out to express a conception of life-issues is not intrinsic to any sport. But I am not convinced that any art form, by contrast, must allow for this possibility. The representational arts seem to do so. Shakespeare's play, *Henry IV,* expresses a certain complex conception of honor, and Goya's famous paintings a certain conception of war. But the situation is different with the nonrepresentational arts. It just seems mistaken, because too intellectualist, to hold that abstract paintings express a conception of life-issues. And how could a piece of music express a conception of poverty, or war, or loyalty, or death, or honor? Architecture, and possibly dance, also seem unfitted to express conceptions of life-issues. At one point (2: p. 354) Best switches to speaking of art forms as necessarily allowing the possibility of the artist's being able, through his art, to comment on life situations. That term "comment" brings out even more clearly the cognitive, even intellectualist, cast of his view of art.[5] Best obviously wants to hold onto the idea that the arts are somehow meaningful, pregnant with significance and force for us. I think he is right to want this. But we do not have to use his terms to capture this feature of the arts. Indeed, it seems we cannot use those terms if we are to acknowledge abstract painting, music, architecture, and even perhaps dance, as forms of art. How else might we register this feature of the arts?

I suggest, by saying that rather than having to be able to express a conception of life-issues, works of art manifest or enact or realize life-values, and that the deepest kind of meaning and value they have for us is grounded in this capacity they possess. This formulation has at least three virtues: It holds onto the idea that the arts are fundamentally meaningful and value-laden; it manages this while avoiding the intellectualist bias of Best's criterion; and it applies as well to music, abstract painting, architecture, and dance as to the representational arts, without foreclosing on the possibility of interesting differences between representational and abstract art. But I must explain the suggestion. On my formulation, works of art are most deeply meaningful or value-laden—in this context these terms are interchangeable—in much the same way a human face is meaningful or value-laden. Faces can realize for us an indefinitely wide range of what I am calling life-values. Compassion, suffering, nobility, dignity, vanity, innocence, evil, complacency, stupidity, wisdom, avarice, for instance (as well as different kinds and compounds of these and many other things), can constitute the life that is manifest in a face.

But am I not simply missing what is central to art in pressing this analogy? For after all, a face is not a work of art. True, but irrelevant to my point. Consider what a portrait is. Is it painting of a face plus a comment on the face, or plus a conception of some social or moral or political issue? No; it is a face painted so as to realize a certain kind of life in the face—certain life-qualities or life-values, to use my earlier term: the blend of delicacy, sensitiveness and weakness in Van Dyck's portrait of Charles I, for example. The good portraitist enables us to see in the painted face something more than, and perhaps different from, what we might have been able to see in the

face itself. The portrait focuses, and clearly reveals, the life in a face. When Hegel (5: pp. 153-154) says that the aim of the artist is to make what he paints "all eye"—he calls art the "thousand-eyed Argus"—he is invoking the idea of the eye as the window of the soul. To make a portrait (for Hegel, any work of art in fact) "all eye" is then to realize as fully as possible a distinctive character of "soul," or in my terms a distinctive cast of life, in the face. The force of the portrait lies not in its presenting us with a face on which it then makes a comment or about which it then expresses a conception, but in the vividness and fullness with which it realizes or makes manifest certain life-values. This distinction is related to a traditional distinction between saying and showing. But my point is not just that portraits show us something rather than tell us something. What we are interested in is the distinctive quality and character of the showing, and in that quality or character the distinctive life of the work of art itself is manifested. That distinctive life animating the work is what is analogous to the distinctive life animating a face. Then we are talking about a distinction not so much between what a work says and what it shows as between what it says and what it most deeply is.

I do not want to deny here that many works of art can express conceptions of life-issues, and make comments on them. But one way of putting my present point is to say that even when a work of art does this there is no good reason to regard what is deepest in the work—what is most valuable to us in it—as consisting in the conceptions it expresses. Notoriously, William Blake said that Milton in *Paradise Lost,* a work intended to "justify the ways of God to man," was "of the devil's party without knowing it." If Blake was right, the conception of life-issues expressed by the work does not take us to the energy center of the poem, for the work manifests or realizes life-values that press against what the author endorses as his conceptions of moral matters. There is a lesson in this example. Our main focus in a work of art is the life embodied in it, and our registering of any conceptions of or comments on life-issues it may contain occurs always within the broader context of our sense of the distinctive life animating it. This is part of what D.H. Lawrence (7: p. 123) meant when he said, "Never trust the artist. Trust the tale." Very often the tension between what a work "says"—the conceptions it explicitly endorses—and the energies we feel to be really animating it is the source of a work of art's greatest attraction and influence. But even when this is not so, our sense of the life that animates a work of art reaches for springs of energy in it which lie deeper than, though they also of course somehow infuse, any conceptions of life issues to which the work gives expression.

My point here reaches back to an earlier comment about the distinctiveness of any artistic or sporting genius. The Best line I am attacking has difficulty in explaining why I should even notice that this is Mozart, let alone why its peculiarly Mozartian vitality and joy should be chiefly what engages me. For if my artistic interest is mainly in the conception of or comments on life-issues contained in a work, this is an interest in the message rather than the medium. But the distinctive Mozartianness of what I hear must surely fall on the "medium" side of this distinction. For the ways I try to characterize that distinctive Mozartian quality make reference not to what the music says—the conceptions of life-issues it expresses, or the comments it makes—but to what it is. It is joyous but shot through with tenderness, passionate yet meditative.[6]

The problem with Best's view is shared by other cognitivist aesthetic theories. They overlook the deep connection between our responsiveness to art and our responsiveness to people, which I have already touched on briefly. Certainly we can be interested in what other people say—including the conceptions of life-issues they may express—but only impoverished intellectualism could lead us to suppose that any person's deepest life is realized only in what he or she says. For that life will have to include the way he/she says it, at least, and even that leads beyond the content of his/her conceptions of life-issues. Of course one's deepest life may be realized not in one's sayings at all, but in one's generosity, or bitterness, or courage, or even in how one tends one's garden; and as Dr. Johnson says, it will always be realized in one's pleasures. Similarly we must realize, if we are to avoid a distorted view of the kind of significance works of art have, that the conceptions or comments on life-issues they express contribute to, but never exhaust, and may even be an insignificant element of, the life-values realized in them. The chief kind of significance and value in art lies deeper than Best's criterion seems to allow.

Thus we can hold onto the idea that works of art are meaningful, without having to articulate this idea in Best's terms. Indeed, we have to reject Best's formulation in order to do justice to various important aspects of our experience of art. But once we characterize the deepest kind of meaningfulness of art in the terms I have suggested, then there no longer seems to be the kind of gap between arts and sports that Best's version of the meaning-content of art implied there to be. For sports quite clearly can have meaning in a very similar way. I once read a critic's description of Jackson Pollock's painting, Blue Poles, as "bountiful, violent and rigid." I think the terms are just right. But the terms also apply, interestingly, equally well to American football. The game has explosive energy and violence as the players burst from the line of scrimmage and launch themselves into tackles and full-blooded running. But the energy and violence is rigidly contained within the structured plays, the preordained movements, the grid of lines on the field, and the absolute precision of the clock. And then the ball suddenly spirals and floats up the field toward a streaming running-back who breaks into the end zone like a wave. The game can suddenly be bountiful too. In speaking of the game in these terms, we are speaking of its human and even emotional meaning, just as when we describe Pollock's painting as bountiful, violent, and rigid. (Of course there is much more to be said about both the painting and the game.) We need not suppose that the players in any game of football think of it in these terms, though many of them might recognize the terms as about right if someone were to suggest them. But Pollock probably didn't think of his paintings as having that kind of force or character either; more likely he just kept on painting until it seemed finished. For all that, however, the painting and the football can still both have that character. And in both cases our sense of them as having that character is central to what we find compelling in them.

So far I have not done full justice to Best's claim that works of art, unlike sports, contain the possibility of expressing a conception of life-issues. For Best underwrites this claim by reference to another feature that he says distinguishes sports and arts. He says the object of our attention, in the case of the arts, is imaginatively constituted. So when we go to the threatre, for example, it is not the actions, character, and sufferings of John Smith to which we attend, but those of Hamlet, the character Smith is playing. What happens to Hamlet, the imagined object of our attention, does not happen to Smith (4: p. 31). Sporting performances do not allow this distinction. What happens to the fullback does happen to the man who is filling that position. Sport affords no imagined objects such as those the theatre generates. As Best puts it, "the possibility of an imaginative portrayal . . . applies only to the arts." Best holds that this extra dimension of imagination in our engagement with art explains the possibility of the expression of a conception of life-issues in art, and its impossibility in sport. For any such issues could be the imaginative subject of art. Best crystallizes his point thus: "sport can be the subject of art, but art could not be the subject of sport. Indeed, the very notion of a subject of sport makes no sense" (4: p. 32).[7]

Thus Best seeks to give a more solid grounding to his distinction between sport and art. It is clear that he wants to tie the most important way in which the arts are meaningful to the imaginative status of the objects of our attention in a work of art. If he is right in holding that the objects of our attention in sports are not imaginatively constituted, then even if sports remain in some sense meaningful, Best will claim that they lack a kind of meaningfulness central to the arts.

Unfortunately, however, there remains a problem with Best's position. In fact, it is just a relocation of the problem we have already identified in his claim that it is essential to art forms that they are able to express a conception of life-issues. Not all art forms have subjects. Indeed, just the same range of art forms that are not fitted to the expression of conceptions of life-issues are not able to have subjects. An abstract painting does not have a subject, nor does a piece of music (even the 1812 Overture), nor does a work of architecture. Of course works of art within these art forms can still have meaning, in that they can (as I put it before) manifest or realize various life-values. But then we saw that sporting activities can do this too. So it seems that to maintain his distinction between sport and these forms of art, Best will have to hold either that abstract painting, music, and architecture are not really forms of art, or that they are somehow secondary or derivative forms of art, the basic or essential forms being those that are able to have a subject matter. Neither option seems plausible.

Let us label as "abstract" those works of art that lack a subject. Does Best think the object of our attention in abstract art works is an imagined object? Certainly he writes as if the imaginary status of the object of our attention in a work of art owes to that work's having a subject. If this is so, then the objects of our attention in abstract art are not imagined objects. In that case, however, the supposed fact that the objects of our attention in sporting performances are not imagined but actual would not support the general distinction of sport from art. At most it would support the distinction of sports from those arts in which the objects of attention are imagined, and these would be the traditionally representational arts: theatre, the novel, figurative painting, and perhaps some dance. The possibility of assimilating sports to non-representational arts would still be open.

But from the tone of Best's thought, I doubt

that this is the way he would want to go. I imagine he would want to insist—in accordance with a long tradition of philosophical thought—that works of art in general (the abstract arts as well as the representational arts) are bound up with the exercise of imagination in a way sports are not. It seems, anyway, that his attempt to keep sports distinct from arts will require this insistence. The problem, however, is that there seems to be just as good a reason to construe the object of our attention in sports as an imagined object as there is to construe the object of our attention in the abstract arts in this way.

Suppose we return to our example of Blue Poles. What I am now taking to be the Best line will have it that it is only as imagined that the object of our attention here is bountiful, violent, and rigid. The implied contrast seems to be with what is really or actually or literally these things. And the further explanation of why the painting cannot literally be these things is perhaps that the painting is not a sentient creature, but only a mass of paint, and a mass of paint cannot be bountiful or violent. And even if it can be rigid as paint—dry and stiff—that is not what we mean in calling the painting rigid. But remember that the football game seemed rightly characterizable in just the same terms, and a football game is not a sentient creature either. So if the insentience of the painting was the reason for the imagined status of its bountiful, violent, and rigid character, then the insentience of the football game should also justify the imagined status of its similar character. ("But the football game is played by sentient creatures and that's why its character is real and not imagined." But this retort fails. For the painting is painted by a sentient creature, and this does not destroy the imaginative status of its bountiful, violent, and rigid character.)

Now perhaps I have simply missed a crucial difference in the kind of basis for ascription of these terms to the painting and to the game, a difference that would sustain the imagined status of the object of our attention in the one case and its reality in the other. But at least this difference needs to be pointed out. The observation by Best

that while what happens to characters in a play does not happen to the actors who play them, what happens to the fullback does happen to the player in that position, does not add up to this difference. All it shows is that in our appreciation of football we do not have to imagine characters. But imagination can be engaged in ways other than that, as I think it is in both these cases.

But I have given one example only, and perhaps I should broaden the suggestion that our engagement with sports can indeed be imaginatively structured. Santayana (9: p. 71) once wrote, "Sport is a liberal form of war stripped of its compulsions and malignity; a rational art and the expression of a civilised instinct." This implies that the meaning and value of sports can be characterized only by reference to our imaginative engagement with it. We see in athletics a suspended "as if" enactment of the "agon" or struggle of war, with a patterning out of those capacities and qualities engaged in that agon, but which can here be appreciated and savored in the bracketing context of sport. American football terminology lends weight to Santayana's claim: military metaphors of bombs, blitzes, defense, attack, holding ground, and so on abound in the game. Of course in one sense the game of football is a struggle, but it is also a game, and appreciating the struggle as engaged in the play of a game is an achievement of imagination. It is said that the Inuit, when first confronted with the game of soccer, could not understand it, and that each team would "generously" kick an own goal to even up the scores whenever it found itself ahead. Now we can say of them that they had not grasped the conventions of the game, but in saying only this we have not yet explained what it is they have not grasped. What they lack is in fact the concept of the game of football, in that they cannot understand the idea of a struggle which is also "only a game." But what this means is that they have not understood the idea of a struggle raised to the level of imagination.

There is a still more general way of expressing the present point. Best remarks that while many people seem to be keen to establish that sports can be art, no one has ever even thought of suggesting that art might be sport. But has he not heard of Schiller's (10) theory of art as play, since endorsed by others? Whatever its virtues as a general theory of art, this view nicely captures the idea that in our response to art our various capacities are disengaged from their normal practical relation to the demands of life. Schiller is building on Kant with his idea that our pleasure in art involves the free play of our faculties elicited by the work of art. But through the connection of sport with play, Schiller's theory also enables us to make sense of the idea that a similar free play of our faculties might be elicited in our response to sport. This, I take it, is just what is implied by our joint awareness of the football match as both a struggle and a game. An actual struggle—itself trivial in its object, a piece of leather—is also a semblance of an enormously significant engagement.

It seems, then, that our involvement with sports can indeed be imaginative, and the imagination's helping to constitute the object of our attention does not itself mark out a difference between our engagement with art and with sport. I repeat that I do not deny some force to Best's original mark of distinction. For it does seem that those arts that do have a subject, and can therefore express a conception of life-issues, are thereby able to realize a kind of meaningfulness unavailable to sports. But we have seen that this is not a possibility available to the arts in general, and also that there is good reason to question Best's assumption that this potential of some art forms crystallizes the deepest sort of significance art can have. So Best's true claim—that sports, unlike some works of art, cannot have a subject—does not seem to undermine a deep similarity in the kind of meaning and significance sports and arts can have. In the experience of each we are able to realize an indefinitely wide range and combination of life-values, and to do this at least partly through the exercise of imagination in both kinds of case.

But this conclusion may now seem so bland, or so wide, as to be useless. For perhaps the fruits of a spectatorial attitude to almost any human activity could be described in this way. Then our argument against one way of trying to draw a deep distinction between sport and art seems to open the gate too wide. The difference between art and almost any human activity, viewed in a certain way, may appear to have been dissolved.

That outcome would indeed be too extreme, and I do not think my view leads to it. My argument has been directed only against some ways of trying to distinguish sports from arts, and thereby perhaps against some ways of thinking about, and valuing, the differences of art from other activities. But nothing I have said dissolves the concept of art, or reduces it to something else. My final task is to go a little further in specifying what I take to be the relation between the two domains of activity with which this paper has been concerned. For the affinity between them noted two paragraphs ago still leaves much to be said.

Echoing Hegel, the English politician Enoch Powell once said that human life is lived almost entirely in the imagination. By this he did not mean that human beings spend most of their time daydreaming or otherwise detached from the real world. He meant that what is human reality is for the most part imaginatively constituted. Our activities and practices are saturated with symbolic value, and this is value realized imaginatively. The ritual and ceremony of the law courts confer a gravity and impressiveness on the institution of the law that is not a function merely of the character or personal makeup of its individual members. Scientists wear white coats in part to keep clean, but the effect is to surround them with an aura of greater than human purity. Doctors are still often regarded with a priestly veneration owing to their connection with what are seen as the mysteries of healing. When we go out to dinner with others, and even more when we invite them to dinner, it is not just that it happens to be time to eat when we want to see them. The sharing of a meal has a symbolic significance; it is a kind of ritual enactment of intimacy. The practice of politics and war, the cultural regulation of sexual activity, the practice of wearing clothes, as well as the particular clothes we wear—the meaning of all these things too is a matter of the imaginative structure in which we communally house them.

This does not make these activities into art, any more than the presence of imagination in our responsiveness to sport makes it art. Still, the prevalence of imaginative activity in our engagement with the social world may suggest that we need to think of the relation between art and various other activities in a slightly different way from that proposed by Best. As I have said, I do not think that a crucial difference between various other human activities and art lies in a sharp distinction between an attention to the real and an imaginative structuring of an object. For that distinction is blurred by the fact that much of the reality of the social world, including much of what we are engaged by in sport, is itself imaginatively structured. I think it is more helpful to think of the activity of art as built upon a capacity for imaginative engagement that we already exercise throughout our lives. The institution of art effects a temporary self-enclosing of that imaginative activity, so that it is not essentially directed toward the bringing about of a change in social or personal relations, as for example a trial or a wedding is (or the confirming of existing relations). The institutional mark of this self-enclosing of the activity of imagination is the spectatorial aspect of art. Works of art are essentially for looking at, listening to, reading. In traditional terms, the idea is that the work of art is an object for contemplation.

This view has several advantages over Best's view. The first is that it enables us to drop the idea that being a real object is incompatible with being an imaginatively structured object. Indeed we must drop this idea once we accept that much of the social world is imaginatively structured, and I have urged that we have good reason to accept this. Second, and relatedly, my view enables us to explain important continuities between our experience of art and other of our activities. We can, for example, explain how it is that we can treat various things—African masks, rain dances,

cave paintings, Australian aboriginal dream-time stories—as if they were art. If the object of our attention in art was always an imagined object where this meant it was not a real object, then it would be difficult to make sense of our ability to treat these things as if they were art. In so treating them I do not cease to think the masks real, nor the drawings; what I do is relate to them other than as functional items—the masks as talismans for frightening away the evil spirits, the cave drawings as ways of summoning the buffalo. Instead I seek to register the character of the life that is realized in these objects. They become objects of contemplation for me.

I do not say that because we can treat these things as if they were art that they therefore are art. For the sophisticated institution of art is one according to which people can create objects for contemplation, and the primitive objects mentioned were (we may suppose) not created for that purpose. But my point does suggest that the value an object not created as art can have for us, if we treat it as art, may be just like the value we find in an object created as art and which we respond to as art. But where does sport fit into this sketch? Clearly, most sports activities are not arts by the criterion of the previous paragraph, for most do not involve the creation of something for contemplation. (For the moment I exclude the so-called aesthetic sports.) But we can still treat them as objects for contemplation. Indeed, the spectator aspect of sports shows us thus treating them, even if other factors (for example a concern with who wins) can interfere with our appreciation of the spectacle. So most sports, while not arts, can nevertheless be appreciated as realizing life-values for us in a self-enclosed domain, as works of art do. If it is the case that almost any human activity can be appreciated in this way, it remains true that only with great psychological difficulty, and what is worse only by a potentially immoral detachment from one's social world, could one come to treat (say) trials at law, religious ceremonies, weddings, and the various rituals of social life in this way. Sport, by contrast, is institutionally structured in such a way that it can be appreciated easily and quite properly like this.

I am not here saying that sports differ from arts in the same way that, for example, African masks, cave drawings, and dream-line stories differ from art. Certainly it is easy for us to appreciate these things as if they were art, as it is easy for us to treat sports as realizing life-values in a self-enclosed domain, but there is a different reason for the easiness in the two cases. In the former case the cultural distance of these objects from us means that there is no great psychological difficulty, nor any danger of an immoral detachment from our social world, in our coming to respond to these things as embodiments of certain life-values. It is thus much easier for us to treat these things as if they were works of art than it is for us to treat the activities and rituals that still define our own social world in this way. (The Bible and the myths of Christianity presently lie about halfway between these two poles for many.) In the case of sports, however, the ease of treating them as objects for contemplation, as if they were artworks, owes not to their lacking for us a specific functional value they once had for some other group—as is true of the masks, the drawing, and the dream-time stories—but to a spectator attitude being institutionally appropriate to sport as it exists in our society. By definition as it were, sport is fitted to be regarded in this way. (As I have emphasized, however, we need not mistakenly conclude from this that sports are arts.)

It may still be felt, however, that African masks, cave drawings, dream-time stories, and the like are somehow closer to being arts than sports (at least the nonaesthetic sports) are. I share the feeling, and a justification of it, compatible with my line of thought, is not hard to find. It is true that the masks and so forth were not made to be contemplated, and this feature they share with sporting activity. But there is still a generic difference in the focus of the creator's attention in the making of those primitive objects, from the focus of attention of sports performers in a nonaesthetic sport. The making of the mask, like the drawing of the cave drawings, does show a primary concern with the appearance of the object: The mask must look frightening (if it is to frighten away the evil spirits or the enemy), and the drawing must summon the buffalo by representing it. The focus of attention in creating is thus the appearance of the object, as the sports performer's attention is not characteristically on the appearance of what he or she does. I think this difference explains our inclination to regard the primitive objects as nearer to art than the sporting performance is, since the primitive objects share with art objects the quality of having been designed to have a certain appearance. They are still not art, however, because they were not designed within the institutional context necessary for them to be so. The appearances the objects were designed to have were not intended to be of interest for their own sake to observers; they were intended to serve the further purpose of, for example, frightening off the evil spirits or summoning the buffalo.

In the last part of this paper I have so far bracketed the so-called aesthetic sports from discussion. Given my line of argument, these sports may seem to create a problem for my insistence that sports are not arts even though what they have to offer us may share a great deal with what the arts have to offer us. For surely the performer of an aesthetic sport is concerned with doing something so that it will have a certain appearance. The gymnast's focus of attention in performing is on the production of a vault or a somersault that will appear fluent, graceful, nicely arched, and so on. This may seem to dissolve the distinction between the gymnast and the performing artist. But this conclusion is insensitive to a distinction drawn in the previous paragraph. What defines the artist's focus of attention in creating is that he or she seeks to produce something not just with a certain appearance, but with an appearance that is to be of interest for its own sake. That is, he/she seeks to produce something for contemplation.[8] The gymnast, or the ice skater, by contrast, wants the appearance he/she produces to be related to, and evaluated in relation to, an antecedently defined purpose or goal; it is to be measured by the standards for a good vault, a good figure 8, or whatever. In this respect the aesthetic athlete is like the maker of the mask or the cave-drawer, in that his or her concern with the appearance of what he/she does is subsumed under its relation to an antecedently defined purpose or goal. The artist's concern is not thus subsumed, and if it turns out to be so, then he/she is a propagandist or an advertiser or an illustrator, and not an artist at all.

Thus even the aesthetic athlete is not an artist. But we can see why his or her performances can seem closer to art than those of the nonaesthetic athlete. The reason is just like the African mask and the cave drawing, what the aesthetic athlete produces is produced with an attention to how it will appear, and this is a feature his or her performance, but not the performance of the non-aesthetic athlete, shares with that of the artist. It does not follow, of course, that the aesthetic sports are likely to be more interesting, even for the ideal contemplative spectator, than the nonaesthetic sports. In fact when we treat the latter as for contemplation, they probably enable us to realize a greater richness and range of life-values than the aesthetic sports do. Given that the attention of performers in nonaesthetic sports is not, however, on how their performance will appear, the value of these sports to the contemplative spectator may be a more hit-or-miss affair.

Finally, I do not suppose that every interpretive or evaluative predicate applicable to some art or other will be applicable to some sport or other. That works of art are created for contemplation fits them for some predicates not applicable to sports. Unlike a play or a novel, for example, a sporting performance can be comic or tragic only if something goes wrong with it. It should not be surprising if the imaginative and emotional range of works of art is greater than that of sports, given that works of art are designed to exploit and foster our capacity for imaginative response. But it should not be concluded from this that the experience of art involves the imagination while the experience of sport does not. It is rather that the institution of art enables the deliberate and systematic exploiting of a capacity for imaginative engagement that the institution of sport caters to but not in the same deliberate and systematic way. Sport is none the worse for that either; it just has partly different allegiances from art.

Notes

1. The scope of the discussion needs to be thus restricted. We cannot assume that an answer to this question would do much to illuminate the connections between, for example, art and athletics in classical Greece, or would help us appreciate the cultural place of the ball game in the Mayan civilization.

2. I do not claim of course that these different motives are found in the same proportions among artists as among athletes. My point is rather that there are no characteristic motives of the one kind of activity that do not also operate in the other sphere.

3. There may be some vagueness about the boundaries. A play in a theatre can spill off the stage, and street theatre may have no precisely bounded stage. There can be debate about where the work of art (or the game) ends and where its everyday-world context begins. But this vagueness does not deny the bracketing of which I speak. Perhaps so-called performance art does seek to deny it altogether. Consider for instance the activity of the woman whose "artwork" was to shake the hand of every sanitation worker in New York. (I owe the example to Jim Young.) But there is a real problem about why such an activity would count as art. Although the problem is too complex to resolve properly here, I think the answer is briefly that the activity's so counting must depend upon its reference to the bracketing conventions of art she seeks to call into question.

4. There is a useful discussion of this point in Kupfer (6).

5. This description of his position may be thought unfair to Best. Certainly it is clear from other things he says that his cognitivist position is not crass. He writes, "it is not a contingent matter that the best way of expressing the content of Solzenhitsyn's *One Day in the Life of Ivan Denisovich* is in the particular form of that novel, i.e., it would make no sense to suggest that its content could be more effectively conveyed in another way." The end or purpose of the novel can be identified as achieved only "in this particular way and no other. And to give a comprehensive account of what is meant by 'in this particular way and no other' one would have to produce nothing less than the whole novel" (1: pp. 102–103). According to this fairly familiar view, the work of art has a particular cognitive content (it says or

expresses something), but this content cannot be abstracted or extracted from the work. It can be identified only by reference to "nothing less than the whole novel" (or painting or a piece of music or whatever). The problem with this view is that if anything and everything in or of the work belongs to its content (what it says or expresses), then the difference between what it says or expresses and what it is has dissolved. The "cognitive" locutions seem to have lost their point. But recognition of this leads into just the view I go on to develop.

6. I leave aside the much-discussed question of whether the music is literally or metaphorically these things. I do not myself think the question is at all clear. But suppose it is. It still does not matter for our purposes which camp our characterizations of Mozart's music fall into. Either we are (literally) describing the music, and so saying what it is, or we are doing whatever the correct theory of metaphor says we are doing. But on no plausible theory of metaphor will it turn out that what we are doing in talking this way is pinpointing the conceptions of life-issues expressed by the music.

7. It should be noted that Best acknowledges that he is not happy with his use of the term "imagined object" here. I think his unhappiness touches on a lack of clarity in a long tradition of discussion of art as imaginative. Still, it is difficult not to feel that the tradition is onto something of importance about art. And Best still thinks that he has his finger on a crucial distinction here, even if he is not satisfied with his own way of articulating it.

8. This is so even if the artist also seeks, say, to bring about political change through his or her work, or if as an architect or potter he/she makes things with everyday functions. But the potter who seeks only to make a bowl that is sturdy and capacious—say, he/she is interested only in its functional properties as a device for eating from—is no artist. Nor is the author an artist who seeks only to produce a tract that will help bring about the revolution, a mere device for persuading. Neither is an artist because neither seeks to produce an object that is to reward contemplative engagement with it. Art can be, and can be intended to be, functional, but it cannot be only functional.

Bibliography

1. Best, D. *Philosophy and Human Movement.* London: George Allen & Unwin, 1978.
2. Best, D. "The Aesthetic in Sport." *Sport and the Body.* Edited by E.W. Gerber and W.J. Morgan. Philadelphia: Lea & Febiger, 1979, pp. 345–354.
3. Best, D. "Art and Sport." *Journal of Aesthetic Education,* 14 (1980), 69–80.
4. Best, D. "Sport is not Art." *Journal of the Philosophy of Sport,* XII (1985), 25–40.
5. Hegel, G.W.F. *Lectures on Fine Art.* Translated by T.M. Knox. Oxford: Clarendon Press, 1975, Vol. I.
6. Kupfer, J. "Purpose and Beauty in Sport." *Journal of the Philosophy of Sport,* II (1975), 83–90.
7. Lawrence, D.H. "The Spirit of Place." *20th Century Literary Criticism.* Edited by D. Lodge. London: Longman, 1972.
8. Reid, L.A. "Sport, the Aesthetic and Art." *British Journal of Educational Studies,* 18 (1970), 245–258.
9. Santayana, G. *Reason in Society.* New York: Collier Books, 1962.
10. Schiller, J.C.F. *Letters on the Aesthetic Education of Man.* Edited and translated by E.M. Wilkinson and L.A. Willoughby. Oxford: Clarendon Press, 1967.
11. Wertz, S.K. "A Response to Best on Sport and Art." *Journal of Aesthetic Education,* 18 (1984), 105–108.
12. Ziff, P. "A Fine Forehand." *Philosophic Exchange,* 1 (Summer 1974), 41–47.

Questions for Consideration

1. To what extent is winning one of the defining features of sport for Cordner? Address this question from both the perspective of player and that of fan.

2. Cordner uses Mozart's music as a counterexample to Best's account of art. What is this counterexample meant to show? Is it effective?

3. Cordner at one point recognizes that his view that both art and sport offer innumerable opportunities to realize life values through imagination seems to dissolve the possibility of any distinction between the two (or even between art and *any* human activity). Does Cordner adequately dissolve this "dissolution" by the end of the reading?

Chapter Three

Ethics and Sport

Sportsmanship

Cheating

Winning

Violence

Performance-Enhancing Drugs

13 Three Approaches Toward an Understanding of Sportsmanship

Peter J. Arnold
Dunfermline College, Edinburgh, Scotland

In this reading, Peter J. Arnold spells out three different views of sportsmanship: (1) sportsmanship as social union, (2) sportsmanship as a means to pleasure, and (3) sportsmanship as altruism.

According to sportsmanship as social union, guided by a notion of fair play, athletes agree to conserve sportive traditions, customs, and conventions. Playing by the rules promotes a sense of community and amicability.

The second view is etymological. While sport essentially aims at fun and diversion, competitive sport, in contrast, involves dedication, sacrifice, and intensity in working toward victory. Along these lines, sportsmanship is a kind of justice as regards sport that has pleasure as its aim. This view is essentially a form of utilitarianism.

The third view, that sportsmanship is altruistic, transcends actions done on account of justice or fairness. The motivation here is genuine concern for another. This view is spelled out in terms either of actions for another that come at some cost to the agent or of actions that contribute to greater overall good (more so than what would have occurred if one had acted merely in accordance with duty or the rules of fair play). This view has affinities to Kant's deontological morality, but differs in that duty or justice for all is not the aim. Instead the good of another is.

Reprinted, by permission, from Peter J. Arnold, "Three Approaches toward an Understanding of Sportsmanship," *Journal of the Philosophy of Sport*, X (1983): 61–70.

It is strange, but true, that few recent attempts to analyze and clarify the concept or nature of sport make any significant reference to sportsmanship. Despite this neglect, however, few people would wish to deny that the connection of sportsmanship to sport is an important one. Certainly in the games playing ethos of the 19th century English Public Schools the use of one term without the other would barely have been conceivable. The same can be said of such terms as "amateurism" and "Olympism." Today, it would seem, especially if contemporary philosophy of sport literature is anything to go by, the matter is quite different. As far as I know, no serious endeavour has been made to look at the phenomenon of sportsmanship for nearly twenty years.[1] Even McIntosh (18: p. 1), who in his book *Fair Play*, sets out "to link an analysis of the ethics of sport with the theory and practice of education," makes only passing comment on it. What follows, therefore, is an attempt to help rectify what I see as a neglected dimension in contemporary debate in the general area of ethics and sport.

Sportsmanship, although most readily associated with particular types of commendatory acts done in the context of sport, is sometimes extended to apply to other spheres of life and living, especially those which are concerned with competing fairly and honestly as well as with good humor. I do not propose to embark upon these latter applications, but to concentrate upon what I see to be its central cases, all of which are to do with the actions and conduct of sportsmen and sportswomen when engaged in sport. There are, it seems to me, essentially three different, if related, views about sportsmanship and I propose looking at each of these in turn. They are:

1. Sportsmanship as a form of social union,
2. Sportsmanship as a means in the promotion of pleasure, and
3. Sportsmanship as a form of altruism.

It should be made clear that, although I shall be looking at each of these views separately and in turn for purposes of exposition, I do not necessarily wish to maintain that they are not to some extent overlapping. In any one person, at different times, (and maybe even at the same time) all three views can be partially represented.

First, I would like to make a preliminary comment. The idea of sport as justice maintains that when a player enters into the institutionalized social practice of a sport he tacitly agrees to abide by the rules which characterize and govern it. It implies that sport involves a proper understanding of and a commitment to the two principles upon which it is based, namely freedom and equality.[2] The idea of sport as a social union reflects these same undertakings and values. It recognizes that if the practice of sport is to be preserved and flourish, a great deal is dependent upon the players, and officials, understanding and acting in accord with what is fair. They will accept and realize that breaches of the rules, especially if flagrant and deliberate, will destroy the very activity that they have agreed to participate in and uphold. They will appreciate further that if "fairness" is interpreted too contractually or legalistically there is always the danger that the aspect of sport known as "sportsmanship" will be construed as being concerned only with these acts which demonstrate a ready acceptance of the rules and a willingness to abide by them. It will be seen, however, that this is a reasonable expectation of all players and the notion of sportsmanship connotes something more. What must be emphasized is that fairness, if understood only in a legalistic or formal rule-following

sense, can only be regarded as a necessary condition of sportsmanship, but by no means a sufficient one. This point applies to all three views of sportsmanship I intend to outline.

Sportsmanship as a Form of Social Union

The idea of sport as a social union takes into account, but goes beyond an agreement to willingly abide and play by the rules in the interests of what is fair. It is also concerned with the preservation and continuation of its best traditions, customs, and conventions so that the community which makes up the social union cannot only cooperatively participate in sport, but successfully relate to one another as persons through an understood, shared, and appreciated mode of proceeding. "The Sportsmanship Brotherhood" (22) which was founded in 1926, while itself indebted to the English Public School ethos of games playing, may be regarded as a forerunner to this view. Its aim was to foster and spread the spirit of sportsmanship throughout the world which it saw, in part at least, as a form of social and moral well-being. By adopting the slogan "Not that you won or lost—but that you played the game," it brought home the point that the *manner* in which sport is conducted is no less important than its outcome, if amicability and brotherhood are to be encouraged and upheld. Rawls (19: pp. 525–526), in speaking of games as a simple instance of a social union, suggests that in addition to it being concerned with its rules, it is also concerned with an agreed and cooperative "scheme of conduct in which the excellences and enjoyments of each (player) are complementary to the good of all." The idea of sport as a social union, then, is not just concerned with getting players to accept and abide by the rules but also with the maintenance and extolling of a way of life in which sportsmen find value, cooperation, and mutual satisfaction. If this view of sportsmanship is to flourish and be furthered, it is not a matter of merely adopting a particular code of etiquette or set of shibboleths, but of having a genuine commitment to the values of fellowship and goodwill which are held to be more important than the desire to win or the achievement of victory. The central purpose of the social union of view of sportsmanship is to preserve and uphold fraternal relationships that can arise in and through a participation in sport. More than this, it sees this purpose as being intrinsically involved with the nature of sport itself. Any attempt, therefore, to characterize the nature of sport without reference to it would leave the conceptual map of sport incomplete and considerably impoverished.

It is important to stress that the social union view of sportsmanship is not to be seen merely as a socially cohesive device in order to help regulate and oil the institutional practice of sport, though this effect may well come about. Rather it should be perceived as a community of individuals united by a particular practice in which the arts of chivalry are practiced in the interests of mutual affection, comradery, and fellowship. It is seen by the participants as the kind of practice which places a high premium upon those qualities and forms of conduct such as good humor, respect, politeness, and affability which are conducive to, rather than destructive of, good interpersonal relations and cooperative, if competitive, endeavor. In other words, the idea of sport as a social union is a particular kind of social system in and by which players and officials come together in order to share a commonly valued form of life, a part of which is concerned with the manner in which one should ideally participate if the system is to flourish.[3] An example of this is provided by an incident at the French Tennis Championships of 1982 when Wilander, a Swedish player, was awarded match point against his opponent Clerc on the grounds that a drive down the line was out. Wilander, instead of accepting the umpire's decision, as the rules state, asked for the point to be played again because he thought the ball was "good and that he didn't have a chance." Mr. Dorfman, the referee, at some

risk to his official position, but conscious of the good of the players and game alike, agreed (3: p. 10).[4] Another example comes from the World Athletic Championships of 1983, when Banks, the American world triple jump record holder, was defeated in the last round by the Pole, Hoffman. Instead of being grieved and withdrawn, as is often the case when victory eludes an athlete by a hair's breadth, Banks demonstrated his delight at Hoffman's success by running around the track with him as an act of respect and comradery. For both, a moment between them had been forged. The system requires of all members a commitment to live out the ideals cherished by the union in a way that predisposes towards its convivial continuance. When sport is viewed in this way, sportsmanship can be seen as an evaluative term which is attributed to those who not only uphold and play according to the rules, but keep faith with their spirit by acts and forms of conduct which are not required by the rules but which are freely made in accordance with the best traditions of competitive, but friendly, rivalry. The social union view of sport then, apart from a ready acceptance of what is fair, sees acts of sportsmanship as chiefly having to do with maintaining the best traditions of sport as a valued and shared form of life. In this view, sportsmanship is more in keeping with a particular kind of socialization or ideology which predisposes group members to act in ways that are supported and admired by the social union of which they are an integral part. Because of this, the social union view of sportsmanship is best understood as having more to do with an idealized form or model of group mores rather than as an individual and principled form of morality.

Sportsmanship as a Means in the Promotion of Pleasure

Keating's (12: p. 265) analysis of sportsmanship, although it has some things in common with the idea of sport as a social union, arises more from the etymological meaning of sport. In essence, he maintains sport is "a kind of diversion which has for its direct and immediate end fun, pleasure and delight and which is dominated by a spirit of moderation and generosity." He contrasts sport with athletics which he says "is essentially a competitive activity, which has for its end victory in the contest and which is marked by a spirit of dedication, sacrifice and intensity" (12: p. 265).

What it is important to realize is that when Keating speaks of "sport" and "athletics" he does not necessarily have in mind a difference between particular activities (i.e., field games and track and field) so much as an attitude or motivation towards them (13: p. 167). With the term "sport," he associates the notion of play and the doing of something for its sake, and with "athletics" he associates the notion of contest and the struggle for victory. I do not intend to dwell upon the difficulties of holding such a simplistic either/or position. Nonetheless in the interests of clarity a few brief comments seem desirable. First, while it may be true that play is more readily associated with some activities than with others, it should not be assumed that play is confined to them or that play can be adequately expressed only in terms of them. Play can enter "serious" activities, like war, just as it can enter "nonserious" ones like games.

Second, the fact that an activity is "competitive" does not necessarily preclude having a play attitude towards it. This point holds true even when recognizing that a preoccupation with winning can sometimes inhibit, even neutralize, a play spirit. To acknowledge this however, is not to say, as Keating suggests, that if an activity is competitive it *necessarily* follows that a given attitude accompanies it.[5]

Third, it is needlessly confusing to imply, as Keating does, that "athletics" is concerned with competition whereas "sport" is not. The fact is most, if not all, physical activities commonly known as sports are competitive in one sense or another. This is a logical, if trivial point, about them. In view of this it might have been said less perplexingly that the "sportsman's" attitude towards that family of physical activities known as sport differs from that of the "athlete's." This difference in attitude, however, stems not from the constitutive nature of the activities themselves, as Keating (12: p. 266; 13: p. 170) suggests,[6] but rather from the way they are viewed by those who participate in them. Fourth, it does not follow either, as is suggested by some other writers,[7] that because an "athlete" is concerned with "victory" rather than with "pleasure" that his motives are necessarily undesirable or immoral in some way. There is a big distinction, for example, between a contestant setting out to gain an honorable victory and a contestant setting out to defeat at all costs (and maybe to humiliate) an opponent.[8]

At this point, I wish to examine and comment upon—accepting for the moment Keating's two ways of regarding competitive activities—what amounts to two ways of looking at sportsmanship. It would seem that for the "athlete" given his goal of "exclusive possession" rather than cooperative endeavor, sportsmanship can never be much more than a means of taking some of the rawness out of competitive strife. Its purpose is to mitigate the effects of what is seen as a confrontation and challenge between two adversaries. Sportsmanship in these circumstances, Keating seems to be saying, can only ease, soften, and in some way make more civilized, what is essentially a contest between two prize fighters. Athletes will see the need for disciplined conduct and self-control, even courtesy, but they will not be inclined towards expressions of cordiality or generosity. Sportsmanship for the athlete above all means achieving victory in a dignified and honorable way. They will see the need for "an impartial and equal following of the rules" and the need for "modesty in victory and quiet composure in defeat," but that is all. "Fairness or fair play," says Keating (13: p. 170), is "the pivotal virtue in athletics." His chief and driving motive, however, will be the outcome of "winning" rather than amicability or joy. In summary, Keating's presentation of sportsmanship in athletics seems pretty commensurate with the idea of sport as justice and which, as I suggested, should be an expectation of all participants. It should not perhaps, therefore be regarded as a genus of sportsmanship at all. It meets minimal requirements, but no more than this.

For the "*sportsman*," on the other hand, sportsmanship becomes something more expansive. Here sportsmanship is more than simply following a legislative code (which the justice theory of sport might be wrongly accused of being); nor is it best understood as being represented by those virtues which often accompany the admired player such as courage, endurance, perseverance, self-control, self-reliance, sang-froid, and self-respect (with which the character theory of sport is largely associated). Rather it is concerned with those "moral habits or qualities" which essentially and characteristically have to do with generosity and magnanimity (12: p. 266). Unlike the merely "just" player, the true sportsman adopts a cavalier attitude towards his/her rights as permitted by the code. Instead he prefers to be magnanimous and self-sacrificing if, by such conduct, "he contributes to the fun of the occasion" (12: p. 266). It is important to see in Keating's account of sport that competition is not seen in logical terms of "exclusive possession," by one or the other of the vying parties, but more in terms of a cooperative enterprise, which is seen to be a potentially shared source of pleasure. For Keating then, sportsmanship for the sportsman, is essentially a desirable or efficacious manner or way of acting in sport which is in keeping with the promotion of pleasure and the spirit of play.

From the moral point of view at least three questions arise from Keating's account of sportsmanship. The first question is: can sportsmanship in relation to sport be considered moral if it is seen only as a *means* or as an instrument in the promotion of pleasure? The answer to this question is very closely related to whether or not he is taking a utilitarian stance towards moral issues and he does not make this clear.

The second question is concerned with the sense in which Keating uses the phrase sportsmanship as a "moral category." If he means it in the sense of being "self-contained"[9] then it cannot properly be said to be moral since it is inap-

plicable to life outside of sport. Similarly, if he wants to regard it as a form of play, as he seems to, then at least at one level of analysis, it is "nonserious" as opposed to "serious" and therefore nonmoral in consequence. If, on the other hand, he is intending that sportsmanship is concerned with the type of actions that fall within the general category of the moral and therefore somehow related to the "business of life," this should have been stated more explicitly. If this is the case, however, the problem remains as to how this interpretation is to be reconciled with the notion of play. One way around this dilemma might be to say that although play is generally regarded as a nonserious affair, this is not to say that players cannot take what they are doing seriously (in the psychological sense) or that serious incidents (e.g., death, injury, or acts of malevolence) cannot occur. To say, in other words, that play as a category is nonserious and therefore nonmoral, is to say that this is the way it is best understood, but recognizing, at the same time, things occasionally occur that transform it momentarily into something else, which may or may not have moral significance.

The third question is related to the first one. Even if utilitarianism is adopted as a general ethical theory, it is not clear why conduct that is conducive to fun is necessarily more pleasurable and therefore more moral than conduct that is conducive to "honorable victory." One is tempted to ask here, is it not the case that the best examples of sportsmanship in terms of generosity and "magnanimity" arise out of the pursuit of "honorable victory?" A case which gives some support to this thesis is when Brasher, at the Melbourne Olympic Games in 1956, was disqualified from winning the 3000 meters steeplechase for allegedly hindering his opponents. The point here is that it was these same athletes (Laresen, Loufer, and Rosznyoi) who protested on Brasher's behalf and got the decision reversed, thus sacrificing the medals they would otherwise have won.

All in all Keating's attempt to look at sportsmanship in terms of "athletics" and "sport" by reference to competition, or its relative absence, it not altogether clear or helpful. It does, however, emphasize the importance of the play spirit of sport and the desirable attributes of magnanimity and generosity.

Sportsmanship as a Form of Altruism

It should be apparent by now that the term sportsmanship and its relation to sport and morality is a more complex and subtle one than is commonly supposed. In the social union view of sportsmanship it was suggested that sportsmanship largely has to do with the preservation and exemplification of a valued form of life which puts a premium upon an idealized and amicable way of participating. The pleasure view of sportsmanship sees sportsmanship as being chiefly and characteristically concerned with generous and magnanimous conduct that is conducive to the promotion of fun and pleasure. The view of sportsmanship I shall now present takes a different stance. This view is concerned more with seeing sportsmanship as a form of altruistically motivated conduct that is concerned with the good or welfare of another. Again it should be stressed that I do not see these three views of sportsmanship as mutually exclusive. I see them rather as providing a different focus or perspective on a form of social phenomenon which is essentially both recognizable and understood.

What then, more precisely, is the altruistic view of sportsmanship and how and in what way, if at all, can it be considered as a moral form of conduct? In order to look at the second part of the question first I propose to contrast the Kantian view of morality with what I shall call the altruistic view. For Kant, morality is primarily a matter of reason and rationality. It resides in and is based upon the adoption of principles which are universalizable, impartial, consistent, and obligatory. It emphasizes choice, decision, will, and thoughtful deliberation.[10] Williams, in writing of Kantian tradition points out that:

The moral point of view is specially characterised by its impartiality and its indifference to any particular relations to particular persons and that moral thought requires abstraction from particular circumstances and particular characteristics of the parties, including the agent, except in so far as these can be universal features of any morally similar situation. (24: p. 198)

Williams continues:

The motivations of a moral agent, correspondingly, involve a rational application of impartial principle and are thus different in kind from sorts of motivations that he might have for treating some particular persons differently because he happened to have some particular interest towards them. (24: p. 198)

It will be seen that the Kantian view of morality has a lot in common with the justice theory of sport as well as with those preconditional features of sportsmanship which are to do with fairness. In stressing the universal and impartial, however, the Kantian view seems to overlook or disregard some aspects of interpersonal relations which are as morally important in sport as in other spheres of life. I refer to such virtues as sympathy, compassion, concern, and friendship. What needs to be clarified is that the "moral point of view," while it is importantly connected with the impartial and obligatory, is by no means totally taken up by them. In speaking of sportsmanship then as a form of altruism, I am particularly concerned to show that sportsmanship in this sense, while obligated to the following of impartial rules which govern play, at the same time gives moral scope to go beyond them. In order to say more about this and at the same time point up the differences between the Kantian view of morality and those aspects of morality and sportsmanship that place greater emphasis upon the importance of personal and particular relationships, I propose to look now at sportsmanship as a form of altruism. At the same time I shall indicate that acts of supererogation are more in keeping with the Kantian view than with the altruistic view.

Altruism is perhaps best understood as having to do with those forms of action and conduct that are not done merely because of what is fair and just in terms of playing and keeping to the rules but because there is a genuine concern for an interest in and concern for one's fellow competitors, whether on the same side or in opposition. At first sight it may seem as if sportsmanship in this altruistic sense has to do with supererogatory acts in that they go beyond duty or what the rules expect. In common with other forms of supererogatory acts, these acts in sport are to do as Hare (10: p. 198) puts it with those acts which are "praiseworthy but not obligatory." Stated another way, to say that an act in sport is supererogatory is to say two things about it. First, the sportsman is not morally (or by role) obliged to perform it. He is, in other words permitted not to perform it. Second, the action is morally praiseworthy; it would be commendable if it were performed. Urmson, in speaking of the need to make room for the moral actions which lie outside the realm of obligation, could well be speaking of the kinds of situation with which the sportsman is confronted. He argues that there is a large range of actions whose moral status is insufficiently expressible in terms of the traditional classification of actions into morally impermissible, morally neutral, and morally obligatory and that it is necessary to allow "for a range of actions which are of moral value and which an agent may feel called upon to perform, but which cannot be demanded and whose omission cannot be called wrongdoing" (23: p. 208).

There seem to be at least two ways in sport in which an act can go beyond duty (or demands of fair play). The first way is by acting out of concern for the other or at some risk, cost, or sacrifice to oneself. An example here might be the marathon runner who, at the cost of victory, stops to help a fellow runner in a state of distress. The second way is by acting on behalf of another so that more good is brought about than if one had merely acted out of duty or in accordance with the rules. An actual case is provided by Meta Antenan, who although leading in a long jump competition against her great German rival, asked of the presiding jury that her opponent have a longer rest period than is provided by the rules, because of her having just taken part in another event (6: p. 8).[11]

Such examples of sportsmanship, it might be thought, are both supererogatory and altruistic in that they go beyond what is required by duty or a proper observance of the rules, but it should be pointed out that although acts of supererogation and altruism have certain things in common—namely that they have moral value and that they are not morally obligatory—they also have certain important differences which prevent one being assimilated to the other. Whereas supererogatory acts tend to stem from a traditional framework dominated by the notions of duty and obligation, and by some writers (9: Chapter 4) are even spoken of as "doing more than duty requires" in a sacrificial or enobling sort of way, altruistic acts are prompted by various forms of altruistic emotion. Whereas "supererogatory" sportsmen may be prompted into acts which, to them, have the force of duty, but they would not recognize as being encumbent on others, "altruistic" sportsmen may be prompted into acts by the emotions of concern and care.[12]

In referring to the two examples of the "going beyond duty" forms of sportsmanship cited above, it will be seen that either or both could be considered "supererogatory" or "altruistic." The correct interpretation would depend upon the considerations or states which prompted them. Moral actions in sport, like other actions, cannot be properly understood only by reference to their external form.

It will be seen then that supererogatory or altruistic forms of sportsmanship are essentially different from those forms which are to do with a conventional set of values to do with preservation of amicability and group harmony or with the successful pursuit of pleasure.

What characterizes altruistic forms of sportsmanship particularly is that sympathy, compassion, and concern are directed towards the other in virtue of his or her suffering, travail, misery, or pain. The altruistic sportsman not only thinks about and is affected by the plight of the other, but acts in such a way that is directed to bring help or comfort in some way. Altruistic acts of sportsmanship stem from a desire for the other's good. This sometimes leads to impulsive or spontaneous forms of conduct that arise from the sporting contest as when, for example, Karpati, the Hungarian fencer, reached out and tried to console a defeated and disappointed opponent. Such acts, it will be seen, are not motivated by such Kantian virtues as obligation and duty so much as by a perceptive and human response to another's plight. On the rationalistic Kantian view such acts based on altruistic emotions would be considered unreliable as moral motives because they are too transitory, changeable, maybe emotionally charged, and not sufficiently detached, impartial, and consistent. Yet the question arises are they less moral on account of this? Blum (5: p. 93), who has addressed himself to this very problem argues, for instance, "that the domain in which morally good action takes the form of universalizable principles of obligation does not exhaust the areas of morally good action." He argues further that there are different kinds of virtues. Some are articulated by the Kantian view such as justice, impartiality, conscientiousness and so on while others, such as kindness, concern, and compassion are articulated better by the altruistic view.

Whereas the Kantian view is predominantly concerned with what is right and what is just for all, the altruistic view is more concerned with the good of the other, even if this sometimes means acting particularly and personally rather than objectively and impartially and/or in a strict accordance with what the rules decree. All in all, the altruistic view of sportsmanship, in contrast to the social union view or the pursuit of pleasure view, arises not from a concern for the preservation of a valued and particular form of interpersonal life or the promotion of pleasure as an ethic, but rather from a particular and genuine concern for another's welfare. When

acts in sport go beyond that which is expected of players generally and are done only out of concern for another's good and for no other reason, they are not only altruistic, but exemplify the best traditions of sportsmanship.

Notes

1. J.W. Keating's article (12: pp. 264–271) first appeared in *Ethics,* 75 (1964), pp. 25–35.

2. For an interesting article along these lines see Keenan (14: pp. 115–119).

3. This conception of the way sport can (or should) be conducted is not out of keeping with what some writers have referred to as the "radical ethic" which recognizes that "the excellence of the outcome as important, but holds equally important the way that excellence is achieved." See Scott (20: pp. 75–77). It also holds that "the winning of the game is subservient to the playing of the game" in which such qualities as "corporate loyalty and respect for others" are encouraged. All in all "The game is viewed as a framework within which various aims may be realized, qualities fostered, needs met, and values upheld." See Kew (15: pp. 104–107).

4. Two points can be made about this incident. The first is that Wilander, on being asked about why he had challenged the umpire's decision, replied that he could not accept a win "like that" by which he was taken to mean not only unfairly but in a way which would have brought dishonor to himself, and discredit from his opponent, who also thought his drive was in, as well as his from fellow circuit players.

5. See Gallie (8: pp. 167–198) who argued that competition is a normative concept and as such is open to being contested since the evaluative frameworks surrounding it (e.g., a "Lombardian ethic," where winning is everything, as opposed to the "radical ethic," referred to in Note 3 above) are sometimes irreconcilable.

6. Fraleigh (7: pp. 74–82) has touched upon some of the complexities of this issue.

7. Bailey (2: pp. 40–50) argues that since competitive games are concerned with winning, especially when they are made compulsory, they are not only morally questionable but morally undesirable in that those behaviors and attitudes that are conducive to the defeat of the other side and all that this implies for both the winner and loser.

8. Arnold (1: pp. 126–130) attempts to refute Bailey's view of competition and point out the difference between "trying to win" when competing and the attitude and outcome of "winning at all costs." He also points out the intrinsic values of competitive games.

9. For an explication of play seen in this way see Huizinga (11: p. 32), Lucas (16: p. 11) and Schmitz (22: pp. 22–29) among others.

10. Consult Beck (3) for a good statement of the Kantian position.

11. As a result she lost the competition by one centimeter.

12. Lyons (17: pp. 125–145), in keeping with the points I am making, speaks about a "morality of response and care." This she contrasts with a "morality of justice," which stems more from the Kantian tradition, grounded in obligations and duty.

Bibliography

1. Arnold, P.J. "Competitive Games and Education." *Physical Education Review,* 5, No. 2 (1982), 126–130.

2. Bailey, C. "Games, Winning and Education." *Cambridge Journal of Education,* 5 (1975), 40–50.

3. Beck, L.W. *Immanuel Kant: Foundations of the Metaphysics of Morals.* Indianapolis, IN: Bobbs-Merill, 1959.

4. Bellamy, R. "Wilander: A Winner and a Gentleman." *The Times,* (June 5th) 1982.

5. Blum, L.A. *Friendship, Altruism and Morality.* Boston: Rutledge and Kegan Paul, 1980.

6. Borotra, J, "A Plea for Sporting Ethics." *Bulletin of the Federation Internationale D'Education Physique,* 48, No. 3 (1978), 7–10.

7. Fraleigh, W.P. "Sport-Purpose." *Journal of the Philosophy of Sport,* 2 (1975), 74–82.

8. Gallie, W.B. "Essentially Contested Concepts." *Proceedings of the Aristotelian Society,* 16 (1955–56), 167–198.

9. Grice, G.R. *The Grounds of Moral Judgment.* New York: Cambridge University Press, 1967, Chapter 4.

10. Hare, R.M. *Moral Thinking.* New York: Clarendon Press, Oxford 1981.

11. Huizinga, J. *Homo Ludens.* Boulder, CO: Paladin, 1970.

12. Keating, J.W. "Sportsmanship as a Moral Category." *Sport and the Body. Second Edition.* Edited by Ellen W. Gerber and William J. Morgan. Philadelphia: Lea and Febiger, 1979.

13. Keating, J.W. "The Ethics of Competition and its Relation to Some Moral Problems in Athletics." *The Philosophy of Sport.* Edited by R.G. Osterhoudt. Springfield, IL: Charles C. Thomas, 1973.

14. Keenan, F.W. "Justice and Sport." *Journal of the Philosophy of Sport,* 2 (1975), 115–119.

15. Kew, F.C. "Values in Competitive Games." *Quest,* 29 (1978), 103–113.

16. Lucas, J. R. "Moralists and Gamesman." *Philosophy,* 34 (1959), 1–11.

17. Lyons, N.P. "Two Perspectives: On Self, Relationships and Morality." *Harvard Educational Review,* 53 (May, 1983) 125–145.

18. McIntosh, P. *Fair Play: Ethics in Sport and Education.* Heinemann, 1979.

19. Rawls, J. *A Theory of Justice.* New York: Oxford University Press, 1973.

20. Scott, J. "Sport and the Radical Ethic." *Quest,* 19 (January, 1973) 71–77.

21. Schmitz, K.L. "Sport and Play: Suspension of the Ordinary." *Sport and the Body. Second Edition.* Edited by E.W. Gerber and W.J. Morgan. Philadelphia: Lea and Febiger, 1979.

22. "A Sportsmanship Brotherhood." *Literary Digest,* 88 (March 27, 1926)

23. Urmson, J.O. "Saints and Heroes." *Essays in Moral Philosophy.* Edited by A. I. Melden. Seattle: University of Washington Press, 1958.

24. Williams, B. "Persons, Character and Morality." *The Identity of Persons.* Edited by A.O. Rorty. Berkeley: University of California Press, 1976.

Questions for Consideration

1. Which of the three views best captures what we mean by sportsmanship?

2. Like view 2, can view 1 be construed as a form of utilitarianism? If so, precisely how does it differ from view 2?

3. Arnold's third view, sportsmanship as altruism, is briefly contrasted to the Kantian view of actions performed by a good will out of a sense of duty. Is this altruistic account sufficiently motivated? Might not the Kantian view (see Glossary of Key Terms) apply equally as well (or even better) to the few examples Arnold gives?

14 Sportsmanship and Fairness in the Pursuit of Victory

Robert Simon
Hamilton College

In this reading, which is an excerpt from his book,
Fair Play: Sports and Social Values, *Robert Simon draws a distinction, taken from James Keating, between "sport" and "athletics." Sport is a diversion aiming at fun that is dominated by moderation and generosity. Athletics, in contrast, is competitive activity aiming at victory and characterized by dedication, sacrifice, and intensity. Sportsmanship, however, is an attitude that promotes the goals of sport, not those of athletics. It is thus conducted with an aim toward maximizing pleasure. Consequently, sportsmanship does not apply to athletics, according to Keating, at least not easily. Simon's aim in this excerpt is to show that sportsmanship does have a place in athletics, and his main vehicle is the topic "cheating."*

What, then, is cheating? Is it at all permissible in sport? Examples from the practice of competitive sport suggest that answers are not so straightforward. Central to the issues throughout, for Simon, is a notion of competitive sport as a "mutual quest for excellence through challenge." Thus, fair athletic competition, as a commitment to sport itself, has implications for sportsmanship, where sportsmanship involves treating others as partners in a cooperative enterprise. With these implications fleshed out, Keating's distinction between sport and athletics seems meaningless.

In early October 1990, the highly regarded University of Colorado Buffaloes were playing a

home football contest against the University of Missouri. Top national ranking was at stake. The final seconds saw Colorado, trailing 31–27 at the time, driving toward the Missouri goal line. Somehow, in the confusion on the field, the seven officials on the field as well as the "chain gang" working the sideline markers, and the scoreboard operator, lost track of the downs. On what should have been the fourth and deciding down, Colorado failed to score, in part because the Colorado quarterback, mistakenly thinking he had another play left, intentionally grounded a pass. In fact, the officials signaled that Colorado had another chance, unaware that the Buffaloes already had used the four chances to score allowed by the rules. Colorado scored on the illegal but unnoticed fifth down to eke out a 33–31 "victory."

Did Colorado really win? Should the final score have been allowed to stand? It was decided that the officials' mistake was not the sort of error that can be overruled. But should the University of Colorado have accepted the victory? Is such a "win" meaningful in any important ethical sense?

Consider another example. Two top college basketball teams are struggling for a conference championship. The score is tied with five seconds to go and the team with the ball calls time out. The noise in the gym is deafening and, in the pandemonium, the defending team does not hear the buzzer signaling the end of the time out. Before they can regroup, the referees, as required by the rules, give the ball to the offensive team. The offensive team drives the length of the court to score the winning basket before the defenders can even leave their huddle to get on the floor.

Reprinted, by permission, from Robert Simon, "Cheating and Violence in Sports," Ch. 3 in Robert Simon, *Fair Play: Sports and Social Values* (Englewood Cliffs, NJ: Prentice Hall, 1985), 37–46.

Did the offensive team behave as they should have? Is their "win" something in which they may properly take pride?

Take a third example. A championship basketball game is tied, with only a few seconds remaining. A player on the defensive team steals the ball and breaks away for the winning basket. Only one player can catch the streaking guard heading for the winning bucket. The defender realizes she cannot block the shot but also knows the opponent is that team's worst foul shooter. She pretends to go for the ball but in fact deliberately fouls her opponent. Is deliberate fouling ethical? After all, fouling is against the rules. Was committing a deliberate foul in this way a form of cheating? Should one take pride in the resulting victory? Why or why not? . . .

. . . What values ought to govern the behavior of competitors in athletic competition? Sportsmanship is one value that often is appealed to in such contexts. Sportsmanship has received relatively little attention by moral thinkers, and probably suffers today because of associations with the morality of an elite "uppercrust" and perhaps by concerns about a male bias being built into the meaning of the term.[1] Nevertheless, sportsmanship is a value frequently cited by coaches, players, and commentators on sports, and ought not to be dismissed without a hearing.

But what is sportsmanship? Does it apply equally to intense athletic competition as well as to informal games among friends?

Perhaps the most influential recent analysis of sportsmanship has been provided by James W. Keating. Keating properly warns us, first of all, not to make our account of sportsmanship so broad as to make it virtually identical with virtue.[2] Not every virtue is an instance of sportsmanship and not every vice is unsportsmanlike. Thus, one dictionary defines "sportsmanship" rather unhelpfully as "sportsmanlike conduct" and continues by listing conduct appropriate to a sportsman as exhibiting "fairness, self-control, etc." Keating tells us that a formal code of sportsmanship promulgated earlier in this century included such diverse injunctions as "keep yourself fit," "keep your temper," and "keep a sound soul and a clean mind in a healthy body." The trouble with such broad accounts of sportsmanship is that they do no specific work. We cannot say conduct is ethical *because* it is sportsmanlike, for "sportsmanlike" has just become another way of saying "ethical." The idea of sportsmanship has been characterized so broadly that there is no particular aspect of morality that is its specific concern.

Keating believes that a more useful account of sportsmanship will develop the rather vague suggestion of the dictionary about behavior expected of a sportsman or sportswoman. To develop this idea, he introduces a crucial distinction between *sports* and *athletics*:

> In essence, sport is a kind of diversion which has for its direct and immediate end fun, pleasure, and delight and which is dominated by a spirit of moderation and generosity. Athletics on the other hand, is essentially a competitive activity, which has for its end victory in the contest and which is characterized by a spirit of dedication, sacrifice, and intensity.[3]

Sportsmanship, then, is the kind of attitude toward opponents that best promotes the goal of sports as defined by Keating; namely, friendly, mutually satisfactory relationships among the players. "Its purpose is to protect and cultivate the festive mood proper to an activity whose primary purpose is pleasant diversion, amusement, joy."[4] In Keating's view, then, the supreme principle of sportsmanship is an injunction to "always conduct yourself in such a manner that you will increase rather than detract from the pleasure found in the activity, both your own and that of your fellow participant."[5]

Sportsmanship, Keating argues, is a virtue that applies to recreational activity of sports, as he understands it, but not to the more serious and competitive activity of athletics. To Keating, sportsmanship and athletics do not fit together easily. "The strange paradox of sportsmanship as applied to athletics is that it asks the athlete, locked in a deadly serious and emotionally charged situation, to act outwardly as if he was engaged in some pleasant diversion."[6]

Sportsmanship only applies to athletics in an attenuated way, then, involving adherence to the value of *fair play*, which to Keating implies adherence to the letter and spirit of equality before the rules. Since the athletic contest is designed to determine which competitor meets the challenge best, fair play requires that competitors not intentionally disregard or circumvent the rules. Broadly understood, perhaps more broadly than Keating would recommend, fair play requires that victory be honorable. So fair play can be expected of the serious athlete in intense competition, but to also require sportsmanship—the attempt to increase the pleasure of the opponent in the contest—normally is to ask too much.[7]

If sportsmanship can be distinguished from fair play, what is cheating? It is natural to identify cheating with violation of the rules of the game but that surely is not enough. Thus, one who *unknowingly* violates the rules is not a cheater. At the very least, the violation must be intentional, and designed to secure an advantage for the cheater or for some other participant for whom the cheater is concerned.

What makes cheating wrong? There is a tendency to assimilate the wrongness of cheating to promise breaking or to deception. Someone who cheats in tennis, for example, by calling an opponent's serves out when they actually are in, deceives the opponent and can be regarded as breaking an implicit promise binding all competitors to play by the rules.

However, as philosopher Bernard Gert has pointed out in a perspicuous analysis, cheating does not necessarily involve either deception or promise breaking.[8] A competitor who has power over the other competitors may cheat quite openly. Similarly, a revolutionary who cheats on a civil service examination in order to attain a powerful position, which can then be used for purposes of betrayal, may deny that he has ever promised, even implicitly, to obey the rules laid down by the very government he despises. More generally, the idea of an "implicit" promise simply may be too vague to support charges of cheating.[9]

Cheating probably is best identified with intentional violation of a public system of rules in order to secure the goals of that system for oneself or for others for whom one is concerned.[10] Cheating is normally wrong, not only because it deceives or violates a promise or contract, although deceit or violation of a promise may contribute to its wrongness in most cases. However, the distinctive element that accounts for the general presumption that cheating is wrong is that the cheater acts in a way that no one could rationally or impartially recommend that everyone in the activity act. Thus, cheaters make arbitrary exceptions of themselves to gain advantages and in effect treat others as mere means to their own well-being. Cheaters fail to respect their opponents as persons, as agents with purposes of their own, by violating the public system of rules that others may reasonably expect to govern the activity in question. Thus, a golf tournament would not be an athletic contest if everyone cheated because it would not determine who was the best player. The rules of golf are the public system under which it reasonably can be presumed that the participants expect to compete. By violating the rules, cheaters arbitrarily subordinate the interests and purposes of others to their own, and so violate the fundamental moral norm of respect for persons. It may be going too far to say that all competitors have implicitly promised to abide by the rules, but the rules nevertheless are part of the publically acknowledged requirements governing the competition, and all competitors have the right that others abide by them.

We now have provisional accounts of sportsmanship, fair play, and cheating. Perhaps they will be helpful in allowing us to analyze the morality of the actions in sports with which we began our discussion. Alternately, perhaps examination of such cases will suggest the need to revise our accounts of these values. Let us see.

Winning versus Sportsmanship and Fair Play

Consider the example with which we began this chapter. It involved a top-ranked university football team winning a game on a "fifth down" play, which was run because officials lost count and didn't notice that the allotted number of downs already had been used up. Should the winning team, the University of Colorado, have accepted the victory or, as many critics of the university suggested, have refused to accept a tainted win?

Proponents of one view might begin by appealing to Keating's distinction between sports and athletics. They might argue, first, that since a major intercollegiate football game is clearly an example of athletics, neither team is under an obligation to make the experience pleasurable or enjoyable for the other. Moreover, generosity should not be expected either. After all, no one would expect the opponent, Missouri, if a referee, say, had made an incorrect pass interference call in their favor, to not accept the penalty.

Second, Colorado did not cheat, at least as we have defined cheating above. There was no *intent* to violate a public system of rules to gain an advantage. Moreover, it probably is unclear just what is required in the situation that occurred, simply because of its rarity. There are unlikely to be even informal conventions that apply to the situation.

Finally, one might argue, it is at best unclear whether principles of fair play apply. Colorado did not intentionally violate either the letter or spirit of the rules, and in fact was unaware of the true situation. Tapes reveal that on the fourth-down play, the Colorado quarterback looked to the sideline, noticed that the play was officially marked as a third down on the official scoreboard, and intentionally grounded a pass to stop the clock. Had the quarterback believed the play was his team's last down, he surely would have gambled by attempting a touchdown pass, perhaps successfully

But while these arguments cannot just be dismissed, other individuals may think that they rest on an indefensible conception of ethics in competition. To begin with, they might reject Keating's distinction between sports and athletics as misleading. In particular, if it is taken as *descriptive,* it may set up a false dichotomy. Activities need not be classified exclusively as athletics or exclusively as sports but may share elements of each.

More important, we need to ask the normative question. Which conception *should* apply to a particular activity?[11] Thus, to assume that the Colorado-Missouri football game should be regarded as an example of athletics rather than sports, in Keating's sense, is to beg the question about whether or not Colorado should have accepted the victory. By assuming the contest *ought* to be like what Keating calls athletics, we would be assuming the very point that is being debated—namely, whether Colorado ought to have accepted the victory.

Second, critics might maintain that sportsmanship, while certainly not an all-encompassing value, covers more than simply generosity towards opponents. In particular, if athletic contests ought to be regarded as mutual quests for excellence . . . implications follow for sportsmanship. Thus, opponents ought to be regarded as engaged in a cooperative enterprise designed to test their abilities and skills, and whether or not they are owed generous treatment, should be treated as partners in the creation and execution of a fair test. To treat them differently is to reject the presuppositions of the very model of athletic competition that ought to be observed.

Arguably, the Missouri team was not treated in such a fashion. The play that won the game was not allowed by the rules of the game. The fact that the officials were mistaken about how the rule applied does not alter the fact that Colorado did not win the test as defined by the rules.[12] By accepting victory, Colorado did not treat its opponents as partners or facilitators in a common enterprise but instead treated them as a means for attaining the kind of rewards that go with victory in big-time college games.

If this point has force, it suggests that the distinction between sportsmanship and fair play may not be as sharp as Keating's account suggests. If by "fair play" we mean adherence to criteria of fairness implied by the idea of a mutual quest for excellence, it is at best unclear if Colorado's decision was truly fair. If its team did not truly demonstrate superiority by the public code of rules that all parties agree applied to the game, in what sense was the assignment of a victory fair?

Indeed, it is worth noting that in a famous game played forty years before the contest between Colorado and Missouri, a similar incident led to a dissimilar resolution. In the late fall of 1940, an undefeated Cornell team, also in contention for the national championship and a Rose Bowl bid, played a Dartmouth team that was hoping for a major upset. Although trailing late in the fourth quarter, Cornell apparently pulled out a victory with a scoring pass on the game's last play. But did Cornell really win? Film of the game indicated without a doubt that the referee, who admitted the error, had allowed Cornell a fifth down! The game should have ended a play earlier and Dartmouth should have pulled off a major upset.

Although no rule required that Cornell forfeit the victory, soon after the game film's release, "Cornell officials (including the Director of Athletics) telegraphed Hanover formally conceding the game to Dartmouth 'without reservation ... with hearty congratulations ... to the gallant Dartmouth team. ...' Another loss the following Saturday to Pennsylvania helped the Cornell team drop from second to 15th in the Associated Press polls, its season ruined but its pride intact."[13] Should Colorado take pride in its victory? Should Cornell be proud of its loss?

What our discussion suggests so far is that some of the distinctions with which we began our discussion may need to be rethought. If we take fair play as a central value, and understand

it, as perhaps Keating also would, to encompass commitment to the principles supported by the idea of athletic competition as a mutual quest for excellence, it has implications for sportsmanship. Sportsmanship would involve treating opponents in a way fitting their status as partners in a partially cooperative enterprise, namely, the provision of a challenge so that skills and abilities may be tested. Finally, we can question whether even intense competition at high levels of performance *ought* to be regarded as pure cases of athletics in Keating's sense. Although some activities, such as major intercollegiate and professional sports, might justifiably tend more in that direction, a strong case can be made that sportsmanship and fair play should both apply, although perhaps with different emphases, at all levels of sports and athletics. "Athletics," in Keating's sense, arguably ought not to exist at all in its pure form, because unless fair play is understood broadly enough to encompass sportsmanship in the wider sense developed above, "athletics" and the ethic of the mutual quest for excellence are incompatible. Accordingly, the terms "sports" and "athletics" will be used interchangeably in what follows, unless otherwise indicated.

We also need to consider the role of officials and referees in sports. Should we conclude that since opponents in many forms of organized competition delegate responsibility for enforcement of the rules to officials in full knowledge that officials sometimes make mistakes, the decisions of officials should be accepted as ethically final? Alternately, do participants have obligations not to accept unearned benefits arising from particularly egregious official errors, especially those that involve misapplication of the rules rather than "judgment calls" about whether a rule was violated?

We can test our intuition on these issues by considering another kind of case: one where the rules are followed rather than broken but so as to give what many would regard as an unearned advantage to some competitors over others. An example of this is provided in basketball, where the rules of some college and interscholastic organizations require that, after a time-out ends, the referee give the ball to the offensive team, even if the defensive team is not yet ready to continue the competition. Presumably, the intent of the rule is to insure that time-outs are equal in length for each team by eliminating delays caused by coaches taking too much time in the huddle. However, the rule can have unintended consequences. For example, suppose it is applied to a team that is late coming out of its huddle, not because of any intent to gain extra time, but because in the excitement of the moment and noise of the crowd, the buzzer signaling the end of the time-out simply was not heard. Should the other team take advantage of this lapse and, as is allowed by the rules, score even before the other team is on the court?

Here, a much stronger case can be made that the behavior of the offensive team is defensible than in the case of the fifth down discussed earlier. After all, the behavior in question is allowed by the rules. Both teams should be aware of the rules and their implications before the contest starts and should take steps to insure that the noise and confusion in the arena where a major contest is played does not affect their poise or analytic acuity during a time-out. After all, it is not one team's business to insure that the other performs efficiently, but rather to take advantage of inefficiencies as allowed by the rules of the game.

But while such points are not unconvincing, they may not be determinate either. Ask yourself the question, "Is a victory earned in this way significant, one I should take pride in?" I suggest the answer is negative. Presumably, one wants to take pride in being the better basketball team, not being better at noticing the end of time-outs.

Again, the model of athletic competition as a mutual quest for excellence through challenge can be helpful here, although admittedly, it is controversial how it might apply in the kind of case under discussion. Scoring when the opposing team isn't even on the floor is not particularly challenging and does not demonstrate excellence at the activity in question. Arguably, then, such behavior is not "fair play," understood

as adherence to the implications of the model of the quest for excellence. Neither does it involve sportsmanship, understood as treatment of opponents as required by their status as partners obligated to present a challenge to one another. One group of competitors, those that come out of their time-out late, are not even given the opportunity to present a challenge. Their opponent in effect is allowing the rules to be used to avoid the challenge the other team otherwise would present. Attainment of victory is seen as more important than what should be the point of the contest: testing oneself against the challenge presented by other competitors.

Such an analysis, critics might retort, needs to take into account the level at which the contest is played. Here Keating's distinction between "sports" and "athletics" may have a point. Although it may be inappropriate for a team in an eighth-grade contest to win a game by scoring before the opponents are ready, it surely is equally inappropriate for a professional team or a major college team that has worked hard all season to qualify for postseason play, to simply toss the ball in bounds and wait for the opposition to get ready. Surely, that is too much generosity to expect, given the opportunities for success and achievement at stake.

Reasonable people of good will may well disagree over this kind of example. Before making up our minds, however, we should ask what "achievement" and "success" mean in this context. If they mean that the winning team has succeeded in meeting the challenge set by an opponent and has deserved to advance, then it is far from clear that taking advantage of the situation to score is the right option. After all, would anyone—players, coaches, or fans—really want an important championship settled in this way? If not, even if it is controversial whether or not we are morally *required* not to score in such a situation, wouldn't it morally be *better* if all teams, at all levels, adopted the qualities of sportsmanship implied by the idea of a mutual quest for excellence and voluntarily refrained from winning a game by such a tactic?[14]

Cases such as those discussed here are likely to be controversial, and discussion of them may generate disagreement, but it is important to remember that such disagreement occurs against a general background of deeper agreement on sports ethics. None of the parties to the discussion endorse cheating or blatant examples of unfair play or unsportsmanlike behavior. Rather, the disagreement concerns "hard cases" that help us define the boundaries of the values we are exploring. Sometimes disagreement over controversial cases is used as a justification for overall moral scepticism, since it may seem as if no rational resolution is possible. This overall drift to moral scepticism should be resisted, however, for often rational adjudication is possible (as application of the model of the mutual quest for excellence to our cases may suggest) or, if it is not, there still remains deeper agreement on the moral fundamentals that are not at stake in the controversies at issue.

Notes

1. As used here, "sportsmanship" will designate a virtue that can be equally exemplified by males and females of all races and ethnic or socioeconomic backgrounds.

2. James W. Keating, "Sportsmanship as a Moral Category," *Ethics*, Vol. 75 (1964), pp. 25–35, reprinted in Morgan and Meier, *Philosophic Inquiry*, p. 244. All page references to this article will refer to *Philosophic Inquiry.*

3. Morgan and Meier, *Philosophic Inquiry,* p. 244.

4. *Ibid.*, p. 245.

5. *Ibid.*

6. *Ibid.*, p. 247.

7. *Ibid.*, pp. 247–249.

8. Bernard Gert, *Morality: A New Justification for the Moral Rules* (New York: Oxford University Press, 1988), pp. 129–133.

9. The idea of a hypothetical social contract can be useful in explaining the obligations of competitors in sports by identifying such obligations with what rational contractors would consent to under fair conditions of choice. However, the obligation here arises from the reasonableness and fairness of the conditions under which choice is made, not from the dubious claim that people who may never have consciously thought of the terms of the contract actually have signed it.

10. Here I adopt part of Gert's definition, but leave out his requirement that the rules contain no explicit penalty for the act so as to not beg questions that arise later. My analysis of the wrongness of cheating draws on and is indebted to Gert's discussion, but I do not believe he would subscribe to all aspects of my approach. In particular, the emphasis on exploitation of other competitors is my own. See Gert, *Morality,* p. 130ff.

11. My discussion here is indebted to Randolph M. Feezel's discussion in his article "Sportsmanship," *Journal of the Philosophy of Sport,* Vol. 13 (1986), pp. 1–13, reprinted in Morgan and Meier, *Philosophic Inquiry,* particularly pp. 254–256, where Feezel makes similar points.

12. Note that the issue here was not the judgment of the referees in applying a rule. Bad calls can be regarded plausibly as part of the game, in that participants play with the expectation that referees will use their own judgment in deciding whether the rule was violated. However, the Colorado-Missouri game did not involve a judgment call, such as whether pass interference was committed by a defender, but failure to apply a rule at all because of confusion about the number of downs that already had been used up.

13. Ken Johnson, "The Forfeit," *Dartmouth Alumni Magazine,* Oct. 1990, p. 16.

14. This does not imply that teams that actually have taken advantage of such a situation should be *blamed* for doing so, even if in fact it would have been morally better for them to have refrained from scoring. After all, they themselves may have been confused by the unexpected situation and simply reacted as they were trained to. However, coaches might well think in advance of the ethics of such a situation, and ones relevantly similar to it, before it actually arises. Moreover, rule-making bodies certainly ought to consider a change in such a rule so as to distinguish between teams that intentionally stall in a time out (they might be given a technical foul if not on the floor within, say, ten seconds of a referee's warning) and those that simply are distracted, who would be warned by the referee that the time-out ended.

Questions for Consideration

1. Everything Simon has to say concerning sportsmanship hinges on his notion of competitive sport as a "mutual quest for excellence through challenge." Do you agree with this notion of competitive sport?

2. To what extent would Simon's notion of "fair play" rule out psychological tactics in competition?

3. Might there be gender differences in the application of sportsmanship and fair play?
4. According to Simon, the football game between Colorado and Missouri in 1990 did not result in a win for Colorado in any meaningful sense. What does he mean by this? Do you agree?

Cheating

15 Can Cheaters Play the Game?

Craig K. Lehman

That cheating in the practice of sport is logically incompatible with winning is a thesis propounded by many in the philosophy of sport. Taken strictly, Craig Lehman states, this amounts to those practices in which cheating occurs as noninstances of sport. This view, he argues, is false.

First, Lehman considers sporting events in which a deliberate violation of rules occurs. Is it right to say in such cases that no event has occurred? There are numerous instances, many of which are famous.

Second, he looks at nonintentional violations of rules. If the logical incompatibility thesis is correct, then these as well should be instances of nonplay.

The problem with the logical-incompatibility thesis, he asserts, is the failure to distinguish conceptual confusion from moral confusion. This thesis is based on moral confusion—on what ought and ought not to happen in sport—and it draws a conclusion about conceptual confusion, that winning and cheating are logically inconsistent.

Sporting events are social practices, Lehman contends. Some violation of rules has always been socially tolerable, even socially expected. Complete disregard for rules is inconsistent with winning, as dictated by our social expectations, but some contravention of rules is not. Rules do define games, but this is not to say that failure to follow all the rules is a failure to engage in sportive activity.

Reprinted, by permission, from C. K. Lehman, "Can Cheaters Play the Game?" *Journal of the Philosophy of Sport* VIII (1981): 41–46.

A number of recent philosophers of sport have endorsed the thesis that it is logically impossible to win, or even compete, in a game while at the same time breaking one of its rules (intentionally, at least). For instance, Suits argues:

> The end in poker is not to gain money, nor in golf simply to get a ball into a hole, but to do these things in prescribed (or, perhaps more accurately, not to do them in proscribed) ways: that is, to do them only in accordance with rules. Rules in games thus seem to be in some sense inseparable from ends. . . . If the rules are broken, the original end becomes impossible of attainment, since one cannot (really) win the game unless he plays it, and one cannot (really) play the game unless he obeys the rules of the game. (5: pp. 149–150)

The thesis that cheating in a game is logically incompatible with winning that game may sound initially plausible. I imagine everyone has a vague feeling of having heard it somewhere before—perhaps in high school physical education—but I am going to argue that it is false. Undoubtedly, following some "framework" rules is essential to playing any particular game as we know it, and even violation of rules covering "finer points" may in some cases lead us to say that no game worthy of the name has taken place, no real winner been determined. But counterexamples to the unqualified incompatibility thesis advocated by Suits and others (1, 4) are not hard to come by.

I

Consider, first, what people ordinarily say about certain sporting events in which deliberate violations of the rules are known (or at least thought) to take place. (I take it for granted that the issue here is the conventional meaning of such phrases as "compete in a game," "win a game," "deliberately violate the rules of a game," etc. Of course someone can stipulate a sense in which it is impossible for cheaters to "really" win, but the nontrivial question is whether this conclusion is implicit in the ordinary meanings of the words.)

For instance, many baseball fans believe that Atlanta Braves' pitcher Gaylord Perry throws a spitball. Throwing a spitball is a violation of the rules of baseball. Suppose these fans are right about Perry. Does anyone seriously want to say that no baseball game is ever played when Perry pitches? Should Perry be ineligible for the Hall of Fame on the grounds that he has never won a game, let alone competed, in baseball? Yet this seems to follow if we accept the unqualified thesis that cheating and competing are incompatible. And, of course, cases like Perry's—many of them more elaborate, some of them legendary—can be multiplied indefinitely.

A second point is as follows: Why, if Suits's argument is sound, should only *intentional* violation of rules be relevant to the question of whether genuine participation in a certain game (and hence victory) has taken place? (In the first sentence of this essay, I tried to be charitable by adding intention as a parenthetical condition of the logical-incompatibility thesis, but it will be noted that Suits himself does not say this.) The major premise of Suits's argument, after all, is just that one cannot play a game without following the rules of that game; or in the words of another proponent (4: p. 117) of the incompatibility thesis, "the rules of a game are the definition of that game." But the failure of something to conform to an established definition or set of rules is not abolished by the absence of an intention to nonconformity on the part of its creator.

If I draw a four-sided figure with sides of unequal lengths, then I have failed to draw a square, even if I intended to make the sides equal. Thus, it seems that even unintentional violations of the rules of a game should lead us to say that no game (and hence no victory) has occurred, if the usual argument for the logical-incompatibility thesis is correct.

This points the way to more counterexamples. Amateurs almost certainly commit unwitting violations of some rule or other in any game they play, especially while learning. Even in major professional sports, sharp-eyed commentators (and instant replays) often expose accidental violations of the rules, but no one is tempted to say that no game has therefore occurred. Indeed, in team sports, the presence of just one secret cheater on a squad whose members otherwise intend to follow the rules religiously would render the whole team logically incapable of winning.

Let me approach the matter from a different direction. In "Some Reflections on Success and Failure in Competitive Athletics," Delattre, another defender of the logical-incompatibility thesis, remarks:

> Both morally and logically, then, there is only one way to play a game. [That is, by the rules.] Grantland Rice makes clear his appreciation of this point in his autobiography, *The Tumult and the Shouting*. For emphasis, he employs the example of a rookie professional lineman. The athlete responds to Rice's praise for his play during his rookie year by observing that he will be better when he becomes more adept at holding illegally without being caught. Of course, to Rice this confused vision of successful competition is heartbreaking. (1: p. 137)

Now, admittedly, I cannot quite work up a broken heart over this incident, but that is not the main point. My question is rather, what kind of confusion did Rice think his lineman had fallen prey to—conceptual confusion, of the sort which fails to notice the impossibility of round squares and married bachelors, or (alleged) moral confusion of the sort which places winning (or, more precisely, "winning") ahead of playing strictly by the rules? The thesis that cheating and competing are logically incompatible would require the former interpretation (and then, perhaps, we should think of the lineman as heartbreakingly stupid), but I strongly suspect that Rice was disappointed in his lineman's alleged moral confusion. I also suspect that the logical-incompatibility thesis draws part of its appeal from being conflated with the moral thesis; Delattre, for instance, speaks of Rice as appreciating "this point," when there are really two points involved.

II

When one cannot see a pattern to them, counterexamples often seem like trivial nit-picking. In this case, however, I think there is a clear pattern, though perhaps not a particularly profound one. The counterexamples all seem to stem from social custom or convenience (i.e., utility). Games are played within a framework of social practices and priorities, and violations of rules must be assessed within this framework to determine whether competition and victory, in the normal sense of the words, have occurred.

Hence, the spitball and offensive holding are a part of the game of baseball and football, respectively, and are techniques sometimes practiced by winners in those sports. Custom seems the primary reason why a game in which the spitball rule is violated is still baseball: The folklore of the game abounds with gleefully told stories of doctored pitches, bats, playing fields, etc., and booing the umpire (i.e., the embodiment of the rules) is a hallowed tradition. On the other hand, the fact that offensive holding can occur in a game of football seems to be mainly a concession to utility: There is simply no practical way for the officials to see everything that occurs in the interior of the line, and the game would

probably be much less enjoyable to watch if all the infractions were punished (i.e., the offense would be continually frustrated by penalties, if not by the defensive line).

Of course, as I conceded at the outset, a game cannot be played if too many of its rules are violated. There would be no point in calling an activity a game of baseball if none of the rules of baseball were followed, and it is certainly hard to imagine the point when only a few of the rules are followed. Admittedly, too, one can imagine a society of sanctimonious sports purists who allow that a certain game is played only if every rule of that game is strictly followed. But perfect adherence to every rule is not usually essential to the occurrence of a given game, with a genuine winner.

Between the two extremes of angelic obedience to rules and destruction of a game by wholesale violation of its rules is an interesting set of borderline cases, as in professional wrestling: Here, rules against punching, kicking, strangling, etc., are routinely violated, so that even if the outcome were not fixed, there would be considerable question about whether the resulting show was wrestling. In the social context of certain ultra-violent science-fiction movies, the objective of sport usually seems to be the provision of spectacles of mayhem; perhaps in those societies, "illegal" biting and choking would seem as innocuous as the spitball does in American baseball. But in the actual context of our society, I am not sure what to say about professional wrestling.

So, although I concede that at some (probably hard-to-define) point, excessive rule violations become incompatible with playing a given game, and that there also may be certain ideal cases in which exacting conformity to rules is essential, I maintain that (due to social custom and convenience) it is not in general necessary to the playing or winning of games that every rule of those games be obeyed. Pearson (4: p. 116), however, yet another defender of the logical-incompatibility thesis, remarks that "a particular game is no more (in terms of its careful definition) than its rules." She then goes on, in best

Lockean fashion,[1] to state the corollary that "problems of identity and diversity of games are decided by the rules for each game. Identical games have identical rules and diverse games have differing rules." But if I am correct, it should be possible to imagine different games with identical rules (because they are played in the context of different social customs and utilities), and identical games with differing rules (because social customs and utilities negate the difference of rules "in practice"). For example, it seems conceivable (although I do not know this to be the case) that Japanese baseball players are much more earnest about following the rules of the game than American players are. If the spitball were more widely used than it is in American baseball, and if its effect were greater than I think it is, I can easily imagine a Japanese player saying that, because of the spitball, Americans play a different game. In my view, this would be the literal truth rather than just a manner of speech. Also, of course, it is simple to imagine the cases of differential enforcement of rules canceling out differences in rules.

III

So far I have been concentrating on the thesis that cheating and competing are logically incompatible. But the logical-incompatibility thesis often serves as a premise (or at least a background assumption) in moral arguments designed to show that cheating is, without qualification, unethical and/or unsportsmanlike. I therefore want to conclude this essay with a brief examination of one such argument.

The most explicitly worked-out version of this argument that I know of is advanced by Pearson:[2]

I have argued earlier that a particular game is defined by its rules—that the rules of a game are the definition of that game. If this is the case, a player who deliberately breaks the rules of that game is deliberately no longer

playing that game. . . . These acts [i.e., deliberate violations of rules] are designed to interfere with the purpose of the game. If the arguments presented here are correct thus far [and it has been asserted earlier that (1) "the purpose of these games is to test the skill of one individual, or group of individuals, against another . . ." and (2) "If an act is designed by a willing participant in an activity to interfere with the purpose of that activity, then that act can properly be labeled unethical"] we can conclude that the intentional commission of a foul ["an act that is not in compliance with the rules"] in athletics is an unethical act. Ordinarily, when we refer to unethical acts on the part of athletes, we call these acts unsportsmanlike. (4: pp. 116–117)

The major premise of this argument [i.e., item (2) in the brackets] is reminiscent of Kant's second illustration of the first form of the categorical imperative; Pearson also speaks elsewhere of players entering into a contract with their opposition. Obviously, however, discussion of such fundamental principles is beyond the scope of this essay. I grant them for the sake of argument. But consider the other premises.

Understood narrowly enough, I would have no quibble with the assertion that the rules of a game "define" that game; my point has only been that in certain contexts, breaking the rules that "define" a game will not entail that one is not playing that game. Suppose, however, that I am wrong, and the logical-incompatibility thesis is correct. It will still not follow that a player who deliberately breaks the rules of a game is deliberately no longer playing that game. For "deliberately" introduces an intentional context, and validity is not preserved in intentional contexts. (The man behind the arras was Polonius, but it does not follow that in deliberately killing the man behind the arras, Hamlet was deliberately killing Polonius.) Similarly, if someone is too "confused" to appreciate the logical-incompatibility thesis, he or she may deliberately violate a rule without deliberately opting out of the game.

Still, someone might reply, this is irrelevant to Pearson's main point. If her ethical major premise is correct, and if the purpose of games is to test the skill of the participants, then if we just add the premise that someone who deliberately violates the rules of a game is deliberately interfering with a test of the skill of the participants, without trying to deduce it from the logical-incompatibility thesis, the conclusion can still be secured. To be sure, some qualifications might be needed to take care of cases in which rules are deliberately broken for some unusual reason, but the idea would be that in deliberately throwing a spitball (or so we suppose), Perry is deliberately interfering with a test of the batter's skill at hitting a (legal) pitch. In general, cheaters know very well that they are trying to minimize an opponent's chances in a test of skill.

Nevertheless, even if these emendations are allowed, I think the argument is still infected with the same disease I was trying to cure in the last section. For how does one establish that the purpose of a game is a test of its participants' skill? So far as I can see, only by supposing a certain romanticized social context in which custom and convenience dictate that games are played solely to test the players' skill within a certain framework of rules. But that, I would argue, is not the social context of most sports as *we* know them. Indeed, to the extent that it is intelligible to talk of sports having purposes at all (an assumption which apparently goes undefended), sports seem to be multipurpose. Baseball, for example, serves the purposes of providing an income for owners and players, an afternoon's diversion for the casual fan, another installment in a unique kind of larger-than-life drama for a passionate devotee of "the national pastime." Of course, competing in or observing an event in which there are tests of skill basically within the framework of a set of (very complicated) rules is a main purpose of almost everyone concerned with baseball, but a pure test of skill featuring saintly observance of every rule is *the* purpose of baseball only to a few purists.

Thus, I think that Pearson's attempt to derive unsportsmanlike conduct from some kind of frustration of the purpose or goal of a game implicitly falls victim to the same oversight as the thesis that cheating and competing are logically incompatible: It assumes that one can read off what a game (or the purpose of a game) is just by examining the rule book. Admittedly, rule books for games do not contain statements of purposes for those games. But they do set down conditions for winning, and they do proceed on the assumption that the rules are rigorously followed; this makes the hypothesis that the purpose of a game is to determine a winner according to its rules by far the most obvious hypothesis.

I suspect, then, that no argument that makes deliberate violation of rules a sufficient condition for unsportsmanlike conduct is likely to apply to many of the sports we know. And this seems to me as it should be: I have no reason to believe that Perry, if he throws a spitball, or offensive linemen, if they hold, are generally regarded as poor sports by their peers or the fans. On the contrary, it seems likely that many of them are regarded as displaying all the essentials of good sportsmanship. Sportsmanship seems to transcend the rulebook, not only in the sense of sometimes requiring more than adherence to the rules, but also in the sense of sometimes permitting less.

Notes

1. See (3), esp. Bk. II, Ch. 27, sec. 8, "Idea of Identity Suited to the Idea it is Applied to."
2. For similar views, see (1, 2). Keating does not defend the logical-incompatibility thesis, but he does tie unsportsmanlike conduct to frustration of the goal of sport.

Bibliography

1. Delattre, Edwin J. "Some Reflections on Success and Failure in Competitive Athletics." *Journal of the Philosophy of Sport* 2 (1975), 133–139.
2. Keating, James W. "Sportsmanship as a Moral Category." *Ethics* 75 (October 1964), pp. 25–35.

3. Locke, John. *Essay Concerning Human Understanding*. Many editions.

4. Pearson, Kathleen. "Deception, Sportsmanship, and Ethics." *Quest* 19 (January 1973), 115–118.

5. Suits, Bernard. "What is a Game?" *Philosophy of Science* 34 (June 1967), 148–156.

Questions for Consideration

1. The logical-incompatibility thesis results from a definition of sport that entails that no cheating can occur in true sport. Do you agree?

2. Lehman argues that the mistake of logical incompatibilists is conceptual and moral confusion. Is there a way out for logical incompatibilists?

3. Lehman's argument against the logical incompatibility of winning and cheating rests fundamentally on social expectation and social toleration. Do we really expect (and enjoy) some cheating? Ought we to expect and enjoy it?

4. Is it ruinous to Lehman's position that he fails to draw a precise line to demarcate an acceptable amount or kind of cheating from that which is unacceptable?

16 Fair Play: Historical Anachronism or Topical Ideal?

Sigmund Loland
The Norwegian University of
Sports and Physical Education

In this reading, Sigmund Loland, while acknowledging cultural pluralism and moral diversity, addresses the possibility of a common moral code in sportive competition. Traditional moral approaches—such as utilitarianism, Kantianism, and ethical relativism—are fraught with problems. Thus, Loland turns to a formulation of discourse ethics for an attempted solution.

Discourse ethics implies a free, equal, and cooperative search for answers and a pledge to work toward the common good. Participants, in full apprehension of the principles being discussed, voluntarily agree to seek rational consensus on some issue. This approach is rooted in Kantian deontology insofar as it begins with respect for the integrity and dignity of others. However, assuming pluralism and moral diversity, discourse ethics does not require agreement on fundamental principles.

In the remainder of his work, Loland establishes a "fairness norm" and a norm for good play, and then summarizes the pedagogical implications of his own discourse. In keeping with the social nature of sport, Loland argues for a notion of "fairness" in competitive sport that is a voluntary commitment to playing to win, while respecting the rules of the game and an opponent's level of skill, and balancing both internal and external goods of sportive play. The reading ends with a pedagogical challenge to athletes to engage in a discourse of fair play that underscores the internal values of sportive endeavors.

"Fair Play: Historical Anachronism or Topical Ideal?" From *Ethics and Sport,* M. J. McNamee and S. J. Parry (Eds.) (1998) E & F N Spon. Reprinted by permission of International Thomson Publishing Services.

Introduction

The close connection between sport and education is a recurring theme in the history of sport. From the practices of the ancient Greek gymnasium, through the rise of modern competitive sport in nineteenth-century England, and up until today, sport has been considered an important element in the socialization of the young. However, as Peter McIntosh has shown, sport's educational value, both in ancient and modern times, has been seen as depending upon sport being practised in a certain manner and with a certain attitude. (McIntosh, 1979, especially chapters 1–4 and chapter 9). The predominant ideal in modern sport is fair play.

What, then, is the content of this ideal? To what norms does "fair play" refer? As Allen Guttmann points out, references to fair play in nineteenth-century England were closely related to class interests (Guttmann, 1987, pp. 9–19). The ideal was built on an obligation to follow the rules, which conformed well to the interests of the upper class and bourgeoisie who took little interest in "new games" in terms of structural changes of society. Norbert Elias presents similar explanations and also points out that the need for impartial and fair outcomes of competitions increased as gambling became more popular (Elias, 1986, p. 139).

The connection between social and cultural norms and understandings of fair play is just as evident today. Kalevi Heinilä has shown how the interpretation of fair play in soccer differs among groups according to, among other things, age, level of performance and nationality.[1] Per Nilsson describes different and to a certain extent incompatible moralities among soccer clubs at the same level of performance and in the same geographic area, findings he attempts to explain by club culture and local tradition.[2]

Cultural pluralism and moral diversity even at a local level represent a challenge to the meaning of fair play as a moral idea. It represents, too, a key challenge in practice to the coach or physical educator who in one way or the other is using competitive games as a means of education. With this background, the following questions arise: Is a common moral code of conduct in sport competitions possible at all, and if so, how?

Rational Ethics in a Setting of Pluralism and Diversity

A traditional philosophical response is one of rationalism: moral diversity represents no serious obstacle in our search for well-founded ethical standpoints. Philosophical ethics is able to transcend local moralities and establish general ethical principles, such as the utility principle, or the Kantian categorical imperative, valid for all human practice. From here, by adding relevant information, we can deduce rational norms for whatever practice in question.

Such an applied ethics approach can be problematic. One problem is that some ethical theories, such as utilitarianism and Kantianism, are built on incompatible philosophical premises and may sometimes lead to conflicting conclusions in practice. Which theory is the right and best one? Moreover, if our aim is to reach common norms for practice, the approach is problematic as the choice of one particular ethical theory or tradition often excludes proponents of other's views at the very outset of the argument. Last, but not least, strict axiomatic-deductive reasoning tends to overlook the historical and social dimension of human practices: their traditions, their "unwritten rules," and their status as lived and experienced.

Quite to the contrary, the ethical relativist rejects the possibility for a rational ethics. Inspired by the fact that there exist different and sometimes incompatible moralities even within a restricted practice such as soccer at a local level, the relativist is led to the conclusion that ethically speaking, any morality is as good as another. One problem here, of course, is the circularity of the argument. It is hard for the relativist to defend his or her position as anything other than a product of the social and cultural context in which s/he lives. This makes relativism as an ethical standpoint trivial and arbitrary. When facing ethical dilemmas, the relativist can neither deliberate nor suggest solutions in a rational way. As Raz points out, the relativist is driven towards value nihilism and moral apathy (1994, pp. 139–158). In addition, ethical relativism is open to misuse and may serve as a legitimating strategy to avoid moral responsibility and to act immorally. "Everyone else is cheating—it is part of the game!" "Everyone else is using performance enhancing drugs—why shouldn't I?"

How, then, are we to proceed in our attempt to articulate a common, moral code of conduct for a practice acceptable to all parties involved? We can follow the relativist to a certain extent as we accept the fact of cultural and social pluralism both in sport and in society in general. At the same time, experience indicates that within particular practices like sport it is possible to agree on common norms for conduct in spite of differences in fundamental value orientations. There seem to be good reasons for the rationalist's arguments as well.

These assumptions cohere with the basic premises of so-called "discourse ethics."[3] Discourse ethics takes the pluralism of modern life seriously and doubts that moral philosophy can give universally valid answers to fundamental questions on how one should live and on the elements of "the good life." Rather, the role of ethics is limited to establishing fair and impartial procedures in which conflicting interests and normative claims can be adjudicated, The aim is reasoned agreement among participants in a practical discourse.[4] Jürgen Habermas formulates "the distinctive idea of an ethics of discourse" (D) as follows:

> Only these norms can claim to be valid that meet (or could meet) with the approval of all affected in their capacity as participants in a practical discourse. (*Moral Consciousness and Communication Action,* Polity Press, 1990, p. 66)

To be able to reach such common approval, however, certain rules of reasoning apply. Habermas attempts to establish a moral point of view by reinterpreting the Kantian categorical imperative in terms of a principle of universalization (U).[5] A valid norm has to fulfill the following condition:

> *All* affected can accept the consequences and the side effects its *general* observance can be anticipated to have for the satisfaction of *everyone's* interest (and these consequences are preferred to those of known alternative possibilities for regulation). (Jürgen Habermas, *Moral Consciousness and Communicative Action,* p. 65)

(U) requires a procedure in which all parties concerned take part, ". . . freely and equally, in a co-operative search for truth, where nothing coerces anyone except the force of the better argument." A practical discourse has to be public and open to everyone ". . . with competence to speak and act" (Habermas, 1990, p. 198). Egocentric viewpoints have to be abandoned in favor of the perspective of the common good. All participants are asked try to put themselves "in each other's shoes" and thus to engage in a public process of "ideal role taking" in which the interests of all are given equal weight and consideration.

Discourse ethics can be characterized as a kind of contractualism, but differs from the more hypothetical variants, such as Rawls', by underlining the importance of a real discourse in a voluntary, democratic setting.[6] The aim is rational consensus among free and equal parties who grasp cognitively the reasons on which the consensus is based and are thus convinced of their validity. In this way, it is assumed, practical discourses will exert a binding force (*Bindungseffekt*) among the participants to adhere to the solutions upon which they have agreed:

> . . . moral justifications are dependent on argumentation actually being carried out, not for pragmatic reasons of an equalization of power, but for internal reasons, namely that real argument makes moral insight possible.[7] (*Ibid.*)

Discourse ethics is not without critics. One line of critique focuses on its idealistic overtones. In real-life discourses, complete honesty and willingness to listen and let oneself be persuaded by the better argument are hard to find. Discussions are never completely free of force, manipulative arguments and social and psychological pressure. But, as Apel notes, in the non-ideal conditions of real life the vision of an ethical discourse becomes an ideal towards which we have a responsibility to strive continuously; to argue and act as if we are in a situation of *Zwangfrei Kommunikation* (communication free of constraints) (Apel, 1988).

Another line of critique concerns the fact that the approach does not suggest substantial ethical principles but only formal rules to be followed in ethical deliberation. This, it can be argued, leaves the way open for arbitrary conclusions and ethical relativism. The critique can to a certain extent be rejected as the implicit premises for discourse stand solidly in the Kantian tradition. The approach is built on respect for the integrity and dignity of individuals as free and equal parties in a rational discourse. Moreover, if our aim is reasoned agreement on norms for action in particular situations and practices, there is no need for agreement on ultimate justifications. As indicated above, discourse ethics suggests a way of dealing with ethical issues in multi-cultural settings with individuals and groups with differences in fundamental value orientations. Hence, it is of particular interest in the development of ethical norms for a global practice like sport.

What follows below, then, is meant to be one contribution to an open, public discourse on sport. The structure of the argument will be as follows: first, the idea of fairness is examined and a fairness norm is established. Second, I discuss what makes a sport competition "good" for everyone engaged and formulate what will be called a norm for play. The chapter concludes with linking norms for fairness and play in a simple norm system and suggests in this way an interpretation of the ideal of fair play.

Fairness

Where are we to begin? A common understanding of fair play includes two norms which are often referred to as formal and informal fair play (Pilz and Wewer 1987, p. 10 ff.). Formal fair play is expressed as a norm on keeping the written rules of the game, whereas informal fair play prescribes a certain attitude towards the game in terms of doing one's best and respecting one's opponents.

Let us start with examining formal fair play, or what we here will call the fairness norm. A preliminary formulation can go as follows:

1. When engaged in sport competitions, keep the rules!

Can this norm be ethically justified, and if so, how?

Rules in Games

Games are rule-governed practices. The predominant view of rules in games is that they define the very practice of game playing. Searle gives rules which define a practice in this way the well known characterization as "constitutive rules." These rules . . . constitute (and also regu-late) an activity the existence of which is logically dependent on the rules." Searle exemplifies:

> The rules of football or chess, for example, do not merely regulate playing football or chess, but as it were they create the very possibility of playing such games. The activities of playing football or chess are constituted by acting in accordance with (at least a large subset of) the appropriate rules. (J. Searle, *Speech Acts. An Essay in the Philosophy of Language,* Cambridge: Harvard UP, 1969, pp. 33–34)

Searle distinguishes constitutive rules from what he calls regulative rules: "rules which regulate a pre-existing activity, an activity whose existence is logically independent of the rules." Reddiford exemplifies how rule systems in sport include both definitions, constitutive rules and regulative rules (Reddiford 1985, pp. 41 ff.).

Definitions provide a framework for an activity in time and space and by defining requirements on facilities, equipment, and so on. The rule system of tennis, for example, starts with definitions of the dimensions of the court and the qualities of the ball.

The constitutive rules stipulate an end and the means, through prescriptions and proscriptions, by which this end can be attained. They stipulate what is play in a particular game. Constitutive rules do not determine what players have to do but constitute the concept of a permitted, prescribed, or prohibited action and have thus the logical form of "X counts as Y in context C." In tennis, rules 4 through 18 determine what is to count as playing tennis: they determine what is to count as serving and receiving, what it is for a ball to be in play, and what it is to win a point. In what follows, constitutive rules will be referred to with the less technical expression "formal playing rules."

Finally, most rule systems include regulative rules which place certain constraints, restraints or conditions upon ongoing human behavior which is logically independent of the game. For example, an Olympic tennis tournament will have in its rule system rules like "During games, players are not allowed to wear commercial advertisements on their clothes" (X) must (not) be done in context C).[8]

To sum up so far: the formal playing rules provide a conceptual framework necessary to realize a game in practice. "Scoring goals" or "winning points" as determined by the relevant rules is a meaningful activity within the contexts of soccer and tennis only. As the fairness norm is supposed to prescribe how to act in play, (1) can be specified as follows:

2. When engaged in sport competitions, keep the formal playing rules!

(2) seems reasonable as rule conformity appears to be a necessary condition to realize the practice of game playing. However, logical arguments provide no justification for moral action norms. Descriptive statements cannot serve as premises for normative conclusion alone. The point that adherence to a set of formal playing rules is necessary to realize a game in practice, provides no moral reason for abstaining from rule violations. To a player who is more concerned with ending on top in the final ranking of competitors than with the process of playing the game, cheating or the use of violence can be rational strategies. Can (2) be justified from a moral point of view?

The Fairness Argument

Formal playing rules are meaningful only within the practice they conceptualize. These rules have no external function. Logically, games have no direct instrumental value. This logical fact corresponds to an empirical fact: Most of us engage in game playing not because of biological necessity or external force of any kind, but because of values realized in or through the playing of games themselves. We engage in games based on our own intentional goals. This, I believe, is a common sense understanding of what it means to be voluntarily engaged.

Realization of intentional goals linked to a game depends upon realization of that very game. Moreover, the fact that adherence to playing rules is a necessity to realize a game means that, in terms of goal realization, we depend upon other competitors' rule conformity just as they depend upon ours. Here we approach an ethical justification of (2). As Rawls says:

> . . . when a number of persons engage in a mutually advantageous cooperative venture according to certain rules and thus voluntarily restrict their liberty, those who have submitted to these restrictions have a right to a similar acquiescence on the part of those who have benefited from their submission.[9] (J. Rawls, *A Theory of Justice*, Cambridge: Harvard UP, 1971, p. 343)

This is, according to Rawls, an intuitive idea of fairness. It is wrong to benefit from the cooperation of others without doing our fair share. When we voluntarily engage in a rule-governed practice, we enter a more or less tacit social contract in which a moral obligation arises: keep the formal playing rules of the game! Here, then, we have the core justification of the fairness ideal.

In the context of sport, we can suggest a further specification of our fairness norm:

3. When voluntarily engaged in sport competitions, keep the formal playing rules!

Formalism

There are several objections to the fairness norm (3). The main objection is linked to the interpretation of (3) as an expression of what d'Agostino calls game formalism. Formalism implies that a game is only realized as such if it is played in every detail as defined by its rules, or, more precisely, that ". . . no activity is an instance of some particular game G if any rule of G is violated during that activity" (d'Agostino, 1981, p. 9). The problem with formalism is that games become ideal types that are never or almost never realized by their particular instances. This seems counterintuitive and against common sense.[10]

First of all, for formalism to be an intelligible position, we have to presuppose clear-cut and unambiguous rules of which there is no need for interpretation in practice. But surely, rules are not always clear cut and unambiguous. In many sports we find rules that are formulated in vague and general terms. One example can be paragraph 11 in soccer, in which the distinction between being on-side and off-side is introduced. If a player is off-side and at the same time actively involved in play, that player breaks the rules. However, no exact criteria for what it means to be actively involved in play are given. The understanding of this rule will always be a matter of interpretation among the parties involved.[11]

A response here could be that unclear rules represent a problem not to the formalist but to the rule maker. Ambiguous rules have to be reformulated to achieve a greater degree of clarity, and in all circumstances we ought to search for exact criteria for their application. But this response ignores the fact that no game can be completely defined by its rules. Game rules constitute a conceptual framework for, in principle, an infinite variety of play actions. Moreover, some rules, such as the off-side rule, or rules defining aesthetic qualities in ski jumping and figure skating, concern constitutive elements of a sport that add to its fascination precisely because they cannot be defined in exact terms but are a matter of judgment by the parties engaged.

A second and even more fundamental objection to (3) is that the formalist's inability to account for ambiguous rules leads to problems in the understanding of rule violations and penalties. Formalism tends to blur distinctions between game actions and games of differing degrees of fairness, and between fair and unfair game actions and games. To the formalist, the only intelligible characterization of games is "games" or "not-games."

Ethos in Games

This characterization arises from the fact that formalism lacks understanding of the distinction between a game as a system of ideas: as a possible form of conduct expressed by a system of rules, and as a system of action: as the realization in the thought and conduct of certain persons at a certain time and place of actions conceptualized by the rules.[12] Games are defined by rules, but these rules have to be interpreted for games to be realized in practice. Moreover, as games consist of two parties or more, there is need for at least a few common norms on how the rules are to be interpreted. Newcomb *et al.* (1966, pp. 240–241) point to the constitutive function of such shared group norms in human interaction:

> Although norms could not develop apart from the interactional processes of perceiving and communicating with other people, the reverse is equally true. The mutually shared field, as the matrix within which interpersonal perception occurs, presupposes perceptual and cognitive norms at the very least, if there is to be correspondence between the perceptual fields of the interacting persons. That is, if they are to interact realistically they must put similar content into the mutual field, and to do this they must have a common body of norms in terms of which they can organize their perceptions and cognitions. (Newcomb *et al.*, *Social Psychology, The Study of Human Interaction*, London: Routledge and Kegan Paul, 1966)

D'Agostino defines a set of shared group norms on the interpretation of the rules in a game as the ethos of that game; as "... conventions determining how the formal rules of that game are applied in concrete circumstances"; as the ". . . unofficial, implicit, empirically determinable conventions which govern official interpretations of the formal rules of a game" (1981, p. 7, p. 13).

The idea of an ethos allows for a more dynamic understanding of a game. From this perspective, it is easier to deal with the problem of rule violations. The point is this: an ethos of a game draws distinctions between permissible acts which are in accordance with the rules, acceptable acts in terms of certain rule violations which are considered as "part of the game," and rule violations which are considered unacceptable.

Now, the fairness norm can be further specified:

4. When voluntarily engaged in sport competitions, keep the shared ethos of the practice!

Ethos and Ethics

Again, questions and objections arise. Perhaps the most fundamental objection is this: our argument is that a game ought to be played the way certain players at a certain time and place think it ought to be played. We deduce normative conclusions from descriptive premises, which again is to commit a logical error: to put more into a conclusion than can be found in its premises. As said above, ethical relativism leads to problematic consequences in practice. For example, it seems wrong to prescribe adherence to the ethos of a game if this ethos accepts cheating or infliction of harm or injury on other players.

Therefore, the understanding of an ethos cannot be a straightforward empirical one. There is a need here for a distinction between obligations which arise when we voluntarily engage in rule governed practices, such as the obligation of fairness, and basic ethical principles, or what we with Rawls may call "natural duties" which ". . . apply to us without regard to voluntary acts." Natural duties

> . . . have no necessary connection with institutions or social practices: their content is

not, in general, defined by the rules of these arrangements, such as the positive duties to uphold justice, of mutual aid, of mutual respect, and the negative duties of not to injure and not to harm the innocent.[13] (J. Rawls, *A Theory of Justice,* Cambridge: Harvard UP, 1971, p. 114)

Apel's example with the medical doctor who interferes and stops a boxing match due to injury to one of the boxers is meant to illustrate the following: if obligations and basic ethical principles conflict, basic ethical principles have an overruling function (Apel, 1988, p. 230).

In other words:

5. When voluntarily engaged in sport competitions, keep the shared ethos of the practice as long as the ethos does not violate basic, ethical principles!

Rawls lists a norm on the upholding of justice as one of his positive natural duties. An ethos of a game may include an understanding of certain rule violations as acceptable. How can an ethos satisfy the demand on upholding justice if it accepts rule violations?

Intentional and Unintentional Rule Violations

To answer this question, we need to distinguish between different kinds of rule violations.

Unintentional rule violations for which no player can be held responsible occur in almost all games.[14] Sometimes they are caused by bad luck, for example when a soccer player accidentally touches the ball with the hands. Other times they are caused by bad luck and by the fact that participants are devoted and attempt to do their very best in the game, for example when a player, eager to tackle, is too slow and "takes the man instead of the ball". As they represent no intentional attempt to play unfairly, unintentional rule violations do not call for any personal penalty. However, these violations can lead to unfair advantages in the game as such. Usually, therefore, attempts are made to restore the initial situation. In most games, complete restoration of the initial situation is impossible. The point then is to compensate for unfair advantages as far as possible. We see now that even if no individual player can be held personally responsible, unintentional rule violations usually result in a reduction in degree of fairness of the game in which they occur.

Intentional rule violations such as cheating (breaking the rules to get an unfair advantage and trying to get away with it without being penalized) are more problematic. First, and similar to the case with unintentional rule violations, unfair advantages have to be eliminated or compensated for as far as possible. But this is not enough. Intentional rule violations imply breaking the fairness norm. Intentional rule violators "sabotage the game," as it is expressed in many rule systems in sport. There is need here for an additional penalty in terms of a warning or a further reduction of game advantage. If rule violations occur repeatedly, the violator will in many cases be expelled from the game.

The additional penalty for sabotaging the game will always be approximate and a matter of judgment.[15] Therefore, compared to unintentional rule violations, intentional violations usually lead to a further decrease in the degree of fairness of a game.

Now we can rank violations of formal playing rules according to increasing negative influence on degree of fairness qualities of a game in the following way:

1. Unintentional rule violations—unfair advantages are eliminated or compensated for.
2. Unintentional rule violations—unfair advantages are not eliminated nor compensated for.
3. Intentional rule violations—unfair advantages are eliminated or compensated for and additional penalty is imposed.
4. Intentional rule violations—unfair advantages are eliminated or compensated for but no additional penalty is imposed.
5. Intentional rule violations—unfair advantages are not eliminated nor compensated for (and no additional penalty is imposed).

When do we cross the line to an unfair game? One answer is that a game becomes unfair when rule violations have significant and/or decisive influence on the outcome. Usually, unfair games are the product of intentional rule violations in category (4) and (5). But of course, there are no clear-cut criteria here. For example, we may think of a minor, unintentional rule violation of category (1) which, through a chain of cause-effect relationships, is the small difference which in the final instance tips an even game. In situations of doubt, the question of whether a game is fair or unfair can only be dealt with in a practical discourse open to all affected parties: a careful and systematic discourse on the consequences of actual rule violations which again will serve the development of the parties' sense of fairness in that game.

A Sense of Fairness

An ethically acceptable ethos of a game, then, includes a sense of fairness based on similar distinctions and conclusions as sketched above. Permissible acts are in accordance with the rules. Some acts in terms of category (1) and (2) are ethically acceptable at an individual level, but unfair advantages in the game arising from such acts have to be eliminated or compensated for. Intentional rule violations within categories (3) to (5) are ethically unjustifiable as they represent a violation of the moral contract underlying the fairness principle. Intentional rule violations must be rejected as part of an ethos of any sport.

Now we can formulate the fairness norm in its final form:

6. When voluntarily engaged in sport competitions, keep the shared ethos of the practice as long as the ethos does not violate basic, ethical principles and includes a sense of fairness!

Problems Linked to Practice

Objections to (6) could focus on possible problems with applying the norm in practice. First of all, how can adherence to vague, tacit, unwritten norms be a moral obligation? How can one demand adherence to an ethos of a game which, especially to newcomers, can be hard to grasp?

An ethos arises in an interactive process between formal playing rules and norms for their interpretation. As a first step, a player ought to take a closer look at the written rules. However, an ethos can only be learned and internalized through practice. A new player has to be socialized into the game. I guess we could argue that, when voluntarily engaging in a new game, we have a moral obligation not only to learn its formal playing rules, but to keep our eyes and ears open for the hidden language expressed through movements, attitudes, and comments among experienced players. We ought to find our way into "the mutually shared field" or the culture of the game as soon as possible.

A second objection is this: contrasting d'Agostino, we exclude from an ethically sound ethos the idea of acceptable intentional rule violations. In some games, however, some intentional rule violations (such as certain forms of body contact in professional basketball, which is d'Agostino's example) have become "part of the game." To violate certain rules intentionally has become a "shared norm" among players. The advantage gained by such violations is, in principle, open to all competitors. This seems fair enough. Why should norms accepting such conduct be excluded from an ethically sound ethos?

The reason is that in any practice in which intentionally breaking certain rules becomes a "shared norm," there is a gap between the practice as a system of ideas and as a system of action. This is a sign of degeneration. The gap ought to be bridged as it confuses the understanding of what a practice is all about and diminishes respect for rules among its practitioners. One consequence is that the view of a practice as a carrier of commonly accepted social norms ("Keep the rules!" "Do not cheat!") becomes problematic.

Another problem is this: if the idea of acceptable intentional rule violations in a sport becomes widespread, different groups may after a while include different rule violations in their ethos. This again will lead to a differentiation of standards of excellence. If parties with differing standards meet, competitions become unfair. What counts as a fair advantage for one competitor might count as unfair for another. If the differences in ethos are significant, we may end up with completely different games. Now competitions between parties with differing ethos become non-intelligible: they cannot be realized in practice at all.

It is important to underline, however, that conflicts between formal playing rules and practice are not always solved by holding on to the rules. Even if they are the stable core of an ethos, rules represent no absolute and static definition of a game. They are the dynamic products of a historical process. Today, new technical and tactical solutions, new technology and rapidly improving levels of performance challenge established rule systems and their ethos in many ways. With strong pressure from external interests aiming at profit and prestige, there is an urgent need for open and rational discourses to evaluate the consequences in games of suggested and actual changes in their rules and practices.[16]

In conclusion, then, the argument is that the fairness norm (6) can serve as a basis for reasoned agreement among free and equal parties in a practical discourse. Thus, (6) can be one element in a common moral code of conduct for sport competitions.

Play

The fairness norm (6) prescribes players to adhere to the ethos of games. (6) is based on the intuitive idea that when we are voluntarily engaged in rule governed practices, we enter a social contract in which we are mutually obliged to follow the rules.

But, as we all know, fair games are not necessarily experienced as good games. A common moral code of conduct for sport competitions ought to include a norm on the realization of good games as well.

Usually, characterization of a game as "good" refers to experiences of that game as exciting, challenging, fun, dramatic, joyful. These experiential qualities seem again to depend upon whether the game is played with a certain attitude: with intensity and devotion. I believe this is the idea underlying the formulation of a norm on informal fair play:

7. Do your best and treat opponents with respect!

How can (7) be elaborated and ethically justified?

The Play Tradition

To a certain extent, the historical background of informal fair play is to be found in the culture of social élites. Liponski has traced the idea of virtuous conduct in games and battle back to élite Roman troops stationed in England in the third century AD (Liponski, 1988). The idea was further developed in the chivalry culture of the Middle Ages and elaborated and linked to sport by the English middle and upper class in the last century.

Norms on a particular "disinterested" play attitude constituted the core of the amateur ideology so dominant in modern sport history in general and in Olympic history in particular. Informal fair play seems to be rooted in a particular tradition linked to a social and economic situation which allowed for non-instrumental and exclusive ideals.

Although justified in a different way, we find a similar view of the moral superiority of play in the theories of authors, historians, psychologists and philosophers such as Plato, Schiller, Huizinga, Maslow, Sartre and Csikszentmihalyi.[17] In play we

are most truly human, play lies at the heart of culture, play offers "peak experiences" and "deep flow," play opens for existential self-realization.

No doubt, the amateur ethos and the many theories of play provide significant insights into the meaning and value of games. However, in an attempt to establish a common code of conduct in a setting of moral diversity, these views simply take too much for granted. It is an empirical fact that many competitors take part with an instrumental attitude. They see sport as a means to external pay off, primarily in terms of profit and prestige. Usually, and probably rightly, such an instrumental attitude is considered the cause of a dehumanization of sport. Competitors become means to external goals only. On the other hand, it should be mentioned that an instrumental attitude can be morally justifiable, for example in extreme situations in which sport success becomes a way out of social, economic and political misery. Is it possible to find a point of departure here acceptable to all affected parties in their capacity as participants in a practical discourse on sport?

Utilitarianism

One premise in the justification of the fairness norm (6) is that competitors are voluntarily engaged. As mentioned above, voluntary engagement can be understood as an expression of certain intentional goals of individual players. It is reasonable to assume, then, that a player experiences a particular game as good if that player's intentional goals have been realized in or through that game. From the point of view of the common good, we may say that a game can be considered as good if all parties, or at least as many parties as possible, get their intentional goals realized to the greatest possible extent.

This line of reasoning is somewhat different from the deontological framework built on consensus among free and rational parties justifying (6). Deontologists believe that "right" cannot be defined in terms of "good."[18] In fact, deontologists see no clear-cut relationship between the two. Of course, consequences of an action are of importance in characterizing it as right or wrong. But as we have seen, ideas of morally binding contracts and of fairness can overrule these considerations. To the teleologist, however, "good" is defined independently of "right," and "right" is what maximizes "good." In order to start our argument on the good game with as few restrictive assumptions as possible, I choose teleological premises by examining the consequences of actions in terms of their potential in realizing intentional goals.

Among teleological ethical theories, utilitarianism, in which ". . . an act is right if, and only if, it can be reasonably expected to produce the greatest balance of good or the least balance of harm," has been one of the more influential (Beauchamp, 1991, p. 129). There are of course different interpretations of the meaning of "good" and how "goodness" ought to be assessed. For example, classical utilitarianism (Bentham, Mill) prescribes the maximization of total happiness among all parties concerned in a calculus in which, according to Bentham's classical rule of reasoning, "everybody (is) to count for one, nobody for more than one."

Classical utilitarianism has been exposed to stern criticism. Critics argue that the theory can be used to justify what seems highly unreasonable and immoral. In certain situations, it is claimed, utilitarianism can justify the suppression of minorities in a society, or the breaking of rules, norms and agreements, with reference to the maximization of "total happiness" among all parties concerned.[19] Modern versions, such as R. M. Hare's, attempt to avoid some of the critique by, among other things, distinguishing between two levels of moral thinking. At level one, we follow intuitions and the socially accepted norms and values of our societies. The need for moral reflection at level two arises in conflicts of interests or in situations in which we are in doubt on what is the right solution. To Hare, the right solution is the one that maximizes average utility among the parties concerned.[20] Utility is understood in terms of preference-satisfaction, or, in our terminology: in terms of the realization of intentional goals.

We will attempt a utilitarian line of reasoning at this second, critical level. Who, then, are to be counted as parties concerned in sport competitions and what are their intentional goals?

Internal and External Goals

In this context, we will concentrate on the goals of competitors who are the parties most directly involved. Intentional goals here are probably as many and as diverse as the competitors themselves. But this does not leave us without analytic possibilities. When we discuss voluntary engagement in institutionalized practices like sport, we may distinguish, logically, between two categories of goals.

Internal goals are realized within the very practice of game playing. They take the character of experiential values such as the excitement of a tight tennis game, the joy of a well coordinated attack in soccer, the kinesthetic pleasure of rhythm in a successful race in alpine skiing. The realization of internal goals depends upon the realization of the game according to the shared ethos that conceptualizes it. Hence, their realization presupposes fairness.

External goals, on the contrary, are realized outside the game but depend on the realization of the practice as a means towards their realization. Examples here can be the wish for prestige and profit. External goals can be realized even if the holder of such goals does not play according to the relevant ethos. Their realization does not presuppose fairness. Let us take a closer look at how these general categories can be specified to sport competitions.

"Play To Win!" or "Win!"

In terms of logical structure, sport competitions can be characterized as *zero sum* games in which two or more parties strive for a mutually exclusive goal. If we talk about two-person games, we may say that what one player gains, the other player loses. The final goal is to end on top in the final ranking of competitors: to win.

Based on our distinction between internal and external goals above, there are two ways to understand what it means to win. First, if a competitor is motivated by internal goals, s/he searches for goal realization within the very activity of competing. As the realization of internal goals depends upon ethos conformity, the competitor plays fair. "Winning" means to end on top in the final ranking of competitors according to performance of the skills defined by the shared ethos of the game. "Play (according to the shared ethos of the practice) to win" is an internal goal in competitive games.

Second, "winning" can be understood as a means towards realization of external goals. Usually, external goals such as profit and prestige depend upon ending on top in the final ranking of competitors. Winning in this respect can be achieved even at the cost of ethos violation and unfair play. "Win (by ending on top in the final ranking of competitors)!" is an external goal linked to competitive games.

A Utilitarian Calculus

Now we are able to match internal and external goals in two-person *zero sum* games to see what goals competitors ought to act upon to maximize average goal realization among all parties concerned. There are three possible constellations:

a. "Win!" against "Win!"
b. "Play to win!" against "Win!"
c. "Play to win!" against "Play to win!"

If we assume that the players in question are at a similar level of athletic skills and of similar motivational (goal) strength, the utilitarian argument goes as follows:

In competition a), both competitors hold and act on external goals prescribing them to win by ending on top in the final ranking of competitors (if necessary, even at the cost of ethos violations). Here, the classical *zero sum* game structure with two parties striving for a mutually

exclusive goal overlaps with the game as "lived" and experienced. Independent of who wins the game, one out of two will experience goal realization. Average goal realization among all parties concerned will be 1:2.

In competition b), competitor X holds and acts on the internal goal of playing to win whereas competitor Y attempts to win by ending on top in the final ranking. To estimate the outcome in terms of goal realization is more complicated. However, assuming that X and Y are at a similar level of skill, it is reasonable to expect Y's chance of goal realization to be higher than X's. The reason is that Y's goal of ending on top in the final ranking of competitors does not require conformity to what X believes is a shared ethos. On the contrary, rule violations and cheating can be an efficient strategy, especially against X who takes the ethos seriously.

Competition b), then, is open to several outcomes. The minimum outcome is similar to competition a): Y wins by violating the ethos if necessary whereas X realizes that the outcome is based on cheating and has no experience of having played a game at all. The outcome is 1:2.

However, even if Y ends on top in the final ranking of competitors, X may experience goal realization. If X does not know of Y's cheating, or if Y wins without cheating, X will probably experience goal realization to a certain extent, or, in the best possible outcome, complete goal realization in terms of having had the experience of "playing to win." In other words, in competition b) average goal satisfaction among all parties concerned will range from 1:2 to 2:2.

In competition c), the situation is yet another. Here, X meets player Z who has internal goals as well. X and Z both "play to win." The final ranking of competitors plays no role in the estimation of goal realization. The decisive point is that X and Z get the experience of having played to win in the very process towards the final ranking. If we assume, as above, that the players are evenly matched in terms of level of skills and goal strength and thus are able to inspire and motivate each other optimally, we will reach full goal realization for both parties: 2:2. This, then, will be a paradigmatic case of a good sports competition.[21]

Now we can suggest a preliminary conclusion:

8. Play (according to the shared ethos of the practice) to win!

(8) is developed with the aim to realize good games in which high average goal realization is reached among all parties concerned. The norm is justified by referring to experiential qualities in the very playing of games in itself: to its autotelic values. As we have seen, play is often held to be the paradigmatic example of autotelic activities. Now, then, we can reformulate the view of the value of play criticized above. But we do so with a different, teleological justification in which, as a point of departure, all parties' intentional goals count as equal irrespective of content. (8), then, is suggested as a norm for play on which free and equal parties in a practical discourse can rationally agree.

A Subnorm on the Matching of Even Competitors

Our utilitarian calculus is a thought experiment. It is indeed simplistic and hypothetical, and it is built on several presuppositions which may seem problematic. For example, the utilitarian argument presupposes that the competitors are at a similar level of athletic skills and that their intentional goals are of similar strength. Are these rational presuppositions, or do they make the reductionist aspects of our thought experiment even stronger?

I believe these presuppositions are reasonable as they reflect sport practice in real life. In non-organized play and games, most of us look for other competitors at a similar level of skill and with similar attitudes to the game as ourselves. A tennis match between a top ranked professional and a beginner would perhaps have some interest as a curiosity, but would hardly turn out as a good game with high average goal realization among all parties concerned. However, a match with players at a similar level of skill and with similar goal strength would have challenged and motivated both players and made both play towards their very best. The chance for high average goal realization would be significantly increased.

A norm on even matching of competitors is followed even more strongly in organized sport. In individual sports, like tennis and golf, players are ranked according to previous performances. The aim is to realize even contests. Team sports like basketball, handball, volleyball, and soccer organize their activities by playing in leagues and series according to performances as well. It is reasonable to assume that level of skill here, at least to a certain extent, correlates with motivational strength. Hence, (8) prescribing competitors to "Play to win!" seems to be based on reasonable premises as the norm on even competitors to a large extent reflects the practicing of sport in real life.

A subnorm to help maximize average goal realization among all parties concerned, then, could be: "Choose competitors at similar levels of athletic skills and motivational strength!"

Utilitarianism—A Critique

The play norm (8) is by no means unproblematic. Several objections may arise due to the very framework for reasoning: utilitarianism.

Utilitarianism has strong intuitive appeal but is built on problematic premises.[22] As indicated above, a utilitarian calculus can be criticized for being reductionist and highly theoretical. Human beings are not just sites in which preferences and their fulfillment or nonfulfillment occur. Moreover, human acts are never determined by one specific preference or intentional goal only. Players have, of course, a variety of motives for engaging and acting in games. Their goals may vary from game to game and from situation to situation. How can our thought experiment say anything of the good game at all?

The aim here is neither to suggest a particular

(reductionist) view of personhood nor to give a complete empirical description of the motivational system of participants in sport. Rather, I have attempted to evaluate, critically and systematically, what kind of intentional goals competitors ought to act upon to realize good games. If (8) becomes the predominant action norm (even if some competitors in real life are motivated by external goals only), goal realization in terms of 1:2 will be the minimum outcome but with significant chances for higher outcomes all the way up to the maximum of 2:2. Therefore, in our search for a common moral code of conduct for sport competitions, we take (8) to be a rational action norm.

Another criticism of utilitarianism is this: a theory demanding conduct which in all circumstances aims at the maximization of average goal realization among all parties concerned, is simply demanding too much. For example, how can one justify ethically fair play norms requiring not only adherence to a shared ethos, but complete devotion in terms of playing to win in all games?

Sport competitions have the logical structure of *zero sum* games in which two parties or more strive for a mutually exclusive goal: to win.

However, to most of us, there is more to a game than an outcome in terms of a final ranking of competitors. Without willingness among all competitors to play to win, competitive games lose not only reliability as skill tests, they also lose their potential of becoming good games. Their logical structure is undermined together with their value as experienced and "lived."

This leads to a similar justification of the play norm as of the fairness norm (6). The general idea is that it is wrong to benefit from the cooperation of others without doing our fair share. We have assumed that we engage in game playing to realize intentional goals of different kinds. The utilitarian calculus has shown that maximization of average goal realization among all parties concerned depends upon all parties "Playing to win." In good games, we depend upon other competitors "playing to win" just as they depend upon us. Our fair share in the cooperative venture of sport competitions includes therefore an obligation to strive for the realization of games which are experienced as good to all parties engaged by adhering to the following norm:

9. When voluntarily engaged in sport competitions, play to win!

Now we see the role played by teleological arguments within the deontological framework of discourse ethics. The view of the play norm (9) as an obligation implies a radical break with a strict utilitarian line of thought. Even if the utility principle and decision theoretical considerations are important, the play norm is finally justified by referring to the binding force of solutions rationally agreed upon among free and equal parties in a practical discourse.[23]

The Sweet Tension of Uncertainty of Outcome

Hence, we have suggested a fairness norm:

6. When voluntarily engaged in sport competitions, keep the shared ethos of the practice as long as the ethos does not violate basic, ethical principles and includes a sense of fairness!

and a play norm:

9. When voluntarily engaged in sport competitions, play to win!

These norms, we believe, can serve as a common moral code of conduct for competitors in terms of being able "to meet with the approval of all affected in their capacity as participants in a practical discourse."

So far, we have been careful with more general formulations of the value of these practices. The reason is that such formulations are easily tied to particular traditions and serve thus to exclude others.[24] At the same time, there is a close relationship between norms and values. The relationship is a complex one and cannot be extensively dealt with here.[25] A common view, however, is that action norms are based on and find their justification in more general values. The question now is if it is possible to point at one or a few values particular to sport competitions which are open for interpretation in the variety of social and cultural contexts in which competitors find themselves.

The fairness norm (6) and the play norm (9) are closely related. (6) requires ethos conformity and constitutes a conceptual framework for the very activity of competing. By adhering to the fairness norm (9), we realize a game element Roger Caillois calls *agon*: "a struggle in which equality of chance is artificially created in order to make sure that the antagonists confront each other under ideal circumstances."[26] In this way, competitive games become predictable practices.

As sport competitions are *zero sum* skill games, *agon* will always be the dominant element. But, at the same time, good games in which competitors "play to win," include an element of chance (*alea*) and unpredictability as well: "...a rupture between merit and reward, ... an incongruence between result produced and the intended action produced from the skill and the effort of the player."[27] The play norm (9) is founded on an analysis of intentional goals and adds content in terms of meaning and value to the conceptual framework defined by (6).

In tight and good games, there will be a thoroughgoing uncertainty at all levels. Does the ongoing technical and tactical choice succeed? Who is in the lead right now? Who will win in the end? To a certain extent, competitive games are, and ought to be, unpredictable practices.

Here, then, in the optimal balance between predictability and unpredictability and between meritocratic justice and chance, a particular experiential structure arises which can be seen as specific for these practices: what we may call "the sweet tension of uncertainty of outcome."[28] This term refers more to the phenomenological structure of the valuable sport experience than

to a particular view on the value of sport for society and education. Tight games in which the outcome is uncertain to the very end are popular in most cultural and social settings, but are interpreted and legitimized differently in different groups and societies.

By pointing at the particular value structure of good competitions, we come close to a general idea of the value of sport in moral education. In sport competitions practised according to the norms of fair play, focus is led away from partial and narrow interests. If competitors play according to the relevant ethos and play to win, a moral community can arise in which "the sweet tension of uncertainty of outcome" becomes a shared, intrinsic goal for everyone engaged.

Possibility for experiences of such a common, intrinsic goal might be the best legitimation of sport competitions as a means in education one can ask for. Through such experiences, we might be able to reach a more general goal of pressing importance in our modern, pluralistic societies: to provide young people with experiences of the possibility for cooperation within a fair framework in particular practices and institutions in spite of differences in fundamental value orientation.

Concluding Comments

I have attempted to demonstrate the possibility for a common moral code of conduct for sport competitions in a setting of cultural and moral diversity. Moreover, I have pointed at what we consider to be the very basis for the educational value of competitive sport: the experience of a moral community in good games in which each player enjoys, and benefits from, fair cooperation with others.

The fair play norms (6) and (9) are not in themselves radical or spectacular. They are reformulations of a common understanding of the ideal sketched out in the introduction. What is of importance here is their justification through a practical discourse in which we search for solutions which parties from different cultural, social and moral traditions can accept as their own. The very framework of this discourse is built on a meta-principle which is a fairness norm in its most general form: when voluntarily engaged in a practical discourse between free and equal parties, a moral obligation arises to follow the conclusions upon which we rationally agree.

As said initially, discourse ethics leads to solutions and moral insights only if the discourse is carried out in practice. The pedagogical challenge in the use of competitive games in education lies, I believe, in engaging students in such a discourse to cultivate their sense of fair play from within. This can be done by using as a point of departure concrete conflicts arising in the course of play, through analysis of the consequences of different action norms in practice, through the staging of role plays in which students play the "cheater," the "fair player," the "spoil sport" who is not putting effort into play, and so on. Any further elaboration of the practical-pedagogical consequences of the fair play-norms and their justification is beyond the scope of this chapter. However, such an elaboration ought to be an intimate part of our practical discourse on sport. It is through its relevance for practice that the fair play ideal can prove its status as something more than a historical anachronism: as a topical ideal.

Notes

1. Heinila examined players between the age of 15 and 18 in Finland, Sweden and England. In England, a distinction was drawn as well between amateurs and players with association to professional clubs. For a review of the study, see McIntosh, 1979, pp. 128–139.

2. Or, to be more precise, by using Bourdieu's (1990, pp. 52–79) concept of *habitus*. Nilsson 1993.

3. Elsewhere, I have suggested a Rawlsian interpretation of the fair play-ideal based on hypothetical contract theory (Loland, 1989). In a practical setting like that of a coach or a physical educator, however, discourse ethics, which sets up rules for and demands real life arguments, might be a more relevant approach.

4. This version of discourse ethics is built an the works of Habermas and Apel. See, for example, Habermas' *Moral*

Consciousness and Communicative Action (1990) (an English translation of *Moralbewusstsein und kommunikatives Handeln* from 1983) and Apel's *Diskurs und Verantwortung. Das Problem des Überganges zur postkonventionellen Moral* (1988) (*Discourse and Responsibility. The Problem of Conversion to Postmodern Morality*). In fact, here Apel gives a contribution to sport ethics too with his essay "Die ethische Bedeutung des Sports in einer universalistischen Diskursethik."

5. The categorical imperative states that one ought never to act except in a such a way that one also will that one's maxim become a universal law. For an introduction to Kantian ethics, see Beauchamp 1991, pp. 169 ff.

6. See, for example, Habermas' critique of Rawls and Rawls' reply in *The Journal of Philosophy*, Volume XCII, No. 3, March 1995.

7. On this point, Habermas elaborates ideas from Ernst Tugendhat. See Habermas 1990, p. 57, pp. 68 ff.

8. This is a simplification of the complex relationship between constitutive and regulative rules. First of all, the distinction itself is much discussed. See, for example, d'Agostino's (1981, pp. 9 ff.) critique of the distinction between constitutive and regulative rules, and Morgan's (1987, pp. 4 ff.) countercritique and defense of the distinction. Moreover, regulative rules can be of different kinds and have different degrees of influence on game practice. For example, rules which specify and regulate eligibility, admission, training, and other activities outside the realm of the competition itself are by Meier (1985, p. 10) called 'auxiliary rules.'

9. Rawls 1971, p. 343. For a discussion of the background of this interpretation of fairness, see Simmons 1979, pp. 307–317. See also Wigmore and Tuxill (1995) who discuss different approaches to the understanding of the concept of fair play. Our approach here will be based on contractarianism and on the view of sport competitions as cooperative enterprises.

10. This problem d'Agostino refers to as game Platonism: ". . . if a rule of G is violated during an alleged instance of G, then this alleged instance is not in fact a genuine instance of G." *op. cit.*

11. See Kristiansen (1995) for an in-depth discussion of these aspects of the off-side rule.

12. For the distinction between systems of ideas and systems of actions, see Eckhoff and Sundby 1976, pp. 22–23, and Rawls 1971, p. 55.

13. A more elaborate discussion of general ethical requirements on social practices is beyond the scope of this chapter.

14. The discussion of rule violations is based on Fraleigh 1984, pp. 71–79 and Loland 1989, pp. 131–136.

15. These judgments are not always as good as they ought to be. For example, insufficient penalties sometimes open

the way for professional fouls: breaking the rules openly and accepting a penalty because the advantage gained on a long term basis is considered to outweigh the immediate costs. Here, then, there is need for modifications of rules or new ways of interpreting them in practice. In a just rule system in which penalties correspond perfectly to the unfair advantages gained by violations, professional fouls would be an impossibility. For a discussion of the moral status of "the good foul," see Fraleigh 1988, pp. 268–269. For further discussion of requirements on a just rule system, see Loland 1989, pp. 71–146.

16. I have dealt extensively with this question elsewhere (Loland and Sandberg 1995) and mention but a few points here. Actual or suggested changes in the rules or practice of a sport ought to be exposed to two tests. The first test concerns whether the change conflicts with basic ethical principles, or what we above have called "natural duties." If such conflicts are apparent, the change ought to be rejected. If not, the change in question ought to be critically and systematically evaluated and rejected or accepted on the basis of what we may call "ludic rationality." The following questions are of relevance: Does the change in question influence in any way what kind of skills are being measured and compared, and if so, is such an influence acceptable ("the question of validity")? What are the influences on the very evaluation process of performance of skills ("the question of reliability")? And: What are the consequences for experiential values (fun, excitement, thrill) among the parties concerned ("the question of play")?

17. For an overview of different views on play in sport, and for a good bibliography on the topic, see Morgan and Meier 1988, pp. 1–76.

18. For the distinction between deontological and teleological ethical theories, see Rawls 1971, p. 30.

19. For a further discussion of weaknesses linked to the classical version, see for example Parfit 1984, pp. 381 ff.

20. Hare's version of utilitarianism, the so-called universal prescriptivism, is developed in Hare 1963, 1981.

21. So far we have dealt with two-person games. However, we may assume that, even if the quantities of average goal realization would be somewhat different, analysis of n-person games would give similar conclusions. If competitors act on external goals, only one can reach goal realization. If, on the other hand, all competitors hold and act upon the goal "play to win," the possibility for goal realization among all parties concerned still exists. But this more extensive decision theoretical argument is beyond the scope of this chapter.

22. For a discussion of utilitarianism and its critics, see Sen and Williams (1982), Scheffler (1988) and Beauchamp (1991, pp. 155–168).

23. What, then, if our utilitarian conclusions had contradicted the fairness norm? If, for example, "Win (even at the cost of ethos violations)!" had turned out to be (in utilitarian terms) the right solution, we would have had to engage in a new process of deliberation and examination. A first step would have been to look for possible flaws in our argument and to search for relevant information which might have been overlooked in the first place. If, however, on due reflection, our conclusions were the same, we would have had to consider the fertility of the utilitarian approach and looked for alternatives. In other words, in case of conflict between teleological and deontological reasoning, we would attribute to deontology the overriding function.

24. In Western Europe and the US, it is often said that sport is of value as an education for life in a competitive society. Former East Germany had as part of their constitution that sport was of value as a means to demonstrate the superiority of socialism over capitalism. In Norway, competitive sport for the young is legitimated by, among other things, its supposed value in education for democracy.

25. For the relationship between norms and values in normative systems, see Tranøy 1988, pp. 144 ff.

26. Caillois 1961, pp. 14–17. The ideal of *agon*, always to strive to be the best among equals, has roots in the heroic myths of ancient Greece (Homer) and is said to have permeated Greek aristocratic culture and Greek sports from which our Western culture has inherited so much.

27. Wachter 1985, pp. 53, 55. For a description of *alea*, see Caillois 1961, pp. 17–19. To a larger or lesser extent, all games include a certain element of chance. Scoring goals in soccer and points in tennis are usually a reliable measure of skill, but might be a matter of chance as well. And, this is a desirable state of affairs. The expression among soccer aficionados "The ball is round" refers not to an unfortunate defect in the soccer rules, but to one of the key qualities of the game.

28. Kretchmar 1975, p. 30, who attributes the expression to Warren Fraleigh.

Bibliography

Apel, K.O. (1988) *Diskurs und Verantwortung. Das Problem des Übergangs zur postkonventionellen Moral.* Frankfurt am Main, Suhrkamp.

Beauchamp, T.L. (1991) *Philosophical Ethics. An Introduction to Moral Philosophy.* New York, McGraw-Hill (2. ed).

Bourdieu, P. (1990) *The Logic of Practice.* Cambridge, Polity Press.

Caillois, R. (1961) *Man, Play and Games.* New York, The Free Press.

d'Agostino, F. (1981) "The Ethos of Games." *Journal of the Philosophy of Sport* VIII, pp. 7–18.

Eckhoff, T. and Sundby, N.K. (1976) *Rettssystmer. Systemteoretisk innføring i rettsfilosofien.* Oslo, Tanum-Norli.

Elias, N. (1986) "The Genesis of Sport as a Sociological Problem," Elias, N. and Dunning, E.: *Quest for Excitement—Sport and Leisure in The Civilising Process.* Oxford, Basil Blackwell, pp. 126–150.

Fraleigh, W.P. (1984) *Right Actions in Sport. Ethics for Contestants.* Champaign Ill., Human Kinetics.

Fraleigh, W.P. (1988) "Why the Good Foul Is Not Good." Morgan, W.J. and Meier, K.V. (eds.): *Philosophic Inquiry in Sport.* Champaign Ill., Human Kinetics, pp. 267–270.

Guttmann, A. (1987) "Ursprunge, soziale Basis und Zukunft des Fair Play." in: *Sportwissenschaft* 1, pp. 9–19.

Habermas, J. (1990) *Moral Consciousness and Communicative Action.* Translated by Lenhardt, C. and Nicholson, S.W. Cambridge UK, Polity Press.

Habermas, J. (1991) *Erläuterungen zur Diskursethik.* Frankfurt am Main, Suhrkamp.

Hare, R.M. (1963) *Freedom and Reason.* London, Oxford University Press.

Hare, R.M. (1981) *Moral Thinking: Its Levels, Method and Point.* Oxford, Clarendon Press.

Johansen, K.E. (1994) *Etikk—en innføring.* Oslo: Cappelen.

Kretchmar, R.S. (1975) "From Test to Contest. An Analysis of Two Kinds of Counterpoint in Sport" in: *Journal of the Philosophy of Sport* II, pp. 23–30.

Kristiansen, K.P. (1995) "Fotballens etiske grunnlag," Unpublished manuscript, The Norwegian University for Sport and Physical Education, Oslo.

Liponski, W. (1988) "Recognizing the Celts: Some Remarks on The British Origins of the Modern Fair Play Concept," Budapest, Magyar Testnevelesi Føiskola, (unpublished manuscript).

Loland, S. (1989) "Fair play i idrettskonkurranser—et moralsk normsystem." The Norwegian University for Physical Education and Sport, Oslo (unpublished Ph.D. dissertation).

Loland, S. and Sandberg, P. (1995) "Realizing Ludic Rationality in Sport Competitions." in: *International Review for the Sociology of Sport* 2, pp. 225–242.

McIntosh, P. (1984) *Fair Play: Ethics in Sport and Competition.* London, Heinemann.

Meier, K.V. (1985) "Restless Sport." in: *Journal of the Philosophy of Sport* XII pp. 64–77.

Morgan, W.J. (1987) "The Logical Incompatibility Thesis and Rules: A Reconsideration of Formalism as an Account of Games." in: *Journal of the Philosophy of Sport* XIV, pp. 1–20.

Morgan, W.J. and Meier, K.V. (eds.) (1988) *Philosophic Inquiry in Sport.* Champaign Ill., Human Kinetics.

Newcomb, T.M., Turner, R.H. and Converse, P.E. (1966) *Social Psychology. The Study of Human Interaction.* London: Routledge & Kegan Paul.

Nilsson, P. (1993) *Fotbollen och moralen.* Stockholm: HLS forlag.

Parfit, D. (1984) *Reasons and Persons.* Oxford: Clarendon Press.

Pilz, G.A. and Wewer, W. (1987) *Erfolg oder Fair Play? Sport als Spiegel der Gesellschaft.* München: Copress.

Rawls, J. (1971) *A Theory of Justice.* Cambridge: Harvard UP.

Raz, J. (1994) "Moral Change and Social Relativism," in: Paul, E. F., Miller, F. D. Jr. and Paul, J. *Cultural Pluralism and Moral Knowledge.* Cambridge UK; Cambridge UP, pp. 139–158.

Reddiford, G. (1985) "Institutions, Constitutions and Games." in: *Journal of the Philosophy of Sport,* XII, pp. 41–51.

Scheffler, S. (ed) (1988) *Consequentialism and Its Critics.* New York: Oxford UP.

Searle, J. (1969) *Speech Acts. An Essay in the Philosophy of Language.* Cambridge: Harvard UP.

Sen, A. and Williams, B. (eds.) (1982) *Utilitarianism and Beyond.* Cambridge: Harvard UP.

Simmons, A. John (1979) "The Principle of Fair Play." in: *Philosophy and Public Affairs* 4, pp. 316–337.

Suits, B. (1988) "The Elements of Sport." in: Morgan, W.J. and Meier, K.V. (eds.) *Philosophic Inquiry in Sport.* Champaign Ill.: Human Kinetics, pp. 39–48.

Tranøy, Knut-Erik. (1986) *Vitenskapen—samfunnsmakt og livsform.* Oslo: Universitetsforlaget.

Wachter, Frans de (1985), "In Praise of Chance. A Philosophical Analysis of the Elements of

Chance in Sports." in: *Journal of The Philosophy of Sport,* XII, pp. 52–61.

Wigmore, S. and Tuxill, C. (1995) "A Consideration of the Concept of Fair Play." *European Physical Education Review,* 1, pp. 67–73.

Questions for Consideration

1. How successfully does Loland avoid the difficulties of utilitarianism, Kantianism, and ethical relativism in his sketch of discourse ethics?
2. Precisely what role does pedagogy play in the overall formulation of Loland's thoughts?

Winning

17   Where's the Merit If the Best Man Wins?

David Carr
University of Edinburgh

David Carr begins this reading by remarking that, in even some of the most meritorious human achievements, it is difficult to say when one should be praised or blamed. In the area of the practice of sports, it has become commonplace to go from "A is better than B at performing some task X" (an evaluative claim about each person's skill at some task) to "A is better than B" (an evaluative claim about each person's character). The athletic achievements in sport, we fail to realize, are seldom as important as, say, those of science.

It is, however, a valid inference to go from "A is better than B at X" to "A can do X better than B." It is this comparative relationship of being able to do something better than another—what Carr calls the "cans of ability"—that he explores here By getting clearer on this relationship, the notion of blame or praise comes more into focus as regards performance in sport.

The principal candidate for evaluative judgments in sport is skill, which can mean innate abilities, mechanically acquired abilities, or deliberately acquired ones. That innate skills deserve no praise is obvious. What, then, of acquired skills? Certain acquired skills may have come about on account of certain dispositions in an athlete. Why should anyone praise these? Moreover, what of skills acquired by work, practice, and effort? These, Carr notes, beg the very question of the value of sports, and so he leaves off talk of these for another time. There is, however, the "can" of opportunity

or luck, which is an ability to seize chance opportunities as they arise. But if this, too, is an admixture of training and native wit, there is no room for praise here as well. In short, no sense of "skill" seems appropriate for judging an athlete praiseworthy or blameworthy.

This leads us to a "moral dimension." Properly speaking, athletes are praised and blamed not because of their slowness or dearth of strength, but because of their courage, self discipline, loyalty, and fair-mindedness—their character. Thus, it becomes clear that the better person is not necessarily the athlete who wins. In spite of this, we tend to applaud whoever wins. This is manifestly morally paradoxical.

Carr suggests pedagogical reform. There needs to be separation between moral and instrumental goals, with the understanding that the latter subserve the former in the practice of sport.

> Praised be God, and not our strength for it! . . . And be it death proclaimed throughout our host to boast of this, or take that praise from God which is his only.
>
> —*Henry V*, Act IV, Scenes vii and viii

Speaking of the Best

After the battle of Agincourt King Henry insists that credit for the English victory should go to God alone, not to the efforts of his men; and, of course, one possible motive behind this sentiment might well have been the belief that— given the French odds against his forces—it is

Reprinted, by permission, from David Carr, "Where's the Merit If the Best Man Wins?" *Journal of the Philosophy of Sport* XXVI (1999): 1–9.

nothing short of a miracle they prevailed. Indeed, at one level, the remark may be no more than an expression of relief at remarkable good luck and a superstitious desire not to tempt fate via undue hubris into terminating that fortune. But, one might ask, under what circumstances is it at all appropriate to claim credit for one's achievements? On a certain perfectly natural view of human endowment and talent, it may seem quite unjustifiable to claim *any* credit for what I do well—though this would not necessarily absolve me of responsibility for some of the things I do badly. This could be called a spiritual attitude, if you like—but it need not be a superstitious one; it may be more a matter of "I have been blessed with good fortune through none of my own doing," than "Phew! that was a close one; I mustn't tempt fate by crowing about it."

If this attitude of refusing credit for one's achievements is intelligible—if, indeed, it may even be held to represent some sort of spiritual achievement (though not, of course, one for which I might claim credit)—there are obvious implications for the ways in which we appreciate and celebrate sporting success and accomplishment. For, to be sure, sportsmen are widely praised for their achievements, their fans and supporters congratulate themselves vicariously on the achievements of their sporting heroes, and of course, athletes are also liable to admire themselves for their successes and triumphs. But while it may seem that nothing could be more natural than to respond to sporting success in such ways, it is worth asking whether all forms of such response are entirely conceptually or ethically coherent. Indeed, perhaps nothing throws into sharp relief the *hubris* of all this—or, some might say, the invidious absurdity—than the overweight couch potato taking xenophobic pride over his bottle of stout and cheeseburger at the prospect on his television screen of another Olympic gold for Britain. Thus, to the end of stimulating inquiry into an interesting issue, it is my aim in what follows to air a number of skeptical, occasionally provocative, questions about the relationship of merit to sporting achievement.

First, then, though I might anticipate widespread agreement that there is much absurdity in the sort of couch potato satisfaction just now caricatured, it is worth considering momentarily how the absurdity hoves into view; for the fact is that we do invariably and uncritically assume the supporters' pride in an away win to be intelligible, though we should no doubt find it merely ludicrous were the chiropodist down the road to express a sense of local pride in the podiatrical breakthrough for which I have just won the Nobel prize. (Another first in feet for Wakefield—hip hurray!) Briefly, I suppose the difference here lies in the competition that is an inherent feature of much sporting (but not other sorts of) achievement; though people might wax excessively nationalistic about our heart research being better than theirs—it is not integral to the quality of such research that it is better than theirs, in the way that such superiority is integral to some sporting success. At any rate, it seems intrinsic to the idea of much elite *spectator* sporting and athletic achievement to involve ascendancy or supremacy over our competitors; here, evaluation and assessment would appear to be to a large extent (though not, of course. exclusively) norm rather than criterion referenced, and to be good at X is often tantamount to being better at X than the next person. Thus, we may at least to this extent be dangerously drawn towards assimilating the idea of being a better person to that of performing better than another person.

But there is another reason why this element of comparison may well render any self-congratulation for my performance more problematic than it might otherwise have been. For if my medical researches lead me to a cure for some serious disease, it remains true—to whatever extent I might be inclined to attribute the discovery to luck or deny any real hand in things—that I am author of a discovery of substantial or *objective* value. There are, as it were, trans-personal reasons for regarding a medical breakthrough as of great human benefit, and it is of measurable benefit to someone to be cured of cancer or HIV. But although one can hardly deny

Golf superstar Tiger Woods celebrates after a successful shot during a match in North Plains, Oregon, in 1996. Do we tend to regard successful athletes as better people simply because they have physical and mental talents that few others have? Ed.
Jack Smith/AP/Wide World Photos

the enormous enjoyment that most of us rightly find in sporting activity, or the personal aesthetic satisfaction of aspiring to goals of psychological or physical self-mastery or perfection—it is not so clear that sporting achievements have value in quite this objective sense. At this point, of course, someone might want to say that there simply cannot be any culture-free or context-independent notion of objective value of this or any other kind, and that even scientific or medical breakthroughs are relative and liable to be overtaken by further advances. But even if such extreme value relativism should be true—which I believe there is strong cause to doubt—it would be beside the point; even a partial or temporary halt to HIV is of measurable benefit to the sufferer, whereas it is not clear what analogous advantage would follow from even the

most perfect and peerless goal—if (for the moment) we "bracket" spectator enjoyment and any satisfactions or benefits of achievement accruing to the scorer. However, if at least some sporting achievements lack any such objective value—if, indeed, they can be said to have no more than personal, subjective, or inter-subjective significance—then the value of my performance may consist *only* in its superiority over another's; thus, much now clearly does depend for the evaluation of my performance as at all meritworthy—and for any meaningful appraisal of me as a marvelous center-forward or spin-bowler—whether I can take genuine credit for the qualities that have enabled me to triumph over my sporting adversaries. If I cannot, then my achievements may be little more than contingent facts about me, which it may be inappropriate to regard as possessing more than aesthetic significance (as objects of enjoyment or whatever).

The Cans of Ability

At all events, insofar as much sporting achievement is implicated in assessments that are, if not relative, at least comparative, we should first distinguish between different senses in which A's goodness at X implies that A is better than B at X—and it is natural enough to interpret these as values of A *can* do X better than B, where the modality expresses some kind of aptitude. And, of course, different senses of ability have been meticulously distinguished by philosophers.[1] With regard to these, "He can lift that Ford Capri" said of Giant Haystacks, would appear to signify largely what one might call the *physical power* sense of ability. To be sure, physical power and brute strength are sometimes relevant to the assessment of sporting quality, but we should not normally regard these as sufficient grounds for judging one athlete superior to another—except perhaps in those instances where physical strength takes on slightly different connotations of persistence or endurance. Indeed, to the contrary, it is usual in those sports where strength gives unfair advantage for different categories of potential physical power to be distinguished in terms of the weight and size of contestants; thus, while it is clearly impossible to eliminate every likely inequality of this kind, it is widely acknowledged that people are hardly due much credit for their natural physical constitution, and that any contest in which natural endowment of this kind is likely to be the decisive factor is not much of a sporting contest at all.

A sense of ability of arguably greater relevance to the evaluation of sporting achievement is that in which it means something more like *skill*. In turn, the idea of skill appears fairly complexly ambiguous between, first, innate and acquired abilities, and second, abilities that are unreflectively acquired—perhaps through hands-on practical experience—and those acquired through the conscious or deliberate acquisition and exercise of various procedural principles or techniques. It should also be clear that these are by no means hard and fast distinctions and that it may often be difficult to classify an ability or skill in some of these terms to the exclusion of others. If, for example, I place a small baby in water and it makes rapid progress at swimming, it may be difficult to know whether this ability should be regarded as innate or acquired, given that without opportunities for exercise the latent power might never be realized. Indeed, perhaps we may follow Aristotelians here in referring to the innate basis of such ability as a potentiality that nevertheless requires practical experiential occasions for its effective actualization. Similar considerations affect the difference between those skills that are acquired largely through rote training—in the absence of much conscious reflection—and those that more obviously require the conscious internalization of rules; for, though it is doubtless possible to identify clear enough examples at the poles of this dichotomy, both kinds of skill are likely to involve the mastery (either explicitly or tacitly) of procedural principles, we readily refer to both forms of skill as expressions of knowing how—and, of course, most skills do involve significant interplay between conscious reflection and practice.

Ownership of Ability and Skill

But to what extent can we take credit for our skills? Surely, one might reply, we may do so to the extent they are mine and that I have worked to develop or perfect them. But is this so obvious? In terms of the distinction lately observed between innate and acquired abilities or skills, it should first be evident that insofar as skills are innate, one is due no more credit for them than one is for the endowment of Goliath-like height or Samson-like strength. Indeed, since we also saw that the distinction between innate and acquired abilities is not a hard and fast one, it may well be that even my acquired skills could only have been acquired on the basis of some sort of innate potentiality; so it is no fault of my own if I lack that basis, and I am due no credit for possessing it. But surely, even if I can take no credit for the brain and central nervous system that has given me superb hand-eye coordination, or the anatomy that has endowed me with appropriate bone structure or muscle organization, I am owed something for the expertise. time, and energy I have invested in the development of my natural endowments. In Lockean terms, might we not say that a man is entitled to that which he has mixed with his labor?[2]

Indeed, this may be regarded as the point at which the second lately observed distinction between orders or levels of ability—between the principled and practical elements of skill—comes into its own. On such a basis, we might argue that sportspersons deserve praise for their skills just to the extent they express expertise that is precisely a matter of personal development or the result of persistent hard work, practice, and effort. We do not applaud Best, Pele, or Gascoigne exclusively, if at all, for their innate endowments, but because we take them to have introduced a certain ingenuity or creativity into the game and (or) for their industry, dedication, and commitment. Taking the matter of expertise first, one might regard natural abilities as only the potential upon which the creative genius of the great athlete goes to work; it is as the inventor of startling new practical technique that the author of the Western Roll or Fosbury Flop is to be applauded for his or her achievements—not for any natural endowment presupposed to the effective execution of the athletic strategy. But to what extent can an athlete or sportsperson *really* be praised for such expertise or creativity? Without endorsing anything in the way of psychophysical determinism—to which, as we shall see, I do not subscribe—what is here liable to mislead us is the thought that responsibility does attach to the possession or otherwise of knowledge in a way that it does not to innate endowments; I can be blamed for my (culpable) ignorance of certain things, as I cannot be so blamed for being too stocky or bandy-legged to be an effective sprinter. However, it does not follow that because I can sometimes be blamed for ignorance—for example, for having had a road accident on the European continent as a result of failing to familiarize myself with the relevant highway code—I am thereby automatically praiseworthy for having acquired this or that specimen of knowledge.

Moreover, even if it is arguable that there are cases in which we should want to regard the discovery of knowledge as praiseworthy—for example, that which results from successful research into a cure for cancer—it may well be, harking back to an earlier point, that we regard the knowledge itself, more than the person who discovers it, as the true logical focus of commendation. But again, despite the enormous cultural significance with which sporting events and achievements are often invested, it is far from clear that athletic expertise *as such* constitutes knowledge of this kind—the more so if we take some forms of such expertise to be concerned primarily with finding ways of besting competi-

tors. To be sure, people have been known to devote inordinate amounts of time to amassing or developing varieties of recondite knowledge (of, say, the mating habits of the bar-tailed godwit) and skill (eating tractors or light bulbs) which they then proceed to exhibit or exploit in various forms of circus; but while we may be temporarily diverted by such displays, such entertainment value is entirely consistent with a certain contempt for what we otherwise regard as futile effort and wasted lives.

I am not for a moment, of course, suggesting that it is appropriate to view the expertise and skill of sportspersons in this way—there are at the very least, as we have already conceded, perfectly sane and sensible reasons of a personal, social, and cultural kind for the pursuit of sporting activities—and, as we shall shortly argue, the mastery of sporting and athletic skill and prowess may be bound up with the acquisition of virtues and values for which I can indeed be praised; I am merely pointing out that no praise or credit attaches immediately to the ownership, discovery, or development of any—even morally or instrumentally significant—knowledge *per se*. Moreover, when all is said and done, are not much the same points we have already made about natural endowment applicable to athletic and sporting knowledge and expertise? Presumably no ambitious athlete could be blamed for shirking pursuit of the technical expertise that would give him or her competitive edge; in all likelihood, all are diligently seeking it. But then, those who find it presumably do so by virtue of greater intelligence and ingenuity than those who do not; and how is one to explain this except in terms of greater natural endowment or the assistance of others—for neither of which, again, they may take much credit?

Effort and Luck

But isn't either a Lesley Welsh or a Sebastian Coe due at least some credit for the enormous effort by the former put into committing all that sporting information to memory, and the great commitment of the latter to developing that athletic expertise on the track? Any notion of effort, however, is clearly ambiguous between ideas of devoting large amounts of time to some activity and being especially resolute, or prepared to undergo great trials, in the pursuit of its goals. In the first sense, of course, whether someone deserves commendation for having devoted much time to the development of a particular body of knowledge or skill will depend to some degree upon whether we take that knowledge and skill to have objective or non-culturally relative value of the kind earlier specified by reference to the benefits of medical knowledge. As regards this, while we do not rule out the possibility that the enormous significance accorded to sporting expertise *as such* by most cultures may be based upon objective, or more than subjective, considerations—we have not as yet managed to discover in this paper what these considerations might be. In the other sense of effort, however, it is not unintelligible to commend someone for their painful endurance of trials and obstacles encountered in the course of pursuing a particular activity—even when we recognize that the activity is well nigh worthless or meaningless in its own right. The point of many heavyweight athletic events may well lie in circumstances having been so arranged that opportunities for such stoicism can be displayed. While this is true, however, it is important to see that such considerations effectively shift the ground of athletic evaluation away from the sphere of any specific expertise and skill as such—and this introduces further complications to which we will shortly return.

Continuing to interpret the basis of our positive athletic evaluations in terms of senses of ability, however, one might express a further kind of sporting accomplishment in terms of the so-called "can" of opportunity; for it seems that much of what we are able to do, in the sense of having the physical power or strength, crucially awaits occasions of exercise which may not always be seen or imagined in advance. It goes without saying, of course, that the fortunes of athletes and sportsmen and -women are enormously dependent on the presentation or realization of such occasions of opportunity. However, even to state matters thus is to encounter another crucial ambiguity. It was, I believe, said of or by Napoleon that the chief quality or ability he demanded of his generals was luck; but, whether or not this is more than a joke depends on what sense of luck is here meant. It may be that Napoleon was indeed looking for commanders who were more likely to be dealt winning hands than their adversaries. But, since it is also true that many a winning hand at poker has been lost to a smarter player with a weaker hand and better nerves, it is equally likely that he meant the capacity to recognize and exploit opportunities to the best advantage. Likewise, while it is certainly true that sport is the ultimate arena of contingency, and that great sporting triumphs have been built upon little more than chance—on unforeseen cracks appearing out of the blue in the opponent's defense—it is equally true that no sportsman worth his salt really enjoys a hollow victory, and that great athletes are not generally so judged entirely on grounds of their opponents' incompetence or ineptitude.

Thus, insofar as the can of opportunity may be held to express a genuine ability, it would have to be construed a kind of tactical or strategic disposition that enables an agent to recognize and take advantage of opportunities as they arise—rather than merely, as it were, a propensity to have good things befall one on a regular basis (though no doubt, in common usage, it means a loose mixture of both). But we are now, once more, in a position to raise a familiar dilemma: If the can of opportunity expresses a species of strategic intelligence possessed by an actual sporting agent, there is no reason—assuming such intelligence to be the usual mixture of training and native wit—to give him or her any special credit for it. If, however, the opportunities to which he or she is prone are simply sporting analogues of the disposition to regular wins on the lottery, this cannot really attract much in the way of substantial praise either. To date, then, no sense of ability—construed as a possible basis for judgments of athletic or sporting excellence—seems capable of providing plausible grounds for regarding athletes themselves as deserving praise for their achievements.

The Moral Dimension

However, there is another sense in which we are inclined to judge athletic and human performances in general as good or better than others, which cuts across—though it may not exclude—considerations of technical expertise, ability, and skill. Indeed, we have already mentioned those qualities of sheer persistence and endurance that may drive an athlete to put up with every kind of pain and fatigue—less, perhaps, in the effort to better an opponent and more in order to display or celebrate the power of human character over adversity. And, though some past social theorists and philosophers may have inclined to aesthetic characterization of such features,[3] I suspect that it is more natural for them to be interpreted—via their apparent relationship to such other qualities as sportsmanship and fair play—in essentially moral or ethical terms. It is commonplace, then, that as well as evaluating sporting performances by reference to the excellence or otherwise of skills of passing, tackling, or dribbling, we also rate them according to whether the play is fair or foul, clean or dirty, courageous or cowardly, generous or ungenerous. Moreover, eschewing determinism, I believe that the sort of character traits for which a sportsperson—or any human agent—is admired in relation to such goodness or badness of play, are qualities for which they are genuinely responsible. Clearly, the sense in which we regard persons as praiseworthy for their courage, self-control, or fair-mindedness is quite different from that in which we praise them for their beauty or intelligence; indeed, it is significant that while we also readily hold people to

account for their meanness, ruthlessness, or disloyalty, we do not generally blame them for their plainness or lack of native wit. The reason for this, none the worse for being obvious, is that while we suppose someone who is behaving badly both can and should behave better, we cannot in the same way suppose that a person who is ill-favored or stupid—or, for that matter, just hopeless at tennis—can and should improve in these respects.[4]

But, while we have at last encountered a range of qualities for which athletes and sportspersons can be praised or blamed for having or lacking (though it should also be noted that even when others elicit our praise for acting decently, we are inclined to take a dim view of any praise they may bestow on *themselves* in such respects), these are qualities in terms of which we assess human agents *in general*, rather than those in which we evaluate people *qua* athletes and sportspersons. Indeed, though much has been made, at least since the time of Plato,[5] of the ethical dimensions of sports and games and their rich potential for moral education and development—and the inherently ethical character of ideas of sportsmanship and fair play hardly requires emphasis here—it is equally true that sports are but one among many contexts in which moral considerations are assumed to be significant. Moreover, as in other spheres of life, qualities of moral character and athletic or sporting prowess cannot always be expected to coexist in the same individuals—and, where they do not, the former mostly take a second place in popular estimates of sporting excellence. Thus, though the champion we applaud may also be a more morally virtuous person than his opponent, it is not hard to think of instances where this is not so—and where a given athlete is off-field and on it as much renowned for his vanity, petulance, cupidity, or spite as for his skill or prowess. And, while the virtuous loser may find a place in our hearts for his virtues, it seems equally true that the successful competitor, often, by virtue of his success, endears the public to his vices; it may well be, for example, that McEnroe was all the more popular for his tantrums than he would have been had he exercised greater self-restraint.

Concluding Remarks and Possible Implications

What, however, might be the possible practical upshot of anything I have said so far? First, I suspect that some philosophers of sport would suggest that widespread separation of moral from instrumental goals, and a certain subversion of the first to the second, has generally followed in the train of that individualism that is a salient feature of developed liberal-democracies. In that event, what is arguably needed in the context of contemporary education about the place of sport in human affairs, is some means to the erosion of both this pervasive pragmatist ethos and those competitive attitudes of egocentricity and vanity about sporting achievement that so often go with it. In this connection, moreover, it is striking that many contemporary moral and social theorists would appear to have sought a panacea for such modern social and psychological ills in some sort of communitarian or collectivist ideal. But while such communitarianism undoubtedly has its positive features and the general appeal to its benefits is often enough well meant, it is not hard to see how its application to the realm of sport might actually make things worse sooner than better via the substitution of tribal or national for merely individual egocentricity and vanity; it is surely evident that much popular interest in and support for local, national, international, and Olympic sporting events is precisely driven by a narrow and divisive tribalism in which the victory of our athletes over theirs becomes a potent symbol of our general superiority over them. But if neither liberal nor communitarian thinking promises much in the way of an answer, what does?

The answer, if there is one, can only lie in some overhaul of the educational, moral, and spiritual ethos—not least our conceptions of what constitute proper attitudes to sporting achievement—in which we teach young people about the place of sport in human life and its contribution to personal growth; we need, I suspect, to promote attitudes of proper disinterested detachment from personal achievement. Am I seriously claiming, however, that such detachment could and should be promoted on the basis of the present far-fetched ethical position to the effect that since athletes are not the sole authors of their (other than ethical) sporting talents and achievements, they can take little credit for them? However, what I have tried to show in this essay is that this thesis is not at all far-fetched, insofar as pre-theoretical usage explicitly acknowledges the serious limits of our claims to credit for what we can do and the justice of criticizing others for what they can't. If we are really willing to try, for example, it is not hard to get the smallest of children to appreciate that their quickness—or others' slowness—at reading or writing, throwing or catching, are not proper occasions for any praise or blame beyond reasonable need for motivation or encouragement. Indeed, it may well be that far from constituting any revisionary attitude, that of a proper disinterested estimate of one's own talents and abilities is the more basic moral or spiritual response—a response that has, however, fallen prey to considerable distortion under pressure from the highly competitive and divisive social and economic circumstances in which we are nowadays often forced to operate.

But, wouldn't any such change of existing attitudes to sporting achievement effectively undermine the point of engaging in athletic or sporting contests, or any satisfaction that might be supposed to follow from spectating them? To be sure, it would redirect the focus of such satisfaction from extrinsic considerations—that his or her sporting success makes me feel good insofar as I can vicariously partake in the pleasure of putting the other fellow in his place—to intrinsic considerations. Such intrinsic fulfillment—broadly, if you like, aesthetic satisfaction—is already a central feature of most people's enjoyment of such "non-competitive" (albeit often competitively pursued) sports as ice-skating. The achievements of a John Curry are by and large apt for celebration, not because they are better than another person's, but in their own right—and appreciation of the high degree of aspiration and ambition inherent in such achievements is certainly compatible with the promotion of such virtues as performer humility and spectator tolerance. The tendency for the participatory or vicarious enjoyment of sport to become unhealthily extrinsic seems to increase the more sport, particularly elite spectatorial sport, takes on a competitive character—perhaps under commercial pressure. Again, however, there seems to be no inherent reason why this should be so—nor any logical impediment to experiencing genuine satisfaction from their sporting triumph over us, when their side has played a good, clean, and skillful game, exhibiting a range of virtues to which we ought all to aspire irrespective of our personal, local, national, or Olympic loyalties. But it may also be that the only secure foundation for the development of such attitudes of disinterested appreciation is widespread cultivation of a proper modesty about the source of our sporting, athletic, and other talents and achievements.

Notes

1. On senses of ability see, for example, Kenny (3, 4) and Carr (1).
2. See Locke (2).
3. Mostly philosophers following strictly in the Kantian tradition of ethics as a matter of the observation of moral duty. An extremely austere version of this position, for example, is defended by the sociologist Emile Durkheim (2).
4. A markedly similar point was, of course, made by Ludwig Wittgenstein (7).
5. Plato's very definite views on the moral educational role of physical activities are, of course, to be found in his major dialogue *Republic* (6).

Bibliography

1. Carr, D. "The Logic of Knowing How and Ability." *Mind.* 88:394–409, 1979.

2. Durkheim, E. *Moral Education.* New York: Collier-Macmillan, 1961.

3. Kenny, A. *Will, Freedom and Power.* Oxford, UK: Oxford Blackwell, 1975.

4. Kenny, A. *The Metaphysics of Mind.* Oxford, UK: Oxford University Press, 1989.

5. Locke, J. *Second Treatise on Civil Government* (P. Laslett, Ed.). Oxford, UK: Oxford Blackwell, 1949.

6. Plato. *Republic.* In: *Plato The Collected Dialogues,* E. Hamilton and H. Cairns (Eds.). Princeton, NJ: Princeton University Press, 1961, 575–844.

7. Wittgenstein, L. "Lecture on Ethics." *Philosophical Review.* 74:3–26, 1965.

Questions for Consideration

1. Carr's argument hinges on an equivocation of our (mis)use of the word *better* as it applies to sport. Do you agree that we tend to perceive winners as moral betters?

2. Do you support Carr's suggestion for pedagogical reform?

18 The Overemphasis on Winning: A Philosophical Look

Joan Hundley

In this reading, Joan Hundley examines the issue of the overemphasis on winning in contemporary sportive practice.

Traditionally, she says, sport has been a striving for physical excellence guided by sportsmanship and fair play. The modern notion, however, is almost exclusively ends-oriented, and this orientation undermines the game. She then goes on to articulate three theories of what went wrong.

Neo-Marxists, like Rigauer and Brohm, have argued that sport is a result of alienated capitalism. Problems with sport merely reflect more inveterate difficulties that are extant in capitalist societies. Our overemphasis on winning is essentially capitalistic: Reform of sport can only come about through reform of society.

In contrast to Neo-Marxists, play theorists like Johan Huizinga argue that at the base of human civilization is the human love of play. Deterioration of modern societies is a sign of corruption in our attitude toward play. Today the emphasis is on work, not play. Inhumanity, violence, and the stress on winning in sports today is, then, a consequence of an unhealthy "work ethic."

Last, radical feminists like Eugene Bianchi and Lucy Komisar insist that overemphasis on winning in sport is linked to male hegemony in social institutions. Male-dominated society rewards aggression, dominance, and violence. Our love of winning, they assert, is a result of a "masculine obsession to dominate."

Reform of sport, from each perspective, involves massive social reform. This involves a change in the very ideologies undergirding competitive sport. Consequently, reform will be slow, but it can come about.

An overemphasis on winning is presently quite visible within athletic arenas. The "winning is the only thing" attitude pervades professional and intercollegiate athletics, and even youth and recreational athletic programs. The overemphasis on winning is often held responsible for much of the corruption and problems that exist within modern sport. It is believed that the corruption within modern sport occurs because winning is overemphasized to the extent that the major objectives of the games themselves (performance, enjoyment, health, and the like) are deemphasized or neglected. When these important objectives of sport are deemphasized, winning by any means may become an acceptable practice. Thus cheating, brutality, and the like may even be encouraged for the sake of winning. When a win-loss record is the only gauge for athletic success, attitudes toward athletic competition may easily shift from "It is not whether you win or lose, it is how you play the game" to "It is not how you play the game, just that you win!"

Because of the overemphasis on winning many of the traditional benefits of athletic competition, such as sportsmanship, seem to have disappeared. Also, great performances, efforts, and special feelings of personal and team achievements are often not acknowledged after a defeat. Therefore, it is not how you play the game, just that you win. The purpose of this essay is to suggest reasons for this overemphasis on winning, and to suggest steps which may be taken to put the fun and games back into fun and games.

This chapter is divided into five sections. Section I presents sociological evidence indicating a deterioration of the play spirit and humanistic nature of modern sport. Section II attempts to explain the deterioration of modern sport from a neo-Marxist perspective. Section III attempts to explain the deterioration of modern sport from a play theorist point of view. Section IV gives a feminist explanation for this deterioration. Section V summarizes and draws conclusions.

I.   The Misuse of Modern Sport: The Overemphasis on Winning

Traditionally, sport has been regarded as an activity in which individuals strive for human physical excellence through sportsmanship and fair play. Such locker-room sayings as "sport builds character" and "it is how you play the game" clearly illustrate these attitudes toward sportsmanship and excellence.

Sport is sometimes even perceived as being an entity which stands outside of our everyday life experiences. Bernard Suits, along with several other sport theorists, regard sport, by definition, as being a rule bound activity. According to Suits, the rules make the game a game. Thus, activities that are not bound by rules or in which the rules are not followed are not games. Therefore, because players play games by following a set of rules, they are no longer playing the game when they break the rules. Hence Suits argues that because the act of playing a game starts with the players agreeing to follow a set of rules, cheating or the intentional breaking of those rules undermines the game itself.[1]

Also, according to Suits, because the act of cheating indicates the termination of the game, it is impossible to have a game in which the victors have cheated. Suits argues that the cheater is the ultimate loser, because not only does the cheater fail to win the game, the cheater fails to compete. Therefore Suits does not regard success as merely

a win-loss record. Suits would argue that it is not just that you win, *it is how you play the game.*

Paul Weiss regards sport as an area in which young people are given the opportunity to attain physical excellence. According to Weiss it is the striving for and the performance of physical excellence which makes sport a unique experience. Weiss therefore argues that the major objective of sport ought not be the mere quest for victory, but the attainment of excellence.[2] Hence, Weiss would argue that it is not just that you win, it is that you attain excellence.

Competition is often perceived as an antagonistic act of aggression in which opponents attempt to dominate one another. However, many sport theorists, such as Drew Hyland, regard competition as an act of cooperation in which participants strive toward physical excellence. Hyland clearly illustrates this aspect of competition, as he states: "Consider . . . the original meaning of the word. *Com-petitio* means 'to question together, to strive together.' Immediately we see that according to the original meaning of the word, competition is in no way necessarily connected to alienation; instead, it is easily tied to the possibility of friendship."[3] Competition can therefore be regarded as something more than the will to dominate an opponent or to win at any cost. Rather, competition may be more correctly regarded as an activity in which competitors aid each other in the act of striving for excellence. Even within a highly competitive situation, it is how you play the game.

So far, I have attempted to demonstrate that sport cannot be reduced to the numbers on a score board, and that the winning-is-everything perception of sport undermines the meaning and objectives of sport. Sport ought to be regarded as an activity in which the will to win is a means to the end of attaining physical excellence, not one in which human excellence is regarded as a means to the end of winning. The latter idea undermines sport because you can "win" without physical excellence, e.g., by "psyching out" opponents.

This improper emphasis on winning (the notion that winning is the only thing) is responsible for much of the corruption in modern sport. In our modern society, people have the attitude that winning is everything; consequently everybody loves a winner. Sport sociologists Stanley Eitzen and George Sage elaborate on this point, stating: "Americans want winners, whether it be in school, or business, or politics, or sport. In sports, we demand winners. Coaches are fired if they are not successful. Teams are booed for ties." Therefore, although winning ought not be the only thing, within modern sport, winning is everything.[4]

The overemphasis on winning is further reflected in the following quotations popularly credited to several very "successful" football coaches.

> "Winning is not everything. It is the only thing."—Vince Lombardi (legendary coach of the Green Bay Packers)

> "Everytime you win, you're reborn; when you lose, you die a little."—George Allen (coach of the Washington Redskins)

> "No one ever learns anything by losing."—Don Shula (coach of the Miami Dolphins)[5]

The notion that winning is everything corrupts sport because it reduces the game itself to its outcome (the numbers on the sports page). Eitzen and Sage reflect on our attraction to the outcome of events as they write: "In learning the culture (through the socialization process), most Americans have internalized values that predispose them to be interested in the outcome of competitive situations—competition is the *sine qua non* of sports."[6] The act of overemphasizing the outcome of a performance and ignoring the performance itself is the key to the corruption in modern sport. This overemphasis on the outcome of an athletic event is quite visible in the sports pages, in which you will find pages and pages of scores or outcomes accompanied by little or no commentary regarding the performances. Consequently, as we have seen, winning is everything within modern sport; however, this overemphasis on winning corrupts sport because it undermines the game itself.

The notion of winning being not everything but the only thing is embedded in the fiber of modern sport. However, we must keep in mind that for every winner there is a loser. If winning is everything, is losing nothing? Are losers nothing? What about the game? Winning ought not be the only thing, because when it is everybody loses. The dynamics of athletic struggle cannot be reduced to a win-loss record. As the improper emphasis on winning increases, modern sport departs more and more from the ideal of an activity which is mainly concerned with human physical expression and excellence.

I shall center the discussion immediately following around youth sport programs, because I believe youth sport ought to be purer than intercollegiate and professional sports, which are subject to corruption by the large sums of money at stake.

No more than ten years ago the concept of the pick-up game was quite common. These usually unscored, untimed, unsupervised games, which ended either at dinner time or at nightfall, epitomized the notion of playing for fun, for the sake of playing. With the onset of organized youth sport, each year the concept of the pick-up game seems to die a little—and with it the notion of play, fun and games. The pick-up game has been replaced with youth Olympic and professional training camps in which each coach aspires to develop future professional and/or Olympic athletes. Youth sport is often regarded not as fun or games, but as serious business.

Youth sport leagues, often run by aggressive parents, place children into highly competitive situations. And although we often criticize Eastern bloc countries for their exploitation of young athletes, four- and five-year-olds are often placed on gymnastic and/or swim teams in this country. As members of these teams, they are required to practice hours daily. Further, these young athletes are taught to play with the attitude that winning is the only thing. What happened to playing for play's sake?

Another problem with organized youth sport programs is the supervision or coaching. Because the coaches of many Little League teams are volunteer parent/coaches and not professional physical educators, many youth sport teams are coached by enthusiastic parents who may possess little knowledge of physiology of exercise, motor development, or child psychology. Therefore, these weekend coaches may push a child beyond his/her physical or mental limit without knowing it. Youth sport teams are also often coached and supervised by weekend "Vince Lombardis," who may be frustrated ex-athletes pursuing their fantasies of NFL or major league success. Lacking adequate knowledge among other things, these imitation Vince Lombardis cleverly disguised as Little League coaches harm their athletes both physically ("Little League elbow" and the like) and psychologically—subjecting young athletes to pain and trauma, and instilling in them a sense of false values. Young athletes are taught that losing is nothing and losers are nobodies. Hence, no matter how hard they work or try, uncoordinated or less athletic children are made to feel inferior. Also, no matter how well these young athletes perform, they may be made to feel sad or guilty if or when they lose. Young athletes quickly learn that success means winning.

An overemphasis on winning also causes fun to become a secondary factor which can be appreciated only after victory. Great plays are remembered only in the context of winning. Hence, without victory great performances are reduced to nothing; great athletes are defined as the ones who score the most points. It clearly follows that high point scoring individuals are often idolized, while defensive players, individuals who assist and/or set up the big plays, are overlooked.

Further, when winning is a prime objective for participating in sport, cheating (without being discovered, of course) may be viewed as an acceptable practice. Why not? All the numbers say is that you won, not how. As a matter of fact, coaches often teach players tricks which enable them to cheat without being detected. These tactics are often considered more strategic than dishonest. In basketball, e.g., players are often taught how to foul without being detected.

Finally, as a consequence of the contest being regarded as a means to an end (winning) it follows that the opponent may also assume the status of a means to an end, rather than a person. Athletes are often taught to regard their opponents as being objects which must be overcome in the pursuit of victory, rather than the friends which Hyland discusses. Moreover, athletes are also taught to believe that physical aggression and brutality are part of the game. Most athletes feel little or no remorse after inflicting injury upon their opponents. In sports such as football, boxing, and hockey, athletes are praised for their ability to dehumanize and brutalize their opponents.

We have seen that there is a clear contrast between how sport ought to be played (emphasizing rules, enjoyment, performance, and excellence) and how it is being played (overemphasizing winning). It is clear that an overemphasis on winning presently undermines the objectives of athletic competition.

II.   The Overemphasis on Winning: A Neo-Marxist Perspective

Ideologically, sport has been regarded as an autonomous institution, characterized by fair play, sportsmanship, courage, excellence, and a host of additional social and individual virtues. Modern sport, however, can be more accurately characterized as a dog-eat-dog, win-at-any-cost, extremely competitive activity in which individuals go to great lengths to win. The athlete's primary objective is no longer the quest to achieve excellence through the physical. Rather, competitors strive to dominate one another. Also, the "good guys finish last" attitude, now present throughout sport, has acted to undermine the notion of sportsmanship, fair play, and the like.

Neo-Marxists argue that sport is not really an autonomous institution, but rather a mere function of an alienated capitalistic society.[7] The attitudes, norms, and values present within sport are the same attitudes, norms, and values present within society. Neo-Marxists further argue that it would be illogical to assume that anything other than dog-eat-dog, highly competitive sport could exist within a dog-eat-dog, highly competitive society. Sport would be unintelligible if its values contradicted those of society. They conclude that the only way to change sport is to change society.

In *Rip Off the Big Game,* a controversial critical analysis of the sport establishment, sport sociologist Paul Hock illustrates this connection between sport and society, stating:

> There is nothing natural or inevitable about the sports we play or the way we play them. Sports would be completely idiotic without a common acceptance of the rules of the game by the athletes and a common social appreciation of the game by large sections of society. . . . The sports most appreciated in a particular society, and the way in which they are played, in turn reflect the past and present development of that society; they are, in fact, a mirror reflection of the society. Thus, as the Vietnam war heated up, the more militaristic game of professional football rapidly surpassed baseball as America's favorite spectator sport.[8]

Hock further illustrates the interrelation between sport and culture, stating: "To 'attack' sports would be like the old witch's attacking the mirror that showed her how ugly she is, for sport is nothing else but a mirror, a socializing agent, and an opiate of the society it serves. To 'reform' the mirror while leaving the society untouched would change nothing at all. We will have humane, creative sports when we have built a humane and creative society—and not until then."[9]

Neo-Marxists argue not only that sport's values mirror or reflect the competitive values of modern society, but also that competitive athletics enhance the competitive nature of society.

Critics Bero Rigauer and Jean-Marie Brohm both argue that modern sport has been reduced to an activity which perpetuates the same achievement principles found within alienated labor. Rigauer clearly expresses this point in his book, *Sport and Work,* where he states: "Within the context of this interpretation of human activity the connection between sport and work is clear: both systems of behavior enhance the status and prestige of the concept of achievement."[10] It is therefore argued that capitalism reduces sport to another form of production or achievement.

The neo-Marxists argue that modern sport is not based on lofty ideals such as sportsmanship, cooperation, excellence, and the like. They explain that these ideals are ideologies which disguise the true dehumanizing nature of sport. It is further argued that sport's true ideals are based on the ideals of production and achievement which are found within alienated labor. Therefore athletic success is reduced to the production of records and the accumulation of victories. Neo-Marxists thus conclude that capitalism transforms sport into a dehumanizing activity in which participants will do just about anything to themselves and/or their opponents to win.

Neo-Marxists further argue that capitalism also reduces sport to a commodity. Rigauer explains what is meant by a commodity: "By 'commodity' we mean an external 'object, a thing that by nature of its attributes satisfies some sort of human need.' An object becomes a commodity or an article of exchange only when it is something produced not to satisfy the producer's needs but to be exchanged in the marketplace for other values (money)."[11]

Taking a cue from the neo-Marxist line of thought, we may suggest here that modern sport overemphasizes winning because winning or success is the article which is exchanged within the athletic arena. Winning is a rare, valuable commodity because within our capitalistic society the sensation of being a winner or successful is rarely if ever experienced. Neo-Marxists give two broad reasons to explain why these sensations are rarely directly experienced. First, dehumanizing factors such as alienated labor, high achievement drives and/or a constant obsession to increase production, deny workers an opportunity to experience a sense of success through their work. Secondly, upward mobility is in fact extremely difficult under capitalism. These two reasons are elaborated in the next three paragraphs.

Alienated labor denies workers the opportunity to experience success because when workers sell their capacity to labor, they also relinquish their rights, ownership, and control of the product they produce. Therefore, workers often do not feel a responsibility for and/or a sense of pride in what they produce. Neo-Marxists further explain that division of labor also acts to undermine an individual's direct experience of success. They argue that when a task is broken down it becomes more difficult for a worker to identify his or her labor with the finished product. Thus the worker is unable to experience a sense of pride or success for his or her labor.

Further, because of high achievement drives and an obsession to constantly increase production, a worker's work is never done; thus workers never experience the sense of success that results from the completion of a difficult task. Within high production-oriented societies each goal achieved is reduced or perceived as a small step toward a higher unattainable goal. Success, therefore, becomes an unattainable entity. Athletic competition tends to act as a release valve at this point, because each game ends, thus providing spectators with a sense of completion. This gives rise to the neo-Marxist complaint that by providing workers with this sense of completion, which is otherwise unattainable, sport acts to perpetuate capitalism.

The second reason suggested for winning being a rare commodity is the conflict between capitalistic ideology and fact. Neo-Marxists argue here that because of the massive labor forces necessary to sustain capitalism it is extremely difficult, if not impossible, for an individual or group to gain significant social or economic mobility. But if workers knew this fact they would no longer work as hard. Therefore ideologies suggesting that work equals success are perpetuated. Because these ideologies maintain high levels of effort and/or production, individuals are socialized into believing them. Individuals are taught that hard work is the root of all success, and that failure to achieve status indicates a lack of work. Unsuccessful individuals often find few if any flaws in the system itself, and they tend to perceive themselves as inferior or losers. Sport is often blamed for perpetuating this ideology. This is because sport is one of the few areas within society in which hard work still counts and the better competitor still wins. Sport keeps alive the dream of working hard and attaining success.

Neo-Marxists argue that winning in sports is a *commodity*. Individuals, groups, businesses, cities, and countries exchange money and/or other valuables for winning. The fact that winning teams or individuals do receive large sums of money and support, while their losing counterparts are almost unheard of, strengthens the notion that winning is the article that is exchanged in the athletic marketplace. It is suggested that individuals support athletics because through the supporting of athletics individuals obtain the opportunity to experience vicariously the success that is denied them in their place of work.

It might be objected that individuals do not support athletics financially because most people do not go to the arena, field, or stadium to support their favorite team; they simply turn on the television. However, we must understand that large sums of money are exchanged in sports broadcasting. When games are viewed on television, individuals do not have to pay the price of a ticket because corporations foot the bill, after purchasing the right to attempt to sell spectators their products during intermissions. When an individual and/or business supports an athletic team it purchases the right to share vicariously in that team's success. The more a team wins, the more individuals will wish to support that team. Also as opportunities of directly experiencing success are reduced, the demand for vicarious winning increases, causing winning to be a more valuable commodity.

According to neo-Marxist arguments, then, winning is overemphasized in the athletic arena because individuals are denied the opportunity to experience winning within their everyday lives. This allows winning to become a valuable commodity, which is then pursued to the neglect of other aspects of sports.

III.   The Overemphasis on Winning: A Play Theorist Perspective

... [M]an, as we said before, has been constructed as a toy for God, and this is, in fact, the finest thing about him. All of us, then, men and women alike, must fall in our role and spend life in making our play as perfect as possible—to the complete inversion of current theory. [Plato, *Laws* VII, 803C][12]

Johan Huizinga, play theorist and author of the classic work *Homo Ludens*,[13] employs this Platonic metaphor to illustrate his notion of play. Huizinga's notions of modern sport have been selected to represent the play theorist point of view because much of modern play theory is a result of Huizinga's work.

Huizinga's theory of play suggests that play is the ideal form of human expression and the basis of human civilization. In *Homo Ludens* (which translated means "Man the Player") Huizinga argues that individuals, cultures, and civilizations best express their creativity and humanity through their play. He further argues that human civilizations have been built from a concept of play rather than a work ethic, and that play is the single element which separates humans from other beings. *Homo Ludens* attempts to demonstrate that art, music, games, rituals, and the like are all fundamental expressions of the human play spirit, and that the deterioration of modern culture is a result of a loss in this play spirit. The purpose of this section is to present the play theorist point of view regarding the overemphasis on winning in modern sport.

Huizinga argues that because play allows individuals to express themselves in a uniquely human manner, the deterioration of play has resulted in the deterioration of humanity. He concludes that the inhuman, violent nature of modern society is due to a lack of a play spirit. Hence, it may be further concluded that the inhuman, violent nature of sport is also a result of this lack of a play-like attitude,

The play theorist's explanation of the overemphasis on winning is fundamentally different from that of the neo-Marxist. The differences rest in each type of theorist's perception of the ideal form of human expression. Work theorists such as neo-Marxists suggest that the ideal form of human expression is work. Work is argued to be ideal because individuals are said to objectify themselves and/or relate to their world through their labor. Work theorists suggest that because human beings have built and rebuilt their world in their attempts to fulfill basic needs, human civilizations were built on the concept of work. Play theorists, on the other hand, argue that work is merely an instrument of survival and/or an act of fulfilling basic needs. They argue that play, rather than work, is the ideal form of human expression because it is a result of an individual's free will, while work is fettered to the fulfillment of needs. It is further suggested that because play transcends needs, it allows human beings to reach beyond the mundanities of everyday life to create things of beauty and spirit which transcend basic need. Play theorists suggest that this beauty and spirit are readily visible in art, music, games, culture, and other play forms which are uniquely human.

Play theorists argue that play is the factor that separates humans from other beings, because only humans possess the ability to play or to act outside of biological or psychological need. They suggest that while other beings' existences are limited to the obtaining of food and shelter, procreation, and other survival-related activities, human beings possess the ability to search for beauty, truth, and other things which transcend mere survival. They infer that when individuals ignore their ability to play, the quality of their lives is decreased to a subhuman level of existence which is fettered to the fulfillment of needs. Extending this line of reasoning, one may conclude that the lack of a play spirit within modern society is responsible for a decrease in the search for beauty and truth and an increase in violence, brutality, inhumanity, and alienation.

According to Huizinga the deterioration of play is the result of an overemphasis on work and/or utility values. He suggests that because work and play are contradictory concepts they cannot exist at the same time. Thus the greater the emphasis that is placed on work, the more play is deemphasized. Play theorists argue that the extremely high value that modern technical society places on work, success, progress and the like, causes play and/or nonproductive activities to be perceived as nonsense. It is therefore suggested that in an attempt to fulfill the productive standards of modern society, traditional play activities such as games have assumed work-like natures. Hence more and more individuals are no longer participating in play-like activities for the sake of play or enjoyment; rather they are playing to obtain fitness, money, education, psychological relaxation, and/or records or other manufactured needs. Play is then perceived as a means of fulfilling some other need; hence play is reduced to another form of work. And, humans are reduced to other forms of beings.

Play theorists argue that play is the only logical form of human existence and that it would be irrational to conduct life in any other manner. They offer three arguments. The first is that play is the function of each participant's creativity and/or intrinsic motivation; thus play is a demonstration of who an individual is rather than what his/her needs are. They conclude that individuals best relate to their world through play. Need forces individuals to work; freedom allows individuals to play.

In *The Grasshopper*, Bernard Suits gives a second argument explaining why the life of a player is a more logical existence than one of a worker.[14] Suits argues that a playful existence is more logical because play is a self-justifying activity while work is not. Work is not regarded as a self-justifying activity because during work the ends, or the fulfilling of needs resulting from work, are separate from the means of obtaining those ends. If an individual could obtain a need (e.g., money) without working, then working would be avoided. In other words, individuals do not work to work—they work to fulfill needs; thus work is not self-justifying. Play, on the other hand, is considered self-justifying because individuals do play for the sake of playing.

In a further, related argument, Suits reasons that it is illogical to regard work as self-justifying activity because during work individuals attempt to eliminate the need to work. Thus if work were the fundamental basis of existence, through work individuals would attempt to eliminate their purpose of existence. Suits illustrates this idea when he compares work to preventive medicine, stating: "The ideal of prudence [work], therefore, like the ideal of preventive medicine, is its own extinction. For if it were the case that no sacrifice of goods [play time] needed ever be made, the prudential actions [work] would be pointless, indeed impossible . . . the true grasshopper [player] sees that work is not self-justifying, and that his way of life is the final justification of any work whatsoever."[15] Play theorists conclude that play is a logical foundation of existence. It is logical for individuals to work to play, or to play to play, but illogical to work for the sake of working.

Play theorists conclude that the winning-is-the-only-thing attitude which pervades modern sport is a result of the illogical nature of a society based on a work ethic. They suggest that the importance placed on work within our present society has resulted in a loss of the play spirit. Hence, even sport has lost its play-like nature. Huizinga explains that modern sport is no longer play, stating: "In the case of sport we have an activity nominally known as play but raised to such a pitch of technical organization and scientific thoroughness that the real play spirit is threatened with extinction."[16] Play theorists therefore suggest that the violent, inhuman nature of modern society and modern sport can be successfully eradicated through a revitalization of the play spirit, which would result from a deemphasis on the present work ethic. If individuals realized that they were God's playthings, and spent their lives making their play as perfect as possible, they would experience the peace and fulfillment necessary to restore humanity to modern society.

IV.　The Overemphasis on Winning: A Radical Feminist Perspective

Like the neo-Marxists and the play theorists, feminists[17] tie the degraded state of modern sport to the degraded state of society. Radical feminists, however, argue that the degradation of society is due to the patriarchal foundation on which it is based. They hold that the downfall of sport is ultimately a result of patriarchy, rather than of alienated labor or an overemphasis on work.

Radical feminists argue that sport, like education, family, economics, and other social institutions, has been manipulated and employed to maintain the power of men over women. They conclude that the violent nature of modern sport and the overemphasis on winning within modern sport are side effects of patriarchal manipulation. In his essay, "The Super-Bowl Culture of Male Violence," sport sociologist Eugene Bianchi supports this feminist argument, stating: "The sexism in football [is] symbolically fundamental to the other evils of our culture. It is also worth noting that in a culture that encourages people to admire and revel in aggressiveness, sports of intended brutality gain the highest appeal both at the box office and on television."[18] Lucy Komisar further explains the

connection between violence and masculinity, stating: "Violence and male supremacy have been companions in the course of civilization. The domination of women by men has been the prototype of the control men have tried to exercise over other men—in slavery, in war, and in the marketplace."[19]

Male-dominated sports are regarded as instruments which are employed to perpetuate male supremacy because they reinforce what I will refer to as the ideal of physical dominance, aggression, and violence. By this I mean quite simply the ideal that supports the antiquated notion that stronger and more aggressive individuals or nations have the right to dominate weaker, less aggressive individuals or nations. Bianchi explains that athletic contests are struggles for dominance, rather than tests of skill, stating: "It is not just a rivalry that helps a person enjoy the contest for the pleasure and skill involved in it; rather it's a confrontation with others in which a man's self-identity, self-respect and public acceptance is [*sic*] at stake. . . . Winning is all even if it means trampling on one's fellows. Hostility and violence are instruments for removing obstacles on the road to the top. . . ."[20] The overemphasis on winning may therefore be explained as the result of a masculine obsession to dominate.

Aside from its other flaws, the ideal of physical dominance is extremely oppressive to women because women as a group are inferior to men in their ability to dominate physically. It may therefore be concluded that support for the ideal of physical dominance is an attempt to sustain women's inferior status. Sport further acts to sustain the idea of feminine inferiority by placing women on the sideline. Bianchi suggests that sport attempts to demonstrate feminine inferiority and women's place by emphasizing masculine ideals such as toughness and insensitivity, and placing women on the outside: "The weekend trek to the arena is not an escape from the world of corporate America; rather it is a weekly pilgrimage to the national shrines where the virtues of toughness and insensitivity can be renewed. This is especially true in the man/woman relationships. In the football spectacle the role of woman in our society is clearly defined against the masculine criteria of value. The important action is male-dominated; women can share only at a distance in man's world. They can shout and squeal from afar, but their roles are accessory to the male event."[21]

From this perspective, the overemphasis on winning in modern sport seems to be the result of an attempt to maintain and perpetuate this ideal of physical dominance. In present industrialized society the ideal of physical dominance is obsolete; using physical strength as a basis of status is as arbitrary as using physical characteristics such as eye color, height, or weight. Males, therefore, in an attempt to retain this masculine ideal, have overemphasized physical dominance within the athletic arena, and then made athletics a model for the remainder of society.

In "The American Seasonal Masculinity Rites," sport sociologist Arnold Beisser explains that sport is a social "safety valve," because it emphasizes masculine physical superiority: "In sports, mates and females are placed in their historical biological roles. In sports, strength and speed do count, for they determine the winner. As in pre-mechanized combat, women can never be more than second place to men in sports. They can cheer their men on, but a quick review of the record books comparing achievements in sports of men and women confirms the distinctness of the sexes here."[22]

Beisser further demonstrates how athletics perpetuate this ideal of physical dominance: "It is a small wonder that the American male has a strong affinity for sports. He has learned that this is one area where there is no doubt about sexual differences and where his biology is not obsolete. Athletics help assure his difference from women in a world where his functions have come to resemble theirs."[23]

Because of its ability to demonstrate an individual's physical strength and violent nature, sport is often considered a means of determining masculinity. The notion of an athletic contest being used to determine the better man and the statement "may the best man win" clearly illustrate how athletics have been employed to maintain this antiquated ideal. Sport determines who is the better man; therefore all that is considered masculine is overemphasized in the athletic arena. Violence, aggression, physical dominance, and an exaggerated will to win are concentrated to the point that athletic contests have become brutal displays of "masculinity," rather than artful displays of skill. Radical feminists conclude that the overemphasis on winning within modern sport is the result of a patriarchal attempt to oppress or suppress women.

V.   Conclusion

Each of the theorists discussed in this essay suggests that the overemphasis on winning within modern sport is the result of some flaw in modern culture. Neo-Marxists blame the deteriorated state of modern sport on alienated labor, capitalistic production, and the achievement principle. Play theorists argue that the overly competitive nature of modern sport is the result of a loss of the play spirit. They suggest that the problems that pervade sport are the result of the irrational respect and admiration which modern society has placed on the work ethic and technology. Radical feminists conclude that the overemphasis on winning is a result of a patriarchal struggle to maintain the ideal of masculine superiority within a society which is becoming increasingly androgynous.

The notion that the deterioration of modern sport is the result of a capitalistic, work-oriented and/or patriarchal society appears to lead sport reformers and sociologists to a dead end. This occurs because it would make little sense to attempt to change a reflection of the brutal, competitive nature of modern society. Therefore, if sport is a mere reflection, the only way to change sport would be to reform the society in which it exists. If the cultural influence on sport were as pervasive as suggested, to participate in a sport while employing countercultural values would be an unintelligible or nonsensical act. It makes no sense, for example, to attempt to lose a contest in a culture where winning and achieving is revered.

Sport, however, does not merely reflect the values of the culture in which it exists. It also perpetuates them. Sport reform is necessary because sport perpetuates the alienated, oppressive, brutal, violent nature of modern society. Furthermore, if sport can be employed to perpetuate capitalistic ideologies, irrational work priorities, and patriarchy, sport may also be used to undermine them. Reforms within the athletic arena may thus result in social changes and reformations. It must be kept in mind, however, that to maintain intelligibility, influence, and viability, athletic reform must be slow and deliberate.

Neo-Marxists, play theorists, and feminists all suggest that the attitudes and structures accompanying modern athletic participation ought to be changed. New game enthusiasts argue that this change can be best implemented by creating less competitive games. They suggest that new cooperative games would aid in the elimination of brutality and violence in sport by deemphasizing winning in the structure of the game itself. In the game of rotational volleyball, for example, players rotate to the opposite team after relinquishing service.[24] I believe, however, that because the structure of games is not solely responsible for the overemphasis on winning, and its violent, brutal nature, the mere creation of new games will not by itself be an effective measure in athletic reform.

Neo-Marxists and play theorists would more than likely agree on similar athletic reforms. Changes would be similar because both groups suggest that the work-like nature of modern sport is responsible for its deterioration. Neo-Marxists accuse modern sport of perpetuating capitalistic values such as alienated labor, production, and the achievement principle. Play theorists argue that modern sport overemphasizes the significance of work. In any case, both argue that sport, games, and other playful activities ought to be participated in with a humanistic, creative, play-like attitude.

Both groups would more than likely suggest that rigid time periods allotted for play be less structured. Neo-Marxists would be opposed to rigid playing periods because they resemble the rigid working hours found within capitalistic alienated labor. Neo-Marxists could argue that rigid time periods perpetuate and reflect the irrational attitudes toward time found within capitalistic society. Because all things connected with production are perceived as sacred commodities within capitalism, time is viewed as sacred. Time's sacred nature is alienating because individuals often rush through lives in their effort to save the precious commodity, time. In an effort to produce as much as possible, most people in capitalistic society never take the time to relax, to find out the meaning of their existences, or to enjoy life.

Neo-Marxists would object to the rigid time periods found within modern sports because the rigid periods allow time to be a significant factor in the outcome of a contest, thus perpetuating an irrational capitalistic attitude toward time. These rigid time periods are also accused of paralleling the rigid working hours found within capitalistic labor.[25] It is suggested here that a 9:00 to 5:00 working day with an hour off for lunch and coffee breaks is extremely similar to a football game with its half time and time outs.

Because play theorists define play as an activity that is engaged in freely, and sport as play, they would attempt to remove rigid playing times which restrict the choice of when to begin and end playing. The notion of an athletic contest without structured playing times may sound nonsensical at first; however, the pick-up game is not bound by time and it makes sense. Therefore, less structured sport could be easily implemented through a reemphasis on the concept of the pick-up game and a deemphasis on organized youth sport programs, intercollegiate athletics, and professional sport.

Work theorists and play theorists would also agree that records and statistics detract from modern sport. The keeping of statistical records is unique to modern sport. Even the Greeks, founders of the first Olympic games, never bothered to calculate exact times and distances.[26] Neo-Marxists argue that the keeping of statistical records perpetuates capitalistic production and the achievement principle, because it stresses attainment and production.[27] Play theorists argue that statistics, records, and extrinsic awards distract from the game, because participants often place more value on the attainment of records than the enjoyment of the game. Record keeping pervades modern sport. Most teams employ at least one statistician who, disguised as a "sports information director" keeps every record from yardage gained on a rainy day to the number of substitutions within a five-minute period. Record keeping also pervades the sports media; presently most athletic contests are reported in terms of game statistics rather than athletic performance.

Our earlier discussion of the radical feminist perspective suggests that equal participation by women in athletics on all levels, including youth sport programs as well as professional athletics, would be significant in the undermining of the patriarchal nature of modern society. It stands to reason that if women are considered equals within the athletic arena, men could no longer use sport as a proving ground for masculinity; this would also undermine the notion of sport being a safety valve for masculine expression.

A further argument, suggested by Jane English, is that if women had an equal place of honor within the athletic arena, especially professional and Olympic programs, they would have the opportunity to enhance the self-respect of all women and to negate the idea of female physical inferiority.[28] English elaborates: "It contributes to a woman's self-respect to see or read about the best women golfers. But this pride is tempered by the knowledge that they are 'only' the best women. The very need for a protected competition class suggests inferiority. The pride and self-respect gained from witnessing a woman athlete who is not only the best woman but the very best athlete is much greater."[29] Thus, although women would benefit[30] as individuals from mere equality of opportunity to participate in sport, the image

of feminine inferiority can be undermined only by equality of honor in sport. English thinks this feasible: "Before we conclude that women are permanently relegated to inferiority, however, let us note that what is a physiological disadvantage in one activity may be an advantage in others: weight is an asset to a Sumo wrestler and a drawback for marathon running. . . . The hip structure that slows running gives a lower center of gravity. Fat provides insulation and an energy source for running fifty-mile races. The hormones that hinder development of heavy muscles promote flexibility."[31] English suggests that new women's sports ought to be developed from these physiological advantages to allow women to achieve this place of honor within the athletic arena.

Bonnie Beck argues that female equality within the athletic area would be impossible without attitude changes. She argues that violence, aggression, and dominance enhance and perpetuate the notion of male-dominated athletics. She further argues that this model of athletic participation is oppressive and ought to be discarded and replaced with a more humanistic model, stating: "NowSport/ManSport oppresses all, even those to whom it gave birth. With life risking conviction we must demand new life-energizing com-test, play days, sport days, Joy-Sport activities for AllSelves in every activity."[32] Play days are suggested as alternative sport models because the whole atmosphere of a play day promotes an emphasis on enjoyment and participation rather than on victory. Brutality is not encouraged, and is almost unheard of. Prizes are nominal, and everyone receives a ribbon. School rivalries are obviated by drawing each team from various schools. Beck would probably agree, however, that play days must not try to abolish competitive drive and the will to achieve athletic excellence.

Feminists would conclude that to lessen the overemphasis on winning in sport, we must 1) allow more women to participate on all levels (thereby lessening sport's attractiveness as a male proving ground and escape valve); 2) change the emphasis on male physiology (thereby fighting the image of women's physical inferiority which supports the masculine identity that men express in sport); and 3) substitute a humanistic model of sport for the old violent attitudes. Changing the attitudes with which sports are played is just as important as changing the participants of the game and the games themselves. As Beck points out in her essay, if women participate in athletics without changing its violent, brutal, dominant nature they will merely be perpetuating their own oppression.[33]

In considering measures for athletic reform, we must keep it in mind that because sport is influenced by society, these reforms must be slow, deliberate and introduced in social institutions outside of sport as well as within sport. Education, through youth sports and physical education programs, is the most logical institution to initiate athletic reform. Because sport acts as a socializing agent, humanism and athletic appreciation (rather than capitalistic, work-like, or patriarchal values) can be taught in educational institutions through athletic participation. A reemphasis on pick-up games, creative free play and other forms of less organized youth sport could allow children to learn to appreciate the joy of participation for the sake of participation, rather than the importance of winning.

Sport reform can undermine the oppressive nature of modern society by demonstrating that the ideologies perpetuated in the athletic arena are false. I believe that no matter what the underlying cause of sport's deterioration, a change in the attitudes and the model of athletic participation can change social attitudes by redefining "success" and demonstrating that success can be attained through humanistic rather than violent means.[34]

Notes

1. Bernard Suits. *The Grasshopper, Games, Life and Utopia* (Toronto: University of Toronto Press, 1980), chapter 4.

2. Paul Weiss. *Sport: A Philosophic Inquiry* (Carbondale: Southern Illinois University Press, 1979). The major argument presented in Weiss's work is that through sport individuals seek excellence.

3. Drew Hyland. "Athletics and Angst: Reflections on the Philosophical Relevance of Play," *Sport and the Body: A Philosophical Symposium,* ed. Ellen Gerber and William Morgan (Philadelphia: Lea & Febiger, 1979), p. 137.

4. Stanley Eitzen and George Sage. *Sociology of American Sport* (Dubuque, Iowa: Wm. C. Brown, 1978), p. 67.

5. *Ibid.,* p. 66.

6. *Ibid.*

7. Most neo-Marxists do not discuss sport explicitly. The positions I present are either implicitly present in their views and/or explicitly advocated by particular authors whom I credit.

8. Paul Hock. *Rip Off the Big Game* (Garden City, N.Y.: Doubleday, 1972), p. 7.

9. *Ibid.,* p. 10.

10. Bero Rigauer. *Sport and Work* (New York: Columbia University Press, 1981), p. 13. Jean-Marie Brohm's book is *Sport: A Prison of Measured Time* (London: Villiers Publications, 1978).

11. Rigauer, p. 67. Rigauer is quoting F. W. Taylor.

12. Translated by A. E. Taylor in Edith Hamilton & Huntington Cairns (eds.), *Plato: The Collected Dialogues* (Princeton, N.J.: Bollingen, 1980).

13. Johan Huizinga. *Homo Ludens* (Boston: Beacon Press, 1955).

14. Suits, chapter 1.

15. *Ibid.,* p. 8.

16. Huizinga, p. 199.

17. All feminists believe that women suffer systematic injustice. Radical feminists believe, in addition, that the oppression of women is the most fundamental of all sorts of oppression. Most feminists do not discuss sport explicitly. The positions I present here are either implicitly presented in their views and/or explicitly advocated by particular authors whom I credit.

18. Eugene Bianchi. "The Super-Bowl Culture of Male Violence," *Jock: Sport and the Male Identity,* ed. Donald Sabo Jr. & Ross Runfola (Englewood Cliffs, N.J.: Prentice-Hall, 1980), 122.

19. Lucy Komisar. "Violence and the Masculine Mystique, *Jock: Sport and the Male Identity,* p. 140.

20. Bianchi, p. 121.

21. *Ibid.,* p. 123.

22. Arnold Beisser. "The American Seasonal Masculinity Rite," *The Madness in Sport* (New York: Appleton-Century-Crofts, 1967. Chapter 16, pp. 214–225). Reprinted in *Sport Sociology: Contemporary Themes,* Yiannakis, et al. (Dubuque, Iowa: Kendall/Hunt, 1976), p. 196.

23. *Ibid.*

24. Terry Orlick. *Winning Through Cooperation* (Washington, D. C.: Hawkins, 1978), p. 166. The number of players on each team remains constant because the team switching occurs only after a player from each side has relinquished service and is thus ready to switch to the other team.

25. Rigauer discusses this parallelism in the work cited in note #10.

26. Rigauer, p. 58.

27. Both Brohm and Rigauer argue that sport perpetuates the achievement principle.

28. There is presently no participation by women at the youth levels of some sports. There is also no professional level at all in women's sports with a few exceptions, such as tennis and golf.

29. Jane English, "Sex Equality in Sports" *Philosophy & Public Affairs,* 7, no. 3 (Spring 1978), p. 5.

30. English's basic benefits are health, self-respect to be gained by doing one's best, the cooperation to be gained from working with teammates and the incentive gained from facing opponents, the "character" of learning to be a good loser and good winner, the chance to improve one's skills and learn to accept criticism, and just plain fun.

31. English, p. 5.

32. Bonnie Beck, "The Future of Women's Sport: Issues, Insights, and Struggles," *Jock: Sports and Male Identity,* p. 301.

33. *Ibid.*

34. I would like to thank Betsy Postow for her very helpful comments and suggestions.

Questions for Consideration

1. Flesh out, then critically discuss Hundley's arguments against the contemporary ends-oriented approach to sports.

2. Evaluate the three different perspectives of the overemphasis on winning. Can you think of any other causally relevant variables left out of these models?

3. Critically assess some of the feminist ideas on reform of sport.

19   On Winning
and Athletic Superiority

Nicholas Dixon
Altma College

Understanding the "better team" as the team that deserves to win, Nicholas Dixon says that a study of the ways in which the better team often fails to win tells us plenty about the practice of sports and how we judge athletic superiority.

Refereeing errors, cheating, gamesmanship, bad luck, and inferior performances by superior players each must be factored into our understanding of deserving to win. Some of these, such as referees' errors, ill luck, and subpar performances, seem a part of sport. Others, such as cheating and gamesmanship, seem morally wrong. Close scrutiny of these factors force us to reevaluate what we mean by "best team," "winner," and "athletic superiority." In other words, how do we determine which team is best? In the United States, the marquis sports determine this by a playoff system. This puts a premium on excellent play under psychological stress. In other countries, the team that demonstrates success over a season's play is recognized as best. This minimizes psychological factors as well as the role of missed or bad calls and chance.

Dixon's argument is that, given refereeing errors, cheating, gamesmanship, bad luck, and subpar performances, no system can guarantee that the best team will always win on a given day. Declaring by fiat that the team that survives a playoff system is "best" ignores such contingencies. The playoff system, emphasizing mental toughness, gives these contingencies a greater bearing on the overall outcome. The best measure of athletic excellence measures skill and strategy as well as psychological toughness. So, the playoff system should

be abandoned in favor of one that does not inordinately weight mental toughness as a measure of excellence. Moreover, the concepts of "winning" and "losing" need to be put in saner perspective.

How do we decide which team or player is better in a competitive sporting contest?[1] The obvious answer is that the winner is the superior team or athlete. A central purpose of competitive sport is precisely to provide a comparison—in Kretchmar's terms (7), a contest—that *determines* which team or player is superior. However, we can easily find undeserved victories in which this purpose is not achieved—in other words, contests in which the player or team that wins is not, according to both our intuitions and plausible accounts of the goal of competitive sport from the philosophy of sport literature, better than the losing player or team.[2] This paper is an examination of several such situations in which competitive sport fails to provide an accurate measure of athletic superiority. For brevity's sake, I will at times refer to such events as "failed athletic contests," meaning contests that have failed in their central comparative purpose, even though they may have succeeded in other goals like entertaining spectators.

My purpose is threefold. First, studying various ways in which athletic contests fail to achieve their central comparative purpose is intrinsically interesting. While the philosophy of sport literature is replete with discussions of the purpose of competitive sport, it does not, to my knowledge, address the question of how well athletic contests fulfill that purpose. An instrumental benefit of this discussion is that a clear delineation of the

Reprinted, by permission, from Nicholas Dixon, "On Winning and Athletic Superioity," *Journal of the Philosophy of Sport* XXVI (1999): 10–26.

wide variety of sources of unjust outcomes in sporting contests, showing that winning is not the be all and end all of athletic superiority, may help to weaken the motivation to resort to morally objectionable means to secure victory. Second, in the process of examining unjust victories, we will deepen our understanding of the concept of athletic superiority. More specifically, we will be forced to confront the issue of how much weight we should give to such psychological traits as guile and poise in our determinations of athletic superiority. Third, consideration of how much weight we should give to one particular psychological trait—the ability to perform well under pressure—in our judgments about athletic superiority will lead to the conclusion that the "playoff" system by which championships are determined in American team sports is a relatively inefficient method of determining which team is best.

For the first four sections, I will use "the better team" as interchangeable with "the team that deserves to win." Both expressions refer to the team that performs better (however we choose to define superior performance) in a particular athletic contest. In Section 5, the two concepts diverge, as I discuss the possibility that the team that performs better and deserves to win may still not be the better team.

Section One: Refereeing Errors

Suppose that a soccer referee is either incompetent or openly biased in favor of the home team. He or she disallows as offside three perfectly good goals for the away team, even though replays clearly indicate that all the attacking players were onside. The home team wins by a single goal after the referee awards a "phantom" penalty, even though replays conclusively show that no contact was made with the attacker who slumped to the ground in the penalty area. Furthermore, the away team was constantly on the attack, pinning the far less skillful home team in its own half throughout the entire match. In this case, I suggest, the home team did not deserve to win. The better team did not win.[3] Several different views on the goal of competitive sport support this claim, assuming that the team or player that best meets this goal is the better one and deserves to win. For instance, Robert Simon's view that competitive sport is "the attempt to secure victory within the framework set by the constitutive rules" (11: p. 15) indicates that the away team is superior, since, had the referee applied the rules of the game correctly, it would have won. The injustice of the home team's victory follows from another of Simon's views, namely "the idea of the sports contest as a test of skill, a mutual quest for excellence by the participants" (11: p. 50), since the away team displays more skill and excellence. For the same reason, the away team's superiority also follows from Kathleen M. Pearson's view that the purpose of competitive sport is

> to test the skill of one individual, or group of individuals, against the skill of another individual, or group of individuals, in order to determine who is more skillful in a particular, well-defined activity. (6: p. 183)

But let us pause to consider some objections that would deny that refereeing errors lead to undeserved victories and, hence, to failed athletic contests.

First, we might insist that the referee's word is final and that, as long as no cheating occurs, any results based upon the referee's decisions are just. As a long-serving baseball commentator in Detroit was apt to point out, when people challenged an umpire's calls, tomorrow morning's box scores will always prove that the umpire was right after all. The problem with this argument is that it clumsily conflates power with infallibility. The jury in the first trial of the LAPD officers who assaulted Rodney King certainly had the power to acquit them. Those of us who disagreed with the verdict believed that, even though the correct *procedures* for a jury trial may have been followed, the *outcome* was unjust.

Similarly, even though the procedural rules of soccer do indeed give the referee the final word, this in no way guarantees that the referee's calls will be correct. And referees' errors can lead to unjust results.

Second, and rather more plausibly, some people argue that a great team should be able to overcome bad calls by the referee and win anyway. There may be some truth to this claim, but it does not undermine my thesis, which is that the *better* team can be prevented by refereeing errors from winning, not that great teams can be. The away team in my example may not be good enough to overcome the referee's poor calls, but it is certainly the better team, and deserved to win, according to the rules of the game.

A third objection takes a very different tack. Rather than denying that the winning team (in my example, the home team) is superior, this final objection consists in arguing that the home team does not win at all. For instance, Suits (12: p. 9) argues that "a player who does not confine himself to lusory means may not be said to win, even if he achieves the pre-lusory goal." Thus the home team's alleged victory, which has been achieved by methods that violate the permitted lusory means, even though the referee negligently failed to punish these violations, is not a victory after all. This approach has an interesting parallel in natural law theory's treatment of unjust laws. In justifying his violation of segregation laws, Martin Luther King cited St. Augustine's view that "an unjust law is no law at all" (6: p. 89). Just as an unjust law, according to natural law theory, is superseded by the moral law that it violates, so an apparent victory by illicit means is nullified by the very rules that have been violated.

A problem with this approach is that, in preserving the justice of the outcome of sporting contests by legislating out of existence victories by inferior teams due to refereeing errors, it creates the suspicion of an ad hoc maneuver designed to respond to a troubling objection by stipulation rather than by argument. More important, in considering the analogy with natural law theory, we need to examine a rival theory, that of legal positivism. According to legal positivism, whether a statute is indeed a valid law, we need only consider its "pedigree" (that is, whether it was enacted in accordance with the constitution or whatever other "rule of recognition" is operative) without deciding on its moral justifiability. So a bad law is still a law. The problem with natural law theory, according to legal positivists, is that it conflates the concepts of "law" and "good law," and fails to allow for the very possibility of a bad law. We would do better, they suggest, to focus our attention on moral evaluation and criticism of immoral laws than to dispute their status as law.[4] The implication of legal positivism for our debate over refereeing errors is that, rather than disputing the fact that the home team won the game, we should instead concentrate on describing the injustice of this victory. Ordinary usage has a meaning for the expressions "hollow victory" and "undeserved victory," and we should be suspicious of an approach that would render these concepts meaningless by fiat.

Showing that refereeing errors can lead to undeserved victories by inferior teams has not required us to make any controversial assumptions about our criteria for athletic superiority. The fact that the visiting team was far superior in terms of physical skills and performance seems sufficient, in our example, to identify it as the better team. In the next section, however, we will have to broaden our concept of athletic superiority beyond mere physical prowess.

Section Two: Cheating

My purpose in this section is not to offer a comprehensive account of cheating, a complex topic that deserves a much more detailed discussion than is possible in the confines of this paper. I offer instead what I hope will be an uncontroversial sufficient condition for cheating—namely, an attempt to break the rules of a game while escaping detection and punishment. Whatever else may count as cheating, we can be sure that anything meeting this description does. My goal is to explore the implications of this minimal definition for my topic of the relationship between victory and athletic superiority.

A victory that depends in large part upon cheating seems neither deserved nor a sign of athletic superiority. This is, presumably, why Ben Johnson was stripped of his gold medal in the 1988 Olympic Games after he tested positive for illegal steroids. Granted, Johnson did outperform his rivals. But he would also outperform them if he spiked their food or drink with a performance-impairing drug. In neither case does Johnson's victory prove him to be a superior athlete, because his violation of the rules gives him an unfair advantage over his opponents, thus subverting the race as a legitimate test of athletic excellence. Cheating can also occur *during* a game: A golfer may move the ball from a bad lie when her opponent is not looking, a pitcher may doctor the baseball, or a player in a tennis match without an umpire may wrongly call a ball out. An especially infamous act of cheating was committed by Diego Maradona, one of the most gifted soccer players of all time, who illegally punched the ball into the net to score a goal for Argentina against England in a 1986 World Cup quarterfinal. The referee did not spot the infraction that replays revealed, and Maradona afterwards boasted that the "hand of God" had scored his goal. In general, the reason why cheats do not deserve to win is that their victories are due not to their athletic superiority, but to their violation of rules which their opponents, in contrast, obey. This claim is based on the assumption that the athlete who deserves to win is the one who performs better *within the game's rules* and *under conditions of equality.*

However, we need to consider an audacious defense of cheating as playing a legitimate role in competitive sport. Oliver Leaman (8) describes cheating as the use of "wits" in addition to skill and strategy and suggests that it adds a new dimension that makes sport more interesting. As long as cheating occurs in the context of *overall*

obedience to the rules by the cheater and other competitors, it will not result in anarchy, and the overall character of games will be preserved. Moreover, if we were to recognize cheating as a *legitimate* tactic for athletes to use, then the cheater would no longer have an unfair advantage, since *all* athletes would feel free to cheat. Indeed, the ability to cheat without being detected might even become a prized aspect of athletic skill. So, if Leaman is correct, even the orthodox view that the best athlete, the one who deserves to win, is the one who displays most skill does not necessarily preclude cheating. Perhaps Maradona's ability to deceive the referee into believing that he had used his head and not his hand to score the infamous goal against England is itself evidence of his genius. Machiavellian conflict between ruthless competitors would be the best test of this new, broader concept of athletic prowess.

Regardless of the merits of Leaman's defense of cheating, he has said enough to indicate that we need to broaden our concept of athletic superiority to include more than mere physical prowess. An excellent athlete must not only have superior physical skills but also the acumen to use them wisely, employing shrewd tactics and strategy that are designed to maximize the benefits of his or her skills while simultaneously neutralizing those of opponents. A soccer team that has exquisite ball control skills, but unwisely commits all 11 players to a constant onslaught on the opposing team's goal will often leave itself vulnerable to fast breaks from the opposition. Should the opponents win the game by virtue of a goal scored during just such a fast break, the technically-superior losers cannot justly claim to be the superior team, since they have failed to exhibit an integral part of athletic excellence. If, as Leaman argues, the ability to cheat is itself a legitimate component of the "strategy and tactics" dimension of athletic excellence, then perhaps the cheating winners listed at the beginning of this section did after all deserve their victories.

Of course, moral condemnations of cheating in sport are easy to formulate.[5] However, Leaman's point is precisely that athletes are protected by a kind of moral immunity to the criticisms that would rightly be directed at them were they to cheat outside the context of sport.[6] We might compare this immunity to that enjoyed by defense attorneys in the U.S. Even when an attorney is convinced that her client committed a despicable crime, she is professionally obligated to mount a zealous defense, trying to get key evidence excluded on constitutional grounds, challenging truthful prosecution witnesses, and trying to persuade the jury of alternative possibilities that she herself believes did not happen. The end product of the attorney's actions may be the acquittal of a dangerous, factually guilty defendant.

Now the attorney's moral immunity is an essential part of the legal adversary system, which is itself justified by the belief that even the most despicable defendant deserves a loyal ally to protect his or her rights. Whether or not Leaman's argument for the moral immunity of athletes succeeds, depends on the existence of a similar rationale for allowing cheating in sport. Is cheating essential to sport the way that an attorney's loyalty to clients is essential to the legal adversary system? The answer seems to be no. Granted, widespread cheating would add an extra layer of intrigue and excitement to sport, but it hardly seems to further any of sport's central values. On the contrary, it sabotages one of competitive sport's least controversial goals: to determine which team has most athletic skill, including, as we have just seen, mental abilities like shrewd tactics as well as physical prowess, *as permitted by the rules of the game.* Certainly, successful cheating requires some skill and cunning and even, in some cases, considerable physical ability, but this is very different from the kind of legitimate use of tactical and physical prowess that competitive sport aims to test.[7]

My goal in this subsection is not morally to condemn cheating, even though good reasons exist for doing so. It is, instead, to evaluate the relationship between cheating and athletic superi-

ority. However, for the same reason that teams cannot claim moral immunity for their acts of cheating—that is, they subvert the test of athletic skill that is a central goal of competitive sport—the claim that the team that uses cheating to win is *ipso facto* the best team and deserves to win is unconvincing. This judgment is reflected in the heavy penalties that sporting federations have imposed on athletes whom they catch cheating. More than the long-term suspension that was imposed on Ben Johnson for his illegal drug use, the fact that his Olympic gold medal was taken away from him indicates the belief that he did not deserve to win. In terms of the abilities that competitive sport is designed to test, Johnson was *not* the best athlete. So, at least in some cases, cheating can prevent competitive sport from providing an accurate measure of athletic superiority.

Section Three: Gamesmanship

Gamesmanship is a slippery concept that is hard to define. Unlike cheating, it does not involve violating the rules of the game in the hope of avoiding detection. Examples include using legal but morally dubious designed tactics to unsettle opponents: trash talking, taking an inordinate amount of time between points in a tennis match, and so on. A different kind of gamesmanship is the so-called "professional foul," which is committed in order to prevent an opposing player from scoring an easy goal or lay-up. Unlike outright cheating, such fouls are committed openly, in the expectation that a penalty will be imposed. Perhaps what all gamesmanship has in common is an apparent violation of the *spirit* of a game.[8] My purpose here is not morally to assess gamesmanship. It is, rather, to argue that an athlete or team that successfully uses gamesmanship as a major weapon in securing victory may not deserve to win in the sense of being the best athlete or team. Gamesmanship, then, provides another category of situations in which athletic contests can fail in their aim of accurately determining athletic superiority. We should note that at this stage we may only call gamesmanship an *apparent* violation of the spirit of a game. Should we conclude that successful use of gamesmanship is one sign of a good athlete, then we must withdraw the judgment that it violates the spirit of competitive sport.

I begin by considering the professional or "strategic" foul. Some philosophers of sport outright condemn such fouls,[9] while Robert Simon has given a nuanced, qualified defense of professional fouls in some circumstances (11: pp. 46–49). He points out that in basketball, for instance, the intentional foul is widely regarded as a legitimate strategy. The only issue, on Simon's view, seems to be the prudential one of whether preventing an easy lay-up is worth the penalty incurred for intentional fouls. For the sake of argument, I will grant Simon's point that a professional foul is sometimes a legitimate strategy. My goal in this section is to show that sometimes it is *illegitimate* and subverts the goal of measuring the relative athletic ability of the contestants.

For such an example, let us consider a soccer game that has been dominated by the home team but that remains scoreless going into the final few minutes. The home team finally mounts a decisive attack, and one of its players is about to tap the ball into an empty net when he is brutally rugby-tackled by an opponent, preventing him from scoring. The goalkeeper then saves the resultant penalty. In the final seconds of the game, the away team mounts a similar attack. The home team, in contrast, refrains from resorting to a professional foul to prevent the attacker from scoring, and the away team scores the winning goal with the last kick of the game. In such a case, I suggest, the away team did not deserve to win, because it did not demonstrate superior athletic skill. Its victory is due, instead, to its cynical willingness to exploit the rules of the game that "permit" the professional foul to teams willing to incur the resultant free kick or

penalty. The recent (but unevenly enforced) decision by FIFA (the Federation of International Football Associations) to automatically penalize the professional foul by ejection from the game (without substitution) indicates that soccer's highest governing body regards it as a violation of the game's spirit.

How we view a professional foul may depend on the type of foul involved: we naturally view hard fouls more harshly that risk injuring opponents. Especially in basketball, we are more apt to condemn such fouls when they occur late in the game, since they are more likely to determine its outcome than those that occur earlier. The difference in attitude to the professional foul in basketball and soccer is arguably attributable to the vastly different impact that it can have in each sport. Basketball is a high-scoring sport, in which preventing a lay-up and requiring the offensive player to earn points from the free throw line normally has a minimal impact on a game's outcome. Soccer, in contrast, is a low-scoring sport, in which a single professional foul can prevent what would have been the decisive winning or equalizing goal. In such sports, a team that wins as a result of a professional foul is not necessarily the best team, in terms of the criteria we have so far allowed as relevant for athletic excellence: physical skill and tactical acumen, both exercised within the rules of the game.

The use of psychological tricks—for example, trash-talking or delaying the game—to try to unsettle opponents is a very different kind of gamesmanship that forces us to confront another dimension of our concept of athletic excellence. We have already widened the concept to include mental as well as physical attributes. We now need to consider whether the mental element of athletic superiority should include such emotional characteristics as coolness under pressure, in addition to the cognitive abilities (for instance, strategy) that we have already added. In favor of such a widening of our understanding of athletic excellence is the view that players who allow themselves to be distracted by such tactics do not deserve to win. Truly great players, one might argue, will use their vastly superior skill to compensate for whatever loss of composure they suffer as a result of opponents' psychological tricks. However, we need to remember that the question here is not whether *great* players always win but, rather, whether the *better* player wins when gamesmanship is a decisive factor. And we can easily imagine examples in which a clearly superior, but not great, player is so rattled by her opponent's gamesmanship that she loses her cool and the game. According to the uncontroversial view that the primary purpose of competitive sport is to determine which team or player has superior athletic skill (understood as including both physical ability and astute strategy as permitted by the game's rules), players who use this kind of gamesmanship to win do not appear to deserve their victory.

In response, apologists for gamesmanship will respond that it is a legitimate strategy in competitive sport. If the ability to use gamesmanship (and to remain impervious to opponents' use of it) is part of athletic excellence, then the technically superior player who allows herself to be unsettled by her opponent's psychological tricks is deficient in one of the mental elements of athletic excellence and is not, after all, the better athlete. The issue, which we may safely leave unresolved at this stage, hinges on whether we include "psychological coolness" or temperament as part of the mental element of our definition of athletic excellence. In Section 5, I will discuss in more depth the relationship between temperament and athletic excellence. I will conclude there that, while repeated defeats due to extreme nervousness may disqualify a team's claim to be the best, we must also allow for the possibility that a team that loses a big game due to nervousness may nonetheless be the better team. What has already emerged from this section is that at least one kind of gamesmanship—the professional foul in low scoring games like soccer—can result in undeserved victories in which the better team does not win, and the athletic contest has failed.

Section Four: Bad Luck

The next set of putative failures of athletic contests to accurately measure athletic superiority involves neither mistakes by referees nor misconduct by players. It arises, rather, in games in which one team dominates the other but still manages to lose the game, because of a succession of strokes of bad luck.[10] The distinction between high- and low-scoring games is relevant here. In a high-scoring game like basketball, a few unlucky breaks are unlikely to sway the outcome. In contrast, in a low-scoring game like soccer, a small number of unlucky breaks can be decisive. Nor do we have to resort to thought experiments: most soccer fans have seen games dominated by one team that hits the woodwork several times and still ends up losing to a single goal scored on one of its opponents' few serious attacks. Suppose further that the dominant team has several goal-bound shots deflected by erratic gusts of wind, others stopped by thick mud on the goal line, and others still inadvertently stopped by a poorly-positioned referee. When, moreover, the winning goal is caused by a freakish deflection by a defender, the dominant team may justly claim that it was the better team and deserved to win. Unlucky losers appear, therefore, to provide another category of failed athletic contests. Let us pause to consider some objections.

First, mirroring an argument we have already considered, one might insist that a great team makes its own luck, and teams that fail to do so do not deserve to win. But this argument is vulnerable to a response already given: While a truly great team may indeed be able to salvage victory despite horrendously bad luck, a less talented team may be unable to do so, while still being clearly the better team and deserving to win. Granted, if a team with a long-term poor record claims that its losses were all due to bad luck, we would suspect self-deception and suggest that its players take a little more responsibility for their performances. Luck does tend to even out in the long run. However, in the short run—for instance, an individual game—we may plausibly say that a team was unlucky and did not deserve to lose.

A second objection reminds us that the purpose of any competitive game is to score more points than opponents. When a team dominates the action, keeping the opponent pinned in its own half, yet still manages to lose, it may be the lack of two legitimate considerations in determining athletic superiority, a killer instinct and good strategy, not bad luck, that accounts for its losses. Such charges were made, for instance, against the French soccer team in the 1982 World Cup, when it played beautiful, crowd-pleasing soccer but was eliminated in the quarter-finals. However, even granting for the sake of argument that some dominant teams do not deserve to win, we can still produce cases in which a team loses undeservedly due to bad luck. In the hypothetical case at the beginning of this section, the dominant team did not play pretty but innocuous soccer. It employed shrewd strategy and displayed a killer instinct, translating its dominance into several accurate shots on goal that were stopped only by the woodwork and by aberrational interventions by the wind, the mud, and the referee. Had these interventions not taken place, had any one of these shots gone just a few inches inside, and had the freakish deflection not occurred, the team would have won. Under these admittedly far-fetched circumstances, the better team did not win. However, more mundane examples of unlucky losses do occur in the real soccer world. Even the best players cannot direct their shots to the nearest inch, and the precise placement of any shot is partly a matter of luck. When a team repeatedly hits the goalpost without scoring, it is usually unlucky.

A final objection draws a line in the sand and insists that, no matter how close a team may have been to scoring several goals, it does not deserve to win if it does not score. According to this defense, the team that wins by a freakish goal on an isolated attack, despite several lucky escapes,

including having its own goal's woodwork rattled repeatedly throughout the game by opponents' shots, deserves to win. The problem with this impregnable-sounding argument is precisely that it is too impregnable. Instead of honestly confronting the role of luck in sport, it tries to legislate it out of the picture by simply *defining* the best team as the one that scores most points. Arguments, not question-begging stipulative definitions, are needed to decide the question. And the arguments that I have presented in this and previous sections indicate that refereeing errors, cheating, unacceptable gamesmanship,[11] and bad luck can all result in undeserved victories by inferior teams.

Before moving on to a different aspect of the relationship between winning and athletic superiority, I pause to consider an argument that stipulative definitions of the kind I have just criticized are not necessarily question-begging. According to this argument, winning is an *operational definition* of the concept *the better team* in the same way that a score on an IQ test is an operational definition of the everyday concept of intelligence, and a legal verdict of guilty is an operational definition of the intuitive concept "that guy did it!" Operational definitions generally provide clear, objectively-ascertainable criteria for concepts whose everyday usage is more ambiguous and complex. (Legal guilt is an exception, in that rules of evidence and burden of proof requirements may make determinations of guilt appear more complex than the intuitive sense of "he did it!" Nonetheless, like all operational definitions, it provides an objective decision procedure—in this case, has the prosecution proven beyond a reasonable doubt that the defendant performed the *actus reus* with the requisite *mens rea*?—for determining a question that might otherwise be subject to arbitrary personal preference.) Since operational definitions do not claim to capture all the connotations of the everyday concepts that they replace, we should not be surprised by divergences between the two. People whom we judge very intelligent may perform poorly on IQ tests, and people who we know committed the act of which they are accused may be *correctly* found legally innocent. These divergences need reflect no fault in the operational definitions but, rather, the mere fact that they are operational definitions.

In support of viewing winning as an operational definition of athletic superiority, one goal of athletic contests is precisely to *determine* which team is better, and they have been designed to provide an accurate measure of excellence. Moreover, we sometimes modify rules in order to make contests a more accurate test of athletic superiority, for instance the offfside rule in soccer, which prevents the tactic of booting the ball upfield to strikers who are permanently camped in front of the opposing goal, and encourages teams to play a more skillful passing game. To the extent that winning the contest is an operational definition of athletic superiority that has evolved over the years in the sporting world, it appears to be immune from the critiques that I have made, since my critiques are made from the point of view of the intuitive, everyday concept of athletic excellence. As we have seen, operational definitions do not claim to coincide with the everyday concepts that they are designed to replace.

In response, I do not deny that regarding winning as the criterion for athletic superiority is, *qua* operational definition, irreproachable. However, critiques of operational definitions from the point of view of intuitive concepts still perform two useful functions. First, too great a divergence between an everyday concept and its operational definition casts doubts on the adequacy of that definition. This is precisely what has happened with the concept of IQ, which has been criticized because of major discrepancies between it and intuitive judgments about intelligence. Victories by inferior teams or athletes, on the other hand, are sufficiently rare to indicate that this particular criticism is not applicable to regarding the winner as the better athlete, which remains a workable operational definition. Second, and most important, "external" critiques

from the point of view of everyday concepts serve to remind us that such concepts as legal guilt *are* only operational definitions. They remind us that a defendant may really have "done it," even though he was correctly found legally innocent. And, in the case of the intuitive concept of athletic superiority,[12] they remind us that, while regarding the winner as the better athlete is generally a harmless convention, on some occasions it leads to inaccurate judgments of athletic superiority. I intend this paper, in part, as just such a reminder.

Section Five: Inferior Performances by Superior Athletes

Steffi Graf dominated women's tennis for several years from the late 1980s until the mid-1990s. Suppose that in the middle of her period of dominance, she plays devastating tennis to reach the final at Wimbledon without losing a set. Her opponent is an unseeded player who has battled her way to the final by means of a series of gutsy three-set victories over technically superior players. And suppose, finally, that the unseeded player continues her string of upsets with a famous victory over Graf in a long, desperately close game. Her victory is fair and square. It involves no refereeing errors, no cheating, no gamesmanship, and no notably good luck. She deserves her victory because, on that day, she is the better player. However, in another sense, she is not the better player. Steffi Graf, who would almost certainly beat the player nine times out of ten, is the better player. She just had an off-day.

So we appear to have found another sense in which an athletic contest can result in an inaccurate measure of athletic excellence: The winning player can deserve to win and yet still be an inferior athlete. Superior athletes do sometimes have bad days and lose. Few people would deny this claim in the case of my Steffi Graf example, but when it comes to other sports, some sectors of the sporting community are surprisingly reluctant to concede the possibility of this source of failed athletic contests. Concurrent with discussing their obvious relevance for my central topic of the relationship between winning and athletic superiority, I will point out the implications of such inaccurate measures of athletic superiority for the playoff system used in the U.S. to determine the winners of team sports championships.

According to a popular approach in the U.S. sporting community, a football team with the best record during the National Football League's regular season and playoffs, winning all its games easily but losing the Superbowl, is not after all the best team in the NFL. The surest sign of the best team, the view continues, is the ability to save its best performances for the biggest occasions, and this is precisely what the winning team does, despite its indifferent play during the regular season and the playoffs. Evidence of the prevalence of this view is provided by the astonishing scorn directed at the Buffalo Bills football team in the U.S. for a series of Superbowl losses in recent years. Even though it had the best record in American football for several years and was agonizingly close to winning one of its Superbowl games, the mere fact that it lost several of these finals not only prevented it from being considered the best team but also made it a despised laughingstock among many sport journalists.

Michael Jordan's status as an all-time great was secured in the opinion of many American basketball fans the first year he led the Chicago Bulls to a National Basketball Association championship, even though his play, both quantitatively and qualitatively, may have been just as outstanding in previous seasons. Once again, the underlying belief is that the best players, especially great ones, are those who come through to achieve victory when it matters most: postseason playoff games.

More generally, the playoff system in the best-known professional team sports in the U.S.—baseball, basketball, football, and hockey—clearly presupposes that victory in the biggest games is the best measure of athletic superiority. The championship is awarded not to the team with the best regular-season record but rather to the team that excels in a relatively brief playoff tournament involving some of the teams with the best regular-season records. Athletic excellence is understood as the ability to perform well under pressure, when the stakes are highest, rather than as the ability to perform well over the course of an entire season.

As a matter of contingent fact, the two rival criteria for athletic excellence—performance over an extended period (a season) versus performance in a brief, high-pressure playoff tournament—usually point to the same player or team. With rare exceptions, playoff winners tend to have very strong regular-season records, if not the best. Strong teams win most of their games, including high-pressure playoff games. The most interesting cases from the point of view of our discussion of athletic superiority, though, are those where a team with a mediocre regular-season record wins the playoffs, for example a wild-card team winning the Superbowl. What reasons exist for the belief that this Superbowl winner is, *ipso facto*, that season's best NFL team? Think back to the example about Steffi Graf, where a single defeat in a major tournament to an unranked player would not have dislodged our belief that she was the best women's tennis player in the world during her years of dominance. By analogy, why don't we also believe that the team with a perfect regular season record, which has dominated its opponents throughout the regular season and playoffs, is still the best team in the NFL, despite its subpar performance in its Superbowl loss to a wild card team? Certainly, a difference of degree exists between the two situations. Whereas a single loss in a major tournament is relatively insignificant in the context of Steffi Graf's dozens of victories in many other tournaments, the Superbowl is clearly the most important game in a very brief NFL season, consisting of a *single* tournament with a maximum of only 20 or so games. However, this difference in degree seems insufficient to support the view that the team that wins the playoffs for the championship is necessarily the best team. My scenario in which the season's dominant football team has an off day and loses the Superbowl makes a strong enough *prima facie* case that it is still the best team in the NFL to require in response an *argument* for, and not just an assertion of, the accuracy of the playoff system in measuring athletic excellence.

And perhaps such an argument is not too hard to find. The ability to perform well under pressure, so the argument goes, is a sign of *psychological toughness*, which is an essential ingredient of excellence in competitive sport. We have already encountered in Section 3 one element of psychological toughness, namely the ability to remain impervious to opponents' gamesmanship. Now little doubt exists that psychological toughness is an important quality for winning athletic contests. The key question is how much weight we assign to it in assessing athletic excellence.

I agree that a claim to athletic excellence would be hollow in the case of an athlete who *always* choked in any competitive game, not just big games in big tournaments. We would suspect that a general lack of athletic ability, and not just a suspect temperament, is responsible for the repeated losses. Furthermore, we could even require a baseline of psychological toughness as a prerequisite for athletic excellence, and concede that, however gifted an athlete may be, repeated losses in major tournaments due to nerves, undue sensitivity to opponents' gamesmanship, or a failure to be "up" for the occasion preclude us from considering her as the best athlete in her field. However, we also need to avoid the danger of setting our standard for psychological toughness so high that only actually *winning* the tournament or playoff series or Superbowl qualifies us as mentally strong enough to be the best athlete or team. In other words, we should leave conceptual space for regarding the team that has shown supreme skill, strategy, *and* psychological toughness throughout the entire regular season and playoffs, before losing the final game in the

playoffs in a subpar performance, as nonetheless the best team. If we fail to allow for this possibility, the belief that the best team always comes though on the big occasions has become an article of faith rather than a hypothesis that is open to confirmation or falsification by open-minded examination of our concept of athletic excellence.

To further challenge the centrality of psychological toughness to athletic excellence, consider, by analogy, the importance that we place on the ability to perform well under pressure in other activities. For instance, is excellence in teaching best judged by a job candidate's classroom performance during a one-day campus visit, or by observing her classes for an entire semester? While we admire the candidate who rises to the occasion to deliver a dynamic guest lecture, most search committees recognize that nerves caused by the momentousness of the occasion can obscure the ability of even excellent teachers. A far better, but logistically impractical, way to evaluate a candidate's teaching ability would be to observe her over a longer period of time in a more relaxed setting. Why should we regard performance under pressure as so much more important in judging athletic excellence when in other fields we regard pressure as a factor that can *obscure* excellence? Of course, important disanalogies exist between teaching and sport, which is by its very nature competitive and tense. However, this does not explain why people regard performance under the greatest pressure as *the best* indicator of athletic excellence.

One reason for this may be that we in the U.S. are accustomed to the playoff system, which puts a premium on performing well in a small number of high-pressure games. And the very fact that we do have such a system may cause teams to approach the season in such a way that does indeed make the playoff system a reasonably accurate measure of excellence. In other words, professional teams in the U.S. recognize that reaching and sustaining a peak level of performance during the playoffs is far more important for winning the championship than compiling the best regular-season record. They may, therefore, regard the regular season primarily as a training period of little intrinsic importance, the main purpose of which is to allow them to fine-tune their skills and strategy for the playoffs for which they reserve their maximum effort. Given that we have such a system, the best teams will successfully channel their talents into developing the ability to produce excellent performances under extreme pressure in the brief playoff period.

However, we should not let this blind us to the more fundamental question of whether the playoff system is the best way of measuring talent in the first place. The force of my arguments in this section is that it is not. We seem to have fetishized the ability to perform well under pressure and given it far more importance as a criterion of athletic excellence than it deserves. It is instructive to compare the playoff system with the organization of professional sports in other countries. For example, in professional soccer leagues in Europe and South America the most prestigious trophy goes to the team with the best record at the end of the season. No post-season or playoffs exist. Single-elimination cup tournaments also exist, but they run concurrently with and independently of the so-called league championship. The underlying belief is that the most accurate measure of athletic excellence is performance against all rival teams over an entire season. Why does the introduction of the high pressure that accompanies playoff series provide a better measure? A further advantage of the "over the entire season" method of evaluation is that it minimizes the impact of refereeing errors, cheating, gamesmanship, and luck, much of which will tend to even out over the length of a season, whereas any one of them may be decisive in a playoff tournament.

In the case of international tournaments such as the soccer World Cup or the Olympic Games, simple logistics require a brief, high-pressure "knockout" or single elimination tournament. A season-long series of games or track meets would not be feasible for such international competitions. And doubtless powerful financial consider-

ations underlie the American playoff system, in that it sustains fans' interest and attendance at games far deeper into the season than does the league table approach, which can effectively eliminate most teams from contention well before the season ends. None of my arguments in this section are intended to diminish the value of success in such tournaments or in post-season playoff series in American professional sports. The ability to rise to the occasion and succeed in competition against the best athletes in the nation or the world is indeed a sign of athletic excellence. In the absence of crucial refereeing errors, cheating, unacceptable gamesmanship, and exceptional luck, winners of these tournaments are fully deserving of our admiration. They are indeed the best athletes and teams, in the sense that they performed best on the days of the tournament and deserved their victories. In most cases, they are also the best athletes and teams, judged on their form throughout the current or past season.

My objections have been directed solely at the view that insists that the winning team or athlete in a playoff or a similar tournament is *by definition* the best one, not just on the day but for the entire season or year. My point has been that a subpar performance resulting in a loss, whether due to nerves, insufficient motivation, or some other psychological factor, does not necessarily negate an athlete's or a team's claim to be the best. Psychological toughness is a legitimate component of the mental element in athletic excellence, and a serious deficiency in it greatly weakens an athlete's claim to athletic superiority. But we should beware giving psychological toughness so much importance in our understanding of athletic excellence that it eclipses all other elements.

The most important consequence of my reasoning in this section is that we should reexamine our attitude toward the playoff system in American professional sport. The best way to measure relative ability in domestic professional sport is the system used in European countries for such sports as soccer: a league championship, which is awarded to the team with the best record after an entire season of play. This system minimizes the impact of unjust results in individual games due to such factors as poor refereeing, cheating, gamesmanship, and bad luck. And while end-of-season games will sometimes involve enormous pressure, and while the ability to perform well under this pressure is a legitimate aspect of athletic excellence, the over-a-season method of evaluation is superior to the playoff system in not placing an inordinate weight on this ability in determining which team wins the championship. Unlike international tournaments like the Olympics and the World Cup, logistics do *not* demand that we base championships in American professional sport on brief tournaments. If we persist in using the playoff system, we need to acknowledge that this is a choice, not a necessity. And this choice involves sacrificing a more accurate measure of athletic excellence—the season-long championship—in order to enjoy the financial benefits of the playoff system. By choosing this system, we decrease the probability that the best team wins the championship.

Section Six: Justice and Results in Sport

Despite the relatively uncontroversial nature of the list of situations I have described in which a sporting contest fails to provide an accurate measure of athletic superiority (Sections 1–4), we are reluctant to concede that sometimes sporting contests may have unjust results. We like to think of sport as a supremely democratic arena where ability and dedication are the only determinants of success, at least in those sports that do not require expensive equipment and country club memberships. And there is some truth in this belief: A child from the shantytowns around Rio may face insurmountable socioeconomic obstacles that prevent him from any realistic chance of becoming a lawyer, but exquisite soccer skills may by themselves be sufficient

to raise him to fame and fortune with the Brazilian national team. My conclusion that even sport is not a pure meritocracy may, therefore, appear to tarnish its image. However, the fact that a conclusion may disappoint us is not a good reason for rejecting it.

A helpful parallel to my thesis about sporting results exists in ethics. A venerable tradition associated with Kant holds that I am morally responsible only for what is within my control. I am not responsible for any consequences of my actions that I did not intend and had no reason to foresee. Strictly speaking, the only human actions that are subject to moral evaluation are our *intentions,* which, unlike the consequences of our actions, seem to be fully within our control. However, in the last 25 years or so, philosophers have realized that *moral luck* may play a significant role in determining our moral "record."[13] Factors beyond our control, including genetics, upbringing, and even where and when we happen to be born, influence what kind of people we become and even what kind of intentions we form. Nor does recognizing the role of moral luck require that one make controversial metaphysical assumptions about the absence of free will. Even if we grant that people have free will, we must concede that two people with exactly similar moral character may be faced with vastly different challenges and obstacles during their lives, resulting in one's leading an unobjectionable life, while the other becomes a moral monster. But for the historical accident of living in Germany during Hitler's rise, a Nazi war criminal might well have led a morally innocuous life, while his morally innocuous counterpart who spent his entire life as a farmer in South America might have played a gruesome role in the Holocaust had he lived instead in Nazi Germany.[14] Yet if we were to try to strip away the unfair influence of these external factors and confine our moral evaluation to the part of ourselves over which we have complete control, we would be left with no subject for our ethical judgments.[15] If we are to have moral assessment at all, we have to concede the role played by moral luck.

Similarly, my arguments show that displaying superior athletic skill, strategy, and mental toughness to those of our opponents—in other words, doing everything that is within our control while obeying the rules and spirit of the game—does not guarantee victory. Poor refereeing decisions, cheating, gamesmanship, and bad luck can all deny us the victory that we deserve. Perhaps the realization that morality itself is sometimes unfair, in the sense that we are not in complete control over our moral record, will soften the blow of the unfairness that sometimes arises in sporting results.

In contrast, my discussion of inferior performances by superior athletes (Section 5) does not indicate any unfairness in the results of sporting contests. After all, the team that plays better on the day against superior opponents *deserves* to win. What my arguments in that section do show is that even a just result is sometimes not an accurate indicator of the relative athletic excellence of the teams. The only sense in which such a result is unjust is reflected in the statement that the losing team did not do justice to itself.

So we have seen many factors that can prevent the better team from winning. Bad refereeing decisions, cheating, gamesmanship, and bad luck can result in a loss for the team that performed better and deserved to win. And a subpar performance can result in a deserved loss by a team that is better than its opponents. The concept of athletic superiority that has emerged from our examination of these situations includes not only physical prowess but also mental attributes. And relevant mental attributes include not only cognitive skills like astute strategy but also affective qualities like poise and toughness. However, we should beware of placing undue stress on these affective qualities in our determinations of athletic superiority. A welcome consequence of our realization that a wide range of situations exists in which the better team or player does not win may be to weaken the obsession with winning that exists among some athletes, especially in the U.S. Putting winning and losing in a saner perspective may re-duce the motivation to resort to cheating, distasteful forms of gamesmanship, and trash talking and other forms of taunting. And, while the desire to win is a necessary ingredient of competitive sport, realizing that winning is not the be all and end all of athletic excellence may help to foster the cooperation that is part of healthy competition and prevent it from degenerating into alienation.[16]

Notes

1. For the sake of convenience, I will refer throughout most of this paper to the "better" team or player. While the comparative "better" applies most naturally to contests between pairs of players or teams, I also intend my discussion to include competitions involving several players or teams. Understanding "better" in such contexts to mean "better than the rival(s)" will enable me to avoid the cumbersome construction "better or best."

2. For the sake of brevity, I will henceforth usually refer only to the better team, except when explicitly discussing individual sports, in which case I will refer to the better player. The reader should understand, however, that my entire paper pertains to both team and individual sports.

3. An actual example of a victory resulting from a refereeing error was the University of Colorado football team's infamous "5th down" win over the University of Missouri in 1990.

4. For an excellent summary of this central tenet of legal positivism, see Hart (4: sec. 1).

5. See, for example, Edwin J. Delattre's critique (2).

6. "Cheating in sport need not be compared morally to cheating in our everyday affairs since sport is 'just a game' and not simply a reflection of our everyday behavior. It may be morally acceptable to do certain things in sport which are not acceptable in everyday life" (8: p. 196).

7. See Simon (11: pp. 37–51) for a very perceptive analysis of the incompatibility between cheating and sport as a test of athletic skill.

8. Fine questions arise concerning whether a professional foul can be such a violation of d'Agostino's concept of the ethos of a game (1) that it constitutes an outright act of cheating rather than gamesmanship. Such questions, while of great intrinsic interest, are beyond the scope of this section. My concern is with whether such acts, *however* we characterize them, can result in an undeserved

victory by an inferior team, and with what implications this has for our concept of athletic superiority.

9. See Warren Fraleigh (3) for a persuasive example of such critiques.

10. By luck I mean factors that are beyond the control of either team and that have, hence, no bearing on the teams' athletic ability, whether understood in purely physical or psychological terms. Uncontroversial examples of bad luck are being on the wrong end of a net cord in tennis or losing a golf game when one's opponent's tee shot on the final hole rebounds freakishly from a tree into the hole.

11. I add the qualifier "*unacceptable* gamesmanship" to allow for my concession to Simon, for the sake of argument, in the previous section—namely, that some gamesmanship may be permissible. By implication, a team that succumbs to opponents who use *legitimate* gamesmanship may have lost the right to call itself the better team.

12. I remind the reader that what I refer to as the "intuitive" concept of athletic superiority is not a blind appeal to intuition. The account developed in this paper is based on uncontroversial views on the purpose of competitive sport by such philosophers of sport as Kretchmar, Simon, and Pearson, and modified in the light of Leaman's radical critique.

13. Two ground-breaking articles are Thomas Nagel (9) and Bernard Williams (13).

14. This is a variation on an example that Nagel gives (9: p. 26).

15. Nagel: "The area of genuine agency, and therefore of legitimate moral judgment, seems to shrink under this scrutiny to an extensionless point" (9: p. 35).

16. For an excellent account of healthy, non-alienated competition in sport, see Drew A. Hyland (5).

4. Hart. H.L.A. "Positivism and the Separation of Law and Morals." *Harvard Law Review*. 71:593, 1958.

5. Hyland, D.A. "Opponents, Contestants, and Competitors: The Dialectic of Sport." *Journal of the Philosophy of Sport*. 11:63–70, 1984.

6. King, M.L. "Letter from a Birmingham Jail." In: *I Have a Dream: Writings and Speeches that Changed the World*. San Francisco: HarperCollins, 1992.

7. Kretchmar, R.S. "From Test to Contest: An Analysis of Two Kinds of Counterpoint in Sport." *Journal of the Philosophy of Sport*. 2:23–30, 1975.

8. Leaman, O. "Cheating and Fair Play in Sport." In: *Philosophic Inquiry in Sport* (2nd ed.), W.J. Morgan and K.V. Meier (Eds.). Champaign, IL: Human Kinetics, 1995.

9. Nagel, T. "Moral Luck." In: *Mortal Questions*. Cambridge, UK: Cambridge University Press, 1979.

10. Pearson, K.M. "Deception, Sportsmanship, and Ethics." In: *Philosophic Inquiry in Sport* (2nd ed.), W.J. Morgan and K.V. Meier (Eds.). Champaign, IL: Human Kinetics, 1995.

11. Simon, R.L. *Fair Play: Sports, Values, and Society*. Boulder, CO: Westview Press, 1991.

12. Suits, B. "The Elements of Sport." In: *Philosophic Inquiry in Sport* (2nd ed.). W.J. Morgan and K.V. Meier (Eds.). Champaign, IL: Human Kinetics, 1995.

13. Williams, B. "Moral Luck." In: *Moral Luck: Philosophical Papers 1973–1980*. Cambridge, UK: Cambridge University Press, 1981.

Bibliography

1. D'Agostino, F. "The Ethos of Games." *Journal of the Philosophy of Sport*. 8:7–18, 1981.

2. Delattre, E.J. "Some Reflections on Success and Failure in Competitive Athletics." *Journal of the Philosophy of Sport*. 2:133–139, 1975.

3. Fraleigh, W. "Why the Good Foul Is Not Good." *Journal of Physical Education, Recreation and Dance*. 53(1):41–42, 1982.

Questions for Consideration

1. Do you agree that playoff systems put undue stress on psychological factors at the expense of skill and strategy?

2. Are Dixon's proposed reforms morally appropriate? In addition, are they practicable in American society?

20 The Dark Side of Competition

D. Stanley Eitzen

D. Stanley Eitzen begins this reading by stating that it is a human propensity to view competitiveness as natural. This may be so to some extent, but so, too, is cooperation.

Our "natural" competitiveness, he suggests, is instilled in us from infancy and groomed thereafter by parents and society alike. Common justifications for instilling competitiveness are increased motivation and greater desire for what is excellent. Unsurprisingly, these values tie in neatly with the productive aims and consumerist mentality of American capitalism.

There are negative consequences of competition, the most inimical being that it makes winning the chief standard of evaluation.

In summary, Eitzen's argument focuses on how a sense of competition is constantly nurtured and developed in us from childhood. In the end, he is not optimistic about the possibility of social reform, though he does offer some suggestions for improvement: renovation of our reward system and removal of competitive sports from schools. The reading ends with an inspiring episode from a Special Olympics competition, where three mentally challenged youths express their understanding of competition as essentially cooperative. If we want progress, we must cultivate cooperation, not competition.

Some believe that competition is the behavioral equivalent of gravity, a natural and inevitable force. A student in one of my classes once remarked that he was very competitive but that no one had ever taught him to be that way. His argument was that competition is part of the DNA of the animal and human worlds, with the best surviving. This is the credo of the Social Darwinists—that is, as people vie for a prize, honor, advantage, space, sex, or whatever, excellence is rewarded and progress is achieved. In the process, the best minds and the best bodies win and rise to the top while the less able lose and sink to the bottom. This logic has been used to justify social inequality with the able seen as deserving of their rewards and the failures deserving of their lesser fate. This school of thought was prevalent in the United States around the turn of the century and remnants are found today, in the White House and Congress, sometimes in editorials, always among racists, and even occasionally by academicians.

My argument is that if competition is "natural" among the human species, so, too, is cooperation. Stated more strongly, I argue that cooperation is more critical to human progress and to get the things we want than competition. A sports team composed of competitive individuals without teamwork is, by definition, relatively ineffective. The most notable human accomplishments, such as the building of railroads or cathedrals, the forming of a constitution, the damming of mighty rivers, and the overturning of tyranny by a Gandhi or a Martin Luther King, Jr., are monuments to cooperative behavior.

My goal in this presentation is to analyze competition, this most central value of American society, focusing on its negative consequences. I'll conclude by presenting some alternatives.

The Pervasiveness of Competition

Recall my student who said that "no one ever taught him to be competitive." Well, I believe that he was so immersed in a competitive environment that he could not see it, just like a fish doesn't understand water because it does not know anything different. Let me elaborate.

Parents instill competition in their children at a young age. There is evidence that first-borns tend to be more bowlegged than later-borns. I do not know the explanation for this but one possibility is that parents are so interested in showing off the prowess of their parenting *and* their progeny that they force their first child to walk earlier than they should. Having proven their point, parents are less demanding of later-borns, at least with early walking. At a more blatant level, some parents enter their children in "diaper derbies" (crawling races for those under one year), beauty contests, baton twirling contests, and the like. Others enroll their preschoolers in music lessons, ballet lessons, swimming lessons, and other efforts to give their children a head start in the competitive world.

At the elementary school level, there are spelling contests, selection of soloists or actors on the basis of tryouts, ability grouping based on test performance, and so on. Outside of school, there are community-sponsored competitions for the very young, such as in Florida where boys age five play tackle football for a three-and-one-half month season. Adults have organized triathlons (where the contestants participate in a three-part race involving swimming, bicycling, and running) for children as young as seven. The Cub Scouts have one event that epitomizes the American emphasis on competition—the Pinewood Derby. Each scout is given a block of wood and some wheels, from which they are to create a model racing car. Each scout (and his father, no doubt) works at making the fastest car. At the big event, of course, there is only one winner, with the rest of the pack losers. Such an event is very American.

During the junior high and senior high school years, youth are exposed even more to competition. At school, there is grading on the curve, trying out for athletic teams, cheerleader, debate, acting roles, competing for valedictorian, acceptance in top colleges, and intense competition for first chair for each instrument in band and orchestra. Outside of school there are community-based sports, including age-group swimming, elite music groups, beauty and talent contests, 4-H judging, and other forms of competition. An egregious example is the "punt, pass, and kick" contest sponsored by Ford Motor Company. In this contest, winners are selected at the local level and proceed through the various state and regional tournaments until a winner is found for each age category. In one year, there were 1,112,702 entrants in this contest and only six eventual winners. An interesting question is why an organization such as Ford would sponsor an event with six winners and 1,112,696 losers. This, too, is very American.

At the adult level, life is often a zero-sum situation where one wins at the expense of others. The business world in a capitalist society, of course, is highly competitive (except among the large corporations where parallel pricing, shared monopolies, and government subsidies reduce competition substantially). At work, employees compete for limited promotions and salary raises. At my university, for example, each academic department ranks its members from "best" to "worst" and the yearly raises are divided accordingly. One year the philosophy department refused to participate in this exercise, arguing that its members were uniformly excellent. The dean insisted that the faculty must be ranked or else no monies would be allocated to the department. Once again, this type of motivational scheme is very American.

Even during leisure, many, if not most Americans engage in competitions, involving all manner of sports, participation in fantasy sports leagues, tryouts for community plays, music groups, gambling, art contests, county fair competitions for best quilt or pickles, and such competitions as the "Pillsbury Bakeoff," and "Mrs. USA." Finally, competition even intrudes into our most intimate of relationships. In families, there are sibling rivalries, parent-child competition, and even efforts by spouses (or lovers) to outdo the other. Eric Berne, the transactional analyst, wrote of the various "games people play" in relationships. One of those "games" employed even among lovers, he called, if you'll excuse his language, "Now, I've got you, you son of a bitch." Isn't it curious, that people in love would find themselves engaged in behaviors that elevate themselves by diminishing their partners.

The Positive Consequences of Competition

I'm sure that we are quite familiar with the arguments supporting competition, so I will merely list them. The two most common reasons given for competition are that it is a strong motivator and it pushes everyone to strive for excellence. These qualities have led American society to greater societal achievements in productivity than found in less competitive societies. This emphasis on competition and its justification of inequality, of course, fit nicely with capitalism.

The Negative Consequences of Competition

I am going to overlook the more obvious negative consequences of a highly competitive society such as war, the arms race, and imperialism. Similarly, I will not consider here the negative behaviors of corporations in a highly competitive environment such as fraud, misleading advertising, cheating, and the like. These are very important, and I have written a book about these political and economic misadventures. Rather, I will focus here on the more subtle negative results of competition, ones that we might be more likely to miss.

One negative impact of the emphasis on competition is that it is unhealthy for individuals. In 1988 over $1 billion was spent in the United States for one drug—Zantac—which combats ulcers. Surely a major source of ulcers is the stress we face daily in our competitive environments. Similarly, those of us who are "Type A" are competitive, combative, impatient, overscheduled, teeth-grinders. "Type B" people, in contrast, are relaxed, without a sense of urgency, and tolerant. They say the equivalent of "que pasa" a lot. With no expertise on this, I can only speculate that while the boundaries of temperament are encoded genetically, a competitive environment brings out the worst in Type A persons, which heightens their tendency for high blood pressure, stroke, and heart disease. These same people living in a less driven culture likely would live longer.

Another problem with competition is that, by definition, people are sorted into a very few "winners" and many "losers." What is the effect on a youngster's self-esteem when he or she is "cut" from the basketball team or when she or he rarely gets to play in games? What is the level of motivation for a junior high school student who is twenty-third chair flute in the school band? Will she or he strive ever more to achieve in music or give up?

When competition supersedes other values, it may be dysfunctional for the participants and even society. Several years ago, an experiment was made comparing ten-year-olds in the United States and Mexico. This experiment involved a marble-pull game. The investigator told pairs of children that they could obtain prizes by playing the game. The object of the game was for each player to pull a string that manipulated a marble holder so that the marble would drop into a goal at their end of the table. However, if both children pulled on their strings at the same time, the marble holder would break apart and neither child could win a prize. The children soon figured out that they could engage in a tug-of-war where no one would win or they could cooperate and take turns winning prizes. The Anglo-American children tended to choose the former route, which meant no one won, while the Mexican children opted for the latter, where they shared prizes. Now which response was the more rational? My interpretation is that the American youth were possessed with an irrational competitive spirit that was dysfunctional. Let me give another illustration of how competition can have irrational consequences, this time looking at medical students. Norman Cousins, an especially keen observer of American life, has criticized the process whereby students are selected for and graduate from medical school. He says:

[Since admission to medical schools is so competitive, grades have become] the most tangible measure on which the school can base its admission decisions. Grades may be an indication of ability to learn, but when they make students fiercely competitive, the end product is not necessarily good scholarship but more often a sharpening of academic predatory skills. . . . It is important to ask whether we really want to foster a barracuda psychology for young people who will have to carry the responsibility for maintaining the health and well-being of the American people. Do we really want them to be trained in an atmosphere that sharpens their teeth even more than it develops their minds?

When winning is the primary standard for evaluation, several negative outcomes result. Let me enumerate these, using sport for examples. First, in a competitive society there is a tendency to evaluate people by their accomplishments rather than their character, personality, and other human qualities. When "winning is everything," then losers are considered just that. One successful university basketball coach once counseled prospective coaches that if they wanted to be winners, then they should associate only with winners. Is this an appropriate guiding principle for conducting our lives?

Second, when winning is paramount, schools and communities organize sports for the already gifted. This elitist approach means that the few will

be given the best equipment, the best coaching, and prime time reserved for their participation, while the less able will be denied participation altogether or given very little attention. If sports participation is a useful activity, then it should be for the many, not the few, in my view.

A third problem with the emphasis on winning is that parents may push their children beyond the normal to succeed. Two examples make this point. Is it appropriate behavior for parents to hire a swimming coach for their twenty-two-month-old daughter, one who has the girl swim one-fourth of a mile three times a week, switching to one-half a mile three times a week when she turned two? This happened for a California youngster in 1980. The parents' goal is for this youngster to be an Olympic champion in 1992. In 1972 the national record for one-year-olds in the mile run was established by Steve Parsons of Normal, Illinois (the time was 24:16.6). Are these instances of child abuse or what?

A fourth problem with the primacy of winning is that coaches may push their charges too hard. Coaches may be physically or emotionally abusive. They may limit their players' civil rights. And, they may play their injured athletes by using pain killers without regard for their long-term physical well-being.

Fifth, when the desire to win is so great, the "end may justify the means." Coaches and players may use illegal tactics. Athletes may use performance-enhancing drugs such as steroids and amphetamines to achieve a "competitive edge" or more subtly, but nonetheless unethical, using such means as blood doping or getting pregnant to get positive hormonal changes, and then having an abortion. Both of these practices occur among endurance athletes. As we all know, big-time college coaches in their zeal to win have been found guilty of exploiting athletes, falsifying transcripts, providing illegal payments, hiring surrogate test takers, paying athletes for nonexistent summer jobs, and illegally using government Pell grants and work study monies for athletes. So much, I would argue, for the myth that "sport builds character."

Sixth, when winning is all important, there may be a tendency to crush the opposition. This was the case when Riverside Poly High School girls basketball team played Norte Vista several years ago. Riverside won by a score of 179–15 with one player, Cheryl Miller, scoring a California record of 105 points. Was the Riverside coach ethical? I think not. Moreover, what were the consequences of his actions on his team and on the players and community of Norte Vista? Will the Norte Vista girls be motivated to improve their performance or will this humiliating experience crush their spirit?

Seventh, many people in a competitive society have difficulty with coming in second. In 1986, Kathy Ormsby, an excellent student and an All-American distance runner at North Carolina State, veered off the track during a race, ran away from the stadium and jumped off a bridge, suffering, as a result, a life-long paralysis. I can only speculate on her motives. I suspect that losing was so abjectly appalling to her that she could fathom no alternative but to end her life. This is an extreme example but it illustrates the intolerance some of us have for losers, even those who came close to winning. Let me illustrate this point with two examples. The Denver Broncos have made it to the Super Bowl three times but they have lost that big game each time. In the minds of the Bronco players, fans, as well as others across the United States, the Broncos were losers in each of those years even though they were second out of twenty-eight teams, which, if you think about it, is not too shabby an accomplishment. My other illustration involves a football team, composed of fifth-graders, in Florida. They were undefeated going into the state finals but lost there in a close game. At a banquet following that season each player on this team was given a plaque on which was inscribed a quote from Vince Lombardi:

> There is no room for second place. I have finished second twice at Green Bay and I never want to finish second again. There is a second place bowl game but it is a game for losers played by losers. It is and always has been an

American zeal to be first in anything we do and to win and to win and to win.

In other words, the parents and coaches of these boys wanted them to never be satisfied with being second. Second is losing. The only acceptable placement is first.

Finally, when "winning is the only thing" the joy in participation is lost. I have observed that organized sports from youth programs to the professional level is mostly devoid of playfulness. When the object is to win, then the primacy of the activity is lost. In this vein, America's premier cross country skier, Bill Koch, has said:

> If 100 people enter a race that means there have to be 99 losers. The worst thing that you can teach children is that so many of them will be losers. Because then they won't even try. It's the striving, the attempt, the fight, that's the important thing.

In other words, it's the process that is primary, not the outcome. White water rafters and mountain climbers understand this. So, too, do players in a pickup touch football game. Why can't the rest of us figure out this fundamental truth?

Alternatives

I am not naive enough to think that we can eliminate competition in American society. We will not become like the Hopi or the Zuni. Competition is built into the fabric of our society. I must admit, too, that I like competition, I thrive on it. But the problems inherent in competition bother me. I would like to find alternatives that would eliminate or at least diminish some of these problems. Let me provide a few possibilities for you to consider as you form families, become active in communities, and establish yourself in occupations.

Can we improve our competitive environment? I suggest that we shift from a competitive reward structure to an individualistic reward structure. The former is what we have—a system that rewards participants in relation to their competitors, such as grading on a curve or crowning a single winner. An individualistic reward structure, on the other hand, rewards individuals as they measure up to some absolute standard. The striving for excellence is still there but the number of winners is limitless. Grading according to a percentage is one example. Karate provides an excellent example as competitors strive to master different levels of achievement as symbolized by different colored belts. In my department in a research university, faculty members receive annual merit raises based mostly on the number of articles and books they publish annually. This system rewards the most prolific individual the most. Why can't we have a reward system based on a standard, which says that everyone who publishes at least one article a year in a refereed journal is judged as "excellent"? Those who publish one article every other year would be classified as "very good," and rewarded accordingly. Such a plan would encourage everyone in the department to be active scholars. The current system, in contrast, discourages some because they will never be labeled "excellent" and rewarded for that achievement. I believe that the department and individual faculty members suffer from our current practice.

The number of winners can also be maximized by rewarding different skills. Suppose, for example, that we engage in a two-mile race. Who might the winner be? In our society, the winner would be established by whoever is the fastest. But Gandhi said that "there is more to life than increasing its speed." Why not reward those who come closest to predicting their finishing time? Or, how about rewarding form, with judges evaluating the stride, arm swing, posture, and pelvic tilt of the runners? How about rewarding everyone who established a personal best? Why not have a number of categories with winners determined for each?

What about removing sports competition from schools. Schools in many European countries, for example, do not have sports. There are sports clubs in the community but the schools stay out of it, leaving the school day for education and not for the defeat of enemies on Friday evenings. This would free the facilities and equipment for maximum use by the students, not just the elite.

Let me conclude with a special example from the Special Olympics. A friend of mine observed a 200 meter race among three evenly matched 12-year-olds at a Special Olympics event in Colorado Springs. About twenty-five yards from the finish line, one of the contestants fell. The other two runners stopped and helped their competitor to his feet, brushed him off, and jogged together hand in hand to the finish line, ending the race in a three-way tie. The actions of these three, especially the two who did not fall, are un-American. Perhaps because they were retarded, they did not understand the importance of winning in our society. To them, the welfare of their opponent was primary. Can we learn this lesson from the retarded? My message is that the successful life involves the pursuit of excellence, a fundamental respect for others, even one's competitors, and enjoyment in the process. Competition as structured in our society with its emphasis on the outcome undermines these goals. I enjoin you to be thoughtful about the role of competition in your life and how it might be restructured to maximize humane goals.

Questions for Consideration

1. To what extent do competition and cooperation relate to a naturalistic or normative understanding of human behavior?
2. How might the cooperation-versus-competition thesis play out on a global level?
3. Does Eitzen underestimate the importance of biological factors in his explanation of aggression (competition) in human behavior?

Violence

21 Into the Endzone for a Touchdown: A Psychoanalytical Consideration of American Football

Alan Dundes
University of California, Berkeley

This reading, by Alan Dundes, is an attempt to explain from a psychoanalytical points of view the overwhelming popularity of American football, especially among males. What is it about football that strikes "a most responsive chord in the American psyche"? That the game is an appropriate outlet for aggression cannot be the reason, since many other sports match football in aggression but are not as popular. That footballs allows for coordinated teamwork, love of competition, and development of specialized skills is an explanation just as faulty in that many other, if not most, sports do this as well. Dundes answers flatly, and controversially, that the game is popular because it is a form of ritualized male homosexuality.

The gist of the reading is an examination of the idioms and metaphors used in folk speech to describe how American football is properly played. These, Dundes argues, are replete with homosexual significance. While the terminology used to describe one's own teammates is that of trust and respect, for the opponents, it is a matter of homosexual emasculinization and penetration. (I caution readers here that Dundes's use of language is frank and to the point. Thus, it may prove to be offensive for some.)

From Alan Dundes, "Into the Endzone for a Touchdown: A Psychoanalytical Consideration of American Football," from *Western Folklore* 37 (1978): 75–88, © California Folklore Society, reprinted, by permission.

In college athletics it is abundantly clear that it is football which counts highest among both enrolled students and alumni. It is almost as though the masculinity of male alumni is at stake in a given game, especially when a hated rival school is the opponent. College fund raisers are well aware that a winning football season may prove to be the key to a successful financial campaign to increase the school's endowment capital. The Rose Bowl and other postseason bowl games for colleges, plus the Super Bowl for professional football teams have come to rank as national festival occasions in the United States. All this makes it reasonable to assume that there is something about football which strikes a most responsive chord in the American psyche. No other American sport consistently draws fans in the numbers which are attracted to football. One need only compare the crowd-attendance statistics for college or professional baseball games with the analogous figures for football to see the enormous appeal of the latter. The question is: what is it about American football that could possibly account for its extraordinary popularity?

In the relatively meager scholarship devoted to football, one finds the usual array of theoretical approaches. The ancestral form of football, a game more like rugby or soccer, was interpreted as a solar ritual—with a disc-shaped rock or object supposedly representing the sun[1]—and also

241

as a fertility ritual intended to ensure agricultural abundance. It had been noted, for example, that in some parts of England and France, the rival teams consisted of married men playing against bachelors.[2] In one custom, a newly married woman would throw over the church a ball for which married men and bachelors fought. The distinction between the married and the unmarried suggests that the game might be a kind of ritual test or battle with marriage signifying socially sanctioned fertility.[3]

The historical evolution of American football from English rugby has been well documented,[4] but the historical facts do not in and of themselves account for any psychological rationale leading to the unprecedented enthusiasm for the sport. It is insufficient to state that football offers an appropriate outlet for the expression of aggression. William Arens has rightly observed that it would be an oversimplification "to single out violence as the sole or even primary reason for the game's popularity."[5] Many sports provide a similar outlet (e.g., wrestling, ice hockey, roller derby), but few of these come close to matching football as a spectacle for many Americans. Similarly, pointing to such features as a love of competition, or the admiration of coordinated teamwork, or the development of specialists (e.g., punters, punt returners, field-goal kickers, etc.) is not convincing since such features occur in most if not all sports.

Recently, studies of American football have suggested that the game serves as a male initiation ritual.[6] Arens, for example, remarks that football is "a male preserve that manifests both the physical and cultural values of masculinity,"[7] a description which had previously been applied, aptly it would appear, to British rugby.[8] Arens points out that the equipment worn "accents the male physique" through the enlarged head and shoulders coupled with a narrowed waist. With the lower torso "poured into skin-tight pants accented only by a metal codpiece," Arens contends that the result "is not an expression but an exaggeration of maleness." He comments further: "Dressed in this manner, the players can engage in hand holding, hugging, and bottom patting. which would be disapproved of in any other context, but which is accepted on the gridiron without a second thought."[9] Having said this much, Arens fails to draw any inferences about possible ritual homosexual aspects of football. Instead, he goes on to note that American football resembles male rituals in other cultures insofar as contact with females is discouraged if not forbidden. The argument usually given is one of "limited good."[10] A man has only so much energy and if he uses it in sexual activity, he will have that much less to use in hunting, warfare, or in this case, football. I believe Arens and others are correct in calling attention to the ritual and symbolic dimensions of American football, but I think the psychological implications of the underlying symbolism have not been adequately explored.

Football is one of a large number of competitive games which involve the scoring of points by gaining access to a defended area in an opponent's territory. In basketball, one must throw a ball through a hoop (and net) attached to the other team's backboard. In ice hockey, one must hit the puck into the goal at the opponent's end of the rink. In football, the object is to move the ball across the opponent's goal into his endzone. It does not require a great deal of Freudian sophistication to see a possible sexual component in such acts as throwing a ball through a hoop, hitting a puck across a "crease" into an enclosed area bounded by nets or cage, and other structurally similar acts. But what is not so obvious is the connection of such sexual symbolism with an all-male group of participants.

Psychologists and psychoanalysts have not chosen to examine American football to any great extent. Psychologist G. T. W. Patrick, writing in 1903, tried to explain the fascination of the game: "Evidently there is some great force, psychological or sociological, at work here which science has not yet investigated"; but he could offer little detail about what that great force might be.[11] Similarly, psychoanalyst A. A. Brill's superficial consideration of football in 1929 failed to illuminate the psychodynamics of the game.[12] Perhaps the best known Freudian analysis of football is the parody written originally in 1955 in the *Rocky Mountain Herald* by poet Thomas Hornsby Ferril, using the pseudonym Childe Herald, but the essay is more amusing than analytic. Actually his interpretation tends to be more inclined towards ritual than psychoanalytic theory. He suggests "football is so much syndrome of religious rites symbolizing the struggle to preserve the egg of life through the rigors of impending winter. The rites begin at the autumn equinox and culminate on the first day of the New Year with great festivals identified with bowls of plenty; the festivals are associated with flowers such as roses, fruits such as oranges, farm crops such as cotton and even sun-worship and the appeasement of great reptiles such as alligators."[13] While he does say that "football obviously arises out of the Oedipus complex," he provides little evidence other than mentioning that college games are usually played for one's alma mater, which he translates as "dear mother." Actually, a more literal translation would be "nourishing mother" (and for that matter, *alumnus* literally means nursling.)

A more conventional psychoanalytic perspective is offered by Adrian Stokes in his survey of ball games with special reference to cricket. Stokes predictably describes football (soccer) in Oedipal terms. Each team defends the goal at their back. "In front is a new land, the new woman, whom they strive to possess in the interest of preserving the mother inviolate, in order, as it were, to progress from infancy to adulthood: at the same time, the defensive role is the father's; he opposes the forward youth of the opposition."[14] Speaking of rugby football, Stokes proposes the following description: "Ejected out of the mother's body, out of the scrum, after frantic hooking and pushing, there emerges the rich loot of the father's genital." According to Stokes, both teams fight to possess the father's phallus, that is, the ball, in order to "steer it through the archetypal vagina, the goal."[15] Earlier, Stokes had suggested the ball represented semen though he

claimed that "more generally the ball is itself the phallus."[16] Folk speech offers some support for the phallic connotation of a ball. One thinks of "balls" for testicles. A man who has "balls" is a man of strength and determination. To "ball" someone is a slang expression for sexual intercourse.[17] On the other hand, while one might agree with the general thesis that there might be a sexual component to both soccer and American football, it is difficult to cite concrete evidence supporting Stokes's contention that the game involves a mother figure or a father surrogate. If psychoanalytic interpretations are valid, then it ought to be possible to adduce specific details of idiom and ritual as documentation for such interpretations. It is not enough for a psychoanalyst to assert ex cathedra what a given event or object supposedly symbolizes.

I believe that a useful way to begin an attempt to understand the psychoanalytic significance of American football is through an examination of football folk speech. For it is precisely in the idioms and metaphors that a clear pattern of personal interaction is revealed. In this regard, it might be helpful first to briefly consider the slang employed in the verbal dueling of the American male. In effect, I am suggesting that American football is analogous to male verbal dueling. Football entails ritual and dramatic action while verbal dueling is more concerned with words. But structurally speaking, they are similar or at least functionally equivalent. In verbal dueling, it is common to speak about putting one's opponent "down." This could mean simply to topple an opponent figuratively, but it could also imply forcing one's adversary to assume a supine position, that is, the "female" position in typical Western sexual intercourse. It should also be noted that an equally humiliating experience for a male would be to serve as a passive receptacle for a male aggressor's phallic thrust. Numerous idioms attest to the widespread popularity of this pattern of imagery to describe a loser. One speaks of having been screwed by one's boss or of having been given the shaft. Submitting to anal intercourse is also implied in perhaps the most common single American folk gesture, the so-called *digitus impudicus,* better known in folk parlance as *"the finger."* Giving someone the finger is often accompanied by such unambiguous explanatory phrases as "Fuck you!" "Screw you!" "Up yours!" or "Up your ass!"

Now what has all this to do with football? I believe that the same symbolic pattern is at work in verbal dueling and much ritual play. Instead of scoring a putdown, one scores a touchdown. Certainly the terminology used in football is suggestive. One gains yardage, but it is not territory which is kept in the sense of being permanently acquired by the invading team. The territory invaded remains nominally under the proprietorship of the opponent. A sports announcer or fan might say, for example, "This is the deepest *penetration* into (opponent's team name) territory so far" [my emphasis]. Only if one gets into the endzone (or kicks a field goal through the uprights of the goalposts) does one earn points.

The use of the term *end* is not accidental. Evidently there is a kind of structural isomorphism between the line (as opposed to the backfield) and the layout of the field of play. Each line has two ends (left end and right end) with a "center" in the middle. Similarly, each playing field has two ends (endzones) with a midfield line (the fifty-yard line). Ferril remarked on the parallel between the oval shape of the football and the oval shape of most football stadiums,[18] but I submit it might be just as plausible to see the football shape as an elongated version of the earlier round soccer or rugby ball, a shape which tends to produce two accentuated ends of the ball. Surely the distinctive difference between the shape of a football and the shape of the balls used in most other ball games (e.g., baseball, basketball, soccer) is that it is not perfectly spherical. The notion that a football has two "ends" is found in the standard idiom used to describe a kick or punt in which the ball turns over and over from front to back during flight (as opposed to moving in a more direct, linear, spiraling pattern) as an "end over end" kick.

The object of the game, simply stated, is to get into the opponent's endzone while preventing the opponent from getting into one's own endzone. Structurally speaking, this is precisely what is involved in male verbal dueling. One wishes to put one's opponent down; to "screw" him while avoiding being screwed by him. We can now better understand the appropriateness of the "bottom patting" so often observed among football players. A good offensive or defensive play deserves a pat on the rear end. The recipient has held up his end and has thereby helped protect the collective "end" of the entire team. One pats one's teammates' ends, but one seeks to violate the endzone of one's opponents!

The trust one has for one's own teammates is perhaps signalled by the common postural stance of football players. The so-called three-point stance involves bending over in a distinct stooped position with one's rear end exposed. It is an unusual position (in terms of normal life activities) and it does make one especially vulnerable to attack from behind, that is, vulnerable to a homosexual attack. In some ways, the posture might be likened to what is termed *presenting* among nonhuman primates. *Presenting* refers to a subordinate animal's turning its rump towards a higher ranking or dominant one. The center thus presents to the quarterback—just as linemen do to the backs in general. George Plimpton has described how the quarterback's "hand, the top of it, rests up against the center's backside as he bends over the ball—medically, against the perineum, the pelvic floor."[19] We know that some dominant nonhuman primates will sometimes reach out to touch a presenting subordinate in similar fashion. In football, however, it is safe to present to one's teammates. Since one can trust teammates, one knows that one will be patted, not raped. The traditional joking admonitions of the locker room warning against bending over in the shower or picking up the soap (thus presumably offering an inviting target for homosexual attack) do not apply since one is among friends. "Grabass" among friends is understood as being harmless joking, behavior.

The importance of the "ends" is signalled by

the fact that they alone among linemen are eligible to receive a forward pass. In that sense, ends are equivalent to the "backs." In symbolic terms, I am arguing that the end is a kind of backside and that the endzone is a kind of erogenous zone. The relatively recently coined terms *tight end* and *split end* further demonstrate the special emphasis upon this "position" on the team. The terms refer to whether the end stays close to his neighboring tackle, e.g., to block, or whether he moves well away from the normally adjacent tackle, e.g., to go out for a pass. However, both *tight end* and *split end* (cf. also *wide receiver*) could easily be understood as possessing an erotic nuance.

I must stress that the evidence for the present interpretation of American football does not depend upon just a single word. Rather, there are many terms which appear to be relevant. The semantics of the word *down* are of interest. A down is a unit of play insofar as a team has four downs in which to either advance ten yards or score. A touchdown, which earns six points, refers to the act of an offensive player's possessing the ball in the opponent's endzone. (Note it is not sufficient for the player to be in the endzone; it is the ball which must be in the zone.) In a running play, the ball often physically touches the endzone and could therefore be said to "touch down" in that area. However, if an offensive player catches a pass in the endzone, the ball does not actually touch the ground. The recent practice of "spiking" the ball, in which the successful offensive player hurls the ball at the ground as hard as he can, might be construed as an attempt to have the football physically touch down in the endzone. In any case, the rise of the word *touch* in connection with scoring in football does conform to a general sexually symbolic rise of that term. The sexual nuances of *touch* can even be found in the Bible. For example, in I Corinthians 7:1–2, we find "It is good for a man not to touch a woman. Nevertheless to avoid fornication, let every man have his own wife" (cf. Genesis 20:6; Proverbs 6:29). Touching can be construed as an aggressive act. Thus to be touched by in opponent means that one has

been the victim of aggression. The game of "touch football" (as opposed to "tackle" football) supports the notion that a mere art of touching is sufficient to fulfill the structural (and psychological) rerequirements of the basic rules. No team wants to give up a touchdown to an opponent. Often a team on defense may put up a determined goal-line stand to avoid being penetrated by the opponent's offense. The special spatial nature of the endzone is perhaps indicated by the fact that it is not measured in the one hundred yard distance between the goal lines. Yet it is measured. It is only ten yards deep; a pass caught by an offensive player whose feet are beyond the end line of the endzone would be ruled incomplete.

Additional football folk speech could be cited. The object of the game is to "score," a term which in standard slang means to engage in sexual intercourse with a member of the opposite sex. One "scores" by going "all the way." The latter phrase refers specifically to making a touchdown.[20] In sexual slang, it alludes to indulging in intercourse as opposed to petting or necking. The offensive team may try to mount a "drive" in order to "penetrate" the other team's territory. A ball carrier might go "up the middle" or he might "go through a hole" (made by his linemen in the opposing defensive line). A particularly skillful runner might be able to make his own hole. The defense is equally determined to "close the hole." Linemen may encourage one another "to stick it to 'em," meaning to place their helmeted heads (with phallic-symbolic overtones) against the chests of their opposite numbers to drive them back or put them out of the play.

A player who scores a touchdown may elect to "spike" the ball by hurling it down towards the ground full force. This spiking movement confirms to all assembled that the enemy's endzone has been penetrated. The team scored upon is thus shamed and humiliated in front of an audience. In this regard, football is similar to verbal dueling inasmuch as dueling invariably takes place before one or more third parties. The term *spike* may also be germane. As a noun, it could refer to a sharp-pointed long slender part or projection. As a verb, it could mean either "to mark or cut with a spike" (the football would presumably be the phallic spike) or "to thwart or sabotage an enemy." In any event, the ritual act of spiking serves to prolong and accentuate the all-too-short moment of triumph, the successful entry into the enemy's endzone.

The sexual connotations of football folk speech apply equally to players on defense. One goal of the defensive line is to penetrate the offensive line to get to the quarterback. Getting to the offensive quarterback and bringing him down to the ground is termed "sacking the quarterback." The verb *sack* connotes plunder, ravage, and perhaps even rape. David Kopay, one of the few homosexuals in professional football willing to admit a preference for members of the same sex, commented on the nature of typical exhortations made by coaches and others:

> The whole language of football is involved in sexual allusions. We are told to go out and "fuck those guys"; to take that ball and "stick it up their asses" or "down their throats." The coaches would yell, "knock their dicks off," or more often than that, "knock their jocks off." They'd say, "Go out there and give it all you've got, a hundred and ten per cent, shoot your wad." You controlled their line and "knocked" 'em into submission. Over the years I've seen many a coach get emotionally aroused while he was diagramming a particular play into an imaginary hole on the blackboard. His face red, his voice rising, he would show the ball carrier how he wanted him to "stick it in the hole."[21]

The term *rape* is not inappropriate and in fact it has been used to describe what happens when an experienced player humiliates a younger player: "That poor kid, he was raped, keelhauled, he was just *destroyed*. . . ."[22] Kopay's reference to *jock* as phallus is of interest since *jock* is a term (short for *jockstrap*, the article of underapparel worn to protect the male genitals) typically used to refer

generally to athletes. Calling an athlete a *jock* or a *strap* thus tends to reduce him to a phallus. A *jocker* is used in hobo slang and in prison slang to refer to an aggressive male homosexual.[23] (The meaning of *jock* may well be related to the term *jockey* insofar as the latter refers to the act of mounting and riding a horse.)

Some of the football folk speech is less obvious and the interpretation admittedly a bit more speculative. For example, a lineman may be urged to "pop" an opposing player, meaning to tackle or block him well. Executing a perfect tackle or block may entail placing one's helmet as close as possible to the middle of the opponent's chest. The use of the verb *pop* strongly suggests defloration, as in the idiom "to pop the cherry" referring to the notion of rupturing the maidenhead in the process of having intercourse with a virgin.[24] In Afro-American folk speech, "pop" can refer to sexual penetration.[25] To "pop" an opponent thus implies reducing him to female-victim status. Much of the sexual slang makes it very clear that the winners are men while the losers are women or passive homosexuals. David Kopay articulates this when he says, "From grade school on, the curse words on the football field are about behaving like a girl. If you don't run fast enough to block or tackle hard enough you're a pussy, a cunt, a sissy."[26] By implication, if a player succeeds, he is male. Thus in the beginning of the football game, we have two sets or teams of males. By the end of the game, one of the teams is "on top," namely the one which has "scored" most by getting into the other team's "end zone." The losing team, if the scoring differential is great, may be said to have been "creamed."

It is tempting to make something of the fact that originally the inner portion of the football was an inflated animal bladder. Thus touching the enemy's endzone with a bladder would be appropriate ritual behavior in the context of a male homosexual attack. However, it could be argued that the bladder was used simply because it was a convenient inflatable object available to serve as a ball.

If the team on offense is perceived in phallic

terms, then it is the quarterback who could be said to be nominally in charge of directing the attack. In this context, it may be noteworthy that a quarterback intending to pass often tries to stay inside of the "pocket," a deployment of offensive players behind the line of scrimmage designed to provide an area of maximum protection.[27] A pants pocket, of course, could be construed as an area where males can covertly touch or manipulate their genitals without being observed. "Pocket pool," for example, is a slang idiom for fondling the genitals,[28] an idiom which incidentally may suggest something about the symbolic nature of billiards. The quarterback, if given adequate protection by his "pocket," may be able to "thread the needle," that is, throw the ball accurately, past the hands of the defensive players, into the hands of his receiver. The metaphor of threading the needle is an apt one since getting the thread through the eye of the needle is only preparatory for the act of "sewing." (Note also that "to make a pass" at someone is a conventional idiom for an act of flirtation.) Once the ball is in his possession, the receiver is transformed from a passive role as he tries to move the ball as far forward as possible.

While it is possible to disagree with several of the interpretations offered of individual items of folk speech cited thus far, it would seem difficult to deny the overall sexual nature of much of football (and other sports) slang. The word *sport* itself has this connotation and has had it for centuries. Consider one of Gloucester's early lines in *King Lear* when he refers to his bastard son Edmund by saying "There was good sport at his making" (I, i, 23) or in such modern usages as "sporting house" for brothel[29] or "sporting life" referring to pimps and prostitutes.[30] In the early 1950s, kissing was commonly referred to by adolescents as a "favorite indoor sport," presumably in contrast to outdoor sports such as football. It should also be noted that *game* can carry the same sexual connotation as *sport*.[31]

I have no doubt that a good many football players and fans will be skeptical (to say the least) of the analysis proposed here. Even academics with presumably less personal investment in football will probably find implausible, if not downright repugnant, the idea that American football could be a ritual combat between groups of males attempting to assert their masculinity by penetrating the endzones of their rivals. David Kopay, despite suggesting that for a long time football provided a kind of replacement for sex in his life and admitting that football is "a real outlet for repressed sexual energy,"[32] refuses to believe that "being able to hold hands in the huddle and to pat each other on the ass if we felt like it" is necessarily an overt show of homosexuality.[33] Yet I think it is highly likely that the ritual aspect of football, providing as it does a socially sanctioned framework for male body contact—football, after all, is a so-called body contact sport—is a form of homosexual behavior. The unequivocal sexual symbolism of the game, as plainly evidenced in folk speech, coupled with the fact that all of the participants are male, make it difficult to draw any other conclusion. Sexual acts carried out in thinly disguised symbolic form by, and directed towards, males and males only, would seem to constitute ritual homosexuality.

Evidence from other cultures indicates that male homosexual ritual combats are fairly common. Answering the question of who penetrates whom is a pretty standard means of testing masculinity cross-culturally. Interestingly enough, the word masculine itself seems to derive from Latin *mas* (male) and *culus* (anus). The implication might be that for a male to prove his masculinity with his peers, he would need to control or guard his buttocks area while at the same time threatening the posterior of another (weaker) male. A good many men's jokes in Mediterranean cultures (e.g., in Italy and in Spain) center on the *culo*.

That a mass spectacle could be based upon a ritual masculinity contest should not surprise anyone familiar with the bullfight. Without intending to reduce the complexity of the bullfight to a single factor, one could nonetheless observe that it is in part a battle between males attempting to penetrate one another. The one who is penetrated loses. If it is the bull, he may be further feminized or emasculated by having various extremities cut off to reward the successful matador. In this context, we can see American football as a male activity (along with the Boy Scouts, fraternities, and other exclusively male social organizations in American culture) as belonging to the general range of male rituals around the world in which masculinity is defined and affirmed. In American culture, women are permitted to be present as spectators or even cheerleaders, but they are not participants. Women resenting men's preoccupation with such male sports are commonly referred to as football widows (analogous to golf widows). This too suggests that the sport activity is in some sense a substitute for normal heterosexual relations. The men are "dead" as far as relationships with females are concerned. In sport and in ritual, men play both male *and* female parts. Whether it is the verbal dueling tradition of the cirum-Mediterrean[34] in which young men threaten to put opponents into a passive homosexual position, or the initiation rites in aboriginal Australia and New Guinea (and elsewhere) in which younger men are subjected to actual homosexual anal intercourse by older members of the male group,[35] the underlying psychological rationale appears to be similar. Professional football's financial incentives may extend the playing years of individuals beyond late adolescence, but in its essence American football is an adolescent masculinity initiation ritual in which the winner gets into the loser's endzone more times than the loser gets into his!

Notes

1. W. Branch Johnson, "Football, A Survival of Magic?" *The Contemporary Review* 135 (1929):228.

2. Johnson, 230–31; Francis Peabody Magoun, Jr., "Shrove Tuesday Football," *Harvard Studies and Notes in Philology and Literature* 13 (1931):24, 36, 44.

3. Johnson, 230.

4. David Riesman and Reuel Denney, "Football in America: A Study in Cultural Diffusion," *American Quarterly* 3 (1951):309–25.

5. William Arens, "The Great American Football Ritual," *Natural History* 84 (1975):72–80. Reprinted in W. Arens and Susan P. Montague, ed., *The American Dimension: Cultural Myths and Social Realities* (Port Washington, 1975), 3–14.

6. Arnold R. Beisser, *The Madness in Sports* (New York, 1967); Shirley Fiske, "Pigskin Review: An American Initiation," in *Sport in the Socio-Cultural Process*, M. Marie Hart ed. (Dubuque, 1972), 241–258: and Arens, 72–80.

7. Arens, 77.

8. K. G. Sheard and E. G. Dunning, "The Rugby Football Club as a Type of 'Male Preserve': Some Sociological Notes," *International Review of Sport Sociology* 3–4 (1973):5–24.

9. Arens, 79.

10. George M. Foster, "Peasant Society and the Image of Limited Good," *American Anthropologist* 67 (1965):293–315.

11. G. T. W. Patrick, "The Psychology of Football," *American Journal of Psychology* 14 (1903):370.

12. A. A. Brill, "The Why of the Fan," *North American Review* 228 (1929):429–34.

13. Childe Herald [Thomas Hornsby Ferril], "Freud and Football," in *Reader in Comparative Religion*, eds. William A. Lessa and Evon Z. Vogt (New York, 2d ed., 1965), 250–52.

14. Adrian Stokes, "Psycho-Analytic Reflections on the Development of Ball Games, Particularly Cricket," *International Journal of Psycho-Analysis* 37 (1956):185–92.

15. Stokes, 190.

16. Stokes, 187.

17. Bruce Rodgers, *The Queens' Vernacular: A Gay Lexicon* (San Francisco, 1972), 27; Dennis Wepman, Ronald B. Newman, and Murray B. Binderman, *The Life: The Lore and Folk Poetry of the Black Hustler* (Philadelphia, 1976), 178.

18. Herald, 250.

19. George Plimpton, *Paper Lion* (New York, 1965), 59.

20. Kyle Rote and Jack Winter, *The Language of Pro Football* (New York, 1966), 102.

21. David Kopay and Deane Young, *The David Kopay Story* (New York, 1977), 53—54.

22. Plimpton, 195, 339.

23. Harold Wentworth and Stuart Berg Flexner, *Dictionary of American Slang* (New York, 1967), 294; Rodgers, 155.

24. Vance Randolph, *Pissing in the Snow & Other Ozark Folktales* (Urbana, 1976), 9.

25. Wepman, Newman and Binderman, 186.

26. Kopay and Young, 50–51.

27. Rote and Winter, 130.

28. Rodgers, 152.

29. Wentworth and Flexner, 511.

30. Wepman, Newman and Binderman, *The Life*.

31. Rodgers, 92; Wepman, Newman and Binderman, 182.

32. Kopay and Young, 11, 53.

33. Kopay and Young, 57.

34. Cf. Alan Dundes, Jerry W. Leach, and Bora Ozkok, "The Strategy of Turkish Boys' Verbal Dueling Rhymes," *Journal of American Folklore* 83 (1970): 325–49.

35. Cf. Alan Dundes, "A Psychoanalytic Study of the Bull-roarer," *Man* 11 (1976): 220–38.

Bibliography

Arens, William. "The Great American Football Ritual." In *The American Dimension: Cultural Myths and Social Realities,* edited by W. Arens and Susan Montague. Port Washington: 1975.

Beisser, Arnold R. *The Madness in Sports.* New York: 1967.

Brill, A. A. "The Why of the Fan." *North American Review* 228 (1929): 429–34.

Dundes, Alan. "A Psychoanalytic Study of the Bull-roarer." *Man* 11 (1976): 220–38.

Dundes, Alan, Jerry Leach and Bora Özkok. "The Strategy of Turkish Boys' Verbal Dueling Rhymes." *Journal of American Folklore* 831 (1970): 325–49.

Fiske, Shirely. "Pigskin Review: An American Initiation." In *Sport in the Socio-cultural Process,* edited by Marie Hart. Dubuque, IA: 1972.

Foster, George M. "Peasant Society and the Image of Limited Good." *American Anthropologist* 67 (1965): 293–315.

Herald, Childe [Thomas Hornsby Ferril]. "Freud and Football." In *Reader in Contemporary Religion,* 2d ed., edited by W. Lessa and E. Vogt. New York: 1965.

Johnson, Branch. "Football, A Survival of Magic?" *The Contemporary Review* 135 (1929): 228.

Kopay, David and Perry Deane Young. *The David Kopay Story.* New York: 1977.

Magoun, Francis P., Jr. "Shrove Tuesday Football." *Harvard Studies and Notes in Philology and Literature* 13, no. 24 (1931): 44.

Patrick, G. T. W. "The Psychology of Football." *American Journal of Psychology* 14 (1903): 370.

Plimpton, George. *Paper Lion.* New York: 1965.

Randolph, Vance. *Pissing in the Snow and Other Ozark Folktales.* Urbana, IL: 1967.

Riesman, David, and Reuel Denney. "Football in America: A Study in Cultural Diffusion." *American Quarterly* 3 (1951): 309–325.

Rodgers, Bruce. *The Queen's Vernacular: A Gay Lexicon.* San Francisco: 1972.

Rote, Kyle, and Jack Winter. *The Language of Pro Football.* New York: 1966.

Sheard, K. G. and E. G. Dunning. "The Rugby Football Club as a Type of 'Male Preserve': Some Sociological Notes." *International Review of Sport Sociology* 3–4 (1973): 5–24.

Stokes, Adrian. "Psycho-Analytic Reflections on the Development of Ball Games, Particularly Cricket." *International Journal of Psycho-Analysis* 37 (1956): 185–92.

Wenthworth, Harold, and Stuart Berg Flexner. *Dictionary of American Slang.* New York: 1967.

Wepman, Dennis, Ronald B. Newman and Murray B. Binderman. *The Life: The Lore and Folk Poetry of the Black Hustler.* Philadelphia: 1976.

Questions for Consideration

1. Given his ritualized-male-homosexuality thesis, does Dundes adequately do away with the alternative explanations put forth for the popularity of American football? Moreover, does he mean to dismiss these alternatives outright, or does he merely wish to assign them a lesser role in explanation? Are there possibilities that he has not considered?

2. If the ritualized-male-homosexuality thesis is correct, why is it that American males meet this need through football and no other aggressive team sports? Furthermore, is the need for this homosexual ritual condemnatory of American society or men in general?

22   Violence and Aggression in Contemporary Sport

Jim Parry
University of Leeds

Jim Parry opens this reading by noting that today's audience for sports is wide and heterogeneous and that contemporary sports are doing what they can to make themselves appealing to this market. Some sports, however, market themselves by appealing to aggression and violence. There is a nasty paradox: Aggression seems a necessary component of sportive practice, yet most people condemn violence in sport. Is this problem soluble?

Parry begins by distinguishing between "assertiveness," "aggression," and "violence." The first is a need to move about in one's environment with or without force. Aggression is assertiveness with force. Last, violence deals with intentional harm or injury to others. Ethical concerns intimate that violence ought not to be a part of sports, yet sports like boxing, where violence is instrumental for its end, pose a challenge.

There are also different philosophical ways of understanding violence. Consequentialists view the moral issue in terms of the good or bad that arises from the results of an action. Nonconsequentialists are essentially interested in intention. The harm done is often due to lack of respect to others—treating them as means to an end and not as ends themselves.

Returning to the problem of violence, Parry asserts that the main issue is that violence interferes with the equality of opportunity in contest and thereby disregards the rules of sport. Types of violence in sport range from brutal bodily contact, endemic to the very practice of some sports, to criminal violence, which is clearly outside of the boundaries of fair play.

In the end, Parry sees sport as an experimental laboratory, where we release aggression and explore the possibilities of dealing successfully with violent behavior. Success or the lack of it may tell us much about our ability to conduct human affairs peacefully.

Introduction

Not all sports are games and not all games are sports. This chapter will concentrate primarily on those games that are sports. So I will not really be concerned with activities such as track and field athletics (a sport that is not a game) nor with chess (a game that is not a sport). I shall have in mind especially various forms of football, but I shall pay some attention to the special case of boxing (which might not be a game, either!).

Let me offer a preliminary attempt to stipulate a rough and ready definition of "sport," so that we might have some idea of the object of my attention: sports are rule-governed competitions wherein physical abilities are contested. They are more formal, serious, competitive, organized, and institutionalized than the games from which they often sprang. Such a definition is useful as a crude starting-point, because it begins to suggest certain characteristics of "sport" as so defined:

- institutionalization (suggesting "lawful authority");
- contest (suggesting "contract to contest");
- obligation to abide by the rules;

"Violence and Aggression in Contemporary Sport," from *Ethics and Sport*, M. J. McNamee and S. J. Parry (Eds.), (1998) E & F N Spon. Reprinted, by permission, of International Thomson Publishing Services.

- that the activity was freely chosen;
- that due respect is owed to opponents as co-facilitators, and so on.

Such an account may begin to indicate the moral basis of sport, and thus suggest arguments that may be raised against violence. For we may ask how violence relates to the practice of sport; and whether one can have a sports practice in which violence occurs. Obviously, the answer depends on the *kind* and *level* of violence involved (and, of course, what we mean by "violence").

A factor in the development of modern sport has been the internationalization of sports competition and the globalization of spectatorship on the back of spectacular progress in the global travel and communication industries. This has required:

1. Ever greater rule clarity (so as to avoid cross-cultural misunderstanding and to resolve variant interpretations, construals, "customs and practices").
2. Ever greater controls (increased surveillance and rule enforcement e.g. rule changes for the Soccer World Cup 94) so as to ensure fairness and lack of arbitrariness (for the "meaning" and "significance" of the event is threatened by "arbitrary" decisions).

So we are in this "new" situation, wherein sports are competing for popularity (for people playing in minor leagues; for children playing at school level or in out-of-school clubs and leagues; for spectators; for sponsors; for national and international success). Sports are now realizing that to survive and flourish in the modern world they must make themselves attractive to this wide and heterogeneous audience, and they are seeking to present themselves as "marketable."

The subject of this chapter is one of the perceived threats to the "marketability" of serious competitive sport: aggression and violence. The "problem of violence" in sport is paradoxical because, some claim, aggression is a quality *required*

in sport (especially at the highest levels); and so it cannot be surprising if sport attracts aggressive people, or if sport actually *produces* aggression. The *results* of violence, however, are widely condemned. How can this circle be squared?

In the last paragraph you will have noticed that I ran together the two ideas: aggression and violence. I did this to illustrate the way in which these two ideas often are confused, or are thought to be related in important ways, and so our first task must be to clarify what is at issue here, so that we can see just what is a threat, and why.

Assertion, Aggression, and Violence

In the standard texts of sports psychology the idea of violence is usually raised in the context of studies of aggression. Such an interest is conditioned by the natural concerns of psychologists—but our topic is often swiftly side-tracked by conceptual confusion. The initial willingness of psychologists to accept a definition of "aggression" as (for example) "direct physical contact accompanied by the intent to do bodily harm" (Cratty, 1983, p. 91), is very unfortunate, eliding as it does the two concepts. Even more confusion follows, since within a few lines we get aggression, violence, assertiveness (Cratty, p. 100), hostility (p. 106), vigorous behaviours (p. 108), etc. with very little attempt to distinguish between them.

We are reminded of an observation of Wittgenstein's (1968, p. 232):

For in psychology there are experimental methods and conceptual confusion . . . The existence of the experimental method makes us think that we have the means of solving the problems which trouble us; though problem and method pass one another by.

Let us begin with some of these basic concepts, and see if some informed conceptual stipulation might be useful.

1. Assertion

Some see the biological organism as active, positive, and see "aggression" as a basic biological drive, or a pre-condition of existence, or human flourishing, or excellence.

Alderman (1974, p. 231) says:

Each person is born with a capacity and a need to move against his environment—to be aggressive.

However, I prefer to call this capacity "assertiveness" or "self-assertion," because there is no suggestion here of a necessary forcefulness. Rather, there is the sense of affirming or insisting upon one's rights; protecting or vindicating oneself; maintaining or defending a cause.

2. Aggression

Aggression, however, *is* forceful. Some see a possibility of defensive as well as offensive aggression, but both are served by force. Aggression is:

- vigorous (trying to gain advantage by sheer force);
- offensive (in the sport context: battling for the ball);
- proactive (striking first).

Such features may all be morally exceptionable or unexceptionable, according to context, in everyday life, but all are usually permitted according to the rules of team sports.

3. Violence

Just as it is possible to be assertive without being aggressive, it is quite possible to be aggressive without being violent. A player can be both forceful and vigorous without seeking to hurt or harm anyone. Violence, however, is centrally to do with intentional hurt or injury to others, as

well as attempts to harm, recklessness as to harm, and negligence. Since such injury is very often seen as illegitimate, legitimacy has often been seen as an important ethical issue in sport. Accordingly, violence in a sport might be seen as: harm or injury to others (or attempted harm) which is against the rules.

But there is a difficulty here. If the above account were to hold for "combat sports," this would require the counter-intuitive notion that very hard punches aimed at knocking someone out do not constitute "violence" so long as they are delivered legally. There are three possible responses to this difficulty.

The first is to highlight the role of "legitimate" violence. This is precisely the site of the most intractable problem over political violence (civil disobedience/revolution/terrorism), for the criterion most often offered for distinguishing violent acts has been their legitimacy. Van den Haag says:

The social meaning of physically identical actions are often distinguished verbally. Thus, physical force is called "force" when authorised and regarded as legitimate, and "violence" otherwise: the arresting officer employs force, the resisting suspect, violence.

This echoes Marcuse's words:

In the established vocabulary, "violence" is a term which one does not apply to the action of the police . . . (1969, p. 75)

Now, we do not need to take a view on who is right here. For present purposes it is enough simply to note that it has often been thought reasonable in the political sphere to reserve the epithet "violent" for illegitimate acts, no matter how aggressive or forceful the legitimate agencies are.

The second possible response to this difficulty might be to acknowledge that boxing is indeed violent, but to refuse to allow that boxing is a "sport," precisely on the ground that its rules provide for such violence. A real "sport," it might be held, would not admit of intentionally inflicted damage. (This was, in fact, the line taken by a BMA spokeswoman in the BBC *Sportsnight* programme following the McLellan title fight incident to be discussed later.) Of course, not all or any violent acts will be permitted; and so there will be rules distinguishing illegitimate from legitimate violence (e.g. the rabbit punch in boxing).

The problem with this is that we would have to stop using the word "sport" in relation to boxing, whereas it is (and always has been) archetypally a sport. However much we disapprove of field sports, we still call them sports. (Some detractors call them "so-called sports"—but this just highlights the issue.)

Let us try to discover a term we might use to describe this category of sports which, because they permit intentionally inflicted injury, are deemed by some to be beyond the pale. "Combat sports" won't do it, since many combat sports outlaw intentional injury. "Violent sports" might be entirely appropriate, since it is their violent nature that is at issue; but I favour the more emotive tag "blood sports" which I define as those whose aim is either to kill, or inflict serious physical damage; or where death or injury is an inevitable or frequent outcome. I'm thinking of hunting, shooting, fishing, bull fighting, bear-baiting—and possibly some forms of boxing.

A third possible response to the difficulty might be to reserve our descriptions for only one class of sports. All team sports allow aggression, whereas boxing allows violence. Clearly, the account of violence as illegitimate harm works only within the class of team sports, not across classes. But the problem with this is that the meaning of the word "violence" would then have to differ across classes, which would be confusing.

This suggests that we should delete the criterion: "which is against the rules" from this category. Let us simply insist that violence is centrally to do with intentional hurt or injury to others, as well as attempts to harm, recklessness

as to harm, and negligence. It also suggests that we need one more category:

4. Illegitimate violence

Sometimes, violence may be justifiable (in war, or revolution, or terrorism; or in boxing, where "violence" within bounds is legitimate). Illegitimate violence must be characterized as the attempt to harm by the use of illegitimate force.

Instrumental and Reactive Aggression

There are other instructive conceptual issues raised in the psychology literature. For example, the distinction between instrumental and reactive aggression, which is reported in many texts. In Martens (1975, p. 111) we read:

> Aggression occurring in the achievement of non-aggressive goals is known as instrumental aggression. In contrast, aggression where the goal is injury to some object is known as anger or reactive aggression. Instrumental aggression is not a response to frustration and does not involve anger.

Now, imagine a player who wants to win a match (a non-aggressive goal, I take it) and resolves, as a means, to injure his opponent. This is not a person striking out in anger or frustration, but a person coldly intent on harm to another. If this is a credible example it collapses the distinction for, on Martens' account, this would be both instrumental aggression (since it is a means to an end), but also reactive aggression (since the goal is injury to someone). If his reply is to insist that reactive aggression is not a means to something else, but only ever an end in itself (a working-out of my anger or frustration), then he must drop the contrast he proposes; for in both cases the "goal" is injury to someone. It's just that, in my example, the intention to injure has a "further intention"—to win.

A second example reinforces the point. Cratty (1983, p. 100) proposes a

> ... discrimination between aggression that is not excessive nor intended to inflict harm, (instrumental aggression) and aggression that is excessive and intended to harm others (reactive aggression).

My example can't be dealt with by using Cratty's distinction, for there, instrumental aggression *is* intended to inflict harm (and so counts as reactive for Cratty). Further, just because, in instrumental intention, I have an "ultimate goal" beyond harming someone, it does not follow that I did not intentionally harm someone when I did so as a means to winning. (This discussion mirrors the discussion in law of the distinction between direct and oblique intention: in order to shoot my victim, I had to fire through the window. Did I intend to break the glass? See Duff, 1990, pp. 74ff.).

The problem is this: given the instrumental nature of sport, a very large proportion of acts of violence will fall into a third category (of instrumental/expressive actions). Instrumental violence will often be accompanied by important affective elements; and expressive violence will often be in the service of instrumental goals. Sports psychologists seem to have taken one of the canons of the literature from the parent discipline related to aggression in humans generally, and simply applied it directly to sport, assuming that it will "fit," and yield productive insights. I think that it has been of some value, but that it obscures more than it reveals.

Gratuitous Violence

One further point is raised: whether or not an act uses "excessive" aggression seems irrelevant to the distinction, for my instrumental aggres-

sion might be excessive in the extreme, whilst still being delivered with cool efficiency (not in anger, etc.). However, there is a genuine moral problem involving what might be called "gratuitous" violence: when violence exceeds what is necessary for its success, whether used instrumentally or not.

Recklessness and Negligence

There are further interesting problems arising from injuries which are caused instrumentally, but not through full-blown intention. Reckless challenges are those whose intent may be to gain advantage, but whose means are taken in the knowledge of risk or foresight of probable injury. Negligent challenges are those undertaken without appropriate due care for others. We need to rely not just on the concept of intention, but on the wider concepts of culpability and responsibility. We should ask questions not just about intention, but also about which acts and omissions we should be held responsible for and for which we are culpable. A reckless or careless (negligent) driver may have no intent to injure someone, but is held to some degree culpable nevertheless. Should the same apply in sport? A reckless or negligent challenge may maim as well as an intentionally injurious one.

Instrumental and Expressive Violence

Dunning (1993b, p. 54) makes a similar distinction (between instrumental and expressive violence) that avoids this problem. After all, for the person who is thumped in the mouth, it doesn't much matter whether it was done instrumentally or reactively, especially if it is difficult in practice to distinguish the two in sporting situations. Dunning's distinction captures this insight. For him, "instrumental" means (p. 54) the use "of physical violence illegitimately in pursuit of success." This kind of violence, he claims, has increased in rugby due to increasing competitiveness and rewards, and may involve "a large element of rational calculation, even of pre-planning" (p. 65).

"Expressive" means (p. 54) "non-rational and affective": for example, gaining pleasure from "the physical intimidation and infliction of pain on opponents." This kind of violence, he claims, has decreased in rugby due to the "civilizing" of the game through a developing system of rules, penalties and controls. Another example is retaliating, which has ". . . a strong affective component" but is motivated "by a desire for revenge rather than by pleasure in the violence per se" (p. 65).

However, this account has its own problems, for the distinction between instrumental and expressive does not correspond to the distinction between the rational and the non-rational. Imagine my getting caught in a tackle and, in struggling to get free with the ball, I experience a sudden burst of anger that impels me to shove my opponent off the ball. Now, this is non-rational and affective behaviour, but it is also clearly instrumental, in the sense that it uses "physical violence illegitimately in pursuit of success." I don't hate my opponent—I just want to get past him.

Now, we can see what both views are getting at. We want to notice the moral difference between various kinds of act, and the above distinctions are attempts to capture that elusive quality. However, I do not think that they are very successful; nor could they be without a more careful analysis of the ideas of intention and responsible agency, to which we now turn.

Violence and Intention

In the standard texts of sports sociology the idea of violence is usually raised in the context of studies of deviance, hooliganism and crowds. Such an interest is conditioned by the natural concerns of sociologists but I am not here concerned directly with the behaviour of non-participants. My central concern will be with the nature and justification of player violence during the match.

The Nature of Violence

Not all acts of violence are violent acts; and not all violent acts are acts of violence (see Harris, 1982, Chap. 1). Almost any human act may be performed in a more or less violent manner—vigorously, forcefully, strongly, energetically, vehemently, furiously, etc. However, an act of violence is identified not by the manner of its execution, but by the human consequences flowing from it, such as injury, distress, suffering, and so on.

We should also posit a parallel distinction between aggressive acts and acts of aggression. Aggressive acts are those acts marked by vigour, offensiveness and proactivity. Acts of aggression, however, are attacks or assaults on others—and these may be performed vigorously or not.

Two issues immediately arise:

1. Psychological violence and intimidation

This means that verbal intimidation, for example—threat of violence, creation of an atmosphere of threat, insecurity, uncertainty, etc.—may be an act of violence, whilst not necessarily being a violent act. However, I shall seek to side-step issues to do with psychological aggression and violence. This is not because the psychological varieties are unimportant; nor because they are rare in sport; but merely because, for reasons of simplicity, I wish to consider here only physical aggression and violence.

Psychological violence and physical intimidation are borderline practices, sometimes acceptable as "custom and practice" in certain sports settings. In some sports, it is regarded as "part of the game" (acceptable within the culture) to "shake them up a bit" so long as that is: (a) within the rules; (b) with no intent actually to harm (although if you hurt the opponent a bit, that's all part of the game!). There's a functional aspect to this (it's a physical contest, and hard challenges debilitate), but also a psychological challenge (let's see whether and how they stand up to it!).

Notice the distinction between "hurt" and "harm." I am using "hurt" here to mean "give pain to," "knock, strike, give a blow to" and "harm" to mean "injure, damage."

2. Intention

All of this raises fundamental questions about intentionality, liability, recklessness, negligence, etc. For example, Duff emphasizes the difference between intending a result; and bringing a result about intentionally. For although intention involves bringing about a result which I intend (or act with the intention of bringing about), it also extends beyond this, to include results which I bring about not with intent, but nevertheless intentionally.

These two aspects of intention are related to two different, conflicting, moral conceptions of responsible agency: consequentialist and non-consequentialist accounts. The consequentialist sees the rightness or wrongness of an action as depending only on the goodness and badness of its consequences, so that harms may be identified independently of the conduct which causes them.

The non-consequentialist finds an intrinsic moral significance in intended action; that is, a significance which depends not on its intended consequences, but on the intentions which structure the act. For example, central to the idea of rape is not the consequentialist idea of an occurrence—but that of a human action (structured by a particular intention) which attacks the sexual integrity and autonomy of the victim. What the rapist intends is not "to have consensual intercourse" but simply "to have intercourse." It is this kind of harm (disregard for the

autonomy and bodily integrity of others) that is the essence of rape.

With other crimes, there are obvious consequential harms which we aim to prevent. But, for example, even in murder, it is not clear that death is the harm which the crime of murder seeks to prevent. It is true that if murdered I die, but I suffer the same consequence if lightning strikes me dead. In murder, the character of the harm is different. In murder, I die, but I do so *because* someone tries to kill me (attacks my life and my basic rights).

Applied to sport, this distinction is instructive. Imagine in soccer a penalty awarded for tripping. Is the harm to be seen in consequentialist terms (my falling to the ground) or in non-consequentialist terms (my being tripped by another)? That is to say: should we be thinking in terms of outcomes or intentions? Think carefully, for the rules actually say that, unless the trip were intentional, there is no foul; and therefore no penalty should be awarded.

However, even in non-consequentialist terms, referees usually give penalties for reckless challenges, and even for negligent ones (i.e. for faults that fall short of intention). And don't you suspect that, in the absence of good evidence about intentions, referees very often judge simply on outcomes? You made contact with me and tripped me. The outcome is that I was denied a proper opportunity to score. Should you not be held responsible for that?

Duff's reply would be that there are indeed occasions on which we should be held responsible for our intentional actions which have results that we did not intend; for we are also responsible for the intentions that structured the act we performed. In cases of alleged recklessness the test of responsible agency proposed by Duff is that of "practical indifference," which can take the forms of:

- choosing to take an unreasonable risk,
- failing to notice an obvious risk;
- acting on the unreasonable belief that there is no risk.

Justification—The Ethics of Violence

Justifications of violence are often to be found in the literature on political violence (see Arendt, H., 1969; Audi *et al.,* 1971; Honderich, T., 1980; Rule, J.B., 1989). But these justifications all refer (as they must) to the ethical limitations of *de facto* political authorities. If there are concerns about the ethical nature of a particular sport, or of a particular rule or practice within a sport, however, it is difficult to see how these concerns might legitimately be expressed through acts of violence during a match.

Violence involves the pursuit of interests in situations where legitimate forms of activity have failed, or seem likely to fail. But it does this in such a way as to fundamentally overturn the expectations on which a game proceeds (rules, fair play, etc.).

It does this in order to:

- gain an advantage;
- intimidate;
- force withdrawal;
- enforce a contest on abilities not specified in the game's constitutive rules;
- challenge the referee's claim to a monopoly on the use of sanctions.

However, there are some possible justifications of the resort to violence (although some in this list might better be seen as defences or mitigations, rather than justifications). There is so much to say here, but I must make do here with a simple list:

- non-intentional ("I went for the ball . . .");
- non-premeditated (spur of the moment, automatic response);
- self-defence ("He was coming for me . . .");
- pre-emptive self-defence;
- defence, of others;

- duress ("My coach insisted that I do that . . . my job was on the line.");
- preventing an offence;
- provocation (retaliation);
- lack of an adequate authority (the referee's "lost it");
- rules are unclear and it's legitimate to push them to the limit;
- it's not a moral issue, because game rules aren't moral rules;
- it works (achieves the end);
- custom and practice ("That's what's expected of a professional.");
- consent ("Everyone knows the risks . . .").

What's Wrong with Offering Violence?

If violence is "against the rules," then what's wrong with violence in sport amounts to:

1. What's wrong (in general) with *rule-breaking*;
2. What's (in *addition*) especially wrong with violence:
   a. intention to harm;
   b. failing to accord proper respect to opponents;
   c. failing to uphold the laws and conventions of the sport;
   d. failing to maintain the institution (breaking the rules of the practice).

That is to say: some forms of violence conflict with the requirements of sport. Violence stands in the way of a proper equality of opportunity to contest; and it fails to respect the rules of the contest.

Types of Sports Violence

Smith (1983) divides sports violence into four types; brutal body contact, borderline violence, quasi-criminal violence, and criminal violence. These types of sport violence include, respectively, violence approved by the rules of the game, violence for which the rules of the game specify appropriate penalties, violence governed traditionally by case law in civil court procedures, and violence governed traditionally by criminal statutes and criminal prosecution (see Hughes, 1984, p. 79).

1. Brutal body contact

It is taken for granted that when one participates, one automatically accepts:

- inevitability of contact,
- probability of minor bodily injury;
- possibility of serious injury.

Practices may strain formal rules of sport but do not necessarily violate them.

2. Borderline violence

These are assaults which, though prohibited by the formal rules of a sport, occur routinely and are more or less accepted by players and fans. They are essentially the province of referees and umpires; penalties seldom exceed brief suspensions and/or a fine; and rationales for virtual immunity from criminal prosecution include:

- community sub-group rationale;
- continuing relationship rationale;
- applying criminal law to sport is judged inappropriate and ineffective.

3. Quasi-criminal violence

Violates not only formal rules of sport, but also informal norms of player conduct; usually results or could have resulted in a grave injury; is brought to the attention of top league officials: penalties range from several games suspension to life-time ban. Court and criminal proceedings, rare in the past, now increasingly follow.

4. Criminal violence

Violence so serious and obviously outside the boundaries of what can be considered "part of the game" that is handled from the outset by the law. Permanent, debilitating injury or death are often involved.

Smith is more concerned with criminal aspects of violence in sport (3. and 4.), whereas my focus has been rather on 1. and 2.; and he looks at sport through the lenses of deviance theory, whereas I'm more interested in a Sport Education and Development approach. Nevertheless, his schema offers a further insight into how we might approach particular examples.

Some Examples

Smith's account needs applying in different situations. How does it help us to understand soccer, rugby, American football, boxing? We must remember, firstly, that whatever we say next will be reliant on certain empirical claims about how those sports *are*—about what is actually happening in them—and there are serious disputes at this level:

- over the current level of violence;
- over whether violence is increasing or not;
- over whether there is reason to suppose that things look set to improve in the near future;
- or whether organized sport is on the decline and facing oblivion, etc.

Secondly, a sport can change its character very quickly indeed. Any sport might already be about to respond with a few simple rule changes to negate the source of whatever criticism we might offer—so what we say might already be out of date.

That said, let's look at a few practical applications of the above thoughts, and see how they fare when tested against examples.

Soccer At every instant in the game of soccer, possession of the ball is being contested. Assertion is necessary at all times, and aggression is permitted in pursuit of legitimate ends. Games like soccer are essentially exercises in controlled aggression. However, violent and dangerous play are strictly against the rules, so the case against acts of violence is simply that they are illegitimate.

Sometimes commentators may be heard to criticize a tackle as "too hard" (for which I think we might read "too aggressive"). But I think that the above analysis means that there is no such thing as a tackle that is too hard. If it is a fair tackle, aimed at the ball, it can't be too hard (i.e. too aggressive), unless the hardness involves intentional injury to another, or is reckless as to his safety (i.e. is violent). "Hardness" and "aggression" are not against the rules—but violence is.

Rugby Here is a game which many see as violent, for part of the game seems to be to overcome others simply by violent force. One way of expressing this thought is to argue that, although rugby might be a violent sport, it is not a sport of violence. People may get hurt in the course of the game due to the extreme nature of honourable physical combat, but the aim of the game (and the way to win it) is to score points, not to hurt people.

Having said that, I am of course referring to what official sets of rules appear to say, in distinction to what "custom and practice" appears to be. Amongst players, for example, there may exist a "code of silence" which prohibits the reporting of acts of violence witnessed. If this is true, then hard questions must be asked about the moral basis of custom and practice. If the rules prohibit acts of violence, then any such collusion risks bringing the game into disrepute, to the disadvantage of all. If the rules actually don't, then perhaps they will require revision.

American Football Hughes (1984) says:

. . . in North American football each play may involve a number of players in violent behaviour that is completely legitimate under the rules of the game and under law.

Now, I'm not well-informed about the game of American football, so it may serve as a good example for us. Perhaps by "violent" Hughes is referring to violent acts, not acts of violence, but if it is true that the rules of this sport allow for the intentional harming of others, then it might qualify as a Type 4 violence sport, along with boxing.

But these things are a matter of degree. I understand that it was formerly often the practice to tackle at or below the knee, so as not only to bring the opponent down, but also to break his knee. In any event, many knees were broken, and a rule change was implemented presumably in order to outlaw those acts of violence previously permitted: intentional attacks on knees.

I suppose its status as a Type 4 violence sport will depend on the amount and kind of acts of violence which remain permitted by the rules of the game; but also those which are condoned by the culture of the sport as played in the NFL. Consider the following description:

You hurt others.
You ignore your own pain.
You lose your capacity for empathy.
It becomes a value to cause pain (it becomes integrated into your personality).
(BBC2,1994)

If this is a correct account of one of the perceived values of the sport, then there do seem grounds characterizing it as being at least at risk of being considered a blood sport. And, if so, we should be asking whether it, too, should either be cleaned up, or become the object of sanctions.

The Special Case of Boxing, Or: Blood Sports Proper! Whilst thinking about these issues only a few, weeks before the Cardiff conference, Nigel Benn ("The Dark Destroyer") beat Gerard McClellan by a 10th round KO on 26 February 1995. McClellan was counted out whilst not unconscious, but down on one knee, obviously distressed and blinking heavily. As soon as he reached his corner it became clear that something was badly wrong and he was rushed to hospital, where he had a blood clot removed from his brain shortly after arrival. His condition was critical.

BBBC officials were very quick on the night to explain the detailed precautions taken, including the presence of four doctors, one an anaesthetist (although the very necessity for such precautions is itself evidence of foreknowledge of risk to life).

On BBC1 *News* the next night (1995a) a promoter, Frank Warren, and a BBBC official mounted a spirited defence of the sport, in the following terms (supplemented by later discussion on BBC1 *Sportsnight*, 1995b):

1. Boxing is a skilled sport, whose aim is to score points, etc.

This is true, but boxing also not only permits, but ultimately rewards the causing of grievous or actual bodily harm. Boxing already has the knock-down and knock-out. Imagine if it were possible with one blow to decapitate one's opponent (let us call this the "knock-off"). Surely this would not be against the rules nor the spirit of the rules. A knock-out is a final knock-down. The knock-off would simply be a more final and spectacular way of ending the fight than a simple knock-out.

If the knock-off were possible, why should it not be permitted? We must say either that it is permissible, which dramatically exposes the sport's rationale, I think; or that it is impermissible for some reason—which reason would, I think, also provide a criterion for banning head punching at all.

2. Boxing should be treated the same as any other risk sport. Many other sports are as dangerous as boxing, and people die every year in many different sports.

The actual facts of the matter are in some dispute. Sports medics argue over the precise nature, degree, effects and probabilities of injury.

The statistics given on the *Sportsnight* programme were that over the previous 9 years in Britain there were 94 deaths in horse riding, 4 in cricket, and only 2 in boxing. Leave aside for the moment the fact that these are not properly weighted statistics (ignoring as they do participation rates, time spent during periods of activity, etc.), for they are simply irrelevant to the point. The argument is not about the facts of injury levels—but it is a moral argument about the aim of the activity. John might hurt someone in cricket, but he won't get runs or wickets for that. In boxing, he might win just by doing that. Indeed, hurting or harming someone so badly that he cannot continue the contest is a sufficient condition of victory—and surely this feature of the sport exposes its false appeal to the skill argument, as in 1. above. It is not as if there is no skill in boxing; but rather that a boxer might rationally aim at inflicting a simple debilitating injury as a means of winning.

Surely other sports take care not only to provide for casualties, but also to avoid those casualties as far as possible. Interestingly, the Professional Boxers' Association argue for better safeguards (more experts at ringside, ambulances on site, all venues within one hour of a properly equipped hospital, etc.) but they don't argue for the only thing that will help avoid these cases: a ban on head punching. Rugby, for example, has (only!) recently taken particular notice of its own restrictions on tackles around the head and neck. So why hot take the head out of the target area in boxing?

3. Answer: you can't have boxing without the head as a target. That's like having rugby without scrums, or the steeplechase without jumps.

Well, these are interestingly different cases. It's quite possible to envisage rugby without scrums. Most boxers would not know the difference between a scrum and a ruck and a maul. But the definitions of each might all change without detriment to the game, and each might be dropped without doing away with the game. Could we imagine Rugby League (which already has no line-outs) without scrums? No problem—it would look just like Rugby League without scrums!

A steeplechase, however, is defined in terms of jumps. It means ". . . formerly, a race having a church steeple in view as goal, in which all intervening obstacles had to be cleared." (SOED). Nowadays, often, artificial hurdles and water-jumps, etc. are created on a racecourse (or a running track, for humans). So you could have rugby without scrums, but you couldn't have a steeplechase without jumps.

Now, what shall we say about boxing? That boxing without the head as target is a logical nonsense? Or that we could easily envisage a simple rule change that would preserve all that is good about the skill, fitness, endurance, etc. of boxing except for that proportion of those things relating to the intentional permanent damage of another human being? I vote for the latter. If boxing is about skill, endurance, etc., then it can survive such a rule change. But if it is really about the thrill and chill of the ultimate snuff sport, then shouldn't we do away with it, and with the promoters who profit from it?

Remember pancration, the forerunner of both boxing and wrestling, a discipline at the Ancient Olympic Games in which allowable body contact was so extreme that gouging, throttling, etc. were allowed, and death was not uncommon. We no longer have pancration, and I think that it would be unacceptable as a modern Olympic sport, for very good reasons. Of course, it is still an open question as to whether boxing (or what kind of boxing) should remain an Olympic sport.

4. The BMA shouldn't moralize, but only advise on risk. There should be freedom of choice. The State shouldn't ban boxing—these are fighting men, and the activity would go underground rather than wither away.

Should boxing be banned? Well, it's not the same thing to argue that something is immoral or unpleasant and to argue that it should be banned. One might think alcohol to be an entirely malign influence but nevertheless think that prohibition would be counter-productive. Remember: those who participate in boxing are different from most of us, who would not dare step into a ring. McLellan keeps pit bull terriers and says he finds knocking someone out better than sex. In "Sudden Impact," the pre-fight publicity document, McLellan said:

> You have to go to war and you have to be prepared to die. That's what boxing is.

Don't such people have the right to make their choices under constraint and ignorance, just like the rest of us? Mill said that we should only prohibit what right-thinking people don't want to do anyway. The measure of that is (presumably) consensus, and there does not seem to be a consensus against boxing. The general situation seems to be as confused as I am!

But, short of banning boxing, there are practical steps internal to the sport that might be taken towards the reduction of head injuries:

a. Going back to bare-knuckle fighting. Gloves were invented for the protection of the hands, not the head. They permit more head punches, and more violent head punches. Without the gloves, fights would be more often stopped for hand injuries.

b. Outlawing blows to the side of the head (just as we now outlaw blows to the back of the head), since these are the blows that cause rotation of the skull, which is the main cause of brain damage.

c. Having shorter bouts, or shorter rounds, or both. Boxers are getting fitter and are punching harder, so the onslaught must be reduced. McLellan took 70 head punches in 10 rounds. If repetition is what does damage, then there should be less opportunity for it. Alternatively, if it were possible to produce a glove (or other protective gear) that really protected not just the head but also its contents, then such equipment should be made compulsory.

And, even if absolute prohibition is not justified, there are many measures short of prohibition; for example, ensuring that there were no boxing in schools, if only on the ground of inadequate consent; or dropping boxing from the Olympic Games programme (which would be enormously important in reducing the amount of state support for boxing in many countries). In addition, there are many "expressive" measures that might be taken in order to make clear our concerns about the activity: e.g. banning the televising of boxing, especially live, and especially before very late at night; enforcing controls on the kinds of advertising and promotion of boxing that rely on incitement (the creation of a violent and antagonistic context for the contest); and so on.

5. One thought: most boxers are (in legal terms) reckless; and especially one who calls himself "The Dark Destroyer."

One account of recklessness describes it as "conscious risk-taking." A professional boxer knows from the outset that it is entirely possible that he will "destroy" his opponent, and perhaps he even hopes that he will. He most certainly appreciates the riskiness to others of his business (as well as to himself), especially after Michael Watson's fate. That is to say, it is almost certain that Benn fully appreciated the risk that he might kill his next opponent, and yet he went willingly and enthusiastically into battle after careful and serious preparation.

This is not true of sportspeople in any other sport. Some have thought that this factor offers a case for arguing that boxing is not, after all, a "sport" (e.g. the BMA spokeswoman on *Sportsnight*). Now we must return to our earlier (albeit sketchy) account of "sport," to see which crite-

rion is unfulfilled. I'd argue, for example, that professional wrestling isn't a sport, because (for one thing) the rehearsal of moves ensures that there is not a proper contest.

In the case of boxing, I think we might rely on the boxer's "willingness to cause intentional harm" as failing to accord due respect to other participants. An objection to this is that boxing is a consensual activity, such that due respect is preserved. My route to a reply (which would have to be worked out in its detail) would both question the validity of "consent" (by analogy with prostitutes or pornographees) and also deny that consent to possible brain injury or death to oneself should be granted as exonerating the other from disrespect.

After all, we do not permit Russian Roulette to be played (and we might imagine "solitaire," "duel" and "team sport" varieties, for fun in argument!) even amongst consenting adults. We do, though, allow ourselves and others to drive cars, even though we are well aware that even careful drivers sometimes kill people. The issues here are difficult ones, but as well as intentionality another facet of culpability is reasonableness. Maybe in the context of our lives driving performs a more useful, essential, reasonable function than does Russian Roulette or boxing—such that the unreasonableness of boxing adds another dimension to the unjustifiability of the harms it intentionally or recklessly inflicts. (On this, see Duff, pp. 143 and 147—especially the case of Shimmen).

But where do I (and you) stand in all of this? Why was I watching the fight at all? Why did I continue to watch, fascinated, gripped, tense, as the 40–1 outsider, Benn, was bashed out of the ring in the first round; lurched around for a while only just surviving and under such intense punching that he might have been knocked out at any time; then gradually worked his way courageously and violently back to a kind of equality in a contest of sustained brutality—and finally won.

I confess to experiencing a classic contradiction: I can see the argument against professional boxing—the simple moral imperative against an activity not only the outcome but also the object of which is too often the injury, incapacitation or even death of a human being.

Yet I also acknowledge the particular virtues of boxing, which seem to differ only in degree from the virtues of many other sports: the courage involved in putting oneself on the line (think of individual compared with team sports); in putting one's entire self on the line (think of boxing as opposed to other individual sports); the facing of injury, danger and risk; the absolute reliance on one's personal resources; the discipline involved in attaining and maintaining extremely high levels of fitness and endurance, and so on.

Summary

This excursion through a series of examples has been most instructive. We can now see that there is nothing necessarily wrong or suspicious about assertiveness or aggression. We can see precisely what is wrong with violence in soccer; what is wrong with rugby or American football, if either their rules or their practices permit violence; and just why boxing is immoral, and perhaps should not be considered a sport.

I believe that boxing will eventually go the way of pancration. But not yet; and not even soon. Meanwhile, we should not prohibit it, although we should signal our disapproval either by selective bans or by other expressive gestures. Despite that, I cannot help thinking that the argument that shows boxing to be immoral is none the less important as a step towards our eventual collective realization that this sort of thing has no place in a society which strives towards the eradication of violence in human affairs.

Meanwhile, too, many of us will remain in the grip of the unresolved contradiction between our sentiments and our moral reason—but that's not such an unusual position for the ethical self to find itself in.

Sport and Education for Non-Violence

I would like to conclude by very briefly exploring the role of aggression and violence in sport in a wider social setting, and especially in education for non-violence. So far I have only toyed with the idea that assertion and aggression may not be wholly bad; but I want to intimate now a much stronger thesis: that aggression and violence in sport present opportunities for moral education and moral development.

When playing sport we exercise our potential for aggression, and we may be tempted by the attractions of violence in pursuit of our aims. I have argued elsewhere (Parry, 1986, pp. 144–5) that, in the educational setting, games function as laboratories for value experiments:

> Students are put in the position of having to act, time and time again, sometimes in haste, under pressure or provocation, either to prevent something or to achieve something, under a structure of rules. The settled dispositions which it is claimed emerge from such a crucible of value-related behaviour are those which were consciously cultivated through games in the public schools in the last century.

I believe that the impetus and opportunity for values education here is tremendous. The questions are: how do we come to terms with our own behaviour and dispositions, motivations and propensities? Is there a route from the potentially risky confrontation that sport sometimes is to the development of a self with greater moral resolution? And, more generally, is there a possibility for peace and the non-violent conduct of human affairs?

As Nissiotis said (1983, pp. 106– 8):

> . . . this is the ethical challenge that faces humanity: how to harness the creative and mo-

tivating forces of aggression into the service of humanity.

Sport in Olympic practice is one of the most powerful events transforming aggressiveness to competition as emulation. Sports life moves on the demarcation line between aggressiveness and violence. It is a risky affair . . . *Citius-altius-fortius* is a dangerous enterprise on the threshold of power as aggression, violence and domination. But this is, precisely, the immense value of Olympic sports: they challenge people to react, to pass the test of power . . .

I find it an attractive and intriguing idea, worthy of further consideration, that the competitive sports situation challenges individuals to develop and use their power and aggressiveness; but not, finally, to use this power to control and subjugate the other. May we see more assertive and aggressive people, and less violent ones. And may sport be an agent of moral change.

Bibliography

Alderman, RB, 1974, *Psychological Behaviour in Sport* (London: WB Saunders Co)

Arendt, H, 1969, "Reflections On Violence" (*NY Review of Books*, 12, Feb 27, pp. 19–31)

Audi, R, 1971, "On the Meaning and Justification of Violence" (in Audi R et al, pp. 45–100)

Audi, R, et al, 1971, *Violence* (New York: D Mackay)

BBC1, 1995a, *News*, 27 Feb 95, 9.00 pm

BBC1, 1995b, *Sportsnight*, 1 Mar 95, 10.20 pm

BBC2, 1994, *On the Line*, ("Aggression in Sport") 5 Sept 94, 8.30 pm

Cratty, BJ, 1983, *Psychology in Contemporary Sport*, Englewood Cliffs, NJ: Prentice-Hall

Duff, A, 1990, *Intention, Agency and Criminal Liability*

Dunning, EG, et al, 1993a, *The Sports Process*, (Human Kinetics)

Dunning, E, 1993b, "Sport in the Civilising Process" (in Dunning et al, 1993a, pp. 39–70)

Harris, J, 1982, *Violence and Responsibility*, (London: RKP)

Honderich, T, 1980, *Violence For Equality*, (Harmondsworth and NY: Penguin)

Hughes RH, 1984, Review of MD. Smith, *Violence and Sport* (*Sociology of Sport Journal* 1, 1, 84, pp. 79–83)

Marcuse, H, 1969, *An Essay On Liberation*, (Harmondsworth and NY: Penguin)

Martens, R, 1975, *Social Psychology and Physical Activity*, NY: Harper & Row

Nissiotis, N, 1983; "Psychological and Sociological Motives For Violence in Sport," *Proceedings of the International Olympic Academy*, pp. 95–108

Parry, J, 1986, "Values in Physical Education" (in Tomlinson, P and Quinton, M, *Values Across the Curriculum*, Brighton: Falmer Press, pp. 134–57)

Rule, JB, 1989, *Theories of Civil Violence*, (Calif: Univ Calif Press)

Smith, MD, 1983, *Violence and Sport*, Toronto: Butterworth & Co Ltd

van den Haag, E, 1972, *Political Violence and Civil Disobedience*, (New York: Harper & Row)

Wittgenstein, L, 1968, *Philosophical Investigations*, (Oxford: Blackwell)

Questions for Consideration

1. What precisely is Parry's stand concerning violence in sport? Does he ultimately concede that some forms of violence in sport are legitimate?

2. How do Parry's views on violence concern the sport of boxing? Do you agree with his proposals for reform?

3. Does Parry adhere to a cathartic model of aggression concerning sports?

23   Sports and Speciesism

Maurice L. Wade
Trinity College

In this reading, Maurice L. Wade takes a look at the use of animals in sportive practices through an examination of the views of three contemporary pro–animal rights philosophers: Peter Singer, Tom Regan, and Mary Anne Warren. Through an analysis of these views, Wade essays to find solid ground for the case for animal rights and some moral restrictions pertaining to the use of animals in sports.

Singer's account is utilitarian. Everyone's interests count, though people come in different shapes and sizes, and those actions are preferred that bring about the most satisfaction and the least frustration of interests. There are differences among species, even differences within species. Yet none of these differences is a reason for regarding the interests of any one group above those of another—for instance, humans over other animals. Interests themselves determine which group ranks above another. Racism, sexism, and speciesism (giving priority to one species over another because of group-related differences) are readily swept away. To accept that the interests of animals are subordinate to ours is discrimination and a denial of equality of interests. Consideration of utility must take into consideration the satisfaction and frustration of animals' interests. The implications for animals in sport are unclear, Wade says, because of the intricacies of the utilitarian calculus.

Wade next turns to Regan's case for animal liberation. Regan rejects Singer's arguments mostly because he repudiates his utilitarianism. Equal moral rights cannot find a basis in utilitarianism because utilitarianism makes no place for equal inherent value of persons. For the utilitarian, it is

Reprinted, by permission, from Maurice L. Wade, "Sports and Speciesism," *Journal of the Philosophy of Sport* XXIII (1996): 10–29.

feelings that are prized, not persons. For Regan, as for Kant, no subject of life can be treated as a means. Animals have moral rights every bit as binding as ours. As regards animals in sports, Regan's account seems to sanction complete abolition.

Last, Mary Anne Warren acknowledges nonhuman animals' moral rights, but argues for their subordination under human moral rights. Human aims and actions, she states, require greater freedom and fuller expression. Other animals may not be imprisoned by the imposition of some restrictions—say, encagement—the way humans are. This is not to diminish the importance of animals' rights at all. Our rights are primary only when our own vital interests are threatened. For sports, Warren would likely mandate no killing of animals for any purpose. Sports involving living animals would perhaps each be judged restrictions of liberty and happiness of those animals.

Millions of people participate in sports with passionate engagement as players and/or as fans and devote large amounts of their time, energy, money, and other resources to these endeavors. Some even risk life, limb, and health for the sake of sports. This means that the interests, indeed the well-being, of very many people are affected by how our sporting practices are conducted. For this reason alone, sports are proper matters of moral reflection. This is why we do, and should, vigorously debate issues such as whether to ban the use of performance-enhancing drugs, whether professional athletes should be held responsible for being role models for young people, whether opportunities for sports participation should be made equal for both sexes, how we can prevent the intensity of competition from degenerating into violence, whether children who play sports are subjected to too much pressure to win, and so forth. This list is, of course, only a tiny sampling of the ethical issues pertaining to sports that are currently being discussed in both popular and scholarly forums. However, no comprehensive account is required for us to admit that our moral concern with sports is largely anthropocentric, is largely focused on how human beings are affected by sporting practices.

But humans are not the only animals involved in sports, though we may be the only ones whose involvement is intentional. Nonhuman animals are also involved in our sporting practices in several ways. We kill them in practices such as sport hunting. Indeed, in this sort of blood sport, the effort to kill is a necessary feature of participation in the sport. In nonblood sports, while one is not required to attempt to kill in order even to be engaged in the sport, the equipment used is often made from materials provided by the dead bodies of nonhuman animals. Leather, for instance, is used in the manufacture of basketballs, baseball gloves, golf bags, and the saddles used in rodeo and horse racing, to list only a few of the forms of sports equipment for the sake of which nonhuman animal lives are sacrificed. In some sports, nonhuman animals are themselves the primary sporting equipment. In rodeo and horse racing, for example, one uses the living animals themselves in order to play the sports. While the animals are not intentionally killed for the sake of these sorts of sports, their bodies and lives are subjected to a variety of forms of control and constraint, some of which cause the animals discomfort and put their welfare at risk. Yet the moral concern expressed for animals used in sport is at best only a tiny fraction of the concern displayed for the effects of sports on human interests.

Proponents of animal liberation would argue that this disparity in moral concern (an abundance for our fellow human participants in sports and much, much less for the nonhuman participants) simply reflects the fact that in sports, no less than in our other endeavors, most

of us, most of the time, don't regard the interests and well-being of nonhuman animals as matters that merit serious moral concern. Animal liberationists recognize, of course, that this does not mean that we generally do not care at all about how animals are treated in sports. Very many of us, even those who kill animals for sport, believe that we have a duty not to be cruel to them, a duty not to cause them gratuitous suffering or harm. That we agree that some level of suffering or harm is gratuitous means that animals *do* count morally for us even while we disagree about just what constitutes genuinely gratuitous suffering or harm and about just how much we ought to be willing to compromise our sporting ends in order to prevent or ameliorate such suffering and harm. This certainly differentiates us from those of our ancestors for whom causing animals, human and nonhuman, to suffer was sometimes itself a sporting aim. Yet, proponents of animal liberation would note that our concern for the interests and well-being of our fellow humans is not limited to avoidance and prevention of gratuitous suffering. We take our fellow human participants in sports far more seriously than this. While we may generally agree on the wrongness of cruelty to animals, that does not prevent us from regarding the nonhuman animals involved in sports primarily as sporting resources. Within the bounds set by noncruelty, we feel free to do with them whatever serves our sporting purposes. Our concern for our fellow human sports participants goes far beyond the limits of noncruelty, as the small sampling of ethical issues in sport previously listed illustrates. And, that is the rub according to animal liberationists, and that is why they have popularized the term *speciesism,* to name this attitude, a term obviously meant to call to mind the invidious departures from equality that constitute racism and sexism.

Are we guilty of a form of invidious discrimination by giving less moral concern to the interests of the animals being used in sports? Should we regard our treatment of them as sporting resources, even within the limits of noncruelty, as evils of no less proportion than racism and sexism? Few, these days, would (openly, at least) disagree with the notion that invidious discrimination has no proper place in sports. We have something of a general consensus on this even as we often find that we cannot agree about just what counts as racist or sexist or which proposed remedies have merit. If we give affirmative answers to the questions just posed, then this consensus ought to extend to how we treat animals in sports. The proponents of animal liberation, while at odds over the supporting reasons, seek to convince us that our answers should be affirmative and that we ought to indict our current conduct toward nonhuman participants in sports as speciesist.

This essay aims to provide an exploration of some of the arguments from the philosophical literature in favor of animal liberation. This literature has become rather large, and the arguments and analyses contained therein are subtle and complex. The account provided in the following pages is far, far from comprehensive and leaves out, by necessity, very much of importance in the arguments that it does cover. It should suffice though to set firmly before us some of the issues and considerations relative to the use of animals in sports that ought to be taken seriously by anyone concerned with the moral quality of our sporting endeavors.

Singer's Case for Animal Liberation—The Principle of Equality

An especially apt place to begin to explore the arguments on behalf of animal liberation is with the utilitarianism of the Australian philosopher Peter Singer. Singer is one of the first contemporary professional philosophers to articulate a sustained philosophical case on behalf of animal liberation and is credited with coining the term *speciesism.*

A useful general characterization of utilitarianism is provided by Tom Regan in the following words:

A utilitarian accepts two moral principles. The first is that of equality: everyone's interests count, and similar interests must be counted as having similar weight or importance. White or black, American or Iranian, human or animal—everyone's pain or frustration matters, and matters just as much as the equivalent pain or frustration of anyone else. The second principle a utilitarian accepts is that of utility: do the act that will bring about the best balance between satisfaction and frustration for everyone affected by the outcome. (2: p. 43)

The first of these two principles is used by Singer to explain the evils of racism, sexism, and invidious intrahuman discrimination generally and provides the basis upon which he elaborates speciesism as a no less invidious form of discrimination. As we shall see, the second principle is the basis for some important criticisms of utilitarianism as a moral theory generally and thus as a basis for illuminating the evils of invidious discrimination of any sort.

Singer begins his explication of the first principle by cautioning against any understanding of equality that denies the many factual differences between human beings.

Like it or not, we must face the fact that humans come in different shapes and sizes; they come with differing moral capacities, differing intellectual abilities, differing amounts of benevolent feeling and sensitivity to the needs of others, differing abilities to communicate effectively, and differing capacities to experience pleasure and pain, In short, if the demand for equality were based on the actual equality of all human beings, we would have to stop demanding equality. (3: p. 34)

Racists and sexists assume, correctly, that people differ in these and many other ways. The case against racism and sexism must fail if it cannot accommodate this. But racists and sexists also assume that these sorts of differences justify treating some people better than others and that these differences are strongly correlated with, perhaps even necessarily linked to, racial and sexual difference, respectively. The racist assumes that the constellation of phenotypic characteristics that constitute race is tightly bound up with those qualities regarded as rendering the interests of some people inferior to those of others. If the racist is a White supremacist, for example, the interest of a Black person in food is of less importance than the very same interest of a White person because, on this view, this racial difference sorts Blacks and Whites into inferior and superior ranks, respectively. The sexist, in similar fashion, assumes that the biological differences that sort us into males and females are tightly linked to characteristics that render some people the natural inferiors of others, so that to know that an individual is male and another is female is to know whose interests takes precedence, even when their interests are the same.

One line of response to the racist and the sexist is to argue that these alleged correlations between race and sex and those qualities that supposedly sort us into inferiors and superiors simply do not hold. Singer argues that this response is inadequate for two reasons. First, the alleged correlations are matters of fact. And, we simply may not have all of the kinds of relevant factual data needed to rule decisively that these allegations are false, that the correlations do not hold. The response leaves open, therefore, the possibility of a factual vindication of racism and sexism. If our objections to racism and sexism persist even in the face of such a vindication, then this reply must fail to capture the heart of those objections. Second, even if the alleged correlations can be decisively shown to be false, this would only remove the ground for racism and sexism. That race and sex are not well correlated with the characteristics that are alleged to sort us into inferiors and superiors does not show that there are no such characteristics. Why not then, let the characteristics themselves sort us into inferiors and superiors rather than something else with which they are supposedly correlated? If discrimination of this sort would nonetheless strike us as invidious, then we have further reason for judging the response to have missed the crux of the matter.

What, then, is the crux of the matter? It is whether the qualities that differentiate us into groups justify treating the interests of some as less important than those of others even when the interests at issue are the same. Can there be differences between person X and person Y that entail that even when they have the same interest in Z, X's interest in Z must be more important than Y's? On Singer's view, there cannot be. What matters about interests is not who has them but rather the nature of the interests themselves. All interests count, and equal interests count equally regardless of who has them and to what group he or she belongs. Singer is clear in admitting that this is not an account of what is or isn't factually true about the world. Rather, it is a moral commitment, a commitment that how we treat people is to be determined not by who or what they are, but instead by the interest they have. What makes racism and sexism, or any scheme that ranks us into superiors and inferiors, *invidious* forms of discrimination is that they base how we are to be treated on who we are rather than on our interests.

This, according to Singer, opens the door to seeing why ranking humans as superior to nonhuman animals and thus giving automatic priority to human interests over the interests of nonhuman animals is also invidious discrimination and deserves the label *speciesism*. One might attempt to block this opening by asserting that the reason our treatment of human individuals should be based upon their interests, and whether those are similar or dissimilar, rather than on who the individuals themselves are, is that they, after all, are all human individuals. If we share a common humanity, this trumps our differences and makes looking to the similarities and dissimilarities of our interests the only reasonable way to proceed. Species difference then is taken to be able to do what race, sex, and other intrahuman differences cannot do. It can sort the world of creatures into superiors and inferiors. All we need to know is which are human and which are not. Can the moral commitment that interests count rather than who has them be kept in this fashion within the bounds of human beings alone? Can this effort to block the charge of speciesism succeed?

Singer argues that it cannot, because what makes our interests the central consideration in how we treat one another is not our common humanity but rather that having interests is what makes how we are treated matter to us. Absent interests, we would not care about how we are treated. What would there be for one to care about? One would lack a well-being, a good, a weal, a welfare, that could be damaged by how one is treated. If our interests are what makes how we are treated matter to us, then, of course, if our interests are similar, we have a similar kind of well-being at stake, whomever or *whatever* we might be. Rather than our common humanity trumping our differences, our common status as beings with interests trumps our humanity. Take away our interestedness and leave our humanity and we cannot care about what happens to us. This is true no matter what one's race, sex, or level of intelligence might be. Accordingly, if nonhuman animals have interests, then how they are treated matters to them and where their interests are similar to ours, the well-being put at stake by how they are treated is also similar to ours.

Singer argues that the fact of interestedness is just as much the case of nonhuman animals as it is of human animals. To have interests, a being need only be sentient. That alone is sufficient to ensure that it has at least an interest in not suffering. This means, according to Singer, that to rank animal interests as lower than human interests, just because they are animal interests, is to violate the same commitment to equality that animates opposition to racism and sexism and any form of invidious intrahuman discrimination. The moral commitment that leads to con-

demnation of these entails, if Singer is correct, condemnation of ranking animals as our inferiors. Hence, we can see the point of his deliberate coinage of the term *speciesism* as the name of a moral evil analogous to racism and sexism. If the analogy holds, then the consensus that racism and sexism have no proper place in sport ought to be extended to speciesism. And, the grounds for denominating all these "isms" as moral evils is the same.

Midgley on Speciesism

Mary Midgley (1), herself a philosophical critic of many of the arguments traditionally used to justify exploitation of nonhuman animals, offers some remarks on the concept of speciesism that can be usefully applied to further clarify Singer's views on interspecies equality. As noted, the term *speciesism* is meant to draw out an alleged analogy between invidious discrimination against nonhuman animals on the one side, and racism, sexism, and invidious intrahuman discrimination on the other. This analogy, in turn, depends on regarding racial and sexual difference as analogous to species difference. Midgley argues that while the analogy between sexual difference and other intrahuman differences, on the one hand, and species difference is generally sound, the analogy between racial difference and species difference is not.

If Singer is correct, we avoid racism when we predicate our conduct toward others on how their interests are affected rather than on what their race is. It would seem to follow then that to avoid speciesism, our conduct toward animals should be based upon how their interests are affected rather than on the species to which they belong. But, Midgley argues, the connection between species and interests is quite unlike the connection between race and interests. She writes:

Race in humans is not a significant grouping at all, but species in animals certainly is. It is never true that, in order to know how to treat a human being, you must find out what race he belongs to. (Cases where this might seem to matter always turn on culture.) But with an animal, to know the species is absolutely essential. A zoo-keeper who is told to expect an animal, and get a place ready for it, cannot even begin to do this without far more detailed information. (1: pp. 98–99). Overlooking somebody's race is entirely sensible. Overlooking their species is a supercilious insult. (1: p. 98–99)

If Midgley is correct, our ability to discern a human individual's interests, and therefore how to treat that individual, is unaffected by whether we know the individual does or does not have the constellation of phenotypic characteristics that constitute membership in a particular race. On the other hand, knowing the species of a nonhuman creature is, Midgely claims, essential to knowing its interests. We do no harm to a human individual when our decisions about how to treat her ignore her race, although to ignore a nonhuman animal's species in deciding how to treat it is very like to cause us to do it harm. Concern for the interests of our fellow humans is quite compatible with race-blindness, while concern for the interests of nonhuman animals requires us to not to be species-blind. Thus, even if the cure for racism is to become blind to the constellations of phenotypic properties that constitute race, an analogous approach to dealing with speciesism would be mistaken. It would simply replace the harms done to nonhuman animals on speciesist grounds with ones done by misguided inattention to the many ways that species difference makes a difference.

This is not say that Midgley believes that no group differences between human beings are importantly connected to their interests. In her view, differences of age, sex, and culture (and when race appears to be important, on her view, it is so only as a stand-in for culture) do have this kind of connection and hence to take them into account when determining a human individual's interests and therefore how to treat her is often quite sensible. "Differences . . . can be real and can need to be respected for the dignity and the interests of those most closely involved in them" (1: p. 101). "Serious injustice can be done to women or the old by insisting on giving them exactly the same treatment as men or the young" (1: p. 100). In the sense that they are importantly connected to interests, in just the way that race is not, these intrahuman differences are, in this respect, analogous to species difference.

Let us suppose that Midgley is correct. Then species, sex, age, and culture are real differences that make a difference to the interests of creatures, while race, as a constellation of phenotypic characteristics, is not and does not. Does this damage Singer's extension of the principle of equality to nonhuman animals? As Midgley herself concedes, it does not. For, Singer's position only requires that group differences, real or not, are never a legitimate basis for ranking the importance of anyone or anything's interest. His view requires only that when interests are similar, they should count similarly without regard for the groups to which the individuals with those belong. If an elephant and a man have the same interest in liberty, then that interest should be given the same weight. The fact that one is an elephant and the other is not is then irrelevant. It may be that an elephant and a man do not have the same interest in liberty and that this would be true of any elephant and any man because of the very properties that define species in each case. Differences in capacities can lead to differences in interests, and species differences will often include differences in capacities. Yet, Singer would hold that it is the difference in interests that matters. Even though knowing the species of the creature can be critical to knowing that difference, it is not the species membership itself that counts morally. He acknowledges as much for both species difference and sex difference in the following words:

There *are* important differences between humans and other animals, and these differences must give rise to *some* differences in the rights that each have. Recognizing this obvious fact, however, is no barrier to the case for extending the basic principle of equality to nonhuman animals. The differences that exist between men and women are equally undeniable. . . . The extension of the basic principle of equality from one group to another does not imply that we must treat both groups in exactly the same way, or grant exactly the same rights to both groups. Whether we should do so will depend on the nature of the members of the two groups. The basic principle of equality . . . is equality of consideration; and equal consideration for different beings may lead to different treatment and different rights. (3: p. 34)

If Singer is correct, then even a real group difference, such as age, sex, culture, or species, is an illegitimate basis for ranking some interests ahead of others. Real group differences may, however, come legitimately into play in determining whether and why different individuals have different interests, and hence, whether equality of consideration requires differences in treatment. Singer's position requires not that we make of race more than it is or species less than it is but only that we give no preference to interests just because their bearers belong to some or another group. The upshot of Midgley's remarks on the difference between race and species is that race is a trivial distinction, while species is not. At worst, then Singer's mistake is one of assimilating invidious discrimination based on a trivial group difference with invidious discrimination based on a real group difference. While the former may be cured by ignoring the difference, the latter requires not that we ignore the difference, but that we take it into account in the right way.

Midgley's comments on the concept of speciesism do not stop here, and her further comments strike closer to the heart of Singer's extension of the principle of equality to nonhuman animals. Like Singer, Midgley rejects any attempt to ground preference for human interests over animal interests on the claim that human capacities and/or lives are more valuable than animal capacities or lives. She sees no nonarbitrary vantage point from which such a claim could be established. But, she does not think that this kind of value judgment is the only source for our longstanding preference for our conspecifics. She argues that this preference is grounded in emotion. It is a matter of sentiment rather than one of value judgment, and as such, it may justify *some* degree of human preference for human interests.

The evolutionary processes that have shaped the various life forms on this planet have rendered some of them social animals, animals that undertake the challenges of life primarily through cooperation with their conspecifics rather than as more solitary individuals. Such animals, including humans, "attend mostly to members of their own species, and usually ignore others" (1: p. 105). Midgley notes that this preference of a social animal for its conspecifics is due in large part to the kind of imprinting upon it during infancy that takes place under normal circumstances. Once this imprinting has occurred, a life-long preference for its own kind is established in a social animal. This preference is critical to the sociability that has been such a successful evolutionary adaptation for social animals. Furthermore, Midgley notes, social animals tend also to be naturally endowed with capacities important to their welfare, which do not get developed and exercised except by way of cues provided in interactions with conspecifics. "Zoology would . . . back our impressions that, for a full life, a developing social creature needs to be surrounded by beings very similar to it in all sorts of apparently trivial ways, which abstractly might not seem important, but which will furnish essential clues for the unfolding of its faculties" (1: p. 107). (In the human case, the capacity for language is a strong candidate for this sort of faculty.) If this is correct, then our longstanding human preference for the interests of fellow humans is a natural disposition that we share with all social animals as a consequence of our and their evolutionary histories, one which has been critical to our survival and our flourishing. It is not then a mere prejudice rooted in an arbitrary partiality to those like us. Midgley writes:

> I think it is important to stress in this way that species-bonds are real, because unless we take account of them, the frequent exclusive attitude of our own species is hard to understand. There does indeed seem to be a deep emotional tendency, in us as in other creatures, to attend first to those around us who are like those who brought us up, and to take much less notice of others. And this, rather than some abstract judgement of value, does seem to be the main root of that relative disregard of other creatures which has been called "speciesism." (1: p. 106)

Looking back at the disparity noted earlier in this essay between the concern that we have for how our sporting practices affect our fellow humans and for how they affect nonhuman animals, Midgley would likely say that, while the question of whether that disparity is morally justifiable is not settled by this fact, it is a fact that the disparity is rooted in the natural disposition previously discussed.

But so what? If Singer is correct, what does it matter how our tendency to give greater importance to human interests than to nonhuman ones originates? If it is a form of invidious discrimination, then we ought nonetheless to be obligated to do all that we can to obliterate or stifle it, unless, it simply cannot be resisted. The point, I take it, for Midgley, is that this tendency, because it has contributed to and continues to contribute to our survival and our capacities, cannot be invidious in all of its expressions. Some range of greater concern for the well-being of our fellow humans over that of nonhumans must be morally permissible. Suppose that Midgley is correct about this, that the fact that a disposition with natural origins contributes to our survival and well-being makes at least some

of its expressions morally permissible. What does this mean for Singer's notion of speciesism? It means, as I see the matter, that if speciesism is invidious discrimination, then it cannot simply be equated with all instances of human preferences for human interests over animal interests. The critical question would be then, which instances of human preferences for human interests over animals' interests constitute invidious discrimination, a question of when such preferences are invidious and why? Thus, if Midgley is right, the matter of determining when we are conducting ourselves in a speciesist manner is rather less straightforward than Singer would have it. How ought we to make such a determination on her view? I confess that I find no help from her on this question. I can only say that if she is correct, animal liberationists such as Singer may have a somewhat harder row to hoe than they might have imagined. They must show us which preferences for human interests over animal interests comprise invidious discrimination, and this is bound to be more difficult than simply setting aside all such preferences as immoral. If Midgley is correct, then to judge our uses of animals in sports to be speciesist, Singer will not have done enough simply by showing that those uses are based upon ranking human interests ahead of animal interests. He will further have to show us that those uses fall outside the range of acceptable human species loyalty. That Midgley should also provide some notion of how to determine the parameters of that range would perhaps not be an unreasonable demand for Singer to make of her as well.

Fortunately, for Singer, Midgley is mistaken as the following argument, suggested by my colleague, W. Miller Brown, shows. Let's grant a disposition in us (and other social animals) to maintain species bonds. Each such species can flourish only by maintaining these bonds. In this way humans differ from elephants. For instance, we seek out and need humans; elephants seek out and need elephants. It does not follow that we can invidiously favor our species bond interests over those of other species any more than men can favor any interests they have over any men have simply by virtue of sexual differences. Our interest in (human) species bonding is morally no more important than an elephant's interest in elephant bonding. These are just additional interests tied to real species differences. Singer can take them into account in his view as it stands. Insofar as human and nonhuman interests in species bonding are equivalent, they are to be counted in the same way. Insofar as they are not, they are not to be so counted.

Singer's Case for Animal Liberation—The Principle of Utility

Let us set aside Midgley's case for permissible human species preference so that we can turn to Singer's use of the second of the two principles accepted by utilitarians: the principle of utility. Once we know which interests count, this principle tells us how to proceed with determining what we should or should not do. Again, Tom Regan's general characterization is useful:

> As a utilitarian, then, here is how I am to approach the task of deciding what I morally ought to do: I must ask who will be affected if I choose to do one thing rather than another, how much each individual will be affected, and where the best results are likely to lie—which option, in other words, is most likely to bring about the best results, the best balance of satisfaction over frustration. That option, *whatever it may be,* is the one I ought to choose. That is where my moral duty lies. (emphasis added) (2: p. 43)

The principle of utility tells us that achieving a particular aim is the definitive business of morality, the aim of generating the best balance of satisfaction over frustration. Extending the principle of equality to animals means that, in calculating this balance, their satisfactions and frustrations count in the same way as equivalent human satisfactions and frustrations. Whatever treatment of animals and/or humans yields the better balance is the morally proper treatment. Consequently, conduct that sacrifices the well-being of a creature, human or nonhuman, is neither intrinsically right or wrong. How well it serves the end that utilitarianism takes to be the only business of morality is what must settle the matter. If we look then at our current uses of animals within sports, those uses might well be unwittingly morally sound from this utilitarian perspective. For, although we have not counted equivalent animal frustration and satisfaction in the same way that we count human frustration and satisfaction, we might nonetheless be treating animals in just those ways that produce the best balance. Whether we are or not is an empirical matter. If we are, we would then be guilty of speciesism, not in how we are actually treating animals in our sporting practices, but rather in our reasons for those uses. We would be doing the right thing but for the wrong reasons.

Because Singer is a utilitarian, his case for animal liberation need not result in any alterations in current practice. I have little doubt that Singer would argue, as he has in the case of factory farming, for example, that the aggregate of satisfactions generated for humans by our current sporting uses of animals is far less than the aggregate of frustrations that animals thereby suffer. Yet, because the issue is one of fact, he must admit that his view might be mistaken. If we could get past the vast problems posed by comparing and quantifying satisfactions and frustrations, a rigorous and detailed examination of our current sporting uses of animals might show just that. Further, even if Singer's factual claim were to turn out to be correct, that we ought not to use animals at all in our sporting practices would not follow. For we might find that we can sufficiently reduce their frustrations and nonetheless produce a high enough quantity of human satisfactions to continue their sporting use on utilitarian grounds.

Perhaps a useful way to understand the principle of utility is simply as a way of giving rigor to the commitment to noncruelty that currently is the consensus on how to treat animals in sports and the other contexts in which we use them. What counts as gratuitous suffering? The principle of utility says any amount beyond that contained in the best available balance of satisfaction over frustration. While this gives rigor to our notion of cruelty, as noted at the outset in this essay, and thereby constrains the uses to which animals may be put, it does not mean that they cannot legitimately be used as resources, sporting or otherwise. On Singer's view, despite what he might like to conclude, such use could not properly be deemed speciesist. Why? Because it is arrived at in the proper way, a way that counts animal frustrations and satisfactions the same as equivalent human frustrations and satisfactions. This point becomes clearer if we remember that the principle of utility also determines how we are to treat our fellow humans. Whether and when the effects of our sporting practices upon human individuals is morally licit will be a matter of the balance of satisfaction over frustration thereby yielded. Any frustrations caused to them that exceeds that amount that would be contained in the best available balance of satisfactions and frustrations would be gratuitous and therefore cruel in just the same way that it would be for nonhuman animals. We might then say that for both humans and nonhuman animals alike, the principle of utility gives us no more than a rigorous noncruelty ethic, one that is nonspeciesist because avoiding and ameliorating cruelty would be our main concern for all sentient creatures. But a noncruelty ethic does not entail that using a sentient creature as a sporting resource is morally problematic. Indeed, it is difficult to see how the list of ethical concerns about the effects of sports on humans listed at the outset of this essay can be reduced to avoiding causing gratuitous suffering. Something else seems to be going on in those concerns, something that maximizing utility seems not to capture. And, for many animal liberationists, that something else is what

should be extended to our decisions about how animals are treated. That is why proponents of a nonutilitarian case for animal liberation such as Tom Regan reject Singer's approach.

Tom Regan's Nonutilitarian Case for Animal Liberation

Like Singer, Regan is a staunch opponent of speciesism and is also one of the first contemporary philosophers to develop a philosophically sophisticated case for animal liberation. We can begin to understand that case by turning to his disagreement with Singer. First, Regan argues that Singer's understanding of equality is mistaken because it locates inherent value in the wrong place. Regan writes:

> The sort of equality we find in utilitarianism . . . is not the sort an advocate of animal or human rights should have in mind. Utilitarianism has no room for the *equal moral rights of different individuals because it has no room for their equal inherent value or worth.* What has value for the utilitarian is the satisfaction of an individual's interests, not the individual whose interests they are. A universe in which you satisfy your desire for water, food, and warmth, is, other things being equal, better than a universe in which the desires are frustrated. And the same is true in the case of an animal with similar desires. But neither you nor the animal have any value in your own right. *Only your feelings do.* (2: p. 43)

The central contention here is that the kind of equality to which utilitarians such as Singer are committed values animals, human and nonhuman, not for what they are, but for what they can feel. We and they are valued, not for ourselves, but as loci of what does inherently have value for the utilitarian, our and their feelings. How we and they should be treated then is not predicated on what we and they are inherently worth but on what will produce positive feelings and remove or avoid those negative ones. Human and animal satisfactions and frustrations therefore count for their own sake, simply because of what they are, while humans and animals themselves count only for the sake of those frustrations and satisfactions. While Regan surely would concede that this does not arbitrarily rank humans ahead of animals, he would nonetheless insist that this kind of interspecies equality denies to both any value except as containers of a special kind. Regan illustrates this claim in the following words.

> Here is an analogy to help make the philosophical point clearer: a cup contains two different liquids—sometimes sweet, sometimes bitter, sometimes a mix of the two. What has value are the liquids: the sweeter the better, the bitter the worse. The cup—the container—has no value. It's what goes into it, not what they go into that has value. For the utilitarian, you and I are like the cup: we have no value as individuals and thus no equal value. What has value is what goes into us, what we serve as receptacles for; our feelings of satisfaction have positive value, our feelings of frustration have negative value. (2: p. 43)

To view us this way, is for Regan, to view us as mere instruments in the same way that a box or cup is a mere instrument. If it were not for what we can contain, we would not count morally. How we are treated would lack moral significance. Regan insists that rather than being valuable as special kinds of containers, we are valuable inherently, valuable for what we are. What are we such that our value attaches to us inherently, according to Regan?

> We are each of us the experiencing subject of a life, each of us a conscious creature having an individual welfare that has importance to us whatever our usefulness to others. We want and prefer things; believe and feel things; recall and expect things; And all these dimensions of our life, including our pleasure and pain, our enjoyment and suffering, our satisfaction and frustration, our continued existence or our untimely death—all make a difference to the quality of our life as lived, as experienced by us. (2: p. 45)

So Regan contends that utilitarians such as Singer fail to see that we are valuable not merely as sites of positive or negative feelings but rather that our positive and negative feelings have value only because of our value. Our feelings matter to us and what matters to us counts because we count. Regan's own commitment to equality resides in his position that this is true of any and every experiencing subject of a life without regard for race, sex, intelligence, culture, or species. Any experiencing subject of a life is inherently valuable and no more or less so than any other. That is why humans are and should be accorded the same basic moral rights regardless of race, sex, intelligence, culture, and the like. It is why, on this view, animals also should be accorded those very same rights. Any subject of a life has the same inherent value as any other, according to Regan, and so each should have the same basic moral rights as all. Before proceeding with further explication of Regan's position, we need to ask whether the criticism here expressed really does apply to Singer's position. Does Singer indeed reduce us to merely containers of a kind?

Singer argues, in the following passage, that he does not.

> When we think of receptacles such as boxes or bottles—considering them *qua* receptacle, and not as objects of artistic or commercial value in their own right—we think of their instrumental value in holding something else, and it is the contents which really matter. So, if utilitarians think of pigs, for instance, as valuable only because of the capacity of pigs to experience pleasure or preference satisfac-

tion, aren't they necessarily denying inherent value to pigs? (4: p. 80)

The analogy is misleading. Sentient creatures are not receptacles for valuable experiences in the way that bottles, for instance, are receptacles for wine. If I have a bottle of wine in my hand, I can pour the wine out of the bottle; but there is no way in which I can separate the valuable experiences of pigs from the pigs themselves. We cannot even make sense of the idea of an experience—whether of pleasure, or preference satisfaction, or anything else—floating around detached from all sentient creatures. Hence the distinction between treating individuals as if their experiences possessed inherent value, and treating them as if their experiences possessed inherent value, is much more problematic than we might at first glance suspect. (4: p. 80)

This response to Regan seems, to me, quite correct. We do not contain our experiences in the way that a container contains its contents. Our experiences *constitute* our subjectivity. We are subjects only insofar as we have experiences. A container remains what it is even when its contents are removed. Remove all of our experiences from us and so long as they are not replaced, our subjectivity is also removed. Nothing can matter to us. Much the same can be said about the characteristics that constitute being the subject of a life on Regan's own account. Remove from us those features that Reagan lists and you progressively remove our subjectivity. Why couldn't one say that on Regan's view we are valued because we "contain" those features as legitimately as one could say that on Singer's we are valued because we "contain" feelings. Either view could be as properly characterized as valuing us as special kinds of containers or we could legitimately say of both that what is at stake is which creatures have subjective existences—existences that can go better or worse for them. The one makes sentience the demarcation be-

tween these kinds of creatures and those which have no moral standing while the other takes the complex subjectivity involved in being the subject of a life to be the proper line of demarcation.

Regan's disagreement with Singer's case for animal liberation does not end here. In addition to questioning Singer's notion of equality, he also finds the aggregative nature of Singer's utilitarianism highly problematic. Here the charge of not adequately capturing the inherent nature of our value can be made to stick as a criticism of Singer's utilitarianism. Regan writes:

Serious problems arise for utilitarianism when we remind ourselves that it enjoins us to bring about the best consequences. What does this mean? It doesn't mean the best consequences for me alone, or for my family or friends, or any other person taken individually. No, what we must do is, roughly, as follows: we must add up—somehow!—the separate satisfactions and frustrations of everyone likely to be affected by our choice, the satisfactions in one column, the frustrations in the other. We must total each column for each of the options before us. This is what it means to say the theory is aggregative. And then we must choose that option which is most likely to bring about the best balance of totaled satisfactions over totaled frustrations. Whatever act would lead to this outcome is the one we ought to perform—is where our moral duty lies. And that act quite clearly might not be the same one that would bring about the best results for me personally, or my family or friends, or a lab animal. The best aggregated consequences for everyone concerned are not necessarily the best for each individual. (2: pp. 43–44)

Any creature with interests should have its interests counted in the same way as the equivalent interests of any other creature on this outlook. But those interests can ultimately be sacrificed by our conduct toward it, if, once the counting has been done, the best sum of satisfactions over frustrations requires it. No kind of treatment of a creature with interests is ruled out on this view so long as the decision justifying it is taken in the correct manner, so long, that is, as equivalent interests are counted equally and the decision aims at maximizing the balance of satisfaction over frustrations. Whereas Singer is correct that his view does not treat human or nonhuman animals as mere receptacles, he is wrong that this response is sufficient to defeat the charge that his utilitarianism fails to treat us as having inherent value. How can a view that is not willing to put any form of treatment of me beyond the pale as long as such treatment serves the goal of utility maximization also be respectful of my inherent value? Isn't that just how we decide how to treat something that has only instrumental value? We figure out what aims we can accomplish with it and then we treat it accordingly. To treat something as intrinsically valuable is to premise what one does to it not on what can be accomplished by means of it, but rather on what shows proper respect for it, what treatment does not degrade it.

Perhaps we can see more sharply how Regan's view differs from Singer's by contrasting the notion of a moral right that we get from each. A rough and incomplete notion of a moral right, but one serviceable for this discussion, is that of a valid claim that is assertable against moral agents. Such a claim places on moral agents at least the duty to refrain from interfering with one's efforts to obtain that to which one has the claim and perhaps sometimes also requires them to provide one with positive assistance in acquiring that to which one has a claim. For a utilitarian like Singer, what one can have a moral right to, when one has a valid claim of this sort, is wholly and solely a matter of whether according such a right is required in order to generate the best ratio of total satisfactions to total frustrations. One's interests are thus accorded the protection of moral rights only insofar as this aim is thereby served. For a nonutilitarian such as Regan, one has basic moral rights, valid moral

claims, on a noncontingent basis. One's possession of those claims is not contingent on what serves any aim other than respect for one's inherent value. Sacrifices of one's interests that fail to serve this aim are ruled out in principle no matter what consequences might thereby ensue.

If we return to the sampling of moral concerns about how sports affect the interests of human beings that was listed at the outset of this essay, Regan would say that we have these concerns, at least in part, because we want to know if our sporting practices are respecting the inherent value of our fellow humans. We are concerned that our sporting goals not be prosecuted in ways that put their basic moral rights in jeopardy. The reason the disparity between our concern for our conspecifics and our concern for other animals is speciesist on this sort of outlook is that it is not matched by a parallel disparity in the nature of our value and theirs, in our basic moral rights and theirs. Because they are subjects of a life no less than we are, how they are treated matters to them and affects their well-being. If noncruelty is insufficient as a standard of concern for humans because it would not be adequate to safeguard their inherent value, then this must hold true as well for any subject of a life. Any subject of a life, on Regan's view, is treated wrongly if it is treated as a resource and since the constraints on our conduct posed by noncruelty would not rule this out, noncruelty is an inadequate standard for our conduct toward both humans and animals when they are subjects of a life. If we remember the point made earlier that we can, without distortion, view the principle of utility simply as a standard for making our notion of cruelty rigorous, we can see why it would be unconvincing to an ethicist of Regan's ilk, one who puts respect for inherent value as the primary business of morality.

How do we avoid speciesism in our use of animals in sports from a standpoint like Regan's? We do so by refraining from violating their basic moral rights, rights to life, liberty, and happiness, for instance. Our sporting use of animals will honor their intrinsic value as subjects of a life only if those uses do not violate these kinds of rights. My guess is that Regan would likely take the same position here that he takes with regard to our use of animals for food and as subjects in medical and other forms of research—an abolitionist position. Blood sports and the making of sports equipment from the bodies of dead animals violates their right to life. Sporting practices that do not involve killing nonhuman animals do often cause them various degrees of discomfort and subject them to constraint and control and thereby violate their rights to happiness and liberty. Using animals in sports without violating any of these rights may be logically possible, but how it is practically possible is very, very difficult to see indeed.

Warren on Animal and Human Rights

Mary Anne Warren agrees with Regan's view that to avoid speciesism the better way to proceed is by recognizing nonhuman animals as holders of basic moral rights rather than by putting their interests into the utilitarian calculus on the same footing as human interests. But, she sees Regan's position as involving a false dichotomy. Regan seems to hold that we have only two mutually exclusive options. Either we are speciesist and thereby guilty of invidious interspecies discrimination or we accord nonhuman animals the very same basic moral rights that we accord to our fellow humans. Warren agrees that failure to accord basic moral rights to nonhuman animals is speciesist, but disagrees that we must accord them the same ones that we should accord to our conspecifics. They and we have lives that can go better or worse and in this regard there is no nonarbitrary reason for not providing them with the protections of basic moral rights. But, they and we are nonetheless different and, Warren argues, those differences should be seen as making a difference between their basic moral

rights and our own. On her view, the basic moral rights that are properly accorded to animals are justifiably weaker than those properly accorded to human beings. So between speciesism on the one side and radical interspecies egalitarianism on the other, she locates a middle position, one which is meant to rule out invidious interspecies discrimination without requiring that animals and humans be accorded the same fundamental moral rights.

Warren offers two reasons for judging the basic moral rights of nonhuman animals to be weaker than those of humans. First, she considers the respective content of these rights. Taking the basic moral right of liberty, Warren says:

> The *human* right to liberty precludes imprisonment without due process of law, even if the prison is spacious and the conditions of confinement cause no obvious physical suffering. But it is not so obviously wrong to imprison animals, especially when the area to which they are confined provides a fair approximation of the conditions of their natural habitat and a reasonable opportunity to pursue the satisfactions natural to their kind. Such conditions . . . need not frustrate the needs or interests of animals in any significant way, and thus do not clearly violate their rights. Similarly treated human beings, on the other hand (e.g., native peoples confined to prison-like reservations), do tend to suffer from their loss of freedom. Human dignity and the fulfillment of the sorts of plans, hopes, and desires which appear (thus far) to be uniquely human, require a more extensive freedom of movement than is the case with at least many nonhuman animals. Furthermore, there are aspects of human freedom, such as freedom of thought, freedom of speech, and freedom of political association, which simply do not apply in the case of animals. (6: p. 191)

So human liberty involves particular forms that simply are unavailable to nonhuman animals because they do not possess the capacities presupposed by those forms of freedom. And, with respect to freedom of movement, for which humans and animals alike are equipped, restrictions that cause harm to humans may not and often will not cause harm to animals. Their interests can be well met, and so their well-being respected, within bounds that would not respect human well-being. Hence, respect for human beings with regard to their liberty means being constrained in our conduct toward them to a substantially greater degree than would equal respect for animals in this regard. Thinking about the use of animals in sports, that they are restrained in ways that would never be countenanced for our fellow humans, does not mean that such restraint is necessarily speciesist. That will depend upon the nature of the animals beings used and whether those restraints deprive them of, in the words that Warren uses in the passage previously quoted, "a fair approximation of the conditions of their natural habitat, and a reasonable opportunity to pursue satisfactions natural to their kinds." As she correctly notes, this leaves open the possibility that some animals may suffer even if they are restrained no more than would be appropriate for a human being. The effect of restraint on the animal's well-being is the issue, and that can't be settled by knowing whether it is human or not but requires instead that we know what capacities and hence interests are at stake with regard to its freedom.

Consider next the basic moral right to life. Here again differences between human and animal capacities lead to difference in the content of their rights. Warren argues:

> Animals . . . lack the cognitive equipment to value their lives in the way that human beings do. . . . In other words, animals appear to lack the sorts of long-range hopes, plans, ambitions, and the like, which give human beings such a powerful interest in continued life. Animals, it seems, take life as it comes and do

not specifically desire that it go on. True, squirrels store nuts for the winter and deer run from wolves; but these may be seen as instinctive or conditioned responses to present circumstances, rather than evidence that they value life as such.

> These reflections probably help to explain why the death of a sparrow seems less tragic than that of a human being. (6: p. 192)

We must be careful not to misconstrue Warren's remarks. She is not arguing that nonhuman animals have no right to life. Indeed, she clearly recognizes that death takes from an animal those future satisfactions that it might have had and further that we simply don't know whether animals have "future-oriented desires," whether they "consciously pursue relatively distance future goals" (6: p. 192).

What does this difference between animals and humans mean for their respective rights to life? It means, according to Warren, that:

> animals do have a right to life . . . that is generally weaker than that of human beings. It is, perhaps, weak enough to enable us to justify killing animals when we have no other way of achieving such vital goals as feeding or clothing ourselves, or obtaining knowledge which is necessary to save human lives. Weakening their right to life does not render meaningless the assertion that they have such a right. For the point remains that some serious justification for the killing of sentient nonhuman animals is always necessary; they may not be killed merely to provide amusement or minor gains in convenience. (6: p. 193)

If we apply this to our use of animals in sports, we again do not necessarily arrive at across-the-board abolition. With respect to blood sports and the construction of sports equipment from the dead bodies of animals, the central matter is whether some vital purpose is served by killing animals. I cannot see that any is. While blood sports participants certainly value their sporting aims very highly, they cannot plausibly claim that their lives cannot go on very well indeed without engaging in killing animals. If pursuit of the kill is a constitutive feature of what they value about their sports, then abolition does seem to be the only morally licit position. As for the use of the bodies of dead animals in manufacturing sports equipment, here too the purposes served may be highly valued but cannot plausibly be regarded as vital. Life can go on, and very well at that, even if equipment using other materials is substituted or even if the sporting practices themselves are ended because no suitable substitutes can be had. The harm done to an animal by destruction of its life may be less than would be done to a human, but it is nonetheless of far greater moral importance, if Warren is correct, than any sporting aims we can thereby accomplish. The constraints placed upon us by recognition of a right to life for nonhuman animals are less substantial than those placed by the analogous human right, but they are substantial enough to merit serious changes in our uses of animals in sports.

That the rights to liberty and life of animals are weaker than those of humans does not mean that their right to happiness, "their right not to be made to suffer needlessly or to be deprived of the pleasures natural to their kind" (6: p. 193), is also weaker, at least not on the grounds of differences between animal and human capacities. Warren points out that:

> Our large brains *may* cause us to experience pain more intensely than do most animals, and *probably* cause us to suffer more from the anticipation or remembrance of pain. These facts might tend to suggest that pain is, on the whole, a worse experience for us than for them. But it might also be argued that pain may be *worse* in some respects for nonhuman animals, who are presumably less able to distract themselves from it by thinking of some-

thing else, or to comfort themselves with the knowledge that it is temporary. (6: p. 193)

So while we may be able, in many instances, on the grounds of content, to judge the rights of nonhumans to life and liberty to be weaker than human rights, content cannot ground the same judgment for their right to happiness.

This brings us to Warren's second reason for judging basic human rights to be stronger than animal rights, a reason that is more important because it provides a basis for "regarding all of the moral rights of animals as somewhat less stringent than the corresponding human rights" (6: p. 193). Again, a difference between humans and animals is at issue; humans are autonomous, "are at least sometimes capable of being moved to action or inaction by the force of reasoned argument" (5: p. 49). Nonhuman animals lack this capacity. Warren notes that this difference does not mean that we are morally superior to animals (whatever that might mean), but rather that we have:

> greater possibilities for cooperation and for the nonviolent resolution of problems. It also makes us more dangerous than non-rational beings can ever be. Because we are potentially more dangerous and less predictable than wolves, we need an articulated system of morality to regulate our conduct. Any human morality, to be workable in the long run, must recognize the equal moral status of all persons, whether through the postulate of equal basic moral rights or in some other way. The recognition of the moral equality of other persons is the price we must each pay for their recognition of our moral equality. Without this mutual recognition of moral equality, human society can only exist in a state of chronic and bitter conflict. . . . But, to the extent that we achieve a mutual recognition of equality, we can hope to live together, perhaps as peacefully as wolves, achieving (in part) through explicitly moral principles

what they do not seem to need explicit moral principles to achieve. (5: p. 50)

. . . for morally autonomous beings such as ourselves, there is enormous mutual advantage in the adoption of a moral system designed to protect each of us from the harms that might otherwise be visited upon us by others. Each of us ought to accept and promote such a system because, to the extent that others also accept it, we will all be safer from attack by our fellows, more likely to receive assistance when we need it, and freer to engage in individual as well as cooperative endeavors of all kinds.

Thus, it is the possibility of *reciprocity* motivates moral agents to extend *full and equal* moral rights, in the first instance, only to other moral agents. I respect your rights to life, liberty, and the pursuit of happiness in part because you are a sentient being, whose interests have intrinsic moral significance. But I respect them as *fully equal to my own* because I hope and expect that you will do the same for me. Animals, insofar as they lack the degree of rationality necessary for moral autonomy, cannot agree to respect our interests as equal in moral importance to their own. . . . Consequently, it is neither pragmatically feasible nor morally obligatory to extend to them the same *full and equal* rights which we extend to human beings. (6: pp. 194–195)

In these passages. Warren is essentially holding that our rationality, and the moral autonomy that it provides, enables us to reduce the dangers and enhance the benefits of living together. Because we are rational, we can agree not to damage, and perhaps also to assist, one another in ways crucial to our well-being. Such agreement is sustainable on the expectation that the rights thereby established are accorded to all parties fully and equally. We cannot make this agreement with nonhuman animals.

Each of us who can should respect the lives, liberty, and pursuit of happiness of each and every sentient creature, according to this view, because the interests involved therein are morally significant for their own sake. But, not every such creature can respect my life, my liberty, and my pursuit of happiness as much as I respect my life, my liberty, and my pursuit of happiness. I can ask that the conditions that justify damaging those interests of mine that are bound up with my life, liberty, and pursuit of happiness be limited to ones of especially great importance. But I cannot ask every sentient creature or even every subject of a life to agree to this. I can ask it only of creatures that are, like me, rational and morally autonomous, just as they can, in turn, ask it of me. Human beings thus can interact on terms that amount to full and equal recognition of each other's basic moral rights and in doing so provide each other with assurances that make life mutually better. We cannot do this with any of the nonhuman sentient creatures that we have so far encountered. And, according to Warren, this entails that we are not morally required to take the basic moral rights of nonhuman animals as stringently as those of humans. In the context of sports, this is not likely to justify killing animals for sport, because we hardly can be said to respect the right to life of animals at all if we kill them for a reason so nonvital. It need not mean that other sporting uses of them must be abolished. That depends upon whether we can pursue our sporting aims, none of which can plausibly be regarded as vital, without restricting their liberty to the point of damaging their interests, and whether we can do so without causing them to suffer. This would constrain our use of animals in sport far more than would mere noncruelty.

Warren's argument is that human beings can reciprocate in our respect for each other's interests. And we all get something out of doing so, which gives us reason to do so. This seems to imply that the main reason for not taking the interests of nonhuman animals equally seriously is that, since they can't reciprocate, to do so would be to accord them a benefit that we cannot get from them in return. But isn't this to say that we have a certain kind of usefulness to each other that can be tapped only on the basis of mutual recognition of full and equal rights, which, in turn, seems to be to say that such recognition is based only in that utility. We and animals gain basic moral rights simply in virtue of being entities whose lives can go better or worse. On this view, we humans should accord one another an extra measure of moral standing though and so regard one another's basic moral rights as more stringent, because of what we can thereby get from each other.

I confess that I am not persuaded by this second reason for regarding the basic moral rights of animals as less stringent than those of humans. We have a reason to extend stringent moral rights to our fellow humans because we reciprocally benefit from doing so. We don't get reciprocal benefits from extending stringent basic moral rights to nonhuman animals. Why does this mean that we are not obligated nonetheless to make this extension? We will not benefit from it, but they will. They will not be subject to whatever harms to their interests that would be allowable if their basic moral rights are less stringent ones. That is surely to their good. Why shouldn't we be obliged to extend those additional protections to them and to bear the burdens of so doing just because we get no gain for ourselves thereby? Isn't this a case of arbitrarily preferring our interests in these benefits to theirs?

Warren's first reason seems to me to be more compelling. It takes the differences between our capacities to be the reason that animal's basic moral rights are less stringent than human ones. Such a reason does not make their moral status turn on what they can or cannot offer us in return for our consideration. It turns instead on what they are and how their lives matter to them as a consequence of what they are. This reason strikes me therefore as avoiding the arbitrariness of Warren's second reason.

Conclusion

What is the upshot of this rather rapid tour through some of the ins and outs of some of the philosophical arguments in favor of animal liberation? First, the kind of utilitarian case proffered by Peter Singer runs afoul of the traditional inability of utilitarianism to give adequate recognition to our intrinsic value and therefore to extend such recognition to nonhuman animals. Its way of avoiding speciesism degrades both humans and animals to mere means by which to generate utility. Second, the nonutilitarian case offered by Tom Regan, while avoiding the inadequacies of utilitarianism, offers a form of interspecies equality that is too radical. It is too radical not because it places heavy demands on us but rather because it does not recognize that there are differences between humans and animals that make a difference in their and our respective basic moral rights. Third, Warren offers two reasons for regarding the basic moral rights of nonhuman animals as less stringent than those of humans, the first of which is more compelling than the second. But the second does support her case that giving the interests of nonhuman animals due moral recognition will mean regarding their basic rights often to be less stringent than our own.

Singer's case, even if it were successful, might or might not require changes in our use of animals in sport. Without some clear sense of what the utility effects of change versus the status quo would be, we can't say with confidence whether it would or not. Regan's case, if it were successful, would probably require abolition of the use of animals in sport. Because such use, even within the limits noncruelty infringes upon one or more of the basic rights of animals and is not, because it cannot be, premised upon their consent, it is difficult to see any course following from this position other than abolition. Warren's case, which seems to me to be successful, would require that animals not be killed for sport, either in blood sports or to make equipment for nonblood sports. As for sporting uses that do not involve killing animals, whether such uses should continue at all or should continue only in changed fashion is dependent upon whether the basic rights to liberty and happiness of animals can be respected within them. That question lies beyond the boundaries of this essay.

Bibliography

1. Midgley, Mary. *Animals and Why They Matter.* Athens, GA: The University of Georgia Press, 1983.

2. Regan, Tom. "The Radical Egalitarian Case for Animal Rights." In *Environmental Ethics: Readings in Theory and Application.* Edited by Louis Pojman. Boston, MA.: Jones and Bartlett Publishers, 1994,

3. Singer, Peter. "All Animals are Equal." In *Environmental Ethics: Readings in Theory and Application.* Edited by Louis Pojman. Boston, MA: Jones and Bartlett Publishers, 1994.

4. Singer, Peter. "Animal Liberation or Animal Rights?" In *People, Penguins, and Plastic Trees: Basic Issues In Environmental Ethics* (2nd ed.). Edited by Christine Pierce and Donald VanDeVeer. Belmont, CA: Wadsworth Publishing Company, 1995.

5. Warren, Mary Anne. "Difficulties with the Strong Animal Rights Position." In *Environmental Ethics: Readings in Theory and Practice.* Edited by Louis Pojman. Boston, MA: Jones and Bartlett Publishers, 1994.

6. Warren, Mary Anne. "The Rights of the Nonhuman World." In *The Animal Rights/Environmental Ethics Debate: The Environmental Perspective.* Edited by Eugene C. Hargrove. Albany: State University of New York Press, 1992.

Questions for Consideration

1. Is the case made against Singer regarding the confusion about the application of utility a decisive one?

2. Is there, following Regan, an equal inherent value of all living things? To what extent do you think Regan extends this to living non-animals?

3. Is Warren's argument for the superordination of human rights over nonhuman animals' rights more speciesism? How would Regan respond?

4. Which of the three accounts do you believe best makes a case for animals' rights?

5. For each of the three accounts, flesh out, in greater detail than Wade gives, the implications for the use of animals in sports.

Performance-Enhancing Drugs

24   Paternalism, Drugs, and the Nature of Sports

W. M. Brown
Trinity College

In this reading, W. M. Brown looks at the moral issue of the use of performance-enhancing drugs in sports.

What has the greatest bearing on deciding the issue is paternalism, both soft and hard. Soft paternalism asserts that restrictions on the liberty of another to act are sometimes justified when such actions are not wholly voluntary (due to youth, limited education, mental impairment, etc.). Hard paternalism, in contrast, maintains that restrictions on liberty are sometimes justified even when someone else is acting in full voluntary control.

Pertaining to sports, Brown argues that we should proscribe the use of performance-enhancing drugs to youths (soft paternalism), since we run the risk of skewing their underdeveloped values by unduly emphasizing winning through drug use. Yet for adults who are in full voluntary control (hard paternalism), the scenario is otherwise. The values of adults are not always the same as those we instill in children. Adult life is more complex and, for some people, winning, fame, wealth, and power are important values.

What is ultimately at stake is human autonomy and self-determination. Each rational person has a right to do what he or she wants to do, so long as his or her actions do not harm others. Risk taking, like the taking of steroids to enhance perform-

ance, is a personal matter. Paternalistic intervention is immoral.

Brown ends by stating that there is no essence of sport and no one conception of it upon which we all need to agree. The values of sport are those values we choose to link to it. Therefore, in denying athletes the use of performance-enhancing drugs, we deny them certain key values adjoined to sport: achievement, self-reliance, and autonomy.

During the marathon run at the 1972 Munich Olympics, Frank Shorter is said to have sipped decarbonated Coca-Cola provided along the route by his assistants as he headed for a gold medal. Clearly, for Shorter, caffeine was the drug of choice for that most demanding of running events. Since that time, caffeine has become one of an increasingly long list of banned drugs no longer permitted by the International Olympic Committee for competing athletes.[1] The list includes both a variety of chemically synthesized drugs as well as naturally occurring substances that are artificially prepared for human use.[2] The central issue of the use of such substances is not their so-called recreational use, the most prominent example of which is probably the widely publicized use of cocaine by some professional athletes. (Alcohol is apparently not currently a prohibited drug for Olympic athletes.) Rather, the issue is the use of drugs to enhance the benefits of training and to improve peak performance in competition.

Reprinted, by permission, from W. M. Brown, "Paternalism, Drugs, and the Nature of Sports," *Journal of the Philosophy of Sport* XI (1984): 14–22.

Controversy on this issue centers on several factors which have both an empirical aspect and a moral one. The empirical questions concern both the effectiveness of drug use for training and competition and the possible harm such use can have for users.[3] The moral questions concern the appropriateness of the use of drugs in sports, especially when their use is seen as a kind of cheating, a breach of principles of fair play. It is sometimes claimed, too, that the use of drugs in sports is somehow unnatural or incompatible with the very nature of sports. I intend to discuss these matters, but from the perspective of the moral principle of paternalism that I believe motivates many people who are concerned with this issue. First I want to look closely at the issue of drug use in sports by children and young people—cases which may appear to justify paternalistic choices—to the harder case of the paternalistic control of drug use by adults in sports.

Even John Stuart Mill (7), in his sustained attack on paternalistic restrictions on individual liberty, limited the application of his principles to mature individuals, adults in the full possession of their cognitive and emotional capacities. In the case of children, and perhaps others whose mature development of these capacities and a wider experience of life's possibilities has yet to be achieved, restrictions on individual liberty may be justified as preventing significant harm that might not otherwise be recognized and avoided. In such cases it seems clear that paternalistic interference is not only permissible but may indeed be obligatory to prevent harm and allow for a full flourishing of the child's potential development. Of course, judgment must be balanced: An important part of growing up is making mistakes and learning from them. All parents know the anguish of allowing failure to help guide the maturation of their children. Following Joel Feinberg and Gerald Dworkin, we can distinguish between "soft" and "hard" paternalism (2;3;4).[4]

Soft paternalism is defined by Dworkin (3: p. 107) as "the view that (1) paternalism is some-times justified, and (2) it is a necessary condition for such justification that the person for whom we are acting paternalistically is in some way not competent." The key element here is clearly the determination that the person for whom we are acting is in fact not acting voluntarily, perhaps due to various circumstances including immaturity, ignorance, incapacity, or coercion. It may be that the nonvoluntary character of the behavior is evident or justifiably assumed on other grounds. This is typically the case with young children; but it is sometimes also true of adults whose situation makes clear that their actions are not fully voluntary. The more problematic cases are those of adult behavior that is not obviously nonvoluntary, but whose consequences are potentially dangerous or serious enough to call for careful deliberation. In these cases, as Feinberg (4: p. 8) suggests, we may be justified in intervening at least temporarily to determine whether the conduct is voluntary or not.

If soft paternalism is most clearly relevant to intervention in the lives of children and incompetent persons, hard paternalism must deal with cases of fully voluntary action and show nevertheless that paternalism is justified. Here we may have every reason to suppose that the action in question is voluntarily undertaken by someone who has carefully appraised the consequences, weighed all available information, is emotionally responsive to the circumstances, but still opts to act in ways that involve the probability of serious harm, degradation, or impairment of opportunity or liberty. The most frequently cited cases are of those who seek to sell themselves into slavery, or persist in ignoring basic safety precautions such as wearing helmets while riding motorcycles. I shall return to the hard paternalistic thesis and its application to the case of adult sports after considering first the view of the soft paternalist and its application to the case of children and young people and their participation in sports. I shall not be directly concerned with the soft paternalist attitude toward adult sports except as an extension of its application to the case of children.

The soft paternalist argues that limitation of one's liberty is justified when one's behavior or actions are not fully voluntary because they are not fully informed, or because one is not fully competent or is in some relevant way coerced. All of these factors may plausibly be seen as present in the case of children's sports. By virtue of their youth, limited education, and inexperience, young people may frequently act in imprudent and potentially harmful ways, ways that may have unforeseen but long-term or irreversible consequences. Before considering the case of drugs, let me review several other cases in which the soft paternalist has what seems to be a strong argument for intervention or control of the young athlete's participation in sports.

The first kind of situation can best be called "safety cases."[5] These involve efforts by coaches, trainers, parents, and others to ensure that young players are provided with proper safety equipment and that they use it while engaged in playing the sport. Especially in contact sports such as football or hockey, such equipment as helmets and padded uniforms may be essential to protect the players against serious injury. Other sports may require other kinds of precautions. For example, swimmers may be prohibited from training alone in a pool, runners may be required to wear proper shoes, contact lenses may be forbidden, and so on. Some of these precautions may simply be prescribed by thoughtful parents or coaches, but others may be written into the rules of the sports by athletic associations, schools, or boards of education, thereby restricting participation to those who are properly equipped, or prohibiting certain kinds of play as too dangerous.

Indeed, most of the rules governing contact between players are formulated with the intention of ensuring the safety of enthusiastic and energetic players. The reasons for these requirements and rules are evident. Young athletes are frequently marvelously competent and talented in performing the intricate or arduous or swift feats called for in their sports. But they are typically equally unaware of their own limitations,

their susceptibility to injury, and the long-term consequences of injuries to their development or effective participation. What justifies intervention in these cases, of restrictions on what young athletes may do, is precisely the belief that they are thus being prevented from harming themselves and that on mature reflection they themselves will come to see the reasonableness of the restrictions now placed on them. As their own experience broadens, and as their knowledge of themselves and their actions deepens and their values mature, they are, we anticipate, likely to join in accepting the restrictions they may have seen before as irksome and unnecessary.

A second set of cases I propose to refer to as "health cases." Insofar as injuries are closely connected with our views of health, there is clearly a considerable overlap between these two types of cases. Nevertheless, I believe there are some significant differences that warrant a separate category. Even in the absence of injuries and of circumstances likely to promote them, other matters of health rightly should concern the parent or coach of young athletes. I have in mind here matters that concern training, medical examinations and corresponding medical treatment or therapy, and nutrition and rest. They may involve the need for periodic medical examinations, the proper treatment of injuries, insistence on adequate nutrition and rest, and thoughtful organizing of training schedules that carefully consider the age, preparation, and health of the athlete.

In these cases, the young person typically lacks information to make adequate judgments—information that may be the purview of specially trained persons with long experience working with athletes and others. Furthermore, the young person is not generally expected even to be aware of his or her own ignorance or of the importance of acquiring medical or other information at an age when health may be taken for granted. Moreover, even when information is available, its significance may not be readily appreciated, habits of restraint and caution may be ill-formed, and self-discipline in maintaining therapeutic or training regimens may be minimal. The opposite may also occur. Youthful determination may manifest itself in excessive restraint, debilitating training, or stubborn persistence. Here ancient wisdom of balance, moderation, measure or variation may be the needed antidote, provided by more experienced people who insist on more wholesome approaches to sports preparation.

Of course, other factors than ignorance and inexperience may need to be overcome in paternalistic control of youthful sports. Peer and perhaps especially adult pressures are often a critical factor that adult advisors must deal with firmly and sensitively. One other important distinction should be mentioned here. So far, I have ignored the difference between health as the absence of disease or injury and health as a positive feature of growth and development. If it is clear that adults are justified in controlling the sports activities of young people in the interest of preventing injuries or speeding recuperation, and in maintaining the health of their children and students in the sense of keeping them injury-free and minimally healthy, it is also plausible that they are justified in seeking a greater degree of health or fitness for them. This seems to involve more centrally an educational function, though this feature is clearly present in the other two kinds of cases I have discussed, and I now turn to consider what might be called "educational cases."

Sports in our schools and universities, even when they involve intercollegiate competition, are almost invariably associated with departments of physical education. I mention this because it seems that a neglected but focal role for parents and coaches is educational, and the educational function goes far beyond the training of skills to include the inculcation of attitudes and values, the dissemination of information, and the formation of habits of mind as well as of body. It is difficult to illustrate cases in which paternalistic issues arise here, because the guidance of parents and coaches is often so subtle and pervasive as to be unnoticed by those it influences.

Its character as interfering with or controlling the behavior of unwilling charges is more difficult to discern. Nevertheless, I think there are some fairly clear cases.

One type of case brings us back to efforts to prevent injury and to foster wholesome development by prescribing training schedules and nutritional standards designed to maximize training effectiveness. The effort here should never be merely to prescribe, but also to educate by explaining the rationale for the requirements, presenting the evidence available to substantiate the judgments, and requiring that the student understand as much as possible how the decisions were made. What can be expected here will vary with the age and educational level of the student; but resistance can often be expected, not only to following the requirements but to making efforts to understand them. I offer no formula for success in these efforts. As in all educational contexts many options are available to gifted teachers: cajolery, punishment, rewards, example, the inducements of affection, friendship, and respect, and lessons of failure and success. But I do wish to stress that these efforts are made because we believe the lessons should be learned, willingly or not, in the gym and playing field as well as the classroom. In doing so we counter the thoughtless or irrational or emotionally immature behavior of our students with paternalistic measures we believe are acceptable to fully rational and emotionally mature individuals.

A second type of educational case involves values. I have in mind instances of cheating or foul play in which adults may intervene to correct unfair, dishonest, or unsportsmanlike actions. Here again the goal is not merely to remedy or referee but is fundamentally educational. We should seek to instill values of fairness and honesty, countering whatever tendencies to the contrary we observe on the grounds that such action is not in the best interest of the players, whatever they may think about it. The development of values like the acquisition of knowledge in general is but one aspect of the central aim of education, which is the discovery of self-knowledge. Since, especially in young people, this is inextricably bound up with what they will become as well as with what they now are, the paternalistic guidance by adults must both inform and shape in light of what the adults believe to be the characteristics of persons in the fullness of their cognitive and emotional powers.

We are now ready to discuss control of the use of drugs by children and young people as an aspect of their participation in sports. Although I think a good general case can be made for proscribing drug use by young people, and even that a recreational use of drugs has some negative relevance to participation in sports, I plan to limit my remarks to a consideration of the use of drugs to influence athletic training and performance. I have not hesitated to offer here what I consider to be defensible moral judgments on the topics and issues I have raised. My point is not to insist that these judgments are unavoidable, but to suggest that they correspond with widely held intuitions relating to the acceptability of paternalism in regard to children and their sports activities.

Two aspects of drug use can be distinguished in advance, one being the use of drugs as medication. When medical treatment does not prevent sports participation entirely, it may significantly curtail that involvement. And when injury or illness requires medication which nevertheless will allow some sports activity, the decisive criterion will be improvement of the participant's health, not athletic achievement. There may also be times when use of medication is unrelated to sports and seems in no way to affect participation, except perhaps to allow it where otherwise it might not be possible. (An example might be drugs used to control mild epilepsy.) Here, too, the primary concern is the health and safety of the child. Such use may enhance participation in the limiting sense of making it possible, but where the purpose and effect of such usage is limited to medically justifiable ones, we may reasonably disregard this trivial

enhancement. In the event that a medication did significantly improve performance over what would otherwise be expected, we could consider it in the next category.

This category involves cases in which drugs are used by otherwise healthy people for the express purpose of enhancing training or competition. There are a number of reasons why such usage should be prohibited. Foremost, of course, are the clear threats to the health and safety of the persons taking them. Among the many drugs available to athletes are some that have a powerful effect on the balance of the hormonal system, such as testosterone and other steroids, or human growth hormone, or L-dopa and ß-blockers which can stimulate such hormones. Psychomotor or central nervous system stimulants can have a variety of powerful effects on the human body. Young people are especially vulnerable not only to the primary effects of such drugs but also to many deleterious side effects and to possible long-range effects that in many cases are only now beginning to be determined.[6] Damaging effects on growth patterns, and on psychosocial development, are probable high risks of such drugs for children and young people—risks far outweighing any possible benefits of temporary superior athletic prowess.

I should mention that in this respect, drugs are not different in kind, though perhaps in degree, from other features of sports which conflict with our values of health for young people. Arduous and extreme training methods, excessively rough contact between players, and insufficient recuperation or recovery from illness or injury, for example, may all violate our reasonable standards of wholesome athletics. Indeed a paramount concern for any tendency to overemphasize achievements in young people's sports is that it encourages a disregard for the health and balanced development of the young players.

I suspect that these judgments are relatively uncontroversial. But I now want to renew our discussion of the relation of such possible drug use and the development of attitudes and values by young players which I have already defended as among the legitimate paternalistic concerns of guardians and athletic supervisors. Drug use of the kind we are discussing (and of course many other features of training and competition) is clearly associated with winning, indeed with winning at virtually all costs. The chief consideration will always be how use of drugs will enable a young athlete to develop more quickly and effectively the strength, speed, or endurance needed to win, and how subsequent use will provide an improved competitive performance. This attitude is one that we can fairly consider to be nearly a defining characteristic of professionalism as it has come to be understood.

This use of drugs therefore carries with it, or encourages the development of, attitudes and values that conflict with those we hope to instill in children and young people through their very early participation in athletics. Among these latter values are sportsmanship, honesty, fairness, self-reliance as well as cooperation, grace under pressure, and health. Others could also be mentioned. But a central value is that of experiencing achievement through personal effort, of responding willfully to challenge, and thereby of coming to realize, that is, both to create and to understand, one's self, the complex bundle of skills, dispositions, beliefs, values, and capacities which constitute a personality.

Merit in a young athlete should reflect factors that are fully within his or her control. Ability and achievement should be a reflection of the amount of effort and self-motivation that are consonant with a normal life not characterized by fanaticism (an unreasonable purposiveness). We seek to stress a history of training and competitive effort that may to some extent cancel the uncontrollable differences among people so that superior skill is the result of a growing strength or personal resolve. In our paternalistic limiting of the freedom of young athletes, we are not emphasizing freedom to do anything or to have anything done to one, but rather the freedom of self-determination which accords with ideals of a reasoned, autonomous, well-balanced life, led in relation to a sensible ranking of values. It is

because success due to some special technique or technology is only marginally reflective of athletic skill or training or motivation that we discount it or forbid it in the repertoire of young athletes.[7]

I want to emphasize that sports are not the only context in which these values are developed; indeed, they may not even be the best one. But they are a place, and for many people a very important one, where this learning process does occur. The conflict raised by drug usage of the kind we are discussing is that, by emphasizing one value over all others, it skews the context of learning and growth so as to deny sufficient credibility to other values. Moreover, it may conflict directly with efforts to encourage the young athlete to grasp the relation between personal effort and achievement so closely tied to both the experience of joy, excitement, and satisfaction of the athletes themselves, and to a similar appreciation by spectators.

It should be clear that we can extend the claims of soft paternalism, which I have so far discussed in regard to children, to various cases of adult behavior which presume incapacity of some sort, for example, ignorance, lack of opportunity or resources, or immaturity. But these are the easy cases for the soft paternalist and I shall not dispute them here. The difficult cases are surely those that give us every reason to believe that the actors are rational, informed, emotionally mature adults. The soft paternalist in turn must dispute such presumptions. We could of course hold that adult athletes who take drugs to enhance training or performance are in some way irrational, that they do not fully appreciate the dangers of such actions or the seriousness of side effects, or cannot adequately weigh the evidence that drug usage is not beneficial to performance. Moreover, we could claim that such athletes, in addition to ignoring relevant information, are unable to resist the pressures of others to succeed at all costs, that their weakness of will warrants paternalistic interference.

But such a reply is unconvincing, at least in many readily imaginable cases. It cannot be the very use of drugs which is the sole evidence for irrationality or self-destructiveness or weakness of will, on pain of begging the central question. And the evidence, once in, is very unlikely to support the claim that all cases of drug use are nonvoluntary in the requisite way. Rather, the truth seems to be that in these cases other values come into play. Adult values and motivations are not always the same as those we may encourage for young people. Adult life *is* more complicated, and though we intend the training in values and skills of childhood and youth to carry over to maturity, we are well aware that they will inevitably compete with other values that are often at odds with those we can reasonably insist on earlier. Often for adults winning *is* more important, and the circumstances of life may encourage a new range of motives: fame, wealth, power, social mobility, patriotism, pride of class, or race or ideology.

We may not accept such values or wish to encourage such motivations but, in a free society they are permissible; we may not deny them, to those who choose them, on grounds of paternalism. Where such values predominate, the risks of drugs may be outweighed by the benefits they may bring. Perhaps we come here to one of the sources of the distinction between "amateur" and "professional." If so, the distinction does not match the one I am suggesting between the values of youth and adulthood. Some professional skills and the knowledge of professional experience are clearly applicable to youth sports, and, conversely, professional values need not conflict with other values. It is always a matter of emphasis, role, age, commitments, and goals that determine which values dominate.

Indeed, even in our approach to sports for children, and especially of youths, we will at some point begin to anticipate some of the competing values that will increasingly vie for their attention and commitment as they grow older. As always, there are important questions of timing, emphasis, role, and age. But teachers and parents must at some point help facilitate the transition to full autonomy at which earlier limits to freedom can no longer be tolerated.

The soft paternalist could of course insist that where drug use or sports activities carry with them high risk, even risk of death or permanent injury, we are justified in intervening to prevent serious costs to the rest of us even when the athletes are willing to take the risks.[8] But society does not typically support the costs of such injury, and we could in any case require proper insurance for the athletes. Moreover, the psychic cost to others is surely minimal and, even in cases such as boxing, it is normally outweighed by the psychic gains of the spectator; the vicarious thrill and excitement, the shared pride, the satisfactions of knowledgeable viewing. In any case the balance of risks and benefits concerning drug usage is not likely to be clear. Efforts are no doubt being made to control for undesirable side effects, and the benefits may often need to be measured only in fractions of seconds. And why should we single out one class of risks when others, perhaps equally great, are already tolerated for the sake of excellence? Finally though it involves interference in the lives of others, such a response does not seem paternalistically motivated.

At this point, we may resort to something like a principle of "hard" paternalism if we are to persist in our efforts to control the choices and options of athletes. We are in effect seeking to impose on those who resist it an alternative set of values. But what would justify such an imposition? There seems no reason to suppose that taking risk in sports, even great risk, is inevitably irrational, self-destructive, or immature, as we have seen. Nor is it plausible to suggest that we forbid all of the sports which involve such risk, such as mountain climbing, sky-diving, or even boxing. As Mill argued, such intervention in people's lives would itself be a greater wrong than the possible injury of activities voluntarily chosen.

It may nevertheless be argued that the use of drugs is somehow inconsistent with the nature of sports, and that sports in turn are linked with a broader set of values—a conception of the good life—which is betrayed by the use of drugs, so that interference in the choices of athletes in this respect is done to preserve a greater good, one they may have lost sight of in their preoccupation with the more narrow concerns of training and competition. Such an argument a priori, as I have argued elsewhere, is not cogent (1). There is, I believe, no single conception of sports on which we need agree. In competitive sports we stress fairness and balanced competition; but in more solitary pursuits these values seem irrelevant. In the case of drugs, fairness may dictate equal access and widely available information. But even this is not clear: athletes and coaches seem justified in keeping secret their training regimens, and even, when permitted by the rules, equipment modifications.

Often, too, we stress human factors such as determination, fortitude, and cooperativeness over risk taking and technology. But in other cases—luge, skiing, mountain climbing, hanggliding—risk and technology dominate. We believe in the capacity of sports to promote health and fitness, but many originated in the practice of war and routinely involve stress and injury, sometimes death. We fashion rules and continually modify them to reduce hazards and minimize serious injury, but few would seek to do so entirely. Perhaps we are tempted to require in athletes only what is natural. But our sports have evolved with our technology and our best athletes are often unnaturally, statistically, endowed with abilities and other characteristics far beyond the norm. It seems artificial indeed to draw the line at drugs when so much of today's training techniques, equipment, food, medical care, even the origin of the sports themselves, are the product of our technological culture.

Nevertheless, something more may be said for the claim that sports reflect a broader set of values. In discussing the justification of paternalism in coaching the young, I have stressed the formation of the values of honesty, fairness, and autonomy, values central to my conception of personhood. But they are not the only ones that might be stressed. Obedience, regimentation,

Philosophers W. Miller Brown (left) and M. Andrew Holowchak, editor, debate the issue of doping in sports at Ohio University, January 19, 2001. Ed. Ed Venrick/The Athens NEWS, Athens, Ohio

service to others, or sacrifice might have been proposed. These, too, in the proper context, might also be developed together with the skills of athletics. The values, perhaps even a conception of what is good for human life, are associated with sports, not because of their nature, but due to the way we choose to play them. We can indeed forbid the use of drugs in athletics in general, just as we do in the case of children. But ironically, in adopting such a paternalistic stance of insisting that we know better than the athletes themselves how to achieve some more general good which they myopically ignore, we must deny in them the very attributes we claim to value: self-reliance, personal achievement, and autonomy.

Notes

1. The current ban on caffeine is defined in terms of a maximum level in urine of 15 µg/mL. For athletes this certainly means no direct ingestion of caffeine tablets, but also a need to avoid combinations of coffee, soft drinks, and over-the-counter medications like Anacin or Empirin which could lead to excessive accumulations of the drug.

2. A good example of such substances is the hormone testosterone. Since it occurs naturally in the body, it has been difficult to detect exogenous testosterone. A new test, however, now measures the ratio of testosterone to a metabolite, epitestosterone, which normally occur in a one-to-one ratio. Since exogenous testosterone isn't converted as readily to epitestosterone, it changes the ratio. The IOC requires the ratio of testosterone to its epimer in urine to be less than six to one. See Zurer (10).

3. Much of the evidence available to athletes in this regard is anecdotal, based on the personal experience of coaches, trainers, a few sports physicians, and the athletes themselves. The research literature is skimpy and the results conflicting. See Zurer (10) for a brief discussion of the conflicting views on the evidence. See also Williams (9).

4. These articles are conveniently reprinted in (8). Dworkin makes the distinction between "soft" and "hard" paternalism in (3). A slightly broader definition of paternalism is defended by Gert and Culver (5). (A version of this article appears in 6: Ch. 7.)

5. Dworkin (3: p. 108) uses this rubric, but for a different type of case.

6. Among the side effects of anabolic steroids are acne and liver tumors. For children and adolescents who are still growing, premature bone fusing and precocious puberty are likely results. See Zurer (10: pp. 73–75).

7. I'm grateful to Bill Puka for discussing this point with me, though in a somewhat different context.

8. Dworkin (3: p. 109) briefly discusses this argument for a different kind of case.

Bibliography

1. Brown, W.M. (1980). "Drugs, Ethics, and Sport." *The Journal of the Philosophy of Sport,* VII, 15–23.

2. Dworkin, Gerald. (1972). "Paternalism." *The Monist,* 56, 64–84.

3. Dworkin, Gerald. (1983). "Paternalism: Some Second Thoughts." *Paternalism.* Edited by Rolf Sartorius. Minneapolis: University of Minnesota Press.

4. Feinberg, Joel. (1971). "Legal Paternalism." *Canadian Journal of Philosophy,* 1, 106–124.

5. Gert, Bernard, and Culver, Charles. (1976). "Paternalistic Behavior." *Philosophy and Public Affairs,* 6, 45–57.

6. Geri, Bernard, and Culver, Charles. (1982). *Philosophy in Medicine: Conceptual and Ethical Issues in Medicine and Psychiatry.* New York: Oxford University Press.

7. Mill, J.S. (1978). *On Liberty.* Indianapolis: Hackett Publ.

8. Sartorius, Rolf. (1983). *Paternalism.* Minneapolis: University of Minnesota Press.

9. Williams, Melvin H. (1974). *Drugs and Athletic Performance.* Springfield, IL: Thomas.

10. Zurer, Pamela S. (1984). "Drugs in. Sports." *Chemical and Engineering News,* April 30, pp. 69–79.

Questions for Consideration

1. Why should the values that adults instill in children be sometimes different from the val-

ues adults embrace? Is it perhaps strange, for instance, that a parent would teach a child that cooperation is much more important than winning and then, in the parent's athletic competition, would focus on winning instead of cooperation? Why are values so malleable?

2. Does Brown employ autonomy as a privileged value? If so, why should this value have a superior status?
3. Do you agree with Brown that the values associated with sport are merely those which we choose to join to it?

25   On Performance-Enhancing Substances and the Unfair Advantage Argument

Roger Gardner
Purdue University

Roger Gardner takes up the issue of performance-enhancing substances in an effort to take a closer look at one of the arguments that comes center stage into the debate: the unfair advantage argument.

He first essays to come clean on the term "unfair advantage." As the term implies, it is not "advantage" that is at issue, but a certain kind of unfair advantage—the manner in which the advantage is gained. In addition, some types of unfair advantage are unobjectionable, such as when the best female tennis player faces off against the 128th seed. Thus, Gardner turns to the manner of gaining advantage.

One easily dismissed instance is advantage that comes through violation of rules. Many flatly proclaim that the advantage of a violation of rules, is immoral. Yet this does little to address the issue of performance-enhancing substances. The interesting scenario is, If all such substances were allowed, then what would be unfair about them?

He then considers two responses: advantage over athletes and advantage over sport. The issue again is reducible to the means in which the advantage is gained. Concerning the first, there are verbal distinctions between good and bad substances, but no criteria to justify these distinctions. Other considerations are equally without warrant. Concerning advantage over sport, no arguments are decisive. Making substances available to all athletes levels the playing field.

Gardner asserts that no arguments for performance-enhancing proscription justify proscription. If performance-enhancing substances should be proscribed, it seems it is not because of unfair advantage gained by their use.

Following the Ben Johnson track disqualification episode at the 1988 Olympics, one of the more common rationales used to argue against Johnson's use of the steroid Stanozolol was that it provided him with an unfair advantage. This notion of unfair advantage is frequently used to support the banning of performance-enhancing substances in sport (1, 4, 5, 10, 13, 16). But whereas this argument is routinely employed and may represent one of our more intuitive objections toward such substances, it has not been subjected to the type of philosophical scrutiny it deserves. Even among those who have addressed the general ethical issues surrounding athletic use of performance-enhancing substances (e.g., 2, 6, 7, 11, 14, 16, 18), and, in so doing, may have commented on the question of unfair advantage (in most cases then maintaining that the argument is problematic), the argument has escaped careful study.

In this paper I explore the ethical status of competitive advantages that might be gained through performance-enhancing substances. I attempt to answer the question of whether such a line of reasoning can offer a compelling justification for prohibiting their use in sport.

Before beginning, several qualifications are in order. First, this essay deals only with issues surrounding those substances used in athletics to

Reprinted, by permission, from Roger Gardner, "On Performance-Enhancing Substances and the Unfair Advantage Argument," *Journal of the Philosophy of Sport*, XVI (1989):59–73.

improve performance. Two of the more identifiable substances are amphetamines and anabolic steroids. I will not be addressing the use by athletes of substances taken for purposes of altering mood or behavior—so-called recreational drugs (e.g., alcohol or cocaine). It needs to be understood, however, that many substances commonly associated with "recreational" usage have been used and can be used as performance enhancers; for example, alcohol has been used to reduce anxiety, cocaine to offset fatigue. The distinguishing feature would seem to be intent. Any and all such substances, when intentionally used to improve athletic performance, are then acceptable examples of performance-enhancing substances.

Second, the jury is still out on whether many of the substances to be discussed do in fact enhance performance. The question of efficacy as well as degree of efficacy would seem pivotal to any opposition to performance enhancers that is grounded in concern for the possible competitive advantages to be gained through use; if there is no advantage to be gained—unfair or otherwise—then there is no reason for concern and no justification for proscription.[1] The importance of efficacy notwithstanding, it is a matter to be left to scientific debate and a matter to be sidestepped here. For purposes of philosophical discussion, this paper will be argued from the standpoint that if a particular substance were to provide its suspected (or hoped for) qualities of enhancement, would it then also provide the athlete with competitive advantages that could be considered unacceptable in sport?

A third stipulation is that my comments are devoted to ethical issues related to unfair advantage only. In other words, as indicated by Fost (6), Brown (2), and Lavin (11), there are at least four ethical arguments around which opposition to performance-enhancing substances is usually centered: harm, coercion, unnaturalness, and unfair advantage. The principal focus in this paper is the unfair advantage argument. And even though it can prove difficult to isolate these four rationales and address each one individually, an attempt to do so would seem an important step toward a better understanding of the overall problem.

Finally, nothing I say should be taken as advocating the use of performance-enhancing substances. The aim of this paper is to subject a common objection to performance enhancers to rational and ethical examination to see if it can offer a compelling justification for prohibiting use.

What Is an Unfair Advantage?

Ben Johnson's steroid-enhanced performance is often viewed as having created a condition of inequality among competitors. Any subsequent advantage Johnson may have gained is thereby characterized as unfair and, in turn, as unacceptable in sport. In what sense though is such an advantage unfair, and does unfair necessarily mean unacceptable or for that matter immoral? Before any determination can be made as to the ethical nature of advantages gained through the use of performance-enhancing substances, it is first necessary to understand what we mean by unfair advantage.

To claim unfair advantage would seem to imply that an athlete's or team's chances for success have been improved in an unacceptable manner. This would suggest, in turn, that if the manner of improving one's chances for success is acceptable, it is a fair advantage. Such being the case, two issues arise. First, it would appear that it is not the advantage per se that we object to, because gaining a competitive edge in skill or strategy is an essential feature of sport. Instead, what we object to is the way in which the athlete acquires the advantage. For instance, one possible way to gain an advantage during competition is to improve one's own capabilities. Yet, depending on the circumstances, we could either accept or reject an athletic advantage so gained. A major league baseball player might want to gain an advantage by improving his ability to hit home runs. If such ability is acquired by increasing upper body strength through weight training, we would tend to classify any advantage gained as fair and acceptable. On the other hand, if the increased ability to hit home runs is secured by using a corked bat (an illegal process of altering the bat's structure in order to increase bat speed), any subsequent advantage is viewed as unfair and unacceptable. So, when we say an athlete has an unfair advantage, it would seem that we are objecting to the actions or circumstances that have created the gained advantage.

The second point is that in order to distinguish between acceptable and unacceptable advantages in sport, it appears that we need simply to determine whether the advantage is fair or unfair. However, unlike the preceding example, unfair may not always be the equivalent of unacceptable. For instance, in international competition athletes from some countries gain an advantage in certain sports due to more favorable climates or sporting traditions. It is often commented in just such a context that countries such as Austria and Switzerland have an unfair advantage over America when it comes to winter sports. Or consider that American athletes, in a similar manner, would seem to have an unfair competitive advantage over third world athletes because of better facilities and sophisticated training techniques. And it could perhaps be argued that some athletes gain a decided and unfair advantage over others due to superior skill or physique. Does it not seem unfair when, say, Steffi Graf, the world's number one ranked tennis player, is matched against the 128th ranked player; or when a basketball team that averages 6'10" in height plays one that averages 6'2"? Such conditions of inequality and any ensuing advantages gained, although intuitively unfair, would appear to fall into a class of unfair but accepted (or at least tolerated) advantages in sport.[2]

Whether the prima facie advantage is considered unfair does not then seem to provide a clear distinction between acceptable and unacceptable advantage. More is required. And, what is needed may have to do with the first point discussed; that is, the way in which the advantage is gained. I would contend that in many instances what determines acceptability is not whether an athlete has an advantage or whether the advantage itself seems unfair but our ethical evaluation of the way in which the advantage is acquired. In other words, depending on the circumstances, although a condition of inequality may indeed be unfair, we might not consider the athlete morally blameworthy for exploiting the resulting advantages.

For instance, returning to the aforementioned examples, the Swiss skier is able to benefit from resources and climatic conditions that are more conducive for training than are those available to the skiers of many other nations. Exposure to such training in turn could provide a significant and seemingly unfair advantage during competition with those other nations. But because the advantage results from geographic location (something we perhaps cannot control), it does not seem unethical for the Swiss skier to benefit from that advantage. Likewise, though it may indeed seem that Steffi Graf has an unfair advantage over the lower ranked players, if the advantage is acquired through, say, genetic endowment, then we might not hold her morally culpable for benefiting from that advantage on the tennis court. The means used to secure an advantage would seem to have quite a bit to say about the eventual acceptability of that advantage. And in that sense, the issue of fairness is perhaps more properly placed with the means and not the resulting advantage. A further example will help to clarify this matter.

In the late 1970s, Bruce Sutter, then with the Chicago Cubs, was perhaps the first pitcher to develop an effective split-finger fast ball. This pitch, due to the way the ball is held and to the imparted spin, makes a drastic and sudden downward movement just as it approaches home plate. Sutter acquired the pitch through the guidance of a pitching coach and countless hours of practice. The split-finger fast ball gave Sutter a decided advantage over the hitter; in fact, some commented that it seemed unfair to have to face such a pitch. During this same time period, a pitcher for the San Diego Padres, Gaylord Perry, had a pitch with the same sharp downward movement as Sutter's. This pitch gave Perry a similar advantage over the hitter and, likewise, opposing hitters may have felt it unfair to have to face such a pitch. In Perry's case, however, it is suspected that he secured his advantage (the drastic and sudden ball movement) by applying a foreign substance to the ball. Though some say Perry used the pretense of throwing spitballs simply as a ploy to break the concentration of the hitter (he was caught throwing a "loaded" pitch only once in his more than 20-year career), let us say for purposes of argument that he did indeed achieve his advantage through the use of a foreign substance. Most would view Sutter's advantage as acceptable, Perry's as unacceptable. What distinguishes the two?

Both pitchers had the same advantage per se: a pitch that was difficult to hit due to its sudden drop. And it would seem we do not object to either pitcher having an advantage over the hitter; trying to gain such an edge is part of pitching. We also do not object if in each case the advantage (or the difficulty of hitting the pitch) seems unfair. But we do object (in Perry's case, not Sutter's) to the way in which the advantage was gained. What determines acceptability is our evaluation of how each pitcher created ball movement. So it is here and not with respect to the advantage itself that "fair" or "unfair" may more clearly indicate both acceptability and morality. That is, Sutter's use of a split-finger fast ball is evaluated as a fair and ethical way to gain an (unfair) advantage over the hitter. Perry's use of a spitball is evaluated as an unfair and unethical way to gain the same advantage.[3] This raises of course the more significant question of what determines our ethical evaluations (in this case, for instance, it might be the rules of baseball—a spitball violates those rules), and still leaves unanswered the critical issue of why, ultimately,

some methods of gaining an advantage are permitted in sport and others are not. What is the initial justification for the rule?

In sum, to object to a specific advantage by claiming that the athlete has an unfair advantage may not provide a clear indication as to whether it is unacceptable. Instead, because it is the way the advantage is gained that concerns us, a better indication might be provided by claiming that the athlete has an unfairly gained advantage. And even though this approach may ultimately encounter similar problems, at this time it would seem to resolve the intuitive difficulties posed by cases such as those previously discussed. In any event, regardless of where one posits the term unfair (whether it is associated with the advantage itself or the method of securing the advantage), the point of agreement and the central issue is that, in each instance, we usually mean to declare the situation unacceptable for reason of fairness. And, in each instance, we are still left with the more significant task of justifying why it should be unacceptable. Understanding this, my attention now turns to whether using performance-enhancing substances to gain an advantage can be justified as unacceptable in sport.

Let me begin by dispensing with an obvious objection to gaining an advantage through currently banned performance enhancers: such advantages are illegally gained. One area of sport in which we desire equality is with respect to following the rules, and illegally gaining an advantage is considered (in most cases) unacceptable and unethical. But although there may be little denying this position, it fails to justify substance prohibitions. If one's only objection to a substance-acquired advantage is that use of the substance is currently against the rules, the problem could be avoided by legalizing the substance. What is ethically required is to establish initial justification for the rule. The question to be addressed is therefore as follows: If all performance-enhancing substances were allowed, what justification could then be offered for prohibiting this attempt to gain an advantage in sport? The unrestricted use of performance enhancers would raise concern in regard to two areas of athletic advantage: (a) an advantage over other athletes, and (b) an advantage over the sport.

An Advantage over Other Athletes

Under a condition of unrestricted use the possibility would exist, due to perhaps unequal access or choice, that both users and nonusers of performance enhancers would be competing on the same playing field. The argument could thereby be made that due to this inequality, performance advantages would be available to some and not to others. Some athletes, for instance, would benefit more than others by having greater access to effective substances and to information and advice about their use. In addition, an individual's financial ability or a nation's technological advancement would lead to inequalities in regard to the availability of the "best" substances. One response to this is that any advantages that might accrue from limited availability could be avoided through equal access (2, 6, 19). But although equal access might indeed suggest a greater sense of fairness, it is not clear that it would be a required condition for permitting performance enhancers.

Athletic performance can be enhanced by the availability of many things, things which would not seem to implicate greater access as an unacceptable means to gaining an advantage. It is advantageous to be exposed to good coaches and trainers, to have access to modern training facilities and equipment, and to benefit from the advice of knowledgeable physiologists and biomechanists. Yet having unequal access to these or similar means for improving performance due to such things as economic standing, technological advancement, or available knowledge does not seem to evoke cries for universal or equal access. As a consequence, many athletes routinely gain a performance advantage over other athletes without raising ethical concerns. So, although we might wish to see such advantages eliminated and may feel that equal access would be the ideal condition of sport (i.e., athletes would then be given an equal opportunity to improve and develop to their true performance capabilities, and outcomes would reflect only the differences in the competitors themselves [5]), equal access to means for enhancing performance does not appear to be a necessary condition of sport. It would follow then that unequal access to performance enhancers and knowledge and advice about their use would not be a sufficient reason for disallowing them in sport.[4]

Irrespective of the degree of accessibility, and even if equal access were achieved, users and nonusers might still be competing against one another due simply to choice. An athlete might have access to performance enhancers but opt (for whatever reason) not to use them to try to gain an edge. Would this in turn result in an unacceptable advantage for those who chose to be users? There are many avenues to improved performance that the athlete may or may not choose to pursue. But merely because some athletes may choose not to utilize a certain (legal) method of improvement, we do not then claim that other athletes, who have so chosen, have somehow unjustly gained an advantage.[5] Any advantages users might gain over nonusers due solely to choice would appear permissible on similar grounds.

Another argument that might be made against unrestricted use of performance enhancers is that inequalities would exist not just between users and nonusers but among users. In other words, even if universal access were achieved and even if all athletes chose to use the same substance, it could still be argued that athletes might not react to substances equally. If all competitors in the 1988 Olympic 100-meter race used Stanozolol, perhaps Johnson would still have gained a performance advantage due to the better physiological ability of his body to utilize the substance. Simon (18: p. 11), indirectly framing this objection, has stated that this probable difference in reaction to substances suggests that competitive success and failure would be determined by the innate capacity of the body to react to a substance, and that this reaction might vary unequally among competitors.[6] It is not clear however that such inequalities would result in unacceptable or unethical advantages over other athletes.

There are many innate differences or inequalities in athletes that might enable some to benefit more than others. In men, for instance, differences in the innate amount of testosterone in the blood can vary over threefold. This considerable variance in testosterone levels predisposes men with high levels to excel and gain an advantage in sports in which muscular strength and size are important. Along similar lines, every athlete has a unique response to the variety of available training stimuli. There are inequalities in the predispositions of athletes to benefit from weight training and endurance training and diet. There are discrepancies in the capacity to physiologically benefit from currently permitted substances, such as caffeine (permitted in limited quantities), bicarbonate (offsets the buildup of lactic acid), and amino acids. Gaining an advantage through inequalities in innate capabilities is unavoidable and it hardly seems unethical; nor from a practical standpoint do such discrepancies seem to be distinguishable.

There would therefore seem no necessity to restrict substance use based on the position that inequalities would exist in the innate capacities of athletes to benefit from a performance enhancer. In fact, when we begin discussing advantages gained over others as a result of differences in the athletes themselves—innate or acquired— we encounter a formidable problem: This is one area of sport where we may not want equality.

To this point, we have been discussing conditions that could lead either to users competing against nonusers or to disparity among users. However, in both cases, the ultimate concern is that through substance use inequalities will be created in the eventual performance capabilities of the athletes themselves. Put another way, the two principal qualities of athleticism that would be most affected by substance use are ability (strength, endurance, speed, power, etc.) and physique (height and weight). Yet, some might consider it illogical to oppose gaining an advantage through differences in these qualities.

It does not seem unreasonable to desire equality in the structure of the game, in respect to following the rules, and even in regard to access during the preparatory phase of a game; but, it might seem unreasonable to desire equality in the ultimate abilities (skills and strategies) of individual athletes.[7] Now we may, in order to see a close contest, prefer competition between participants who are relatively even in ability but, in the end, the idea is not for all to come out equally or to have equal ability. Sport in fact would seem dependent upon differences in performance capabilities. After all, if we wanted to avoid the accumulation of advantages and disadvantages due to inequalities in ability, then we would try to equalize individual skill levels by allowing those lacking in ability to compensate for their disadvantage through the structure of the game (e.g., a 5-yard head start), or we would build and program robot athletes as equals. And although there are some attempts to equalize skill levels through such things as handicapped golf tournaments, this is not the case in true athletic competition. Any disparities that substance use might create in abilities such as strength or speed would not seem to suggest sufficient cause for proscription.

Substance-gained advantages in either height or weight would also seem permissible. There are no attempts in elite sport—that is, the highest levels of competition—to equalize or limit the heights of competitors. If, then, certain substances (e.g., human growth hormone) could influence an athlete's height, any advantages gained over other athletes would seem allowable. With respect to weight, though there are branches of sport in which possible advantages gained through weight discrepancies are eliminated (e.g., boxing, crew, judo, amateur and Olympic wrestling, and weight lifting), there are also those activities in which weight is not legislated and any advantages so gained are accepted (e.g., lacrosse, football, gymnastics, etc.). In either case, regardless of one's weight and regardless of whether one acquires that weight (loss or gain) through a substance, differences could be accommodated for (equalized) through weight classes, or, as they are in sports with no weight limitations, simply permitted.

As before, objecting to performance enhancers on grounds that inequalities would be created among athletes does not provide strong justification for banning their use. Advantages gained due to differences in the performance capabilities of athletes are not only accepted in sport, they are usually desired. This point would seem crucial, and it serves to reestablish the contention made at the beginning of this essay: It is not the advantage per se that we object to but the action or circumstances that have created the gained advantage. What has made justification of prohibition problematic up to this point is that whatever possible (objected to) advantages can be gained through substance use, can be and are gained through currently accepted means. Therefore, in order to determine the permissibility of certain substances, perhaps the focus should not be on the potential advantages; instead, the focus should be on the use of performance enhancers as a means for gaining an advantage.

Perhaps securing an advantage through the use of proscribed substances can somehow be distinguished from gaining the similar advantage through accepted modes of enhancement. Consider the following two cases: (a) One way to gain an advantage over other competitors in endurance events is to increase the oxygen transporting capacity of the blood. Two theoretical ways this can be achieved are high-altitude training and blood boosting. Blood boosting is a process by which athletes increase their blood volume and hemoglobin count through injecting supplemental blood—either their own or a donor's (usually a blood relative)—prior to an event. Receiving a transfusion from a donor was the method used by U.S. cyclists during the 1984 Olympics. (Seven riders have either admitted to this or were named by witnesses; 15: pp. 32-35). (b) Another way to gain an advantage in some activities is to increase body weight through adding muscle. Muscle mass can result from such things as genetic endowment, arduous training and diet, or human growth hormone (HGH). HGH is a hormone produced by the pituitary gland and shown to affect the growth of skeletal muscle and bone as well as visceral organs and tissues. Previously extracted from the pituitary glands of human corpses, it can now be produced synthetically. HGH is used to treat children with stunted growth; it is also used (since at least 1983) to promote muscle growth in athletes (4: p. 113).

In the first case, we do not object to differences in the endurance capabilities of athletes resulting from increased hemoglobin count, provided that increase is the result of high-altitude training. In the second case, we do not object to discrepancies in the size of skeletal muscles, provided that size results from genetic endowment or training (e.g., weight lifting). In each case, we are not objecting to the advantage, but to the way in which the advantage is gained. So what is there about blood boosting and human growth hormone that somehow distinguishes these methods of securing an advantage and seems to render their effects unacceptable? The most obvious difference is that the advantages gained by blood boosting and HGH are achieved through the use of a (supplemented) substance. However, if the basis of our objection is to be that using a substance is an unacceptable means to gaining an advantage, then the inconsistencies are more than apparent.

There are many legal substances used by athletes in their attempt to gain an advantage over competitors—for example, amino acids, protein powders, vitamin and mineral supplements (sometimes injected), caffeine (legally limited to 12 micrograms per milliliter of urine, about seven cups of coffee), glucose polymer drinks, and injections of ATP (a naturally produced chemical involved in muscle contraction). The list could go on and on. Clearly we do not object to gaining an advantage through the use of a substance; it is only particular substances to which we are opposed. This being the case, it seems that some form of definitive criteria would have to be established in order to differentiate between permissible and prohibited substances. Yet, such criteria do not seem to exist.

Others (6, 11, 12) have indicated the difficulty (and perhaps interminability) of attempting to establish a working distinction between "good" and "bad" substances that relies solely on characteristics or properties of the substances themselves. For example, trying to distinguish food from nonfood, restoratives from additives, or drugs from nondrugs is fraught with ambiguity. Likewise, the notions of naturalness and/or harm have thus far proven incapable of providing principled distinctions between acceptable and unacceptable performance enhancers. The problem is that regardless of the criteria or morally objectionable properties we try to use to define proscribed substances, permitted substances either fit the same criteria or possess similar properties.[8]

Given this difficulty, instead of focusing on the substance itself, perhaps there is something about the way a substance allows one to acquire an advantage that will provide a compelling acceptable/unacceptable distinction. For instance (as is often suggested), maybe substance use represents a shortcut to improved performance; that is, the advantages gained (enhanced capabilities) are not actually earned by the athlete.

Returning to the above cases, it seems through blood boosting and HGH that the athlete is indeed provided a shortcut to endurance and muscle mass, respectively. For instance, whereas in high-altitude training the athlete is perhaps putting in long hours of hard work in order to gain a competitive edge, in receiving a blood transfusion from a donor no such training effort is required; therefore, any subsequent advantage would seem unearned. Would discrepancies created in the amount and intensity of required training render substance use an unac-

ceptable or unethical means for seeking a competitive advantage?[9]

To the contrary, in sport the notion of effort would not seem to carry sufficient moral weight for justifying prohibition. The amount and intensity of effort required to become an elite athlete greatly varies among competitors. But because it may be "easier" for some, we do not then claim that they have unethically gained any ensuing competitive advantage. Due to genetic predisposition and endowment, Nancy Lopez may have developed her golfing abilities in a rather accelerated and effortless fashion; Jose Canseco of the Oakland A's baseball club may have developed his large physique in the same manner. Although not actually earned through effort, any resulting advantage they gain over their competitors is permitted. We do not accuse Lopez and Canseco of immorally gaining an advantage simply because others may have to work twice as hard and long to acquire ability or size.[10]

In a related fashion then, though some may work long and hard to gain an advantage in endurance or muscle size, the fact that others might gain such advantages through the effortlessness of blood boosting or HGH (or genetic endowment) would not seem to render the method of acquiring those advantages unacceptable.[11] Much the same could be said for using other performance enhancers as well.

Another distinction that might be offered is that the acquired capabilities are somehow separate or external to the athlete. Perhaps the body weight and endurance promoted through the respective uses of HGH and blood boosting is analogous to using lead-filled water bottles in cycling (to increase the weight, and thus the speed, of the rider and bike during mountainous descents) and using the subway during New York City marathons. The objection now being that the extrinsically gained capabilities (advantages) are not directly related to the ability or physique of the athlete per se (or related to the athlete's legal equipment). And it would appear some proscriptions could be justified along these lines (e.g., spit or scuffed balls and corked bats in baseball, stickum in football, and weighted gloves in boxing). But in order for this rationale to be applied to substance-enhanced advantages, the acquired capabilities must somehow be shown to be independent of the athlete (like lead-filled water bottles) in ways that similar capabilities acquired through permitted modes of extrinsic enhancement are not. How do the capabilities and accompanying advantages that result from training techniques, running shoes, or legal substances differ? Before addressing this issue, it needs to be pointed out that the focus of the overall argument may now have shifted.

To this point the discussion has centered on those circumstances that might result in one athlete having a competitive edge over another. It has been shown that any inequalities that might surface among athletes due to unrestricted use of performance enhancers would not provide justificatory grounds for proscription. Whether an athlete could gain an advantage through greater access, choice, better physiological response, or improved ability or physique would not in turn seem to create unacceptable or unethical situations in sport. Further, it has been suggested that there is perhaps no defensible distinction between using proscribed substances as a means to gain an advantage and using other currently accepted methods to gain the similar advantage (e.g., high-altitude training, weight lifting, permitted substances, or genetic endowment). However, in all instances the overriding moral consideration has been that one athlete might unjustly gain an advantage over another. With the justification proposed above (i.e., enhancement extrinsic to the athlete), this may no longer be the concern.

In each preceding example of extrinsically enhanced capabilities the method for gaining the advantage could have been permitted, thereby avoiding any subsequent (prima facie) inequality among athletes. We could allow all wide receivers stickum, or all cyclists lead-filled water bottles, or, following from this, all athletes HGH and additional blood. So it would seem that

more is involved here than just a concern for possible advantages one athlete might gain over another. And as before, justifying prohibition along these lines would prove problematic. Instead, perhaps what renders a substance-gained advantage unacceptable, and what we may be ultimately objecting to, is not that an advantage is gained over other athletes but that one is gained over the sport itself—either its intended purpose or its conceived obstacles.

An Advantage over the Sport

Consider again the Ben Johnson incident. One might object that the capabilities Johnson acquired through Stanozolol infringed upon the purpose of the 100-meter race or somehow made the activity less demanding than it should have been. In this case, what makes gaining an advantage through substance use unacceptable is not that Johnson had an edge over other competitors, but that he had one over the activity. The purpose of the 100-meter race is to determine who can cover that distance fastest on foot. In the process, the competitors encounter and attempt to overcome certain obstacles, such as depletion of leg strength. If the competitors decided to use, say, motorcycles, then both of these intended conditions would be compromised. Would allowing unrestricted use of steroids in the 100 meters be somewhat like providing the participants with motorcycles? More generally, does the use of performance-enhancing substances somehow alter the intended purpose or difficulty of an activity (i.e., does it change what the sport was originally designed to test) and, if so, would this provide sufficient justification for prohibiting use?

It would seem that some rules have been enacted to prevent the athlete from gaining an advantage over the activity or, in other words, from in some way threatening the integrity of the sport. Such rules revolve primarily around performance-enhancing equipment (innovations, modifications) and, to a lesser extent, changes in athletic technique (e.g., using a mid-air somersault in the long jump). The most recent example comes from the sport of golf. Square- or U-grooved irons were banned from the PGA tour as of January 1, 1990. Tour players can now use only those clubs with traditional V-shaped grooves. The reason behind the ruling is that tests and anecdotal accounts of players suggest that U grooves give the golfer an advantage, especially out of the rough (9). They create a higher spin rate, which translates into better ball control (3: p. 54) The fact is, since U grooves first came on the scene in 1985 many touring professionals have been opposed to their use because of a concern that they devalue true golf skill and consolidate the talent (3).

We have here two related objections. First, square grooves make shots out of the rough easier (or less a matter of true golfing ability) than they should be, for all players. Gaining an advantage in such a manner is unacceptable not because it provides one golfer an advantage over another (although it might do so),[12] it is unacceptable because an advantage is gained over the sport itself—the intended "test" of the rough, for example, is avoided. Second, and as a consequence, the quality of golf (or the difference between various skill levels) is being equalized. This second objection represents the reverse of an earlier argument. That is, what is being objected to here is not that performance enhancement will create inequality among athletes, but that it will lead to parity. In the end, U grooves are more responsible for the performance than is the golfer.

Now it could be argued that a similar line of reasoning could be used to justify the banning of previously mentioned and parallel cases of extrinsic enhancement (e.g., corked bats, stickum, etc.). Employing this as a general rationale, however, is problematic.

It is not always the case that creating and altering equipment or technique (consider the Fosbury Flop) in order to gain an advantage is prohibited. Golf itself offers a clear example of this. In 1932 Gene Sarazen invented the sand wedge. Like U grooves, the sand wedge made it easier for the golfer to contend with a designed obstacle, in this case sand. In point of fact, there have been many changes and innovations in equipment that have resulted in the enhancement of athletic performance (e.g., tennis rackets, baseball gloves, vaulting poles, archery bows, bicycles, etc.). Such extrinsic enhancement, while assuming greater responsibility for the athlete's performance, and perhaps making the task in question less difficult,[13] has nevertheless been permitted. At the same time, it would seem an argument could be offered that athletic skill remains at a premium, diverse levels of talent are still displayed (i.e., equality has not been created), and the purpose or test of the sport, although perhaps altered somewhat from its historical beginnings, appears to maintain its (perhaps evolving) integrity.[14]

Returning to the context of performance-enhancing substances; it is not always the case then that extrinsic advantages gained over a sport are prohibited. But for purposes of argument let us contend, along the lines of U-grooved golf clubs, that this is our justification for banning certain performance-enhancing substances. That is to say, gaining enhancement (speed, endurance, strength, power, physique, etc.) through certain substances is unacceptable because it threatens a sport's integrity. The substance, in the end, is more responsible for any gained advantage than is the athlete, and hence we are no longer testing the athlete but the substance. Even if this is to be the main objection to performance enhancers, there are several ways in which the argument proves problematic, ways that relate to the by now familiar dilemma of trying to establish principled distinctions.

How does attempting to gain an advantage over the physical and mental obstacles of a sport through the use of prohibited substances differ from trying to do so through training, coaching, diet, technology, use of physiologists, biomechanists, and psychologists; or, for that matter, how does it differ from using permitted substances such as amino acids or (loading) carbohydrates? Whereas many athletes reach their level of performance due directly to the use of a coach, sport psychologist (biofeedback, hypnosis), or special diet, others may reach theirs through the use of substances such as steroids. It could thereby be argued that the extrinsic assistance of the psychologist or diet, like the steroid, is responsible for the resulting performance of the athlete. And, in turn, the purpose of the sport becomes not just a test of the athlete but of the athlete's scientists or diet and how efficiently the athlete can utilize what each has to offer. Is this not comparable to the claim that with the use of substances such as steroids we are no longer appraising the athlete but the substance and the efficiency with which the athlete's body can utilize that substance?

It seems that the responding argument would rely upon the notion of sport as a measure of human performance and attempt to claim that the capabilities provided athletes through substance use are nonhuman, or unnatural. So, one might want to argue that the psychologist, biomechanist, diet, and so on are simply bringing out the best in the athlete, and the athlete (qua human) is still ultimately responsible for the performance and any gained advantage. The resulting capability is not external to the athlete, like U-grooved irons, but inherent within the athlete. The enhancement allowed for through the scientist or diet simply permits the athlete to overcome some "undesired inhibitor" (16: p. 42) to better performance (e.g., anxiety, poor technique, or glycogen depletion in the muscles), and thereby reach his or her full potential. Yet, it would seem the similar argument could be made with respect to the use of substances such as amphetamines or steroids. That is, the substance brings out the inherent ability of the athlete by assisting him or her to overcome certain performance inhibitors, in this case perhaps passiveness and muscle exhaustion. If the limiting condition is to be humanness, then the objectionable enhancement must be shown to be nonhuman.

We thus return to the basis for the original objection: capabilities separate from the athlete. Because, clearly, the burden confronting the U-groove argument is the need to establish that the substance-influenced advantage gained over a particular sport is independent of the athlete's human capabilities (like using a motorcycle in the 100 meters). Moreover, and even if this could be shown, it would still have to be made clear how this form of extrinsic (unnatural) capability or advantage differs from those which, although they seem independent of the athletes, we accept (e.g., those resulting from running shoes or carbohydrate loading).[15] And it is at this point that we must look to an entirely different line of philosophical and ethical reasoning; that associated with trying to define and understand the natural/unnatural distinction.

In summary then, I have suggested that our primary concern regarding performance-enhancing substances may be that athletes would unjustly gain an advantage over the intended purpose or test of a sport. Such an argument, however, is problematic and would seem contingent upon the need to show that the capabilities acquired through a (proscribed) substance are extrinsic to the athlete and in some way unnatural (i.e., did Ben Johnson have "corked" legs?).

To conclude, the purpose of this essay has been to demonstrate that arguments opposing the use of performance-enhancing substances that are grounded primarily in a concern for the athletic advantages that might be gained through such use are, at the least, problematic and, at the most, unable to provide a compelling justificatory defense for proscription. Given a condition of unrestricted use, any moral concern that users may unjustly gain advantages over other athletes appears to be unwarranted. Such being the case, it has been suggested that the critical area of concern in this matter may not be opposition to one athlete gaining an advantage over another but that, through substance use, an athlete may gain an advantage over the sport itself. Yet, this line of argumentation also proved problematic and, at this stage, does not seem to offer sufficient justification for banning performance-enhancing substances.[16]

Notes

1. At least no justification on grounds of unfair advantage. One might still search for justification on other grounds, say, for instance, harm.

2. Some may have a philosophical objection with this and want to argue that such things as geography, ability, and technology, though certainly advantages, are not necessarily unfair. This claim, however, would at least seem to suggest more analysis; because, at this point in time, such advantages do not seem to be *clearly* fair either.

3. As to the morality of Perry's suspected actions, consider that in February of 1989 the Baseball Writers Association of America succeeded in keeping Perry out of the Hall of Fame on moral grounds. Several writers have admitted to ignoring Perry because they evaluated his accomplishments as morally questionable (8).

4. The fundamental mode of argumentation throughout this essay will be to indicate contradictions and inconsistencies in current policies and rationales. To point out these inconsistencies is not to advocate tolerance for any of them or to suggest that because we allow *a* we should then allow *b*. Further, as one anonymous referee put it, "it does not follow from the fact that people would not regard *X* as unfair that *X* is indeed not unfair." Because these are philosophically important matters, addressing them would seem to be the next step. The first step is to point out inconsistencies and to thereby suggest that concern over performance enhancers may involve other issues, in this case, issues other than fairness. (My thanks to W. Fraleigh, S. Kretchmar, and the anonymous referee for bringing this to my attention.)

5. Fraleigh (7) and Murray (14) argue that when it comes to harmful performance enhancers, athletes confront not just choice but coercion. Such an objection is dependent upon the issue of harm and is more properly couched in the harm and coercion arguments. If, for instance, relevant substances were harmless, then clearly the simple act of choice would not represent an unacceptable means to gaining an advantage over others.

6. The basis for Simon's objection is not so much that athletes will react to substances unequally, but that such differences are athletically irrelevant. This ultimately is more a concern for changes in the nature of sport than it is for inequality and advantages some athletes might gain over others.

7. Brown (2: p. 17) and Foldesi and Földesi (5) make the similar point.

8. Fost (6), in general, and Lavin (11: p. 39), more specifically, also identify this dilemma. In Lavin's case, he then wants to offer "consensus disapproval" as the distinguishing criterion. Although this is not the place to address Lavin's position, it might be said that accepting an argument that seems practically (democratically) strong but is nonetheless logically weak seems more like resignation than justification; it merely satisfies the status quo.

9. Some maintain that the ability of anabolics to aid in muscle recovery allow one to increase the intensity and frequency of workouts; in effect, permitting the athlete to work harder.

10. In fact, genetic endowments would seem to suggest moral neutrality. Rawls (17) argues that an individual does not deserve the products of genetic endowments, as such endowments are bestowed by a blind genetic lottery.

11. Of course one might argue that although it may be true that genetically determined advantages are unmerited, they are at least the result of natural occurrences; substance-enhanced advantages are not. This is a significant objection but one that seems little concerned with effort and more properly placed within the unnaturalness argument.

12. That is, square grooves might provide the lesser player with an advantage over the better player. It could be argued that the lesser player does not need golfing skill to equal the performance of the better player. This points out that there may not be an absolute line of distinction between an advantage over the sport and an advantage over other athletes. It would seem, however, that the two can be sufficiently separated.

13. In some cases an equipment change may not make an activity necessarily less difficult, but it may still improve performance; that is, the same effort may be required but a better performance results (e.g., solid disk wheels in cycling, fiberglass vaulting poles, artificial track surfaces).

14. There may be a sense that there is a baseline beyond which, but only beyond which, the intended purpose of a sport is sufficiently challenged. So, in the sport of cycling we may allow titanium components, solid disk wheels, and aerodynamic helmets and handle bars—

which Greg LeMond credits for having significantly contributed to his winning of the 1989 Tour de France—but we will not allow a motor to be attached to the bicycle. It is not clear where exactly this baseline may be, but it might be found in the distinction that surfaces later in the essay, the notion of testing *human* ability.

15. Perry (16) argues for such a distinction. The critical elements of his argument, however, are unnaturalness and harm.

16. My thanks to Bill Harper, Larry May, and three anonymous *JPS* referees for their input into this project.

Bibliography

1. Beckett, A. "Philosophy, Chemistry and the Athlete." *New Scientist,* 103 (1984), 18.

2. Brown, W.M. "Drugs, Ethics, and Sport." *Journal of the Philosophy of Sport,* VII (1980), 15–23.

3. Diaz, J. "Has Golf Gotten Too Groovy?" *Sports Illustrated,* 67, No. 5 (August 3, 1987), 52–59.

4. Donohoe, T., and Johnson, N. *Foul Play: Drug Abuse in Sports.* New York: Basil Blackwell, 1986.

5. Földesi, T., and Földesi, G. "Dilemmas of Justness In Top Sport." *Dialectics and Humanism,* 1 (1984), 21–32.

6. Fost, N. "Banning Drugs in Sports: A Skeptical View." *Hastings Center Report,* 16 (1986), 5–10.

7. Fraleigh, W. "Performance-Enhancing Drugs in Sport: The Ethical Issue." *Journal of the Philosophy of Sport,* XI (1985), 23–29.

8. Gammons, P. "Morals and Immortals: Ferguson Jenkins and Gaylord Perry Should Be in the Hall." *Sports Illustrated,* 70, No. 10 (March, 1989), 78.

9. Hershey, S. "A Groovy Decision: PGA Told to Rough It Without U-Grooved Irons." *USA Today* (March 1, 1989), 2C.

10. Hyland, D. "Playing to Win: How Much Should It Hurt?" *Hastings Center Report,* 9 (1979), 5–8.

11. Lavin, M. "Sports and Drugs: Are the Current Bans Justified?" *Journal of the Philosophy of Sport,* XIV (1987), 35–43.

12. Michels, R. "Doctors, Drugs Used for Pleasure and Performance, and the Medical Model." In *Feeling Good and Doing Better.* Edited by T. Murray, W. Gaylin, and R. Macklin. Clifton, NJ: Humana Press, 1984, 175–184.

13. Moorcroft, D. "Doping: The Athlete's View." *Olympic Review* (October, 1985), 634–635.

14. Murray, T. "Drugs, Sports, and Ethics." In *Feeling Good and Doing Better.* Edited by T. Murray, W. Gaylin, and R. Macklin. Clifton, NJ: Humana Press, 1984, 107–126.

15. Pavelka, E. "Olympic Blood Boosting." *Bicycling,* XXVI, No. 3 (April, 1985), 32–35.

16. Perry, C. "Blood Doping and Athletic Competition." *International Journal of Applied Philosophy,* 1 (1983), 39–45.

17. Rawls, J. *A Theory of Justice.* Cambridge, MA: Harvard University Press, 1970.

18. Simon, R. "Good Competition and Drug-Enhanced Performance." *Journal of the Philosophy of Sport,* XI (1985), 6–13.

19. Torrey, L. *Stretching The Limits.* New York: Doss, Mead & Company, 1985.

Questions for Consideration

1. Clearly define the range of Gardner's line of argument. What is Gardner *not* trying to demonstrate?

2. Is Gardner's notion of "unfairness" exhaustive, or are there other relevant types of unfairness that he fails to consider?

26   "Aretism" and Pharmacological Ergogenic Aids in Sport: Taking a Shot at the Use of Steroids

M. Andrew Holowchak
Ohio University

The issue of the use of steroids has been one of the longest running and most volatile issues in the philosophy of sport, and it sheds much light on the issue of what sport is and ought to be. Critics of the current ban on steroids, whom I call "liberals" in this reading, argue that proposing limits to performance enhancement by disallowing steroids in competitive sport runs contrary to regard for autonomy—one of the chief values, if not the chief value, of sportive morality. Therefore, the ban on steroids in formal athletic competition is wrongfully paternalistic, and fairness and regard for autonomy requires that all athletes have access to them.

Fairness itself dictates only that sport has a level playing field: Either all or no athletes should have access to steroids. Placing athletic performance above athletes' health (since there is good reason to believe at this point in time that steroids are dangerous) devalues sport, whereas maintaining the ban on steroids balances concern for health with athletic excellence. Failure to maintain the ban on steroids is itself wrongful because it pressures athletes either to take steroids and risk harm or to abandon hope of competing at the highest levels of competition.

I call this view of sport "Aretism" (from the Greek word arete, *"excellence"). Aretism is based on the view that competitive sport is essentially a social phenomenon and ought to be a quest for excellence at three levels of integration: personal, political, and cosmic integration. Athletes practicing competitive sport gain a greater sense of self through cultivating perseverance and patience; they gain regard for other competitors and develop genuine affective bonds; and they gain respect and love of sport.*

Introduction

We take a greater interest in sport today than perhaps we, as fans, have ever taken before. Decades ago, we might have contented ourselves with spirited interest in our local baseball team, but today, our love of sport has evolved into frenzied and omnivorous lust. As sports fans today, it seems, we involve ourselves in one sport or another most, if not all, of the time. We live through our sports, and shall accept nothing less than our favorite athletes and teams being the best. Success in sports, more then ever, is today measured wholly in terms of being "number one."

With the frenzied omnienthusiasm for today's sport, sport itself has become big business. Professional athletes' salaries have gone up nearly at an exponential rate, and even successful "amateurs" often make considerable money through product-line endorsements. It is no large shock to find that athletes are increasingly encouraged or pressured to do whatever they can in order to win, and the means to winning most often includes a plan toward improved athletic performance.

One way of facilitating improved athletic performance is through the use of ergogenic (work-

Reprinted, by permission, from M. Andrew Holowchak, "'Aretism' and Pharmacological Ergogenic Aids in Sport: Taking a Shot at the Use of Steroids," *Journal of the Philosophy of Sport* XXVII (2000): 35–50.

engendering) aids in athletic competition. At the highest levels of competition, athletes employ the most scientifically sophisticated ergogenic aids—mechanical (e.g., improved equipment or technique), pharmacological (e.g., diuretics or anabolic steroids), psychological (e.g., imagery or arousal techniques), physiological (e.g., altitude training's effects), and nutritional (e.g., antioxidant vitamins)—in an effort to enhance performance. Yet many of us find the use of some of these ergogenic supplements, like amphetamines or anabolic steroids, morally objectionable. Certain ergogenic aids, like the practice of blood doping, are even banned by the International Olympic Committee (IOC, hereafter).

Yet just what is it about these banned "supplements" that we find objectionable? In addition, what is it about those that are not banned that makes them acceptable? We hold on to our beliefs quite obdurately, but we find, upon the least bit of critical reflection, that these questions do not admit of simple answers.

The perceived immorality of ergogenic aids in sport is intriguing and deserves much more attention than I can give in this undertaking. My goal here is modest. I hope to go some ways toward clearing up this matter through focusing on what may be the most famous pharmacological ergogenic aid: anabolic steroids.

Anabolic steroids were among the first drugs customarily used (and abused) in sport, especially where training with weights was common in the 1960s. Yet when their anabolic effects and health risks were disclosed, steroids were soon banned by the IOC (9: pp. 400–401). The rule dealing with such kinds of "doping" is stated as follows.

> Doping is the administration of or the use by a competing athlete of any substance foreign to the body or of any physiological substance taken in abnormal quantity or by an abnormal route of entry into the body, with the intention of increasing in an artificial and unfair manner his performance in competition. When necessity demands medical treatment with any substance which because of its na-

ture, dosage, or application is able to boost the athletes performance in competition in an artificial and unfair manner, this is to be regarded as doping.

Thus far, the IOC has banned substances such as narcotic analgesics, anabolic steroids, beta blockers, diuretics, peptide hormones, human growth hormone, and certain stimulants (e.g., amphetamines and large amounts of caffeine) along with the practice of blood doping.

Since its inception, there has been vigorous debate concerning the IOC's doping policy. On the one hand, there are many supporters of the list of banned substances and practices. Arguments of supporters are many and varied, but they are mostly based on a notion that there needs to be some philosophic vision of sport to decide issues like the use of steroids in sport. Hereafter I shall refer to supporters as "conservatives." Dissenters, hereafter "liberals," counter that *no* arguments in favor of the bans on such substances are evidentially cogent and that, therefore, the list itself is unwarranted. Their view is that sport is in no need of "paternalistic" philosophic guidance because sport mostly, if not wholly, defines itself through its practice. To provide "guidance" where none is necessary is a matter of encroaching upon the autonomy of the very athletes engaged in athletic competition, when athletes themselves know what is best for themselves.

Limiting myself to the issue of anabolic steroids, in what follows I argue that there is better reason to think that regard for autonomy in competitive sport supports the view that the current ban of steroids should be *maintained*, instead of lifted.

Liberalism and the Argument from Autonomy

"Paternalism," roughly understood, is the view that we are sometimes warranted in interfering with the liberties of others when there is evidence that their actions will result in harm to themselves.

J.S. Mill has forcefully argued that regard for an individual's autonomy—especially in areas of social, political, religious, and moral concerns where there is no consensus regarding truth—must reign supreme over paternalistic influence. In a very famous passage, he writes:

> [T]he sole end for which mankind are warranted, individually or collectively, in interfering with the liberty of action of any of their number is self-protection. That the sole purpose for which power can be rightfully exercised over any member of a civilized community, against his will, is to prevent harm to others. His own good, either physical or moral, is not a sufficient warrant. He cannot rightfully be compelled to do or forbear because it will be better for him to do so, because it will make him happier, because, in the opinions of others, to do so would be wise or even right. These are good reasons for remonstrating with him, or reasoning with him, or persuading him, or entreating him, but not for compelling him or visiting him with any evil in case he do otherwise. To justify that, the conduct from which it is desired to deter him must be calculated to produce evil to someone else. The only part of the conduct of anyone for which he is amenable to society is that which concerns others. In the part which merely concerns himself, his independence is, of right, absolute. Over himself, over his own body and mind, the individual is sovereign. (20: pp. 68–69)

In other words, interfering in others' activities is only justified when the harm of agents' actions extends beyond them (unless it can be demonstrated that agents are mentally incompetent or acting under coercion). When mentally competent and uncoerced agents harm only themselves, force is never warranted. This has come to be known as Mill's "principle of harm."

Over the years, the issue of paternalism concerning sporting events has become weighty. Liberals have argued that the looming specter of paternalism is warrant enough for informed athletes being able to do as they so desire with their own bodies, whatever the risk to themselves, to gain any advantage that they can over competitors. No actions taken by informed athletes are inappropriate just because they may result in harm to these same athletes. In short, liberals argue for an extension of Mill's principle of harm to sporting events. I agree.

To illustrate, let us hypothetically introduce a highly successful female bodybuilder, Roxanne. Roxanne has reached a plateau after many years of successful drug-free competition and now decides to take steroids as a means of getting to the next level. Her decision comes only after having deliberated long and hard on the potential dangers of taking such drugs. Following Mill, to show that Roxanne's decision is consistent with the principle of harm, we must be sure that her decision is rational (that she is fully aware of the risks involved) and that it will result in no (at least no significant) harm to others.

For the purpose of this undertaking, I shall not invoke paternalistic intervention in this case (or any other) by supposing that Roxanne's decision is irrational. The most reasonable option—the one that does not beg the very question we are raising—is to assume that many, if not most, athletes who choose to take steroids have control over their decision-making abilities. The question now becomes: "Does Roxanne, by taking steroids, harm others?"

Debunking Liberalism: Injury and Fairness

An issue that is much discussed among both conservatives and liberals alike is fairness, for our purposes: Steroids are injurious because they offer those who use them an "unfair" advantage. The issue of "fairness" here is cashed out in terms of an advantage that the user of steroids has that other competitors, who do not take steroids, do not have.

That "advantage" itself is not the issue Roger Gardner has shown. Many athletes have advantages of all kinds over others that we, as spectators and critics of sport, nowise find objectionable. We do not object when one football team has a decided advantage of strength over another. The Washington Redskins had a decided strength and size advantage, especially when it came to their offensive line, over the Miami Dolphins in the 1993 Super Bowl, yet this made for an exciting game. We do not object when a triathletic champion like Julie Moss improves her performance through greater attention to diet. We *do*, however, object to competitors, like Ben Johnson and Roxanne, who gain an advantage through the use of steroids. In the first two instances, the advantage is judged acceptable or "fair." In the last, the advantage is deemed "unfair." The issue of "fairness," then, has everything to do with the manner in which the advantage is gained and little to do with "advantage" itself.

To illustrate, Gardner goes on to contrast two former major-league pitchers with two pitches having similar effects: Gaylord Perry's spitball and Bruce Sutter's splitfinger. Both the spitball and splitfinger fastball take a sudden dip before reaching the plate and are extraordinarily difficult to hit. In Sutter's case, the advantage was gained by well-planned work. In Perry's, the advantage was due, presumably, to foreign substances on the ball. Gardner writes:

> This raises of course the more significant question of what determines our ethical evaluations (in this case, for instance, it might be the rules of baseball—a spitball violates those rules), and still leaves unanswered the critical issue of why, ultimately, some methods of gaining an advantage are permitted in sport and others are not. *What is the initial justification for the rule?* (my italics; 13: p. 62)

In other words, if we should legalize the spitball, then on what grounds would we argue that spitters are unfair, for then every major-league pitcher would then have the option to use the spitball? Similarly, if we should allow all athletes equal access to steroids, then in what sense would they be unfair? The unfairness, if any, is not advantage over other competitors, so it must be advantage over sport itself.

Gardner next examines the issue of unfairness to sport itself. If this is the issue, then there must be some means of distinguishing between the fairness of steroids and the fairness of other "external" performance enhancers such as diet, technology, coaching, and methods of training. So those who would argue that the ban on steroids should not be lifted need to show how steroids differ from these other external ergogenic aids (to which we voice no objection). There are, he states, no criteria to differentiate, and so steroids offer no advantage over sport itself. Gardner concludes that the unfair-advantage argument is unavailing at all levels (13: p. 70).

Nevertheless, we must entertain scepticism with due caution. Gardner is by no means putting forth arguments *in favor of* athletes taking anabolic steroids. Steroids, as we have seen, are among the IOC's list of banned substances. This itself is sufficient to show that taking steroids is immoral, for to do so would be to cheat. Gardner is, however, taking the debate to another level: If the taking of steroids by itself is morally wrong (here, because of unfairness), then we ought to be able to clearly articulate why this is. Our inability to do this shows that our intuitions against steroids may not be stable. This, however, is *not* the same as saying that steroids should be legalized.

With respect to the issue of steroids and fairness, there are two means of leveling the playing field. On the one hand, steroids and information concerning their possible health-related risks could be made accessible to all athletes. Athletes, then, would have to choose between taking them or refraining from taking them. On the other hand, sport could continue as it currently is. Steroids could remain banned and athletes who choose to use them would continue to suffer the consequences, if caught. My argument is simply this: Given the proven health-related risks of taking anabolic steroids, the burden of proof ought to be foursquare on those who want them legalized.

By leveling the playing field in the direction of legalizing steroids, what would athletes gain by taking them that they would not gain by not taking them? More importantly, what would *sport* gain? Sport, I shall show, has nothing at all to gain. Instead, by putting the degree of performance head-and-shoulders above any consideration for the health of its athletes, sport has everything to lose.

Injury and Coercion

The most persuasive line of argument concerns harm due to coercion. Steroids should be banned because, if legalized, many athletes would be forced to use them and unwillingly exposed to undue health-related risks. Paternalistic intervention is warranted, the argument runs, since the great health-related risks involved with the use of steroids overrides the assistance athletes would get through their use.

Of course, there are two kinds of harm to be considered at the level of individuals through taking steroids: harm done by individuals to themselves and harm done by individuals to others. I agree with liberals who say that risk of harm to individuals who freely choose to take steroids does not justify paternalism, in light of the other possible risks that these very same athletes already knowingly accept. Regard for autonomy requires that we allow others the opportunity to decide for themselves what is right for them, even if it ultimately results in great harm to them.

The more interesting scenario concerns harm done to others by those, like Roxanne, who "freely" choose to take steroids. Athletes certainly have a right to do with their bodies what they so choose as long as the harm that they do has no impact on others. The real question is this: Does the taking of steroids for performance

enhancement by some competitive athletes put coercive pressures on others to take them and risk their health?

Justifying intervention in such cases depends crucially upon whether or not we actually have examples of coercion here. After all, isn't information concerning the risks involved with steroids widely available to all athletes and, thus, isn't the taking or not taking of such drugs a matter of deliberate and free choice and not coercion?

The answer, I suggest, is not so cut-and-dried as philosophers have traditionally made it out to be. On the one hand, it is clear and trivially true that athletes always have a choice: They can choose to take steroids or they can refuse. On the other hand, athletes who are inclined not to take steroids face tremendous external pressures to consider taking them in order to remain competitive with those who do. In most cases, the *complete* freedom to choose is illusory: By choosing not to take steroids, most athletes also choose to give up competing at the highest levels of their sport. In many cases, athletes may choose to risk great harm to their bodies so that they may compete with others who do take steroids, when this need not be the case.

Simon, however, disagrees that the issue is one of harm to others. What is the difference, he asks, between the coercion generated by use of steroids and that, say, generated by training heavily with weights? After all, a heavy routine with weights may be more dangerous to some athletes than steroids. He sums up:

Arguably, the charge that drug users create unfair pressures on other competitors begs the very question at issue. That is, it presupposes that such pressures are morally suspect in ways that other competitive pressures are not, when the very point at issue is whether that is the case. What is needed is some principled basis for asserting that certain competitive pressures—those generated by the use of performance enhancing drugs—are illegitimately imposed while other competitive pressures—such as those generated by hard training—are legitimate and proper. It will not do to point out that the former pressures are generated by drug use. What is needed is an explanation of why the use of performance-enhancing drugs should be prohibited in the first place (25: p. 9).

The "principled basis" that Simon seeks is legitimate. The answer, however, is right under his nose: Steroids should be banned because, given what we know, they are dangerous to the athletes who take them. As such, steroids place regard for enhancement of athletic performance above regard for the health of athletes themselves, and ergogenic aids that do just this do not properly belong in sport. There is no such reasonable suspicion concerning heavy weights. Athletes do get hurt while training with heavy weights, but, done cautiously, such training is more helpful than hurtful. In fact, experts today advocate the use of training properly with heavy weights to significantly *reduce* the risk of injury to athletes involved in rigorous physical activities, such as playing football or wrestling. Such training is necessary to strengthen the muscles, tendons, and ligaments involved in explosive muscular contractions and serve as a deterrent to injury. There is no such consensus on steroids. I agree with Simon, however, when he says that risk is a very part of the fabric of sport and the goal of sport is not necessarily to reduce risk in sport (25: p. 10). Nonetheless, ergogenic aids that risk the health of athletes *above and beyond* their performance-enhancement capacities ought to be left out of sport. And this applies to all ergogenic aids that are unduly injurious, such as training techniques or new equipment, not just those which are pharmacological. If Simon insists on a principle, and he is right to do so, let us give him one.

Ergogenic aids, which place enhanced performance before the health of athletes themselves, are risks that have no proper place in the practice of sport.

The question now becomes: What grounds do we have for entertaining reasonable suspicion concerning the dangers of steroids? The issue is now empirical.

An Issue of Evidence

Over the past 15 years, research on steroids has admittedly been inconclusive as regards the long-term effects on those taking them. Nonetheless, research is beginning to disclose the harmful effects of such use. Steroids are linked to cosmetic defects, heart disease, liver toxicity and tumors, and reproductive problems. Cosmetic defects include acne, loss of hair on the scalp, breast enlargement, and acromegaly (exaggerated growth of bone, especially in the skull, jaw, and extremities). Concerning the liver, they are believed to be causal factors for jaundice, blood-filled cysts, cancerous tumors, hyperinsulinemia, and impaired glucose tolerance. Steroids are also strongly suspected to be causally linked to pulmonary (and related) problems such as blood-cholesterol increase (because steroids affect how sugars and fats are handled), increased blood pressure, hypertension, and, consequently, stroke, and heart attack. There are definite causal relationships between use of steroids and decrease in the production of testosterone, shrinking of testes, low sperm counts, and infertility in males as well as masculinization, enlargement of the clitoris, and irregular menstruation in females—most of which lead to impaired reproductive ability. Many athletes these days prefer human growth hormone (HGH, a polypeptide hormone produced by the pituitary gland). HGH may cause hepatitis, antibody formation directed against the hormone, hyperglycemia and diabetes, and acromegaly (9: p. 395–418; 22: p. 175; 30: pp. 108–111).

The main problem with gleaning conclusive evidence that steroids are dangerous is that their very illegality makes those who take them shun from experiments involving their long-term effects. Moreover, studies in laboratories cannot mimic the doses that many athletes take. Some athletes take dosages of *more than 100 times* their body's own replacement level (30: p. 98). No such studies are ethically permissible today in American laboratories due to public hostility concerning the perceived dangers.[1]

Obviously, it may be argued that many athletes take steroids in reasonably low amounts and the likelihood of injury to self is, thus, minimal. This will not work, however. Steroids are hormonal drugs and, judged by their effects alone, *extremely* potent. For example, after having worked around a shoulder injury and not having bench pressed for over a year, I moved my bench press from 300 to 460 pounds in a matter of 6 months through training and taking *only* 15–20 mgs. of dianabol in 6-week cycles in 1983. My personal best at the same bodyweight without steroids is 405 pounds. This is roughly a 15% difference in strength, and I strongly suspect that, if I had taken the more potent growth hormones that athletes are taking today, I would have made an even greater gain in strength. Now, with a significant increase in hormone levels in the blood, it is reasonable to assume a corresponding increase in the likelihood of injury to the body over time, especially those organs—such as the heart, liver, and kidneys—that are most intimately involved with growth hormones. This is exactly what studies are beginning to disclose. Consequently, even though conclusive evidence of the dangers of steroids may be lacking, *there are incontestably good reasons to be chary!* This is enough to suggest due caution.

There are many celebrated examples of death or serious harm that are suspected to be strongly linked with steroids: Steve Courson's heart disease at age 32, Lyle Alzedo's inoperable brain cancer and death at age 42, bodybuilder Steve Valley's heart attack in a Phoenix gym and subsequent death (at age 21!), and U.S. weightlifting coach, Dr. John Zeigler, who was responsible for the development of the steroid, dianabol, which transformed American weightlifting. Zeigler himself used steroids and died in 1983. Before his death, Zeigler warned others in a taped message: I wish I had never heard the word "steroid." . . . All these young kids . . . don't realize the terrible price they are going to pay" (9: pp. 395–401). The list could go on.[2]

Thus, given the serious dangers involved in taking anabolic steroids, it would be incautious, unwise, and immoral to advocate their use in competitive sport. Legalizing steroids to accommodate those who want to take them, in spite of the great risks to their health, would coerce many other serious athletes to take them, who otherwise would not, in order to compete at the highest levels. This, quite clearly, is injurious to these others by interfering with their autonomy, if fairness dictates a level playing field, common sense dictates that we level it by maintaining the current ban on steroids.[3] Warren Fraleigh agrees:

> Under current historical conditions of sport, why, morally speaking, should a highly competent athlete be forced either to lower his/her expectancies or discontinue sport involvement because he/she cannot compete with drug users? Why should the effective coercive force not be in the opposite direction against drug users? The effect of more people harmed by coerced drug use . . . amounts to tacit social approval of coerced self-harm of athletes. To me the forced choice of either coerced self-harm or of dropping out or lowering one's expectations is a morally unconscionable choice. (11: p. 28)

As an example, let us assume that a certain athlete, say Alexander, competes as a nationally ranked powerlifter. After a few years in the sport, Alexander finds that most of the very best powerlifters in the world in his weight division exceed him in overall strength by no more than 15%—a difference that he figures exists only because of performance-enhancement drugs. Alexander's strong desire to compete as efficiently as possible, however, is matched by an equally strong desire not to take great risks with his body. In other words, his goal of international recognition is tempered by great concern for his physical health. Since be has reached a certain level of notoriety without the drugs, he faces a dilemma: Does he rest content with what he has achieved or does he risk serious health problems to gain the notoriety that those who take drugs have gained?

The dilemma is real and acute.[4] Athletes who have always avoided performance-enhancement drugs for health reasons will never really know if indeed they are as good as or even better than those taking steroids unless they play by the pharmacological rules, which could even have *lethal* consequences. The "values" of a minority of athletes, who would willingly sacrifice their own health for a moment of glory, are thus imposed on the majority, who are being penalized for having self-regard and a higher notion of athletic competition. Those few who would subject themselves to serious health risks are trying to impose their *dangerous* standards upon the many who would rather compete without such risks. Again, if the playing field can be leveled by minimizing health-related risks to competitors without any compromise to the integrity of sport, why should we risk the health of athletes senselessly? Harm, through coercion, dictates that the ban on steroids be maintained, not reversed. Such sober legislation does more to preserve than destroy autonomy, rightly apprehended.[5]

A Normative Turn in the Debate

Athletic performance and competition has evolved through the centuries to its present practice. Those who argue that we can impose no "paternalistic" restrictions on sporting behavior, such as imposing a ban on steroids, often appeal to the lack of consensus on the nature of "sport" itself. W.M. Brown, for instance, argues thus (my italics throughout):

It may nevertheless be argued that the use of drugs is somehow inconsistent with the na-

ture of sports, and that sports in turn are linked with a broader set of values—a conception of the *good life*—which is betrayed by the use of drugs, so that interference in the choices of athletes in this respect is done to preserve a *greater good,* once they may have lost sight of in their preoccupation with the more narrow concerns of training and competition, such an argument . . . is not cogent. *There is, I believe, no single conception of sports on which we need agree.* (6: p. 20)

Just what Brown means by this final sentence is unclear, though I suggest that he adds it in order to keep the debate from taking a normative turn.

Brown does go on to outline certain values that are held in high repute in athletic competitions: honesty, fairness, autonomy, obedience, regimentation, service to others, and sacrifice. He adds:

We can indeed forbid the use of drugs in athletics in general, just as we do in the case of children. But ironically, in adopting such a paternalistic stance of insisting that we know better than the athletes themselves how to achieve some more *general good* which they myopically ignore, we must deny in them the very attributes we claim to value: self-reliance, personal achievement, and autonomy. (6: p. 21)

The "values" that Brown endorses are all centered around a concept of sport where, under the guise of autonomy, individuals and their own performance are everything. The tenor of Brown's paper makes it clear that his reference to values such as honesty, fairness, service to others, and sacrifice is mere lip service to those who otherwise might object.

Similarly, powerlifter and editor, Dr. Frederick Hatfield, says this concerning drugs (my italics throughout):

Drugs are not inherently evil—misuse and abuse by people give them that connotation. I believe that drugs have been, are and will continue to be an important source of man's *salvation*. I also believe that there can be *no nobler use* for drugs that improving man's performance capabilities. Society demands bigger, faster and stronger athletes. The *sacrosanctity* of the sports arena, however, has been a hindrance to meeting this demand. (14: p. 321)

Hatfield's notion of (performance-enhancement) drugs as "an important source of man's salvation" is exaggerated to absurdity. For Hatfield, athletes are first and foremost entertainers, and this presumably justifies *anything* that improves their performance, regardless of how it affects them. The religious metaphors here are misplaced and ludicrous.

Why liberals' arguments, like those of Brown and Hatfield *seem* persuasive as regards sport is because we lack and always have lacked an intelligent consensus of what sport *ought to be*. It is only in light of this glaring defect that their reasons seem cogent, when instead they themselves are constructed from a certain myopic vision. Competition is not merely, as liberals seem to intimate, an anything-goes quest for number one. Sport, like everything else that humans engage in, is laden with values, and these values exact more than just a vision of "self."

Ethical issues of sport are matters that have not been resolved mostly because they have never been earnestly and satisfactorily explored. Serious scholarship on such issues is in its infancy. Liberals are wrong in maintaining that it is the relatively arbitrary evolution of sport that determines what sport is. Athletes, critics, and philosophers of sport must have some say. To decide ethical issues in sport, we must appeal to a set of rules that apply to all sports across the board at a given time. It is true that no such rules presently exist, either implicitly or explicitly. The interesting questions are these: Can any such rules exist? Moreover, ought they to exist?[6]

Rules of ethical athletic performance can and ought to exist, I shall argue next. We need only to come to a *rational* consensus concerning the aims of the practice of sport. It is to this issue that we now turn.

The Concept of "Competition"

Any attempt to grapple with the issue of what sport ought to be for us today, I believe, should first come to terms with what sport has hitherto meant to us from its earliest times. Thus, if we look back to this early history, we shall be able to construct an agreeable normative picture for us today. This takes us back to ancient Greek practice.

For the ancient Greeks, athletic competition was significantly linked to a type of physical excellence recognized by ancient philosophers and poets alike. "Excellence," from the ancient Greek word *arete,* is a term that has to do with what someone or something does best. *Arete* was applied to human excellence both at the physical level and at the moral (psychic) level. A wrestler or runner who won at the ancient Olympic or Pythian Games would be said to have *arete,* that is, excellence of physical character. Likewise, *arete* applied to moral excellence. A courageous soldier and just citizen would both have *arete* or excellence of moral character.[7] And so any normative concept of "competitive sport," the ancient Greeks teach us, must deal with *human excellence*. This seems to accord with much of the literature today.

Of further etymological significance, our word "athlete" comes from the Greek word *athlein,* which means principally "to contend for a prize," and, secondarily, "to suffer" or "to endure hardship." This implies that athletic excellence of character is also a measure of an athlete's ability to endure hardship. It is a form of *athlein* that Homer uses to describe the Greeks' ten-years war with Troy and that we find used to describe Herakles' local and worldly labors. Historian of sport E. Norman Gardiner writes concerning the importance of this ancient element of the athletic spirit for us today:

The athletic spirit cannot exist where the conditions of life are too soft and luxurious; it cannot exist where conditions are too hard and where all the physical energies are exhausted in a constant struggle with the forces of man or nature. (12: p. 2)

And so, for the ancient Greeks, sport was a measure of excellence gained through enduring hardship for the sake of contending for a prize. And though the ancient Greeks loved their winners (perhaps almost as much as we do today!), the focus here must be on the striving for and not the attainment of victory. For it is not victory itself that should be prized most, but the manner in which it is attained.[8] This view I shall call "Aretism," and I offer a fuller account below.

In linking "sport" with "excellence," we gain a sense of continuity: We link the present practice of sport with its past. We join ancient values with contemptorary values.[9] The difference here is that excellence is not just the excellence of any particular athlete or any distinct manner of doing something in athletic competition. Aretism is rather the excellence of sport itself, the values to which all athletes who consent to engage in competition with others at least implicitly agree. If, then, sport demands the greatest regard for excellence, the normative challenge is to come to a fuller understanding of "excellence" as regards sport. I can, for the present, do no more than offer a brief and inchoate sketch.

What Classical Greek philosophers, such as Plato and Aristotle, have taught us is that individual expression and self-interest, without regard for community, is destructive of a community. As Plato says in *Republic,* for instance, "Is there any greater evil we can mention for a city than that which tears it apart and makes it many instead of one? Or any greater good than that which binds it together and makes it one?" (462a)

Liberals' views of competitive sport reduce its practice mostly, if not exclusively, to individual and autonomous expression:[10] The actions of those individuals within a particular sport define that sport for a given time. Sport exists for the sake of the individuals in it; there is no requirement, or even expectation, that athletes give anything in return. This ridiculous view of sport insidiously erodes the very communities in which athletes live.

In contrast, Aretism recognizes that competitive sport is essentially social practice. Its practice, as a quest for excellence in sport, works at three levels of integration: excellence through personal integration, political integration, and cosmic integration. Taking the last first, athletes integrate with competitive sport itself by contending in a manner consistent with the set of values that define its practice at a given time. They come to understand that their own athletic expression in sport, as a celebration of human perseverance and creativity, takes on meaning because of these values. Individual autonomy is thereby not quashed, but suitably nurtured, by appreciation and regard for sport itself as a social instution. At the level of political integration, competitive sport is a recognition of "other." While competitively and creatively distinguishing themselves from others in a particular sport, athletes acknowledge the contributions of other autonomous athletes who also accept sport as a social institution. Politically integrated athletes agree to conduct themselves in a manner respectful and appreciative of the efforts of other competitors. Last, personal integration involves athletes' own autonomous striving for a greater sense of self. Athletes come to see sport as a vehicle for both physical and moral self-betterment, especially the latter. This focus on and tripartitioning of excellence is what distinguishes Aretism from other normative accounts of sport.

Moreover, "excellence" itself implies that there is an ineliminable aesthetic component to sport. Sport is excellence principally because sport is beautiful. From the simplest to the most complex movements and arrangements of movements involved, what moves us *most* about sport is not our bestial, unslakable thirst for victory, but rather our appreciation of the values involved in superior or peak performance: the passion, sedulousness, focus, drive, planning, and patience involved in working by oneself or with others toward a worthwhile, but seemingly unattainable goal. Such work is play, when motivated by love of sport itself.

To truly love sport is to recognize that sport is more than merely contending for a prize. It involves more than just winning or losing. Sport is excellence and excellence is integration. Contrary to liberals like Brown and Hatfield, if developing and nurturing a broader aesthetic view of sport forces us to reevaluate our way of looking at ourselves and at the world in which we live, then let it be so.

Innovation, Social Justice, and Sport

So far I have shown that none of the liberals' arguments against the ban of steroids from formal athletic competitions show that steroids should be legalized. Fairness requires that athletes each perform on a level playing field. This is done by either legalizing or banning steroids, and since the former places coercive constraints upon athletes to compete at considerable risk to their health, maintaining the current ban is the most sensible option as regards true concern for autonomy. In addition, maintaining the current ban on steroids is consistent with a philosophy of sport that balances individual competitiveness with a concern for other competitors and sport itself.

Because of the current controversy about steroids, arguments proposing that the ban on steroids is without philosophic merit amount to a tacit endorsement of their legalization. As such, any proposal to legalize steroids in sport, then, amounts to a *methodological innovation* in sport itself. The question now becomes "When should an innovation of sport be adopted?" (It is important to note that here we are not arguing about innovation within any particular sport. There have been several instances of this. Here we are arguing about innovation in *sport itself*.)

Burke has recently argued that our moral condemnation of drug use in sport is a result of a confusion resulting when an oral culture (and morality) of sport gets fixed into a "written culture of constancy" that is inconsistent with human nature, Sport is dynamic and flowing, and this dynamism and flow are constantly responsible for innovation in and redefinition of sport. He writes:

> Drug users test the latitude of the rules in a way that is not as far removed from the change that Dick Fosbury produced with his new technique as we would like to think. New knowledge, technical innovation, training methods, new materials, and stronger, faster athletes all create redefinitions of games.... All testing of the latitude involves egocentric attempts by players to shape the practice. No one attempt is more morally condemnable than any other. All attempts, whether successful or not, involve the production of beneficiaries and victims. The drug user in modern times is a victim, much as the exponents of the scissors method of high jumping were also victims. Both are victims of aesthetic sensibilities of the community. (8: p. 60)

The definition and redefinition of "sport," he believes, is to be found in the actual practice of sport and not in any written culture, for the latter quashes autonomy in order to preserve constancy of practice.

In keeping with his misuse of Mill's principle of harm, Burke asks whether the drug law attempts to "impose an essentialist and written logic an the freedom of the athletes?" His answer is clearly affirmative. There is a conspiracy, it seems, to keep "game conditions as constant as possible," and this conspiracy is rooted in the false notion that the proposition "drugs are, by nature, evil" is capable of rational demonstration (20: p. 60). Those responsible for the ban on drugs in sport are the very conspirators who, presumably, would have us keep the rules of all sports fixed for all times.

Of course, as I have taken myself to have shown, nothing of the sort follows. In agreement with the liberals, I believe that there is nothing *inherently* wicked about drugs. Yet I am also quite sure that there is no underlying conspiracy by conservatives to do away with creativity and innovation. Drugs like steroids are wrong because they make personal performance everything, elevating it above concern for the health of athletes themselves. The Fosbury Flop, just like the splitfinger fastball, was a technical innovation without such harmful, widespread implications.

If we ignore such absurd notions about conspiratorial conservatism, we find that there is nothing inconsistent between innovation and a philosophy of sport that stresses social responsibility. This also does not imply stasis and lack of innovation.

There is, nonetheless, a more striking reason for not taking what Burke has to say too seriously. In "Drugs in Sport," Terrence Roberts and he acknowledge the widespread disapprobation of athletic use of drugs. "[T]he *pervasive dislike* [my italics] of athletes using drugs is not explained entirely by the 'good' practice of sport and fairness, and that it also has something to do with the fear of transgressing socially constructed, gender boundaries" (7: p. 100). Later they endorse "the *rational* as nothing more than a commitment to think in the ways that the rest of the community at this historical moment thinks" (7: p. 111). Well, if the lion's share of the community tends to regard the use of performance-enhancing drugs as anathema, one is "rationally" committed to embracing one's community's views *against* taking such drugs. The weight of Burke's many arguments fail to add up to anything in light of this postmodernistic notion of "rationality"[11] and his acknowledgement of his community's abhorrence of performance-enhancing drugs.

W.M. Brown takes a different line of argument in another defense of liberalism that takes innovation into consideration. He states that sports and their goods, being predominantly expressions of individual character, invite exploration of difference and change that pave the path for "new ways of being human." The worthwhile price for this, he thinks, is that sport will reflect, though not solve, problems of social justice (6: p. 246).

What Brown fails to mention is that many of these new ways of being human do more to harm than help communities or societies—that is, they neither reflect, nor solve, but create grand problems for social justice. The rampant use of steroids, as I have tried to show above, is one such instance.[12]

The view of sport that I have outlined, "Aretism," puts no stranglehold on human expression. It merely invites us to temper our exploration of our own humanity through sport by sensible and appropriate moral guidelines. It acknowledges that sport transcends individual expression and has undeniable social implications, which bind each athlete in a triad of normative, "aretic" relations: one of athlete with self, one of athlete with other athletes, and one of athlete with sport. In this way, sport is a vehicle of creative human expression with an aim (at least indirectly) toward the health of community. Though it may be no part of philosophy of sport to endorse the view that sport, through its practice, must aim to solve problems of social injustice, sport, as a social institution itself, cannot be wholly indifferent to such problems. Sport must at least strive to steer clear of social injustice.

A rational and relatively fixed notion of "sport" is philosophically highly desirable and does not preclude innovation, change, novelty, and autonomy. It merely challenges us to come up with a view of sport that reflects timeless values, such as respect for self and others and love of challenge. Aretism, as I have sketched above, is just such a view.

Let me now summarize the issue of steroids. I have taken myself to have shown that none of the arguments directed against the ban on steroids is evidence that the legalization of steroids would be good for sport. Moreover, I have argued that lifting the ban on steroids would create a coercive environment that promotes injury to others and, thus, injury to sport itself. On account of this, neutral scepticism cannot be maintained. Regard for autonomy demands that no athlete be allowed to engage in behavior that puts fellow competitors at risk. Conservativism must win the day.

Notes

1. Such experiments are, however, conducted in Europe, though these focus on changes in athletic performance or lean body-mass, instead of long-term effect to health (9: p. 404).

2. In my own sport, powerlifting, there have been many noteworthy deaths of young athletes, especially among the big men, that were undoubtedly related to heavy use of steroids over years. Reports of such deaths in weightlifting magazines are strangely silent about each athlete's use of anabolic aids, while hereditary factors and environmentals stressors are always suggested as principal causal factors. Mill's Method of Agreement I suggest, would be sufficient to clear up any mystery.

3. See also Yesalis and Wright (30: p. 310).

4. Breivik argues cleverly that the coercive element plays itself out in the form of a prisoner's dilemma, where rational self interest winds up self-defeating (2: p. 3).

5. I shall develop the argument later that liberals' anything-goes notion of autonomy, making each individual his own best judge of what is right for him, is cardinally responsible for the rampant relativism of today's postmodernism For an excellent exposition of this thesis, see Brecher (1).

6. See also Fraleigh (11: p. 25).

7. In addition, it was not inappropriate for Greeks to talk of the *arete* of, say, a carriage that could do what it was made to do and do it quite well.

8. Similar to the point made by Schneider and Butcher, who argue that proper practice of sport should center on internal goods, which are defined by the relationship between the prelusory goals of the sport and the rules that delimit these goals. Victory is important, of course, but not merely or even mostly because of the external rewards it brings. *How* one wins is especially important (24: pp. 69–72).

9. For other links of sport with "excellence," see Simon (25: p. 10; 26: p. 30), Farichild (10: p. 76), and Schneider and Butcher (24: p. 65).

10. For example. see Brown (3: p. 22), Burke (7: p. 48), and Burke and Roberts (9: p. 111).

11. The mistake, of course, is equating "rationality" and "liberality." They write, "This is the desire of liberal communities: to open up our freedoms to other people. This is the hope of all liberal philosophies that claim a rational base to freedoms, which is transhistorical and transcultural, and therefore appropriate to any human being. If these freedoms are rational and, therefore, human, anyone at anytime will accept this philosophy. Failure to accept it is the hallmark of irrationality. Such people cannot be accepted as part of the negotiating committee of freedoms until they are educated" (8: p. 107).

12. The absurdly gross amounts of money that owners and athletes alike make is another.

Bibliography

1. Brecher, B. *Getting What You Want: A Critique of Liberal Morality.* New York: Routledge, 1998.

2. Breivik. G. "The Doping Dilemma: Some Game Theoretical and Philosophical Considerations." *Sportwissenshaft.* XVII: 83–94, 1987.

3. Brown, W.M. "Ethics, Drugs, and Sport." *Journal of the Philosophy of Sport* VII: 15–23, 1980.

4. Brown, W.M. "Paternalism, Drugs, and the Nature of Sports." *Journal of the Philosophy of Sport,* XI: 14–22, 1985.

5. Brown, W.M. "Comments on Simon and Fraleigh." *Journal of the Philosophy of Sport.* XI:33–35, 1995.

6. Brown, W.M. "Practices and Prudence" In: *Philosophic Inquiry in Sport*, W.J. Morgan and K. V. Meier (Eds.; 2nd ed.). Champaign, IL., Human Kinetics, 1990.

7. Burke. M. "Drugs in Sport: Have They Practiced Too Hard? A Response to Schneider and Butcher." *Journal of the Philosophy of Sport.* XXIV:47–66, 1997.

8. Burke, M., and Roberts, T.J. "Drugs in Sport: An Issue of Morality or Sentimentality?" *Journal of the Philosophy of Sport*. XXIV:99–113, 1997.

9. Colgan, M. *Ultimate Sports Nutrition: Your Competitive Edge*. Ronkonkoma, NY: Advanced Research Press, 1993.

10. Fairchild, D.L. "Sport Abjection: Steroids and the Uglification of the Athlete." *Journal of the Philosophy of Sport*. XVI:74–88, 1989.

11. Fraleigh, W.P. "Performance-Enhancing Drugs in Sport: The Ethical Issue." *Journal of the Philosophy of Sport*. XI:23–29, 1985.

12. Gardiner, E.N. *Athletics of the Ancient World*. Chicago: Ares, 1997.

13. Gardner, Roger. "On Performance-Enhancing Substances and the Unfair Advantage Argument." *Journal of the Philosophy of Sport*. XVI:59–73, 1989.

14. Hoberman, J.M. "Sport and the Technological Image of Man." *Philosophic Inquiry in Sport*. W.J. Morgan and K.M. (Eds.). Champaign, IL: Human Kinetics, 1986.

15. Holowchak, M.A. "The Early Greek Influence on Sport III: Legendary Figures of Greek Sport." *Milo*. IV(3):44–46, 1996.

16. Lavin, M. "Sports and Drugs: Are the Current Bans Justified?" *Journal of the Philosophy of Sport*. XIV:34–43, 1987.

17. Lee, H.M. "Athletic Arete in Pindar." *The Ancient World: Athletics in Antiquity*. VII(12):31–37, 1983.

18. McNamee, M.J., and Parry, S.J. *Ethics & Sport*. New York: E & FN Spon, 1998.

19. Meier, K.V. "Fields of Dreams and Men of Straw: Philosophical Reflections on Performance-Enhancers in Sport." *Journal of the Philosophy of Sport*. XVIII:74–85, 1991.

20. Mill, J.S. *On Liberty*. New York: Penguin Books, 1985/1859.

21. Morgan, W.J. and Meier, K.V. Editors, *Philosophic Inquiry in Sport*. Champaign, IL: Human Kinetics, 1990.

22. Ringhofer, K.R., and Harding, M.E. *Coaches Guide to Drugs and Sport*. Champaign, IL: Human Kinetics, 1996.

23. Sansone, D. *Greek Athletics and the Genesis of Sport*. Berkeley: University of California Press. 1992.

24. Schneider, A., and Butcher, R.B. "Why Olympic Athletes Should Avoid the Use and Seek the Elimination of Performance-Enhancing Substances and Practices from the Olympic Games." *Journal of the Philosophy of Sport*. XX–XXI:64–81, 1993–1994.

25. Simon, R.L. "Good Competition and Drug-Enhanced Performance." *Journal of the Philosophy of Sport*. XI:6–13, 1985.

26. Simon, R.L. "Response to Brown and Fraleigh." *Journal of the Philosophy of Sport*. XI:30–32, 1985.

27. Thompson, P.B. "Privacy and the Urinalysis Testing of Athletes." *Journal of the Philosophy of Sport*. IX:60–65, 1982.

28. Wertz, S.K. "The Varieties of Cheating." *Journal of the Philosophy of Sport*. VIII:19–40, 1981.

29. Williams, M.H. "The Use of Nutritional Erogenic Aids in Sports: Is It an Ethical Issue?" *International Journal of Sport Nutrition*. 4:120–131, 1994.

30. Yesalis, C.E. and Wright, J. "Social Alternatives." *Anabolic Steroids in Sport and Exercise*. Champaign, IL: Human Kinetics, 1993.

Questions for Consideration

1. Do you agree that autonomy in competitive sport is best realized through an understanding of sport as essentially a social phenomenon?

2. Do you find the argument of harm (that legalizing steroids creates a coercive environment that does more harm than good) compelling?

3. Is Aretism a viable account for what sport ought to be, or do you agree with liberals, who argue that sport is a genuine expression of individuality?

4. Assess the argument against Burke's charge that nonliberal views of sport quash creativity.

Chapter Four

Epistemological Issues in Sport

27 On Reaching First Base with a "Science" of Moral Development in Sport: Problems with Scientific Objectivity and Reductivism

Russell W. Gough
Pepperdine University

In this reading, Russell W. Gough begins by applauding the efforts of psychologists and sociologists in the sports milieu. Nonetheless, there is one area, he says, where their empirical efforts have done more harm than good: moral investigation.

Beginning with the groundbreaking work of Lawrence Kohlberg on moral development, a vast body of empirical research into the topic has accumulated. However, there is good reason to think that this body of research is contaminated, Gough feels, for it rests on certain (generally implicit) assumptions on an accepted or correct moral paradigm.

Most of these moral studies proceed as follows. First, they assume that moral development occurs through a series of well-defined and empirically verifiable stages. Next, they tend to equate moral maturity with formal features of their responses, not content. Last, they smuggle in a certain notion of moral correctness as the standard by which their evaluative judgments are made. It is this last feature that Gough finds offensive and mistaken.

There are two questions that bear on the possibility of an objective science of moral evaluation. First, can there be in sport an objective science of what is naturally and ineliminably value-laden and normative? Second, to what extent can a science of moral development be reduced to the language of science?

Reprinted, by permission, from Russell W. Gough, "On Reaching First Base with a 'Science' of Moral Development in Sport: Problems with Scientific Objectivity and Reductivism," *Journal of the Philosophy of Sport* XXII (1995): 11–25.

That there can be a science of morality in (or outside of) sport is uncontroversial, so long as this science remains at the level of describing athletes' responses to moral questions or comments on moral issues. Yet when scientists begin to categorize athletes evaluatively, they leave off doing science and begin to do philosophy. It may be that the "naturalistic reductivism" required for a science of moral development is possible, Gough asserts, but the present state of scholarship is in a state, to borrow a phrase from Robert Bellah (whom he quotes at the end), of "plain moral confusion." Until then, Gough concludes, the burden of proof is on the shoulders of those who "practice" such a science to justify their practice.

I

Judging from the relevant social scientific literature of the past forty years or so, the character of moral inquiry in sport has taken a pronounced empirical turn, with researchers attempting to discover scientifically objective, law-like generalizations concerning what has been described variously as the "moral development" or the "character development" or the "moral reasoning abilities" of sport populations.[1] That the character of moral inquiry in sport has become so markedly empirical is somewhat unsurprising given at least two factors: (1) the historically preponderant influence of social scientists in this particular moral inquiry, and (2) the positivistic paradigm of social science as science that continues to undergird and motivate investigations into most of what ostensibly falls under the rubrics of moral development, character development, and moral reasoning in sport (or in any particular investigative context, for that matter).

With respect to (1), it is to their credit that social scientists such as sports psychologists and sports sociologists seem to have regarded the sport milieu as a bonafide object of scholarly inquiry much earlier and in greater numbers than philosophers and ethicists. A perusal of the relevant literature helps bear this out. Nonetheless, I want to suggest in this essay that despite this now well-established body of social scientific research, there remain deeply compelling philosophical reasons for questioning the extent to which the character of moral inquiry in sport can be "scientific." More specifically, I will argue that in certain fundamental respects this inquiry can be neither scientifically objective nor scientifically reductive as the social scientific research concerned with moral development in sport has presumed for the past few decades.

With respect to (2), it is significant that this social scientific research has invariably been cultivated by an unflinching faith in positivistic paradigms of social science as science. These positivistic paradigms, which have undergirded the actual mainstream practice of social science from the seventeenth and eighteenth century Enlightenment to the present day, assume that social science is (or can be) a nonideological, value-free (or predominantly value-free),[2] traditionless, explanatory science. While it is beyond the scope of this essay to take issue with this modern conception of social science, I do want to challenge in part the degree to which moral development research can even be true to its positivistic underpinnings. Indeed, given the already well-documented theoretical and methodological obstacles confronting positivistic paradigms of social science as science, one might justifiably suspect *a fortiori* that the obstacles confronting positivistic conceptions of social science as moral development science might

be unmanageably numerous, if not insuperable, given the inescapable normativity, variability, and complexity of the subject matter.[3] As we shall see below, at the very least it appears the burden of proof is on researchers to demonstrate how and in what ways their investigations into moral development in sport are in fact *not* ideological, value-laden, and tradition-bound— in sum, normative—projects.

II

There are, of course, certain fundamental respects in which the empirical turn in sport moral inquiry has been relatively noncontroversial and genuinely scientific. Insofar as it has generated statistical data concerning, for example, patterns of competitive attitudes among coaches and athletes or actual incidences of illicit drug use among Olympic athletes, the empirical turn has indeed been revealing and beneficial. With respect to these sorts of empirical investigations into what might be called sport morality or sports ethics,[4] I have no qualms, only thanks. Further, and more to the point for present purposes, I also do not wish to challenge the general way in which a science of sport morality could be developed insofar as it merely observes and describes the kinds of moral rationales given by individual athletes and coaches to justify their actions. Given this particular kind of social scientific inquiry, the investigator might discover, for example, that Athlete A tends to reason like a utilitarian; that Athlete B tends to reason like a pragmatist; and that Athlete C not merely tends to reason but unfailingly reasons on the basis of biblical authority and precedent.

However, aside from these relatively unproblematic, descriptive kinds of investigations, the empirical turn has heralded many other findings concerning what is described ubiquitously in the literature as moral development in sport that are at once deeply problematic and presumptively scientific. Consider the following claims typical of this moral development in sport literature:

- "Athletes do not [morally] reason as well as nonathletes" (2: p. 53).
- "Participation in collegiate (but not high school) basketball is associated with lower level moral reasoning in both sport and life" (3: p. 15).
- "Sports that are typified by . . . [aggressive] acts may tend to attract participants with lower levels of moral reasoning . . ." (3: p. 25).
- "Within some sports there is a relationship, generally negative, between participation and level or stage of moral reasoning development" (4: p. 190).

One overarching aim of this essay, of course, is to suggest how and in what ways conclusions such as these, and especially the moral development inquiries that generate them, cannot be scientifically objective insofar as they will be inescapably normative. Far from merely describing how Athletes A, B, and C reason according to a particular moral point of view, conclusions of the variety "Athlete A morally reasons at a higher/lower level than Athlete B" or "Athlete A is more/less morally mature than Athlete B" are invariably generated from a family of theoretical constructs that entail substantive moral assumptions. Indeed, the arguments of this essay have arisen primarily in response to this family of theoretical constructs that in fact continues to undergird most of the recent social scientific studies concerned with moral development in sport.[5] These moral-theoretic constructs are essentially those of developmental psychology and retain at least three significant features found most notably in the late psychologist Lawrence Kohlberg's widely influential, precedent-setting studies (17, 18).

First, these constructs construe moral development as a process of moving through a series of distinct, qualitatively different, and empirically verifiable stages or levels of moral maturity. While developmentalists may disagree concerning how certain stages or levels of moral development are to be characterized, they invariably postulate a starting point and an endpoint of development, with the latter prescribing the ultimate goal of moral development.

Second, these constructs construe moral maturity itself largely, if not exclusively, in terms of moral reasoning ability (i.e., in terms of the reasons that can be given to justify one's moral opinions or actions). Importantly, it is not the content but the logical form of the reasoning that is said to determine whether a given person is more or less morally mature. Thus, an analysis of a given person's moral development will turn primarily not on *what* that person believes but on *why* that person believes it.

Third, and most significantly for my arguments these constructs invariably assume the moral correctness—or at least the moral superiority—of a general moral point of view, which itself entails the correctness or superiority of some particular form of moral reasoning. The contours of a given moral point of view can usually be identified quite readily by examining a construct's final stage or highest level of moral development, wherein will be found the norms by which moral development is to be evaluated. (For example, according to the Kohlbergian framework, a person has reached the highest level of moral development—is most morally mature—when he or she can reason according to something very much like Kant's deontological framework.) This way of putting the point, of course, may not sit well with many researchers who conduct investigations into moral development. Or at least one could suggest that it *should not* sit well with them if researchers are to genuinely and meaningfully see themselves as conducting scientifically objective investigations into moral development. The fact remains, however, that the majority of what is or has been described as moral development research in and out of sport has proceeded from within this tradition of developmentalism that explicitly or implicitly prescribes deeply normative responses to questions such as, "Development towards what?" or "What is the ultimate goal of moral development?" or "What is it to morally reason well?"

Thus, in light of these prevailing features, to argue against the possibility of an objective science of moral development in sport, while at the same time allowing for the possibility of an objective science of sports ethics, is not merely to engage in terminological gymnastics. It is much more than mere terminology, at least insofar as moral development continues to be a theoretically loaded term inextricably intertwined with the moral assumptions and methods of developmental psychology.[6]

Three additional provisos: First, although I couch my misgivings with the notion of moral development science within the milieu of sport—providing as it does a most provocative context for exploiting issues about the nature and scope of applied moral analysis—it will become clear at the outset that I take my arguments as entailing a range of application far greater than moral inquiry in sport. Indeed, I believe they extend beyond the character of moral inquiry in any particular context to the character of moral inquiry as such. Second, although these misgivings will be described primarily in philosophical terms, it would be a mistake to infer that my arguments are primarily philosophical and not scientific. For at stake will be foundational scientific issues of test validity—especially construct validity, the most significant kind of test validity because of its inextricable linkage to theoretical assumptions.[7]

Finally, the arguments in what follows will be largely negative. That is, they will be concerned not so much with the ways in which the character of moral inquiry in sport can be genuinely scientific as much as with the ways in which it *cannot* be genuinely scientific. Thus, rather than exploring the legitimate foundations and horizons for what might be described as a science of sports ethics, I will exclusively focus on two general reasons why moral inquiry in sport cannot be scientific as a number of moral development researchers have presumed, and on the basis of which their research has been conducted, for the past few decades.

III

I would suggest that there are at least two general types of foundational "Home Plate" questions that must be addressed adequately before one can proceed to first base, as it were, with the notion of a science of moral development in sport:

> *HP1:* How can a science of moral development in sport arrive at scientifically objective, value-free (or predominantly value-free) conclusions about that which is by nature so deeply and inescapably value-laden and normative?
>
> *HP2:* To what extent can a science of moral development in sport be scientifically reductive?

Put bluntly, it strikes me as methodologically and philosophically, even ethically,[8] imperative that these two Home Plate questions should be addressed adequately before researchers presume to engage themselves in the business of *scientifically* quantifying and ranking the moral development of athletic populations. Strikingly, the vast majority of the social scientific literature to date has either glossed or ignored altogether these foundational "meta" questions. Thus, to defend moral development research at this point in time by appealing to its forty-year or so history and its extensive body of longitudinal data will not do. It is quite beside the point; it merely begs the question. Given the deeply normative nature of the subject matter, it would appear that the burden of proof does indeed remain squarely on moral development researchers to formulate adequate responses concerning basic issues of objectivity and reductivism.

HP1 asked, How can a science of moral development in sport arrive at scientifically objective, value-free (or predominantly value-free) conclusions about that which is by nature so deeply and inescapably value-laden and normative? In one sense, the way HP1 has been framed admittedly seems to stack the deck against the possibility of an objective science of moral development. For insofar as the object of inquiry is in fact inescapably normative, HP1 seems to imply that any inquiry into what is inescapably normative will itself be normative. This, of course, does not necessarily follow, nor is this necessarily implied by HP1. Again, to the extent that researchers might merely observe and describe the moral rationales employed by Athletes A, B, and C, there would appear to be no normativity necessarily involved in the process of so observing and describing. Since such non-normative investigative possibilities clearly exist, it should also be clear that HP1 need not be interpreted as implying categorically that any inquiry into what is inescapably normative will itself be normative.

However, in large measure HP1 is indeed meant to draw special attention to the inescapable normativity of moral development research in sport as it is presently understood and practiced. To sharpen this point, the force of HP1 for present purposes could be expressed as follows: To the extent that this research continues to be undergirded by developmentalism's paradigms of moral development, there is a genuine sense in which this research will continue to stack the deck against itself in regard to scientific objectivity.

To see in part why this is the case, consider the example of basketball's widely accepted notion of the "good foul." A good foul occurs when a defensive player intentionally yet unmaliciously fouls an offensive player to prevent an easy basket. The foul is called "good" because it is thought to be strategically good. But is it ethical? Ethically good, as it were? Warren Fraleigh (10) has most notably made the argument that the good foul is not good. On the other side of the

issue, I, for one, do not find the good foul so ethically problematic. As I have written elsewhere, albeit in passing, "Though fouls are 'against the rules,' . . . [an] unwritten rule holds no one ethically suspect for committing 'good fouls'" (11: p. 8).

Consider further what would happen if Fraleigh and I were to take a moral reasoning "test" that presumes to measure and rank our respective moral reasoning abilities, such as the Hahm-Beller Values Choice Inventory does (2). (The copyrighted HBVCI has been used to evaluate the moral reasoning abilities of over 10,000 athletes and coaches throughout North America. The conclusion cited above—that "athletes do not [morally] reason as well as nonathletes"—is said to be supported by studies using the HBVCI [2: p. 53].) While taking the HBVCI, suppose we came across a question that poses a morally dilemmatic scenario concerning whether or not it is ethical to commit good fouls.[9] The point here, of course, is not to debate the ethics of the good foul. Indeed, it is important at this juncture that we need not be so concerned with how either Fraleigh or Gough, as test-takers, would answer this question. What should primarily concern us is how Fraleigh and Gough's answers would be evaluated and ranked—scientifically and objectively evaluated and ranked, that is—by the moral development researchers who created and administered the HBVCI. The evaluation and ranking process, of course, will depend on what moral point of view these researchers bring to bear on our respective responses.

The HBVCI is expressly said by its designers to have a deontological moral foundation and thus is said to accord "higher scores" to those responses that "reflect a consistent use of principles and reasoning which can be universally applied" (2: p. 48). Given this deontological moral point of view, it would be unsurprising for us to conclude here that Fraleigh's (10) response would be accorded a higher score than mine, which, suffice it to say, would not be deontological in character. What are we to make of this conclusion? In one sense, of course, it is quite beside the point which of the two individuals actually ends up scoring higher on the HBVCI. The fundamental point remains the same whether we simultaneously evaluate two differing points of view or evaluate just one point of view in isolation: What are we to make of HBVCI-generated conclusions regarding a given individual's moral reasoning "score" on a given question, much less a given test? Will these scores be scientifically objective? Insofar as a deeply normative moral point of view—deontology—was used to evaluate such a question, it appears virtually tautological to conclude that the scoring process cannot be scientifically objective.

Moral development researchers in general do not in fact always make their moral points of view apparent as the HBVCI researchers themselves do. My point here is not at all to impugn or second guess motives, however, as if some researchers, unlike HBVCI researchers, conceal their moral points of view from us. Rather, my claim is simply that many researchers do not seem to see their theoretical constructs as entailing normative moral points of view. And in those cases when researchers, like those who developed the HBVCI, make their moral points of view apparent, they invariably argue (as did Kohlberg) that embracing a general moral perspective does not necessarily commit one to specific normative moral assumptions and thus does not preclude scientific objectivity. This argument, of course, is in large measure what HP1 is intent on challenging. Indeed, contrary to this argument, it seems if anything argued thus far comes close to being unarguable, it is this: Any moral evaluation process, scientific or otherwise, that involves measuring and *ranking* moral development according to a predetermined hierarchy of moral maturity necessarily entails inescapably normative moral assumptions that preclude scientific objectivity.

Nonetheless, we should inquire further: Is a theory of moral development in fact available, devoid of normative moral assumptions, that would allow researchers to evaluate responses to moral reasoning test questions in a value-neutral, non-normative, scientifically objective manner? This question does *not* merely ask whether researchers can give an objective description, for example, of Athlete A's point of view concerning the ethics of the good foul. Rather, it inquires whether a theory of moral development is available that can enable researchers to assess objectively whether Athlete A gave a more or less morally reasoned response (and then perhaps goes on to conclude more generally whether Athlete A is more or less morally developed). It would appear that *if* such a theory devoid of normative moral assumptions exists, it is either (a) a theory that would be useless at best and absurd at worst as it pertains to the evaluation of moral reasoning, or (b) a truly view-from-nowhere theory known solely to the mind of God.

Glossing (b) and focusing solely on (a), why would such a theory devoid of moral assumptions be useless at best and absurd at worst regarding the evaluation of moral development? We can begin to answer this question by noting that the typical line of argument given by moral development researchers in the developmentalism tradition in defense of objectivity usually involves an appeal to the distinction previously described between the *content* of moral reasoning and the *form* of moral reasoning. Thus it is purported by researchers that a theory of moral development can evaluate objectively in virtue of formal patterns of moral reasoning, without reference to or entailment of any specific normative moral content.

While there are a variety of effective ways to challenge this form/content line of defense, I will suggest one rather straightforward approach. We can begin by noticing with Carr (8) how this distinction can easily lead to

a quite perverse or bizarre view of moral reasoning, for surely the only really intelligible purpose that moral reasoning might be seen to have is to arrive at conclusions which are right rather than wrong or true rather than false; our judgments in moral matters . . . do not have the goal of exhibiting valid or invalid reasoning but that of guiding us towards conduct which is morally correct. (8: p. 163).

On one level, of course, there is little doubt that researchers can make good on the distinction between the moral content and the formal patterns of moral reasoning, especially in the sense of distinguishing between, for example, that Athlete A believes good fouls are unethical and that Athlete A gives deontological reasons in support of this belief. Hence I see no necessary and insuperable reasons why researchers would be debarred from the possibility of describing objectively that Athlete A so believes and so reasons. There is certainly nothing bizarre about this level of description.

However, it is crucial to notice that contemporary moral development research, perhaps in virtue of its commitment to developmentalist assumptions, is seldom content to leave the analysis at this descriptive level. Instead, this research invariably seeks to determine how well Athlete A morally reasons as such, or how well Athlete A morally reasons in comparison to Athletes B and C. But to justify this fundamentally different move by continuing to appeal to the form/content distinction is misleading, for it obscures the fact that the researcher is no longer merely describing that Athlete A defends his or her view of the good foul on deontological grounds. The researcher is now engaged in the deeply normative process of judging the form of the reasoning as good or bad, higher or lower, more or less mature on the basis of the correctness or the superiority of deontological standards of moral reasoning. The upshot here, of course, is that the researcher's "scientific" judgment(s) will necessarily entail normative moral assumptions concerning the correctness or the superiority of a given form of moral reasoning.

Thus, the moral development researcher would appear to be engaged most fundamentally in moral philosophy, not science. To avoid repeating further what has already been described concerning developmentalism's hierarchical schemes of moral maturity, suffice it here to ask: How else is one to meaningfully interpret the force of morally reasoning "well"—as in "athletes do not [morally] reason as well as nonathletes" (2: p. 53)—but in this deeply normative way?[10]

We can sum up the force of HP1 as follows: To the extent researchers attempt to determine how well Athlete A morally reasons concerning a given moral dilemma, their evaluation process will be inescapably moral theory-dependent. Importantly, to make such a determination, moral development researchers will necessarily embrace a normative moral theory that not only determines (a) the individual's evaluation of the correctness or incorrectness of a particular mode of reasoning but that also determines (b) whether or not a particular scenario is even to be seen as morally dilemmatic in the first place. Pincoffs (23) has argued convincingly concerning the latter insight that there are no theory-independent criteria of a moral problem. To embrace any moral theory—including the two most well-known modern moral theories, utilitarianism and deontological ethics—is "to hold to criteria that determine what is to count as a moral problem, not just to provide [a supposedly value neutral] means for approaching moral problems" (21: p. 50). (It is worth noting further that, for Pincoffs, since moral theory is necessarily tied methodologically to the presentation and evaluation of moral dilemmas in this deeply normative way, there can be no moral development "experts.")

Insofar as researchers in the developmentalist tradition are attempting to judge how well Athlete A morally reasons, it seems reasonable to suggest further that any given moral reasoning test designed by these researchers might suffer from deep-seeded systematic bias merely because of its normative design (i.e., the process of choosing which questions are to be deemed morally relevant and useful for test purposes). Any such test might be biased both in terms of its evaluation, and, more fundamentally, in terms of its morally value-laden design. If the claim is made that its design is *not* morally value-laden, then it appears the test's "construct validity" (as social scientists describe it)[11] would cease to exist; it would not—could not—involve a moral measuring.

Moreover, it will do no good for researchers to suggest that only very straightforward, cut-and-dry questions could be chosen, the answers to which are universally agreed upon. Even if one were to concede that such questions could be formulated—and there is very good reason to doubt they could be; *universal* agreement is very hard to come by—one could nonetheless deny the presumption of scientific objectivity. Indeed, even if one were to embrace the researchers' moral theory and accept both the moral relevance of the test questions and the moral scientist's evaluation of the respondents' answers to those test questions, one could still reject the researchers' claims of scientific objectivity. The enterprise would remain inescapably normative.

One last caveat in this regard worth noting: I am not implying, nor do I believe my arguments thus far entail, either moral subjectivism or moral relativism. The issue at stake with respect to HP1 most fundamentally involves the moral development researcher's presumption of scientific objectivity, not moral objectivity. At the very least, it must be admitted that there are no simple or unarguable segues between notions of moral objectivity and scientific objectivity. Neither would seem to follow necessarily from the other.[12]

IV

Intimately connected with the first Home Plate question, HP2 asks: To what extent can a science of moral development in sport be scientifically reductive?

In certain respects HP2 seems to be more fundamental than HP1 insofar as it asks us to consider the degree to which the reductivistic methods of science can even penetrate our moral lives—much less be objective about it—outside of discovering such things as incidences of drug abuse among Olympic athletes or merely describing the moral rationales given by athletes to justify their actions. The moral development researcher would seem to be confronted with a most daunting, if not insuperable, interweave of questions concerning scientific reductivism. In this final section, I will pose two sets of such questions, involving what I will term, on the one hand, "moral-theoretic reductivism," and on the other, "naturalistic reductivism." Both terms are meant to convey different aspects of scientific reductivism, the latter term merely being used to suggest how that science essentially seeks to explain in the simplest of ways and solely in terms of natural phenomena, and the former term being used to suggest the ways in which modern theories of morality tend to reduce morality to unitary, bedrock notions such as duty or utility. While moral-theoretic reductivism may not ordinarily be connected with issues of scientific reductivism, it is inextricably so connected as regards contemporary moral development research (and in largest measure for reasons described above concerning the inextricable relationship between developmentalist projects and normative moral theory).

Even prior to problems arising from the scientific method's overarching goal of explaining things solely in naturalistically reducible terms, there are considerable problems we can exploit arising from the reductive nature of the underlying moral-theoretic constructs appropriated by researchers for their moral development analyses. We may begin by noticing once again the way in which, for example, developmentalism's notions of higher and lower levels of moral reasoning—made popular by Kohlberg (19, 20)—are themselves significantly reductive concepts, circumscribing as they do moral development and moral reasoning in terms of a fixed and deeply presumptive hierarchy of moral growth.

Legions of writers have challenged such theoretically reductive concepts. To offer just two recent examples: James Q. Wilson has argued in his recent book, *The Moral Sense*, that "ranking moral stages from low to high does not capture the reality of many moral problems, which often involve choosing which of several moral sentiments ought to govern one's actions"; moreover, "the problem with . . . Kohlberg's stages is that they presuppose general agreement as to what constitutes the relevant universe within which a rule is to operate" (25: pp. 182, 183). Or, as Carr (8) has argued concerning Kohlberg,

> it is worth asking in relation to the features of moral development which Kohlberg claims to be invariant across cultures and universal in nature, why this should be so? Is this really a conclusion to which Kohlberg comes by empirical inquiry; is it indeed something that *could* be confirmed by empirical inquiry? . . . This seems unlikely. . . . There is an ineliminable *a priori* dimension to the character of . . . Kohlberg's purportedly empirical investigations into the growth of moral reasoning. (8: p. 163)

The point in citing these two examples is not merely to exploit the problematic nature of Kohlberg's own model but to challenge all such modern moral-theoretic reductions entailing crystallized, hierarchical stages of moral reasoning. Indeed, given the apparent "ineliminable *a priori* dimension" associated with developmentalism's empirical research, it would appear that these theoretical reductions themselves are quite unlikely to ascend any "higher" epistemologically than the "stage" of moral-philosophical assumption. What we are presented with in the name of science appears to be ideology in scientific guise.

Taking another cue from Pincoffs (23), we can further call attention to the problematic reductive nature of modern moral-theoretic constructs by noticing the ways in which they reduce moral reasoning to bedrock notions such as duty or utility, and, consequently, determine by theoretical fiat what is morally relevant—and eliminate by fiat what is not—thereby legislating the form that moral reflection should take (23: p. 5). Pincoffs sums up the problem by concluding:

> Ethical theory is essentially a modern invention. To say that one has a theory of ethics is to say . . . that one has a systematic account of the 'foundation' of moral judgment. Theories are made to be applied to cases, to provide the principles and procedures by which moral problems can be resolved. . . . [These] theories are more threats to moral sanity and balance than instruments for their attainment. They have these malign characteristics principally because they are, by nature, reductive. They restrict and warp moral reflection by their insistence that moral considerations are related in some [fixed] hierarchical order. (23: p. 5)

Given this reductivistic character of modern moral theory and especially moral development researchers' employment of it, we can begin to ask several questions concerning what moral considerations were and were not eliminated by researchers in the process of drawing their conclusions. Consider, for example, another ongoing moral development in sport research project focusing on athletes' moral reasonings about athletic aggression (3, 4, 5, 6). The moral-theoretic construct undergirding this project is essentially liberalist and contractarian in its moral assumptions: "Moral maturity is marked by an ability to consider and integrate varying moral perspectives in a dialogical process oriented toward reaching consensus about moral rights and responsibilities" (3: p. 20). Thus, an athlete would be said to have reached the highest level of moral development when he or she "gives equal recognition to all parties' interests" (4: p. 70). Based on this theory of moral development, these researchers have concluded that, for instance, "sports that are typified by . . . [aggressive] acts may tend to attract participants with lower levels of moral reasoning . . ." (3: p. 25).

What moral considerations were and were not eliminated by these researchers on the way to reaching this "scientific" conclusion? In the final analysis, the only moral consideration that was *not* eliminated for the purpose of quantifying an athlete's moral maturity was the degree to which an athlete gave equal consideration to the interests and needs of all relevant parties. Within this particular moral-theoretic construct, fair and balanced compromise—based on a liberalist conception of equality—is the sole overarching criterion of moral evaluation (3, 4, 13, 14).

Aside from obvious questions regarding how one is to construe a "fair" compromise or "relevant" parties or even an "aggressive" act,[13] we can press the following sorts of questions concerning the justification for reducing moral development to a liberalist, contractarian notion of "equal recognition to all parties' interests": Did the moral-theoretic construct employed by these researchers deem any specific contextualities of a given dilemma involving athletic aggression as morally relevant (e.g., what if a particular aggressive act is an accepted part of the game's ethos, like the "bean ball" in professional baseball once was)? If a coach reasoned consequentially about aggressive acts, would consequences even count in the researchers' analysis (e.g., what if a coach justified a personal act of aggression against one of his or her players on the grounds that it was in that player's long-term best interest)? Were an athlete's religious convictions considered morally significant (e.g., what if an athlete's competitive rationale is "an eye for an eye")? What if an athlete appealed to a sense of duty or loyalty to his or her coach (e.g., what about an athlete who reasons, "As a player on this team, I have a responsibility to do what my coach tells me to, even if someone else finds it questionable")?

These questions, of course, can take us right back to the objectivity issue: How does one go about choosing, for scientifically objective ends,

among competing, fundamentally incompatible, and variously reductive moral-theoretic constructs? Is this anything that can be decided on empirical grounds? Even philosophical grounds? Aside from the objectivity issue, however, we can press this basic concern with moral-theoretic reductivism itself: What evidence is there—empirical or philosophical—for assuming that moral reasoning (or moral development, for that matter) can be or should be reduced by philosophical fiat to a hierarchy of moral stages, much less to any one unitary common denominator such as equality, duty, or utility? What if moral reasoning ultimately cannot be reduced in these ways? What if, for example, moral reasoning is in fact far more intimately bound together with moral character, resulting in an extremely complex moral psychology, as many moral philosophers throughout history have believed? How could unitary notions of equality or duty or utility possibly account for this complex moral psychology on the way to concluding, in scientifically objective fashion, that sports involving aggressive acts tend to attract participants with lower levels of moral reasoning?

Seguing to issues of naturalistic reductivism, we can begin by making an interesting historical observation about the great deontic, moral-theoretic reductivist, Immanuel Kant. For the sake of argument, let us assume for the moment that Pincoffs' argument about moral-theoretic reductivism is overdrawn, that there does exist for the moral development in sport researcher a moral theory that provides reasonable justification for its particular reductivistic explanation of moral reasoning. Let us assume further that this moral theory is Kant's own deontological moral theory. What is striking is that while Kant's moral theory does indeed represent one of the great exercises in moral-theoretic reductivism, reducing moral reasoning to a notion of duty to universal principles, Kant's own moral theory unequivocally precludes attempts to scientifically measure moral development as developmentalists presume to do.

According to Kant (16, 17), morality and

moral reasoning are *not* empirically ascertainable; they are part and parcel of our "noumenal" selves that lie beyond any empirical knowledge we may have of our inner "phenomenal" nature.[14] In Kant's view, any attempt to scientifically measure, for example, moral reasoning ability would constitute an attempt to force a reduction onto a realm of inquiry for which purely naturalistic concepts would be grossly inadequate and distortive. Kant's own misgivings with empirical investigations into moral development brings to light the following question: What consequences follow, for example, when a methodology based on reductivistic naturalism is employed to evaluate a complex state of affairs that many believe entails nonnatural or supernatural phenomena?

For the long list of those who embrace the existence of such phenomena—and such a list would certainly include the diverse and towering names of Plato, Aristotle, Aquinas, and Kant, among others—much of the skepticism that can arise with respect to the possibility of scientifically evaluating moral development arises precisely because the prevailing paradigms of moral development research so often deny, ignore, or, at best, underemphasize, non-naturalistically reducible entities and concepts that are at the heart of many moral frameworks: freedom, conscience, soul, God, mind, moral consciousness, moral purpose, practical wisdom, states of character, virtues, and the like. If there are indeed grounds, as many believe, for embracing notions such as these within one's view of morality generally and of moral development or moral reasoning in particular, then *ipso facto* there will likely be good grounds for suggesting that the conclusions of modern moral development research are grossly myopic at best and (especially when combined with issues concerning HP1 above) ideologically pseudo-scientific at worst.

It is admittedly quite difficult to ascertain in the moral development in sport literature (as in the moral development literature generally) precisely to what extent credence is given to the possible existence and casual importance of non-naturalistically reducible notions such as these. I suspect, however, that for the present argument there is no great need to so ascertain. For insofar as contemporary moral development research continues to see itself as "science" (conventionally understood), it will by definition continue to restrict the scope of its investigations to what (presumedly) can be reduced and explained in purely naturalistic terms.

Of course, nothing I have argued concerning HP2 has shown that Kant was correct, that researchers are debarred from the possibility of reducing and explaining moral development in purely naturalistic terms. But HP2 has been offered in part for the purpose of showing (or perhaps reminding) that a view such as Kant's still remains a distinct and viable possibility. Indeed, arguments against the possibility of reducing and explaining moral development in purely naturalistic terms need not even proceed from metaphysical commitments as sharply dualistic as Kant's— or Plato's or Aquinas' for that matter. Such arguments may, for example, proceed generally along less dualistic lines not unlike Aristotle's: Ethics does not admit of the kind of quantitative precision and exactness that is possible in other sciences, if for no other reason than that the very nature of ethical inquiry resists quantitative analyses;[15] it invariably resists, and at times precludes, scientific reduction because the moral life, even a state of character, is an extraordinarily complex entity that simultaneously and necessarily requires reference to several different aspects of human experience, including emotion, reason, and self-determination, as well as the overall complex social character of that experience.

V

Toward the end of a provocative essay entitled "The Ethical Aims of Social Inquiry," sociologist Robert Bellah trenchantly and summarily criticizes the contemporary paradigms of social science as moral science in the following way:

The sterility of much sociological research is due to moral infantilism and not to the fact that "our science is still young." In particular, reductionism as an explanatory device is due to moral timidity or cowardice or—this is why reductionism and determinism are so attractive to the young—plain moral confusion. That people are "animals maneuvering for advantage" or that "ideals and beliefs . . . are to be explained in terms of . . . interests" are assertions that are often enough true. But in the interesting and decisive cases, these reductionistic statements are false, and as generalizations they are worthless, if not pernicious—pernicious because to the degree that they are rhetorically persuasive, they act as self-fulfilling prophecies. They help create the moral cretinism they describe. . . . Power and meaning always go together in human action, and we forget it at our peril. (15: pp. 379–80)

Bellah's incisive words offer a resounding exclamation point to the questions I have raised. At the very least, the burden of proof seems to be overwhelmingly on researchers to demonstrate how and in what ways a "science" of moral development in sport can be *either* scientifically objective *or* can be meaningfully susceptible of reductivistic methodologies. Until that time when the moral development researcher can so demonstrate, I would suggest, first, that we regard reductivistic generalizations like "athletes morally reason at lower levels than nonathletes" not unlike Bellah encourages us to regard them, and, second, that we proceed ever so cautiously with our inquiries lest we force the character of moral inquiry in sport to be scientific in ways that it cannot.

Notes

1. For a sampling of the more recent social scientific literature treating morality and sport, see especially Bredemeier and Shields (3, 4, 5, 6), as well as Beller and Stoll (2), Kleiber and Roberts (18), Ogilvie and Tutko (22),

and Stevenson (24). Bredemeier and Shields (4) provides, among other things, an excellent, up-to-date discussion of the literature.

2. Bredemeier and Shields (3, 4, 5, 6), whose extensive social scientific investigations into sport and moral development are based on Norma Haan's constructivist approach, concede that values are implicit in moral-scientific inquiries but argue that these values are methodologically and manageably "thin," and, thus, do not preclude scientific objectivity. See especially Bredemeier and Shields (3: pp. 17–18), as well as Haan (13, 14). In a forthcoming paper, "Moral Development Researchers' Quest for Objectivity: On Whether the Judgment-Passing Hurdle Can Be Cleared" (in press), I reject the Haanian-cum-Bredemeier/Shields approach by arguing there are always "thick" values invariably present in moral scientific investigations that preclude scientific objectivity.

3. For an excellent general discussion of the issues surrounding positivistic notions of both social science-as-science and social science-as-moral science, see Haan, Bellah, Rabinow, and Sullivan (15).

4. As I shall henceforth use the terms and their cognates, "morality" and "ethics" are used synonymously.

5. See, for example, Beller and Stoll (2) and Bredemeier and Shields (3, 4, 5, 6). For an extensive bibliographic listing, see Bredemeier and Shields (4: pp. 227–57).

6. For a recent, critical treatment of development psychology, see Burman (7). Of particular interest is chapter 13, which exploits several of the moral assumptions permeating developmentalism's models of moral development.

7. In this regard, see Cortese (9: p. 80).

8. I include "ethically," even at the risk of sounding a bit morally pedantic, primarily to suggest that the business ("scientific" or otherwise) of evaluating or judging moral behavior can itself always and justifiably be open to substantive ethical evaluation and scrutiny.

9. I have chosen to illustrate my point here using the good foul primarily because of the notable discussion regarding it among philosophers of sport. I am unaware as to whether or not the HBVCI has in fact ever posed a question involving the good foul.

10. An anonymous reviewer suggested that perhaps researchers could objectively determine, say, that Athlete A's reasons are more "morally sophisticated" than Athlete B's, but it seems to me we would be confronted with precisely the same situation just described, for we would still be in the position of appealing to a given norm or set of norms to evaluate Athlete A and B's level of moral sophistication. Who decides which formal pattern of moral sophistication is correct or the most superior? How could one decide this in scientifically objective fashion?

11. As Cortese (9: p. 80) defines it, "Construct validity, the most significant kind of test validity, measures the extent to which the fundamental structures or constructs that the instrument is believed to measure do in fact explain a subject's efficiency on the test."

12. Contrary to Kohlberg (19).

13. As these researchers inform us, "when the word [aggressive] is employed by social scientists it definitely carries negative moral connotations," (3: p. 15). One can, of course, ask why it should have a negative connotation, but, aside from this line of inquiry, one can especially press the issue of normativity: Is this not a clear example of researchers embracing and employing assumptions with deeply normative moral content?

14. Take Kant's notion of moral duty, for example, entailing as it does freedom of the will. For Kant, any attempt to apply empirical method to the notion of moral duty will be an attempt to put free will under certain reductivistic, casual laws that would preclude the will from being free, and, hence, would preclude the possibility of moral action.

15. See Aristotle (1: pp. 1094b12–28).

Bibliography

1. Aristotle. *Nichomachean Ethics.* Translated by Hippocrates Apostle. Grinnell, IA: The Peripatetic Press, 1984.

2. Beller, Jennifer M., and Stoll, Sharon K. "A Moral Reasoning Intervention Program for Student Athletes." *Academic Athletic Journal,* (Spring 1992), 43–57.

3. Bredemeier, Brenda Jo, and Shields, David L. "Athletic Aggression: An Issue of Contextual Morality." *Sociology of Sport Journal,* 3 (1986), 15–28.

4. Bredemeier, Brenda Jo, and Shields, David L. *Character Development and Physical Activity.* Champaign, IL: Human Kinetics, 1995.

5. Bredemeier, Brenda Jo, and Shields, David L. "Divergence in Moral Reasoning About Sport and Everyday Life." *Sociology of Sport Journal,* 1 (1984), 348–357.

6. Bredemeier, Brenda Jo, and Shields, David L. "Moral Growth Among Athletes and Nonathletes: A Comparative Analysis." *The Journal of Genetic Psychology,* 147:1 (1986), 7–18.

7. Burman, Erica. *Deconstructing Developmental Psychology.* New York: Routledge, 1994.

8. Carr, David. *Educating the Virtues.* New York: Routledge, Chapman and Hall, Inc., 1991.

9. Cortese, Anthony. *Ethnic Ethics.* Albany, NY: State University of New York Press, 1990.

10. Fraleigh, Warren. "Why the Good Foul is Not Good." *Journal of Physical Education, Recreation & Dance,* (January 1982), 41–42.

11. Gough, Russell. "Moral Development Researchers' Quest for Objectivity: On Whether the Judgment-Passing Hurdle Can Be Cleared." In *Ethics and Sport.* Edited by M.J. McNamee and S.J. Parry. London: Chapman and Hall, 1996 (in press).

12. Gough, Russell. "Ranking Athletes' Moral Development: The Hubris of Social Science as Moral Inquiry." *The National Review of Athletics,* (January 1994), 1–15.

13. Haan, Norma. "Can Research on Morality Be 'Scientific'?" *American Psychologist,* 37:10 (October 1982), 1096–1104.

14. Haan, Norma. "Two Moralities in Action Contexts: Relationships to Thought, Ego Regulation, and Development. *Journal of Personality and Social Psychology,* 30 (1978), 286–305.

15. Haan, Norma, Bellah, Robert N., Rabinow, Paul, and Sullivan, William M. (Eds.). *Social Science As Moral Inquiry.* New York: Columbia University Press, 1983.

16. Kant, Immanuel. *Critique of Practical Reason.* Translated by Lewis White Beck. New York: Macmillan Publishing Co., 1985.

17. Kant, Immanuel. *Foundations of the Metaphysics of Morals.* Translated by Lewis White Beck. New York: Macmillan Publishing Co., 1985.

18. Kleiber, Douglas A., and Roberts, Glyn C. "The Effects of Sport Experience in the Development of Social Character: An Exploratory Investigation." *Journal of Sport Psychology,* 3 (1981), 114–122.

19. Kohlberg, Lawrence. "From Is to Ought: How to Commit the Naturalistic Fallacy and Get Away With It."In *Cognitive Development and Epistemology.* Edited by T. Mischel. New York: Academic Press, 1971, 151–235.

20. Kohlberg, Lawrence. *The Philosophy of Moral Development: Moral Stages and the Idea of Justice.* New York: Harper and Row, 1981.

21. Nagel, Thomas. *The View from Nowhere.* New York: Oxford University Press, 1986.

22. Ogilvie, Bruce C., and Tutko, Thomas A. "Sport: If You Want to Build Character, Try Something Else." *Psychology Today,* (October 1971), 61–63.

23. Pincoffs, Edmund. *Quandaries and Virtues: Against Reductivism in Ethics.* Lawrence, KS: University of Kansas Press, 1986.

24. Stevenson, Christopher L. "Socialization Effects of Participation in Sport: A Critical Review of the Research." *The Research Quarterly,* 46:3 (1975), 287–301.

25. Wilson, James Q. *The Moral Sense.* New York: Macmillan, 1993.

Questions for Consideration

1. Explain precisely what Gough means by "moral-theoretic reductivism" and "naturalistic reductivism."

2. What is the normative (or "is-ought") fallacy? How does it relate to Gough's overall argument?

3. If you find Gough's overall argument persuasive, what changes should be made to the empirical literature that is presently investigating moral development? If not, where does Gough go wrong?

28 An Epistemologist Looks at the Hot Hand in Sports

Steven D. Hales
Bloomsburg University

In this reading, Steven D. Hales critically examines much of the relatively recent literature on having a hot hand in sports that essays to explain away the phenomenon completely. This research is informative, he concedes, but the conclusions drawn by researchers are consistent with another, more attractive, interpretation.

Hales breaks up the "evidence" against hot hands into a series of three separate arguments. Each of the arguments has a flawed premise. Two of the arguments stack the deck in defining "success" as a gross statistical anomaly. The other assumes that "success breeds success" is an indispensable condition for having a hot hand. Neither of these, Hales argues, is necessitated.

What the evidence does show is that past success in sport is no guarantee of future success. In this sense, shooting baskets differs little from rolling dice. Still, this merely exacts that certain conceptualizations of hot-hand performance be ruled out by fiat. This does not, however, preclude having a hot hand. What is essential to hot-hand performance is its deviation from mean performance. Though this is coextensive with chance performance, it is not fully explicable by it. There is a crucial, phenomenological element that we miss. The phenomenon of hot-hand performance is every bit as real as the feeling of heat when molecules frantically move around.

Recently psychologists and statisticians have mooted a surprising thesis: Despite nearly uni-

Reprinted, by permission, from Steven D. Hales, "An Epistemologist Looks at the Hot Hand in Sports," *Journal of the Philosophy of Sport* XXVI (1999): 79–87

versal beliefs to the contrary, there is no such thing as streak runs of success in sports; no one has ever been on a roll or had hot hands. Here are some sample statements of the view. According to Stephen J. Gould, "Everybody knows about hot hands. The problem is that no such phenomenon exists" (4: p. 465). Thomas Gilovich, Robert Vallone, and Amos Tversky write, "Probably . . . most players, spectators, and students of the game believe in the hot hand, although our statistical analyses provide no evidence to support this belief" (3: pp. 302–303). Robert M. Adams concurs, "Even though virtually any basketball player, fan, or commentator would scoff at the notion that the 'hot hand' is only an illusion, the present data confirm that" (1). Skeptical claims that no one knows as much as they think they do are a very familiar theme in epistemology. It is noteworthy, then, that no epistemologist has heretofore investigated the criticisms of the hot hand doubters named above. Moreover, this skeptical view about hot hands has burst the seams of scholarly arcana and into the public eye.[1] Getting the matter right is thereby doubly important. In this paper, I will defend the view that there is such a thing as hot hands in sports, that they are ubiquitous, and that players and observers are often right in identifying them.

Stephen J. Gould writes, "We believe in 'hot hands' because we must impart meaning to a pattern—and we like meanings that tell stories about heroism, valor, and excellence . . . and we have no feel for the frequency and length of sequences in random data" (4: p. 468). While this may be true at some deep level, it is certainly not the reason sports participants cite on behalf of hot hands. Anyone who has ever played a sport will cite internal, phenomenological, felt experience in favor of hot hand phenomena. An interviewer once asked five-time Wimbledon champion Bjorn Borg, then at the height of his powers, what it felt like for him when he was playing at the top of his game. Borg replied that he felt that he could do anything—put the ball on a dime at any angle, anywhere on the court, at the speed he chose, with the spin he wanted. Similarly, Purvis Short, of the NBA's Golden State Warriors, has said, "You're in a world all your own. It's hard to describe. But the basket seems to be so wide. No matter what you do, you know the ball is going to go in" (9: p. 16). A seemingly natural understanding of these attitudes is expressed in saying that a player has a better chance of making a shot after having just made his last two or three shots than he does after having missed his last two or three shots. Ninety-one out of 100 basketball fans polled believe this statement; that is, they believe that success breeds success (3: p. 297).

This idea is the driving force in the first argument against hot hands, an argument endorsed by all the skeptics (1, 3, 4, 9, 10).[2]

Argument I: Success Does Not Breed Success

1. Someone has a hot hand only if they are performing in a way that success breeds success.[3]
2. Empirical study indicates that success does not breed success in sports.
3. Therefore there are no hot hand phenomena in sports.

Players on the Philadelphia 76ers believed that success breeds success, just as the fans did. When they feel hot, their confidence increases. In interviews the 76ers often said that after making a few shots in a row they "know" that they are going to make their next shot, that they "almost can't miss." This has a plausible a priori explana-

tion: When a player realizes that he is hot, his confidence in his subsequent shots increases. He relaxes and doesn't overplay his shots. He just gets in the groove and hits them smoothly and cleanly. Regrettably (and remarkably) the data fail to bear this out. In fact, they show a slight negative correlation between a hit and the following shot.[4] The 76ers were just a little bit likelier to miss after hitting three in a row. The converse is true too—they are likelier to hit after a cold period of zero or one hit in the last four attempts than they are to continue missing. Moreover, this finding held true for both field goals (shot under defensive pressure) and free throws (shot without such pressure), and in studies of the New Jersey Nets and the New York Knicks (3: pp. 303–304). Knowing this, we can refit our a priori explanations: When a player realizes he is hot, he tends to push the envelope and attempt more difficult shots, believing that, as Borg said, he can do anything he wants. Such a strategy then leads predictably to failure. How wonderfully malleable a priori explanations are!

One might conclude that the empirical results show that the internal phenomenology of being hot is unreliable. As one group of researchers puts it, "The sense of being 'hot' does not predict hits or misses" (3: p. 310). Other critics have intimated even more strongly that since one's own felt experience is not wholly trustworthy, it adds nothing to the statistical study of the hot hand.

This is not the best explanation of the data. A more plausible interpretation is that the 76ers are mistaken in thinking they can tell when their streaks of success will end. That is, either they erroneously believe that their prior success is casually efficacious into the future, or they reason inductively that having made several shots in a row is compelling evidence that they will make the next one. It is of course interesting that neither form of reasoning turns out to be reliable, but this does not undercut the players' beliefs that they are hot. The problem isn't that their internal feelings of having a hot hand are wrong, but rather that they have a misguided optimism about how long their streak will last, and where they are in it. They believe that they are towards the beginning or in the middle of a success streak. In fact, they may well be at the end of one, and their next shot will be a miss. The streak could be 3 successful shots in a row, or it could be 10. Upon sinking the 3rd basket, a player may well feel confident about hitting the 4th, believing hopefully that he is at the beginning of a 10-streak instead of at the close of a 3-streak. What the data show here is not that one's internal sense of being hot is wrong but that there is no telling how long one will remain hot. The streak could end at any time, and induction from past success fails. Joe DiMaggio couldn't feel a cold front coming in as he walked onto the baseball field on July 17, 1941. In fact, maybe he felt pretty optimistic about making a hit. Who wouldn't, having made a hit in each of 56 previous games?[5] Does this positive attitude, however statistically mistaken or epistemically unjustified, show that Joe wasn't hot during his streak? Of course not.

The second skeptical argument tries a different tack: Hot hands are not undone by the failure of streaks to cause or predict future success, but by the very predictable nature of the streaks themselves.

Argument II: Streaks Are Predictable

1. Someone has a hot hand only if their streak of success is statistically unlikely.
2. Empirical study has shown that there are no statistically unlikely streaks of success in sports.
3. Therefore, there are no hot hand phenomena in sports.

Supporters of this argument include Gould (4) and Gilovich, Vallone, and Tversky (3). There has been much fervor over whether the second premise of this argument is true. Gould endorses

it except for "one major exception, one sequence so many standard deviations above the expected distribution that it should never have occurred at all: Joe DiMaggio's 56-game hitting streak in 1941" (4: p. 467). Debate over this "exception" has generated a small cottage industry devoted to computing the exact probability of DiMaggio's streak (e.g., 2, 7, 11). The noteworthy thing about Gould's claim concerning the DiMaggio streak is that unless one accepts the first premise in Argument II, there is no reason at all to take the streak's statistical unlikelihood as proof of hot hands. It is this premise that requires critical scrutiny.

Precisely how unlikely does a streak of success need to be before we are prepared to count it as a legitimate instance of hot hands? Gould sets the bar extremely high, admitting only what he calls "the most extraordinary thing ever to happen in American sports" (4: p. 467). But why should we follow suit? It is not as if DiMaggio's streak was somehow so momentous that its description is beyond the reach of probability. Every run of success will be more or less probable given the average skill of the player involved. Let us suppose that DiMaggio's streak was very improbable—one recent estimate is that there was only a 1/3700 chance of its occurring (11). So not only did DiMaggio have hot hands, they were white hot. Yet is there no room for red hot hands, or even mildly warm ones? Suppose someone achieves a sports success with only 1/100 chance of its occurring. The only reason to think that it does not have every bit as much of a claim to being a case of hot hands as the DiMaggio streak is the acceptance of Gould's arbitrarily high standards. Every sporting event will fall somewhere on the curve, whether it is four standard deviations from the mean or only one. It is nonsense to suppose that there is something "off the chart." There is no principled way of parsing the above-average portion of the curve into "hot hand" and "not hot hand" zones.

Thus if "unlikely" in premise one is made strong enough, a la Gould, then the argument is bound to be right. Yet this smacks of thievery. If "unlikely" is weakened enough, then every positive deviation from the mean will count as a case of hot hands—some are just hotter than others—premise two will be false, and the conclusion will not follow. We could fix our improbability standard for hot hands at some precise level by fiat, but there is no principled way of doing so. Argument II is therefore of little interest. It is sound only if we agree to a purely arbitrary account of how statistically unlikely a streak of success must be to count as an instance of hot hands.

Argument III: The Frequency of Streaks Is Predictable

1. Someone has a hot hand only if the number of successes in a row exceeds that predicted by chance.
2. Empirical study has shown that there are no success streaks whose frequency exceeds the number predicted by chance.
3. Therefore, there are no hot hand phenomena in sports.

Defenders of this argument maintain that a run of success "can be properly called streak shooting only if their length of frequency exceeds what is expected on the basis of chance alone" (3: p. 296). Each sequence of hits (successful field goals in basketball, for example) or misses (unsuccessful ones) is counted as a "run." In any random process, there will be such runs. For example, suppose I flip a fair coin a dozen times. Despite the fact that the probability of tossing heads is .5, if I were to get exactly HTHTHTHTHTHT, this would be quite surprising, as the probability of this sequence is only .00024, whereas the probability that it is some other sequence is .99975. If I do the flipping and get a sequence other* than strict heads/tails alternation, this should be completely expected, because it is so enormously

likely that I get such a result. Suppose I do the flipping and get, say, HHHTHTHTTHHT. While this specific result is not so likely, it is very probable, as we have seen that a result like this one is obtained. Such sequences are noticeably "clumpy," containing bursts of heads and runs of tails. In addition, the example just given shows more heads than tails. In the long run, the number of heads and tails will approach equivalence but not in short stretches like this.

In defense of the second premise of Argument III, Gilovich and his colleagues studied field goals made by the Philadelphia 76ers during 48 home games in the 1980–1981 season, and also conducted a controlled study of 26 Cornell University basketball players. In examining these data sets, the question posed was whether any player had more success runs than one would expect from flipping a coin. The answer was no.[6]

Suppose the chance of making each basket is .5 (obviously this value has to be computed on a player-by-player basis). If a player shoots 16 rounds of four shots per round, on average only one of these rounds will be a run of four hits ($.5^4$ = 1/16). The same is true of coin tossing; on average four heads will come up once every 16 rounds of four flips. This does not mean that making baskets is nothing but chance. To borrow an example from Gould, Michael Jordan will get more runs of four in a row than Joe Airball because his average success rate is higher, and Jordan's average success rate is higher because of his superior skill, effort, talent, and the usual sporting virtues. Suppose Jordan shoots field goals with a .6 probability of success. About one out of eight sets of four shots will be four hits in a row ($.6^4$). If Joe, on the other hand, is only half as good from the field as Jordan, making .3 of his field goal attempts, he will get four straight roughly only once every 125 attempts ($.3^4$). Nothing besides probability is needed to explain the pattern of runs. Therefore, Argument III concludes that there is no such thing as a hot hand.

While these are interesting empirical findings, Argument III is unsound. The problem is neither the way the study was concluded, nor the way the numbers are calculated. As in the second argument, the error is in the first premise, which is problematic in several ways. First, prima facie, this is a strange requirement for a hot hand. One might instead conclude that an unusual number of success streaks shows *streakiness*—a player who runs hot and cold. Gilovich and his colleagues also conclude that contrary to popular perception, players are never streaky, but this is a different matter from having hot hands. The other, more vital problem with the first premise is that it incorporates the same arbitrariness that we saw in Argument II. To what extent should the number of streaks deviate from statistical expectations in order for it to count as hot hands? There seems to be no nonarbitrary place to draw the line. Do we draw it at statistical significance? At three standard deviations from the expected distribution? As with the "statistically unlikely" criterion of Argument II, any number of streaks can receive a statistical modeling. Some patterns of success runs are just considered less probable than others. The common thread in Arguments II and III is that essential to the hot hand is success beyond what is to be expected from a chance process. This is the root error.

Arguments II and III are on the right path in one sense: They correctly link having a hot hand with the nature of streaks. My contention is that a hot hand just *is* a streak or run of success, with no arbitrary restrictions on how rare or improbable it must be. If Michael Jordan hits 10 free throws in a row, he *does* have a hot hand, even if statistically this is a reasonably likely occurrence given his skill as a player and the large number of free throws he shoots. Even if after hitting those 10 free throws in a row Jordan misses the 11th, and empirical study tells us that his success with the first 10 made it no likelier that he would make the 11th, this is no reason to think that he didn't have a hot hand. Gilovich and his colleagues write, "Evidently, people tend to perceive chance shooting as streak shooting" (3: p. 311). This is entirely right. There are then two possible

conclusions to draw: (a) The skeptics are mistaken in distinguishing between chance and streak shooting, and (b) everyone else is wrong in thinking that there is such a thing as streak shooting. The skeptics, naturally, opt for the second. But I argue that there are good reasons for choosing the first conclusion, not the least of which is that such a view preserves and explains the widespread belief that players have hot hands.

The hot hand critics have to assume an error theory. They maintain that people are just uniformly mistaken in believing that they ever have a hot hand and always wrong in believing that others do. The skeptical view is not just that success makes people too optimistic about future success, or that the internal sense of being hot is sometimes wrong. Rather, the skeptics maintain that it is always wrong. This is a bitter pill to swallow. Sure, sometimes people are universally wrong about things that seem compelling; the history of science is replete with instances. The sun's motion in the sky and the evidence of design in the universe are familiar examples. Nevertheless the preservation of widespread antecedent belief is one desideratum in theory choice (6. pp. 66–67). Conservatism is not a *sine qua non*, but we should jettison widely held, intuitively plausible beliefs only if this is mandated by a clearly superior theory to the one in which our beliefs are embedded. The hot hand skeptics have not met this condition.

To take another example, suppose I flip a fair coin a dozen times and get three tails in a row. This is better than average, since the mean is .5. There is a clear sense in which it was luck that I tossed three tails in a row (good luck if that's what I wanted, bad luck if not). I had a "hot hand" for tossing tails and can detect my hot hand through observation. Of course this does not imply that the fourth toss was likelier to be heads or that probability cannot explain why I got three tails in a row. The fact that success in sports has been shown to be assimilable to a coin-tossing model gives an interesting conceptual result: Certain potential analyses of hot hand are shown to be empirically inadequate. This does not show that all analyses of hot hand are empirically inadequate. Indeed, Gould's recognition that being hot has to do with the nature of streaks, and the admission of Gilovich and colleagues that ordinary people do not discriminate between chance and streak success runs are important indicators of the correct analysis.

One possible objection here is that a distinction should be drawn between above-average success runs due in some identifiable sense to the player's skill and effort, and those runs due to fortuitous deviant casual mechanisms. Only the former, goes the objection, are genuine examples of hot hands. Tossing five consecutive tails in a row with a fair coin is not an act of skill. Neither is birdieing several holes in a row at golf through a series of bizarre shots and circumstances. Are these legitimate examples of hot hands? I feel the pull in both directions. My inclination is to say that hot hands are simply above-average success runs, however they are accomplished. I think this accords best with our everyday expressions of running hot or being on a roll. Yet even if one insists on adding a clause requiring this success to be the result of some appropriate causal mechanism, my central point remains untouched. The core element of having hot hands is deviation above mean performance—not success breeds success, extreme statistical unlikeliness, or somehow outpacing chance, as the skeptics contend.

What of the phenomenology of hot hands? Does my analysis of hot hands give short shrift to the importance of the basket seeming wider or the sense of things slowing down? I do not think so. Unlike the skeptics, I take seriously the phenomenology of hot hands and the observation of hot hands. When people believe they have a hot hand, they may well be usually right. When they are right, their internal sensation of being hot represents the world: They are shooting above their norm, serving better than average, punting deeper than usual, deviating above

the mean. This may all be within the bounds of normal statistical variance, but that only serves to explain the phenomenon. I am arguing that the nature of hot hands involves above-average success, whereas at best the phenomenology of feeling hot constitutes evidence for having hot hands. Whether the sense of being hot is an all-or-nothing quality, whether it comes in degrees, and how well it correlates to actual success in performance are matters for further study. We should not assume a priori either that the internal phenomenology of hot hands is an infallible indicator of actually being hot, or that every episode of hot hands is accompanied by an internal recognition of it. The empirical studies are right in taking hot hands to be an empirical, quantifiable matter.

There are also valuable practical lessons to be learned from the studies. For example, coaches who give instructions that a hot player be given the ball more or see more court time may be making a costly error. Statistically the hot streak could end at any moment. Thus the strategy of "give it to the hot player" is no better than that of a Vegas gambler who, having won her last three blackjack hands, bets the house on the fourth. However, the lesson the authors of these studies draw—that there are no hot hands—is wrong. Gamblers often speak of streaks of luck or running hot or being on a roll. Does this imply that they think some force other than chance (skill, or perhaps divine intervention)[7] is at work? Some may, although surely professional gamblers would not think of such a streak as anything other than a chance distribution of success. This hardly prevents them from reasonably commenting on a night's success as being a run of luck or referring to themselves as having been hot. In other words, they knowingly assimilate streak shooting (of dice, say) to chance shooting. The two may be coextensive, but the former is not eliminable in favor of the latter. Rather, the latter is an explanation of, or an analysis of, what is understood by "streak."

Nietzsche wrote, "Because something has become transparent to us, we think it will no longer offer us any resistance—and are then amazed when we discover we can see through it but cannot go through it! It is the same folly and amazement as overcomes the fly in the face of a pane of glass" (5: p. 444). The skeptics have done much to make hot hand phenomena transparent, but the glass is still there. They argue that empirically there is no more to hot hands than a predictable distribution of success runs that receives an easy statistical modeling; hence, hot hands are a "statistical illusion." This professed view is similar to arguing that temperature is nothing but the frenetic motion of molecules,[8] and therefore, there is no such thing as heat, nor can humans tell when something is cold by touch alone. The explanation of a phenomenon alone does not eradicate it, as we should have well learned from recent philosophy of mind and cognitive science.

In sum, there are three prominent arguments that conclude there are no hot hands in sports. The first argument of the hot hands critics creates a tradition in the very act of destroying it. By making "success breeds success" a necessary condition of having hot hands, the critics have established a previously undefended and barely articulated account of hot hands, only to demolish it. Instead I have argued that there are good reasons to reject "success breeds success" as a requirement for having hot hands. While it is true that many players believe that future success is more likely when they are already hot, either this is only a belief that their current "hot" state has causal efficacy into the future, or it is inductive reasoning that their current high rate of success is evidence of future success. Yet neither disjunct makes "success breeds success" part of the concept of having hot hands.

The second two arguments offered by the hot hand critics are of a well-known skeptical pattern: Set the standards for knowledge of X extremely high, then show that no one meets those standards. The canonical reply to this strategy, of which I availed myself, is to reject those standards in favor of more modest ones that charitably preserve our claims of knowledge. The skeptical insistence upon exceedingly rare streaks or statistically remote numbers of streaks as being the only legitimate instances of hot hands is arbitrary and severe. I have argued that "being hot" denotes a continuum, one that is nothing other than deviation from the mean itself. And this obviously comes in degrees.

So what is proven by the hot hand studies? Some conclusions correctly drawn by the skeptics include (a) having a hot hand does not increase the chance of success for one's upcoming shot; (b) players who believe that their recent run of successful shots increases the chance of making their next shot are unjustified in this belief; (c) players perceived as streaky do not have more success runs than is statistically expected; and (d) having a hot hand is not the result of a causal mechanism beyond the laws of probability. Unfortunately, the skeptics erroneously infer that the previous results mean that there are no hot hands and that everyone is wrong in thinking otherwise. Instead, I have argued that being hot does not have to do with the fecundity, duration, or even frequency of streaks. It has to do with their existence. The conclusions to be drawn are (a) one has a hot hand when one is playing better than average; (b) players often known when they are playing better than average; and (c) observers can often tell when players are playing better than average. This judgment of countless fans, coaches, and players is vindicated.

Notes

1. It made the front page of the *New York Times*'s science section (8), for example.

2. It should be noted that Waldrop accepts the analysis of hot hand as success breeds success, but he gives a somewhat different explanation of what accounts for fans' belief in the "statistical illusion" of hot hands. This difference is not relevant here.

3. The authors on this topic do not make the logical status

of this premise clear. In particular it is hard to tell whether statistical unlikelihood is supposed to be both necessary and sufficient for having a hot hand or just a necessary condition. In this and subsequent proposals, I assume, weakly, that the proposal is offered as a necessary condition.

4. Following several authors on this topic, I am using "hit" as a generic term for successful performance.

5. Don't think that DiMaggio's failure to get a hit in the 57th game was to be expected because his long streak of luck increased the probability that he would soon miss. This is the Reverse Gambler's Fallacy.

6. To be fair, in a later article, Tversky and Gilovich back off a bit and say that their data only shows that there is no hot hand in basketball and that they are not generalizing to all sports (9: p. 21). This modesty is not shared by all the hot hand skeptics and is not relevant to the arguments I will make against the skeptical view. So, for simplicity, I am slightly overstating their latest view.

7. Perhaps we shouldn't underestimate the popularity of providential appeals to explain what is obviously chance. Recently the local paper recounted a highway accident in which a truck driver was killed. The police blocked off the area, preventing traffic until the accident site was cleaned up. During the cleanup, a small plane in distress crash-landed on the strip of cleared-off highway. The pilot of the plane was quoted as saying that God had saved them by providing a place to land when they needed it. The pilot apparently found it unremarkable that God would regard assassinating a hapless truck driver to be the most expedient way of saving the plane's passengers. I sometimes wonder what the truck driver's family thought about the divine will.

8. A view, by the way, that must be in error—at least if we take seriously physicists' claims that the very early universe was quite hot, and it was only after it cooled a bit that molecules could form.

Bibliography

1. Adams, R.M. "The 'Hot Hand' Revisited: Successful Basketball Shooting as a Function of Intershot Interval." *Perceptual and Motor Skills.* 74:934, 1992.

2. Berry, S. "The Summer of '41: A Probabilistic Analysis of DiMaggio's 'Streak' and Williams's Average of .406." *Chance.* 4(4):8–11, 1991.

3. Gilovich, T., Vallone, R., and Tversky, A. "The Hot Hand in Basketball: On the Misperception of Random Sequences." *Cognitive Psychology.* 17:295–314, 1985.

4. Gould, S.J. *Bully for Brontosaurus.* New York: W.W. Norton, 1991.

5. Nietzsche, F. *Daybreak.* (R.J. Hollingdale, Trans.). Cambridge, UK: Cambridge University Press, 1881.

6. Quine, W.V.O., and Ullian, J.S. *The Web of Belief.* New York: Random House, 1970.

7. Short, T., and Wasserman, L. "Should We Be Surprised by the Streak of Streaks?" *Chance.* 2(2):13, 1991.

8. Staff, Science Desk. "'Hot Hands' Phenomenon: A Myth?" *The New York Times.* April 19, 1988: C1.

9. Tversky, A., and Gilovich, T. "The Cold Facts About the 'Hot Hand' in Basketball." *Chance.* 2(1):16–21, 1989.

10. Wardrop, R.L. "Simpson's Paradox and the Hot Hand in Basketball." *The American Statistician.* 49(1):24–28, 1995.

11. Warrack, G. "The Great Streak." *Chance.* 8(3): 41–43, 60, 1995.

Questions for Consideration

1. Of the two possible interpretations of the data, that streak shooting does not exist and that streak shooting is just a matter of chance, Hales opts for the latter. Reconstruct fully and assess Hale's reasons for this interpretation.

2. Does Hales's phenomenological interpretation salvage our commonsense notion of just what is involved in having a hot hand?

Chapter Five

Sport and Society

Heroism
Gender
Race
Pedagogy
Sport in Society

29 Is Our Admiration for Sports Heroes Fascistoid?

Torbjörn Tännsjö
University of Göteborg, Sweden

Torbjörn Tännsjö argues in this reading that his excitement over sporting events like the Olympic Games is based not on respectable enthusiasm but on fascism—a fascism that is at root nationalistic. What is worse, he says, is that this "fascistoid" enthusiasm is the very root of our admiration of individual athletes also.

The basis of nationalism, Tännsjö states, is a focus on abstract entities, such as flags, emblems, and even nations. In celebrating such entities, individual athletes acquire a secondary status and they become replaceable.

The problem, Tännsjö argues, is that only individuals, not abstract entities, have value. In placing entities over individuals, as when we endorse nationalism, we indulge a fetishism that gives life to lifeless symbols. Thus, he asks, is nationalism concerning sports of this nature?

Tännsjö argues that nationalism in regard to sports is only harmful when political nationalism is strong. But commercialism and the money accessible to individual athletes have begun to render the nationalism of sports innocuous. Our interest is now in individuals and their personal accomplishments. Herein lies a more dangerous fanaticism, he declares, which is at bottom nazi: love of strength and contempt for weakness. While nationalism is only accidentally associated with Nazism, contempt for weakness (and praise of strength), in contrast, are at its very core.

In celebrating our winners and condemning our losers, we morally evaluate athletes. Winners are better people; losers, inferior. The former deserve more of the good things in life, while the latter do not. This is nazi ideology.

To remedy this severe problem, Tännsjö believes, we ought to resist moral evaluation of athletes—especially our praise of strength and condemnation of its lack. And even though our immediate feelings toward winners and losers may have their roots in human constitution, we should look to education in order to stay such dispositions.

Reprinted, by permission, from Torbjörn Tännsjö, "Is Our Admiration for Sports Heroes Fascistoid?" *Journal of the Philosophy of Sport* XXV (1998): 23–34

Introduction

Already looking forward to the Olympic Games in Sydney at the turn of the millennium, I try to recollect what happened last time in Atlanta. How did I react? I realize that once again I was swept away with enthusiasm and admiration for those heroic athletes who had stretched the limits of what is physically possible for humans to achieve. Some have run faster than anyone has done before. This is true of Michael Johnson. Others have excelled and shown that, contrary to what should have been expected, they are—still—invincible. This is true of the greatest of them all, Carl Lewis. My query is: Is my enthusiasm for Johnson, Lewis, and all the other athletic heroes, respectable? Upon closer examination, my answer is *no*. My enthusiasm is not respectable. On the contrary, it is of a fascistoid nature.[1] So the problem is really what to do about it. The problem is pressing, for my attitude toward the Games is not exceptional. I share it with a great many other people who walk this planet. This is why the games were so widely broadcast.

Many people have pointed out that there is something unhealthy in much of the public interest in team sports on an elitist level. There was a time in many European countries when the Workers' Movement fought actively against the growing interest in sports. This concern has withered, but the rationale behind it remains relevant. As a matter of fact, team sports have often been used by nationalist governments to create a chauvinist zeal in their own populations. This zeal has rendered easier the formation of totalitarian government, oppression of minorities at home, and imperialist adventures abroad. National sports teams have become emblems of their respective nations. These facts are rather obvious. It is also obvious that some of the interest that most people take in elitist sports events is nourished by these kinds of nationalistic sentiments. The interest as such reinforces the nationalism. This is indeed a vicious circle. But what about the public interest in the individual athletes in the Olympics? Should it be condemned because it reinforces an unhealthy nationalism?

To some extent it certainly does. Even individual athletes may become the target of these kinds of sentiments. Johnson and Lewis have reinforced U.S. nationalist sentiments. I am, on my part, more interested when a Swede succeeds in the Olympics, than when someone else does. But this cannot be the only source of my interest in the Olympic Games. For my main interest is in the achievements of people like Johnson and Lewis. So perhaps much (the main part) of my admiration for their achievements is, after all, respectable? Perhaps much of the general interest taken in the games is respectable?

If this were the case, there would be room for optimism. For it seems to be part of the received wisdom that nationalism within sports withers. When big business in the form of international enterprises enter the arena, in the manner of sponsoring, advertising, and selling and buying television rights, national governments have to go. Often, the foreign NHL professionals do not bother to take part with their respective national teams. Instead of nationalism and interest on the part of the public in one's "own" team, admiration comes for the achievement of the outstanding individual. Local teams turn into corporations. And these corporations are seen as places where the outstanding individual can excel. However, this interest in the achievement of the outstanding individual is really no better than our (perhaps outmoded) nationalistic interest in the fate of "our" own team. Or so I will argue in this paper.

My thesis is that our admiration for the achievements of the great sports heroes, such as the athletes that triumph at the Olympics, reflects a fascistoid ideology. While nationalism may be dangerous and has often been associated with fascism, what is going on in our enthusiasm for individual athletic heroes is even worse. Our enthusiasm springs from the very core of fascist ideology.

Note that my thesis is not that there is anything fishy about the motives of the athletes themselves. I say nothing about this. Nor do I condemn those who organize sports events, those who train young people to become members of the athletic elite, or those who profit from the games, and so forth. In the present context, the *exclusive* target of my criticism is what goes on within the enormous, world-wide public, watching sports, usually through television. My interest is in the values entertained by you and me, we who tend, over and over again, to get carried away by such events as the Olympic Games.

Traditional Team Sports on an Elitist Level

Before developing my main argument, let me briefly comment on why it is a bad thing to have nationalistic values expressed and reinforced by publicly broadcast sports events. If this is a kind of danger in relation to elite sports that is becoming outmoded, and so it seems to be, it might be interesting to reflect on what it is we are getting rid of. When we see this more clearly, we are on firmer ground in our investigation of the new kind of danger we exchanged for the old one.

The main problem with nationalism is its orientation towards abstract symbols: the flag, the team (seen as an emblem), and yes, even the nation conceived of abstractly. When such entities are celebrated, the individual tends to become replaceable. The nation can get strong, it can be successful, even if each and every one of its citizens suffers. This individual suffering need not matter in the very least to the nationalistic ideology. In a similar vein, when the team becomes a representative of the nation, *its* individual members tend to become replaceable. When our football or soccer heroes are successful, we cheer for them. When they fail "us," we despise them.

This way of regarding our sports stars as representatives of our country, conceived of abstractly, fits with a common view of the military force. It may easily spread and permeate all the relations between people in a country. Young women are treated as potential instruments that shall safeguard the strength and survival of the nation; young men are viewed merely as potential soldiers, and so forth.

One might object that this is only a description. What is actually *wrong* with celebrating abstract symbols? Why not stress the interests of the nation rather than the interests of individual beings? Why not stress the survival of a race or species rather than of individuals making it up?

The answer is, as far as I can see, that abstract entities as such are of no value. What matters, ultimately, from a moral point of view, is what

happens to individuals capable (at least) of feeling pleasure and pain. Only *individual* values are genuine. In order to be good absolutely, something must be good *for* an individual, capable of feeling (at least) pleasure and pain.

This is not to say that there exist no positive examples of nationalism. The U.S. struggle, say, for national independence was a worthy aim. But in those times, nationalism had a content. It was possible to see over and above the flags and the marches a point to the struggle, a point relating, in the final analysis, to respectable individual interests (in avoiding oppression, of various kinds). Even so, the flags and the marches are dangerous things. When the struggle is over, they tend to stay with us and live their own lives in the form of fetishes.

I will not try to argue the point in the present context that all respectable values are individual. I have discussed it in detail in *Hedonistic Utilitarianism* (2). It is here simply taken for granted. This means that if someone claims that the strength of his or her nation is of value in itself, he or she makes a value mistake. This mistake is dangerous if it leads to actions where individual interests actually get sacrificed for the sake of abstract, symbolic values. And this kind of sacrifice is the rule rather than the exception when a nationalistic ideology gets a firm hold of the members of a nation—in particular, if the nation in question does not face the least *threat* from any other nation.

Even if this be conceded, it might perhaps be argued that the kind of nationalism fostered by the public interest in team sports events is innocent. It might even be argued that nationalism in relation to sports is a good replacement for political nationalism (i.e., the kind of nationalism that is truly dangerous). It is better if people live out their nationalism in front of their television sets or on the seats around the sports arenas, than if they channel their nationalism through political parties and movements. Only in the latter case does their nationalism pose a real threat to important values.

I do not believe that this argument is tenable. The nationalism fostered by our interest for our "own" national team, and the nationalism we exhibit on the political arena, tend to reinforce each other. In particular, in periods where political nationalism is strong, what happens on the sports arenas tend to become politically important. There is only a small step from being a soccer hooligan to joining a fascist organization modeled on the Hitler Jugend. I will not develop this line of thought, however. The reason for not developing it has already been adumbrated. I think the common observation, that nationalism is becoming less and less important in relation to sports, is correct.

Why is nationalism within sports becoming less important? This has to do with commercialization and internationalization. The best sportsmen and the best teams earn enormous amounts of money. They can afford to allow themselves a considerable independence from political authorities and interests. They can take liberties with their own sports organizations. They rely rather on their own impresarios than on elected authorities of the Olympic Committee. However, when the old nationalism gives way, it gives way to something no less problematic. Let me now develop this main theme of my paper.

Contempt for Weakness

Nationalism, or chauvinism, has sometimes been thought to be a defining trait of nazism. However, in his seminal book, *Our Contempt for Weakness,* Harald Ofstad has argued, convincingly it seems to me, that the nationalism of the Nazis was only a contingent fact. To be sure, Hitler put the German nation before all other nations. And he put the so-called Aryan race before all other races. However, the hard core of nazism was different. The hard core of nazism was a contempt for weakness. This is shown by Hitler's reaction when the Third Reich broke down. In Hitler's own opinion, the defeat showed, not that there was something basically wrong with the Nazi ideology, but that there was something basically wrong with the German Nation. The German

Nation had proved to be weak rather than strong. So eventually Hitler came to feel contempt for it (1: p. 24).

My thesis is: When we give up nationalism as a source of our interest in elite sports activities, when we give up our view of individual sportsmen and teams as representatives of "our" nation, when we base our interest in sports on a more direct fascination for the individual winners of these events—we move from something that is only contingently associated with nazism (nationalism) to something that is really at the core of nazism (a contempt for weakness).

Obviously, in my argument, a premise is missing. It is one thing to admire the person who wins the victory, who shows off as the strongest, but another thing to feel contempt for those who do not win (and turn out to be weak). I believe, however, that in doing the one thing, we cannot help but do the other. When we celebrate the winner, we cannot help but feel contempt for those who do not win. Admiration for the winner and contempt for the loser are only two sides of the same Olympic medal.

This is not to say that those who win the contest feel contempt for those who don't. It is one thing to compete and to want to win and quite a different thing to admire, as a third party, the winner. My argument relates to those who view sports, not to those who perform. Those who perform may well look upon each other as colleagues. They may feel that they are doing their job, and that is all. The winner may well feel respect for the loser. Or the winner may entertain any other feelings. It is not part of my project to speculate about this at all. My argument does not relate to the responses of the athletes; it relates to *our* responses to what they are doing. We, who comprise the public *viewing* the sports events, are the ones who admire the winner and feel contempt for the loser. If we are sincere in our admiration, and we often are, we cannot *help* but feel contempt for the losers. We would be *inconsistent* if we did not feel any kind of contempt for the losers, once we sincerely admire the winner.

To see why this is so we ought to think critically about *why* we admire those who excel in the Olympics. Our feeling is based on a value judgment. Those who win the game, if the competition is fair, are *excellent,* and their excellence makes them *valuable;* that is why we admire them. Their excellence is, in an obvious manner, based on the strength they exhibited in the competition. And the strength they exhibit is "strength" in a very literal sense of the word.

But our value terms are comparative. So if we see a person as especially valuable, because of his excellence, and if the excellence is a manifestation of strength (in a very literal sense), then this must mean that other people, who do not win the fair competition, those who are comparatively weak, are *less* valuable. The most natural feeling associated with *this* value judgement is—contempt. It is expressed in the popular saying: Being second is being the first one among the losers.

Contempt can take very different forms, of course. It may be of some interest in the present context to distinguish between three forms of contempt. First, contempt can take an aggressive form, as was the case with the Nazis. They wanted to exterminate weakness (by exterminating those who were weak). Second, contempt can take a negligent form. We try not to think at all about those for whom we feel contempt. We "think them away." We treat them as nonexistent. We do not care about them at all. Third, contempt can assume a paternalistic form. We want to "take care" of those "poor creatures" for whom we feel contempt. Common to all these reactions (all based on the idea that some individuals are of less value than others) is a tendency not to treat those who are considered less valuable with respect. They are not treated as full persons.

The surer we are that "we" are among the strong ones, among those who are valuable, the more prepared we are, I conjecture, to adopt the paternalistic reaction to those whom we consider weak. The more we fear that we might really belong to the weak ones, I also conjecture, the stronger our inclination to treat the weak ones negligently, as nonexistent—or even aggressively, with hatred: We want to exterminate them (i.e., *make* them nonexistent).

This is what is going on when enthusiastically we stay up half the night watching the athletes compete. To be sure, to some extent what takes place does so only in a symbolic way. We admire Carl Lewis for his excellence, and we feel some contempt for those who fall behind. However, we know that we would never stand a chance of beating Carl Lewis. Does this mean that we realize we are among those who are weak? It means, probably, that we fear this. But many of us believe we have other skills that compensate for those Carl Lewis possesses. Even if we are not physically as strong as he is, we may possess other kinds of strength. We may excel in respects that are (in our own opinions) more valuable than "strength" in the literal sense of the word.

But what if we do not? I believe that some of us may fear that we might fall on *all* relevant accounts. Those of us who do, I conjecture, are those who cheer most loudly for people like Carl Lewis.

What respects are relevant? This question is not possible to answer in a general manner. The Nazis had one (rather vague) notion about what kind of strength was important. We may have a differing view. As a matter of fact, each person may have his or her own opinion about this. But there is really no *need* to give a general answer to the question: What kind of strength is important to exhibit? As soon as we hold one opinion or another about it, we are vulnerable to the kind of argument I want to level in the present paper. Any person who is eager to be strong, who is prepared to feel contempt for those who are weak, and who fears that he or she may belong to those who are weak—any person who feels that those who are in any sense "strong" are better than those who are "weak"—are open to the criticism that he or she has fallen prey to the core of Nazi ideology.

There is a kind of betterness that is moral. A person, S, is (morally) better than another person, P, if and only if S is more praiseworthy, admirable, or deserving of the good things in life than is P. This notion is given a fascistoid twist when moral betterness is conceived of in terms of *strength*.

But must we feel contempt for those who are less successful (valuable)? Can we not just admire them less? I think not. For there are normative aspects of the notion as well. Those who are less valuable have to stand back when some goods (and evils) are to be distributed. And when resources are scarce, treating one person well is tantamount to treating another person badly. In a sports situation, this is clearly the fact. The setting is competitive. Olympic medals (and the money and reputation that go with them) are a scarce resource.

If we want to be sure that we do not get carried away by our admiration for winners, we ought to resist the very idea of moral excellence and betterness. In particular, we ought to resist the idea that moral excellence consists of *strength*.

To be sure, the idea of moral excellence in general and of moral excellence as (at least partly) a matter of strength of some kind, is an idea with deep roots in the history of philosophy, playing a crucial role for example in the ethical thinking of Aristotle. Yet an ethical theory can be constructed without having recourse to it. The utilitarian tradition, for example, bears witness to this.

Of course, even a utilitarian must concede that a life can be better or worse, for the person who lives it, depending on the content of the life, as experienced "from inside"; but this does not mean that a *person* can, as such, be (morally) better or worse. A certain kind of character can be more conducive to happiness than another kind of character, and should for this reason be encouraged; however, this has nothing to do with moral worth. In particular, it has nothing to do with strength of any kind. And the idea that strength is a proper grounds for admiration, the idea that underlies our fascination for the winners of sports events, is one that we ought to resist.

Objection: Similarities in the Arts and Science

Those who are prepared to concede that there is something to the argument stated above may still want to protest. They may want to argue like this. Even if there is something fishy about the reaction of the sports public to athletic achievements, it is unfair to single out sports for exclusive concern. After all, even within science and the arts we meet with the same phenomenon. Some people exhibit an unusual scientific or creative skill (strength). They make important contributions to science or create valuable pieces of art. They are then met with admiration. Does that not mean we value these persons in a manner similar to the way we value successful athletes? And if we do, does this not mean we think of those who are less successful in these areas as less valuable? Do we not exhibit contempt for weakness, then, when, for example, we give Nobel Prizes and the like to some "outstanding" persons?

At least to some extent I think this argument sound. And to the extent that it is sound, we ought to be ashamed of ourselves. But I think it sound only to some extent. For, to be sure, when we become enthusiastic about scientific and cultural achievements, we *need* not have scientists or artists as the focus of our attention. We can admire Frege's theories and Mozart's operas without feeling that Frege and Mozart are valuable persons. We can value the *products* of their ingenuity, not their genius itself. We can say truthfully that what they produced is of the utmost value but still retain the view that *they* are not more valuable than anyone else. They are merely *instrumental* to things of importance in themselves.

To be sure, even within science and the arts there are ugly manifestations of the phenomenon I have criticized within sports. Some people tend to get carried away with their admiration for lonely, heroic "geniuses" in the development of human science and art. Philosophy is not free of this phenomenon. There are people who speak with admiration of philosophers such as Nietzsche, Heidegger, and Wittgenstein, not because of any clear thoughts they have absorbed from the writings of these philosophers, but because they feel confident that these philosophers are especially "deep" and "inspired" thinkers. All this, like the actual Nazi ideology, is part of the legacy of the romanticism of the 19th century. However, while this phenomenon within science and the arts may be seen as a kind of corruption, it belongs in a more essential way to sports.

We can and we ought to admire the *products* of skillful scientists and artists, not these persons themselves, at least not because of their skill. (Perhaps some of them deserve our admiration because of their moral qualities, but Frege is not among those.) However, we cannot but admire the winning athletes themselves or else give up our interest in watching sport. Or can we? Why not consider the sports as simply a (very popular) part of human culture, where the results (products) of the individual achievements are what count?

Objection: We Admire Results, Not Athletes

I believe that there may be something to the objection that sport is not very different from art. In both cases there is excitement over the results of people's strivings. However, while the results are often, and should always be, the main focus of our attention within the arts, sports are different. There is an aesthetic aspect even to sport, to be sure. Some people are met with admiration not only because of their strength, but also because of the beauty with which they perform. Juantorena ran more beautifully than anyone before him. Why not say that it is the beauty of his running we admire, not himself? We admire the beauty in his running in the same way that we admire the beauty in a piano concerto by Mozart.

This line of argument is tenable to some ex-

tent. The Juantorena example is not a very good one, however. Had Juantorena not also been, for the time being, the fastest, we would not have remembered him for the beauty in his way of running. In the final analysis, what counts is who breaks the tape. But in some team sports, such as soccer, the aesthetic dimension may be considered more important. I believe that it might be of considerable importance, particularly among skilled audience members. After a match, they can discuss for hours the beauty in a single rush, irrespective of the outcome of the match. Remember that during the Chinese Cultural Revolution, there was a period when soccer competitions were reviewed with no mention of the outcome. At least among the majority of the sports public, this policy met with little approval and soon had to be changed.

As a rough approximation, then, we may say that, though there is room in science and the arts for admiration both of scientists and artists for their skill (their metaphorical "strength") and for their results, within sports there is room only for admiration of performers. The "results" they produce are not genuine; they are mainly results of measurements, measurements intended, first of all, to establish who won. But winning (a fair competition) is only a means. It is a means to prove excellence. So what we admire in sports is really the excellence shown by the winner.

Take away our admiration for the winner of the genetic lottery, who has proved his superiority in a big sports manifestation, and you take away most of our interest in the manifestation. This is true in particular for those of us who are not experts in the field and who tend to get carried away only now and then when we are informed by media that something remarkable is going on in a sports arena (like the Olympics).

But could it not be argued that what we admire is not really the *excellence* of the winner but what the winner has achieved *given* his natural endowments? And would not this kind of reaction on our part be morally more acceptable?

There is a grain of truth in this objection. And this grain of truth explains that there is a public interest in such things as female competition, competition between seniors, competition between handicapped persons, and so forth. When someone wins the Olympics for handicapped persons and we admire him or her for winning, we admire the achievement (given the constraints). In spite of the obstacles, this person made quite an achievement, we concede. However, the relatively weak public interest in such competitions, as compared to the interest in competitions of the absolute elite, shows that this kind of public interest in sports is of minor importance.

As a matter of fact, I suspect that there is even an element of contempt for weakness underlying many people's interest in this kind of handicap sport—but that it takes a paternalistic form. We do not take those who perform in handicap competitions seriously. We encourage them to go on but only in order that they develop into something less worthy of our contempt. In any case, if we are forced to choose, what we, the vast majority of us, want most to watch, are competitions involving the *absolute* elite, not the Olympics for handicapped people.

Moreover, even if we are prepared to admire people who have worked hard, at least if they succeed in the competition (and the ability to work hard need not be anything that must be explained with reference to genes), I believe we will admire even more a person who excels *without* having worked hard for it. If a middle aged member of the audience who never exercised unexpectedly walked down from the stadium and joined the Olympic 10,000-meter race and, because of superior natural talent, defeated all the finalists, the success would be formidable. Our admiration for this person would be unlimited. It is talent (which can be genetically explained), not achievement, we admire most. The point of the contest is to show who has the most superior talent.

This elitism of ours is also revealed by our way of reacting to doping. We want the competition to be fair. We are not prepared to admire Ben Johnson only because he has run 100 meters faster than anyone before or after him. Why? We suspect that Carl Lewis is genetically more fit than Ben Johnson. This is why we condemn Ben Johnson. He cheated.

But how do we know that Carl Lewis did not cheat too? Perhaps he was only more clever and got away with it. If doping were allowed, we would avoid *this* problem. We would not need to fear that the winner was not the strongest individual. If everybody were free to use whatever drugs they find helpful, then the crucial test, the competition, would show who is most fit. The competition is then fair.

For this reason, it is not at all implausible that doping, the deliberate use of drugs intended to enhance our strength, will rather soon be permitted. At least it is plausible to assume that drugs that do not pose any threat to the health of those who use them will be allowed. This seems only an extrapolation of a development that has already taken place. After all, there was a time when training was looked upon with suspicion. No one questions training today, and all athletes engage in it. Then came a time when *massive* training, on a professional basis, was condemned; I can vividly recollect the disdain with which swimmers from Eastern Germany were regarded by Western media during the 1960s. These days are also gone. Today, all successful athletes train on a professional and scientific basis. To the extent that all have the same resources at their disposal (an ideal we are far from having realized, of course, because of social differences or differences between nations), the competitions remain fair. But if training, even on a professional and scientific basis is all right, then why not accept doping as well, at least so long as the drugs used are not especially dangerous to the user?

If we were to permit such performance-enhancing drugs, we would no longer need to entertain the uneasy suspicion that the winner used prohibited drugs and managed to get away with it. We could then watch the games in a more relaxed manner.

A special problem, of course, is posed by the

possibility of genetic engineering. What if those who win the Olympic Games in some not too distant future are not winners in a natural genetic lottery but genetically *designed* to do what they do? Would we still be prepared to stay up half the night to watch them perform? Would we still be prepared to admire those who make the greatest achievements? Would we still be prepared to cheer for the winners?

My conjecture is that we would not. Interestingly enough, then, genetic engineering may come to pose a threat not only to elitist sport but to the fascist ideology I claim underlies our interest in such sports.

Objection: Contempt for Weakness Is Human Nature

A fourth objection to my thesis that our admiration for sports heroes is at its core fascist needs to be addressed. Is not our admiration for strength, and a corresponding contempt for weakness, only natural? Are these feelings, moreover, not natural as well? Hence, is not a criticism of them misplaced? Since our nature is given to us by evolution, and since that nature dictates that we admire strength and feel a contempt for weakness, it hardly seems fair to criticize the possession and expression of these kinds of feelings.

This objection is flawed, but it renders necessary some important distinctions. It may be true that most of us are, by nature, competitive. We compete with each other, and we enjoy doing so. But there is nothing wrong in this, or at least, this competitiveness is not the target of my criticism. The competitiveness might go to an unsound extreme in certain circumstances, of course, but I do not intend to say that our competitiveness, as such, is immoral. Our competitiveness engenders important achievements, and it is a source of excitement and joy. It is also, of course, a source of disappointment and dissatis-

Is our admiration for sports heroes like former tennis great Billy Jean King and our contempt for nonwinners based on a natural instinct or disposition? Ed. David Ashdown/Hulton/ Archive

faction. However, this is only as it should be; without *some* disappointment and dissatisfaction our lives would feel rather empty. I can readily concede this, for my criticism, in the present context, is not directed against competitiveness as such, nor to competitiveness in sports. I accept that scientists compete in a struggle to be the first to solve a certain problem, and I accept that athletes compete to win an important race. What I protest against is the admiration we show for the winner, be they scientists or sports heroes—and the corresponding contempt we feel for the losers. This reaction of *ours*, not the natural pride felt by *the winner himself*, is immoral. And the stronger our enthusiasm for the winner (and the stronger our corresponding contempt for the losers), the more immoral our reaction.

However, is not also this admiration for the winner, and the corresponding contempt for the loser, only natural? Well, this may depend on what we mean by calling a disposition "natural." Here we need another distinction.

One way of talking about "natural" dispositions is as follows. A certain disposition is "natural" if nature (evolution) has provided a species with it in the form of a blind *instinct*. If this is how the disposition is given to the species, then there is no room for blame when individual members of the species act on it. There is no point in blaming the lion for preying on the antelope. Under the circumstances, the lion can't help doing what it does. And it cannot help finding itself under the circumstances, either.

Another way of taking the idea that a certain disposition is "natural" is as follows. Evolution has provided the species with the disposition, but not as a blind instinct. Individual members of the species tend to act on it to be sure. And there exists a good evolutionary explanation *why* they do. However, sometimes they do not. When they don't, we need an explanation for this fact, an explanation cast, not in terms of evolutionary biology, but rather in cultural or psychological terms.

It seems highly implausible that our admiration for strength and contempt for weakness is natural in the former sense. Human beings are not driven by instinct when they cheer for the winners of the Olympics. If people choose not to do so, then they often succeed. Some people do choose, for one reason or another, not to join in, when the public hysteria is raised by main sports events. And they succeed in not joining in. So this is a possible course of action.

However, it might well be that we need an explanation why they do not join in, and the explanation may have to be cast in psychological or cultural terms. For snobbish reasons, say,

they do not want to go with the crowd. Be that as it may, they *can* stay out of the events and they *do*.

So it might well be that our admiration for strength and our contempt for weakness, exhibited most prominently in our reaction to sports, is natural in the sense that it has been given to us by evolution: It takes education of some kind to avoid developing it. From the evolutionary perspective, it might have been advantageous to show contempt for weak individuals. It might have been advantageous to cheer for those who are skilled in aspects that relate to human survival. To borrow a phrase, if you can't beat them, join them. In particular, it might have been advantageous, alas, to despise handicapped children, not to feed them—and even to kill them, rather than to raise and nurture them.

This does not show, however, that such admiration for strength and contempt for weakness is morally acceptable. On the contrary, such kinds of contempt are *not* acceptable. They are morally evil. And to the extent we can through education counteract the influence of them, we ought to do so.

This raises an important and strongly contested question. If contempt for weakness is immoral, in particular when it is directed against individuals who are "weak" in a very literal sense of the word (people who are physically or mentally handicapped), does this mean that selective abortion (of fetuses with defective genes) is not acceptable?

It does not. It does mean, however, that some grounds for selective abortion are not respectable. It is not respectable to abort a fetus because one feels a "natural" contempt for the kind of handicap one knows it will be born with. Instead, one ought to convince oneself to accept and treat with respect individuals with this handicap. However, in rare circumstances, it can be obligatory to abort a fetus selectively, because one knows that the child it will develop into, if carried to term, will lead a miserable life, one filled with pain and devoid of pleasure. But then the abortion should not be carried out because of contempt for this (possible) child but, rather, out of compassion.

There may also exist selective abortions that are morally legitimate on the account that they save the family from unnecessary burdens, or, simply, because it allows a healthy child to be born rather than a handicapped one.

However, in all these kinds of selective abortions, as has been repeatedly and correctly noted by representatives of the handicapped people's movement, there is a risk that we might well be acting on an immoral contempt for weakness, rather than on a morally admirable compassion. Selective abortions provide much room for rationalization and wishful thinking. This is something we should always keep in mind.

Conclusion

I conclude, then, that our enthusiasm for our sports heroes is fascistoid in nature. It is not respectable. Our admiration for strength carries with it a fascistoid contempt for weakness. There are relatively innocent (paternalistic) forms of this contempt, but there is always a risk that they might develop into more morally problematic kinds, where we choose not to acknowledge those who are weak, or to reject them as unworthy of our respect, or worse yet, to seek their extermination (as did the Nazis).

It is true that sports are not the only place where this admiration for strength and a corresponding contempt for weakness is exhibited. We see the same phenomenon in the sciences and the arts as well. And when we do, what we see is no less morally depraved than what is exhibited in our enthusiasm for the winners of the Olympics. However, there is a rough but crucial difference between sports, on the one hand, and science and the arts, on the other. In sports, admiration of the winner is essential. If we do not admire the winners, and admire them *qua* winners of a genetic lottery, there is no reason to

watch the games at all. For the aesthetic dimension of sports, however important it might be as an additional value, commands very little interest of its own. If our admiration for strength and contempt for weakness were somehow purged from sports, there would, I contend, be little reason to watch them. There will be little reason to watch sports competitions.

This is not to say, of course, that there will be little reason to take part in sports. We can all take joy in the exercise and excitement they provide. There is always someone to compete with. (If with no one else, one can always compete against oneself.) But if we get rid of our unhealthy enthusiasm for strength and corresponding contempt for weakness, no one will be able to arrange the kind of Summer Olympic Games that we witnessed in Atlanta in 1996.

Recommendation for the Future

Suppose we are now convinced that there is something wrong with our enthusiasm for sports heroes like Carl Lewis and Michael Johnson—what should we do about it?

Well, our enthusiasm for sports is much like an addiction. How do we defeat addictions? There is little help in imposing sanctions and using force. We cannot compel a person not to smoke, at least not if there remains a physical possibility for him or her to continue the habit. The only way to make someone give up a bad habit is to *convince* the person in question that the habit *is* bad. Then a possibility opens up that this person might, himself or herself, overcome the habit. This may take a lot of strength, skill, time, control, and cunning. However, eventually many people succeed in giving up even deeply entrenched bad habits. I suppose that something of the kind is what we ought to do with regards to our enthusiasm for sports heroes.

In sum, we ought to realize that our enthusiasm for sports heroes is fascistoid in nature. That is why it is no exaggeration to say, in closing, that if we are to grow as moral agents, we need to cultivate a distaste for our present interest in and admiration for sports.

Bibliography

1. Ofstad, H. *Our Contempt for Weakness. Nazi Norms and Values—And Our Own.* Stockholm, Sweden: Almqvist and Wiksell, 1998.

2. Tännsjö, T. *Hedonistic Utilitarianism.* Edinburgh, Scotland: Edinburgh University Press, 1998.

Note

1. My neologism *fascistoid* should be understood in analogy with the word *schizoid*. Just as something schizoid tends to or resembles schizophrenia, something fascistoid tends to or resembles fascism.

Questions for Consideration

1. Do you think our attitude toward competitive sport today is nazi in the manner Tännsjö states?

2. What are the three main objections Tännsjö anticipates toward his thesis? Does he adequately address them?

3. Why does Tännsjö believe that the contempt-for-weakness thesis may have its roots in biology? What would be the *moral* implications of this thesis?

30 *Sports, Fascism, and the Market*

Claudio M. Tamburrini
University of Göteborg, Sweden

This reading is a response to Tännsjö's thesis that our enthusiasm for sports heroes at the elite level is based on the fascistoid ideology of loving winners and despising losers. In turn, Claudio Tamburrini argues that there is nothing necessarily fascistoid about our admiration of winners. Moreover, this very admiration can be used to furnish positive role models in an effort to fight racism and other fascist manifestations.

First, Tamburrini questions the "mutual reinforcement" thesis: the suggestion that political and sportive nationalism via hooliganism reinforce each other. Tamburrini argues that the word hooligan *begs the question. What needs to be shown is that a common soccer fan is a step away from being a political fascist.*

In addition Tamburrini claims that Tännsjö's picture of the esteem in which we hold elite athletes is exaggerated. Instead of contempt for failure, we likely have a resistance to disappointment and defeat. Yet does this same resistance hold for ordinary athletes? Perhaps not, but this is no different from our disappointment of ordinary people outside of sports who fail at some task in which they were expected to succeed. Athletes are different, the argument continues, because of their public stature. Thus our criticism of them is stronger than it is for ordinary nonathletes.

We may concede that there is stronger criticism for athletes than nonathletes, but this does not prove that we have contempt for nonwinning athletes. Admiration for winners does not imply contempt for losers either.

There is a more fundamental problem with Tännsjö's thesis. Tännsjö's claim that we hold losers in contempt is a descriptive claim, not a normative one. In final analysis, it is incumbent upon him to show that this descriptive claim is true.

Introduction

Sports have a grip on our lives. Either as active practitioners or as weekend athletes, as active spectators at the stadium or as passive audience members at home, we all come in daily contact with sports in one way or another. Sports affect society in different ways. Social attitudes and character traits are framed by the values derived from—many would even say embedded in—sports. Some of these are positively judged: self-discipline, teamwork, fair play. Others are seen as clearly negative: uncritical obedience to the team authority, a disposition to beat or even hurt rivals to secure victory, an exaggerated competitive spirit. Critics of sports tend to draw a clear distinction between mass sport activities and *élite sports* competitions. While they ascribe the positive traits to the former, these declared enemies of élite sports strongly underline the (some of them admittedly) negative features of the practice. This resistance to élite sports is often expressed with the help of a variety of arguments, ranging from a (more or less concealed) snobbish contempt for massive celebrations or for physical activity (or both), to pointing out the fact that enormous resources are invested in élite sport activities (seen by these critics as completely useless) that could instead be diverted to other, more important areas of social life. And, to be honest, we should grant to those critical voices that there probably is something morally dubious about a practice whose most conspicuous element is victorious athletes being raised to

Reprinted, by permission, from Claudio M. Tamburrini, "Sports, Fascism, and the Market," *Journal of the Philosophy of Sport* XXV (1998): 35–47.

the level of heroes by a cheering crowd. In a word, élite sports seem to provide an ideal forum for fruitful ethical discussion.

Torbjörn Tännsjö also belongs to the group of people who are morally troubled by the way we react to élite sports and athletes. According to Tännsjö, the public's (often exaggerated) enthusiasm for sports heroes is morally dubious. As a matter of fact, he expresses his worries in far more alarming terms than that. His thesis, in his own words, is that

> Our admiration for the achievements of the great sports heroes, such as the athletes that triumph at the Olympics, reflects a fascistoid ideology. While nationalism may be dangerous, and has often been associated with fascism, what is going on in our enthusiasm for individual athletic heroes is even worse. Our enthusiasm springs from the very core of fascist ideology. (4: p. 24)

Tännsjö's attack is comprehensive: It is directed against all kinds of sports—individual or team—carried out on an élite level. However, he is not aiming to stigmatize the motives that lead top athletes to compete. Nor is he condemning games promoters or coaches who motivate young people to become top sportsmen. Rather, his objections to élite sports concentrate *exclusively* on "what goes on within the enormous, world-wide public, watching sports, usually through television." The target of his criticism is "the values entertained by you and me, we who tend, over and over again, to get carried away by such events as the Olympic Games." Thus, what turns élite sports into a morally problematic matter is the kind of reaction it seems to evoke in us, the spectators. These reactions can be summed up in the following manner: (a) Élite sports events reinforce undesirable nationalistic sentiments in the public; and (b) our (the public's) admiration for winners in élite sports competitions is an expression of our contempt for weakness (which, according to Tännsjö, is an essential element of Nazi ideology).

I intend to examine Tännsjö's arguments in that order. In doing so, I will not only aim at showing that there is nothing fascistoid about our admiration for sport heroes, but will also argue that, properly supplemented by professionalization and commercialization, élite sports might provide us with positive social models to be used in the struggle against fascist manifestations, such as racism and the discrimination of ethnic minorities.

Sport Events Reinforce Nationalistic Sentiments in the Public

One could begin by asking why we should worry about nationalism being reinforced by competitive sports. After all, national feelings in sports do not necessarily have to lead to political chauvinism. It has even been argued that sport nationalism not only is a rather innocent sort of patriotism but even a replacement for more dubious versions of political nationalism, as well. Tännsjö is well aware of this fact, but he thinks otherwise. According to him, political and sport nationalism reinforce each other.

> The nationalism fostered by our interest for our "own" national team, and the nationalism we exhibit on the political arena, tend to reinforce each other. In particular, in periods where political nationalism is strong, what happens on the sports arenas tend to become politically important. (4: p. 25)

This "mutual reinforcement" thesis is a rather strong one indeed. However, the only support Tännsjö provides for it is the assertion that "(T)here is only a small step from being a soccer hooligan to joining a fascist organization modeled on the Hitler Jugend." (4: p. 25) The example is clearly biased. If you are a hooligan, you already are a violent person. It would then not be surprising if you are inclined to join whatever organization is suitable to manifest your violent character. The relevant example here would be showing that there is a small step from being a *common soccer fan* to joining a (politically undesirable) nationalistic organization. Correctly formulated, this "mutual reinforcement" thesis seems false.

So if we have to worry about nationalism in sports, this worry would have to depend on negative consequences of the activity, rather than on its presumed connection with less desirable expressions of national feelings. Tännsjö points out one such consequence: Sport nationalism orientates people towards *abstract symbols,* such as "the flag, the team (seen as an emblem), and yes, even the nation conceived of abstractly," and this is why we should reject it. According to him, celebrating abstract symbols is wrong because

> abstract entities as such are of no value. What matters, ultimately, from a moral point of view, is rather what happens to individuals, capable (at least) of feeling pleasure and pain. . . . This means that if someone claims that the strength of his or her nation is of value in itself, he or she makes a value mistake. (4: p. 25)

As a meta-ethical statement, this latter claim is uncontroversial. However, as an objection to our interest in sports, the argument is flawed on two grounds. First, it could be asked, what does it mean to see the team "as an emblem," or the nation or the flag, as "abstract symbols"? In the context of sports, these symbols stand for thousands and thousands of people who share the dream of seeing their team succeed. A sport team, for instance, is in part driven to win by the encouragement provided by its supporters. Victorious teams often acknowledge this support by dedicating the victory to their supporters. A particular kind of discourse is thus established between the team members and the public. This seems to me to be the sense to be ascribed to the traditional ritual—indeed, a popular and massive celebration—in which a crowd receives its

local team in a public place after a meritorious performance abroad. And even in those cases in which the victory is offered to more abstract entities than an exhilarating crowd, the symbol thus honored (the flag, the City house, etc.) might reasonably be seen as representing the people who identify themselves with it.[1] We should not forget that, *in the context of sports,* abstract symbols refer to people of flesh and bone.

Secondly, there is no reason to suppose that if a sport fan cares about the strength of his team or his nation, he must necessarily be considering it as valuable in itself. He might reasonably see this strength as instrumental to sentiments of pride, joy, or whatever pleasurable state of mind the feeling of belonging to a team or a nation might bring about.

Therefore, it seems to me that the problem here, if there is a problem, cannot be the abstractness of the entities celebrated: After all, symbols usually are implemented in real life arrangements and affect actual people. The relevant issue here is what these symbols stand for. Being generally accepted as natural, historical symbols of a community, a flag, a City house, even a religious figure, can hardly be said to represent *in themselves* fascist ideals as soon as they are advocated in the context of sport events.

Another reason why Tännsjö finds spectator orientation on abstract symbols morally problematic is due to the priority given to group interests over those of individuals. Thus, he says that "when such entities are celebrated, the individual tends to become replaceable. . . . When our football or soccer heroes are successful, we cheer for them. When they fail 'us,' we despise them." Thus, according to Tännsjö, when all we care about is the strength of a nation, a team, or a flag, individuals are sacrificed for the sake of the collective. This ideology, he argues, accords with a view that is common in the military: There, "young women become seen as potential instruments that shall safeguard the strength and survival of the nation, young men are being seen merely as potential soldiers, and so forth" (4: p. 24).

Now, it can hardly be denied that there is something, to put it mildly, morally problematic about a practice that, first, raises a person to the level of a hero, then discards her as soon as she fails to fulfill our expectations of victory. Such an attitude might reasonably be said to violate the Kantian principle that we should always treat other human beings as ends in themselves, never merely as means. So perhaps Tännsjö is right after all in exhorting us to reflect upon our attitudes towards top athletes and the kind of values we might be expressing through them. However, his account of what's going on when we express such disappointment misses the mark.

First, Tännsjö's description of the esteem in which spectators hold *top athletes* is simply inaccurate. The Swedish boxer Ingemar "Ingo" Johansson and soccer player Diego Maradona are examples of such sports heroes. Both "Ingo" and Maradona reached the pinnacles of athletic success and attracted adoring fans. In 1959, Johansson defeated the American boxer Floyd Paterson in a fight for the heavy-weight world championship, thereby giving Sweden its first (and hitherto only) world championship title in boxing. In 1986, Maradona led the Argentinian soccer team to an outstanding victory in the International Association of Federated Football (FIFA) World Cup in Mexico. On the way to the final game against West Germany, Maradona scored a couple of goals (in the matches against England and Belgium) of such quality that more than 10 years after, they still are shown on TV-sport shows from time to time. (The goal scored against England has even been recorded with both classic music and tango tunes in the background with the intention of emphasizing the plasticity of its conception.)

In both cases, however, the outstanding sport performances were followed by defeats. "Ingo" clearly lost two return matches against Paterson, and Maradona has never again reached the top level he showed at the Mexico tournament in 1986. In Maradona's case, rather than mere sport defeats, one could even talk of disappointing the

wider expectations of the public by having been sanctioned twice by the FIFA's disciplinary committee for using performance-enhancing drugs. Both "Ingo" and Maradona, perhaps to different degrees and in different manners, can be said to have disappointed the expectations of victory of their supporters. This notwithstanding, they still enjoy the almost unconditional love and admiration from their numerous fans. Although no generally valid and definitive conclusions can be drawn from only two cases, I believe that they exemplify something typical about the relationship between sports heroes and the public. In that sense, the particular personal bond that is born between them in victory seems to be more resistant to defeat and disappointment than Tännsjö's argument assumes.

But what about ordinary athletes, those who have not been blessed (if it is a blessing) by the public's unconditional devotion? Standard performers are often strongly questioned by supporters. The recognition and admiration they might come to enjoy on favorable occasions is rapidly withdrawn in defeat. Would it not then be warranted to say that these athletes are loved and admired in victory but criticized and slandered by the public when failing to live up to its demands? And would this not be tantamount to using those athletes simply as means to express our (rapidly changing) states of mind?

To begin with, I do not think this particular criticism affects élite sports more than it affects any other profession. In our professional life, our work is expected to satisfy certain standards. If we do not live up to these demands, we get criticized. And when we still fail, in spite of criticism, to react in an adequate manner (that is, if we do not improve our work), the trust we might have enjoyed before from employers and work-mates is withdrawn, we are deprived of certain benefits and, in some cases, get fired. From a moral point of view, this situation is no worse than that depicted for common athletes who do not live up to the expectations of the public. Far from being an essential trait of élite sports, responding negatively to shortcomings in performances belongs to all kinds of professional activity.

To this it could be objected that, owing to the public and vivid manner in which they are rejected, criticism of not-up-to-the-mark athletes is much stronger than what other professional categories normally experience.

My answer to this argument is twofold. First, there is no necessary link between contempt and the publicness and vividness of a critical reaction. A person can publicly and vividly criticize her best friend's conduct without this having to imply she despises her friend. And contempt can indeed be expressed in very subtle manners. Indifferent work-mates, for instance, can turn out to be much more cruel and contemptuous than a hilarious crowd at the sport arena.

Secondly, especially in the context of sports, the vividness of the situation, the emotions experienced in a competition, yields a particularly intensive communication between the athletes and the crowd. Through it, the previous bond between performers and audience—the particular discourse that takes place between them and the public—now reaches a higher level of directness and interaction. Their bond, in other words, becomes more personalized and humanized, independent of the final result of the athletic performance.[2] A similar situation seems to occur in other emotion-laden professional activities, such as the performing arts. But even when an unsatisfactory result hinders the development of such a bond, there is no reason to underestimate an athlete's capacity to handle that failure. In sports, as well as in other areas of life, we have to accept that human relationships sometimes simply do not work out in a manner we would wish. This should not bother sports supporters any more than it does devotees, say, of opera.

So, concerning common athletes, I also believe that it would be an overstatement to characterize the public's reaction as one of scorn or contempt. Even when overtly showing disappointment for an athlete's performance, the interactive relationship that is attained between sport audiences and the athletes contains elements of human communication that go far beyond (and are essentially different from) the expression of contempt.

Admiration for Victorious Athletes Expresses Contempt for Weakness

According to Tännsjö, nationalism in sports is no longer a threat to society. He points out, in my opinion, correctly, that the commercialization and internationalization of élite sports have turned the best athletes and teams into independent, transnational, social phenomena. Rather, the problem with élite sports is the admiration we—the public—feel for the winner. Tännsjö formulates his second objection to élite sports in the following terms:

> My thesis is: When we give up nationalism as a source of our interest in élite sports activities, when we give up our view of individual sportsmen and teams as representatives of "our" nation, when we base our interest in sports on a more direct fascination for the individual winners of these events—we move from something that is only contingently associated with nazism (nationalism) to something that is really at the core of nazism (a contempt for weakness). (4: p. 26)

Tännsjö's argument is descriptive, not normative. As such, it does not tell us how spectators *should* behave but rather how they *actually* react towards victorious athletes. When we feel admiration for the winner of a competition, his argument runs, our feelings are based on a value judgment:

> Those who win the game, if the competition is fair, are *excellent,* and their excellence makes them *valuable;* that is why we admire them.

Their excellence is, in an obvious manner, based on the strength they exhibit in the competition. And the strength they exhibit is "strength" in a very literal sense of the word. (4: p. 26)

A natural objection to this argument is that admiring the winner for his strength does not necessarily mean feeling contempt for the weak. The link between these two attitudes needs to be substantiated. Tännsjö's attempt to support that link goes as follows:

> If we see a person as especially valuable, because of his excellence, and if the excellence is a manifestation of strength (in a very literal sense), then this must mean that other people, who do not win the fair competition, those who are comparatively weak, are *less* valuable. The most natural feeling associated with *this* value judgment is—contempt. (4: p. 27)

In order to criticize Tännsjö's position, I will first argue that our admiration for top athletes may rest on other grounds than plain fascination for their excellence, literally understood in terms of "strength." Hence, this argument will allow me to affirm that the supposedly necessary link is, at best, a contingent one. (Tännsjö even goes so far as to affirm that "we would be *inconsistent* if we did not feel any kind of contempt for the losers, once we sincerely admire the winner" [4: p. 26].) Finally, I will also argue that, when properly implemented, the public's admiration for top athletes, far from being an alarming social manifestation, might even yield socially desirable effects.

As a kind of introduction to my counter argument, let me first briefly comment on the fact, correctly pointed out by Tännsjö, that personal admiration can even be present in such areas as science and the arts.[3] As talented artists and prominent scientists make important contributions to society's cultural and scientific development, they (the "strongest," in a metaphorical

sense of the word, in these areas) also become objects of our admiration. In relation to this, Tännsjö actually wonders if this

> does not mean we value these persons in a manner similar to the way we value successful athletes? And if we do, does this not mean that we think of those who are less successful in these areas as less valuable? Do we not exhibit contempt for weakness, then, when, for example, we give Nobel Prizes and the like to some "outstanding" persons? (4: p. 28)

However, even if disposed to grant this argument at least some weight, Tännsjö rejects it on the grounds that, unlike the excitement felt by spectators for top athletes, our admiration for scientific and cultural feats does not *necessarily* mean that we admire the scientists or artists who are responsible for them. In Tännsjö's own words:

> When we become enthusiastic because of scientific and cultural achievements, we *need* not have scientists or artists as the focus of our attention. We can admire Frege's theories and Mozart's operas without feeling that Frege and Mozart are valuable persons. We can value the *products* of their ingenuity, not their genius itself. We can say truthfully that what they produced is of the utmost value, but still retain the view that *they* are not more valuable than anyone else. They are merely *instrumental* to things of importance in themselves. (4: p. 28–29, Tännsjö's emphasis)

Now, why could we not come to consider Frege or Mozart as more valuable persons than average people on grounds of their achievements? After all, the fact that some people are "instrumental" to the achievement of intrinsically important things is not necessarily a hindrance to admiring them as *persons*, and sometimes even rightly so (recall Mother Theresa). Furthermore, why could we not admire Carl Lewis' or George Foreman's sport achievements without seeing them as (more) valuable (than ordinary) persons at the same time? Tännsjö believes that, while we can (and ought to) "admire the *products* of skillful scientists and artists . . . we cannot but admire the winning athletes themselves or else give up our interest in watching sport" (4: p. 29). In that sense, he considers this personal admiration as essential to sports activities in a way that is not prevalent in the sciences or the arts. Unfortunately, his only support for this assertion is his rather vague characterization of scientific and artistic products as "things important in themselves," as contrasted with sports results, labeled by Tännsjö as "not genuine" on grounds that "they are mainly results of measurements . . . intended, first of all, to establish who won. . . . But winning (a fair competition) is only a means . . . to prove excellence" (4: p. 30). Therefore, what we actually admire in sports, he concludes, is the excellence in terms of strength shown by the winner.[4]

That characterization of excellence in sports strikes me as elitistic and gender-biased. It is elitistic because it does not even consider ranking athletic achievements culturally on par with scientific or artistic ones. However, it seems unreasonable not to rank at least some athletic achievements on par with some cultural and scientific ones. Outstanding sports performances demand not only personal sacrifices, strenuous efforts, and courage to stand up to challenges, but also the capacity to execute an effective strategy and to realize it in practice. Provided it is deserved, an athletic victory offers, therefore, testimony of skills and excellences (both of physical and mental character) that go far beyond mere strength.[5]

Thus, our admiration for victorious athletes might very well depend on the ascription of a *wider* kind of excellence to the winner, rather than on a (admittedly) dubious admiration for the strongest. On this line of reasoning, it might then be argued that what we actually admire is not necessarily the strength ("in a very literal sense") of élite athletes, but rather their *achievements, as cultural expressions of excellence.*

Tännsjö's characterization is also gender-biased, because it focuses exclusively on strength. It is plausible to affirm that, at least in some sports, qualities other than strength are celebrated by the public as tokens of excellence. In rhythmic sports such as gymnastics (a well-established sport with its own world championship), for example, women are recognized as excellent, sometimes even superior to their male counterparts, for skills and qualities other than strength. Ice-skating is another example. Moreover, some of the most successful female gymnasts and skaters have almost reached the category of celebrities (recall, for instance, Nadia Comaneci, Olga Korbut, Katarina Witt, and many others). It is true that the public interest in sports where women excel and surpass male athletes is still low compared with male-dominated ones. And women are still poorly represented in most sports.[6] This, obviously, needs to be changed. But to emphasize strength as the only aspect of a sport performance capable of arousing our enthusiasm is to make a regrettable concession to the "status quo," not only in élite sports, but in sports activities in general. In that sense, Tännsjö simply glosses over some positive features of sports practices that make them worthy of pursuit.[7]

Tännsjö does not discuss in his article the role played by gender in élite sports. But he actually has a reply to my former argument about wider excellence. He says that if top performances (and the various kinds of excellence they indicate) were the real reason for our admiration of élite athletes, then we should feel equally enthusiastic about the top performances of handicapped athletes or those of female athletes. Some of these athletes must surmount more difficult obstacles in order to produce a top performance. But the fact is that we do not feel equally enthusiastic over their performances. In any case, Tännsjö points out, "If we are forced to choose, what we, the vast majority of us, want most to watch, are competitions involving the *absolute* élite, not the Olympics for handicapped people" (4: p. 30). And, according to Tännsjö, the only reasonable explanation for this asymmetry in our interest is that these sorts of athletes are not as capable as their Olympic counterparts: In other words, in our eyes, they are not as powerful and physically complete as male, top athletes. Might not Tännsjö then be right after all?

I do not think so. In assigning excellence to an athlete, the result obtained in the contest is obviously of utmost importance. It is true that, sometimes, the public honors an athlete who, though defeated, did the best he could to reach the top (recall the different kinds of qualities excellence includes). And sometimes the public denies this recognition to a victorious athlete who, although he is a legitimate winner, lacks some of the moral qualities required by excellence (for instance, he did not practice "fair play"). However, *in general terms,* the result achieved by an athlete is a central element in the attribution of excellence. Tännsjö is right when he points out that handicapped athletes can be equally excellent in physical and mental qualities as their élite counterparts.[8] However, they differ in the *results* they attain: Their *performances* are not as good. Granted that they have achieved top results *within their class.* But however deserved their victories may have been, they have not reached a top result *in absolute terms.* By this I simply mean that there exists another athlete who, also deservedly (he too has demonstrated excellence), has achieved a *better* athletic result.

In my opinion, this fact allows us to explain why our interest for handicapped or for female athletes is not as pronounced as the interest we feel for male élite athletes. It is true that society values excellence, in the wider sense outlined above. But it is equally true that results matter. So it would not be surprising to see that the best results arouse the most excitement.[9]

I am not arguing that relative performances should not be praised or admired; they might

even become the proper object of our (exaggerated) admiration. But this fact does not turn our admiration for the best performances (in absolute terms) into a morally dubious one. Granted that the backside of our admiration for excellence is often a lack of interest for everything that falls short of it. *Yet lack of interest can hardly be ranked on the same level as contempt for the weak.* There is no inconsistency in admiring the winner and not despising the loser. We just might not be as interested in "second bests"!

But excellence is a comparative term. And so is the notion of best results. Thus, it could be asked, how much has been gained by this argumentative move? After all, as long as a relative ranking takes place, the best will be admired and seen as more valuable than the next bests. By the very act of identifying winners, we define losers. Tännsjö's crusaders might therefore argue that next bests are nonetheless *implicitly* despised by us, even if not consciously. So, they will probably stress, there is after all some inconsistency between ranking someone as more valuable and not expressing (in this implicit manner) contempt for next bests.

However, provided we adopt a suitably broad characterization of excellence, I see no difficulty in ranking an athlete as best without feeling contempt, not even implicit, for others. In Tännsjö's unidimensional ranking (where excellence is defined exclusively in terms of strength), there is no possibility for next bests to excel: Only one athlete, the winner, can be celebrated as the strongest. Contrary to Tännsjö, I have argued that the ideal of excellence in sports involves a plurality of qualities. The most excellent athlete will naturally excel over others on the whole (that is, in most qualities and most of the time). But (at least some) next bests might excel in some particular quality.[10] As a matter of fact, next bests sometimes can even surpass the most excellent in this limited sense. Two examples might help to clarify what I have in mind here. A losing athlete may have made more sacrifices or shown more dedication and courage than the winner. Or, to focus on the athletic result, both the winner and the second best might have broken the former world record for the sport in question. The fact that next bests too can show this kind of *partial* excellence might, in my opinion, neutralize the implicit contempt suggested by the present objection.

So, if it still has to have any bite, the argument of implicit contempt must be limited to those athletes who never show any sign whatsoever of excellence. As their performances always fail, they cannot compensate for their shortcomings by excelling in a particular quality or by winning a contest from time to time. Perhaps about them it could then be said that they are submitted to the implicit contempt that might be embedded in value rankings.

Maybe. However, no matter how contemptuous, the public's attitude towards these athletes does not seem directly related to admiring excellence. Such a complete lack of valuable qualities results on its own in negative reactions. Besides, within the realm of élite sports, we just do not see this kind of athlete. One simply cannot get to the top without excelling in at least some way.

I do not want to leave the subject of our admiration for the best athletes without calling attention to the role that professionalism can be said to have played, and can reasonably be expected to play in the future, in the re-appraisal of ethnic minorities. Social ideals are not usually dictated by standards and prototypes belonging to ethnic minority groups. Heroes, and the corresponding ideal picture of success that youths aspire to, are commonly depicted in terms of characteristics—racial, social, cultural, and economic—of the dominant groups in society. The spread of élite sports—mainly due to professionalism and the intensified commercialization that followed in its wake—has in my opinion undoubtedly contributed to counterbalance this trend. Unlike Tännsjö, I cannot see anything morally troublesome in our admiration for the best skilled athletes. But even if he were right in his negative account of athletic admiration, this should be seen in the light of other positive effects that might follow from it.

To put it crudely: When condemning the public's admiration of élite athletes, we should not neglect the fact that the winner might, for instance, be a member of an ethnic minority. This appears to me to be of the utmost relevance in the current political situation where racist trends threaten to distort the values inculcated in society.[11] Any serious discussion of the moral status of élite sports must pay attention to this matter.

Conclusion

Is Tännsjö right, then, when he affirms that "if we rid our interest in sports from admiration for strength and contempt for weakness, there will remain little point in upholding it. There will be little reason to watch sports competitions."? Is this admiration for strength and contempt for weakness, as he puts it, "morally evil" (4: p. 32)? In the course of this article, I have tried to show that Tännsjö's arguments are flawed or, at best, not sufficiently developed to sustain his thesis.

To support my claim, I made a distinction between admiring athletic excellence (as it is shown in victory), and despising the weak. We often get excited over top performances, both within and outside of sports. Most of us feel more devoted to top sports events, because this is where the most outstanding athletic performances occur. This, however, does not mean that our lack of interest for average sport performances should be interpreted as a sign of contempt for those who do not manage to reach the top. In my view, there is no reason to assume the existence of such motives. As a matter of fact, sports promote, perhaps as no other human activity does, all kinds of excellences in the Aristotelian sense. Physical skills and strength are developed to their maximum; excellences of character (such as discipline, temperance, self-sacrifice, even righteousness—a central ingredient in "fair play"—are both a requisite for and a result of sport practices. And, finally, the capacity to plan a strategy for victory and implement it successfully requires all the intellectual skills (understanding, judgment, cleverness, etc.) that are characteristic of that excellent state of the soul which Aristotle calls practical wisdom.

Thus, provided we adopt a plural notion of excellence, I see no inconsistency in admiring the most excellent athletes without feeling contempt for the less skilled. Tännsjö has failed to show any substantial link between this admiration and contempt for next bests. That link, however, is essential to his argument.

My disagreement with Tännsjö's thesis, however, is deeper than that. I do not want to deny that, for some people, admiration for winners may have its roots in undemocratic social ideals. However, I do not think this constitutes a serious objection to élite sports events. First, such social phenomena must reasonably be seen in a wider social context. Undemocratic sports fans are surely in the minority. As I see it, elite sports can even be enlisted to combat racism in sports and in society at large. Through the influence of commercialization on sports, members of ethnic minorities might become social prototypes for young people. In my opinion, this possible effect of élite sports would greatly outweigh the feared excesses of undemocratic sports fans.

Secondly, the skills and qualities included in excellence are socially valuable. Some of them (such as, for instance, respect for competitors and "fair play") might even be regarded as expressing a praiseworthy moral attitude. In that sense, it is perfectly understandable to admire top athletes because we know, or at least can imagine, what it takes to reach those heights in sport activities. And, even more importantly, this admiration is rational on a general social level as well, as it can lead to fostering desirable character qualities among the public.

The social rationality of the admiration for excellence extends also to one of its main components: the achievement of a top result. An in-

dividual cannot reasonably be celebrated as excellent in his specific activity if he never succeeds in implementing his strategy. This factor, in my view, explains why spectators feel more enthusiastic about top sports performances. Handicapped athletes, for instance, only achieve relative top performances. However, this does not necessarily imply that they are despised by the public. As a matter of fact, they might even be admired for the excellence they show within their class. But it is socially rational that the absolutely best performers are admired most.

To sum up: The positive results of the public's admiration for sports heroes seems to outweigh the eventual negative consequences of the practice.

Finally, one could object to my claims by arguing that the public does not actually embrace a plural notion of excellence. Along with Tännsjö, a critic might maintain that a majority of sports spectators admire victorious athletes on no other grounds than their strength, in a literal sense of the word. This, however, is a factual statement. Tännsjö has not provided any support for it. Contrary to Tännsjö, I have argued for the possibility of other skills and qualities evoking our admiration for top athletes. It should be granted that this is a speculative statement. Obviously, it would be unwarranted to affirm that all spectators, or even that most of them, actually feel the way I have described them. Sports audiences are still not that educated. However, I believe my views are supported by some of the reactions of the public. In some women's sports, for instance, we see a similar admiration for their most excellent practitioners as we find in men's sports. Further, next best athletes also sometimes receive the admiration and enthusiasm of the public. Maybe these are not conclusive arguments. But the ones advanced in Tännsjö's article are not substantiated enough to justify dismissing mine. And if we are to condemn a whole range of generally accepted social practices, it seems more reasonable to me that the burden of proof be put on those who wish to reject them. This would be sufficient to save élite sports from wholesale condemnation.

Notes

1. In the city of Barcelona, for instance, there is an ancient custom consisting in city teams dedicating their victories to the patron saint of the village by placing a flower arrangement depicting the coat of arms of Catalunya. Such practices might be related to the tradition of armies paying tribute to the city by dedicating to it the victory in a public ceremony. The example of Barcelona is not an isolated one. Unlike ancient communities, we no longer make soldiers the object of our admiration in our societies. Their place has been taken by athletes. The hero worship of athletes might in that sense be seen as a sign of higher culture.

2. We often see the public honor a failing athlete who, though not winning, has at least "done his or her best."

3. Thus, he says, "to be sure, even within science and the arts there are ugly manifestations of the phenomenon I have criticized within sports. Some people tend to get carried away with their admiration for lonely, heroic 'geniuses' in the development of human science and art" (4: p. 29).

4. At some point in his text, Tannsjö seems to attempt a broader interpretation of "strength" in terms of "[natural] talent." Thus, he suggests that we would feel a boundless admiration for a middle aged spectator at the Olympics who, without previous training, "walked down from the stadium and joined the Olympic 10,000-meter race and, because of superior natural talent, defeated all the finalists" (4: p. 30). Perhaps—but I have the intuition that most of us would feel even more excited in front of a much less talented individual who, motivated by that event, decided to submit himself to hard training and personal sacrifices and, 4 years later, joined the race and clearly won it. I am not so convinced of the accuracy of Tannsjö's intuition as he advances it here, nor am I convinced of its relevance to the present discussion. However, he does not pursue this line of reasoning in the rest of his article.

5. The element of desert demands roughly that the challenges presented by the athletes to their competitors must be advanced within the rules (that is why cheating cannot yield excellence). Desert also means that victory has been achieved as a consequence of the athlete's previous choices concerning how to maximize his or her athletic ability. (That is why lucky winners are not viewed as excellent ones.)

6. It has been argued that the reason why women are so poorly represented in the world of sports is that most sports, especially "big time" sports, have been designed and developed to favor those abilities that characterize male musculature and body type: strength, height, speed, and size. Some authors, for instance Betsy Postow (2: pp. 359–365), has even asked whether women should refuse to engage in sports clearly unfitted for their physiological characteristics and instead concentrate upon sports in which they can more easily achieve excellence (i.e., gymnastics, diving, or ultra-marathoning).

7. Furthermore, even in those sports where women's performances are lower than men's, they may arouse spectators' interest precisely because they display other skills than mere strength. Take, for instance, basketball. Female basketball players are physically weaker than their male counterparts. This results in the fact that women's basketball is more of a team game than men's basketball. As such, it could be seen as displaying, not *lesser,* but a *different* excellence than the men's game. It is true that the majority of the public gets more excited by men's basketball. But once the character of women's game is properly understood, we should not neglect the possibility that a more sophisticated audience would find as much to admire—and to get excited about—in women's basketball as in men's.

8. It could be objected that handicapped athletes, by definition, cannot be ascribed physical excellence. I think they can, if the notion of being at the top of one's physical form is made relative to one's physical capacity. Why not, it could be asked, simply explain the asymmetry simply by saying that the public is less interested in handicapped athletes, because they are not physically excellent? Because I believe it is the result that matters, rather than the athlete's physical constitution. If a handicapped athlete had defeated Carl Lewis, we would not hesitate to ascribe *absolute* excellence to him in spite of his physical handicap.

9. Again, this seems to be confirmed by female rhythmic gymnastics. Though physically weaker than their male counterparts, female gymnasts get most attention from the public, probably due to the fact that they achieve the best results within the discipline.

10. We can also think of other configurations in this regard. For instance, some among the next best athletes may *always* be superior concerning a particular quality while not on the whole. Or he may *temporarily* become the most excellent (for instance, in connection with a particular competition). Similar possibilities are open in team sports. Given a high level of performance, the public seldom despises a losing team. And, for instance, in a low-level soccer match, spectators usually show their discontent with both teams, not only with the losing one. Once again, Tannsjö seems not to have paid sufficient attention to the fact that the admiration or disap-

proval of the public is evoked by a variety of qualities and circumstances.

11. However, this positive effect does not ensue automatically. Drew A. Hyland calls our attention to the fact that victories by racial minorities in sports sometimes might be turned into arguments for racist purposes. He mentions, for instance, the common claim that "blacks are natural athletes" as an assumption that, ironically, "has been turned against them as implicit or explicit evidence that they do not need to exhibit, and therefore need not be praised for, such virtues as discipline, commitment, and sustained effort for which white athletes are regularly praised." (1: p. 15).

Bibliography

1. Hyland, D.A. *Philosophy of Sport,* New York: Paragon House, 1990.

2. Ofstad, H. *Our Contempt for Weakness, Nazi Norms and Values—And Our Own.* Stockholm, Sweden: Almqvist and Wiksell International, 1989.

3. Postow, B. "Women and Masculine Sports." In: *Philosophic Inquiry in Sport,* W.J. Morgan and K.V. Meier (Eds.), Champaign, IL: Human Kinetics, 1988.

4. Tännsjö, T. "Is our admiration for sports heroes fascistoid?" *Journal of Philosophy of Sport,* 25: 23–34, 1998.

Questions for Consideration

1. Considering the destructive part of Tamburrini's thesis, he argues that there is nothing *necessarily* fascistoid about our views of winners and losers. In doing so, does he take Tännsjö as holding (1) a necessary connection between admiration for winners and contempt for losers (that is, Tännsjö's "blind instinct" hypothesis), or (2) a dispositional tendency to admire winners and hold losers in contempt? (Recall that Tännsjö rules out one of these.)

2. Considering the constructive part of Tamburrini's thesis, what is his argument for using our admiration for winners to fight racism?

3. Tamburrini argues that admiration for winners results from our tendency to rank competitors in terms of how they have finished overall. This has implications for handicapped and female athletes, who may have as much physical and mental excellence as elite males, but cannot perform as well "in absolute terms." Do you think this sufficiently explains our present overall less enthusiastic interest in handicapped and female sports?

4. We can salvage Tännsjö's argument by decking it out normatively. Clearly our responses to nonwinners is *sometimes* contemptuous (as was the case with the Buffalo Bills, who lost the Super Bowl four times, as well as the Denver Broncos, until they finally managed to win it twice). Can you build an argument to show that this attitude of contempt is always immoral?

31 Television Sport and the Sacrificial Hero

John Izod
University of Stirling, Scotland

In this reading, John Izod examines the role of television in creating and promoting heroism in individual athletes. Competitive sport today is the ideal arena for construction of heroes, since competitive individualism is the received view in cultural and political ideology. Viewers have a need for heroes, and these heroes, as television coverage shows, are almost always winners.

According to Jung, Izod elaborates, a narrative of a hero's journey is one of separation, initiation, and return. Along the way, numerous obstacles are overcome and the overall result is heightened self-understanding.

Our attachment to heroes is libidinal. We search to strengthen ourselves by identifying with a hero. When the attachment is collective, the bond is similar to a religious experience. A hero's triumphs and failures are our own.

Yet athletic heroes today seem to fall as quickly as they rise. As such, they are similar to ancient sacrificial heroes, whose sacrifice was to guarantee a good harvest. In this manner, heroes too mark off the passage of time, and their strength, fertility, vitality, and youth are our own. Identification with athletes, then, is a triumph of physicality and desire of youth. It is the triumph of consciousness over the unconscious in that our love of heroes postpones analysis of our unconscious self as we enter our golden years.

It is rare for the television coverage of sporting heroes to be concerned with aspects of their behavior and thoughts beyond matters strictly relating to their physical performance. Sometimes sports reports also refer to the psychological preparations that enable athletes to improve that performance, but there is very little else. The main exception to these constraints is found in interviews with sports personalities in which the hopes and fears of the heroes are discussed. Often this format masks a somewhat prurient interest in the emotions experienced by winners and losers. Only very occasionally in the television sports calendar does the commentator's near total concern with physical achievements give way to an uneasy sense that something might be left out by so fixated an approach. However, mainly because a compulsory cultural element accompanies the Olympic Games, such doubts do surface regularly in coverage of their opening and closing ceremonies. On these occasions, broadcasters find themselves obliged to join with the Olympic Games' organizers to make much of the supposed connections between sport and culture. It certainly does disturb momentarily the usually complacent routines of sports reporting.

This article takes the ceremonies that bracketed the 1992 Barcelona Olympics as the stimulus prompting a reexamination of the television sporting hero. It begins with a review of familiar territory. This includes a short account of the nature of modern competitive sports and the values typically inherent in television coverage of them. It considers briefly the pressures that encourage broadcasters to build the most successful athletes into stars, and it addresses some of the main elements propagated in the mythic figure of the sporting hero on the small screen.

Turning to the 1992 Olympics, the article of-

From John Izod, "Television Sport and the Sacrificial Hero," *Journal of Sport and Social Issues* (May 1996): 173–193. Reprinted by permission of Sage Publications, Inc.

fers a speculative reading of the myths presented to spectators in the Barcelona stadium during the opening and closing ceremonies. It then shows what happened to those myths (and the image of a legendary sporting hero) when they were passed through the filters of live coverage to the British television audience. It is not hard to see that the attempt by the on-site organizers to bring traditional mythic stories and images alive for today's audience did not weather intact the dominant values of television sports reporting.

In the final section, the perspective of the article is altered to afford a view of the hero of both the Olympic ceremonies and routine televised sport that takes its source from the work of C. G. Jung. This analysis of the sporting hero's image suggests that, notwithstanding the findings concerning coverage of the Olympic ceremonies, the dominant mode of sports reporting does in its own right throw up myths around the athletic hero. These mythic images, far from being entirely unknown to history, actually renew certain ancient uses to which such idolized figures were always put.

The Nature of Sport

Before speculating on how sport transfers to the small screen, we need to consider briefly its nature.

Play

We may begin by noting that participation in sports differs from the behavior of the individual playing alone. This is because in the latter case, the person playing can choose to either observe or break the rules. Further, the rules do not have to be preexistent but may be made up on the spot. Samuels (1990) extrapolates from this idea the thought that "the essence of [solitary] play is that the rules of the ego may be broken" (p. 130). Where norms, hierarchies, and clarity can be ignored, the unconscious rather than the ego system is dominant. As Jung (1973) recognized from his own experience, the instinct to play is closely linked to the drive toward self-discovery

and exploration of the unconscious. In this respect, it has a religious quality (pp. 197–198).

Games

The case is rather different with games. They resemble play in being nonutilitarian, but differ, as Guttmann (1978) says, in that they are regulated and rule bound. "Games symbolize the willing surrender of absolute spontaneity for the sake of playful order. One remains outside the sphere of material necessity, but one must obey the rules one imposes on oneself" (p. 4). The unconscious yields in part to a greater intensity of conscious control precisely because most games are social, and so the players submit to rules that the group or community imposes. Such rules often function in a technically inefficient manner (like the off-side rule in soccer) because they are designed actually to make it harder to achieve the goal and thus prolong the play itself (pp. 4–5).

Modern Sports as Contests

Although many games (such as leapfrog) are not competitive and players neither win nor lose, modern sports belong to a wider class of activity that is normally rule bound. This is the contest, which apart from sport includes things such as elections, legal proceedings, and war. "We can . . . define sports as 'playful' physical contests, that is, as non-utilitarian contests which include an important measure of physical as well as intellectual skill" (Guttmann, 1978, pp. 5–7). Triumph through contest or conflict is a prerequisite to becoming a hero.

Ideology and Sport

The Past

Several writers show how the history of sport can be traced not only in terms of the progression from play to contest but also (among other factors) through shifts in the values that dominated it. There is abundant evidence that, although not all sports of every nation were once dominated by religious significance, a great many were. Some were part of a yearly fertility rite (Guttmann, 1978, cites the sports of the Jicarilla Apaches of the Southwest Plains). Others enacted rites of passage from puberty to adulthood. Yet others, such as the ball game of the Mayans and Aztecs that celebrated the birth of the sun and moon, appear to have invoked creation myths (pp. 17–20). The ancient Olympic Games were thus not unusual in celebrating the sacred. However, after a long period of evolution, sport ceased to be consecrated and became predominantly secular in nature. "Modern sports are activities partly pursued for their own sake, partly for other ends which are equally secular. We do not run in order that the earth be more fertile. We till the earth, or work in our factories and offices, so that we can have time to play" (pp. 25–26).

As sports evolved, so did their rules. Dunning (1971) and Elias (1971) demonstrate that the characteristics of sports, including the degree to which they were governed by rules, should be viewed in the context of the kind of society that fostered them. For example, the pancration, a form of wrestling that was popular in the ancient Olympic Games, was both far less rule bound and far more physically violent than are the make-believe and theatrical televised wrestling contests of the late 20th century. "To be killed or to be very severely wounded and perhaps incapacitated for life was a risk a fighter in the pancration had to take" (Elias, 1971, p. 99). Elias endorses an idea in circulation among the ancient Greeks that such contests were a training for war and, conversely, war prepared men for victory in the Olympic Games. In that context, and in a society where the transformation of private conscience into general social principles of justice was still the exception rather than the norm, regulation of physical contests was of less importance than their execution with honor (pp. 98–101).

Games still were expressive of social custom and ritual in medieval Britain when an early and riotous form of football was played by whole communities in frank defiance of the authorities. The organization of the game was much looser and a good deal more dangerous than it is today. People did not play according to nationally agreed rules (which did not yet exist) but rather contested the issue in the light of local customs. Yet, in many places, this wild form of play formed part of annually observed and solemn folk rituals. Nothing was seen to be incongruous in the conjunction of riot and ritual (Elias & Dunning, 1971, pp. 116–126).

The Present

Today's sports are no less firmly embedded in their social structures, as Lipsky (1975) has observed. "Sport is the symbolic expression of the values of the larger political and social milieu" (p. 351). One indicative factor is the quantifying of performance through the recording of data. Another is the burning ambition of athletes to break records by exceeding the achievements of the past. Both objectives have become obsessive foci for those interested in sports. Yet Guttmann (1978) shows that this was not always so; measurement was once almost irrelevant to the reckoning of sporting success. Today, quantification of sporting achievements is ideologically of a piece with the dominant work practices of late 20th-century economies. The latter depend for survival on recording and calculation. Few people employed in the industrialized nations during the 1980s and 1990s have escaped the constant pressure to perform their tasks faster or more efficiently than they have been performed before. Arguably, our "Faustian lust for the absolutely unprecedented athletic achievement" (p. 54) stands in compensatory relation to the daily experience of millions of workers. The obsession with quantifying sporting achievement indicates a massive investment of psychic energy. Thus we express through statistics, a language we have endowed with magical power, a new way of attaining an ancient goal. "Once the gods have vanished from Mount Olympus or from Dante's paradise, we can no longer run to appease them or to save our souls, but we can set a new record. It is a uniquely modern form of immortality" (p. 55).

The Construction of Heroes

Competitive Individualism

A number of converging factors encourage television sports programs to build star players into heroes. We may begin with what Clarke and Clarke (1982) describe as apparently the most natural characteristic of contemporary sport.

> Sport provides the opportunity for individuals to pit themselves against others and be judged by their competitive performance. It appears as the most primitive and natural form of interaction between humans. This may seem "self-evident," but it is connected to propositions about this as the natural state of society—that social life is "competitive individualism." From this standpoint, it is possible to see the cross-connections that are constructed between sport and social images. (p. 63)

It follows that images drawn from the sports field serve to affirm that competitive individualism, which is in fact a cultural and political ideology, is the natural human condition. Therefore, the strongest, fittest, and (above all) most successful athletes are lionized as exemplars. Among them, the most outstanding become media personalities, and as such they reveal their hopes and fears as well as their thoughts about their game to the viewer. The process is not restricted to the cultivation of personality, however, because the heroes are usually cast as individuals who have succeeded while obeying the rules. Meanwhile, those who are perceived to be bending or breaking the rules become stereotyped as villains. Thus, on the face of things, television sport shows a pronounced moralizing tendency in its construction of heroes, although some villains may be sneakily admired for

challenging authority (p. 72; also see Hargreaves, 1986, p. 147).

Characters and Stories

As is well known, television stations use sport as a means of enhancing their power by increasing their audience share, income, and status. Broadcasters have to appeal to an audience far larger than the number of fans for each specific sport to gain these ends. In creating heroes, sports programs satisfy what appears to be an incessant audience need. That is one reason why broadcasters lionize stars. Another is that the practice marries with the sports reporter's need to create a story.

Although the forms of narrative employed in the coverage of sporting events are rather different from those employed in fiction, commentators are still required to create "characters" to people them. This is another reason why today's sporting heroes are required to have distinctively marked individual personalities. But even so, their production as images has to conform with the requirements of routinized, cost-effective television production. This economic factor, together with the desire of audiences to get to know personalities with easily recognized qualities, exerts a strong stereotyping force on the construction of sporting heroes.

An instance is the fact that the characters most frequently discovered through sports coverage are usually winners. Winners, rather than losers, receive the most attention because, as we have said, the constant pressure to compete in most 20th-century societies encourages the adulation of victors. Those who come in second or after do not arouse the same media interest unless they are representing the viewer's nation. However, if they happen to be doing so, a distorting effect can result as conflicting stereotypes collide. For example, since the World Cup of 1990, Paul Gascoigne has been famous in the United Kingdom not only for his soccer-playing skills but also for what was in fact a momentary outbreak of tears at being shown the yellow card. He had committed a foul that would have kept him out of England's following game—hence his disappointment. In fact, England lost and was knocked out of the competition. The tabloid press and television worked on the episode for several days, after which the tears came to signify something else altogether. Gascoigne's devout patriotism—the sorrow of a man who cannot bear his country losing. In this case, a member of the losing team was turned into a national hero.

Predictability

Because most sporting contests result in triumph for an individual or a team, there is a constant stream of winners. This feeds television's need for the predictable occurrence. Of course, it is seldom possible to foretell the outcome of any particular contest. Despite this, commentators and experts constantly try to do so as a means of giving continuity to the characters in the event by drawing on their athletic histories. However, the difficulty of foretelling results is actually welcome because it feeds television's equally strong need for the unpredictable—for the dramatic surprise. It follows that the institution of sports broadcasting is indifferent to the fact that individual heroes may come and go because, just as in pop music or the movie business, there are always new stars to replace those that disappear.

All these factors provide a framework for the emergence of sports heroes in routine television coverage. Before we consider their nature from a fresh perspective, let us turn to one of the comparatively rare instances in which mythology has been consciously promoted in the context of televised sport.

Myth, Spectacle, and the Olympic Ceremonies

The opening and closing ceremonies of the Olympic Games have for some years been conspicuously costly spectacles. Designed to entertain a vast global television audience, they both celebrate the games themselves and promote the venue that is hosting them. During the days leading up to the event, some of the attractions that the city elders want shown to the world (as well as others that they would prefer were not publicized) are communicated by a variety of programs. These include sports features; documentaries on the history, culture, and life of the locality; and holiday programs exploring the promise it holds for tourists.

During the actual ceremonies, the city's marketable qualities are depicted through a display of performing and other arts associated with the region, presented with an entertaining panache to attract an international television audience. In the Olympic Games in Los Angeles (1984), the opening ceremony exploited the city's close associations with Hollywood. Similarly, performances based in local culture that showcased both the host cities and nations were mounted in Seoul (1988) and Barcelona (1992). However, the organizers in both the latter venues did much more than market their regions to potential tourists. They exploited the antiquity of their civilizations in a way that Californians had not found possible. And they introduced a new element to the ceremonial mix by entwining certain ancient myths of the regions into their dances and spectacles.

The Ceremonies at Barcelona, 1992

What follows is a two-part analysis centering on the episodes in the opening ceremony that featured Hercules. The first part represents a speculative attempt to interpret the mythology in the way the Catalan organizers appear to have wanted television audiences to perceive the performances in the Montjuic stadium. The second part gives an account of the way the myths became obscured in coverage provided by the two channels that transmitted the ceremony to the United Kingdom.

A tentative interpretation of the themes governing the performances in the stadium can be drawn from two sources. First are the live images fed to participating networks by the television company set up in Barcelona specifically to cover the Olympic Games. The networks were entitled to add their own live or prerecorded images, but a comparison of BBC coverage to that of the satellite channel Eurosport shows that, for the duration of the opening and closing ceremonies, both took the feed without interruptions other than those for commercial breaks on Eurosport. The second source is fragments of the narration. Careful attention to the verbal texture of the commentaries on both these channels suggests that in places the scripts were not written by the reporters. It seems reasonable to deduce the existence of an official explanatory text designed by the authorities in Barcelona to help sports commentators explain what they were witnessing. Commentary teams appear to have sampled this text with varying degrees of success.

Hercules, the Ancient Hero

The scriptwriters in Barcelona took advantage of their Mediterranean site to recall not so much the history of the ancient Olympic Games (which is obscure) as the mythology surrounding their origins. In the opening ceremony, they made Hercules the main protagonist of a vast drama. The mythical inaugurator of the games, he was represented as a gigantic god-like figure—literally a hero made of steel who towered meters above the human operator who was working him. In the metaphoric terms, it created an image in which the myth was larger than the man beneath but intriguingly also dependent on him.

In this rendering of a fragment of Hercules's ninth labor, the founding of the Olympic Games was shown to be integral to his creation of Mediterranean civilization. In the first place, he challenged the sun by running a race through its gorgeous but dangerous flames, accompanied by his team of athletes. This test was said (by the BBC's commentator) to have made it possible

for him to divide the column of civilization. The idea seems to be a double reference both to his erecting the Pillars of Hercules at the Straits of Gibraltar and (as the Eurosport commentary team mentioned) to his parting good from evil. These events were seen as both the source of and model for the Olympic Games.

Hercules's heroic powers were called on again as a ship laden with Greek mariners sailed across the arena, now transformed into the Mediterranean Sea. Presently, the ocean grew hostile and great waves hurled monsters up from the deep. (The imagination of Barcelona's artists and designers showed itself to brilliant effect with sun and sea represented by hundreds of costumed dancers. The ship resembled an iron relic of the industrial age, its attackers a rabble of sea demons, among them animated claws and knives, a nightmarish globe of corpses and weaponry, and an etiolated black octopus.) When the vessel broke and the demons threatened to overwhelm them, the crew prayed to the gods for help. And they were answered when, under the tutelage of Hercules, the sun returned and the waves lost their force. Guided by the sun, the ship then reached the shore where, offering the gods thanks for their salvation, the voyagers built an altar with a flame like the Olympic beacon. There they settled and established a community—the future Barcelona.

The spectators in 1992 seem, then, to have been invited by these performances to recall the long-forgotten ritualistic celebrations of the ancient Olympic Games. They were encouraged by the narrative to use them as a mental backdrop to the modern games, the televised rituals of which would otherwise have centered almost exclusively on the athletes' physical prowess. Thus, despite its surface appearance as an opulent and startlingly original performance (features that television extravaganzas require to attract vast audiences), the spectacle allowed one to see that beyond the exuberant blend of modernist Catalan imagination, artifice, and high technology, there were connections to be drawn to an older tradition of drama. This was a matter of not just the story's antiquity but also its structure.

An Allegory Concerning Conflict

First, the characters and story line functioned in an allegorical mode comparable to that of the Renaissance masque. They existed not only in their own right but also as keys to an interpretive text. For example, in addition to being a striking visual representation of a man of iron, Hercules acted as mediator in the age-old conflict between the elements. Then again, neither the sun nor the sea alone was shown to be a benign influence. In isolation, either could destroy humanity; in cooperation, they brought peace and new life so that Hercules's labor symbolically defeated the forces of death and fostered life. Taken a step further, the peaceable resolution of elemental battle was shown to be a model for the Olympic Games. This reading is confirmed by the perilous voyage of the ship that (as the commentators for Eurosport explained) represented in dramatic form the long and difficult journey of Olympism from ancient Greece to Barcelona.

Like the allegories of old, this narrative was also intended to function on a less abstract level. This became evident when, in his welcoming speech, the mayor of Barcelona expressed the hope that the Olympic spirit could expand across the world and help bring an end to conflict in the war-torn states of the former Yugoslavia.

Fertility and Rebirth

The theme of conflict was worked through a number of segments in both the opening and closing ceremonies. So too was another related theme, the invocation of fertility. Hercules's own mythological line of descent is strongly marked with this association. Although he had been demoted to the rank of hero by the Greeks, in his prior incarnation he had been a Minoan fertility god. In addition, as Guttmann (1978) shows, the theme provided the common thread linking every version of the Olympic Games' origins. And a ritual intended to ensure continued fertility constituted an integral element of the ancient games, a sacrifice being made to Zeus to persuade him to return from the dead "in the form of a new shoot emerging from the dark womb of the earth into the light of day" (p. 22). Looking at the obverse of this, defeat in an athletic contest was regarded as the symbolic equivalent of death (pp. 21–22).

This theme extended into the closing ceremony in which fertility myths were again invoked. This time fire was used to extend the elemental imagery that in the opening ceremony had been provided by the sun. Fire now became a unifying motif signifying both creation and rebirth. In this register, it fused together the symbolism of many elements in the final show. These included a performance of De Falla's *Fire Dance*; the extinguishing of the Olympic flame; and a festival of fire in which, while the sun gamboled among the planets in a universal dance, flames blazed in the bowels of the universe where cheerful devils worked the smithy of creation. In the end, something with a new and benign purity sprang from the raw energy of these demons' unexpurgated flames. An aerial ship of shining steel, a refulgent creation forged in the fire, arose from the stadium floor. A massive fireworks display coincided with its launch and carried it high on the updraft of 100,000 rockets. It was said to take with it an invisible flame, the spirit of the Olympics, bound for the 1996 Summer Games in Atlanta, Georgia. The rebirth motif could hardly have been more clearly stated.

The themes remarked on in the proceeding subsections—the god-like stature of Hercules; his achievement of heroism through conflict; and the links between his acts, sporting rituals, and ideas of fertility and rebirth—were plainly indicated in the dramaturgy in Barcelona. The question is, Why did they not penetrate the U.K. television coverage more effectively?

Construction of the Foregoing Narrative

Whether or not the reading offered in the preceding text might find favor with the producers of the ceremonies or the Catalan television directors, it is not one that many U.K. viewers of the ceremonies could have made. It would be an exaggeration to suggest that the BBC and Eurosport commentaries did not aid my understanding in any way, but they did leave large gaps and serious confusion. So the interpretation sketched out in the preceding subsections also required careful consideration of the images' potential meanings. This was augmented with readings in mythology and with Guttman's (1978) history of early sports.

Ideological Constraints on Sports Coverage

When one listens to the commentaries at leisure, it sounds as though the reporters are editing the script as they go along. They seem to do this in part to fit it into events on screen but mainly because too much explanation of the spectacle is thought likely to bore many viewers. For example, Archie MacPherson, in his live commentary on the closing ceremony for Eurosport, felt that at times the ceremonies were "a little bit heavy." From this perspective, the good side of the elaborate rituals in the arena was found in the entertainment and emotional pleasure they gave. Meanwhile, the bad aspect was anything that was "pompous," which it was if it contained "a good deal of symbolism." That seemed to refer to anything beyond the routine experience of the commentator in his familiar role as the representative of British television viewers.

Thus, for MacPherson, there developed a split view in which the closing ceremony was both pleasing and dull, simultaneously joyous and pompous. Conceivably, this view arose simply from his own predilections. Because he had taken up a similar no-nonsense attitude in his sports reporting for BBC Scotland over many years, this thought is not implausible. But he might equally well have been reflecting an institutional rather than a personal set of values. That is, his attitude may have been intended to meet the supposed preferences of the majority in the audience—those alleged to dislike anything not obvious to the uninitiated. Because an average of more than 11 million people in the United Kingdom were estimated to have been watching each ceremony (about 20% of the population), the producers' concern for the mass audience is understandable. It was, and remains, the always compelling justification for domesticating anything foreign to render it recognizable and comfortable to the home audience.

As a consequence of the commentators cutting down explanation of the spectacle to less than the bare bones, the information actually given was so fragmentary as to be incomprehensible. There were even occasions during coverage of the ceremonies when the British presenters appeared not to understand the words they were uttering. No surprise, then, that they were unable to clinch meaning for viewers.

Far from being an exception, incidentally, the presentation at Barcelona conformed to the usual pattern of coverage of Olympic ceremonies on British television. For example, according to O'Donnell (in press), David Coleman's BBC commentary on the opening ceremony of the Lillehammer Olympics in Norway appears to have used a good deal of locally inspired text. Not all of it made sense.

Entertainment and Spectacle

Something more than the protection of the audience from boredom is at work here. It relates to the well-documented fact that television coverage of the Olympics is dominated by the entertainment requirements of the world's richest nations. A ceremony of this kind is designed to depend on extravagant spectacle to guarantee the mass audience in these countries, and thus it inevitably solemnizes conspicuous wealth. Sporting and other myths become subsumed to a dominant idea of market-oriented capitalism, namely the myth that we find our main pleasure in consumption to excess—be it of goods or of orchestras and choruses supported by casts of thousands dressed in all the colors of the rainbow. Thus a principal object of television presentation of the ceremonies is to give the viewers satisfaction through the richest sensuous pleasures that aesthetic plenitude can offer in the spectacle. This practice has certain consequences.

As MacAloon (1984) argues, the aggrandizing ethos of spectacle that is designed to reach a mass audience has licensed passive watching. This undermines the requirement of all rituals that those who watch them be engaged. He finds that games, insofar as they are embedded within a spectacle, tend to be taken as "mere games," or "mere entertainments," rather than as "metaphors that are meant" (p. 263).[1]

The analytical psychologist Jung (1976) commented on this kind of tendency in connection with drama and painting. It amounted to taking art as if it were merely an aesthetic exercise. The advantages of such a tendency were not far to seek.

> The aesthetic approach immediately converts the problem into a picture which the spectator can contemplate at his ease, admiring both its beauty and its ugliness, merely re-experiencing its passions at a safe distance, with no danger of becoming involved in them. The aesthetic attitude guards against any real participation, prevents one from being personally implicated, which is what a religious understanding . . . would mean. (p. 142)

That is exactly the way that British coverage of the Olympic ceremonies functioned for its viewers.

The Slighting of Hercules

What happened to Hercules, the bionic hero, in the British commentaries? The short answer is, of course, that he was treated as a colorful component of the vivid spectacle, but nothing more. His image was not used to augment our understanding of today's sporting heroes. At first glance, this slighting of a heroic figure might seem strange because, in the abstract, the parallels with the modern athletic hero are clearly marked. Both test themselves through contests. Both have something superhuman about them. And both offer the commentator lively stories.

When one considers the routine naturalization of sports reporting, however, it is not so surprising that Hercules was ignored even despite the seductive appeal of spectacle. He was neither predictable in terms of television routine nor readily adapted to its realist register. He was a figure from the distant past who could not be interviewed. And although constructed as a character in a narrative, he was given no personality. More significantly, allegory is not a mode to which sports commentators are accustomed, as MacPherson's unease with the idea of symbolism showed. Finally, the Olympic Games are now heavily marketed as gatherings for peace, and so the ancient association with warfare was an alien concept. Thus, from the perspective of the sports reporter, the differences between Hercules and the athletes gathered around him would have been more striking than the likenesses. Not only have the gods vanished from Mount Olympus, but we have lost the habit of thinking about human activities as shadowing their deeds.

Our loss may seem trivial, but from the perspective of Jungian analytical psychology, the gods and heroes aided not only individuals but also communities to gain a better intuitive understanding of their predispositions and needs.

We can see this by looking both at what might have been made of the Barcelona spectacle and at the values that attach to the sporting hero in routine television coverage.

Hercules's Missed Potential as a Hero: A Jungian Reading

The mythical journey of the hero recognized by classical Jungians represents a pattern of transformation long since rendered familiar by repetition in numerous guises across many forms of narrative art. It entails a process of separation, initiation, and return. Heroes usually leave the familiar world of the ego to enter a dangerous territory. Often they descend into the dark underworld of the unconscious, but any menacing situation can symbolize the terrors of the unknown. There they face extreme danger or defy monsters, and they usually suffer in the process. Some would-be victors fail or allow themselves to be seduced into staying in the other world. Thus, to finally claim their place as heroes, they must return to the familial world, bringing with them the fruits of their conquests.

Jung describes this transformation as symbolizing their separation from an earlier state of consciousness. In the process, heroes have to confront the parameters of the unconscious inherited from their parents. They do so with the intuitive goal of emerging renewed from this encounter with the innermost self. Marked by suffering inflicted by the split from the old self, they are rewarded in bringing back either the grail itself or some knowledge of it. In other words, heroes have made entries into and have been altered by the renewed self-knowledge found in the unconscious psyche.

This is the figure that the Barcelona Hercules could have been. Embedded as he was in conflict, exposed to monsters and other dangers, he had potent associations with the kind of rebirth motifs that often express the renewal of the psyche. But these quasi-religious associations latent in the performance in the stadium were exactly what television's concentration on spectacle ensured most spectators would overlook. The organizers' attempt to offer a spiritually or psychologically regenerative hero for our time did not succeed.

Jungian Hero in Routine Sports Coverage

Popular Choice

Accepting that many of the mythological elements embedded in Olympics ceremonies were ignored or suppressed in the process of mediation to television audiences is one thing. Finding traces of ancient myths in the routine coverage of sporting activities is a rather different challenge because their presence is not consciously indicated in any way, whereas it was signaled boldly by the organizers in Barcelona.

Consider, for instance, the forming of heroes. As with all popular media icons, members of the public—in this case a large sector of the audience for television sports—choose their own heroes from the many candidates offered them. The process, although fostered knowingly by broadcasters and marketing departments, depends only to some extent on their activities and far more on the devotion of fans and the demand of the television audience. It is clear that many spectators (e.g., the Welsh with rugby and the Australians with all sports) devote themselves to their sports with passionate enthusiasm. As Guttmann (1978) says, for some people sports have become religions in themselves, and the best practitioners are heroes who are worshipped (pp. 25–26). Heroes are not created without a surge of popular desire for what they represent.

The fact that people buy clothing and equipment merchandised by sports stars and enjoy the association with the image they market implies that the creation of heroes is urged by the libido. That is, the adulation of sporting heroes arises in part from unconscious desires and impulses. Because the search for personal power through identification with the image of a hero is often led by the libido in this way (no less in the 20th century than in other eras), it could be described as a quasi-religious activity. The description fits when the activity has the devotion of very large numbers of people, for where a psychological search through mythological experience becomes a collective enterprise, it embodies significant elements of popular intuitive needs.

This indeed is the point. Whereas Guttmann (1978) is plainly correct in asserting that all the surface signs demonstrate the evacuation of the sacred from 20th-century sport, we can also detect exceedingly strong contraindications in them. The latter are sufficiently strong to suggest that Heraclitus's psychological law that sooner or later everything runs to its opposites is still current.

The Task of the Sporting Hero

As we have seen, the great tasks of the contemporary sporting hero are against all odds to win contests and to strive to break records. In some sports physical danger has to be confronted, and in all of them athletes have to face painful difficulties. These include lack of physical or mental fitness, the technical difficulties of the sport and rules that often make the task harder, and the strength of the competition. Equally devastating are the private hells of self-doubt and the public hell of failure and humiliation.

The sportsman or sportswoman, as opposed to the solitary games player, acts in a rule-bound world—the world of the ego where will and consciousness dominate. It is that which allows such an individual to gain recognition as a hero, something that the solitary games player who has ready access to the personal unconscious can never be. Like every other hero, the sporting hero has to be seen to have confronted not only every conceivable external hardship but also all his or her deepest fears and doubts.

Linford Christie is a British national sporting hero much lauded on television. He captains the men's team of track athletes. There is no ques-

tion that he has completed all the external tasks of the athletic hero, winning countless sprint championships (including the 100-meter sprint in the Barcelona Olympics) and breaking world records. When he runs, his face becomes a totally focused mask. This expression, often featured in slow-motion close-up recordings of his races, can be read as the haunting sign of his knowledge of the internal hells through which the supreme champion must pass. Thus he is an obvious repository of the heroic archetype.

Sacrifice and the Popular Hero

The television sporting hero differs from those whose triumph seems eternal. We have seen ample evidence of the way television practice invites sports spectators to celebrate the increase of human vitality. But time has another inescapable dimension in sports aside from the measuring of speed and records—namely, the short professional life cycle of most athletes. Indeed, few sports commentators fail to mention whether an athlete is still improving, has reached his or her peak, or is in decline. So the waning of human energies is simultaneously implicated in every celebration of their waxing. In 1995, Christie announced his immediate retirement in a fit of pique; although he later changed his mind, it was impossible not to be aware (with the champion in his early 30s) that his top-level running career must be nearly over.

The Year King

The fact that our sporting idols rise and fall across the screen in swift succession makes them resemble in some ways the archetypal image of the year king or a sacrificial hero. As such, they belong to a line that reaches back to the vegetative gods and goddesses. Their intense but brief lives are dedicated to us as spectators and invested with our libidos, as the inflated fees they earn demonstrate. We accept their heroic feats as our due, and they celebrate for us the triumph of our desire for strength and vitality. They also mark the years' passage. Therefore, to some degree they perform a function like that of the dying kings and heroes of old whose sacrifice was intended to ensure the harvest's fertility. However, today's sporting heroes do not wax and wane in accordance with the year's farming seasons but do so in a rhythm that embodies in stark miniature the rising and ebbing of life. At one fairly obvious level, then, they hallow human fertility and vitality; this is confirmed by the way in which sportswear designed for a number of activities (e.g., swimming, tennis, gymnastics, and track events) shows off the physique of the athletes who help market it. Not only does such clothing display athletes' strength, but it also often enhances the sexuality of their images. Christie, for example, started wearing a new style of Lycra running suit during the 1990s that did just this. The effectiveness of this appeal is evidenced by the numbers of people who seek to empower themselves vicariously by copying their heroes' appearances.

Magical Space

The special quality of television sporting heroes is confirmed and complemented by the magical nature of the space they occupy. Contrary to MacAloon's (1984) belief that the loss of frame boundaries blurs the impact of the Olympic ceremonies (p. 263), it can be argued that conditions for the production of myths are met in televised sporting events in that they are often carefully set up to prepare audiences for their quasi-religious significance. On the sports field itself, as Guttmann (1978) observes, the progression from play (through games and contests) to sports seems to involve an increasing degree of spatiotemporal separateness from ordinary space and time (pp. 5–7). Thus, in the minds of many fans, their home stadium becomes a sacred place, no matter whether it be a national monument or an almost unknown venue. This is true of many sports on both sides of the Atlantic (Bale, 1991, p. 131; Trujillo & Krizek, 1994).

The kind of separation to which Guttmann

(1978) refers is typically developed further in television coverage of sporting events. The viewers are introduced to a place and time analogous to a magical zone. Everything, including the scheduling of programs into clearly demarcated slots, the glamour of their title sequences, their modes of address, and the lionizing of star performers, lets the audience know that the televised arena is a place in which the extraordinary can almost always be anticipated and is often delivered by heroes with seemingly superhuman qualities (see Clarke & Clarke, 1982, pp. 70–72).

This is clearly demonstrated when the magical arena is violated. When, early in 1995, Eric Cantona responded to provocation during a game in the English soccer league by jumping into the terraces and kicking a fan, it was more than just the assault that shocked television audiences. He had breached the frame boundaries surrounding the sacred and in so doing cast off the hero's invisible mantle. Because it entailed the descent of a hero, it was a desecration more abhorrent than that of the fans whom from time to time run the other way onto the pitch in the vain hope that entering the sacred space will enable them to touch the glory of their heroes.

Reading the Myth of the Sacrificial Sporting Hero

The year gods were sacrificed to ensure human survival and the continuity of the seasons. Herein lies their most obvious distinction from today's sporting heroes, even though the lives of the latter as television performers are short. How, then, can the myth of sporting heroes be read? Jung would remind us that images that seem to have magical qualities are invested with energies rising from the unconscious. Finding their archetypal sources helps us perceive more clearly the values that the present-day myth expresses. But before we see what readings that produces, a word of caution is necessary.

Although gratifications research into the

pleasures people take from televised sports is still in the early stages of exploration, we know from the work of Wenner and Gantz (1989) that audience experiences are diverse. They tend to vary according to the sport watched and the social positions of the viewers. As it happens, Wenner and Gantz's research demonstrated that viewers experienced the strongest feelings when their favorites did well (p. 266). But although this conclusion complements my account of the sporting hero's significance, it needs to be emphasized that what follow here are speculative readings that have not been tested by audience research. If, as Jhally (1989) says, images of competition are appropriated differently by groups in different social positions (p. 88), many more readings of the sporting hero will be possible than those spelled out in the following.

The Wise Old Man or Woman

There seem to be two opposing ways in which television spectators might read the myths projected by their athletic heroes, depending on the stage in life and personal development of the individual viewers. The first is found where recognition of the inevitable decline in athletes' sporting prowess furnishes people with a psychological role model. It could conceivably support them through a time of crisis brought on by the changes with which the aging process inevitably confronts the individual. Instances of athletes providing such a role model include some of those former sporting heroes who have a continuing screen life as commentators or experts. At their best, they recall the archetypal image of the wise old person. Jung said such figures represent knowledge, reflection, insight, wisdom, cleverness, intuition, and positive moral qualities (Jung, 1968, pp. 219–230). They may occur in dreams of "psychopomps"—guides offering the dreamer hints, clues, or even direct instruction concerning the nature of the inner life. In life, the archetype might attach to an image of an older doctor, teacher, or spiritual leader.

In general, however, it has to be said that the archetypal image of the wise old person does not fit the case of most television sports personalities particularly well. Whatever their private off-screen qualities, it is rare for them to express wisdom reaching beyond the technicalities and occasionally the morality of sporting practice. A few do play this role, but of course most sporting heroes do not "survive" at all after their athletic careers have ended. Some are lionized in a final valedictory appearance, some join the developing professional circuits for veterans, but many simply slip off the screen into obscurity. Their going hardly troubles the ceaseless celebration of the young in the televising of sport.

Eternal Youth

This observation indicates the second dominant way in which such mythic figures may be used by viewers. The glorious eternal youth of the endless stream of sporting heroes will be what makes them the cynosure of most spectators' eyes—not the grace and wisdom of their aging. Such a reading of the heroic image fits with the expression of the desire for power often associated with sport. Freud noticed that the playing of sports can represent the desire to achieve mastery through more than just the physical contest because a wish to gain the upper hand through psychological conflict may also be acted out. Meanwhile, televised sport offers viewers role models for their own psychological exploration of power relations in society. (If it did not, there would not be the need for sports commentators to scourge foul play as obsessively as they do.) Roberts and Sutton-Smith argue, "Games are . . . models of ways of succeeding over others, by magical power (as in games of chance), by force (as in physical skill games), or by cleverness (as in games of strategy)" (cited in Guttman, 1978, p. 9).

But what does fixation on youth imply for the culture that is locked into it? One answer is prompted by the main factor that all sports seem to have in common: the requirement that participants exercise the will and focus it intensely on their goal. Jung (1985) said the following of the will:

> It is of the greatest importance for the young person, who is still unadapted and has as yet achieved nothing, to shape his conscious ego as effectively as possible, that is, to educate his will. . . . He must feel himself a man of will, and may safely depreciate everything else in him and deem it subject to his will, for without this illusion he could not succeed in adapting himself socially.
>
> It is otherwise with a person in the second half of life who no longer needs to educate his conscious will, but who, to understand the meaning of his individual life, needs to experience his own inner being. (p. 50)

Jung often focused his readers' attention on the second half of life because he saw it as the time when the well-rounded person needed to get in touch with and respond to the unconscious. Not so long ago, religion (and to a lesser degree myths) initiated people in the second half of their lives into an awareness and understanding of the archetypal images. The latter are for Jungians the symbols older than the individuals that make up the groundwork of the human psyche and give access to the unconscious. Through the religious archetypes, people were once able to reach a measure of intuitive knowledge of their inner lives. However, for most people, religion has now lost that important cultural function (Jung, 1981, pp. 396–403).

Therefore, contemporary propagators of myths and enduring symbols (among which the media are probably the most powerful) carry the burden of this work, whether they know it or not. The significance of routine television programming is that it can relay myths and images that resonate in tune with the ancient archetypes (such as that of the athletic hero). It then reworks them into symbols that convey variations on those older values in forms adapted to today's needs.

What then of our cultural fixation on youthful heroes? In Jung's experience, the desire of people in the second half of life to hold on to youth frequently indicated a failure to look toward the unconscious and acknowledge the prompting of primordial images. He thought it was caused by a fear of facing the inevitable decline of physical energies and a reluctance to prepare for the eventual approach of death (Jung, 1981, pp. 396–403). Thus the ceaseless collective celebration of youth in television sport seems to exalt the triumph of physicality and will. Read metaphorically, it claims the victory of consciousness over the unconscious and covers a marked collective fear of the inner life.

That is the dominant perspective, but a thorough Jungian analysis will respect the principle he drew from Heraclitus and called enantiodromia. This is the idea we have already encountered, that all things carry within them the seeds of their opposites and eventually run to them. In our case, this has a bearing on the nature of the hero as a mythical image. As we have seen, the distinctive characteristics of heroes are locked into their classic narrative. They regress, they battle with their dark side, and in the process they may suffer injury. If they succeed, they emerge changed by the encounter with the opposites and are more completely adapted to their present stage in life. What is more, they have to expose themselves to the danger not once but many times. It is a lifelong process. "What we seek in visible human form is not man, but the superman, the hero or god, that *quasi-human* being who symbolizes the ideas, forms, and forces which grip and mould the soul" (Jung, 1956, p. 178).

As a figure who represents the willingness to undergo repeated transformations to explore wholeness, the hero is analogous to the priest (Samuels, Shorter, & Plaut, 1986, p. 66). Thus, masked beneath our overriding absorption with the youthfulness of television's sporting superstars, there lie concealed the seeds of a rather different desire. Perhaps one day televised sports will provide a platform for heroes with the potential to offer viewers role models for more challenging explorations of the self than those restricted to developing physical power and the control of will. Christie is now too old for viewers to project the image of eternal youth onto him. As he moves toward and eventually into retirement, will he be taken up by sports reporters as the transformative hero? There could hardly be a better candidate for the role than this gentle, majestic man.

Note

1. A further diffusion takes place in countries such as the United States, where NBC interrupts coverage with not only commercials but a great deal of material that lionizes U.S. national heroes. Larson and Rivenburgh (1991) record that, in covering the Seoul Olympics, NBC interrupted the opening ceremony 25 times for nearly 52 minutes of commercials and another 21 times for news breaks, interviews, and background segments averaging more than 3 minutes in length. Most of the inserted material cut into coverage of the cultural performances in the stadium.

Bibliography

Bale, J. (1991). Playing at home: British football and a sense of place. In J. Williams & S. Wagg (Eds.), *British football and social change: Getting into Europe* (pp. 130–144). Leicester, England: Leicester University Press.

Clarke, A., & Clarke, J. (1982). Highlights and action replays: Ideology, sport and the media. In J. Hargreaves (Ed.), *Sport, culture and ideology* (pp. 62–87). London: Routledge & Kegan Paul.

Dunning, E. (1971). *The sociology of sport: A selection of readings*. London: Frank Cass.

Elias, N. (1971). The genesis of sport as a sociological problem. In E. Dunning, *The sociology of sport: A selection of readings* (pp. 88–115). London: Frank Cass.

Elias, N., & Dunning, E. (1971). Folk football in medieval and early modern Britain. In E. Dun-

ning, *The sociology of sport: A selection of readings* (pp. 116–132). London: Frank Cass.

Guttmann, A. (1978). *From ritual to record: The nature of modern sports*. New York: Columbia University Press.

Hargreaves, J. (1986). *Sport, power and culture: A social and historical analysis of popular sports in Britain*. Cambridge, England: Polity.

Jhally, S. (1989). Cultural studies and the sports/media complex. In L. A. Wenner (Ed.), *Media, sports, and society* (pp. 70–93). London: Sage.

Jung, C. G. (1956). *Symbols and transformation: The collected works, 5* (rev. ed.). London: Routledge & Kegan Paul. (Originally published 1952)

Jung, C. G. (1968). *The archetypes and the collective unconscious: The collected works, 9* (rev. ed.). London: Routledge & Kegan Paul. (Originally published 1948)

Jung, C. G. (1973). *Memories, dreams, reflections* (rev. ed.). Glasgow, Scotland: Collins. (Originally published 1961)

Jung, C. G. (1976). *Psychological types: The collected works, 6* (rev. ed.). Princeton, NJ: Princeton University Press, 1976. (Originally published 1921)

Jung, C. G. (1981) *The structure and dynamics of the psyche: The collected works, 8* (rev. ed.). London: Routledge & Kegan Paul. (Originally published 1931)

Jung, C. G. (1985). *The practice of psychotherapy. The collected works, 16* (rev. ed.). Princeton, NJ: Princeton University Press. (Originally published 1935)

Larson, J. F., & Rivenburgh, N. (1991). A comparative analysis of Australian, U.S., and British telecasts of the Seoul Olympic opening ceremony. *Journal of Broadcasting and Electronic Media, 35*(1), 75–94.

Lipsky, R. (1975). *Sports world: An American dreamland*. New York: Quadrangle.

MacAloon, J. J. (1984). *Rite, drama, festival, spectacle: Rehearsals towards a theory of cultural performance*. Philadelphia: Institute for the Study of Human Issues.

O'Donnell, H. (in press). *Lillehammer 1994: The reception of the Norwegian image in the British media*. London: John Libbey.

Samuels, A. (1990). *Jung and the post-Jungians*. London: Routledge.

Samuels, A., Shorter, B., & Plaut, F. (1986). *A critical dictionary of Jungian analysis*. London: Routledge & Kegan Paul.

Trujillo, N., & Krizek, B. (1994). Emotionality in the stands and in the field: Expressing self through baseball. *Journal of Sport & Social Issues, 18*, 303–325.

Wenner, L. A., & Gantz, W. (1989). The audience experience with sports on television. In L. A. Wenner (Ed.), *Media, sports, and society* (pp. 241–269). London: Sage.

Questions for Consideration

1. Is the libidinal model of heroic identification helpful or harmful to individuals?
2. Does competitive individualism promote proper values in today's heroes?
3. Why do you think we look to find many of our heroes especially in competitive athletics?

Gender

32   Women and Masculine Sports

B. C. Postow
University of Tennessee, Knoxville

Antiandrogynists maintain, according to B.C. Postow, that distinct gender roles in sport must be maintained either because of natural differences between males and females or to preserve socially cultivated gender roles. Against antiandrogynism, Joyce Trebilcot has argued for a distinction between monoandrogynism (M, where males and females should develop masculine and feminine traits and compete in both traditionally masculine and feminine activities) and polyandrogynism (P, where individuals of both sexes are encouraged to develop along masculine or feminine lines exclusively, or according to the guidelines of M). Trebilcot's distinction, Postow argues, is unavailing in that it sweeps away the larger social issue of genuine differences in genders, while it focuses on the issue from the perspective of individual excellence.

Postow then distinguishes four different senses in which sports may be labeled "masculine": (1) masculine$_a$ (sports characterized by physical aggression, power, and effectiveness); (2) masculine$_b$ (sports in which the attitude of aggressiveness, competition, stamina, and discipline combine in a focus on winning and setting records); (3) masculine$_c$ (sports that serve and have served as a vehicle for masculine identification); and (4) masculine$_d$ (sports in which certain masculine biological advantages such as strength and speed are factors). The question she addresses in the remainder of the reading is, Do any of these senses of masculine offer women a moral reason for refraining from sports or, at least, for participating in them in a manner different from men?

Of the four types of masculinity in sports, only the latter is problematic, since by participating with males in sports where males have an obvious statistical advantage, women perpetuate the image of female inferiority. One way to rectify this is by selectively competing in sports in which females have a statistical advantage or, at least, have no disadvantage.

A problem emerges. Fairness and freedom of opportunity seem to dictate that women who can compete with men in masculine$_d$ sports ought to be able to do so. But if allowed, then men ought to be able to compete freely with women in such sports. This may be fine for the few women who can compete with males, but what of the many others who cannot? Thus, the scarce available resources, such as facilities and coaching, would go preferentially to men, and this seems unfair.

Reprinted, by permission, from B. C. Postow, "Women and Masculine Sports," *Journal of the Philosophy of Sport* VII (1980): 51–58.

Supporters of the antiandrogynist, or "vive la différence," ideal of gender identification may understandably find encouragement and reassurance in the contemplation of sports. Sports have traditionally been regarded as an unequivocally masculine endeavor—a training ground for manly skills and attitudes. Nature itself seems to support the antiandrogynist position, for in sports anatomical differences between men and women are undeniably relevant, giving men a very considerable statistical superiority over women. I shall investigate the various senses in which sports may plausibly be called masculine, and I shall argue that the fact that sports do qualify as masculine in these senses yields no support to the antiandrogynist ideal. The antiandrogynist position holds that people ought to maintain a distinction between the masculine and the feminine either to conform to some good natural order or to foster and preserve distinct gender identities for reasons of mental health or social welfare. My investigation will reveal no natural order which is *prima facie* worthy of efforts for its preservation. I shall also argue against the view that the desirability of preserving distinct gender identities justifies maintaining any sort of distinction between men's and women's sports (e.g., by subtly discouraging women's participation, or even by maintaining sex segregation in teams). I shall also argue, on the other hand, that the natural male advantage in most sports must be acknowledged and dealt with in a way not provided for within well-known androgynist ideals of individual excellence.

Joyce Trebilcot (9: pp. 71–72) distinguishes between two androgynist ideals: monoandrogynism, or M for short, and polyandrogynism, or P for short. According to M, each individual should develop both traditionally masculine and traditionally feminine personality traits and should engage in both traditionally masculine and traditionally feminine activities. According to P, it is desirable for any individual who is inclined to do so to conform to the ideal approved by M, but it is equally desirable for an individual who is inclined to do so to develop only "masculine" or only "feminine" personality traits and to engage only in "masculine" or only in "feminine" activities. With respect to women and sports, M would naturally lead us to believe that it is desirable for women to participate in "masculine" sports; P would naturally lead us to believe that it is equally desirable for women to participate in "masculine" sports as not to participate in them. Both M and P seem to lead us astray here because they are limited to ideals of individual excellence and do not deal with the larger social reality. I shall argue that unlike most activities,

some sports are masculine[1] in a sense that I shall call masculine$_d$, which does give women a moral reason *not* to support or participate in them.

First, I will define the senses in which sports may be called masculine and then inquire whether the fact that a sport is masculine in any of these senses provides a reason for women not to engage in it or to engage in it differently or separately from men. At least four different features or clusters of features of a sport might reasonably be referred to in calling a sport masculine. One such cluster of features was isolated by Eleanor Metheny, who analyzed those sports (e.g., wrestling, weight-lifting, long-distance running, and most team sports) from which Olympic rules have excluded women. She lists these features as follows:

> An attempt to physically subdue the opponent by bodily contact
>
> Direct application of bodily force to some heavy object
>
> Attempt to project the body into or through space over long distances
>
> Cooperative face-to-face opposition in situations in which some body contact may occur. (7: p. 49)

Perhaps these features are believed to be especially appropriate physical expressions of aggression, power, and effectiveness, which are seen as especially masculine. Whatever the explanation, however, it does seem that a native speaker would be likely to call sports which possess these features masculine or even supermasculine, although sports may also be characterized as masculine on other grounds. Metheny has shown that some features which identify a sport as masculine are characterizable solely in terms of the behavior required of participants by the rules of the game. To determine whether a sport has these features, one should refer to the rules of the game rather than to the characteristic attitudes of participants or to the societal function served by the sport. Any sport requiring the behavior depicted by Metheny's list or some similar list,[2] then, will be called masculine$_a$.

A second cluster of features which may prompt people to call a sport masculine concerns the attitude with which the sport is characteristically played and which is thought to be necessary for playing the sport well. This attitude includes "aggressiveness, competitive spirit, stamina, and discipline" all focused on winning or setting records.[3] Devotion to a team is also a contributing factor. These elements of attitude constitute a "mode which is understood to conform to an image of masculinity no less strong in contemporary America than in ancient Greece" (6: pp. 184; 187). Sports which are characteristically played in this mode and which it is commonly thought must be played this way to be played well, will be called masculine$_b$ sports. All sports may be masculine$_b$ to a greater or lesser degree, but sports such as football, in which approved aggressiveness includes a readiness to injure an opponent, seem to qualify as masculine$_b$ to an especially high degree.

Another feature which may be thought to qualify a sport as masculine is its use as a vehicle of masculine gender identification. A sport will be termed masculine$_c$ if participation in it in our society functions to engender or reinforce a feeling of identity and solidarity with men as distinct from women. Baseball and football are two sports which have traditionally served this function in our society, largely by being designated as activities especially appropriate for boys and men and inappropriate or questionably appropriate for girls and women. Swimming and volleyball would not qualify as masculine$_c$ sports.

Of course, masculine$_b$ sports and masculine$_c$ sports are somewhat related in that masculine$_b$ sports are by definition well suited to socialize males in accordance with the particular ideal of masculine gender identity embodied in the masculine$_b$ attitudinal mode. Nevertheless, an activity which is masculine$_b$ to the highest degree would fail to be masculine$_c$ if it were approved for women and men equally and without role differentiation.[4] Such a sport would socialize both women and men in accordance with the masculine$_b$ attitudinal mode, but it would not socialize men as a group distinct from women. Little League baseball has traditionally been masculine$_c$, but sex-integrated Little League baseball should cease to be masculine$_c$ even if it remains masculine$_b$.

Another reason for which sports may be thought masculine is their definition of athletic excellence in terms of developed capacities, such as strength and speed, in which men naturally have a considerable statistical advantage over women. A sport will be called masculine$_d$, then if it is such that due to biological factors, most men are significantly better at it than most women, and the best athletes in it are men. Examples of masculine$_d$ sports are football, baseball, basketball, and tennis, which strongly emphasize upper-body strength (10: p. 96). Not all sports are masculine$_d$. On the balance beam, "small size, flexibility and low center of gravity combine to give women the kind of natural hegemony that men enjoy in football" (5: p. 275), and in long-distance swimming women have the natural advantages of long-term endurance, buoyancy, insulation, and narrow shoulders (10: p. 98). Still the vast majority of our sports, including the most prestigious ones, are masculine$_d$.

Does the fact that a sport is masculine in any of the senses explained above provide a moral reason for women not to engage in it or to engage in it differently or separately from men? The features which make a sport masculine$_a$ seem generally to be morally neutral,[5] and insofar as they are neutral, I take it to be uncontroversial that these features per se provide no moral grounds for women to observe any limitations on participation, or to participate separately from men. Of course, masculine$_a$ sports are generally also masculine$_d$;[6] this fact is arguably grounds for sex segregation and will be subsequently dealt with.

In my opinion, there is nothing intrinsically immoral in participating in masculine$_b$ sports in a masculine$_b$ way, but if there is a superior ideal, there is a moral reason to pursue that ideal

The incomparable Babe Didrikson leaps over a hurdle in a race. Perhaps as much as any other female athlete, Didrikson opened many doors for women who wanted to compete in sports that were traditionally open only to men. Ed. Hulton/Archive

rather than the masculine$_b$ ideal. Mary Duquin (4: pp. 101–102) depicts a superior ideal of sport which combines instrumental and expressive attitudes and behavior. In ideal sport, "the participant feels a sense of fulfillment when participating, as well as when winning. She feels joy, strength, thrill, competence and control when sporting whether in practice or competition. She performs ethically, drawing her ethics from her own self-conscience. . . . She performs with confidence and comradeship." Now, all masculine$_b$ sports seem capable of being played in a non-masculine$_b$ way.[7] Therefore, those with moral objections to the masculine$_b$ attitudinal mode have no reason to refrain from masculine$_b$ sports, but only (at most) to refrain from participation with those who subscribe to that ideal. This might well preclude participation in profes-

sional or even subsidized athletics,[8] but it need not preclude mixed teams of men and women, for not all men subscribe to the masculine$_b$ ideal. Nothing that has been said supports the anti-androgynist position, for women have not been shown to have any less right than men to play masculine$_b$ sports in a masculine$_b$ way against men. Insofar as Duquin's ideal is accepted as superior to the masculine$_b$ ideal, however, M must be preferred to P, for P would approve of the masculine$_b$ ideal equally with Duquin's ideal.

I shall assume for the sake of argument the positive value of masculine orientation and solidarity for males. It may be thought that women should refrain from participating in masculine$_c$ sports, or at least be relegated to second-class status in them, for we have seen that a sport ceases to be masculine$_c$ if women are fully integrated in it. But sport is not the only way to forge masculine orientation and solidarity,[9] and exclusion from the dominant sport culture is directly and indirectly detrimental to women in many ways.[10] Thus, even if masculine orientation and solidarity for males are of undoubted net value, women would betray their own dignity as agents with rights as important as those of men by accepting limitations on participation or second-class status for the purpose of preserving popular sports as masculine$_c$ male preserves. Those who disagree with me may object that sport is not, as I have alleged, merely one of many possible vehicles of masculine orientation in our society. Arnold R. Beisser (2: pp. 194–195) argues that sport's emphasis on strength, together with its separation of male from female roles, makes it uniquely suited to relieve the tensions created by the facts that men have lost much of their fatherly authority and their status of sole breadwinner and that male strength is almost obsolete, even though "the cultural expectations of masculinity have remained fixed as they were in pioneer days." Notice, however, that the function of sport to which Beisser is here drawing our attention is not merely the formation or reinforcement of masculine gender identity, but rather the relief of a tension generated by the dissonance between reality and the ideology of "pioneer days" that men deserve respect and authority because of their physical strength. Insofar as sports serve as a safety valve to relieve the pressure caused by the dissonance between this ideology and reality, they help to preserve the ideology. Because this ideology is patently unworthy of preservation, Beisser's observation cannot be used to show that the fact that sports are masculine$_c$ is a good reason for women to refrain from participation in them or to accept second-class status in them.

As I indicated at the beginning of the paper, the fact that a sport is masculine$_d$ does, I think, provide some reason for women not to support or engage in it. The number and prestige of sports in which men have a natural statistical superiority to women, together with the virtual absence of sports in which women are naturally superior, help perpetuate an image of general female inferiority which we have a moral reason to undermine. An obvious way to undermine it is to increase the number and prestige of sports in which women have a natural statistical superiority to men or at least are not naturally inferior. Thus, there is reason, at least where this can be done without undue personal sacrifice, for women to withdraw energy and support from masculine$_d$ sports and to turn instead toward other sports—preferably ones in which women naturally excel. It seems clear, however, that women who enjoy or are well-suited to masculine$_d$ sports are not obligated to abstain from them in order to popularize sports in which women excel, for that end can be achieved without such sacrifices.

My moral intuitions become less definite when we turn to a problem of current interest raised in school athletics by the male advantage in masculine sports. It seems unfair to bar from men's teams those women who can make the grade, for this would deny those women equality of opportunity to compete, defined as freedom from legal or other socially imposed restrictions. But if women should be free to compete against men, then it seems that men should also be free to compete against women. In masculine$_d$ sports, allowing men to compete against women would expose women to a drastically reduced probability of receiving the moderately scarce athletic resources, such as access to facilities and coaching, that go with making a team. This too seems unfair. Equality of opportunity *qua* freedom from socially imposed restrictions on one's ability to compete seems to work against equality of opportunity *qua* probability, given the same level of effort, of actually receiving the benefits of the sport. The first kind of equality of opportunity seems required by the ideal of fair competition; the second kind of equality of opportunity seems required by the students' *prima facie* equal rights to what Jane English (5: p. 270) calls the basic benefits of sports, such as health and fun. A scheme supported by Richard Alan Rubin that each sport should have three independent teams offers a possible compromise. The varsity team "would consist of the best male and female athletes. . . . The remaining two teams would consist of athletes of lesser ability and would be separated by sex" (8: p. 566). In Rubin's scheme, women interested in participating on a team in a masculine$_d$ sport would still have roughly half as much probability of making some team (i.e., either varsity or second string) as men have, because men would make up all or almost all of the varsity and all of the men's team, whereas women would be almost exclusively confined to the women's team. This might be acceptable, however, if Rubin is right that "virtually everyone interested would be able to compete." Preserving one team for women and one for men would, at any rate, avoid the drastic reduction in women's chances of participating that would result from having only mixed teams. Rubin's scheme also avoids the drastic denial of formal equality of competitive opportunity for men that would result of a team were reserved for women but not for men. Of course, one might wish to strike the compromise differently, sacrificing men's rights to formal equality of opportunity in favor of women's right to equal probability of receiving the benefits of sports. This could be done by having only one second string team which either barred men completely or put a quota on them.

A possible problem with both these compromise schemes is that they are probably illegal under the ERA (8: 573–574).[11] Another objectionable feature is that they tie probability of receiving the basic benefits of a sport to natural aptitude. Men and women with unsuitable physiques do not have an equal probability of receiving the basic benefits of sports, compared with more athletically gifted men and women. A way to grant fully everyone's *prima facie* claim (even those with unsuitable physiques) to an equal right to the basic benefits of participating in the school sports which she or he most enjoys, and still to grant fully everyone's *prima facie* claim to equal formal freedom to compete, would be to sever the connection between winning a place on a team and being granted access to moderately scarce athletic resources. In team sports, either enough teams could be available at every ability level to accommodate everyone who wanted to play and who was willing to turn out for practice (with scarce athletic resources simply spread as thinly as necessary to go around), or there could be at least one team for each ability level, with membership in the teams determined by some form of lottery that equalized the probability of being on a team for everyone who wanted to play and was willing to turn out for practice. There would, in these schemes, be no apparent need for sex separation, because women would not be deprived of an equal chance for athletic benefits by being made to compete with men. Of course, the best athletes would stand to lose a great deal compared with the usual arrangement which makes access to scarce athletic resources a reward of winning competitions. Perhaps a sound argument could be made that the social desirability of helping the best athletes develop to their fullest potential overrides the *prima facie* claim of athletically ill-endowed people to an equal right to the benefits of the sports they enjoy. In this case, a scheme like Rubin's would be preferable.

In professional athletics, there may appear to be a special reason for maintaining single-sex teams in masculine$_d$ sports. Jane English (5: p. 273) argues that "when there are virtually no female athletic stars, or when women receive much less prize money than men do, this is damaging to the self-respect of all women." But this argument is open to several objections. Raymond A. Belliotti (3: pp. 68, 71) seems correct in stating that "we should not respect ourselves because of our own or our group's attainments of fame and fortune in professional sports," and that "as an empirical matter of fact, these attainments *are not* an important factor in the way the vast majority of women determine their respect for themselves." Furthermore, if women's self-respect were dependent on the existence of female athletic stars, it would seem more helpful to have stars in female-biased sports, where the very best athletes are women, than in masculine sports, where the very best athletes are men.

In closing, let me recapitulate the major positions I have taken in this paper: (1) The anti-androgynist position is incorrect: women have as much right as men to engage in any masculine sport in any sense of that term and do not have any duty to accept second-class status; (2) sex segregation is not morally required in sports on grounds of its usefulness in preserving masculine$_c$ sports, nor is it morally required on grounds of its usefulness in maintaining women's equality of opportunity in masculine$_d$ sports, or on grounds of serving women's self-respect by making possible female stars in masculine$_d$ sports; (3) because they are ideals of purely individual excellence, both forms of androgynism discussed by Trebilcot lead us astray concerning the desirability of women participating in masculine sports. Neither form of androgynism takes account of the fact that men do naturally have a very considerable statistical advantage over women in performing prestigious activities such as masculine$_d$ sports, and that women have reason to counter the general image of male superiority fostered by those activities by withdrawing support from the activities and promoting activities in which women have a natural advantage over men.

Notes

1. I intend the word "masculine" itself to be neutral between the androgynist and antiandrogynist ideals. I shall at this point cease to put the word in quotes. This may seem to favor the antiandrogynist position, but it would have favored the androgynist position to use quotes at every occurrence. I have decided that it is fairest to err, if err I must, by allowing my choice of punctuation to favor the position with which I have least sympathy.

2. One suggestion for tinkering with the list is to delete Metheny's third item and to add "the use of deadly force against animals" to capture bull-fighting and hunting.

3. Duquin (4: pp. 97–98) is here speaking of the instrumental orientation (i.e. focus on winning) which she says has characterized sports up to the present. She argues that sports have been regarded this way because they have been regarded as masculine, and "society has traditionally expected males to be instrumental, not expressive."

4. The fact that females must be excluded for a sport to be "masculine$_e$" is obvious also to the promoters of sports as a vehicle of masculine socialization. Duquin (4: p. 90) cites the following examples: A. Fisher, "Sports as an Agent of Masculine Orientation," *The Physical Educator*, 29 (1972), p. 120, and P. Werner, "The Role of Physical Education in Gender Identification," Ibid., p. 27.

5. The use of deadly force against animals (see note 2 above) seems morally objectionable to me—equally objectionable for men as for women, of course.

6. Possible exceptions are sports in which there is an "attempt to project the body into or through space over long distances," for if the distances are long enough male strength may be countered by female endurance, light weight, and tolerance for heat (10: p. 98).

7. It seems that if soccer can be played noninstrumentally, then any sport can. I know that soccer can from my participation in a series of soccer games played by a mixed-sex faculty group at my own institution. Although we played our best and cheered enthusiastically when our team scored a goal, most of us did not keep track of the number of goals scored, and did not know which team had won the game when it was close.

8. Duquin (4: p. 102) cites a psychological study which supports the view that extrinsic incentives in athletics may impede a noninstrumental approach: M. R. Lepper, D. Greene, and R. Nisbett, "Undermining Children's Intrinsic Interest with Extrinsic Reward: A Test of the Overjustification Hypothesis," *Journal of Personality and Social Psychology*, 8 (1973), p. 129.

9. Some other ways are the wearing of clothing socially defined as male attire, behavior which is demanded of and reserved for males by etiquette, the different roles assigned to men and women in dancing and other mixed-sex activities, participation in groups and ceremonies from which women are excluded, and participation in activities in which males and females engage separately (e.g., sex-segregated clubs). I do not wish to defend all of these as morally unobjectionable.

10. This is argued in detail by Iris Young in an unpublished manuscript, "Social Implications of the Exclusion of Women from Sport." Drawing on Beauvoir, Merleau-Ponty, and Eleanor Metheny, she argues (to put her argument very roughly) that because sport is activity *par excellence*, to be regarded as an inappropriate participant in sport is to be regarded as less than a human subject or conscious agent. Furthermore, she argues, exclusion from the dominant sport culture carries serious cultural disabilities in business, politics, and everyday life.

11. Other possible drawbacks of the plan favored by Rubin are expense, dilution of talent, and difficulty of finding schools to compete with at the lower levels. See (1).

Bibliography

1. Association of American Colleges, Washington, D.C. Project on the Status and Education of Women. "What Constitutes Equality for Women in Sport? Federal Law Puts Women in the Running." April 1974.

2. Beisser, Arnold R. "The American Seasonal Masculinity Rites." *Sport Sociology: Contemporary Themes*. Edited by Andrew Yiannakis et al. Dubuque, IA: Kendall/Hunt Publishing Co., 1976.

3. Belliotti, Raymond A. "Women, Sex, and Sports." *Journal of the Philosophy of Sport*, 6 (1979), 67–72.

4. Duquin, Mary E. "The Androgynous Advantage." *Women and Sport: From Myth to Reality*. Edited by Carole A. Oglesby. Philadelphia: Lea & Febiger, 1968.

5. English, Jane. "Sex Equality in Sports." *Philosophy & Public Affairs*, 7 (1978), 269–277.

6. Felshin, Jan. "The Dialectic of Women and Sport." *The American Woman in Sport*. By Ellen W. Gerber et al. Reading, MA: Addison-Wesley Publishing Co., 1974.

7. Metheny, Eleanor. "Symbolic Forms of Movement: The Feminine Image in Sports." *Connota-*

tions of Movement in Sport and Dance. Dubuque, IA: Wm. C. Brown Publishing Co., 1965.

8. Rubin, Richard Alan. "Sex Discrimination in Interscholastic High School Athletics." *Syracuse Law Review,* 25 (1974), 535–574.

9. Trebilcot, Joyce. "Two Forms of Androgynism." *Journal of Social Philosophy,* 8 (1977), 4–8. Reprinted in *Feminism and Philosophy.* Edited by Mary Vetterling-Braggin et al. Totowa, NJ: Littlefield, Adams and Co., 1977.

10. Wood, P.S. "Sex Differences in Sports." *The New York Times Magazine,* May 18, 1980.

Questions for Consideration

1. Do you agree with Postow's argument that Trebilcot's androgynous solution to anti-androgyny is flawed?

2. Postow's own solution to inequality of gender in sport seems radical. It suggests that women who want to play masculine$_d$ sports and who cannot compete with men in them ought to seek other sports in which they are competitive or superior. Is this solution fair? Will it eliminate the notion of female inferiority or perpetuate it?

3. Is the having of *athletic* role models so critical for female (or even male) self-respect? Might it not be the case that much of American male gender uncertainty and instability is on account of having aggressive and violent role models such as many male sports figures?

33   Title IX and Gender Equity

Jan Boxill
University of North Carolina at Chapel Hill

In this reading, Jan Boxill argues that Title IX is an important first step in establishing gender equity in sports. Nevertheless, more needs to be done.

Women have traditionally been barred from competitive sports through the many biases that exist both culturally and within sports themselves. Women who desire to compete are often still considered manly or lesbian. Moreover, most competitive sports are structured in such a manner as to favor masculine traits such as height, weight, strength, and speed. Much of the issue of equality centers on eradicating these biases—a redefinition of sport.

Sport itself is an expression of morally heroic virtues and beauty. Athletes develop courage, grace, and self-discipline. Sport also allows for self-expression. Nothing in the nature of sport is gender specific. Women, Boxill argues, should have equal opportunity to participate in sports.

Since sport has traditionally been viewed as male activity, the various sports themselves are mostly designed to suit males and favor male attributes. Winning at all costs is not the aim of sports, nor are opponents to be considered as enemies, but rather as challenges to overcome. Overall, athletes ought to strive for excellence in cooperative competition with others.

For Boxill, the value of sport is unquestionable. Sport, she asserts, "is the single most available, unalienated activity that provides autonomous agents a vehicle for self-expression, self-respect, and self-development." Sport is freely chosen and allows creative energy of both body and mind in agreement with aesthetic standards.

Reprinted, by permission, from J. Boxill, "Title IX and Gender Equity," *Journal of the Philosophy of Sport* XX–XXI (1993–1994): 23–31.

Title IX is the portion of the Education Amendments of 1972 that prohibits sex discrimination in educational institutions receiving any federal funds. Title IX states:

> No person in the United States shall, on the basis of sex, be excluded from participation in, be denied the benefits of, or be subjected to discrimination under any educational program or activity receiving federal financial assistance. (8: p. 3)

One of the main targets of Title IX has been sports and athletic activities. Before its passage, athletic scholarships for women were nonexistent. Now, there are over 10,000 scholarships for women athletes (8: p. 4). Today, Title IX guarantees two major areas of high school and college athletics: financial assistance and effective accommodation of student interests and abilities.

Since the passage of Title IX in 1972, great strides have been made in girls' and women's sports. The 1994 Women's Basketball Championship made that clear to me. In an atmosphere usually seen only in the men's "Final Four" games, the women's "Final Four" games were played before a packed Richmond Coliseum in Richmond, Virginia; tickets were sold out months in advance. Also like the men's games, the women's games were nationally televised. And to top it all, the 1994 Women's National Championship team, the University of North Carolina (UNC) Tar Heels were treated to a visit to the White House for an audience with President Clinton. All this is a far cry from when I played college basketball in the days before Title IX. The progress has been great, but there is more to be done, for along with the gains have come some losses and a great deal of misunderstanding. The integration of women into the traditionally male domain of sports, as with any integration, is not without conflict, compromise, and confusion. Men tend to see sports as their territory and the mere presence of women in the arena as a violation. But not only can sports benefit from the integration, so too can the men and women who participate. In this paper I will attempt an analysis of the gain, the benefits, the losses, and the misunderstandings of women in sports and will conclude with some recommendations.

With the Civil Rights movement and women's liberation, calls for equality have often been heard. Women and minorities have argued for equal access to education, to economic opportunities, to political opportunities, and to opportunities for social equality. But the meaning of equality in these claims was, and still is, controversial. In education it seems relatively clear that equality means essentially that men and women are treated the same with regards to admissions policies. On the surface, quantitative grades and Scholastic Aptitude Test (SAT) scores are easy to compare in admissions applications; however, controversy has arisen because these grades and SAT scores do not reveal the possible hidden biases beneath that surface.

In the sports world, women not only have to contend with hidden biases, they also have to compete against the more firmly entrenched biases based on observable physical attributes such as height, weight, strength, muscle mass, and speed—all attributes admired in men. Because sports are seen as activities designed to develop these attributes, women's exclusion from sports was not seen as the result of bias, but as mere fact. As a result, attempting to gain equality in sports requires more than eradicating the hidden biases in how people think about sports; it requires a recognition of the physical differences between men and women and a rethinking of the value of sports. The value of sport is not only about achieving a goal, it is also about determining what that goal should be. I will approach the topic of equality by examining why women want

to participate, why they ought to participate, and thus why women ought to have equal access.

Women wish to participate in sports for essentially the same reasons that men want to participate, though this does not necessarily mean they wish to be men. The reasons are closely related to why sports are so pervasive in the United States and the world.

What accounts for the fascination with sports? Sport fascinates for many reasons. Its beauty and its display of morally heroic virtues are just a couple of reasons. Human beings admire the beauty and grace of sport; they are moved by the discipline it requires. Often it is the heroism and the courage in sport we applaud, not the violence that occasions the display of these virtues. Both men and women want to participate for these reasons.

There are further reasons why both men and women ought to participate. Because of the nature and design of sport, it provides a significant moral function both for the individual and for society at large. It does so first because it provides autonomous agents with a vehicle for self-expression—a means to self-respect and self-development. Sport in this sense serves as what John Rawls (7: p. 523) calls "a social union in a society of social unions, a community of shared ends and common activities valued for themselves, enjoying one another's excellences and individuality as they participate in the activities." These virtues, shared ends, and common activities are not gender specific; that is, they are not exclusively male.

To understand the issues involved, a working or paradigmatic notion of sport may be helpful. In its paradigmatic form, sport is a freely chosen, rule-governed activity in which one is physically challenged through competition. The first two features certainly are gender neutral; the last two may give us hints as to why sport was traditionally male. Competition is often claimed as a male domain, first because it involves the physical body and second because it engenders a "macho" aggressive image.

Physical challenges are usually associated with the male body. This may explain why there are sports available for almost every male body type. We have been socialized to think that men's bodies are to be developed and challenged to be made strong, while women's are to be admired for their beauty. Indeed when we think of someone as "athletic," we think of this in terms of men's bodies.

One of the most controversial, and perhaps most misunderstood, features of our society is "competition." Competition is seen to be driven by selfish motives and involves competitors treating others as means, as enemies to be defeated, or as obstacles thwarting one's victory or success—all of which are to be removed by any means possible. Competition places an emphasis on winning, leading to the "win-at-all-costs" syndrome. These characteristics are associated with men. On the other hand, cooperation, the unselfish treatment of others as partners sharing in the ends, places no emphasis on winning. These characteristics are associated with women. It has been stated, "Athletic competition builds character in our boys. We do not need that kind of character in our girls"[1] (1: p. 135). This mentality has served to keep women out of sports. And since sports competition has been viewed as preparation for the business world, excluding women from this competition has also served to exclude them from the business world.

While competition can lead to the win at all costs syndrome with all its evils, it need not and most often does not. While we see instances of cheating, injuring others, and steroid use to win at all costs, we more often see fair competitions in which the participants respect each other for the challenge. Examples can be seen in almost all women's competitions, in the Olympics, and in most high school and collegiate competitions. The desire to win is no less strong, but not at all costs. We do indeed see clear instances of the evil consequences of competition, but they are made clear because sport dramatizes the virtues and vices of our society. While virtues and vices are both dramatized, vices are not more noticeable because they are more prevalent, but because they make better headlines.

Athletic competition need not be seen as combat where opponents are viewed as enemies. Rather, one's opponents are seen as challenges to make one better and to achieve excellence. Each agrees to do her best to test herself against her opponent. Each tests her capabilities against the other. The emphasis is not solely on defeating her opponent, but on striving for excellence through a desire to win within the rules of the game. In playing tennis, for example, if I wish to test my abilities, I choose a partner of similar or slightly better ability who has a similar desire to win within the rules. To complete the challenge, competition requires a great deal of cooperation. Indeed competition is a cooperative challenge for each participant. Viewed in this way, sport competitions are neither evil nor "for males only." Rather, sport competitions serve to develop both men and women, with the result that they benefit everyone.

It is true, and perhaps some may say unfortunate, that sports plays a significant role in the social and business worlds. Sport is a means for providing opportunities, jobs, promotions, for understanding society, appreciating both its benefits and burdens. Education also provides these same opportunities, which is why Janice Moulton (5: p. 220) eloquently and effectively argues that everyone deserves a sporting chance. "Like education," Moulton concludes, "sport is a means, and participation in our civilization is the end. This is why equal opportunity in both is important." This sentiment is the impetus behind Title IX.

I wholeheartedly agree with Moulton but would also like to go further. I maintain that sport is the single most available, unalienated activity that provides autonomous agents a vehicle for self-expression, self-respect, and self-development. An unalienated activity is freely chosen and exemplifies human creativity requiring both the energy of the mind and the body, in accordance with aesthetic standards. It is an activity designed specifically to provide room to express and develop oneself. Though it may serve other purposes, it has as its end the activity itself. It need not have a product nor provide a service. Sports are such activities. Sports are ends in themselves, and as such are included in Marx's "realm of freedom." Both men and women need such activities, and since sports are readily available, they must be made available for both men and women. What is interesting and significant is that different sports are designed to exploit the different bodily excellences that correspond to the different body types of men; this not the case for females. To achieve this end, females must be allowed access to more kinds of sports. This may require opening traditionally male sports to women, modifying these traditionally male sports, or creating new sports. While this is possible, it raises further difficulties.

One of the gender equity's goals is equal access to sports for girls and woman. Title IX is the means to that end. Women cannot, as a rule, compete in football or boxing, nor can they compete with men in most other sports.[2] Although there are exceptions, because they are *exceptions,* they reinforce society's prejudices and thus perpetuate the inequalities of opportunities. Therefore, there is a case for developing sport activities that exploit women's body types. In some cases this may simply be done by modifying the rules of existing sports; in other cases it might require the development of entirely new activities.

Some have argued, among other things, to create new sports for women that emphasize traditionally female attributes such as flexibility, balance, and grace (3). This has been done in the Olympic Games with the addition of rhythmic gymnastics and synchronized swimming. Now, while many of us find these appropriate and competitive additions to the Games, many have still heard sarcastic comments that they are not "real" sports. This is not unusual; often when something new is added, in any area, it is not readily accepted. It must be time tested; some

new activities make it and others don't.[3] Creating new activities for specific purposes is certainly not new. Basketball was originally created for men to play during the winter months, in between the fall and spring sports, to keep them fit. Interestingly, both men and women participated in the early days of basketball. This testifies to the truth that sport can be a fresh creation made to satisfy definite purposes; so other sports could be similarly created. The rules of the game have changed a great deal over time, but the essential concept of basketball still remains.

This brings us to another avenue of allowing access, namely, modifying established sports specifically for women. This is where we hear the complaints that if women want equality, then they should have to compete using the same rules, standards, and equipment as men. For instance, women should use the same ball as men in basketball and the same tee as men in golf. Why change the rules to suit women? But we might ask, why do we ever change the rules of any sport? And further, if the rules were created to favor attributes men tend to have, why not create rules to favor attributes women tend to have? As I mentioned previously, basketball is a very different game today from when it was first invented by James Naismith. The point is that sport governing bodies modify rules all the time for all kinds of reasons, but the main one is to make the game as challenging as possible for all participants. The college game is different from the professional game; international rules are different from U.S. rules; NCAA rules are different from USABA rules; college rules are different from high school rules; and yes, women's rules are different from men's. Yet it is all competitive basketball. There has been discussion for years about lowering the height of the basket for women. Given that in general women are shorter than men, it makes sense to consider this proposal. The women's ball is smaller in diameter than the men's ball by one inch to suit the generally smaller hands of women. I believe this rule has improved the game and made it more challenging for the participants, just as the dimensions and design of the basket have been modified to make the game move more quickly and be more challenging.[4] I could mention a great many other modifications, but the point is that sport activities have been modified for all kinds of reasons for men; there is no reason not to accept modifications for women. Some modifications are to permit equal opportunities for all men to participate; we can do the same for women.

Gender equity seeks the equal opportunity for women to participate in the goods of our society. And as in any aspect of our society, we treat similarities similarly, and the differences differently. This certainly holds true in sports. The obvious problem is to determine just when this is appropriate. In examining the issues in sports, we see all kinds of different treatment especially designed to promote equal opportunity as well as safety. We don't require the same equipment in all sports; in fact, we don't even require the same equipment within sports. In baseball, different gloves are used for the positions, and all the present day gloves are significantly different from those used even 20 years ago. Even different bats are used by the players on the same team. Different equipment is used to protect different areas of the body that are vulnerable in different sports. For example, shin guards are worn in soccer but not in football; in football the helmets worn by the linesmen are different from those worn by the place kicker or the quarterback; the catcher's gear in baseball is different from all the other positions. I could go on, but the point is that the different treatment is based on relevant factors. Thus, it makes good sense for men to wear protective cups and women perhaps to wear protective bras.

One might say here that all this is fine, but if women want to compete with men, then they must compete against them on the same level, using the same rules and standards. But, we don't even require this of men. There are many different classifications based on age, weight, and size within men's sports, most specifically in boxing and wrestling, and not only do we not re-

quire them to compete against each other, we do not sanction it. For example, a heavyweight boxer may not fight a lighter classed boxer unless the lighter classed boxer promotes the challenge. Again, this is to allow equal opportunity for all male body types to develop and be challenged physically. In general, sports, like everything else, are most satisfying when played among people with similar body types and skills.

Could women simply integrate in the established sports and classes? They could and should be allowed to in some sports (e.g., equestrian, archery), but there are good reasons for gender specific classes or sports, some based on physical differences and others not. There are obvious and significant differences between men and women. Those relating to reproduction are the most obvious, but there are others such as body fat content, strength, and height. These differences may need to be taken into consideration when promoting challenges. It is still unlikely that the UNC women's basketball team, though the NCAA National Champions, could successfully challenge the UNC men's basketball team. Size, strength, and speed differences are too great, although there may be individuals on the team who could successfully compete on a one-on-one basis or for a spot on the team.

The gender equity question is: Should women be allowed an opportunity to play on the men's team? At this time I would argue that until women's sports provide the same opportunities as those available for men, women should be allowed to play on a men's team. If for example, a female player of any sport is so far superior to any other female and thus has no significant challenges, then she should be allowed to compete with the men. It would be similar to a "cruiser weight" boxer finding no more challenges in his own weight class and thus wanting to be challenged by a heavier weight boxer. As I mentioned previously, the converse is not permitted; that is, a heavyweight unable to compete successfully in his own weight is not allowed to fight a lighter weight.

Title IX is an attempt to provide opportunities for women to develop in activities previously denied them. To integrate sports fully before women have been given full opportunity to develop in the traditionally male sports would be disastrous and would serve initially to reinforce stereotypes and prejudices and worse, would yield fewer opportunities and would discourage women from participating in the activities at all. The hope is that there will come a time when the best athletes, male and female, compete together, but that time has not yet been reached. Thus, a policy of separate but equal is still necessary. The question is: Is separate but equal ever equal?

Traditionally, separate but equal was never equal, and still is not—but it can be. The NCAA Gender Equity Task Force adopts this premise in advocating equal scholarships and budgets for men's and women's sports. While more money and scholarships are given to women's sports today than in 1972, an NCAA gender equity study conducted in 1992 showed that three-fourths of the money spent on athletics nationally goes to men's programs. These figures are not much different today (2).

In the more than twenty years since the passage of Title IX, strides have been made. There are more scholarships, bigger budgets, more women participating, more television coverage, and more role models for young girls. But along with these strides have come some losses. In 1972, 95% of women's sports were coached and administered by women; in 1990, less than 20% were (6: p. 159). Several explanations come to mind. First, prior to 1972, women were paid very little to run their programs. When more money was put into the programs, men became more interested in positions that paid them to coach and administer programs. In addition, men as coaches reinforced the traditional biases.

There is a belief that men know more about sports and are more capable, so they are naturally more qualified to run and coach sports no matter who is playing. Unfortunately, women collude in this belief, as do parents of girls who wish to participate. Further, since the programs became integrated and thus were automatically subsumed under departments run by men, the "old boy networks" took hold. The women who had coached and run their programs did it because they loved it. (They had to love it, since they did it for little or no monetary compensation!) This was taken to mean by many that they weren't really serious. If sports are to be taken seriously, they must be run by men. And since resources are limited, if money is to be distributed, it must go to those who are the most serious.

Another factor that serves to perpetuate male dominance is homophobia. Homophobia serves to prevent women from participating. As Jackie Joyner-Kersee (6: p. 145) put it: "It used to be you couldn't play basketball or any sport without, 'Oh, she's a lesbian.' Now it's a little better. But it's something they do to keep you from playing sports. That's all it's about." This turns participants into sexual beings and misunderstands the whole concept of sports participation. "Homophobia in sports serves as a way to control women, both gay and straight, and it reflects a gross misunderstanding of who women are as physical and sexual beings" (6: p. 145). Thus homophobia undermines the joy of participating. It still takes courage to be female and athletic.

Homophobia also serves to control the resources, and thus, the administrative and coaching positions. As a coach, this was made very clear to me. First of all in recruiting, when talking with parents about their daughters playing basketball for me, almost all of them asked about whether my assistant and I were married, and whether there were lesbians on the team. The first time this was asked of me I was quite unprepared for the question and went away thinking it was just these parents. Little did I know. As married coaches, we were able to allay many of the parents' fears. If they inquired further about the team, we responded that sexual orientation was not an issue with us, and this usually satisfied them.

Homophobia was again made clear to me in a case in which a coach resigned her position in 1985 to go to another school. The administration made it clear that they wanted either a married woman or a man, single or married, for the coaching position. What is more interesting in this case is that the search had been narrowed to three candidates—two women and one man. Both women had been members of national championship teams and were successful head coaches; one was married and one was single. The man was an assistant coach and was single. The first candidate was made an offer which she turned down because it was significantly less than the salary she was making at her current school; further, she was asked to coach not just basketball, but tennis or another team as well. She could not take such a deep cut, so she negotiated for a salary still below her current one, but one she could live with. The administration refused and went to the second candidate with the same proposal; she countered with a similar request and was refused. They then offered the third candidate, the man, even more than the salary the women had asked for and indicated that he would be required to coach basketball only. When asked why they went with a man, the answer was that it had been offered to two women and they both turned it down. This case arguably has both to do with homophobia and with the bias that women either do it for love or the fun of it and are not serious. In either case, money should not be an issue. Two very good coaches were denied a chance for advancement and even more, women participants were denied the opportunity to learn from positive role models. It also "soured" both women applicants toward college coaching.

Like all the prejudices held about women participating in sports, homophobia will begin to disappear when more women are participating. Both men and women not only can learn more from and about one another but also about themselves as well. Sports can serve to show that many of the old ideas about women are simply prejudices. It is time the established programs realize that women want to gain access to the goods of sports, that women don't want power over men, but instead they want power to participate. Women don't want to be men or even de-

feat men, although they may want to play with men. "If women's athletic potentialities are taken with as much seriousness as a man's it will become more evident that sport concerns not only *man*kind by *human*kind and deserves to be viewed as a basic human enterprise" (9: p. 228).

Though Title IX has done a great deal toward achieving gender equity, there is still more to do. The debate is quieter than before, but it is no less important. The fact that it is not on the front pages of national newspapers does not mean it is no longer an issue. Ninety-five percent of colleges still do not comply with Title IX (2: p. C1). The push for gender equity has now moved to the legal courts. This is unfortunate because it wastes valuable resources and it serves to make enemies of potential partners.

There is no easy way to settle the issue, but I believe that once we recognize that men and women are partners rather than adversaries, then we can achieve a great deal through cooperative endeavors. One approach may require creating more women's programs and even some women's sports, or modifying others. As already mentioned, we make such changes all the time with no loss to the game. We need to educate all people that sports participation has value, not just for men, but for all of us. It is not simply a male activity. Through education we will come to realize that strength is important in some sports, but is overrated and not the decisive factor in most sports.

Another approach toward achieving gender equity has been to cancel men's sports. But this is both dramatic and causes animosities. Revenue shifts can be done with less fanfare; digging in one's heel prevents sensible compromise. An approach taken by legislators in Washington state was to commit 1% of the state universities' tuition revenues to achieve equality for women in sports.

That everyone is entitled to self-respect and self-esteem is undisputed. That everyone has capacities that ought to be developed is also undisputed—capacities that include the moral, the rational, and the aesthetic, what many refer to as "uniquely human attributes." What is required for self-respect, self-esteem, and the development of these attributes is a certain kind of activity. A particularly important kind of activity in this respect is "unalienated activity"—activity that is not a means to an end outside itself. For the vast majority of people, sport is the most available form of unalienated activity and consequently is an important way that people develop their uniquely human attributes, their self-respect, and their self-esteem. In this way, sport serves to humanize the individual. Thus, gender equity is essential in order that women may take advantage of this humanizing activity, just as men have for centuries. Providing women with access to sports allows them to participate in the joys and excellences of a significant social activity, and it allows them to share those joys with others. As such, participation serves not to separate the sexes but to integrate them as partners in a true social union.[5]

Notes

1. A judge ruling against allowing a girl to compete on the boy's cross country team made this statement.

2. I asked a hundred tenth-grade girls how many of them would like to play football and not powder puff. All but five said they would.

3. For example, motorball, motorcycle soccer, was added in the Moscow Olympics. It has not caught on and it is unlikely we will see it again in any Olympic Games.

4. The original basket was a peach basket, 15" in diameter, with a closed bottom. For other changes consult Naismith's original rules (4: pp. 14–15).

5. I wish to thank Bernard Boxill for comments on earlier drafts of this paper.

Bibliography

1. Addelson, Kathryn Pyne. "Equality and Competition." In *Women, Philosophy and Sport,* Metuchen, NJ: Scarecrow Press, 1983, p. 135.

2. Dame, Mike. (1994, August 21). "Many Lawsuits Later, Women Still Not Equal: The Push for Gender Equity Has Stirred Courts—But Not Playing Fields." *Orlando Sentinel.*

3. English, Jane. "Sex Equality in Sports." *Philosophy and Public Affairs,* VII (1978), 269–277.

4. Fox, Larry. *The Illustrated History of Basketball.* New York: Grosset & Dunlop Publ., 1974, pp. 14–15.

5. Moulton, Janice. "Why Everyone Deserves a Sporting Chance: Education, Justice, and College Sport." In *Rethinking College Athletics.* Edited by Judith Andre and David N. James. Philadelphia, PA: Temple University Press, 1991, pp. 210–220.

6. Nelson, Mariah Burton. *Are We Winning Yet? How Women are Changing Sports and Sports are Changing Women.* New York: Random House, 1991.

7. Rawls, John. *A Theory of Justice.* Cambridge, MA: Harvard University Press, 1971.

8. Reith, Kathryn M. *Playing Fair: A Guide to Title IX in High School & College Sports.* (2nd ed.). East Meadow, NY: Women's Sports Foundation, 1994.

9. Weiss, Paul. *Sport: A Philosophic Inquiry.* Carbondale: Southern Illinois University Press, 1969.

Questions for Consideration

1. Do you agree with Boxill that the current practice of sport is masculinely biased? If so, to what extent is it biased?

2. What are Boxill's ideas for reform in sport? Do you favor such reform?

34 The Men's Cultural Centre: Sports and the Dynamic of Women's Oppression/ Men's Repression

Bruce Kidd
University of Toronto

Bruce Kidd's two-pronged thesis is as follows: (1) Sport as it has been traditionally practiced from ancient to present is the "legitimation of male power" in which different masculinities compete, and (2) sport's perpetuation of the sexual division of labor disadvantages women and delimits the opportunities for personal male growth.

With the rise and spread of women's participation in male-dominated societies, men take refuge in sport and find in it a haven where they can be secure in their gender identity. Still sport itself is stratified. At the "lower" level, there are the feminine sports where intrinsic satisfaction and aesthetic sensibility predominate. At the "higher" level, there are the manly sports, where force, dominance, cunning, and might mix together in a fixed effort to win. Male dominance in sport, Kidd argues, is due to a host of psychosexual fears stemming from women's involvement in male-dominated society as well as men's lack of self-understanding.

In the end, Kidd proposes that sport itself is a societal good, but its current practice warrants "democratic" reforms. First, we ought to change the masculine bias of sport itself. Second, we need to address locker-room homophobia and sexism. Third, there ought to be democratic redefinition of the values and rules of sport. Fourth, we must quit regarding contests as battlefronts. Last, we must address sexism in sport by supporting gender equity campaigns by active feminists.

Like many North American cities, Toronto has a strong feminist movement. During the most recent wave of activism, which began in the mid-1960s, women have mounted imaginative, well-organized campaigns for reproductive rights, publicly funded day care, and equal pay for work of equal value as well as against discriminatory hiring practices and sexist stereotyping in the media. These struggles are supported by a broad network or organizations, shelters, periodicals, bookstores, cultural groups, educational activities, and several archives. Feminist leaders have successfully linked their own efforts to other struggles in the workplace and community, especially those struggles for trade union rights and against racism. Yet these campaigns have been only partially successful in contesting and reducing women's historic disadvantage. The dominant, patriarchal institutions—the corporations, the state, and the mass media—have effectively contained women and marginalized their importance in mainstream discourse (Maroney & Luxton, 1987).

Sport as Legitimation of Male Power

An extremely fertile field for the reassertion and legitimation of male power and privilege has

Reprinted, by permission, from Bruce Kidd, "The Men's Cultural Centre: Sports and the Dynamic of Women's Oppression/Men's Repression," in *Sport, Men, and the Gender Order*, edited by Michael A. Messner and Donald F. Sabo (Champaign, IL: Human Kinetics, 1990), 31–43.

been sports. In fact, although its character is rarely admitted, the most successful cultural intervention in the realm of gender politics in Toronto during the two decades of second-wave feminism has been a men's project—a domed stadium. Ever since 1969, a group of male politicians, businessmen, sports writers, and media entrepreneurs have lobbied for a publicly financed covered stadium. Thwarted in the early 1970s, they were later successful and the new stadium opened in 1989. It already dominates the downtown skyline and the mass media, and it constitutes a massive subsidization and celebration of the interests of men.

I make no bones about linking the uphill battles of the Toronto women's movement to a new stadium. To be sure, both efforts have been influenced by a complex of social structures, institutions, and events, and in a fuller account, they could not be ignored. But the dynamic of gender . . . has been paramount. I call the stadium the "men's cultural centre" (MCC). It was initiated by male politicians well known for their hostility to feminist causes, and it was developed by an almost exclusively male provincial crown corporation. At a time when women's crisis centers go underfunded, the developers obtained 25 acres of prime downtown public land and $85 million in public funds for the stadium. Its primary tenants will be the local franchises of the commercial baseball and Canadian football cartels, the Blue Jays and the Argonauts, which stage male team games for predominantly male audiences. The other major beneficiaries will be the public and private media corporations that sell male audiences to advertisers through their broadcast of male team sports (Jhally, 1984), the advertisers, and the businessmen who will stay in and entertain clients in the adjoining hotel.

No doubt the MCC is popular among women as well as men. It will be a great improvement over the existing stadium, increasing the pleasure derived from watching gifted athletes. But in many ways, the MCC will serve to buttress male power and privilege. It has directed public and private investment and consumption to largely male activities, preventing the alternative use of these resources in programs that would redress the disadvantagement of women. In the absence of comparable opportunities for female athletes, coaches, managers, and sports impresarios, the MCC will provide almost daily ideological justification for patriarchal power. Women as well as men are capable of difficult, dramatic, and pleasing feats of grace, agility, and teamwork, but we will never know it from this stadium. Women will be either rendered invisible ("symbolically annihilated"; Boutilier & SanGiovanni, 1983, p. 185–215) or reduced to handmaidens and sex objects (cheerleaders) along the sidelines. The effect is to reinforce the male claim to the most important positions in society and to a significantly larger share of the fruits of social labour. This effect is especially powerful because it is rarely acknowledged. If a city gave pride of place to a stadium where only Anglo-Saxons could play, there would be howls of protest, but in the matter of gender and sports, such favouritism is usually taken for granted. The only thing that might communicate this male orientation is appearance. Standing at the foot of a tall telecommunications tower, the development will be a giant Klaes Oldenberg–like sculpture of the male genitals.

Despite the suggestiveness of feminist scholarship, the question of gender and sports is widely considered only a "women's issue" and is reduced to a problem of distribution (i.e., females "lack" opportunities). The gendered nature of the activities themselves and the consequences for men are rarely examined. The purpose of this paper is to contribute to this long-overdue analysis. I will argue that in their origins and essential characteristics, sports must be considered a form of male practice through which different "masculinities" compete. I will also argue that by perpetuating the sexual division of labour, sports not only contribute to the ongoing disadvantage of women but severely limit men's opportunities for personal growth. Such an expedition is not without its terrors—it requires radical questioning of that which many of us have found joyously validating—but it is essential if we are to understand fully what it means to "be a man." I do not advocate the abolition of sports, for they can empower humans of both sexes in beneficial, exhilarating ways. But I contend that sports should be transformed, and I will suggest some initial steps.

Deconstructing the "Naturalness" of Sports

My starting point is the social history insight that sports as we know them today are not the natural, universal, and transhistorical physical activity forms they are commonly thought to be, played in roughly the same way by all people in all periods of human history; rather, sports comprise a family of different activities developed under the specific conditions of rapidly industrializing 19th-century Britain and spread to the rest of the world through emigration, emulation, and imperialism. Although modern sports are popularly equated with the athletic events of the ancient Olympic Games, for example, scholars now argue that the differences between the contests of antiquity and those of our own era significantly outweigh the similarities. We must seek to understand each of these competitive forms in its own terms (Elias, 1971; Guttmann, 1978).

Few of us would recognize what we call sport in the athletics of classical Greece. By modern standards, these athletics were extremely violent. The combative events—the most popular contests—were conducted with little concern for fairness or safety. There were no weight categories to equalize size and strength, no rounds, and no ring. Bouts were essentially fights to the finish, which is not surprising when you consider that these competitions began as preparations for war. The modern Olympics are widely admired for their encouragement of participation for its own sake and personal growth through constant self-testing, but the ancients did not hold such ideals. Competitors prayed "Give me the wreath (of victory) or give me death!" because victory alone brought glory. Placings other than first were rarely recorded, because defeat brought undying shame. Although the Greeks had the technology to measure records in running, jumping, and throwing events, they rarely did so; performance for itself—pursuing a personal best despite one's placing—was meaningless to them. In fact, champions tried to psyche their opponents into withdrawing so the champions could boast they had won without even having to compete. There were no team events because competitors did not want to share the glory of victory. No competitor would have congratulated an opponent for a fairly fought or outstanding triumph. Today's handshake would have seemed an act of cowardice to the ancient Greeks (Finlay & Pleket, 1976; D. Young, 1985). Nor were these fiercely competitive games common to all cultures living along the Mediterranean in this period. In fact, anthropologists have established that only warlike peoples have used their leisure for combative events (Sipes, 1973).

Contrary to widespread belief, the ancient Olympic Games were inextricably bound up with the prevailing system of power. To be sure, the Games stood above city-state rivalries, enabling all free Greeks to compete. The "Olympic truce" was one of their most ingenious accomplishments. But practically and symbolically, athletics heavily reinforced gender and class domination. The classical Greek citizen's wealth and culture largely depended upon the exploitation of women and slaves. Although the origins of this system of power are not fully understood, it is clear that many subordinates were kept in submission through the force of arms, with which the classical events were closely associated. Even when athletic training became specialized and lost its direct connection to military skill, the Games celebrated the subjection of women and slaves at the level of ideology by excluding them from eligibility and the glory of victory (Kidd, 1984).

Sports as Male Practice

Armed with this insight about the social specificity of physical activity forms, we can begin to take a closer look at our own. Pierre de Coubertin did not revive the Olympics, as he liked to claim; he appropriated and recast the symbols of the ancient Games for a project of his own. He sought to combat the decadence and militarism of *fin de siècle* Europe by inculcating in young men the values he admired in English rugby and cricket (MacAloon, 1981). These activities had their beginnings in the rural folk games of the late Middle Ages. In the mid- to late 19th century, these activities were fashioned into the first modern sports (characterized by standard rules, a bureaucratic structure, the privileging of records, and the concept of fair play) by middle- and upper-class males in the increasingly elitist institutions of public school, the university, and the private club (Dunning & Sheard, 1979). Innovators, organizers, and creative publicists like de Coubertin consciously regarded sports as educational, preparing boys and young men for careers in business, government, colonial administration, and the military by instilling physical and mental toughness, obedience to authority, and loyalty to the team (Mangan, 1981). When working-class males began to take up sports too, some groups refused to accommodate them; at the Royal Henley Regatta, for example, working-class oarsmen were excluded by definition until 1933 (Alison, 1980). But most groups eventually adopted the strategy of "rational recreation," in other words, incorporating working-class males as players and spectators under strict middle-class leadership as a means of fostering respect for the established order and reducing class tension (Bailey, 1978). As Richard Gruneau (1983) has written, sports "mobilize middle-class bias" to this day (p. 134).

Education and socialization through sports were consciously understood to be masculinizing. According to Thomas Hughes's influential *Tom Brown's Schooldays* (1867/1979), the romanticiza-tion of all-male Rugby School under Thomas Arnold, the most important thing to learn is what it takes to be a man. In the course of 6 years of rugby, cricket, cross-country running, and impromptu fistfighting, Hughes's young protagonist acquires courage, stamina, ingenuity, close friendships, and leadership, attributes traditionally associated with dominant class norms of masculinity. Hughes's best-seller inspired Coubertin to develop the ideology of the modern Olympics, and the book persuaded parents, schoolmasters, and youth leaders throughout the English-speaking world to encourage sports to combat effeminacy. When Theodore Roosevelt feared that his asthmatic son, Theodore Jr., was becoming too heavily influenced by his mother and sisters, the father persuaded his son to take up boxing as an antidote (Pringle, 1931; Silverman, 1973). Working-class men also imbued sports with notions of masculinity (Palmer, 1979). The most popular 19th-century games and contests—football, lacrosse, hockey, track and field, and boxing—were termed "manly sports." Although they have now lost the epithet, they continue to be encouraged for the same reason.

Sports as Male Preserves

The men who developed and promoted sports were careful to ensure that only males were masculinized in this way. These developers maintained sports as male preserves by actively discouraging females from participation. These men denied women adequate facilities and programs, ridiculed their attempts, and threatened them with the spectre of ill health and "race suicide." Male doctors and physical educators proposed that people have only a finite quantity of energy, which in the case of women is needed for their reproductive organs. If women consume this energy in vigorous athletic activity, went the argument, they not only undermine their own health but the future of the white race. Working-class men generally shared these prejudices and contributed to the exclusionary practices, which suggests that sports participation helped males strengthen and extend cross-class masculinist bonds. Economic and social conditions—long hours of domestic labour, differential and generally less adequate diets, and restrictive dress—also deterred many girls and women from sports participation (Atkinson, 1978; Lenskyj, 1986).

Response to Feminism

These exclusions and the emphasis upon manliness in sports can also be considered a response to the rising voice of women. In 19th-century Canada and the United States, men introduced sports to public schoolboys and to the adolescent members of organizations such as the YMCA to overcome "the feminization of teaching" (Kett, 1977; D. MacLeod, 1986). The increased numbers of women teachers and their expanding feminine influence over boys' psychosocial development was a cause for manly concern. British sociologists Kevin Sheard and Eric Dunning (1973) have suggested a direct relationship between the boorish, sexist subculture of rugby—the public "moonings," songs of male sexual conquest of women, and the exaggerated drinking—and first-wave feminism:

> The historical conjuncture represented by the simultaneous rise of rugby football and the suffragette movement within the upper and middle classes may have been of some significance with respect to the emergence of the specific pattern of socially tolerated taboo breaking. For women were increasingly becoming a threat to men, and men responded by developing rugby football as a male preserve in which they could bolster up their threatened masculinity and at the same time, mock, objectify, and vilify women, the principal source of that threat. (p. 12)

When women persisted, especially during the 1920s and 1970s, males continued to exclude women from their own games and contests, requiring women to play on a sex-segregated basis with inferior resources. Despite the available examples from agriculture, industry, and sports of women performing arduous "men's" tasks, many persisted in the belief that a distinct women's biology prevents them from competing in the male realm. (The argument assumes—falsely—that all males are the same in size, strength, and fitness. For most of the population, including trained athletes, those ranges overlap; Hubbard, Henifin, & Fried, 1982). Organizers have also tried to confine females to those sports believed to enhance middle- and upper-class concepts of femininity, such as swimming, tennis, and gymnastics, and to devise "girls' rules" to discourage the ambitious and aggressive play expected of boys and men.[1] Female athletes have also faced inordinate pressures to conform to the heterosexual expectations of most males (B. Kidd, 1983).

The Distributive Problem

One legacy of this pattern of development is the well-known distributive problem—the significant inequalities that continue to plague females seeking sporting opportunities and careers. In most countries, despite a decade of "progress," males still have access to more than twice the number of opportunities and public resources available for sport. The Olympic Games still hold more than twice as many events for men as for women. But the effect of sports is also relational—sports perpetuate the patriarchy by powerfully reinforcing the division of labour. By giving males exciting opportunities, preaching that the qualities males learn from sports are masculine, and preventing girls and women from learning in the same context, sports confirm the prejudice that males are a breed apart. By encouraging us to spend our most creative and rewarding moments as children and our favourite forms of recreation as adults in the company of other males, sports condition us to trust each other much more than women. By publicly celebrating the dramatic achievements of the best males in public stadia while marginalizing females as spectators, sports validate the male claim to the best jobs and the highest status and rewards. Sports contribute to the underdevelopment of the female majority of the population and the undervaluing of those traditionally "feminine" skills of nurturing and emotional maintenance, which are essential to human growth and survival.

Competing Masculinities

Although men have created a sporting culture that sharply distinguishes between masculine and feminine, they also express different and frequently competing masculinities through sports. The preferences we express for different sports and positions within sports (e.g., individual vs. team, body contact vs. non–body contact, or games requiring spontaneous creativity vs. those relying upon set plays) are in part statements about what we value "in a man" and what sort of relations we want to encourage between men. When Charles Dickens championed boxing in *The Pickwick Papers* despite the 19th-century prohibition, he endorsed a method for men to settle their disputes that was more scientific, humane, and democratic than the duel (Marlow, 1982). The current debate about boxing—under radically different social conditions—is still about competing masculinities: Should we admire men who risk their most valuable and most distinctively human parts—their heads and their hands—to test themselves in a dramatic contest, or should we condemn them for stupidity? Hockey loyalties can be read in the same way. I know a number of Torontonians who cheer for the Montreal Canadiens because this team has never systematically practised the "beat-'em-in-the-alley" tactics of the Toronto Maple Leafs. These fans value a particular masculinity—one that prefers skill and artistry to physical force and intimidation—more than geographical community.

There is little scope for the full expression of different masculinities in sports, however. As in every other sphere of Western culture, the broad range of actual masculinities is subordinated in public discourse and institutional expectation to a single dominant or hegemonic masculinity, which is highly competitive, technological, and homophobic (Kinsman, 1987). Given the inordinate pressure to win, the emphasis upon measurable achievement as opposed to intrinsic satisfaction and aesthetic creativity, and the well-established dependence of the commercial sports upon male audiences, hegemonic masculinity in sports has been difficult to combat. Several years ago, Wayne Gretsky skated away from a fight in a nationally televised play-off game, clearly rejecting the dominant code of hockey masculinity (which emphasizes defending your honour by dropping your stick and gloves to fight) in favour of the intelligence and self-discipline of staying out of the penalty box. Although his action won him the admiration of hockey reformers, he was attacked as a "wimp" by most media commentators. More recently, he has begun to argue that fighting in hockey is a "natural" part of the game.

Men's Fears

Social biologist Ken Dyer (1982) has shown that women's records in the measurable sports like track and field and swimming are now being broken significantly faster than men's records in the same events, and he has concluded that lack of opportunity—not biology—is the primary reason why female performances have always lagged behind. Projecting his findings into the future, he suggests that if opportunities for women can be equalized, in most sports the best females will be able to compete on a par with the best males. Imagine a woman winning the open 100 metres at the Olympics or playing in the National Hockey League!

Character Change of Sport

Performances once considered impossible are now commonplace in virtually every sport, but most men balk at Dyer's suggestion. Not only do they not believe it could happen, but the idea that it could frightens them. Men fear the changes in the character of sport that would come about if females played with men. "You have to play softer with women," a softball official testified during an Ontario Human Rights Commission inquiry in explaining why he felt integrated competition, even in which the female players had made the team on ability, would reduce the satisfaction for males (Re Ontario Softball Association and Bannerman, 1978). But although this is unspoken, I believe men also fear the profound social and psychological changes that would result if women were understood to be fully competent in the special domain of men. For years, the Ontario Hockey Association (OHA) refused to allow females to play on any of its teams. In the most recent case, it refused to register 13-year-old Justine Blainey, even though she had made a team in a competitive tryout. The OHA went to court four times in an effort to stop her. In 1987 it lost, largely because of the equality provisions in the 1982 Canadian Charter of Rights and Freedoms ("Girl Wins." 1987). Was one 13-year-old female, or even 200 female players, going to topple the male hockey leadership and disrupt a 500,000-male strong, century-old organization? Hardly. There must be something deeper.

Disorientation of the Male Psyche

In part, what men fear is the disorientation of the male psyche. As Nancy Chodorow (1978) has argued, male children develop their identities positionally, by differentiating themselves from their mothers. Because the major tasks of child rearing have been performed by women, the primary interaction for young males has been with women, with the result that boys have great difficulty in identifying with their fathers. So, Chodorow says, in developing masculine identities, males are essentially learning to differentiate

themselves from their mothers and from women in general. Males rehearse and strengthen this positional masculinity in activities that accentuate male-female differences and stigmatize those characteristics generally associated with women.

Although Chodorow does not discuss sports, it is clear that sports were developed for—and serve—that very purpose in the industrial capitalist societies with which we are most familiar. This was certainly my experience growing up in Toronto in the 1940s and 1950s. I played sports endlessly as a child. I simply gobbled up the rules, skills, strategies, and lore, none of which seemed to interest my mother, her friends, or girls of my own age. Certainly my peers and I rarely involved girls. I also learned to accept (rather than question) physical pain, to deny anxiety and anger, and to be aggressive in ways that were clearly valued as manly. I realize now that I gained an enormous sense of my own power when I could respond to challenges in this way and be emotionally tougher than my mother and younger sister. Yet this shows how shaky such positional identity can be, because when I put myself into the emotional state I remember from that period, I realize that I would have been devastated if a girl—no matter how gifted—had played for any of the teams I was so proud to make. Such a situation would have proclaimed to the world that I was "like a girl" and inadequate. At the deepest psychological levels, the blurring of sex roles undermines not only the male-privileging sexual division of labour but also the very process by which males raised within sexually segregated sports have gained personal validation and confidence. The vulnerability of positional identity also helps explain why so many athletes fear gay men: Because of the widespread but false perception that all gay men are effeminate (Kleinberg, 1987), gay men appear to betray "masculinity."

Loss of Nurturing

Males also fear the loss of traditional nurturing that might result if females were socialized through sports (and other predominantly male activities) to be as hard and unyielding as males. This helps explain why so many men are determined to keep sports a male sanctuary, why in the quintessentially masculine sport of boxing many jurisdictions still prohibit females from competing at all, even against other females. It also helps us understand the psychological weight of the pressures on female athletes to be what is considered feminine. To be sure, many females share these fears and support the status quo. As Dorothy Dinnerstein (1976) points out, males and females actively collaborate to maintain the existing gender arrangements—"nostalgia for the familiar is a feeling that has so far been mobilized in opposition to social change" (p. 229). But the price of such collaboration is extremely high.

Men's Problem

The patriarchal nature of sports has harmed men, too. By encouraging and reinforcing a positional identity, sports have led us to limit our options as humans.

Inability to Express the Feminine

Sports have led us to deny feelings and to disparage—and therefore not to learn—interpersonal skills stereotypically associated with females. By teaching us a form of strength and assertiveness disconnected from emotional understanding and the skills of emotional maintenance, sports have encouraged us to close ourselves off from our own inner feelings and those of others. Through sports, men learn to cooperate with, care for, and love other men in a myriad or rewarding ways, but sports rarely teach men to get close to each other or to open up emotionally. On the contrary, the only way many of us express fondness for other men is by teasing or mock fighting (the private form of what has become a public form of tribute—the "roast"). Anything more openly affectionate would be suspect.

Inability to Value Intrinsic Reward

Chodorow and Dinnerstein argue that the development of positional identity has also contributed to the process by which males privilege abstract achievement, which in sport has meant victory and records. Because sports elevate external goals over intrinsic ones, sports have encouraged athletes to treat their bodies instrumentally, to undergo physical and psychological injury, and to inflict it upon others. The active repression of pain is an everyday part of the sports world ("No pain, no gain!" is a common slogan), but this ethic has ruined the careers of countless athletes and left many crippled for life. There are also psychological scars; the constant emphasis upon external goals leaves many unable to identify their own needs, let alone pursue them. At the same time, the sports culture labels as failures those who cannot make increasingly higher standards of performance (Butts, 1976).

Inability to Interact Appropriately with Other Men

Sports may well poison the athlete's dealings with other men. Connell (1983) has defined masculinity in terms of power and has suggested that sports instruct men in two aspects of power: the development of force ("the irresistible occupation of space"; p. 18) and the perfection of skill ("the ability to operate on the objects within that space, including other humans"; p. 18). The rules of football (all codes), basketball, boxing, hockey, and others for which territorial control is important almost literally conform to this definition, and I can't think of any sport where it doesn't fit.[2] Sports encourage athletes to treat each other as enemies, when in fact athletes are coplayers without whom the rewards of playing cannot be obtained. This is the other side of "that sweet spot in time," "walking tall," or the exhilaration of doing it right. Psychologists

Tutko and Bruns say that "to be a champion, you have to be the meanest son-of-a-bitch in the valley" (1976). Such mental and physical competitiveness wins championships, but it also throws up enormous barriers to the development and maintenance of close relationships.

Toward More Humane Sporting Practices

There are no magic solutions to the situation I have described. It is deeply rooted in long-established patterns of child rearing and human interaction, and it is perpetuated by powerful economic and political interests. We cannot dismiss or abolish sports, nor should we want to. Potentially, sports can help all humans acquire self-mastery in pleasurable, health-strengthening, and popularly validated skills and rituals. Such opportunities are particularly important in societies in which work is increasingly automated and alienating. Sports can also provide highly accessible popular dramas in ways that strengthen community and confirm widely shared meanings. Hockey may be a puberty rite for male Canadians, but it is also a celebration of creativity, energy, and élan of the human spirit in the depths of winter, the season of death.

The contradictions of modern sports can sometimes undermine the very privilege that they enshrine. In their claim to be democratic, sports organizations provide the arguments— and sometimes the playing surfaces—for the disadvantaged to demonstrate their rights to a better future. In the Olympic Games, for example, the universalist aspirations of the ruling International Olympic Committee (IOC) have paved the way for athletes from the poorest and smallest countries to compete, even when they have had little chance of winning medals. In turn, the overwhelming presence of Third World nations (there are now 164 national Olympic committees) has pressured the elitist, Europe-dominated IOC to support the international struggle against apartheid and racism and to begin a program of technical assistance to have-not countries.

Liberating sports from patriarchal (as well as class and First World) structures of domination will be a long and complex process. It will have to be undertaken in conjunction with similar efforts in other areas of everyday life. The outcome—how humans will pursue sports in a more egalitarian, less oppressive age—will largely depend upon the nature of those struggles because, as we have seen, forms of physical activity, including sport, are historically grounded. But that should not dissuade us.

Question Masculinist Bias

We can start by actively questioning the pervasive masculinist bias in the sports world. The language is rife with words and phrases that unconsciously reinforce the male preserve: *jock*, the popular metonym for athlete: *tomboy* to describe any bright, active girl who likes physical activity and is good at sports; and *suck* and *sissy* to condemn anyone who betrays fear or anxiety. These all remind us that sports were designed to harden males. We should question the use of these terms the way the civil rights movement did with *nigger* and *boy* and the women's movement has with *mankind* and *girl*; develop inclusive substitutes (such as *athlete* for *jock* and *young athlete* for *tomboy*); and then campaign to remove the offending terms from usage. It will also be necessary to change the practices as well. Although we will always admire physical courage, we do ourselves a disservice if we continue uncritically to condemn the expression of pain and uneasiness that is usually associated with being a "sissy."

Challenge Sexism and Homophobia

We should challenge the gross sexism and homophobia of that inner sanctum of patriarchy, the locker room. Allen Sack, who played on the

1966 Notre Dame championship football team, has said that in many ways football is a training ground for rape. In the game, players learn to control the field and dominate other players, and in the dressing room they endlessly fantasize and celebrate the male conquest of women (Burstyn, 1986). Gay bashing has also been encouraged and plotted in the locker room. It takes a different kind of courage to contest such explicit, omnipresent misogyny and homophobia. Much of what is said is often rich in humour. Yet it contributes to our own repression, as well as the denigration of others. If you contest locker-room talk, you'll get denial and anger— "it's just a joke, I'm not a pig!"—but you will also start a reconsideration.

Redefine the Rules and Values of Sports

We can also contribute by redefining the rules and values of sports to make them more inviting to everybody. Physical educators, coaches, and community groups of both sexes have amended rules to make games safer, more accessible, and more genuinely educative. In Canada, parents, players, teachers, and government leaders have contributed to the effort to eliminate the gratuitous violence of ice hockey. In my neighborhood, a community softball league has recently added a second first base (immediately adjacent to the original base, but on the other side of the foul line) and eliminated the necessity of tagging the runner at home, both of which reduce collisions between players. These changes often involve trade-offs (I was sorry to see the softballers discourage the slide) but they subtly reduce the premium on physical dominance. (When I was 9 years old, I was taught to throw a cross-body block at second, third, and home. "There's ten dollars on every bag," our coach would tell us, "and if you don't get it, he will.") These experiments, especially when they result from open discussion about the purpose of sports, should

be encouraged. To opponents who appeal to tradition, we can point out that the rules of games have been continually changed for other reasons, so why not make them more humane?

Make Sports More Than Contests

We should also struggle to change the way sports are regarded. Too frequently, they are characterized as battlefronts. Competitions are viewed as zero-sum contests, and athletes are expected to treat each other as enemies. Military metaphors abound: Players "throw the long bomb" and teams "whip," "punish," "roll over," and "savage" each other. This imagery is hardly coincidental: Throughout the century, sports have frequently been associated with military training. Instead, I suggest we consider sports glorious improvisations, dialectical play, or collective theatre; although competing athletes are cast as antagonists, they need each other if the discoveries and pleasures of the contest are to be enjoyed at all. As athletes, we should respect and care for each other as coplayers. The pregame friendship ritual of basketball rivals Isiah Thomas and Magic Johnson is a welcome example in this regard. As spectators, we should applaud the winner but not at the expense of other members of the company.

There are powerful incentives structuring games as contests, fueling the tremendous exhilaration of triumph. In North America, the mass media and governments have monopolized the interpretation of athletic performance, and the participant's voice has been distorted, if not silenced. But other cultural performers—painters, dancers, actors, filmmakers—and their audiences have begun to contest the corporate media's interpretation of their work, and athletes could well learn from their example. A sports culture that de-emphasized winning and emphasized an exploration of artistry and skill and the creative interaction of rival athletes would be much less repressive.

Support Feminists Working for Change

Finally, we should actively support those feminists struggling to combat sexism and inequality in sport, and we should admit to the privilege men enjoy in public projects like the domed stadium. We should not only support advocacy groups like the Canadian Association for the Advancement of Women and Sport (*and Sport* rather than *in Sport* was a conscious recognition that increasing opportunities will not be enough), but we should take the initiative in struggling with men. It is necessary to assure males who resist integration on the basis of ability that we are strong enough to survive an "invasion" of outstanding female athletes. Where the implementation of affirmative action programs will bring about cuts in existing male opportunities, we should strive to find additional resources and make more efficient use of the existing ones. The most difficult task will be persuading other men that gender-divided sports are not just a "women's problem" but in dialectical interaction harm us as well. Once there's a shared understanding of that, the critical redesign of sports can really begin.

Notes

1. Many women contributed to the development of girls' rules. Atkinson (1978), Lenskyj (1986), and others have argued that in part this represented a tactically necessary defence against male control of women's institutions and a creative attempt to avoid the most brutalizing features of male sport, and that without these rules, girls and women would not have been allowed to play at all. Nevertheless, girls' rules confined most females interested in sports to a ghetto of inequality and left unchallenged the existing stereotypes about female frailty.

2. There are, of course, lots of cooperative games in which this does not necessarily occur. My favourite is the Mbuti tug-of-war from Zaïre, where winning happens when, through the exchange of players, both teams achieve equal strength.

Questions for Consideration

1. Is male dominance within sport as extreme as Kidd states?
2. To what extent is the fragility of male identity an issue here?
3. What is Kidd's explanation of male dominance in sport? Is this explanation compelling?
4. Are Kidd's proposals for reform adequate, too extreme, or insufficient for the magnitude of the problem? If too extreme or insufficient, what would you add or change?

35 Title IX: Equality for Women's Sports?

Leslie P. Francis
University of Utah

The passage of Title IX in 1972 is generally viewed as a positive move in the direction toward equality for competitive women's collegiate sports. In this reading, Leslie Francis argues that there is good reason to cast doubt on the overall benefits for women. College academics, she argues, is becoming increasingly contaminated by moral corruption in college athletics. If so, her argument runs, then Title IX may be merely introducing females to a morally venal practice. This shines a different light on the issue of equality.

Should athletic competition be a part of academic institutions? Francis evaluates some of the more forceful arguments that have been advanced on its behalf. She finds none of these cogent. On the other hand, arguments against competitive athletics at colleges are themselves unavailing.

In effect, Title IX is an affirmative-action policy instituted to right past redresses, to correct ongoing injustice, and to promote distributive justice in collegiate athletics. What, she asks, if collegiate athletics on account of "vanity sports" (i.e., football and basketball) is itself morally corrupt? Her answer is twofold. If society is essaying to discourage collegiate athletics, then no argument for affirmative action is tenable. If on the other hand there is no societal pressure to eliminate competitive athletics, then there is still a case for affirmative action. She sums, "In short, universities that stick with football are stuck with Title IX."

There may be reasons that "vanity" sports ought to be eliminated from academic institutions, but coordinating such an effort would be difficult

and unfair to existing athletes. The most sensible of the reasonable options is to keep vanity sports and increase support for women's sports. In conclusion, she offers some suggestions to facilitate this option.

Since their beginnings in 1859 with a crew race between Harvard and Yale, intercollegiate athletics have been central to the mythology of American universities. Varsity football dominates the fall social calendar of student life; "homecoming," timed to coincide with an important football game, evokes alumni nostalgia. Winter is the season for varsity basketball, culminating in the National Collegiate Athletic Association (NCAA) national championship tournaments in early spring. Until quite recently, the participants in intercollegiate varsity sports were nearly all men.

The entry of women competitors into the apparently glorious haze of intercollegiate athletics has been belated and awkward. With the passage of Title IX in 1972, universities were required to provide equal opportunity in all of their federally funded programs. Most moved quickly to establish varsity sports teams for women in numbers roughly equal to their offerings for men. The near similarity in numbers of teams, however, belies important continuing differences. Football remains a major source of attention, revenue, and expenditure. Men's basketball is also a high-profile activity; women's basketball, particularly with the NCAA tournament and television exposure, recently has taken some steps toward success on the male model. In non-revenue sports, from skiing and ice hockey to swimming and water polo, although teams are fielded in roughly equal numbers, participation

Reprinted, by permission, from L. P. Francis, "Title IX: Equality for Women's Sports?" *Journal of the Philosophy of Sport* XX–XXI (1993–1994): 32–47.

and expenditure rates remain higher for men, in ratios that far exceed the proportions of men in overall enrollments.

The rosy glow of college athletics, perhaps always exaggerated, has been fading of late. Even football is a losing proposition on most campuses. Sperber (27), Thelin (29), and others report mismanagement, overexpenditure, and corruption. The National Collegiate Athletic Association, the private body that regulates intercollegiate athletics, has been criticized for behaving as an economic cartel by Fleisher, Goff, and Tollison (8), Hart-Nibbrig and Cottingham (11), and Lawrence (13), among others. Colleges are rebuked for exploiting, not educating athletes; premier athletes themselves exit early, in increasingly greater numbers, to professional opportunities. Faculties and even university presidents seek, with uneven success, to establish greater control over intercollegiate athletics. As universities confront shrinking academic budgets, athletics expenditures, often more than 5% of the institution's total, are viewed with mounting concern (30). Universities are urged to sell off their money-making sports teams as separate businesses and to abolish the remainder, leaving only intramural activities that all can enjoy. Older and working students may view intercollegiate athletics as part of a romanticized past that never really was and may resent the dedication of large proportions of student fees to their continued support.

Given this critical picture of the current state of intercollegiate competitive sports, there is something of a paradox to women's claims for equal participation. These claims might be viewed as efforts to participate in a practice that is morally problematic on many counts—that is perhaps bad for, and most likely not beneficial for, participants; bad for their fellow students and the universities; and bad for society in general. If intercollegiate athletics in their current state are indeed an activity that universities should discourage, radically alter, or even eliminate, how should claims to equality on behalf of women be evaluated? In this paper, I take

women's athletics as a problem about the morality of affirmative action within a social practice that is significantly morally flawed. I argue that within such a context, the case for affirmative action is limited but powerful, at least until there are serious social efforts to improve or eliminate the flawed social practice. I begin with an assessment of the case to be made for the current practice of intercollegiate athletic competition.

Why Intercollegiate Athletic Competition?

Since Greek times at least, sports have been thought to be an important part of the process of education. Athletic endeavors, it has been argued, promote discipline and health. They clear the mind for other learning, it is said. For women, athletic participation may also be important in counteracting historical images of weakness and passivity. If this or a similar paean to the educational glory of sports is to be believed, then there are arguments for physical education, health, and intramural sports activities on university campuses. Arguments for the general educational importance of athletics, however, do not necessarily provide support for intercollegiate competition. Indeed, if the development of intercollegiate competition draws money and enthusiasm away from more widespread participation in sports, education and intercollegiate sports may come into conflict. The critical analysis that follows is aimed at intercollegiate sports competition of the kind found in schools offering athletic scholarships, not at the general educational value of sport or at the intramural or club programs open to the entire student body.[1]

Universities typically offer both intrinsic and instrumental arguments for the promotion of intercollegiate varsity competition. Some arguments are based on the value of the activity itself to those involved. Athletics on the competitive level, it is said, develop skills and self-discipline to the highest degree possible for those participating. Team sports are an enjoyable, even a thrilling, activity. Without further support, however, these arguments do not explain why universities ought to provide such intrinsically valuable activities. Skill development and teamwork surely can be learned outside the university; and there are many valued activities, from good parties to good horse racing, that universities are not generally expected to offer. More complete defenses of intercollegiate competition rely either on the benefits it provides to athletes—benefits which are thought in some way to be relevant to the educational function of the university—or on overall benefits to the university as an institution.

One quite traditional, and perhaps rather quaint, argument for intercollegiate competition is that it develops character traits in athletes—and, by example, in other students—in a way appropriate to the function of the university. The "Battle of Waterloo was won on the playing fields of Eton," the Duke of Wellington once opined.[2] Some recent empirical work by sociologists, however, questions whether the kinds of character traits that are developed in intercollegiate competitive athletes today are appropriate sequelae of a liberal education. Chu (4) and Stevenson (28) report data suggesting that as athletes become more successful, they increasingly value winning rather than fair play, and that coaches tend to model authoritarian rather than autonomous behavior patterns. Both the focus on winning for its own sake, and the authoritarian coaching behavior might seem to be at odds with the values of a liberal education.

An argument that relies heavily on the social role of the modern university is that intercollegiate athletics are a source of upward mobility for otherwise disadvantaged participants. Varsity athletes receive scholarships and academic support that often are not generally available to other students. Premier athletes may parlay their college success into lucrative professional athletic careers. The experience of intercollegiate competition may also prove a useful basis for job opportunities more generally. Unfortunately, the data indicate that these claims are unjustifiably optimistic. Although varsity athletes do receive scholarships and other support, Purdy, Eitzen, and Hufnagel (23) report that graduation rates are low, particularly for minority students in the sports of football and basketball. Women athletes graduate in rates comparable to rates of students overall, but the picture is worsening for women playing basketball as their sport becomes increasingly successful and emulates the model of a male, revenue-earning sport. Dubois's (6) study of post competition occupations of male varsity athletes in comparison to occupations of male students who did not participate in varsity sports shows no advantage for the athletes, whether white or minority. Intercollegiate sports have also been argued to be an important source of opportunities in professional sports. College football and basketball serve to some extent as a farm system for the professional leagues, although professional opportunities are limited. For women, there are few professional sports opportunities, and even fewer lucrative possibilities. If increasing numbers of women are well trained in college competition, however, perhaps they will become a source of pressures for changes in professional sports. Thus the desirability of pressures for increased professional athletic opportunities for women might be an argument for increased opportunities on the university level.

Another argument for varsity competition is the positive contribution it makes to attitudes toward athletes. Successful competition may be a source of self-esteem for the athletes themselves. Competition may also help change attitudes towards historically underappreciated groups. Both university and professional sports have been important forums for the admiration of minority male athletes. Female sports heroes such as Jackie Joyner-Kersee have also emerged from the college ranks into professional and Olympic competition. They are exemplars of achievement and strength, rather than weakness and passivity. If intercollegiate competition contributes to changes in attitudes toward women and minorities, it is arguably linked to the social role of the university in opening opportunities for underrepresented groups in society and should be supported on that ground.

Intercollegiate athletics are also thought to be of significant instrumental benefit for universities. The "big game" is part of the mythology of campus life. Defenders of intercollegiate competition argue that winning sports teams garner respect for the institution, encourage better potential students to apply, and augment alumni donations. One recent survey of the data (30) suggests that this optimism is not borne out. Evidence for the contention that successful teams increase alumni gifts is very mixed. Contributions to booster clubs go to underwrite athletics rather than to bolster academic budgets. In a few cases, the investment in revenue-producing sports is profitable; in most schools, however, even high-profile sports are a losing proposition. In the end, claims that intercollegiate athletics contribute to an overall aura of institutional success are very difficult to pin down.

Finally, defenders of intercollegiate sports competition argue that it fosters university identification and community. Students, who may lead very fragmented and separate lives, come together to cheer on their teams. They are joined by alumni reliving their loyalties to alma mater. Members of the local community may also identify with university sports teams and town-gown conflicts may thus be mitigated (4). Sports are a "safe" vehicle for affiliation, cutting across at least some religious, cultural, racial, and generational lines, and even linking students with alumni and members of the local community. Chu (4: p. 162) has argued that students who attend university athletic events are more likely to be involved with the institution in other ways, although the study does not indicate whether these are dependent or independent variables. Even so, however, overall student community might be fostered more successfully by an intense intramural system such as the one in place at the University of California at Davis. When they attract visitors from afar, university athletic events surely bring money into local businesses; but there may be other, more successful ways for universities to contribute to local economies.

The case for intercollegiate competition on its current scale is thus tenuous. The best case that can be made for the current practice of intercollegiate sports is that they are sought after by their participants and may open opportunities for them, although the empirical evidence in support of this is slim. Varsity competition may also contribute to changed social perceptions of women and minorities, and to an enhanced sense of university community. Many continue to believe that, despite their flaws, university intercollegiate sports make important contributions to institutional glory and community, besides being just plain fun. At the same time, others charge that varsity competition exploits athletes, drains revenue, and detracts from the educational programs of the university. Efforts to remedy discrimination against women and minorities in university athletics thus take place against a background of at best mixed support for the enterprise generally.

Title IX and University Athletics

Enacted in 1972, Title IX[3] prohibits discrimination in any educational program or activity receiving federal financial assistance. In part because of debates about Title IX's impact on athletics, universities were given six years from its adoption to develop compliance programs. Despite the phase in, Title IX was met with resistance from coaches of men's teams, from university athletics directors, and from the National Collegiate Athletic Association. For example, the athletic director of the University of Maryland told a congressional subcommittee in 1975 that his department stood in staunch opposition to women's varsity sports because they did not want to market an inferior product (30). The NCAA lobbied Congress to exempt athletics from Title IX, and, when this effort failed, brought suit challenging the regulations issued by the Department of Health, Education, and Welfare (HEW) to implement Title IX.[4]

At the time Title IX was enacted, university athletic programs were heavily dominated by men's varsity sports. With the impetus of Title IX, many universities moved quickly to add a number of women's varsity teams. By the late 1970s, the typical pattern was for a university to offer roughly equal numbers of men's and women's teams in nonrevenue sports, men's and women's basketball teams, and a football team. Football of course consumed—and, in at least a few cases, produced—immense amounts of revenue. But differences persisted in the patterns of participation in, and support for, other men's and women's varsity teams. In 1985, the percentage of athletic budgets devoted to women's sports in Division I schools offering football was 12%; in nonfootball Division I schools, it was 23% (4: p. 103). Although expenses for women's sports rose after implementation of Title IX, Chu (4) reports that expenses for men's sports also rose by multiples of two to five times as much at different institutions during the same period. As late as 1993, NCAA (19) statistics indicate that only 34.8% of varsity university athletes were women, up from 31.3% in the 1984–85 academic year. In 1992, the NCAA (19) reported that only 30% of athletic scholarship money, 23% of operating dollars, and 17% of recruitment funds went to women. Nationally, the NCAA (19) calculated that the most frequently offered women's sport was basketball (289 schools; 3,873 athletes) and the sport with the most female participants was outdoor track (249 schools; 6,250 athletes). At individual institutions, participation rates over the entire period since the enactment of Title IX have departed noticeably from enrollment rates. At the University of Illinois in the Big Ten Conference, for example, although 56% of the student body was male, over 75% of the varsity athletes (including football players) were male.[5] Pieronek (20) reports that these rates were typical in the Big Ten Conference, which in 1992 proposed to require a proportion of at least 40% female athletes by 1997. At Colorado State University in the Western Athletic Conference, there was a better than 10% disparity in participation rates, a quite low difference by national and Big Ten standards, but insufficient for Title IX.[6] Moreover, with the merger of men's and women's programs at many institutions, Acosta and Carpenter (1) and Lapchick and Slaughter (12) have reported that the number of women coaches and women athletics administrators has dwindled.

By the early 1980s, over 100 Title IX challenges to gender differences in university athletics had been filed with the Office of Civil Rights or the Department of Education (32). In 1984, however, the United States Supreme Court held that Title IX applied only to specific program(s) receiving federal funding, rather than to entire institutions.[7] Because university athletics programs rarely received federal funding on their own, this holding largely deflated the Title IX challenges to them. In 1988, however, the program-specific interpretation of Title IX was superseded by Congress in the Civil Rights Restoration Act.[8]

Since 1988, a new set of Title IX complaints has been brought against university athletics programs, by both male and female athletes. These complaints have forced courts to rule directly on what is meant by nondiscrimination in athletics programs under Title IX and, ultimately, to confront difficult ethical questions about the meaning of equal opportunity in university athletics.

The renewed ability to challenge athletics programs under Title IX coincided with a period of significant retrenchment in university athletics budgets specifically and university budgets more generally. Much of the Title IX litigation was instigated by athletes seeking to block their school from dropping their chosen sports. Female members of varsity teams objected to cutbacks that eliminated the teams in equal numbers for both sexes. Male members protested cutbacks that were imposed unilaterally on men's teams. In several other cases, women members of club teams sought to compel their university to upgrade their teams to varsity status, a step that the university was unwilling to take for financial reasons.

Judicial analyses of these Title IX claims have followed a pattern set out in the federal regulations and interpretive policy manuals.[9] Athletics programs must not discriminate in awarding financial aid—although they may structure awards differently for separate male and female teams provided that reasonable and proportional aid is available for each.[10] Second, programs must provide equal opportunity in a range of important supportive services: equipment, practice times, travel and per diem allowances, coaching and tutoring, locker rooms, medical and training facilities, housing and dining services, publicity. Finally, programs must offer a "selection of sports and levels of competition [that] effectively accommodate[s] the interests and abilities of members of both sexes."[11] Relying on a policy interpretation issued by the Office of Civil Rights of the Department of Education,[12] courts have developed a three-prong test for effective accommodation of the interests of a sex that has been underserved historically in an athletic program: universities must offer varsity opportunities in proportion to representation in the student body; or, universities must demonstrate continuing progress in adding opportunities for the underserved sex; or, universities must demonstrate the interests and abilities of the underserved sex are in fact fully met.

This structure of analysis reflects an uneasy compromise between exactly equal levels of participation and the historical differences between men's and women's sports. First, it allows football to remain a sport apart, as long as there is equal opportunity in the program overall, by allowing separate teams in contact sports, along with separate scholarship and revenue functions for those teams. Second, this analysis also permits ongoing, quite large differences between percentages of participation by sex in varsity sports and percentages in the overall student body, that is, if the uni-

versity can bear the burden of proving that existing interests and abilities are met for the underrepresented sex. This allowance, too, is important to the perpetuation of large football programs.

On the other hand, where there are ongoing disproportionalities between participation rates and the student body, the university will be virtually compelled to accede to demands by women for a sport to be upgraded, or for a sport to be protected from cuts. In the view of the Department of Education (32),

> Institutions where women are currently underrepresented in the athletics program will have a difficult time maintaining compliance with Title IX while eliminating women's teams unless they make comparable cuts, and, in some cases, deeper cuts in the men's program. . . . Institutions that plan to eliminate the same number of sports for men and women may also have compliance problems if women are already underrepresented in the athletics program.

Women ice hockey players, for example, obtained a court order in line with this analysis, compelling Colgate University to upgrade their club team to varsity status, against a background of differential participation in varsity sports by women and men.[13] Women gymnasts and field hockey players at Indiana University of Pennsylvania successfully fought elimination of their varsity teams (in tandem with the elimination of men's tennis and soccer), despite a university proposal to replace them with women's soccer.[14] At Colorado State University, women blocked the elimination of fast-pitch softball;[15] at Brown University, they fought off cuts in women's gymnastics and volleyball.[16] On the other side, male athletes have not found Title IX a particular ally in their efforts to stall cuts, even when the counterpart women's team was spared. Male swimmers at the University of Illinois, for example, failed in a challenge to their team's elimination despite the continuation of the women's team, because the Illinois athletics programs were predominately (75%) male.[17]

Thus as Title IX is currently implemented, unless a university provides varsity opportunities in proportion to enrollments (which schools fielding football teams are unlikely to do), women's varsity sports are virtually guaranteed protection when women express interest in varsity competition. This bottom line has been characterized by Thro and Snow (31) as a form of affirmative action and criticized as an unfair burden on straitened athletics budgets. A quick but facile reply to this criticism is that universities can do much to end participation rates that are disproportional to enrollments by cutting football rosters.[18] A deeper set of concerns is prompted by the observation that mandated varsity teams may be quite expensive yet benefit only the few athletes who participate in them. Pieronek (20) estimates that in order to achieve proportionality with enrollments but still leave men's varsity sports untouched, universities would need to add on average six sports (and 128 varsity spaces) for women. Is Title IX, as currently interpreted to barter football for women's varsity teams, a desirable model for equality in athletics? Is it an example of affirmative action at all, much less of justifiable affirmative action? Should universities cut football, cut other men's sports, or add women's sports? Should revenues from football, when football is profit-making, be dedicated to football or be used to underwrite the remainder of the academic program?[19] Would models of equality that require major changes in the organization of intercollegiate athletics be morally preferable within the current context?

Affirmative Action in University Athletics

The term *affirmative action* encompasses a wide range of positive steps that might be taken in response to discrimination.[20] In university athletics, in addition to the provision of varsity sports opportunities for women, affirmative action might include efforts to evoke women's interest and develop their skills, to encourage intramural participation by more women, to form coeducational teams, and even to reassess the entire way that intercollegiate competition is structured and understood. In comparison, affirmative action in employment has ranged from reassessment of frankly biased selection criteria, to job training and recruitment, to redefinition of entire job categories.

I have argued elsewhere (10) that the case for affirmative action in education can be made on at least three different moral grounds. Affirmative action may be used to compensate identified victims of past injustices; the creation of remedial programs for individuals who have been unjustly denied opportunities is an example. In athletics, Lapchick and Slaughter (12) suggest the example of providing enhanced scholarship opportunities for women who have been discriminatorily denied them. It may serve to correct ongoing discrimination; faculty recruitment or hiring goals may be required when patterns of selection indicate subjective, difficult-to-eradicate bias. An example here might be the recruitment of more women coaches and athletic administrators. A third moral justification for affirmative action is that it may be a method for improving overall distributive justice in society. The United States Supreme Court had held, however, that a concern for social justice is not a legally compelling interest that can justify the state's use of reverse racial preferences in such areas as government contracts.[21] Nonetheless, educational diversity may remain a legally compelling state interest that justifies university consideration of multiple factors, including race, in making admissions decisions.[22] An example from athletics might be increasing participation by women to further the likely development of women's opportunities in professional sports.

These arguments for affirmative action typically are made within contexts in which the activity at issue is thought to be worthwhile both to the individuals seeking increased access and to society more generally. Compensatory affirmative action gives victims something of value, such as a training opportunity. Moral objections to compensatory affirmative action generally rest on the claims of others to the means of compensation, such as admission to a training program, or on whether the source from which compensation is sought is any way responsible for the past victimization, not on whether the means of compensation is itself a good. Corrective affirmative action roots out continuing bias in order, it is hoped, that everyone is treated fairly. Here, the chief moral objection lies not with what is being distributed, but with the risk that affirmative action will introduce new forms of bias. Redistributive affirmative action aims to move society towards more just distribution of the benefits and burdens of social living. Here, too, objections that affirmative action is unjust rest on who wins and loses under the change and why and how they lose, rather than on whether it is a good thing for anyone at all to experience the benefits being redistributed.[23]

What happens to these justifications for affirmative action if an historically disadvantaged group seeks fuller participation in an activity that is socially problematic or that should be reduced or eliminated for good social reasons? If criticisms of the current practice of university athletics are to be believed, this is the problem posed by affirmative action for women in intercollegiate varsity competition. I will argue here that the case for affirmative action is limited, but not entirely vitiated, under such circumstances. Moreover, how the case is changed depends on the nature of the reasons for discouraging the activity; several importantly different reasons are that it is risky to participating individuals, that it is costly but unlikely to yield any benefits to participants, or that it has undesirable consequences for others in society.

First, take activities that are risky to participants. Such risks have been offered as objections to including women in high-injury or high-stress sports.[24] They may be at least part of the explanation for the continued accommodation of separate teams for men and women in contact sports.[25] Risks to participants are, however, unjust reasons for exclusion, so long as the activity is left open to men. Medical experiments with human subjects are an illuminating analogy.[26] Some experiments simply are not permitted by federal regulations because their risks outweigh their potential benefits. Researchers may not enter any subjects in such experiments, even with the subjects' informed consent. In medical research, however, there has been a long-standing practice of routinely excluding women from experiments, allegedly because of the risks of pregnancy or the need for a uniform subject population. This exclusion has been criticized as unwarranted paternalism, because it substitutes the experimenter's risk judgments for the judgments of the excluded group of women subjects, but not for the included men subjects. It thus continues stereotypes of women as less capable of responsible decision-making. Moreover, as Merton (15) and others have argued, the insistence on exclusion to ensure a uniform patient population is misguided because it significantly limits the information that is available about the responses of women to new medical therapies and limits women's access to the therapies themselves in their developmental stages. The National Institutes of Health (NIH) have recently issued policy guidelines requiring equal participation of women in studies it sponsors and analysis of relevant differences in results by gender, unless there is a compelling justification to the contrary.[27] Thus, in medical research, affirmative action has not been required when experiments are prohibited across the board, but is demanded when a study is open to men but not to women. Applying this analogy to sports, the concusion would be that universities may decide that some sports are too risky to offer at all, but not that their risks warrant limiting them to men.

A second concern about the assumption that it is desirable to increase opportunities for varsity competition is that there is little evidence that such competition benefits participants with increased educational or job opportunities. This lack of evidence at least undercuts the argument that affirmative action in women's varsity athletics will give more women these benefits and thus increase overall social justice. The fact remains, however, that Title IX only requires a university to protect women's varsity sports when its athletic program is disproportionate, when it has not made continued progress towards improvement, or when there is unmet need among able women competitors. A university can avoid a Title IX order if it can show that there is insufficient interest or ability to field a given women's team. Nonetheless, a university with a problematic history will need to respond to expressions of women's interest despite a lack of evidence that the women will ultimately benefit. Such universities will be ordered to make quite substantial expenditures because a few women want the opportunities. In times of tight budgets, there is something unfortunate about costly expenditures that respond to the desires of a few. This argument could be the basis for the elimination of all varsity sports that respond principally to the interests of their participants—all of what might be called "vanity" sports. The trouble with applying this argument to the present situation, however, is that universities continue to offer at least some low-interest varsity sports for both men and women. As long as universities continue the pattern of funding for "vanity" sports, it is wrong for them to offer this desired benefit disproportionately to men. Title IX's requirements are therefore justified. At the same time, it might be preferable from the point of view of justice to eliminate all "vanity" programs and spend the money saved on more important opportunities for a larger group of students such as intramural sports, an issue to which I shall return in the final section.

Universities opting to eliminate all intercollegiate competition in "vanity" sports, however, would also confront the problem of whether they could choose, legally or ethically, to retain football as a revenue-producing sport.[28] Under current legal standards, they probably could not make this choice; although Title IX permits differently structured and financed programs, it also requires that there be equal accommodation of the interests of women athletes, including provision of teams at competitive levels and efforts to develop women's teams as revenue-producers on the model of men's teams. It would also be ethically troublesome to retain football while abolishing the remainder of the intercollegiate program for both men and women. This choice would leave the university with a high-profile, highly sought after (albeit most likely not beneficial) showcase for male athletes, with no comparable opportunities for women. An alternative might be to take up the suggestion of critics of university athletics that some allegedly profitable sports enterprises be privatized.

Finally, what are the consequences for affirmative action if the activity to which increased entry is sought is one that there are good social reasons for discouraging entirely? As the initial section of this paper argued, intercollegiate athletic competition might well fall into this category because it is expensive, provides little or no educational benefit, and may foster problematic images of excellence and fair play. If society is genuinely discouraging the activity, then the argument for affirmative action would be undercut. But if society is not working to discourage the activity, the case for affirmative action remains. It is worse from the point of view of justice to continue sponsoring the activity, but leave women out, than to sponsor it without women. It is worse still if one of the concerns about the activity is that it contributes to problematic images of women or other disadvantaged groups. Thus even if it would be best overall to phase out intercollegiate athletic competition, it is better to make serious efforts to include women, even if they increase the resources committed to the enterprise, than to continue it with disproportionate participation by men. In short, universities that stick with football are stuck with Title IX.

There are, to be sure, moral difficulties with phasing out intercollegiate competition, just as there are with phasing out any cherished benefit. Athletes, both male and female, have been recruited with promises of scholarships and competition. They have what I have argued elsewhere (9) might be viewed as legitimate expectations that these opportunities will continue during their time as students; at least, they have been encouraged to form these expectations by those providing the benefits—they have had no reason to believe the assurances were dubious or that they themselves were benefiting as perpetrators of injustice. These expectations might be the basis for constructing a phase-out so as to cushion the impact on present athletes, while not creating a new set of expectations for incoming students. Recruited athletes might, for example, be able to keep their scholarships for four years; or, universities might continue to field competitive teams at least through the junior years of recruited athletes in sports slated for discontinuation.

Phase-outs such as the abolition of all or most "vanity" sports face tremendously difficult issues of coordination, however. Unless all of the schools within a conference—or, perhaps, within a region—adopt similar phase-out strategies, athletes recruited by one school will find themselves left out, while athletes at other schools will continue to compete. They may well believe that they have been treated unfairly by their own schools. While they have no entitlement to continue to compete, and of course are free to transfer, it is true that they are losing a cherished benefit that others just like them continue to enjoy. The situation is perhaps worst when a men's sport is cancelled and women at the same school continue to enjoy the opportunity to compete in that sport.[29] The alternative that voids the apparent unfairness of differential treatment of athletes with similar expectations is to continue to provide the competitive opportunity until a coordinated system of cuts is in place. Athletes already recruited could continue to enjoy their sport until it was gradually phased down in a coordinated way, and new recruitment efforts would cease. Such coordination strategies are difficult to implement, however, because as Fleisher, Goff, and Tollison (8) argue, individual athletic departments have incentives to keep their budgets as large as possible. Thus the fairest of the likely outcomes is to continue to support men's "vanity" sports, while increasing support for women's sports—an outcome that is expensive and that may lead universities in the long run to reconsider the wisdom of their support for intercollegiate competition.

Beyond the Title IX Model of Equality

The strong protection given women's varsity sports by Title IX is thus justified despite—and perhaps even because of—the flaws of the current system of competition. A better alternative, however, might be to consider ways of radically restructuring intercollegiate athletic competition. In this concluding section, I explore four possibilities for reconstruction and argue that all are preferable, from the point of view of justice, to affirmative action with the current context.[30] None, however, are explicitly supported by the current interpretation of Title IX.

First, universities might increase efforts to encourage women to participate in skills training and sports activities. If women's historical underrepresentation in competitive athletics is in part a result of earlier educational programs and attitudes that discourage them from participating in athletics at all, such efforts are an important form of affirmative action. Because the aim would be to increase exposure to a real benefit, the focus of such encouragement would be fitness and skills activities that are of a lifelong importance and simply not short-term competitive opportunities. An analogy might be the programs at many universities to increase interest and training in science and mathematics among women and minority students. The focus of the Title IX regulations, however, is the provision of levels of competition that "effectively accommodate the interests and abilities of members of both sexes."[31]

A second initiative for universities might be the development of intramural sports programs that expand participation and competition widely throughout the student body. A typical pattern of universities today is the contrast between lavish support for varsity athletics and little support for intramural activities.

An alternative would be to improve intramural facilities, to make educational opportunities (such as skills training) available in conjunction with them, and to increase the amenities associated with them. The University of California at Davis is an example of how widespread intramural programs can help to develop a sense of community among students. While Title IX requires the provision of appropriate levels of competition at all levels, including the intramural level, its emphasis, as it has been interpreted in litigation, has been varsity teams, not the overall expansion of athletic participation across the student body.

A more radical option might be the reconsideration of what are considered sports. Sports today emphasize physical characteristics such as bulk (football) and height (basketball)—characteristics that are predominately male—rather than characteristics such as finesse, agility, or endurance. Women athletes confront what Martha Minow (16) has called the "difference dilemma": either they play by historical rules, which fail to acknowledge differences between women and men, or they are stigmatized for calling attention to differences. Women basketball players, for example, have moved into a sport constructed for tall bodies. Although they have in many respects been successful in constructing a different kind of sport—one that emphasizes ball movement, for example—they might have constructed an even more exciting sport had basket height or angle been adjusted. Nonetheless, there have been some encouraging signs in the direction of changed sports emphases. For example, women's soccer has become far more popular, as have endurance track events such as the marathon for women. Gymnastics tests different skills for men and women; women's gymnastics has become a popular sport on some campuses, although sometimes one that advertises based on the sexuality of the women athletes involved. Title IX, as it has been interpreted, however, does not require implementation of new sports for women, except in response to demand; it may even be an obstacle to new sports to the extent that in protects established ones.[32] Moreover, there is no mandate in Title IX for the identification or development of entirely new sports.

Finally, university sports programs might consider the introduction of coeducational teams. Such teams are of course a mainstay of recreational and intramural programs. They emphasize teamwork and complementary skills— both characteristics that are arguably beneficial and useful educationally. Such teamwork opportunities might also be highly useful in acculturating women and men to work together in other contexts, especially if the opportunities are spread widely throughout the student body. Yet no intercollegiate competition today features coeducational teams, although parallel teams are fielded in such sports as tennis, swimming, diving, track, golf, and skiing. Even mixed doubles, a staple of both professional and recreational tennis, is ignored on the college level. Title IX accepts the separation of men's and women's teams outright, with one exception: in noncontact sports in which no team is fielded for the underrepresented sex, members of the excluded sex must be permitted to try out on a skills basis for the team of the other sex.[33]

Conclusion

In this article, I have argued that university athletics for women should be treated as a case of affirmative action within a morally flawed practice. So long as the practice continues in its present form, the case for affirmative action remains.

But there is a stronger case to be made for radical changes in the current practice. Title IX, the statue requiring equality in federally funded educational programs, does not propose such radical changes and may even in some contexts be a roadblock to them.[34]

Notes

1. As such, my criticism is directed principally at NCAA Division I and Division II schools, which mount large-scale competitive programs. It may not apply to Division III schools, which do not offer athletic scholarships per se, and which adhere to much more stringent limits on funding and other participation in intercollegiate athletics. However, to the extent that Division I practices operate covertly in Division III schools (for example, by using school tours to recruit athletes and suggest the possibility of athletic scholarships), the analysis applies to them also.

2. Quoted in Chu, Segrave, and Becker (5: p. 215) Martin (14) also examines the argument that sports build character.

3. 20 U.S.C. § 1681 (a) (1993).

4. *NCAA v. Califano*, 622 F.2d 1382 (10th Cir., 1980).

5. *Kelley v. Board of Trustees of Univ. of Ill.*, 832 F. Supp. 237 (C.D. Ill. 1993).

6. *Kelley v. Board of Trustees of Univ. of Ill.*, 832 F. Supp. 237 (C.D. Ill. 1993); *Roberts v. Colorado State University*, 814 F. Supp. 1507 (D. Colo.), *aff d* sub nom. *Roberts v. Colorado State Bd. of Agric.*, 993 F.2d 824 (10th Cir.), cert., denied, 114 S.Ct. 580 (1993).

7. *Grove City College v. Bell*, 465 U.S. 555 (1984).

8. 20 U.S.C. § 1687 (1993); P.L. No. 100–259, 102 Stat. 28 (1988).

9. Policy Interpretation, 44 Fed. Reg. 71413 (December 11, 1979; United States Department of Education, 33).

10. 34 C.F.R. § 106.37(c) (1993).

11. 34 C.F.R. § 106.41(c) (1993).

12. 44 Fed. Reg. 71413 (December 11, 1979).

13. *Cook v. Colgate University*, 802 F. Supp. 737 (N.D.N.Y. 1992), vacated and remanded on other grounds, 992 F.2d 17 (2d Cir. 1993). (The other grounds were graduation of the athletes involved in the suit.)

14. *Favia v. Indiana University of Pennsylvania*, 812 F. Supp. 578 (W.D. Pa. 1993), *aff d* 7 F.3d 332 (3d Cir. 1993). Although the undergraduate population at IUP was 55.6% women, only 38% of the varsity athletic slots and 21% of the athletic scholarships went to women. The

court suggested in dicta that Title IX probably not only forbade the cancellation of women's varsity sports when interested athletes were available but also mandated the addition of further women's varsity sports.

15. *Roberts v. Colorado State University*, 814 F. Supp. 1507 (D. Colo.). *aff d* sub nom. *Roberts v. Colorado State Bd. of Agric.*, 993 F.2d 824 (10th Cir.), cert. denied, 114 S.Ct. 580 (1993).

16. *Cohen v. Brown University*, 809 F. Supp. 978 (D.R.I. 1992), *aff d*, 991 F.2d 888 (1st Cir. 1993).

17. *Kelley v. Board of Trustees of Univ. of Ill.*, 832 F. Supp. 237 (C.D. Ill. 1993).

18. The NCAA allowed 88 football scholarships in 1993; at many universities, this is equivalent to the total number of scholarships awarded members of women's teams. When nonscholarship players are allowed to join football teams, squad size may balloon to 145. In comparison, National Football League teams are allowed only 45 players. See Pieronek (20).

19. *Blair v. Washington State University*, 740 P.2d 1379 (Wash. 1987) held that the state's equal protection clause and nondiscrimination statute did not require football revenues to be shared within the athletic program; this approach is endorsed by Pieronek (20).

20. The term comes from the remedy section of Title VII of the Civil Rights Act, 42 U.S.C.§ 2000e-5 (1993).

21. *City of Richmond v. J.A. Croson Co.*, 488 U.S. 469 (1989).

22. *Regents of the University of California v. Bakke*, 438 U.S. 265 (1978).

23. Where there are no common paradigms of social benefits and burdens, it may be impossible to find agreement on basic principles of justice, much less on when redistribution is justified under conditions of injustice. The theoretical shifts from Rawls (24) to Rawls (25) are instructive on this point.

24. An example is the rejection, until quite recently, of the women's marathon in Olympic competition.

25. Or are concerns about sexual contact the real explanation?

26. Another analogy might be inclusion of women in combat positions in the military.

27. "NIH Guidelines on the Inclusion of Women and Minorities as Subjects in Clinical Research," 59 Red. Reg. 14508 (March 28, 1994).

28. Basketball isn't really an issue here, since women's basketball is so well established and a university could achieve equality by retaining both women's and men's basketball.

29. Cases that are examples are *Kelley v. Board of Trustees of Univ. of Ill.*, 832 F. Supp. 237 (C.D. Ill. 1993), and *Gonyo v. Drake University*, 837 F. Supp. 989 (S.D. Iowa 1993).

30. These possibilities are suggested in English (7), Moulton

(18), and Postow (21, 22). They have been criticized by Belliotti (3) and Simon (26).

31. 34 C.F.R. § 106.41(c) (1) (1993).

32. In *Roberts v. Colorado State University,* 814 F. Supp. 1507 (D. Colo.), *aff'd* sub nom. *Roberts v. Colorado State Bd. of Agric.,* 993 F.2d 824 (10th Cir.), cert. denied, 114 S.Ct. 580 (1993), for example, the university sought to substitute women's soccer—a sport that included more athletes and afforded more competitive opportunities—for women's fast-pitch softball. The court refused to allow the substitution and suggested in dicta that CSU might be required to provide both sports for women. If budgets are tight, however, the result might be continued protection of the fast-pitch team, with little development of soccer. For criticism of this outcome, see Chu (4).

33. 34 C.F.R. § 106.41(b) (1993).

34. I am grateful to the University of Utah College of Law for a faculty summer stipend that supported the research on this project. I am also grateful to Peggy Battin, Frances Garrett, and Bob Simon for helpful comments on earlier drafts of this article.

Bibliography

1. Acosta, R.V., and Carpenter, L.J. "Women in Sport." In *Rethinking College Athletics.* Edited by J. Andre and D. James. Philadelphia: Temple University Press, 1991, 313–325.

2. Andre, J., and James, D. (Eds.). *Rethinking College Athletics.* Philadelphia: Temple University Press, 1991.

3. Belloitti, R.A. "Women, Sex & Sports." *Journal of the Philosophy of Sport,* VI (1979), 67–72.

4. Chu, D. *The Character of American Higher Education and Intercollegiate Sport.* Albany: State University of New York Press, 1989.

5. Chu, D., Segrave, J.O., and Becker, B.J. (Eds.). *Sport and Higher Education.* Champaign, IL: Human Kinetics Publishers, 1985.

6. Dubois, P.E. "The Occupational Attainment of Former College Athletes: A Comparative Study." In *Sport and Higher Education.* Edited by D. Chu, J.O. Segrave, and B.J. Becker. Champaign, IL: Human Kinetics Publishers, 1985, 235–248.

7. English, J. "Sex Equality and Sport." *Philosophy and Public Affairs,* 7 (1978), 269–277.

8. Fleisher, A.A., Goff, B.L., and Tollison, R.D. *The National Collegiate Athletic Association: A Study in Cartel Behavior.* Chicago: University of Chicago Press, 1992.

9. Francis. L. "Consumer Expectations and Access to Health Care." *University of Pennsylvania Law Review,* 140 (1992), 1881.

10. Francis L. "In Defense of Affirmative Action." In *Affirmative Action in the University.* Edited by S. Cahn. Philadelphia: Temple University Press, 1993.

11. Hart-Nibbrig, N., and Cottingham, C. *The Political Economy of College Sport.* Lexington, MA: Lexington Books, 1986.

12. Lapchick, R.E., and Slaughter, J.B. *The Rules of the Game: Ethics in College Sport.* New York: American Council on Education, 1989.

13. Lawrence, P.R. *Unsportsmanlike Conduct: The National Collegiate Athletic Association and the Business of College Football.* New York: Praeger, 1987.

14. Martin, W.B. *A College of Character.* San Francisco: Jossey-Bass, 1982.

15. Merton, V. "The Exclusion of Pregnant, Pregnable, and Once-Pregnable People (a.k.a. Women) from Biomedical Research." *American Journal of Law & Medicine,* XIX (1993), 369.

16. Minow, Martha. *Making all the Difference.* Ithaca, NY: Cornell University Press, 1990.

17. Miracle, A.W., Jr., and Rees, C.R. *Lessons of the Locker Room.* Buffalo, NY: Prometheus Books, 1994.

18. Moulton J. "Why Everyone Deserves a Sporting Chance: Education, Justice, and College Sport." In *Rethinking College Athletics.* Edited by J. Andre and D. James. Philadelphia: Temple University Press, 1991, 210–220.

19. National Collegiate Athletic Association. *Gender Equity Task Force Report.* 1993.

20. Pieronek, C. "A Clash of Titans: College Football v. Title IX." *Journal of College and University Law,* 20 (1994), 351.

21. Postow, B. "Women and Masculine Sports." *Journal of the Philosophy of Sport,* VII (1980), 51–58.

22. Postow, B. (Ed.) *Women, Philosophy, & Sport: A Collection of New Essays.* Metuchen, NJ: Scarecrow Press, 1983.

23. Purdy, D.A., Eitzen, D.S., and Hufnagel, R. "Are Athletes Also Students: The Educational Attainment of College Athletes." In *Sport and Higher Education.* Edited by D. Chu, J.O. Segrave, and B.J.

Becker. Champaign, IL: Human Kinetics Publishers, 1985, 221–234.

24. Rawls, J. *A Theory of Justice.* Cambridge, MA: Harvard University Press, 1971.

25. Rawls, J. *Political Liberalism.* New York: Columbia University Press, 1993.

26. Simon, R. *Fair Play: Sports, Values, and Society.* Boulder, CO: Westview Press, 1991.

27. Sperber, M. *College Sports Inc.: The Athletic Department vs. The University.* New York: Henry Holt, 1990.

28. Stevenson, C.L. "College Athletics and 'Character': The Decline and Fall of Socialization Research." In *Sport and Higher Education.* Edited by D. Chu, J.O. Segrave, and B.J. Becker. Champaign, IL: Human Kinetics Publishers, 1985, 249–266.

29. Thelin, J.R. *Games Colleges Play.* Baltimore, MD: Johns Hopkins University Press, 1994.

30. Thelin, J.R., and Wiseman, L.L. *The Old College Try: Balancing Academics and Athletics in Higher Education.* Washington, DC. Clearinghouse on Higher Education, 1989.

31. Thro, W.E., and Snow, B.A. "*Cohen v. Brown University* and the Future of Intercollegiate and Interscholastic Athletics." *Education Law Reporter,* 84 (1993), 611.

32. United States Department of Education., *Technical Assistance Documents for Title IX Intercollegiate Athletics, National Enforcement Strategy.* 1993.

Questions for Consideration

1. If college athletics is a "morally flawed practice," as Francis says it is, why favor the possibility of integrating women in such practice instead of working toward eliminating college athletics completely?

2. To what extent do Francis's four possibilities for reconstructing college athletics work toward *moral* reform as well?

3. Title IX has certainly created greater opportunities for women at schools since its inception. A major flaw is that, because of the importance of revenue-generating sports at institutions, it has been unfair to male athletes in nonrevenue generating sports. Can you think of any practicable way to remedy this defect?

Race

36   White Men Can't Run

Amby Burfoot
Editor in Chief Runner's World

In this reading, Amby Burfoot states that black runners are coming increasingly to dominate Olympic running races, both aerobically and anaerobically. Moreover, black athletes are enjoying tremendous success in American sports. What is astonishing, however, is the incurious attitude of American society as a whole to this phenomenon. Part of the problem, Burfoot acknowledges, is that black athletic success sparks racist notions that greater physical skills are counterpoised by lesser mental abilities. While such notions are unfounded, Burfoot claims, fear still rules American society. As a response to such fear, he quotes the renowned geneticist Claude Bouchard: "I have always worked with the hypothesis that ignorance fosters prejudice. And that knowledge is the greatest safeguard against prejudice."

Unfairness is a fact of sport and a fact of life, Burfoot says. On the one hand, women cannot compete on a level playing field with men, and Japanese rarely succeed in sport, in spite of their great work ethic, because they are short. On the other hand, West African runners dominate sprinting competitions and Kenyan men are increasingly doing so in long-distance races. Africans are coming to monopolize the most nontechnical sports both aerobically and anaerobically.

Burfoot then goes into much of the research that is attempting to explain the performance advantages of blacks. Blacks on average are ever-so-slightly constitutionally different from whites. What is even more astonishing is that East Africans differ from West Africans more than either group itself differs from whites. The interesting question for Burfoot is not, Why are blacks so different from whites? *but,* Why are some blacks so different from other blacks? *In other words,* Why are Africans so diverse? *The answer, Burfoot suggests, is probably some combination of nature and nurture. Kenyans, after all, have an unusual genetic endowment, but they also have a unique environment and are taught both aggressiveness and toughness.*

This month in Barcelona, for the first time in the history of the Olympic Games, runners of African heritage will win every men's running race. West Africans, including American blacks of West African descent, will sweep the gold medals at all distances up to, and including, the 400-meter hurdles. East Africans and North Africans will win everything from the 800 meters through the marathon.

These results won't surprise any close observer of the international track scene. Ever since America's Eddie Tolan won the 100 meters at the 1932 Los Angeles games, becoming the first black gold medalist in an Olympic track race, black runners have increasingly dominated

Olympic and World competitions. An analysis of the three World Championships paints the clearest picture. In 1983, blacks won 14 of the 33 available medals in running races. In 1987, they won 19. Last September in Tokyo, they won 29.

What's more surprising is the lack of public dialogue on the phenomenon. The shroud of silence results, of course, from sour societal taboo against discussing racial differences—a taboo that is growing stronger in these politically correct times.

A good example: *Sports Illustrated*'s changed approach to the subject. In early 1971, *Sports Illustrated* published a landmark story, "An Assessment of 'Black Is Best'" by Martin Kane, which explored various physical reasons for the obvious success of black athletes on the American sports scene. African American sociologists, particularly Harry Edwards, wasted little time in blasting Kane's article. Wrote Edwards, famed for orchestrating black power demonstrations at the 1968 Olympics: "The argument that blacks are physically superior to whites is merely a racist ideology camouflaged to appeal to the ignorant, the unthinking and the unaware."

Edwards was right to question arguments attributing sport success primarily to physiology. American blacks fear that such an overemphasis on their physical skills may call into question their mental skills. Besides, sport success clearly demands more than just a great body. It also requires desire, hard work, family and social support, positive role models, and, often, potential for financial reward.

For these reasons, the University of Texas' Bob Malina, Ph.D., the country's leading expert on physical and performance differences among ethnic groups, has long argued for what he calls a "biocultural approach." Nature (the overall cultural environment) is just as important as biology (genetics).

Because Edwards and others attacked so stridently, mere discussion of the subject grew to be regarded, ipso facto, as a racist activity and hence something to be avoided at all cost. In 1991

Sports Illustrated returned to the fertile subject of black athletes in American sports, devoting dozens of articles to the topic in a multi-issue series. Not one of these articles made even a passing mention of physical differences between blacks and whites. Likewise, *USA Today* barely scratched the surface in its own four-day special report "Race and Sport: Myths and Realities."

When NBC television broadcast its brave "Black Athletes: Fact and Fiction" program in 1989, the network had trouble locating a scientist willing to discuss the subject in the studio. Instead, host Tom Brokaw had to patch through to two experts attending a conference in Brussels. In beginning my research for this story, I contacted one of America's most respected sports scientists. He didn't want to talk about the subject. "Go ahead and hang yourself," he said, "but you're not going to hang me with you."

Fear rules. Why? Because this is a story about inherited abilities, and Americans aren't ready for the genetics revolution that's sweeping over us. In the next 10 years, scientists worldwide will devote $3 billion to the Human Genome Project. In the process they will decipher all 100,000 human genes, cure certain inherited diseases (like cystic fibrosis, Tay-Sachs, and sickle-cell anemia), and tell us more about ourselves than we are prepared to know, including, in all likelihood, why some people run faster than others.

Tom Brokaw, moderator of "Black Athletes: Fact and Fiction," talking with geneticist Claude Bouchard: "A lot of people, when I told them we were doing this program, kept saying to me: 'Why would you even want to do this?' So let me ask you: What do we gain from these studies of blacks and caucasians?"

Dr. Bouchard: "Well, I have always worked with the hypothesis that ignorance fosters prejudice. And that knowledge is the greatest safeguard against prejudice."

Sport: The Illusion of Fairness

Many casual sports fans mistakenly believe that athletic competitions are fair. In fact, this is one reason so many people enjoy sports. Politics and corporate ladder-climbing may be rotten to the core, but sports at least provide a level playing field.

This simple notion of fairness doesn't go very far. Just ask any female athlete. Women excel in law school, medical practice, architectural design, and the business world, but they never win at sports. They don't even want to compete side by side with men in sports (as they do in all other areas of social, cultural, and economic life). Why not? Because sports success stems from certain physical strengths and abilities that women simply don't have. We all acknowledge this.

But we have more trouble understanding that what is true for women is also true for some male groups. In some sports, certain racial groups face overwhelming odds. Take the Japanese. The Japanese are passionate about sports and surely rank among the world's most disciplined, hardest working, and highest achieving peoples. These qualities have brought them great success in many areas and should produce the same in sports.

Yet the Japanese rarely succeed at sports. They fall short because, on the average, they *are* short. Most big-time sports require size, speed, and strength. A racial group lacking these qualities must struggle against great odds to excel.

Of course, a few sports, including marathoning, gymnastics, and ice-skating, actually reward small stature. You've heard of Kristi Yamaguchi and Midori Ito, right? It's no mistake that the Japanese are better at ice-skating than, say, basketball. It's genetics.

On their trip to the 1971 Fukuoka Marathon in Japan, Kenny Moore and Frank Shorter asked athlete coordinator Eiichi Shibuya why the Japanese hold the marathon in such high regard. "We made the marathon important because it is one event in which a man needs not be tall to be great," Shibuya said. "In the marathon we can do well against the world."

In a recent "first," molecular biologists discovered a single amino acid, just a small part of a gene that controls the eye's ability to see the color red. In Olympic archery events, competitors with this gene presumably have an advantage over those without it.

Track: The Perfect Laboratory

A scientist interested in exploring physical and performance differences among different racial groups couldn't invent a better sport than running. First of all, it's a true worldwide sport, practiced and enjoyed in almost every country around the globe. Also, it doesn't require any special equipment, coaching, or facilities. Abebe Bikila proved this dramatically in the 1960 Olympic Games when—shoeless, little coached, and inexperienced—he won the marathon.

Given the universality of running, it's reasonable to expect that the best runners should come from a wide range of countries and racial groups. We should find that Europeans, Asians, Africans, and North and South Americans all win about the same number of gold medals in running events.

This isn't, however, what happens. Nearly all the sprints are won by runners of West African descent. Nearly all the distance races are won, remarkably, by runners from just one small corner of one small African country—Kenya.

Track and field is the perfect laboratory sport for two more important reasons. First, two of the most exciting events—the 100 meters and the marathon—represent the far reaches of human physical ability. A sprinter must be the fastest, most explosive of humans. A marathoner must be the most enduring. Any researcher curious about physical differences between humans could look at runners who excel at these two events and expect to find a fair number of differences. If these differences then broke down along racial lines . . . well, so be it.

Second, since running requires so little technique and equipment, success results *directly* from the athlete's power, endurance, or other purely physical attributes. This explains why drug testing is so important in track. If a golfer, tennis player, gymnast, or even basketball player were to take steroids or to blood dope, we'd be hard-pressed to say that the drugs helped the athlete. In these sports, too much else—rackets, clubs, specialized moves—separate the athlete's physiology from his or her scoring potential.

Runners find, on the other hand, that if they improve the body (even illegally), the performance has to improve. Some scientists even acknowledge that a simple running race can measure certain physical traits better than any laboratory test. The results we observe in Olympic Stadium are as valid as they get.

On the all-time list for 100 meters, 44 of the top 50 performances are sprinters of West African origin. The highest ranking white, Marian Woronin of Poland, stands in 16th place.

At the Seoul Olympics, Kenyan men won the 800 meters, the 1500 meters, the 2000-meter steeplechase and the 5000 meters. Based on population percentages alone, the likelihood that this should have happened is 1 in 1,600,000,000 (one billion, six hundred million).

Human Physique: The Differences

The evidence for a black genetic advantage in running falls into two categories: physique and physiology. The first refers to body size and proportions, and the second to below-the-surface differences in the muscles, the enzymes, the cell structures, and so on. To appreciate the significance of either, you must first understand that very small differences between two racial groups can lead to very dramatic differences in sports and performance. For example, two groups, A and B, can share 99 percent of the same human genes and characteristics. They can be virtually identical. Nevertheless, if the 1 percent of variation occurs in a characteristic that determines success at a certain sport, then group A might win 90 percent of the Olympic medals in that sport.

Over the years, numerous studies of physique have compared blacks of West African heritage with white Americans and consistently reached the same conclusions. Among these conclusions: blacks have less body fat, narrower hips, thicker thighs, longer legs, and lighter calves. From a biomechanical perspective, this is an impressive package. Narrow hips allow for efficient, straight-ahead running. Strong quadriceps muscles provide horsepower, and light calves reduce resistance.

Speaking a year ago at the American College of Sports Medicine's symposium on "Ethnic Variations in Human Performance," Lindsey Carter, Ph.D., observed: "It appears that the biomechanical demands of a particular sport limit the range of physiques that can satisfy these demands." Carter, a San Diego State professor who has conducted a series of studies of Olympic athletes, concluded: "If all else is equal, can a difference in ethnicity confer advantages in physical performance? From a biomechanical point of view, the answer is yes."

A number of direct performance studies have also shown a distinct black superiority in simple physical tasks such as running and jumping. Often the subjects in these studies were children (for example, fourth graders in the Kansas City public schools), which tends to mute the criticism that blacks outrun and outjump whites because society channels black youngsters into sports.

A few studies have even looked beyond simple muscle performance. In one of the first, Robert L. Browne of Southwestern Louisiana Institute showed that black college students had a significantly faster patellar tendon reflex time (the familiar knee-jerk response) than white students. Reflex time is an important variable to study for two reasons. First, because many sports obviously require lightning reflexes. And, second, because classic biological theory holds that faster reflexes will tend to create stronger muscles, which will tend to create denser bones. All of these have been observed in blacks, whose denser bones may make it particularly hard for them to succeed in one major Olympic sport—swimming.

From a 1934 edition of a black-owned newspaper, the *California Eagle:* "We had no colored swimmers in the last Olympic games or the ones before that. Isn't it high time we show the world that we can swim as well as spring, jump and box?"

Fact: No black swimmer has ever qualified for the U.S. Olympic swim team.

Muscle Fibers: Some Slow, Some Fast

Since the study of black-white differences frightens off many U.S. scientists, it's no surprise that the best research on the subject comes from other laboratories around the world. In the last decade, scientists from Quebec City, Stockholm, and Cape Town, South Africa, have been leading the way.

Claude Bouchard, Ph.D., of Laval University in Quebec City, is perhaps the world's leading sports geneticist, as well as a foremost expert in the genetics of obesity. When the *New England Journal of Medicine* published a Bouchard study on human obesity two years ago, it made headlines around the world for its finding that the degree of fatness and locale of fat deposition (hips, waist, etc.) was largely determined by heredity.

Bouchard achieved these and many of his other remarkable results through carefully controlled studies of twins who live in and around Quebec City. From such experiments he has determined the "hereditability" of many human traits, including some relating to athletic performance. Bouchard has shown, for example, that anaerobic power is from 44 to 92 percent inherited, while max VO_2 is only 25 percent inherited. From these findings, we might quickly conclude that sprinters are "born" but distance runners are "made," which, loosely, is what track observers have always thought about sprinters and distance runners.

What "makes" distance runners, of course, is their training, and Bouchard has also investigated "trainability." It's surprisingly easy to do. You simply gather a bunch of out-of-shape people, put them on the same training program, and follow their progress according to certain key physiological measures. The results are astonishing. Some subjects don't improve at all or take a long time to improve; some improve almost instantly and by large amounts. This trainability trait, Bouchard has found, is about 75 percent inherited.

This means that potential for distance-running success may be just as genetically determined as potential for sprinting success. Which is why many coaches and physiologists have been saying for years that the best way to improve your marathon time is to "choose your parents carefully."

Bouchard is now examining physiological differences between white French Canadians and black West Africans, both culled from the student population at Laval. In one study, the only one of its kind ever performed between these two groups, the researchers compared muscle-fiber percentages. The West Africans had significantly more fast-twitch fibers and anaerobic enzymes than the whites. Exercise physiologists have long believed that fast-twitch muscle fibers confer an advantage in explosive, short-duration power events such as sprinting.

Two Bouchard disciples, Pierre F. M. Ama and Jean-Aime Simoneau, next decided to test the two groups' actual power output in the lab. On a 90-second leg extension test (basically the same exercise we all do on our weight benches), the black and white subjects performed about equally for the first 30 seconds. Beyond 30 seconds, the whites were able to produce significantly more power than the blacks.

This experiment failed to show what the researchers expected—that West African blacks should be better sprinters. It may, on the other hand, have shown that these blacks generally wouldn't perform well in continuous events lasting several minutes or longer.

Of course, a leg extension test isn't the same thing as the real world of track and field. In particular, it can't account for any of the biomechanical running advantages that blacks may have—which could explain the curious findings of David Hunter.

Two years before Ama and Simoneau published their study, Hunter completed his Ph.D. requirement in exercise physiology at Ohio State University by writing his thesis on "A Comparison of Anaerobic Power between Black and White Adolescent Males." Hunter began by giving his subjects—high schoolers from Columbus—two laboratory tests that measure anaerobic power. These tests yielded no difference.

Then he decided to turn his subjects loose on the track. There the blacks sprinted and jumped much better than the whites. These results apparently disturbed Hunter, an African African, whose dissertation concluded that the laboratory results (no differences) were more significant than the real-world results (big differences).

In attempting to balance his results, Hunter noted that a 1969 study in the journal *Ergonomics* found that blacks actually had *less* anaerobic power than whites. What he failed to point out, and perhaps even to recognize, was that the *Ergonomics* study compared a group of Italians with a group of *Kenyans*. Indeed, many of the Kenyan subjects came from the Nandi and Kikuyu tribes, famed for their distance running but scarcely noted for their sprinting (anaerobic power). From running results alone, we would expect these Kenyans to score low on any test of anaerobic power.

I mention this only because I believe it highlights an important point: the word "black" provides little information about anyone or any group. Of the 100,000 genes that determine human makeup, only 1 to 6 regulate skin color, so we should assume almost nothing about anyone based on skin color alone. West Africans and East Africans are both black, but in many physical ways they are *more unlike each other* than they are *different from most whites*.

When it comes to assumptions about Africans, we should make just one: That the peoples of Africa, short and tall, thick and thin, fast and slow, white and black, represent the fullest and most spectacular variations of humankind to be found anywhere.

Stanford track coach Brooks Johnson: "I'm going to find a white Carl Lewis. They're all over the place."

Sports columnist Scott Ostler in the *Los Angeles Times*: "Dear Brooks—Pack a lunch. And while you're out there searching, bring back a white Spudd Webb, a white Dominique Wilkens, a white O. J. Simpson, a white Jerry Rice, a white Bo Jackson and a white Wilt Chamberlain."

Endurance: The Muscle Component

Tim Noakes, M.D., director of the Sport Science Centre at the University of Cape Town Medical School, has spent the last 30 years researching the limits of human endurance, largely because of his own and, indeed, his whole country's passion for the 54-mile Comrades Marathon. Noakes's book *Lore of Running* (Leisure Press, 1991) stands as the ultimate compilation of the history, physiology, and training methods of long-distance running.

In recent years, Noakes has been trying to learn why South African blacks, who represent only 20 percent of their country's road racing population, nevertheless take 80 percent of the top positions in South African races. (South African blacks are related to East African through their common Bushman ancestors. West African blacks, representing the Negroid race, stand apart.)

In one experiment, Noakes asked two groups of white and black marathoners to run a full marathon on the laboratory treadmill. The two groups were matched for ability and experience. While they weren't among South Africa's elite corps of distance runners, subjects from both groups were good marathoners with times under 2:45.

When the two groups ran on the treadmill at the same speed, the major difference was that the blacks were able to perform at a much higher percentage of their maximum oxygen capacity. The results, published in the *European Journal of Applied Physiology,* showed that the whites could run only at 81 percent of their max VO_2. The blacks could reach 89 percent.

This same characteristic has previously been noted in several great white marathoners, including Derek Clayton and Frank Shorter. Clayton and Shorter didn't have a particularly high max VO_2, but they were able to run for long periods of time at a very high percentage of their max. This enabled them to beat other marathoners who actually had higher max VO_2 values.

Among white runners, a Clayton or Shorter is a physiologic rarity. Among black South Africans, however, such capacity may be commonplace. Even though the blacks in Noakes's lab were working very hard, their muscles produced little lactic acid and other products of muscle fatigue. How can they do this?

Noakes speculates that the blacks have a muscle fiber quality, as yet unnamed in scientific circles, that he calls "high fatigue resistance." It's pretty much the opposite of what the Canadian researchers found in their 90-second test of West Africans.

Despite their country's longtime ban from international competition, black distance runners from South Africa rank first and second on the all-time list for half-marathons (with identical times of 1:00:11) and hold two of the top 10 positions in the marathon (with times of 2:08:15 and 2:08:04).

Outside the laboratory, Tim Noakes has found that African distance runners train at extremely high intensities, much higher than those observed in most white distance runners. "But what we have here is a chicken or egg situation," says Noakes. "Can they train harder because they have a genetic gift of high fatigue resistance, or can they train harder because they have trained hard to train harder?"

Kenya: Nature Meets Nurture

Sweden's renowned exercise physiologist Bengt Saltin, Ph.D., director of the Karolinska Institute in Stockholm, has spent most of his professional career investigating the extraordinary endurance performances of nordic skiers, multiday bicyclists, orienteers, and distance runners. Since all distance-running roads now lead to Kenya, Saltin decided to travel there two years ago to observe the phenomenon firsthand. He also took a half-dozen national-class Swedish runners with him. Later, he brought several groups of Kenyans back to Stockholm to test them in his lab.

In competitions in Kenya, at and near St. Patrick's High School, which has produced so many world-class runners, the Swedish 800-meter to 10,000-meter specialists were soundly beaten by hundreds of 15- to 17-year old Kenyan boys. Indeed, Saltan estimated that this small region of Kenya in the Rift Valley had at least 500 high schoolers who could outrace the Swedes at 2,000 meters.

Back in Stockholm, Saltin uncovered many small differences between the Kenyan and Swedish runners. The results, not yet published in any specific journal, seemed most extraordinary in the quadriceps muscle area. Here, the Kenyans had more blood-carrying capillaries surrounding the muscle fibers and more mito-chondria within the fibers (the mitochondria are the energy-producing "engine" of the muscle).

Saltin also noted that the Kenyans' muscle fibers were smaller than the Swedes. Not small enough to limit performance—except perhaps the high-power production needed for sprint-ing—but small enough to bring the mitochon-dria closer to the surrounding capillaries. This "closeness" presumably enhances oxygen diffu-sion from the densely packed capillaries into the mitochondria.

And when the oxygen gets there, it is burned with incredible efficiency. After hard workouts and races, Saltin noted, Kenyans show little am-monia buildup (from protein combustion) in the muscles—far less than Swedes and other runners. They seem to have more of the muscle enzymes that burn fat and "spare" glycogen and protein. Sparing glycogen, according to a classic tenet of work physiology, is one of the best ways to improve endurance performance. Added to-gether, all these factors give the Kenyans some-thing very close to what Tim Noakes calls "high fatigue resistance."

Saltin believes Kenyan endurance may result from environmental forces. He told *Runner's World* "Fast Lane" columnist Owen Anderson, Ph.D., that the Kenyans' remarkable quadriceps muscles could develop from years of walking and running over hills at high altitude. Saltin has observed similar capillary densities among ori-enteers who train and race through hilly forests and similar small muscle fibers among nordic skiers who train at altitude.

Of course, Peruvians and Tibetans and other people live at altitude and spend all their lives negotiating steep mountain slopes. Yet they don't seem to develop into great distance run-ners. Why the Kenyans?

The only plausible answer is that Kenyans from the Rift Valley, perhaps more so than any other peoples on Earth, bring together the per-fect combination of genetic endowment with environmental and cultural influences. No one can doubt that many Kenyans are born with great natural talents. But much more is also at work. Consider a few of the following.

Boys and girls from west Kenya grow up in a high-altitude environment of surpassing beauty and good weather conditions. From an early age, they must walk and jog across a hilly terrain to get anywhere. They are raised in a culture that emphasizes both stoicism (adolescent circumci-sion) and aggression (cattle raiding). Indeed, the British introduced track and field in Kenya as a way to channel tribal raiding parties into more appropriate behavior. Kip Keino and others since him have provided positive role models, and the society is so male-dominant that Kenyan men are quick to accept their superiority (an as-pect of Kenyan society that makes things espe-cially tough for Kenyan women). The financial rewards of modern-day track and road racing provide an income Kenyans can achieve in al-most no other activity. In short, nearly every-thing about Kenyan life points to success (for men) in distance running.

At the World Cross-Country Championships, often considered distance running's most competitive annual event, Kenya has won the last seven senior men's team titles and the last five junior men's team titles.

While a student at Washington State Uni-versity, Kenyan Josh Kimeto once heard a teammate complaining of knee pain. Kimeto quickly replied: "Pain is when you're twelve years old and they take you out in the jungle, cut off your foreskin and beat you for three days. That's pain."

Barcelona: The Inside Track

Any close inspection of international track results yields one incontrovertible fact: Black-skinned athletes are winning most races. This phenomenon is likely to grow even more pro-nounced in the future. Many African athletes and countries have barely began to show their potential.

Yet it would be incredibly myopic to conclude, simply, that blacks are faster than whites. A more accurate—albeit admittedly speculative—phrasing might go something like this: West African blacks seem to be faster sprinters than whites, who are better than East African blacks; and East Africans seem to have more endurance capacity than whites, who are better than West Africans.

Whites, always in the middle. Maybe this explains why whites have managed to hold on the longest in the middle-distance races, where Seb Coe still holds the world record for 800 meters and Steve Cram for the mile.

In the past, discussion of racial-group success in sports has largely involved the relative success of blacks in basketball, football, and baseball and their relative failure in tennis, golf, and swimming. The "country club" aspects of the latter three sports guaranteed that these discussions centered on social and economic status: Blacks weren't good at tennis, golf, and swimming because they didn't belong to country clubs. Does an analysis of running add anything new to the discussion?

I think so. Where pure explosive power—that is, sprinting and jumping—is required for excellence in a sport, blacks of West African heritage will excel. The more a sport moves away from speed and toward technique and other prerequisites, like hand-eye coordination, the more other racial groups will find themselves on a level playing field.

The Kenyans and other East Africans, despite their amazing endurance, will hardly come to dominate world sports. As many of us distance runners have learned the hard way—from a lifetime of reality checks on playgrounds and various courts and fields—endurance counts for next to nothing in most big-time sports.

While sports aren't necessarily fair, we can still take heart in the many exceptions to the rule. The truly outstanding athlete always fights his way to the top, no matter what the odds, inspiring us with his courage and determination.

In the movie *White Men Can't Jump,* the hero, Billy Hoyle, wins the big game with a slam-dunk shot that had previously eluded him. Billy's climactic shot stands as testimony to the ability of any man, of any race, to rise high, beat the odds, and achieve his goal. The marvel of the human spirit is that it accepts no limits.

Of course, *Jump* is only a movie. The Olympic track races in Barcelona are for real.

Notes

1. S. L. Price, in a 1977 *Sports Illustrated* piece, "Is It in the Genes," touched on many of the same arguments and names involved that appear in Burfoot's thesis, namely, that science is beginning to identify certain physical differences that may explain the differing performances between blacks and whites. Yet to underscore the sensitivity of such a position, scientists refuse to make a firm stand on genetics versus nurture.

2. Edwards reiterated this position in a 1988 NBC television broadcast, "Black Athletes: Fact and Fiction," in which he said performance and style of African Americans are "culturally linked."

3. Malina is now at Penn State University.

4. *Sports Illustrated* returned to the subject of black and white sports performance and participation in a 1997 issue, "What Ever Happened to the White Athlete," 87, no. 23; 30–51.

5. Wilson Kipketer broke Coe's long-standing 800 meter record in 1997. Kipketer is now a Danish citizen but is of Kenyan ancestry.

Questions for Consideration

1. To what extent does Burfoot argue that blacks are better athletes than whites?
2. Evaluate the evidence Burfoot cites in support of black athletic superiority.
3. Do you agree with critics such as Edwards that research based on physical differences is racist?
4. Do you think that any of Burfoot's comments are racially motivated?

37   Racial Differences in Sports: What's Ethics Got to Do with It?

Albert Mosley
Smith College

*This reading, by Albert Mosley, is a critical exami-
nation of the research that purports to show racial
differences between blacks and nonblacks in athletic performance. Principally, Mosley addresses
the research undergirding a recent book by Jon Entine titled* Taboo: Why Black Athletes Dominate
Sports and Why We Are Afraid to Talk about It.

*Mosley retraces Entine's story of the racist eu-
genics behind the Darwinian revolution as it cul-
minated in the Nazism of the early twentieth
century. This story as well as the "research" that
comes after it, Mosley essays to show, are examples
of attempts to rationalize existing stereotypes and
to keep certain groups of people cut off from social
opportunities.*

*Mosley's main argument is that the conclusions
Entine and others draw are flawed because the
data are contaminated: Researchers are looking
only for evidence to bolster preexisting stereotypes.
Yet this is inevitable, Mosley believes, since history
shows clearly that the practice of science is itself inescapably contaminated by our construction of
what we take to be the facts of the matter. There is
no value-free notion of fact: Our research interests
are symptoms of a current but ever-changing social ideology.*

*Finally, Mosley asks, why is the research ques-
tion of black superiority in athletics, if true, even
interesting? Social justice entails social equality.
Scientific research with an aim to establish slight
natural differences among groups too often leads to
injustices—one of which is the uneven distribution
of social goods, especially social opportunities for
personal growth and development.*

Albert Mosley, "Racial Differences in Sports: What's Ethics
Got to Do with It?"

In his book *Taboo: Why Black Athletes Dominate
Sports and Why We Are Afraid to Talk about It*
(NY: BBS Public Affairs, 2000), Jon Entine presents what he considers to be incontrovertible
evidence for black superiority in athletics, and
addresses our ambivalent reception of this "fact."
The evidence derives from facts produced in the
laboratory and, most importantly, on the playing fields.[1] Elite black athletes have a phenotypic
edge over athletes of other races, Entine argues,
and this edge derives from genotypical differences between the races.[2] While Asians make up
57% of the world's population, they "are virtually invisible in the most democratic of world
sports: running, soccer, and basketball."[3] On the
other hand, Africans, who make up only 12% of
the world's population, dominate running, soccer, and basketball.

Superior athletic performance occurs most
noticeably where the contribution of cultural
and socio-economic factors are least, Entine
holds.[4] This is why he focuses on sports based on
running. Presumably such sports offer performances that are least dependent on extensive
training and equipment. In this, he follows the
views of Amby Burfoot (a senior editor of *Sports
Illustrated*). Running, wrote Amby Burfoot,
"doesn't require any special equipment, coaching, or facilities."[5] Currently, "every men's world
record at every commonly-run distance belongs
to a runner of African descent."[6] Nonetheless,
Entine warns us that this achievement is not
proportionally distributed throughout Africa:
"West Africa is the ancestral home of the world's
top sprinters and jumpers; North Africa turns
out top middle stance runners; and East Africa is
the world distance running capital."[7]

Entine believes the refusal to recognize racial differences in athletic aptitude is a derogation of our duty to seek truth. "Measured by fractions of a second, or wins and losses, sport comes as close as we can get to an objective, racially neutral scoring system."[8] In order to dispel the suspicion that acknowledging racial differences is tantamount to endorsing racism, he presents the views of numerous prominent black spokespersons that have also been led by the evidence to acknowledge the superior ability of black athletes. Thus Arthur Ashe, while militantly anti-racist, was forced to concede that, in terms of athletic performance, "we blacks have something that gives us the edge."[9] Testimonials of this nature from black athletes and intellectuals are cited by Entine as a way of showing that acknowledging racial differences is not tantamount to accepting racist explanations of those differences.

In order to account for our fear of acknowledging black superiority in athletics, Entine provides an overview of eugenic thinking in the early and middle nineteenth century, when prominent American intellectuals such as Charles Davenport, Robert Bean, and many others advocated racist beliefs as a matter of public policy. As a result of the work of Henry Goddard, Lewis Terman, Robert Yerkes, and others, IQ tests were developed as a means of ranking human beings in terms of their cognitive capacity. Using the evidence so provided, Henry Fairfield Osborn, paleontologist at Columbia University and president of the Board of Trustees of The American Museum of Natural History wrote: "The standard of intelligence of the average Negro is similar to that of the eleven-year-old youth of the species *Homo Sapiens*."[10] Even European immigrants from eastern and southern Europe were considered inferior races, and in 1924 Congress restricted immigration from "biologically inferior areas."[11] Sterilization, miscegenation laws, and segregation were some of the hygienic racial policies designed to limit the transfer of bad genes. Such measures were considered necessary to ensure progressive human evolution.

The defeat of Nazi Germany brought about a repudiation of the ideological basis of racist views. "Sports became a highly visible way to demonstrate to the world that Americans took their government's pronouncements on freedom and equality to heart," and universities were in the forefront of putting Negro athletes on the field to compete on equal terms with the white athletes.[12] Association with the racist ideology of Nazism tainted the study of racial differences, and the very concept of races differentiated by biological features was rejected in favor of the notion of "ethnic groups" differentiated on the basis of cultural factors. It became plausible that, if the Jews were not a separate race, perhaps Africans weren't either.

On the other hand, Entine argues that there is a biological basis for genuine racial differences. He surveys polygenecist and monogenecist explanations of the evolution of *Homo sapiens*, and opts for the view that the transformation to modern *Homo sapiens* occurred in an already subdivided population, "with one group giving rise to the modern African and the other to all modern non-Africans."[13] Entine concludes that "the ancestors of a Nigerian, a Scandinavian, and a Chinese have traveled significantly different evolutionary paths," and that races are reliable ways of classifying people in terms of the geographical area they or their immediate ancestors derive from.

After the defeat of the Axis powers, UNESCO of the United Nations issued a number of studies showing that the concept of race had no biological validity. But Entine considers the UNESCO position on race to be an example of "flawed science" and accuses it of having replaced biological determinism with environmental determinism, in which all relevant differences are acquired through experience.[14] Despite attacks on the biological validity of racial concepts, Entine recounts how eminent scientists such as Sir Ronald Fisher, Prof. Henry Garrett, and Nobel Prize laureates Herman Muller and William Shockley continued to hold that blacks had less intellectual ability on the average than whites. In an article published in *Science* in 1962, the past president of the American Psychological Association and chair of the anthropology department at Columbia University wrote: "No matter how low . . . an American white may be, his ancestors built the civilizations of Europe, and no matter how high . . . a Negro may be, his ancestors were (and his kinsmen still are) savages in an African jungle. Free and general race-mixture of Negro-white groups in this country would inevitably be not only dysgenic but socially disastrous."[15]

In 1969 Arthur Jensen argued in the *Harvard Educational Review* that genetic factors rather than environmental ones (e.g., socio-political status) were the primary causes of differences in average IQ among the different races.[16] As recently as 1994, *The Bell Curve* argued that those who were least well off were so because they had lower intellectual potential; while those who were best off were so because they had, on the average, higher intellectual potential.[17] From this perspective it is a short distance to the view that brains vary in inverse proportion to brawn, and those with least intelligence depend most on athletic performance and physical labor while those with most intelligence dominate in intellectual performance and mental labor.[18] We are reinforced to believe that just as the genetic makeup of Europeans predisposes them to have higher IQs, the genetic makeup of Africans and African Americans predisposes them to greater manual dexterity and athletic potential.

Of course, attributions of higher and lower intelligence presuppose that we know what we mean by intelligence, and Entine's survey, to its credit, demonstrates that this is not the case. Instead of intelligence being, as Jensen held, a manifestation of a central processing capacity labeled *g*, others have viewed it as a catchword for distinct types of competence: analytic, creative, practical, emotional, linguistic, musical, logical/mathematical, spatial, bodily/kinesthetic, interpersonal, and naturalist. This might suggest the racialist argument that "each group is intelligent in its own special way," a view espoused by black intellectuals such as W.E.B. Du Bois and Leopold Senghor. But it is equally susceptible to the racist rejoinder

that some "modes of intelligence" are more important than others: on this view, the way Africans think and act may have been valuable in the jungle, but they are dysfunctional in the modern world, where bodily performance is routinely surpassed by that of the machine. Entine recognizes that his view might be interpreted as supporting this racist option, but disclaims that "the data that conclusively links our ancestry to athletic skills have little or anything to say about intelligence."[19] But I find his disavowal unconvincing: if athletic skills can be conclusively linked to ancestry, why can't intellectual skills be as well? Conversely, if intellectual skills cannot be conclusively linked to ancestry, how can we be so sure that athletic skills can?

Entine reports the position of prominent social scientists such as Ashley Montagu and Harry Edwards, who argue that the concept of race has questionable biological validity. They point out that average differences between races are little different from the amount of variation within races. Races, they argue, have a political rather than biological utility, that of continuing a racist agenda. Citing alleged innate differences between groups has historically been a principal justification for supporting existing differences in the distribution of wealth and power. On the other hand, environmentalists typically stress the extent that black athletic achievement is the result of intelligence, hard work, and the lack of opportunities in other areas. The belief that members of certain groups are "naturally better" athletes devalues the importance of training, access, early exposure, social reinforcement, and the like.[20] By encouraging black youth to believe that their natural domain is sports, their energies and talents are channeled away from technical and academic areas. In this regard, Harry Edwards argues that sports is a negative image that merely transfers the black male from the cottonfields to the playing fields, and construes him as good for little else. It is no excuse that many African Americans have romanticized black athletes as realizing the natural potential of the race.[21] Despite the myth of John Henry, we should ask whether African Americans in the southern United States were better cotton-pickers than their Scotch-Irish counterparts, and whether their progeny ought to be proud of it?

But for Entine, stereotypes that portray blacks as naturally better athletes are distillations of commonly recognized truths. And particular stereotypes such as "blacks can't swim" and "whites can't jump" reflect genotypically based propensities of whites and blacks. Entine dismisses the fact that swimming pools and training facilities are in short supply in poor black neighborhoods in favor of "the fact" that blacks have denser skeletons and lower levels of body fat among elite athletes. And while the races may share most genes in common, as environmentalists argue, what matters is not *how many* genes differ but *which* genes. Just as different breeds of dogs have distinctive personalities, behavioral tendencies, and afflictions, Entine suggests that the same is true with different races of human beings: "canine stereotypes are both reasonably accurate and critical information for pet-shopping parents." And he concludes: "it is not far-fetched to assume we will soon locate alleles for herding and guarding in dogs, as well as faster reflexes or more efficient energy processing in humans."[22]

While Entine raises the question of "why it even matters whether blacks are better athletes," he provides no discussion of the question.[23] Yet, why it matters is equally as important as whether it is true. If it is true that "within the performance range in which most of us fall, the environment may be critical," then why shouldn't most of us be concerned about what might be done to improve the performance of most people.[24] Instead, our attention is directed to the few exceptional members of recognized groups, as if these exceptional individuals were exemplars of the group. Entine consecrates the common mistake of taking the most outstanding members of a group as ideal types representative of the group, and this allows him to conclude that "when we talk about people such as Einstein and Mozart—or Mark McGwire, Jim Brown, and Pele—genes count a lot."[25]

The belief that black athletic ability is inversely proportionate to black intellectual ability has been used to justify slavery, colonialism, and segregation. And though Entine acknowledges that biological determinism has been used to defend racist social agendas, he does more to reinforce than challenge racist stereotypes of the innate basis of athletic and intellectual performances. While acknowledging white dominance in sports such as golf, rugby, swimming, gymnastics, wrestling, and tennis, nonetheless Entine stresses the sports in which blacks dominate or in which they are making new excursions, such as bobsledding. But even in sports involving running and jumping, it is debatable whether the evidence so clearly indicates black superiority. He cites the studies of David Hunter, which showed that, when adjusted for body fat, sprint times between similar blacks and whites was statistically insignificant. But, Entine objects, "Blacks have much less fat, a tiny physiological advantage that can translate into a huge on-the-field advantage. This difference may be one key variable that provides black males with an advantage in sprinting."[26] But he does not tell us whether it is true that black people generally have less body fat, or whether it is premier black athletes that have less body fat, perhaps because of hard work and training.

Entine glosses over such difficulties, and instead takes these "facts" to show that "sprinters are born, not made," the same holding true of elite soccer and basketball players.[27] It might be an exaggeration to suggest that, for Entine, Africans take to running the way fish take to swimming. Nonetheless, the conclusion he draws is no less an exaggeration: "Since the first known study of differences between black and white athletes in 1928, the data have been remarkably consistent: in most sports, African-descended athletes have the capacity to do better with their raw skills than whites."[28]

This is an outrageous overgeneralization. Do African and African descended athletes do better in most sports? Or is it rather that they do best in sports based on running and jumping? What about sports such as swimming, wrestling, gymnastics, and judo instead of running and jumping? Using these as the standard, we might find that black athletes do not perform as well as whites. By choosing running and jumping as exemplary of athletic activities, the deck is already stacked, and we are predisposed to the conclusion that blacks are naturally better athletes than whites.

As a matter of fact, in many sports blacks are not the superior athletes they are made out to be. Whites continue to dominate in hockey, skiing, bicycling, gymnastics, fencing, wrestling, as well as track and field events such as the discus, the javelin, the shot put, and the pole vault. As University of the Pacific sociologist John Phillips argues, if we were to look at all the sports, and not just running and jumping ones, we would see that blacks do not dominate, except in the high profile activities central to spectator sports.[29] While duly reporting this position, Entine makes no response to it. Instead, he concludes that "the scientific evidence for black athletic superiority is overwhelming." His evidence is black dominance in running, jumping, and boxing. This may be an example of an innocent inductive fallacy, but I would suggest that it is more likely an example of uncritical stereotypical thinking reflecting an institutionalized racist etiology.[30]

Entine reports that, since 1996, a group making up 1.8% of Kenya's population has produced 20% of the winners of major international distance running events. And 90% of the top Kenyan athletes come from a 60-mile radius around the town of Eldoret in the Nandi Hills.[31] Entine recounts how, because the men of the Nandi area of Kenya were notorious offenders of colonial authority, they were channeled into athletic games as a way of co-opting their energies.[32] But he does not address why this does not remain a plausible explanation for the attention focused on athletic games in the modern world. By diverting the energies of black youth to the least productive areas of modern culture, more lucrative opportunities are reserved for those who are not black. He quotes Brooks Johnson: "The whole idea is to convince black people that they're superior in some areas—sports—and therefore by definition

Is the claim that black athletes have natural advantages in sports involving running and jumping based on well-documented science or racist ideology? Here world-record holder Michael Johnson runs the 400 meters at the 1996 Olympic Games in Atlanta. Ed. Liaison Agency, Inc.

must be inferior in other areas. It's interesting that white people always have the best talent in the areas that pay the best money."[33]

Entine points out that "all of the thirty-two finalists in the last four Olympic men's 100 meter races are of West African descent." But he offers no explanation as to why, if genes rather than training are the crucial variable, no West Africans were among the finalists. And where the finalists were African Americans, he gives no indication as to how he established that they were primarily of West African rather than East African or Central African descent. Entine never attempts to explain why West Africans are not as good or better than African Americans at short distance running, or why descendants of East Africans have not become dominant in the marathons. In order to make his case, Entine is forced to ignore such subtleties.

Just as measurements of skull shape (cephalic index) and brain size were taken as indications of intellectual potential, Entine reports that anthropomorphic measurements of body types and physiological reactions reveal the prerequisites for superior athletic performance. Such observations have shown that sprinters are muscular mesomorphic types capable of explosive energy, while marathon runners are slender ectomorphic types capable of endurance over long distances. Entine also cites empirical observations showing that black babies exhibit superior coordination at an earlier age than white babies[34] and that black teenagers have a "faster patellar tendon reflex time—the knee jerk response—and an edge in reaction time over whites."[35] Facts such as these, Entine concludes, derive from genetic predispositions that also explain the superior performance of black athletes.

But such facts have too often been shown to be artifacts of our social system, reflecting how investigators think things ought to be more than how things are. The conclusion that Africans are naturally better athletes is an unwarranted inductive generalization that reinforces the view that the way things are is the way they are supposed to be. West Africans do not dominate in sprinting, African Americans do. Africans and African Americans do not dominate in all sports, only some.

The "facts" Entine cites follow a long history of anthropomorphic measurements on Africans, women, and the lower classes. *The Mismeasurement of Man* by Stephen Jay Gould and *Myths of Gender* by Anne Fausto-Sterling are but two works that show the extent to which science has not been an objective, value-free enterprise.[36] Instead, the historical record suggests that the biological and social sciences have typically been more instrumental than descriptive: "They do not carve nature at the joints but break it up at places that reflect human needs—the need to control our environment in order to secure food, fiber, health, amusement, and so forth."[37] From a pragmatic perspective, ethics is the attempt to secure the good life for ourselves and others, and the facts of biology and human performance have been constructed to accomplish this, as well as possible given the circumstances.

Entine is best understood in the context of others who argue that current racial and sexual disparities in social achievements (athletic and intellectual) are the result of "natural" genetic predispositions. The usual argument has been that European and Asian achievements outstrip African achievements in the sciences and mathematics because Europeans and Asians are naturally smarter than Africans, that is, have a higher IQ. Entine has merely turned this argument around: African achievements outstrip European and Asian achievements in athletics because they are naturally faster and stronger, that is, have a higher proportion of fast twitch muscle fibers and more efficient metabolic pathways.

But I believe biological determinism of either stripe is misguided, for it presupposes ideal types for existing groups, and encourages members of those group to actively construct themselves on analogy with those ideals. Stereotypes of Africans have been justified by reference to biblical texts, evolutionary theory, mental tests, and now by measurements in laboratories and athletic contests. Allegedly unbiased scientists and contest judges are supposed to base their pronouncements on fact rather than fantasy. Yet, one of the main contributions of the new wave in the philosophy of science is in emphasizing the extent to which all facts are theory-laden, and rest on tacitly held beliefs. In this light, facts that purport to justify current distributions of opportunities and rewards require special moral scrutiny.

For Entine, the facts prove that Africans and people of African descent are naturally better athletes than whites and Asians. If this were the case, then it would seem to make sense for parents of African descent to encourage their children to cultivate athletic skills, rather than intellectual and mathematical skills. This line of argument has appealed to many blacks, and even more whites. It is a view that I believe is damaging. It promotes stereotypes that have been developed to justify the exclusion of whole groups of people from opportunities they are not considered naturally endowed for.

The fact that such stereotypes might contain

a grain of truth is no redeeming feature. To analogize Entine's argument, short people might be better at entering small holes than people of normal height, and that is something short people might learn to be proud of. Indeed, those that consistently win entering-small-holes contests might be very good at it indeed. Short people might then be encouraged to develop their abilities to compete in entering-small-holes contests because they are naturally better at it than most other people. This might be documented by "objective measurements," and provide for exciting entertainment, but it is counterproductive to the expenditure of time and energy by people of short stature. Other than as entertainment, skill at entering small holes is as unlikely to improve the general social and economic status of short people as running skills are likely to improve the general social and economic status of black people.[38]

The odds that a high school athlete will play at the professional level are about 10,000 to 1. Yet a recent survey estimated that 66% of African American males between 13 and 18 believed they could become professional athletes, more than double the number of similar white youth. And black parents were four times more likely to believe it than white parents. Athletics is not even a good way of getting a college education. While colleges gave away some $600 million in athletic scholarships in 1997, $49.7 billion was available from other sources.[39]

A commitment to social justice requires that we appreciate the extent to which notions of biological determinism have been used to limit opportunities for people of African descent, women, the poor, and other socially marginalized groups. We need to better appreciate the extent to which ideas are tools that can be used to help or hinder, rather than view them as descriptions of how God or nature have designed things. Encouraging members of a particular group to cultivate skills of limited utility precludes them from the full range of opportunities available to the wider population. As such, I believe Entine has a special moral obligation to show how his conclusions do not contribute more to maintaining barriers of the past than to constructing a more open and just future.

Notes

1. Jon Entine, *Taboo: Why Black Athletes Dominate Sports and Why We Are Afraid to Talk about It.* (New York: BBS Public Affairs, 2000), p. 4.
2. Ibid., p.18.
3. Ibid., p. 19.
4. Ibid., p. 4. Where differences of a hundredth or thousandth of a second make the difference between winner and loser, "The decisive variable is in our genes."
5. Ibid., p. 30.
6. Ibid., p. 31.
7. Ibid.
8. Ibid., p. 79.
9. Ibid., p. 80.
10. Ibid., p. 166.
11. Ibid., p. 167.
12. Ibid., p. 209.
13. Ibid., p. 92. This is a view he associates with Carleton Coon.
14. "It implied the mutability and perfectibility of humankind. The inexorable forces of evolution and heredity receded into the background, to be replaced by a moral dimension: it was now suggested that prehistoric humans had adapted to austere climates through clever discoveries of fire, clothing, and artificial shelters, not through chance, natural mutations, and the survival of the fittest. Shadowed by the racist ideologies of fascism, common sense was sacrificed to a new ideology: environmentalism." Ibid., p. 215.
15. Ibid., p. 217.
16. Arthur Jensen, "How Much Can We Boost IQ and Scholastic Achievement?" *Harvard Educational Review* 39 (Winter 1969), pp. 1–123.
17. Richard Herrnstein and Charles Murray, *The Bell Curve* (New York: Free Press, 1994).
18. Phillip Rushton, in his book *Race, Evolution, and Behavior* (New Brunswick, NJ: Transactions Publishers, 1995), puts it more crudely: brain size varies inversely proportionally to genital size (pp. 5, 162, 166–169, and 231). Presumably, this makes blacks better at genital sex.
19. Entine, op. cit., p. 245.
20. Carole Oglesby, quoted in Entine, op. cit., p. 333.
21. For a critique of this tendency, see John Hoberman, *Darwin's Athletes: How Sports Has Damaged Black*

America and Preserved the Myth of Race (New York: Houghton Mifflin, 1997).

22. Entine, op. cit., p. 281.

23. Ibid., p. 6.

24. Ibid., p. 8.

25. Ibid.

26. Ibid., p. 252.

27. Ibid., p. 256: "It appears that for Blacks from West Africa, innate ability may be more critical than training in turning out great leapers and sprinters."

28. Ibid., p. 268.

29. "If blacks were dispersed across all sports their apparent superiority would largely disappear." Ibid., p. 273.

30. Ibid., p. 341.

31. Entine dismisses the explanation that the town's high elevation contributes to increased lung capacity and metabolic efficiency because many communities at similar elevations do not produce exceptional runners. Ibid., p. 47.

32. Ibid., p. 49.

33. Ibid., p. 77.

34. Who made the measurements? What was the sample? Was it representative? Instead of raising these questions, Entine accepts these claims as aspects of human nature that are given to us as facts, and only need a proper explanation.

35. Ibid., p. 251. It is interesting that Entine fails to cite Arthur Jensen's "evidence" that, for complex stimuli, blacks generally have slower reaction times than whites. See P. A. Vernon and A. R. Jensen, "Individual and Group Differences in Intelligence and Speed of Information Processing," *Personality and Individual Differences* 5 (1984); 423. For an excellent review of such "evidence," see William H. Tucker, *The Science and Politics of Racial Research* (Chicago: University of Illinois Press, 1994), pp. 264–268.

36. Stephen Jay Gould, *The Mismeasure of Man* (New York: W. W. Norton, 1996); Anne Fausto-Sterling, *Myths of Gender: Biological Theories of Women and Men* (New York: Basic Books, 1985). These works warn us that we ignore the social context of scientific research at our peril. "Science does not always serve the collective *we* or the generic *man,* but particular men often those who control the means of production and application. Science is not different from other aspects of culture in this sense." Robert N. Proctor, *Value Free Science? Purity and Power in Modern Knowledge* (Cambridge, MA: Harvard University Press, 1991), p. 268.

37. Alexander Rosenberg, *Instrumental Biology, or the Disunity of Science* (Chicago: University of Chicago Press, 1994). Rosenberg argues that if biology is instrumental, so is psychology, anthropology, and every other science that builds on it (pp. 15–16).

38. From the perspective Entine has provided, the fact that there are few small holes a person of normal height is going to be interested in entering is irrelevant to the fact documenting which group tends to win more such competitions.

39. John Simon, "Improbable Dreams: African Americans Are a Dominant Presence in Professional Sports—Do Blacks Suffer As a Result?" *U.S. News and World Report*, 3/24/97.

Bibliography

Jon Entine. *Taboo: Why Black Athletes Dominate Sports and Why We Are Afraid to Talk about It.* New York: BBS Public Affairs, 2000.

Anne Fausto-Sterling. *Myths of Gender: Biological Theories of Women and Men.* New York: Basic Books, 1985.

Stephen Jay Gould. *The Mismeasure of Man.* New York: W. W. Norton, 1996.

Richard Herrnstein and Charles Murray. *The Bell Curve.* New York: Free Press, 1994.

John Hoberman. *Darwin's Athletes: How Sports Has Damaged Black America and Preserved the Myth of Race.* New York: Houghton Mifflin, 1997.

Arthur Jensen. "How Much Can We Boost IQ and Scholastic Achievement?" *Harvard Educational Review* 39 (Winter 1969), 1–123.

Robert N. Proctor. *Value Free Science? Purity and Power in Modern Knowledge.* Cambridge, MA: Harvard University Press, 1991.

Alexander Rosenberg. *Instrumental Biology, or the Disunity of Science.* Chicago: University of Chicago Press, 1994.

Philippe Rushton. *Race, Evolution, and Behavior: A Life History Perspective.* New Brunswick, NJ: Transactions Publishers, 1995.

John Simon. "Improbable Dreams: African Americans Are a Dominant Presence in Professional Sports—Do Blacks Suffer as a Result?" *U.S. News and World Report* 3/24/97.

William H. Tucker. *The Science and Politics of Racial Research.* Chicago: University Of Illinois Press, 1994.

P. A. Vernon and A. R. Jensen. "Individual and Group Differences in Intelligence and Speed of Information Processing." *Personality and Individual Differences* 5 (1984), 412–423.

Questions for Consideration

1. Do you think that Mosley has given grounds either for doubting or for outright rejecting the evidence purported on behalf of black athletic superiority? In other words, is the evidence contaminated by the selective and bias interests of researchers?

2. If there is no notion of fact independent of social ideology, then why should research into physical racial differences be any more biased (or unbiased) than any other type of research?

3. Is Mosley's argument on behalf of social justice compelling?

Pedagogy

38   Education for Peace in Sports Education

Frans De Wachter
Katholieke Universiteit Leuven

*Drawing from the UNESCO International Char-
ter of Physical Education and Sports, Frans De
Wachter looks at the practice of sports as a possible
vehicle for world peace. The "spirit of sport," he argues throughout, should be grasped as a normative
ideal. Specifically, the ideal is sportive education to
promote world peace.*

*Peace, though often understood in terms of a
utopia, is better apprehended as nonviolent conflict resolution. Conflict may be a fact of life,
though violent resolution of conflict is not. Sport
here has a role. Instead of sport itself being sufficient to bring about peace, sportive education
can and should be developed and used to teach
conflict-resolution skills.*

*To bring this about, education needs to focus on
four areas: reduction of militaristic attitudes
toward sport, diminution of aggressiveness in
sport, abolition of the notion of an opponent as an
enemy or threat, and the cultivation and institutionalization of conflict-solving skills in athletes.
There are definite obstacles toward the realization
of such strategies, but the goal is worth the effort.*

The International Charter of Physical Education
and Sports approved at the 20th UNESCO General Conference in 1978 includes this sentence:

Through cooperation and the pursuit of mutual interests in the universal language of
physical education and sport, all peoples will
contribute to the preservation of lasting
peace, universal respect and friendship, and
will thus create a propitious climate for solving international problems.

This statement indicates how this charter applies the general object of UNESCO to the world
of sport. The objective is to put education, science, and culture to the service of the promotion
of the respect for human dignity and of better international understanding. This same concern
can be perceived in the activities of the International Council for Sport and Physical Education
(ICSPE), which is actually a suborganization of
UNESCO. Let us not forget that Philip J. Noel-
Baker, who was awarded the Nobel Prize for Peace
in 1959, was president of the ICSPE for sixteen
years. And under the auspices of the same organization, a major congress was organized in
Helsinki in 1982 on "sport and international understanding." The specific intention was to apply
the ideas of the Helsinki conference, of 1975, for
security and cooperation in Europe to the world
of sport. And in the Olympic movement, there is
also a long tradition of glorifying sport as a contribution to peace; thus, in 1983, in Osaka, Japan,
an international symposium was held on the
Olympic movement and world peace.

However, sport is a very rich but also a varied
activity. It can signify, reinforce, or create very

different kinds of human interaction: blind robotization as well as play experience, coercive drive for profit as well as convivial bodily awareness, social antagonism as well as cooperation. Sports is too ambiguous an interaction process and does not simply promote, by its naked presence, peaceful relationships, no more than every science serves social progress, all music improves character, or every religion unites people as brothers and sisters. It is my view that "the spirit of sport" may best be understood as a normative idea or an ethical task.

For this reason, the UNESCO text should not be read as a descriptive text in which an actual relationship between sport and peace is established. The text is more meaningful if it is read normatively and educationally. If sport is not automatically a factor for peace, it can only become such a factor on the basis of a conscious educational intervention. This makes use of certain potentials in sport to form attitudes that create a favorable climate in which something like peace can be established. This is, therefore, my point of departure. It is possible that athletic *education* offers a fruitful educational opportunity for education for peace. It is to this question that I want to restrict myself. To what extent is this possible? What are the positive elements that sport-education can use when we are interested in promoting peace attitudes in the educational process? What precisely are these attitudes? In order to answer these questions, I must first define with more precision the concepts of "peace" and "peace education."

Peace and Peace Education

The concept of peace can have two meanings. First, it could refer to a situation without conflicts, that is, a situation without private interests that must be defended. This is a situation where specific interests are no longer at stake or where the interests of each individual would coincide with the general interest. This is a *utopian* notion of peace, which is meaningful as long as it does

not lose its theological roots. Typical of the Biblical concept of peace is that this condition is situated beyond history, in the heavenly paradise where the lion lies down with the lamb. But when the utopia loses this theological context and is considered an objective that must be achieved in human history, it will probably produce its very opposite: oppression and violence. For the negation of the opposition is the negation of individual differences. This would lead to the elimination of everyone who does not identify with one viewpoint. This suppression of the dissident is the way to a totalitarian vision of society.

Peace in its *operational,* non-utopian meaning is not defined as a condition without conflicts but as a situation where people are capable of rational, non-violent conflict resolution. One does not eliminate conflicts, but learns to live with them in a reasonable way. For reasonableness is non-violence. Reason permits problems and differences of opinion to be reasonably discussed and resolved instead of being assailed in the immediacy of physical or ideological violence. Non-violent conflict resolution is then the opting for a solution that does not consist of the elimination or suppression of the weaker party.

Our notion of peace education must also renounce premature utopian expectations. Here, too, a warning is appropriate against too-utopian haste. Peace education is not a direct peace factor. World peace must be achieved in the hard reality of international situations by politicians who conclude treaties and secure precarious balances of power. Education can only develop subjective attitudes in individuals. These attitudes include the readiness and the competence to resolve conflicts non-violently, without victimizing the weak. Now such an attitude is not a sufficient condition for peace. Wars, for example, are caused by very complex social mechanisms without individuals needing them or nourishing mutual hate.

Nevertheless, such an attitude for peace is a necessary condition. Political decisions, treaties, better world structures, and so on, also assume that they are subjectively desired. Peace education intends that many people, on the basis of their own peace attitude, will increasingly want politicians to increasingly want peace.

This describes my intention clearly. It is humble and realistic. The question is not whether sport is functional for peace. That seems to me to be a question that is too ambitious. The realistic question is whether sport education can be functional in the context of peace education.

This does not exclude its having many other goals, including the goal of developing the physical prowess that enables individuals and groups to defend themselves. This does not contradict the aims of peace education, since I have defined peace in a non-utopian way. The idea is not that people should learn to give up the defense of their legitimate interests, nor does it imply an extreme pacifism, e.g., unilateral individual or collective disarmament. This would create situations of such unbalance that aggression would become even more likely. Peace education is not an education for pacifism in this extreme sense. It should teach people that, while defending their own interests, they can be creative in inventing non-violent solutions when their interests conflict with those of others. Precisely because sport interaction is conflictual, it is suited for exercising and reinforcing this creativity.

How can sport education be a fruitful occasion for peace education? What follows is certainly not an exhaustive reply, but rather a form of brainstorming. I will start from four objectives that are constantly cited in the traditional European literature on peace education, and examine then the possibilities sport education has to offer in this regard. These four objectives are: reducing attitudes of militarism, reducing aggressiveness, demolishing enemy images, and development of conflict-solving competence.

Reducing Attitudes of Militarism

Militarism should not be understood as the readiness to offer legitimate self-defense, which implies the need for an efficient military organi-

zation. But a military organization is not necessarily militaristic. Militarism as an attitude means the one-sided faith in problem solving by means of military violence and thus, also, the one-sided promotion of virtues related to the specific goals of that violence: obedience, discipline, courage, and the like. It is the one-sided faith that problem solving in conflict situations is best achieved by the elimination or suppression of the weaker party by means of fighting or war.

Can sport education mean anything here? Apparently, there is precisely a striking analogy between sports and the military. The same virtues, just mentioned, are also important for the sports team. The same language is used: attack, defend, escape, shoot. Historically and anthropologically, sport games can often be interpreted as war rituals or as learning processes for masculine military qualities, or even as physical preparation for the military game. The examples are numerous and are not limited to the Homeric or the medieval knights, or to the sport ideology of Nazism, or times of cold war. The Victorian British sport language was also warlike, and even Coubertin sang in the same choir: "How will the young man acquire manliness. There are only three ways: by war, by love, and by sport. War is the way of former times, the most noble for the individual and perhaps the most useful for the society" (2: p. 196). The matter is relatively innocent insofar as there presently remains only a kind of war metaphor within the semantic of the game ritual. Less innocent is the reversal of the analogy, where war is presented as a game, a supreme game of "strategy, skill and chance" (15). This happens in almost all war films, which are almost always propaganda films to the extent that they conceal violence by using the game analogy.

Now sport education seems to me to be educationally interesting precisely because of these martial analogies, for its task is to bring the truth of the sport game to light. And this truth is that the sport game, however much it has a win-lose structure, still is the structural reverse of the war game. Sport is not "war without weapons," not "war minus the shooting," as George Orwell wrote in *The New York Times,* in 1959. War is a conflict where the one wins completely and the other loses completely. It is a procedure of conflict resolution by the elimination of the weaker party. Peace is rational conflict resolution so that there are no true losers. In the sport game, there are winners and losers; otherwise, it would not be a sport game and the losers, too, would have no fun. But the losers do not lose themselves. As players, they are not eliminated. They are the players of the next game and have won from the game. Good play education is not so much that which replaces sport by "new games" in which there are no losers, but that which sees to it that the losers are not real losers. By this I mean losers in the social sense of the word, losers of identity and self-respect. Militarism, ultimately, is a danger that threatens education in general. Each teacher, even the mathematics teacher, who plays on competition so that the weaker lose, has a potential militaristic attitude. And good physical education must see to it that the physically less gifted will not experience themselves as "losers" and develop negative body images.

Reducing Aggressiveness

This is the only one of the four objectives for which sport is occasionally cited in the literature on peace education. The assumption is that highly competitive and even aggressive play is a relatively safe channeling of inborn aggressive energy, and that therefore, it would reduce the probability of later aggressive acts. This viewpoint is related to the catharsis theory of Konrad Lorenz and others. Many social psychologists, however, do not agree. According to them, aggression is an acquired personality trait and aggressive behavior is learned. Actually, it has not been scientifically demonstrated whether one of the two conceptions embodies the entire truth. In a review by Russell (10), it is shown that some experiments confirm the catharsis function, while others show the opposite. Perhaps, both conceptions reflect part of the truth. It could be that aggression is in-

born to a certain extent, but not in the same unambiguous way that we inherit the color of our eyes. Human beings live partially from instinct, but still much more from what is learned. In contrast to the animal, the human being enters the world helpless and relatively instinct-poor. His primary capacity is his capacity to learn. And with aggression there is unmistakably present a learning process that occurs in interaction with the environment. Children learn from their environment. If aggression is not a purely inborn instinct, discharge via sport will not necessarily diminish later aggression in real life. Sport could also be a school for aggressive behavior.

The sport literature that is critical of the catharsis function generally appeals to the well-known counterexamples that have been provided by Sipes (13) and by Sherif (12). Sipes studied 20 tribal societies that were selected because it was unambiguously clear that they had or did not have a warlike character and that combative sports were or were not present. Of the ten very warlike tribes, nine practiced combative sports. Of the ten peaceful tribes, only two knew combative sports. According to the catharsis theory, this situation should be just the reverse. Obviously, such research must be qualified for its scope is very limited. A correlation is not yet a causal explanation. And perhaps these nine tribes would have even more wars if they did not have sport competition. But still, such studies keep us from imagining that sport is automatically functional for the reduction of aggression in real life. The sociologist C. W. Sherif also reported a positive correlation between intergroup aggression and competition. Since her report to the Olympic Congress of Munich in 1972, the experiment is sufficiently well-known in the sport world. It concerned a situation of twelve-year-old boys at a youth camp. When competitions were set up in this homogeneous group, conflicts, severe enmity, and even physical aggression developed. The aggression could not be eliminated by negotiations, by the appointment of a neutral judge, or by the giving of delicious communal meals. The conflict was only resolved by introducing a collective need situation. An artificial drinking water problem was created, so that the boys had to move heaven and earth to get drinking water. However methodologically disputable this experiment might be, the hypothesis is plausible and interesting. Conflict is most efficiently resolved when one finds reason to cooperate. The message for sport is that one may certainly not expect an automatic reduction of aggression. Such a reduction is only possible if a superstructure of cooperative objectives is constructed around it. In this sense, it could be that the Olympic peace discourse, ritually interwoven around sport, is not merely idle rhetoric but hard educational necessity.

Demolishing Enemy Images

Sociologists know that the acceptance of a negative orientation toward the "out group" can be constitutive for the differentiation of a social group into "in groups" and "out groups." Individuals or groups build their own identity by means of a negative mirror image, "the bad other." Around this image a number of negative stereotypes are constructed, an enemy image against which one can set off one's own identity. Two characteristics are typical of an enemy image. First, it is not necessarily linked with the objectivity of a threat. If there is no true threat, then it is created in an imaginary way. For the enemy is necessary for the sake of one's own identity. And the more horrible the enemy, the closer the cohesion on one's own group. Second, enemy images are almost not falsifiable. They have a built-in mechanism that refutes every refutation. Suppose, for example, that one considers somebody else a very evil person. Should that person suddenly appear to be friendly and helpful, the conclusion tends to be what he is even worse than was thought: he is not only bad but he is also hypocritical. Who knows what he is up to? Festinger has worked out this notion in his theory of cognitive dissonance (5).

Can sport education mean something in the dismantling of enemy images? For the active sport participant, it would seem plausible to assume that he will question a stereotypical enemy image when he comes in contact with players of other nationalities. This assumption, however, seems to have been proven false by many studies. I refer, for example, to the work of the German sociologist, H.D. Schmidt, who has specialized in research on nationalistic prejudices and has also involved sport in his research (11). He concludes that prejudices are not automatically eliminated when groups with mutually negative feelings are brought together in games and sport. Two reasons can be given for this. First, the attitude change does not depend on the contact as such, but on the function and the nature of the activity by which the contact is made. Now the sport activity is very antagonistic. It is oriented to the establishment of distinction, and can, therefore, obscure the communal and the binding element between the in group and the out group. And, from my own experience, I know that a number of coaches, even with youth clubs, try to denigrate the opposing team and to stimulate feelings of hate. They use the construction of an enemy image as a stimulus. Second, social perception is insufficient to dislocate enemy images. Our perception of other people follows precisely our orientations and expectations with relation to these people. It tends to exaggerate the behavioral traits that concur with these expectations. Perhaps, in sport, it might also be that when the enemy image is not affected by social perception it offers a better alibi for explaining a possible defeat. When Belgian football teams lose to East European teams, stereotypical explanations emerge: the opponents were poorer players but were perfectly disciplined robots, as you would expect from a collectivistic system. In sport, too, experiences that deviate from prejudicial expectations do not seem to be powerful enough to disturb the mechanism of the enemy image.

Can we be more optimistic with regard to the spectators? Passive sport consumption is important in relation to the problem of the enemy image because here large populations are involved.

May one expect that the sport information from the media changes the attitudes of the public toward other nations? Some say yes (9), but there has been as yet no thorough research on the subject, although there is a special commission within the ICSPE on "Sport, Mass Media and International Understanding." This commission has already published a professional code for sport journalists. Halloran, too, of the Center for Mass Communication of the University of Leicester, has compiled a report on the existing literature for this commission. The conclusion of most surveys (6, 8), however, seems to be that no firm conclusions can be drawn. Television, for example, seems to have a very restricted influence on the formation of attitudes toward other nations, and within the television package no influence of sport broadcasts has been demonstrated, neither favorable nor unfavorable. There is no proof of the notion that my image of Russians or Italians would change by the observation of their repeated fair or unfair behavior in televised soccer games. This is not so surprising. Research has shown that, for example, the influence of TV on children is often overestimated. Children are not purely passive recipients of TV images. They interpret them within frameworks that have been created in their education. TV images only have influence if they are reinforced by how things are thought about and discussed in the school and the family. Finally, enemy images are rooted in an entire socio-cultural environment. It is, therefore, very improbable that they will change under the influence of a one-time media event.

Nevertheless, there might be a way of qualifying our skepticism on the basis of an idea that is more intuitive than demonstrable. The more sport is expanded *internationally,* and for the public at large via the media, the more it may be able to acquire a *supra-national* image. Athletes would then no longer simply represent a nation, but a kind of supra-national sport culture with its own code and value scale that break away from nationalistic enemy images. Thus, McIntosh suggests that certain athletes like Owens, Bikila, or Bannister have, in fact, transcended their own nationality (8: p. 280). Finally, it is promising that a Russian sport poll sponsored by Tass, selected the American swimmer Debbie Myers as sportswoman of the year in 1967, at the height of the Vietnam War. Here we touch the heart of the Olympic ideology, which rests on the fundamental hypothesis that internationalism leads to supra-nationalism.

Development of Conflict-Solving Competence

Such competition implies the acceptance of conflicts and the capacity to handle them nonviolently. Educators recommend role playing as an efficient strategy to learn how to make compromises, to accept arbitration, and so on. But, of course, such role playing already exists in the sport game. Play, as Sutton-Smith has convincingly demonstrated (14) is "information processing." It is a learning process whereby members of a group adapt to the values of that group. In competitive games, players learn how to behave in conflict situations with an uncertain outcome. It is not by chance that modern sport arose in England. It is the role playing of the modern democratic society that found its first expression in England with John Locke.

Its basic idea is the acceptance of the mixed character of social life. Totalitarianism understands society as a uniform totality. Democracy is based on the multiplicity of individuals, on their differentiation. The society is conceived on the basis of the idea of a contract whereby individuals delegate authority and agree on all sorts of procedures for decision making when opinions differ. The intention is not to suppress differences in an urge to achieve consensus. That something like voting is provided in parliament means a recognition of the difference.

Democracy is a kind of game, the sticking to agreed upon game rules in decision making. The authentic game is, therefore, the appropriate "information processing" for this. One learns to accept opposition, to make agreements on procedures (the rules of the game), to respect them (fairness), to delegate authority (the referee), to subject oneself to whatever the result is of the accepted procedures (to be a good loser). In short, one acquires peace competence. For one learns how to deal with opposition by means of agreed upon procedures (4: pp. 273–265). Or as Coubertin expressed it: "It is childish to demand that people love each other. But it is not utopian to demand that they respect each other" (3: p. 133). It is striking, however, that this statement was made in a speech entitled *Pax Olympica,* which was given over Berlin radio in 1935 and was published by the Organizing Committee of the Olympic Games of Berlin in 1936.

The great French philosopher and sociologist Raymond Aron expressed a similar idea in a text that he wrote over the world soccer championships in Spain, 1982: "Let us not be ironic over this great feast, not of friendship but of competition between the nations. Subjecting competition to rules supervised by referees, is this not the picture of the only conceivable reconciliation between peoples that is compatible with the nature of communities and perhaps of the person himself" (1)?

Possible Negative Effects

Good education must also be concerned about the possible negative side-effects of the means employed. I want to offer here for consideration the principal danger that arises from the varied character of sport. Sport interactions are both associative and conflictual, cooperative and competitive. This conflictual content is very high, and this for two reasons. First, the conflict is not purely indirect. This would mean that opponents fight for the same prize with efforts that occur in parallel. They would then not interfere directly with each other. An example of indirect conflict is economic market competition. In sport, the conflict is also direct. A good performance often means that one has succeeded in hindering the opponent in his play (4: p. 261).

Second, sport embodies a very special type of opposition, namely what sociological jargon calls "inconclusive competition." In conclusive competition one only wants to know who won the game here and now (e.g., a Miss World contest). Sport games, however, are never concluded. The ending of today's game is the beginning of tomorrow's. The winner sets new norms and new performance levels. The losers of today have to surpass these levels if, tomorrow, they want to have a chance of winning. And the winner, in his turn, must accept this challenge if he still wants to be considered the winner tomorrow. This creates a spiral of continuous shifting of performance norms and of the drive to succeed. And this spiral endangers the four objectives of peace education I have given. In particular, it could threaten the democratic capacity of sport from within. The Finnish sport sociologist Heinilä calls this the threat of totalization (7). This implies two things.

First, the effort of the individual no longer suffices to meet the compelled performance level. All available means must be employed, and for this the total social system must be mobilized: economy, education, technology, scientific research. Thus, oppositions (e.g., East-West) are not dismantled but rather reinforced. The athlete represents only a social system.

Second, totalization also occurs inwardly. Athletes become only pawns of a system (a club, an organization, a nation). Totalitarian pressure on the individual increases. In crisis situations, a group tends to totalization, in equilibrium situations, more to democratization. Now, inconclusive competition is to be seen as a permanent situation of tension or crisis. The danger of totalizing pressure or violence on the individual is, therefore, structurally present in sport, particularly where great size, internationalism, media publicity, etc., generate the increasing drive to succeed. Good sport education must be aware of this danger. Only one who is so aware can resolve the danger. Under this condition, the close human interaction that marks sport can be a powerful opportunity in education for those who want to promote attitudes of peace.

Conclusion

And perhaps this educator may offer one last consideration. It could be that in sport still richer capabilities are involved than those I have mentioned here. Indeed, I have worked with a very realistic definition of peace. I defined this notion not as a conflict-free situation but as a situation where people have conflict-solving skills. Indeed, it would be wonderful if people could cope with conflicts in a reasonable manner. And sport education can teach this. But in our hearts we long for a peace that is still richer than that—a paradise of universal equality, solidarity, and fraternity. This is precisely the theological concept of peace. I have called this utopian because its direct achievement in history is not possible. Still, it is an ideal that can provide an important degree of dynamism to each concrete striving for peace. And, perhaps, this dynamic can be experienced under the surface of sport itself. Perhaps sport can contribute not only to the acceptance of opposition and procedures. Perhaps there is room for other experiences. We should be able to learn more from it than how to cope with conflicts in a reasonable way. We learn also that performance is brief and fame ephemeral. We learn how capacities are developed to the point of failure, as in high jumping. We learn that we all share in losing. And we discover that, in this human inadequacy and deficiency, we are more essentially equal than unequal in the winning.

Bibliography

1. Aron, R. "Confession d'un fan." *L'Express*, 16 April 1982, 67.

2. Coubertin, P. *Essais de psychologie sportive*. Lausanne: Payot, 1913.

3. ———. *L'idee Olympique. Discours et essais*. Schorndorf: Hofmann, 1967.

4. De Wachter, F. "Are Sports a Factor for Peace?" in *Topical Problems of Sport Philosophy*. Edited by H. Lenk. Schorndorf: Hofmann, 1983.

5. Festinger, L. *A Theory of Cognitive Dissonance*. Stanford, CA: Stanford University, 1966.

6. Halloran, J. D. *Mass Media, Sport and International Understanding. A Summary of a Review of Literature and Research*. London: ICSPE, 1981.

7. Heinila, K. *The Totalization Process in International Sport*. Jyvaskyla: University of Jyvaskyla, 1982.

8. McIntosh, P. C. "International Communication, Sport and International Understanding." In *Sport and International Understanding*. Edited by M. Ilmarinen. Berlin-Heidelberg-New York-Tokyo: Springer, 1984.

9. Milhstein, O. A., Molchanov, S. V. "The Shaping of Public Opinion Regarding Sport by the Mass Media as a Factor Promoting International Understanding." *International Review of Sport Sociology*, 1976, 3, 71–85.

10. Russel, G. W. "Psychological Issues in Sports Aggression." In *Sports Violence*. Edited by J. H. Goldstein. New York: Springer, 1983.

11. Schmidt, H. D. "Sport und Vorurteile, insbesondere nationalistische Einstellungen." In *Soziale Einflusse im Sport*. Edited by D. Bierhoff Alfermann. Darmstadt: D. Steinkopf, 1976.

12. Sherif, C. W. "Intergroup Conflict and Competition." In *Sport in the Modern World—Chances and Problems*. Edited by O. Grupe et al., Berlin-Heidelberg-New York: Springer, 1973.

13. Sipes, R. "War, Sports and Aggression: An Empirical Test of Two Theories." *The American Anthropologist*, 1973, vol. 75, 64–68.

14. Sutton-Smith, B. "Games, the Socialization of Conflict." In *Sport in the Modern World—Chances and Problems*. Edited by O. Grupe et al., Berlin-Heidelberg-New York: Springer, 1973.

15. Veitch, C. R. "Play Up! Play Up! And Win the War! The Propaganda of Athleticism in Britain, 1914–1918." In *Sport and Politics*. Edited by G. Redmond. Champaign, IL: Human Kinetics Pub., 1984.

Questions for Consideration

1. What does De Wachter mean by sport being the "structural reverse" of the war game?

2. Would De Wachter's agenda of using sportive education for social reform, if implemented, strip the practice of sport of its richness and autonomy?

John Corlett
University of Windsor

John Corlett argues that, while theory and practice of sport have much to say about fear, they have little to say about courage as an antidote to it. Traditional psychological approaches to fear stress desensitization to fear or fearlessness, without cultivating courage. His thesis is pedagogical: Courage can and should be used as a tool to overcome fear in sport.

For the ancient Greeks, courage was a part of virtuous living. Plato wrote a dialogue, Laches, *on it. Courage was a part of Aristotle's broader notion of excellence of character in his works on ethics. Courage came easily to these ancients because their very notion of living included courage. In contrast, courage today is not perceived as a virtue, but a skill. It is seen as an instrument, not an end. One of the aims of philosophers of sport today could be the introduction of means to show how courage can be used to overcome fear. Of course, doing so would involve reevaluation of courage itself.*

How might this come about? Corlett suggests a couple of ways. First, sport must be promoted "as a social practice worthy of true courage." Second, there ought to be a reevaluation of purely psychological approaches to addressing fear that emphasize fearlessness instead of courage, for these are not the same thing.

Overall, the passion of sport, he maintains, must be counterbalanced by the application of reason. A philosophical approach to the problem of fear in sports discusses a much deeper layer of issues such as "Who are we?" and "Where are we going?" Thus, he states, we need philosophical counseling, not psychological counseling, to truly understand and overcome fear.

I

Fear is a central theme in the theory and practice of sport. The subject indices of books prominent in the literature of sport regularly make reference to it. Athletes and coaches talk about it frequently. Courage, on the other hand, seldom appears as a topic of discussion in those same texts or conversations. It is curious that so much time is devoted by participants in sport to what they perceive as an important problem and so little time devoted to a powerful alternative.

There is a biological and psychological explanation why this might be so. Fear is a state for which we have been "designed" by evolution. It keeps us alive, as individuals and as a species. Humans carry with them at all times the potential to be afraid, even to the sports arena where its presence is troublesome. Athletes cannot lay down their evolutionary baggage simply because, at times, it is inconvenient to carry it. They are keenly aware of fear because, on a grand evolutionary scale, it is advantageous to be so (15).

The decline of traditional courage as a central virtue also contributes to the influence that fear exerts on athletes. I will argue that the philosophical establishment of courage as a feature of sport pedagogy could provide a basis for assisting athletes to break free of fear's effect. There exists a long tradition in Western thought to guide a discussion of courage in the context of athletics. That tradition begins in the heroic societies of the pre-Socratic Greeks.

Reprinted, by permission, from J. Corlett, "Virtue Lost: Courage in Sport," *Journal of the Philosophy of Sport* XXIII (1996): 45–57.

II

Life was a simpler and more brutal proposition in the time of Homer's epic *Iliad*. Weil (33) captured succinctly its essence, suggesting that impersonal, brute force was central, reducing spirited humans to spiritless objects, whether they be victors or vanquished:

> Force is as pitiless to the man who possesses it, or thinks he does, as it is to its victims; the second it crushes, the first it intoxicates. The truth is, nobody really possesses it. The human race is not divided up, in the Iliad, into conquered persons, slaves, suppliants, on the one hand, and conquerors and chiefs on the other. In this poem, there is not a single man who does not at one time or another have to bow his neck to force. (p. 228)

Not just force, but extreme force, was the norm of everyday life for those living in heroic societies, as Weil further explained:

> A moderate use of force, which alone would enable man to escape being enmeshed in its machinery, would require superhuman virtue, which is as rare as dignity in weakness. Moreover, moderation itself is not without its perils, since prestige, from which force derives at least three quarters of its strength, rests principally upon the marvelous indifference that the strong feel toward the weak, an indifference so contagious that it infects the very people who are the objects of it. (33: p. 235)

Each person, warrior or not, had a well-defined and determinate role to play in heroic society. Primitive courage, understood simply as doing whatever was necessary to survive, was the central virtue, bound inextricably to one's obligations to kin and ally. It was neither a weapon to be drawn only when required, nor a skill used only to escape the consequences of living in difficult and violent times. Courage was seamlessly woven into culture, deeply embedded in a way that mitigated strongly against any individual's fearful decline of duty. Pervasive and therefore transparent, courage permeated the cultures of the pre-Socratics—and later the Irish Celts and Norse saga men, among others—in a way quite foreign to modern humans.

It was Plato who most remarkably steered the ship of Greek thought away from the poetic world view of the great Homeric epics and toward an organized system of philosophy. In doing so, he extricated courage and other "excellences" from their resting places deep within the human character and made them visible to the analytical powers of the intellect. It is in the Socratic dialogue, *Laches*, where Plato addresses directly the matter of courage (20). The question upon which the dialogue focuses is deceptively simple. What is courage? Simple answers, however, are quickly found to be deficient.

When Laches offers that "He is courageous who remains at his post" (20: p. 103), Socrates points out that some armies fight in a highly mobile manner in which staying at one's post is counterproductive. Laches concedes that a judicious retreat in battle can often lead to subsequent victory, again making a rigid defence of one's post undesirable. It becomes clear that a behavior, by itself, cannot be interpreted in absolute terms as courageous or not, a conclusion that has stood firmly in many subsequent philosophical analyses. The dialogue then examines the more general aspects of courage as a virtue, characteristics that transcend particular circumstances such as armed combat.

Laches states that "courage is a sort of endurance of the soul" (20: p. 105). However, after considering that some forms of endurance might be foolish and harmful, the other dialogue partner, Nicias, suggests that courage is intelligence. On a previous occasion, he had heard Socrates say that "every man is good in that in which he is wise, and bad in that in which he is unwise" (20: p. 109). However, no agreement can be reached on what the wisdom underlying true courage would have to be, and the dialogue ends without firm resolution. Socrates admits that "we have not discovered what courage is" (20: p. 117), thus emphasizing the difficulty of grasping the truth in moral matters.

Schmid (25) has described the *Laches* as more of a dramatic demonstration of the power of traditional philosophy over sophistry rather than a vehicle for expressly defining the virtue of courage. What does emerge, however, is the notion that courage and knowledge are linked, placing courage squarely in the cognitive domain. Santas (24) maintained that by doing so, Plato did not appreciate the importance of the emotional and behavioral features of courage. Devereux (8), on the other hand, argued that Plato was describing courage as a combination of quality of intellect and quality of temperament rather than a Socratic form of knowledge alone.

Whatever our current interpretation of Plato's intentions, in Books II and III of the *Nicomachean Ethics*, Aristotle (3) firmly rejected any purely rational view of courage. The foundation of the Aristotelian position is the idea of the mean in which virtues such as courage are dispositions to feel or act in ways that are neither excessive nor deficient. For Aristotle, courage was a middle state:

> The observance of the mean in fear and confidence is Courage. . . . he that exceeds in confidence is Rash; he that exceeds in fear and is deficient in confidence is Cowardly. (3, Book II vii, p. 2)

Aristotle saw that courage does not exist where extreme conditions of fear or confidence dominate. Unlike Plato, he also saw that courage is more than a form of knowledge. Affective states, in addition to cognitive ones, are also important in defining it (22). To illustrate, Aristotle identified several kinds of people who act in ways that appear to be courageous, but which are not. There are those who act through knowledge and skill in the sometimes false belief that these will protect them. Others act through ignorance, not realizing the danger and rushing into difficult situations as though they were not difficult. (By identifying such cases, Aristotle stands in contrast to those sport pedagogists who assume that an athlete can never be too confident and for whom the unbridled building of self-confidence is the cornerstone of the counseling process.) Still others act on emotional impulse, whether depression which they wish to shed, or anger. Finally, there are those who act in order to gain worldly advantages such as honor or gain or avoid disadvantages such as disgrace or loss (3, Book III viii, pp. 1–16).

Aristotle had claimed that courage is a mean with regard to fear and confidence. Thomas Aquinas (1), however, considered fear and confidence to be two very different emotional states and believed that courage concerns not a single emotional continuum with fear at one end and confidence at the other, but two continua, each with its own polar and mean regions. Aquinas argued that the Confidence Continuum has timidity at its deficiency end and rashness at its excess end. Its mean state is discretion. The Fear Continuum has cowardliness at its deficiency end and fearlessness at its excess end. Its mean state is bravery. One's positions on these two continua can interact in many ways to predispose one to courage or the lack of it. Timidity and cowardliness need not always coexist, nor must rashness and fearlessness be necessarily linked.

Despite their complexity, the emotional states represented by these two continua were not, to Aquinas, sufficient to define courage. Aquinas regarded a virtue as "a disposition to act, desire and feel that involves the exercise of judgment, leads to a recognizable human excellence, and involves choosing virtue for itself and in light of some justifiable life plan" (35: p. 53). Emotional state alone, therefore, is not enough for a virtuous capacity to flower. The potency of dispositions requires practical wisdom that can guide and inform them. It is this rational side that shapes our emotional states and it is this rational side guiding emotion that determines virtue: "Courage is chiefly concerned with fears of difficulties likely to cause the will to retreat from following the lead of reason" (1: pp. 2–2.123.3).

An acorn will always grow inexorably to be an oak. It has no decisions to make in the matter. Aquinas realized that humans, on the other hand, require reason in their pursuit of the good because it involves choices made in situations in which the good's character is never entirely clear, the proper mode to realize it is never completely evident, and the ability to follow reason is never sure. It is practical wisdom that considers what needs to be accomplished and chooses between possible alternatives to achieve these ends. Courageous people carefully consider what is to be legitimately feared, while also taking into account their grounds for confidence. They recognize that states of both fear and confidence can be illegitimate and rely on practical wisdom to inform them of appropriate and inappropriate emotional states that influence action.

Like Plato and Aristotle, Aquinas recognized that there are no simple rules that allow us to specify whether an act is courageous or not. Retreating, advancing, or holding firm to one's position all may or may not be instances of courage. Judgments about those actions always will depend on one's evaluation of the circumstances and the person in action. Acts of courage can be evaluated only in terms of an actor's intentions, dispositions, and emotional states. True courage always involves a focus on an actor's internal goals to achieve real goods and never on external goals that lead only to illusory goods. Otherwise, what one exhibits is not true courage but what Aquinas called "counterfeits" or semblances of it that can be mistaken for genuine virtue. For Aquinas, those who are courageous do not find it difficult to be so because they think and feel that "we should not only do what is good, but also that we should do it well" (1: pp. 2–1.65.4). Genuinely courageous people act in accordance with their virtue easily and well because to behave in any other way would be inconsistent with justifiable internal goals that are shaped by emotional states guided by reason. This view, grounded in the ideas of Aristotle, holds considerable potential for sport pedagogists who use goal-setting strategies to enhance performance. However, it is a position that has declined in philosophical prominence and is now poorly understood and unappreciated.

III

From archaic Greece to the European middle ages, Western philosophical debate about virtues assumed that they were universal goods. Arguments about courage concerned how it might be best defined or how it interacted with other virtues. The intrinsic value of courage or any other virtue was never at issue, nor was its role in shaping a whole, good, human life. This unassailable status of the traditional virtues began to deteriorate with the Cartesian call to rationality in the early seventeenth century, then unravelled more dramatically during the European Enlightenment a century later. Hume (14) argued forcefully that belief in courage (or any virtue) as a good, was merely a convention, a matter of habit. Reason could not support the inherent goodness of an act of courage because it is not reason, but passion, that is the basis for moral judgement or belief (14). Plato had argued that courage was a matter of knowledge. Aristotle and Aquinas had added emotion to intellect in their analyses. Hume then removed reason altogether, leaving only emotion.

MacIntyre (17) asserted that Hume's moral philosophy possessed three critical features that influence the way in which those living in modern times conceive of traditional virtues. First, in abandoning the longstanding agreement that people existed for some purpose beyond individual acts, no framework remained within which virtues had meaning. Courage had become optional in a way that would have been unimaginable to Aquinas, Aristotle, Plato, and especially Homer.

Second, virtues became attached more closely to rules or laws. If commanded by law to be courageous, one would be virtuous if one possessed not courage, but the disposition to obey the rule requiring courage. Kant formalized this relationship by linking moral behavior to acting in accordance with one's duty (16). Unfortunately, unlike justice, courage is a virtue seldom mandated in modern societies, and its role became increasingly less clear, if not obliterated altogether, under such circumstances.

Third, virtues, conceived as a plurality of individual excellences in traditional thought, became reduced to a singular idea: virtue. In particular, to be virtuous came to possess a narrow connotation associated with sexual behavior. As MacIntyre (17) noted, the Victorian era "Society for the Suppression of Vice did not have among its interests the suppression of either injustice or cowardice" (p. 233).

After Hume, courage metamorphosed from a virtue to a skill, valuable to a few who chose to cultivate it and whose lives could make use of it, but neither required nor prominent. This was a considerable transformation. Aristotle had taken care to differentiate between skills and virtues, even though he and Plato had categorized them both as excellences. Wallace (31) expressed the difference in this way: "The sort of difficulty that a skill is the capacity to overcome—technical difficulty—is not some contrary inclination that opposes action" (p. 45). He further stated that virtues, in contrast, "are not masteries of technique; technique has very little to do with being brave, generous, or honest; nor do these necessarily involve being proficient at any particular thing" (p. 46). Hume effectively dismantled this Aristotelian distinction.

Utilitarian theories of the nineteenth and early twentieth centuries further altered our conceptions of the virtues of traditional Western philosophy. Kant had echoed Plato, Aristotle, and Aquinas by arguing that whether an act was courageous should be determined not by the action taken, but by the intent underlying it. To utilitarians, the reverse was true. Intent was not the proper measure of courage or any virtuous behavior: The results of the action taken were. As Mill (18) wrote, "Actions are right in proportion as they tend to promote happiness; wrong as they tend to promote the reverse of happiness"

(p. 7). Because utilitarian happiness was synonymous with the presence of pleasure and the absence of pain, an action's moral worth could be measurable only by its utility in increasing pleasure and reducing pain. Risking one's life to save another and failing (or perhaps even dying in the attempt) neither increases pleasure nor reduces pain; indeed, it accomplishes the opposite. By utilitarian standards, it would be a morally worthless act.

Modern utilitarian accounts of virtue have attempted to address such apparent paradoxes. Slote (27), for example, has argued that a unity of cardinal virtues, including courage, can be achieved through conformity to the principle of utility. Still, Walton (32) has expressed doubt that duty-based theories of virtue, including utilitarianism, can account for acts of courage and the fundamental criticisms of utilitarianism made by Smart and Williams (28) remain powerful ones. It is in the context of these critiques that one notes how far Western philosophy in its utilitarian forms had diverged from the Homeric Greeks, to whom tragic failure often highlighted courage in a way that success could not.

It has often been the sacrificial display of fairness, the grand failure, or the futile act of unproductive brilliance, that has most clearly illuminated courage in sport. Will (34: p. 328) illustrated this while exposing the bankruptcy of utilitarian philosophy applied to the everyday, common practice of sport:

One afternoon, during Andre Dawson's 1987 MVP season, he was in right field in Wrigley Field, and the Cubs were clobbering the Astros, 11–1. In the top of the sixth inning Dawson ran down a foul fly, banging into the brick wall that is right next to the foul line. In the seventh inning he charged and made a sliding catch on a low line drive that otherwise would have been an unimportant single. When asked after the game why he would risk injuries in those situations when the outcome of the game was not in doubt, Dawson replied laconically, "Because the ball was in play."

Dawson probably found the question unintelligible. The words and syntax were clear enough, but the questioner obviously was oblivious to the mental (and moral) world of a competitor like Dawson.

Will does not mention Dawson's chronically bad knees nor the Cubs' chronically bad finishes in the National League pennant race as part of the story's context. He does, however, illuminate the failure of at least some forms of moral philosophy to recognize the unique role of traditional virtues in sport.

IV

Alfred North Whitehead suggested that all sophisticated philosophies possess the same essential elements and differ only in what is emphasized and what is not. If this is true, then the ongoing philosophical revision of courage need not be of concern because it will have been reformulated or de-emphasized, presumably in favor of substitutes more in keeping with current and relevant modes of thought. Dent (7), for example, argued for better explanations of courage as a virtue because it could be seen through modern eyes to possess both sexist and aristocratic overtones, associated as it is with the military manliness of the ancient Greeks.

Expressing similar sentiments, Rorty (23) has suggested that courage, defined as it traditionally has been, is not necessarily a virtue at all. In fact, it might as easily be considered dangerous, because of its tendency to cause those who possess it to see the world and those in it as obstacles to be overcome, risks to be taken, and opponents to be conquered. Where these challenges are not readily available, the traditionally courageous will seek them out, or create them because those who possess certain virtues will "form a life that sustains and enlarges their particular excellences, creating situations in which their virtues can be given the fullest play" (23: p. 153). This is ultimately undesirable because courage "tends to slide into its excessive forms" (23: p. 155). She offers an option: "We can either stop promoting it as a virtue, or reform it by reconstituting the range of dispositions that identify it" (23: p. 155).

Falk (10) showed little patience with such modern reformulations of virtue when he referred to their "distorted visions which are less convincing than the unsqueamish common sense of the philosophers and divines of earlier times" (p. 119). However, modern sport does appear to sustain and enlarge particular virtues in their most "excessive forms." The kaleidoscope of trash talking, taunting, and thuggery on the field combined with the parade of strikes and scandal off the field certainly seem to embody Rorty's description of loyalty, honor, and courage gone bad. Arnold (2) has pointed out, however, that sport, like other forms of human endeavor, are practices valued by our society and that they are defined by moral standards even when those moral standards are contravened. It would be an error, in Arnold's view, to assume that the corruptions of traditional virtues by participants in sport necessarily mean that sport itself is morally corrupt and the virtues it showcases in need of a complete overhaul. It does not necessitate a reformation or reconstitution as much as it requires a better understanding of virtue in action in sport.

The project of modern moral philosophers is to clarify and organize our perceptions of courage more appropriately for the time in which we live. Those moral philosophers with a particular interest in sport can contribute to this by examining the athletic context for the presence of excessive forms and for examples of how sport is shaped to accentuate particular virtues. While they do so, athletes and sport pedagogists face a substantial practical challenge. Courage as a virtue has retreated to the background of the contemporary moral scene, but fear remains in the foreground. The society from which sport arises, while presenting ample opportunity to learn fear, offers few lessons about courage. As a result, athletes find themselves cast in the role of the Cowardly Lion in the *Wizard of Oz*, lamenting that, "I could show my prowess. Be a lion, not a mow-ess, If I only had the nerve." But where, in an impoverished courage culture, can they find the nerve?

V

The major characters of the novels of Tolstoy or Pasternak, the tragic heroes of Shakespeare's histories, and the deceptively strong female characters of Jane Austen's books or Henrik Ibsen's dramas have all known what it means to be in a state of courage, and what it means not to be. Courage, as portrayed in fiction, does not entail behaving well while quaking in one's boots. It is a matter of embarking on a course of action that one knows to be right, accompanied by the composure that conjoins the satisfactory resolution of a moral conflict. Duff (9) from an Aristotlelian perspective, described it as a unity of reason, passion, and action. Rather than overcoming fear, it is the transformation of fear into willing sacrifice.

Thus the literary Joan of Arc exudes an inner calm and complete certainty of purpose: "I am not a daredevil. . . . My heart is full of courage, not of anger. I will lead; and your men will follow; that is all I can do. But I must do it: you shall not stop me." (26:p. 92). Thus the literary Thomas More endures unjust persecution in a state of tranquil inner peace that makes a mockery of the political power wielded by those who put him to death: "As a spaniel is to water, so is a man to his own self. I will not give in because I oppose it—*I* do—not my pride, not my spleen, nor any other of my appetites, but I do—*I.*" (5: p. 66). The simplemindedness of the Nike slogan, "Just do it," is not comparable to the depth of mind associated with the state of courage in which these characters exist. Theirs is the hard-won understanding of self and of what actions are necessary that a solidly grounded philosophy provides. The corporate marketing phrase, in contrast, induces one to engage the world in an unreasoned, ungrounded philosophical vacuum in which new shoes replace old virtues as the basis for action.

Courage, as reason, passion, and action in concert, does feel like something, and affords great accomplishments in the face of threats to one's physical, mental, or social well-being of the kind perceived regularly by competitive athletes. As Samuel Johnson wryly remarked about the improved death row writing of the unfortunate Thomas Dodd, "Depend upon it, sir, when a man knows he is to be hanged in a fortnight, it concentrates his mind wonderfully." Athletes are not hanged, except, perhaps in effigy, but need wonderfully concentrated minds to achieve great performance, nevertheless.

How, then, might sport pedagogists counsel fearful athletes in the ways of traditional courage? First, they must advocate sport as a social practice worthy of true courage. To treat sport performances and the personal fears they spawn as circumstances below the dignity of genuine courage leaves athletes with all the disadvantages of being afraid and none of the advantages of being courageous. This exacerbates performance problems tremendously, as Queen Victoria recognized in her remark that "Great events make me quiet and calm; it is only trifles that irritate my nerves." Sport as play may stand outside the great events of real life, but it is also very serious in the playing itself (12). Courage is not out of place in any activity, including sport, whose personal meaning is so profound to its participants. Athletes need to believe that, and sport pedagogists need to foster that belief.

Having established sport as an arena in which traditional courage might properly thrive, sport pedagogists must reconsider their reliance on psychological technique when addressing fear. The way they define courage will determine the way in which they seek, literally, to encourage athletes. Examples from sport help to illustrate this, beginning with a discussion of courage as it pertains to the competitive setting itself. Smith (29) remarked that "the most common sources of anxiety in athletes are fears of failure and resulting social disapproval or rejection" (p. 160). Smith's point was that much of the general fear that athletes experience can be understood in very specific terms as fear of negative evaluation. Many athletes look out over the field of play and see looming there the spectres of failure, loss of dignity and prestige, and injury. They often perceive their physical, mental, and social survival to be threatened and the fear that results lurks in the shadows of every competition.

All this occurs despite the self-imposed nature of the perceived threat. Athletes choose to participate in the circumstances that produce the fear that debilitates them. They actively seek the opportunity to challenge themselves and know beforehand that if the challenge were trivial, there would be no point. The difficulty of achieving is the reason for playing. Sport philosophy, on its own, would focus immediately on such nonempirical matters and try to bring reason to bear on the emotions, to create the conditions in which a state of courage can arise and remain.

Conversely, the response of sport pedagogy to the fear that negative perceptions produce is usually to attempt to neutralize it, to manage it using techniques designed to produce immediate, yet temporary, changes beneficial to performance. The extensive list of methods used to combat the symptoms of this form of anxiety includes biofeedback, relaxation, cognitive behavioral therapy, mental preparation routines, and goal setting strategies (30). The purpose of all of these, however, is to create a state of fearlessness, not a state of courage, and Aristotle cautioned that they are not the same thing. Someone who fears nothing, who is fearless, is "mad or insensitive to pain" (3, Book III vii, p. 7). Fearlessness is, to Aristotle, an impediment to courage because one who is courageous "endures or fears the right things and for the right purpose and in the right manner and at the right time" (3, Book III vii, p. 7).

Rachman (21), taking a psychological view that would find favor in current practices in sport pedagogy, argued that one can practice courageous behavior and that ultimately, "Courage turns into fearlessness" (p. 249). This presupposes a completely different view than that offered by Aristotle and Aquinas, one in which fear and fearlessness exist at the poles of a continuum with courage as a middle state between the extremes. Such an understanding of courage as psychological trait rather than virtue portrays fearlessness as a more desirable state than courage. It fails to account for concerns about semblances and counterfeits of courage expressed by both Aristotle and Aquinas. Both would argue that a change from courage to fearlessness is a descent rather than an ascent, as Rachman appears to suggest.

One who is truly courageous does not seek to eliminate fear by burying it with technique or practice. Barrett (4: p. 117) argued that our culture is totally enamored with method at the expense of any underlying philosophy but warned that "Every technique is put to use for some end, and this end is decided in the light of some philosophic outlook or other. The technique cannot produce the philosophy that directs it." The usual approach of sport pedagogists to fear in athletic performance reflects Barrett's concerns. By implication, the unrecognized philosophical basis for their dependence upon fear management techniques is the belief that courage is a virtue lost. Our intellectual history has provided good reason for such a belief, but what is in exile need not be irretrievably so. Courage, if restored in its traditional form, would be a valuable ally to sport pedagogists.

By way of analogy, not to courage itself, but to the difference between the rigidity of a technique-driven approach to behaving as one would like and the flexibility of a principle-based strategy, consider an example from basketball. It illustrates the difference between those who teach athletes to deal with the world using specific methods and those who teach them to navigate through it using just a few fixed stars. When attacking a zone defense, several questions arise: What kind of zone is it? Where are its seams? How do players in different positions in the zone shift when the ball moves? There are many different kinds of zones to overcome, each with its own unique combinations of strengths and weaknesses, each demanding different behaviors in order for the offense to achieve success. One solution to this problem of multiplicity for coaches is to have a number of offense patterns and set plays, each suitable for attacking a particular kind of zone. A second solution is to give offensive players basic principles that, if adhered to, create opportunities to read the specifics of a situation moment by moment, and then respond by doing what is right under the circumstances. Most coaches would prefer the second approach, but many opt for the first, concerned that their players are not smart enough or skilled enough to fend for themselves, to adapt and create using just a few basic rules. Yet watch great players and teams. Theirs is the second strategy, one earned the hard way by the athletic equivalent of rigorous Socratic self-examination. The metaphor is obvious. Fearlessness is relatively easy and can be accomplished with careful attention to pedagogical technique alone, but produces by-the-book performances that can break down when confronted by even small differences in performance conditions. Courage is difficult and can be accomplished only through experience and thorough commitment to understanding one's self and one's general principles. Its great advantage is its resilience in affording appropriate, if more demanding, responses to any performance condition. Cultivating fearlessness when the seeds of courage should be planted and nurtured denies athletes the opportunity to explore their full potential by short circuiting virtue via technique.

Given the high profile of professional sport's labor problems, it is appropriate to consider next, circumstances off the field of play. A complete rendition of the history of baseball's reserve clause is not needed to understand the case of Curt Flood. In 1969, Flood was traded by St. Louis to Philadelphia. He refused to go, arguing that he was not property that could be bought and sold, nor an indentured servant whose labor could be traded by one plantation owner to another. Legal advice cautioned that his was not a fight that could be won under the conditions present at the time. He persisted nevertheless, certain that when one is right, one must act accordingly. Three successive legal challenges, including one to the Supreme Court, failed to uphold Flood's position. This occurred despite the obvious rightness of his position that, as an American worker, he was not a slave and that the reserve clause contravened the Thirteenth Amendment that banned slavery. Curt Flood never played baseball again, his successful and lucrative career sacrificed to moral principle.

Not one other active player appeared to testify on Flood's behalf in any of the three cases, though a retired and aging Jackie Robinson did. It is inconceivable that Flood was the only player of his generation who took issue with the wrongness of the reserve clause. His colleagues, presumably possessing the moral freedom to act on behalf of what Flood believed to be the good, opted not to do so. The apparent contrast is Flood's courage with his colleagues' cowardice. Yet, a closer examination of courage offers an alternative explanation. Certainly, other players remained on the sidelines despite their considerable aversion to the reserve clause. However, just a few years after the Flood–Supreme Court decision, baseball's reserve clause was dead, killed in a duel with the players' union that had served up two test cases for a well-organized arbitration procedure. Timing and planning had succeeded where merely being right had previously failed.

To experience the courage described by Aquinas is to have a clear sense of what one's valued ends are and a thorough understanding of what the legitimate challenges to one's confidence are. When the death blow to the reserve clause was struck, the players were solidly behind the protagonists in the free agency test case. Unlike the Flood challenge, this was a fight that had been carefully orchestrated and one that practical reason determined to be the correct front on which to wage the decisive battle. It is too easy to accuse the players of cowardice in their failure to support Flood in court. The goodness of the end Flood pursued was not, and is not, in doubt. There was, in his mind, a sufficient chance of success to warrant making the attempt. From a Thomist standpoint, however, his decision viewed retrospectively appears to tend to rashness, and therefore lacking an essential element of true courage. It might be interpreted, instead, as a semblance of courage, conjuring the words of Bosquet at Balaclava who, while watching the charge of the Light Brigade, remarked, "C'est magnifique, mais ce n'est pas la guerre." Accordingly, the other players' courage need not be cast into doubt if practical reason informed them that the Flood case was not one to win and that willing sacrifice on behalf of the good would better wait for the conditions for success to be more favorable. Courage can create heroes, but should not create unnecessary martyrs.

Not every athlete faces dilemmas of the magnitude of Curt Flood and his fellow players. However, all athletes face challenges to their moral courage in less notorious circumstances. They experience flawed power relationships with coaches and sport administrators; make decisions about whether to cheat or not, or to address the cheating of other athletes; and, cope with the demands made on the very best athletes to sacrifice life for sport. Athletes can and, in modern sport culture, must, acknowledge sport as a moral arena, one in which they are sometimes challenged to display courage in ethical matters that transcend the playing of the game itself. The need for a balance of reason and passion shown by the example of the Curt Flood case is a strong starting point when taking action under such circumstances.

A final example of the need for courage comes from the sport therapy clinic in which so many athletes spend at least a part of their careers. Injury is a considerable challenge to athletes, not just because of its physical demands, but because of the psychosocial difficulties associated with it (11). During rehabilitation, there is no media coverage, no audience, and greatly diminished association with coaches and teammates who constitute an athlete's usual support system. Injured players are not altogether abandoned, but they are given up for temporary adoption, fostered to a biomedical environment whose priorities, methods, and standards of success and failure are very different from those of the gym,

arena, or playing field. Worst of all, the simple denial of opportunities for skilled physical activity severely undermines an athlete's sense of self in a way that is fundamentally different from the experience of injured or ill nonathletes (13). It is an experience well-disposed to produce fear. It is an experience in need of a courageous response.

Whether athletes have greater pain tolerance than nonathletes is irrelevant to the philosophical point in this context. Animals in their natural habitats who are hurt and in pain simply lie down in a sheltered place, conserve their energy, and heal as quickly and comfortably as they can. Their failure to suffer when in pain as humans do could not be construed as courage, however. They merely do what evolution has programmed them to do. Injured athletes have more imaginative minds, capable not just of pain sensation but suffering because of what the pain is thought to mean. For them, recovery is much more difficult. Courage is necessary, again in a form in which practical reason identifies the specific valued end of maximum possible recovery. Bravado and fearlessness, timidity and fear are both counterproductive combinations for an athlete engaged in rehabilitation.

Therapeutic techniques such as physical manipulation and mental imagery are the direct and indirect agents of change in an athlete's playing condition. But, philosophy, by addressing fundamental questions about who we are and where we are going, can form the bedrock upon which healing can proceed without being a terrifying experience. Bill Moyers noted in *Healing and the Mind* (1993, p. 332), ". . . if I feel deep and unrelieved fear over the diagnosis, . . . that's who I am, and I need to express that fear. But if I don't express it, although I feel it, I'm pretending to be something other than what I am." Courage can serve admirably as the rudder by which one's own energy and that of others is propelled undeterred in the proper direction of healing, steering a course between the uncritical optimism that obscures what must be done and fatalistic pessimism that undermines the will to do what one knows is required.

VI

Like his Greek predecessors, Aquinas found courage rooted in the facing of death, primarily in warfare. However, he also saw that facing death in war was a model for more common occasions in which people risk their immediate well-being, accept insecurity, and abandon their usual self-centered hold on life. In such situations people must overcome their powerful desire for self-interest. Therefore, courage can be manifest in less obvious situations than death in war. Sport is one such modern practice that demands a full appreciation of the meaning of justifiable internal goals, governed by practical reason, set in the context of a moral environment that values the needs of friends and allies, and of one's culture—in this case, sport itself—above one's own.

I have attempted to build an argument that courage should not be understood merely as a solution to the problem of fear. Sport pedagogy already has many alleged solutions at its disposal, and I (6) have argued that sport pedagogy built upon insecure philosophical foundations is akin to the sophistry of Socratic Athens, focused on results at whatever cost, and never addressing athletes' real needs. Rather than being considered a solution, courage should be conceived as an alternative to fear. To accomplish this, sport pedagogists need to appreciate the value of philosophy to sport in the same way that they accept the role of other disciplines and reframe their practices accordingly.

Philosophical counseling is very different from the more current and fashionable forms of psychological counseling, as Moore (19) has noted:

Shallow therapeutic manipulations aimed at restoring normality or tuning a life according to standards reduces—shrinks—that profound mystery to the pale dimensions of a social common denominator referred to as the adjusted personality. Care of the soul sees another reality altogether. It appreciates the mystery of human suffering and does not offer the illusion of a problem-free life. (pp. 19–20)

A demanding alternative, perhaps, given the emphasis on immediate, individual self-improvement that athletes convey to sport pedagogists and the relative ease of relying upon technique alone. Given the difficulty of the task for pedagogists, moral philosophy has an important contribution to make to modern sport if sport philosophers can inform sport pedagogy with the same effectiveness as do psychologists, physiologists, and biomechanists. The meaning of traditional courage, and perhaps the other traditional virtues that have escaped mention in this paper, would be worthwhile messages with which to begin.

Bibliography

1. Aquinas, Thomas. *Summa theoloaiae,* 60 volumes. Edited by T. Gilby and T.C. O'Brien. London: Eyre and Spottiswoode; New York: McGraw-Hill, 1964.

2. Arnold, P.J. "Sport as a valued human practice: A basis for the consideration of some moral issues in sport." *Journal of Philosophy of Education,* 26 (1992), 237–255.

3. Aristotle. *The Nicomachean Ethics* (Trans. H. Rackham). Cambridge, MA: Harvard University Press, 1934.

4. Barrett, W. *The Illusion of Technique.* New York: Anchor Books, 1979.

5. Bolt, R. *A Man for All Seasons.* London: Samuel French, 1960.

6. Corlett, J.T. "Sophistry, Socrates, and Sport Psychology." *The Sport Psychologist,* 10:1 (1996), 84–94.

7. Dent, N.J.H. "The Value of Courage." *Philosophy,* 56 (1981), 574–577.

8. Devereux, D.T. "Courage and Wisdom in Plato's Laches." *Journal of History of Philosophy,* 15 (1977), 129–141.

9. Duff, A. "Aristotelian Courage." *Ratio,* 29 (1987), 2–15.

10. Falk, W.D. "Prudence, Temperance, and Courage." In *Moral Concepts*. Edited by J. Feinberg. London: Oxford University Press, 1970, 114–119.

11. Heil, J. *Psychology of Sport Injury*. Champaign, IL: Human Kinetics, 1993.

12. Huizinga, J. *Homo Ludens: A Study of the Play Element in Culture*. Boston, MA: Beacon Press, 1955.

13. Pargman, D. *Psychological Bases of Sport Injuries*. Morgantown, WV: Fitness Information Technology Inc., 1993.

14. Hume, D. "An Enquiry Concerning Human Understanding." In *Great Books of the Western World*, Vol. 35. Chicago: Encyclopedia Brittanica, 1952.

15. Kalin, N.H. "The Neurobiology of Fear." *Scientific American*, (May 1993), 94–101.

16. Kant, I. *Critique of Pure Reason* (Trans. by N.K. Smith). London: Macmillan Press, 1968.

17. McIntyre, Alasdair. *After Virtue* (2nd Ed.). Notre Dame, IN: Notre Dame University Press, 1984.

18. Mill, J.S. *Utilitarianism*. Indianapolis: Hackct Press, 1979.

19. Moore, T. *The Care of the Soul*. New York: Harper-Collins, 1992.

20. Plato. "Laches" (Trans. by B. Jowett). In *The Dialogues of Plato*, Vol. 4. Edited by B. Jowett and M.J. Knight. New York: Bigelow, Brown, & Co., 1910.

21. Rachman, S. *Fear and Courage*. San Francisco: W. H. Freeman & Company, 1978.

22. Roberts, R.C. "Aristotle on Virtues and Emotions." *Philosophical Studies*, 56 (1989), 293–306.

23. Rorty, A.O. "The Two Faces of Courage." *Philosophy*, 61 (1986), 151–171.

24. Santas, G. "Socrates at Work on Virtue and Knowledge in Plato's Laches." *Review of Metaphysics*, 22 (1969), 433–460.

25. Schmid, W.T. *On Manly Courage: A Study of Plato's Laches*. Carbondale, IL: Southern Illinois University Press, 1992.

26. Shaw, G.B. *Saint Joan*. Toronto: Longman, 1992.

27. Slote, M. "Utilitarian Virtue." *Midwest Studies in Philosophy*, 13 (1988), 384–397.

28. Smart, J.C.C., & Williams, B. *Utilitarianism: For and Against*. Cambridge, MA: Cambridge University Press, 1973.

29. Smith, R.E. "Theoretical and Treatment Approaches to Anxiety Reduction." In *Psychological Foundations of Sport*. Edited by J.M. Silva & R.S. Weinberg. Champaign, IL: Human Kinetics, 1984, 157–170.

30. Vealey, R. "Current Status and Prominent Issues in Sport Psychology Interventions." *Medicine and Science in Sports and Exercise*, 26 (1994), 495–502.

31. Wallace, J.D. *Virtues and Vices*. Ithaca, NY: Cornell University Press, 1978.

32. Walton, D.N. *Courage: A Philosophical Investigation*. Berkeley: University of California Press, 1985.

33. Weil, Simone. "The *Iliad* or the Poem of Force." In *Revisions*. Edited by S. Hauerwas and A. MacIntyre. Notre Dame, IN: University of Notre Dame Press, 1983, 222–248.

34. Will, George. *Men at Work: The Craft of Baseball*. New York: Harper Perennial, 1990.

35. Yearley, L. *Mencius and Aquinas: Theories of Virtue and Conceptions of Courage*. Albany: State University of New York Press, 1990.

Questions for Consideration

1. How does courage in sport differ from courage in areas outside of sport?

2. What is the difference between considering courage as a virtue (an end itself) and courage as a means (an instrument to some end)?

3. Can Corlett's point about a philosophical approach to the problem of fear also be appropriately applied to other problems in sport that concern other virtues, such as friendliness, generosity, moderation, justice, and practical wisdom? If so, what type of rational therapy could be utilized for which problems?

40 Aggression, Gender, and Sport: Reflections on Sport as a Means of Moral Education

M. Andrew Holowchak
Ohio University

In this reading, I examine the data on aggression and gender in an effort to take a fresh look at the issues of aggression and violence in sport and society. My project has both an empirical dimension as well as one that is normative.

Empirically, the reading looks at three types of models of aggression in humans: one that favors strong biological dispositionalism, another that maintains that learning is the chief causal factor, and a third that argues nature and nurture cannot be separated. Current research heavily favors the third. Concerning aggression and sex, the overwhelming historical tendency of males to aggress cannot be explained without recourse to biological factors. To date, study of sex differences and aggression through physiology has been rich and yields the promise of great future reward.

Philosophically, the issue of moral education to overcome aggression has been marred by the widespread belief that exposure to aggression leads to a catharsis of aggressive impulses. The data, however, are mostly inconsistent with such an explanation and heavily favor the hypothesis that aggression leads to aggression. What this suggests is that we seriously rethink the inclusion of overly aggressive sports and violent sportive behavior in contemporary society. Instead of condoning aggression and violence, a condemnatory attitude is more in keeping with the aim of conflict resolution through moral education.

M. Andrew Holowchak, "Aggression, Gender, and Sport: Reflections on Sport as a Means of Moral Education."

Sport and Conflict-Resolution

In a paper titled "Violence and Aggression in Contemporary Society," philosopher Jim Parry argues that assertion, aggression (assertive behavior that need not be violent), and violence (behavior that aims at harm) in competitive sport allow opportunities for reflection on moral education and moral development. Competitive sports, he asserts, are "laboratories for value experiments."[1] He states:

> I find it an attractive and intriguing idea, worthy of further consideration, that the competitive sports situation challenges individuals to develop and use their power and aggressiveness; but not, finally, to use this power to control and subjugate the other. May we see more assertive and aggressive people, and less violent ones. And may sport be an agent of moral change.[2]

Frans De Wachter too sees sport as a possible vehicle for moral progress—specifically, regarding education in conflict-resolution and peace. "The question is not whether sport is functional for peace. That seems to me to be a question that is too ambitious. The realistic question is whether sport education can be functional in the context of peace education."[3] Citing four objectives related to peace education that could be instrumental to that end—reduction of militaristic attitudes, diminution of aggressiveness, eradication of "enemy images," and development of conflict-resolving skills—he encourages work in each of these areas.[4]

The issue of sportive activity for moral betterment and social improvement is engaging. As one can imagine, however, there is not an abundance of contemporary philosophical and sociological speculation on this issue. We are soured perhaps by what we have seen in the past under the rubric "morality and sport," such as the politically vicious fascism that sullied athletic competition at the 1936 Olympics in Berlin. Our attitude today seems to be: *Let's keep sport as value-neutral as possible.* We seem content to let athletes do their own thing.

In agreement with Parry, competitive sport does seem to be a large-scale experiment concerning human aggression and violence with normative implications. The empirical dimension concerns the extent to which we as human beings are aggressive animals. Attending upon the empirical issue is one that is philosophical: To what extent can sport be an instrument of moral change?

Thus, in this paper, I look first at various scientific models of aggression in human beings and then at gender-related differences in aggressive behavior. After evaluating the empirical findings, I consider normative pathways for sport as a means of lessening or channeling aggression and the violence that is often linked to it.

Models of Aggression

In an effort to tackle these issues, I distinguish between three traditional explanations of aggression: strong dispositionalism, culture-pattern models, and weak dispositionalism.

Based upon the seeming universality of aggression, strong dispositionalists posit that aggression is instinctive or inherited and that our propensity to aggress is inevitable. If these theorists are correct, then there is little we can do to overcome aggression, other than releasing aggressive impulses or deciding on strategies to deflect it in less harmful ways.

According to strong dispositionalist models that are cathartic, aggression is a force or impulse that builds up within each person and requires periodic release, if it is not to be debilitating to an organism. If not for the existence of cathartic mechanisms for purging ourselves of aggression, normal human functioning would be greatly impaired. Examples of cathartic models of aggression include Freud's thanatic model, Lorenz's hydraulic model, and the frustration-aggression model.

If the main premise behind cathartic models is correct, then aggressive play in sport is merely a salubrious vent for the natural buildup of aggression. Exposure to and participation in such sports, then, should result in an overall reduction in personal aggression.

Though data are not unambiguous, current research indicates strongly that exposure to aggression leads not to catharsis, but to more aggression. Yet catharsis is as popular as ever in the minds of lay people and those investigators who fail to undertake a careful review of the current literature on it. Psychologists Brad Bushman, Roy Baumeister, and Angela Stack write:

> The scientific community has largely disconfirmed and abandoned catharsis theory and, if anything, is looking to understand why the opposite effect occurs (i.e., venting anger leads to higher subsequent aggression). Meanwhile, the popular mass media continue to suggest that catharsis theory is true and has scientific support, so the message reaching the general public is that catharsis is an effective, desirable way of handling angry impulses.[5]

Of course, this certainly does not mean that catharsis cannot enter into the overall explanation in *some* capacity. If it does, however, it is likely a small part of the overall picture.

In contrast to cathartic models, strong-dispositional, non-cathartic models are built upon the identification of specific biological mechanisms that incite aggression. Since these are principally gender-based models, I leave off talk of these until a later portion of this project. It is sufficient here to say that such models, assuming predominantly biological causes of aggression, leave little room for overcoming aggressive tendencies.

Concerning assessment of non-cathartic, strong-dispositional models, I show in what immediately follows that they cannot be maintained in light of what we currently know about the impact of environment on aggression and even physiological development.

In stark contrast to strong-dispositional models are culture-pattern models of aggression. According to such models, aggression is predominantly learned behavior. Exposure to aggressive play tends to make people more aggressive in other aspects of interpersonal relationships. If this view is right, then aggression leads to aggression and involvement in aggressive play has socially deleterious consequences. In keeping with this school of thought are social-learning theorists, who posit aggression is learned behavior in individuals, and culture-learning theorists, who argue that the basic unit of study is culture, not individuals.

The main problem with culture-pattern models is obvious. In explaining human aggression as essentially learned behavior, it cannot have anything interesting to say about current physiological research on aggression, which is providing us with important new data on bio-physiological links to aggression.

A third, conciliatory path to explaining human aggression has been forged by those who posit aggression is a disposition that can be inflamed or held in check through learning.

Within the last forty years, it has become increasingly apparent that models that overwhelmingly favor either biological predestination or cultural and environmental factors in explaining aggression are flawed. Researchers are now coming to see that the two factors are inseparably conjoined. Biological factors predispose individuals to react to particular circumstances in certain ways, but upbringing and other environmental factors have an impact on aggression and even affect physiological structure itself.

For instance, psychologist Harry Harlow has shown that lack of early nurture is a strong predictor of aggressive behavior in later life.[6] In addition, neurophysiologist James W. Prescott, one of the pioneers on the effect of environmental circumstances on physiology, has argued convincingly that violent upbringing changes the very structure of the brain.[7] In all, such studies show that attempts to isolate the precise roles of biology and learning are futile. As Gene Bylinsky states:

The most recent research suggests that the biological and environmental causes of violence are so closely intertwined as to require a less fragmented search for remedies. The research is showing, among other things, that the environment itself can leave a physical imprint on a developing brain. The wrong kind of upbringing can make a young animal, and probably a child too, more inclined to violent behavior as an adolescent or an adult. The hopeful augury of this research is that such behavior can be prevented if steps are taken to assure that young brains develop properly.[8]

Van der Dennen agrees:

That instincts produce aggression, that drives generate aggression, that learning creates aggression—each proposition, standing by itself, is a simplistic theory. All dimensions are present to some degree and are simultaneously part of the field of relationships and dynamic forces that can modify, dampen, or inflate aggressive impulses, attitudes and behavioral dispositions. The whole is a complex of perception, personality, behavioral dispositions, and expectations. To emphasize one without the others within the field is to forget that man is always a feeling-thinking-doing, integrated totality.[9]

The correct approach to an understanding of aggression must be a weak dispositional model of some sort that allows for biology and learning to factor importantly into explanation.

Sex, Aggression, and Culture

Whatever the model of human aggression, what strikes even the most casual observer as a real difference between men and women is the predominance of aggression in males.[10] As E. E. Thorndike wrote nearly 100 years ago:

> The most striking differences in instinctive equipment consists in the strength of the fighting instinct in the male and of the nursing instinct in the female. . . . The out-and-out physical fighting for the sake of combat is pre-eminently a male instinct, and the resentment at mastery, the zeal to surpass, and the general joy at activity in mental as well as physical matters seem to be closely correlated with it.[11]

The question becomes, How can we best explain this?

Contemporary culture-pattern approaches to such issues are unavailing. Many theorists, by one fell swoop of the hand, want to explain away all sexual differences in behavior by social constructions or learning. They contend, with complete assurance, that biological factors, if they do come into play, do so in a causally irrelevant fashion.

For example, M. Ann Hall, in her work *Feminism and Sporting Bodies,* defines differences of sex in such a way that excludes the possibility of natural or biological factors. She writes:

> Biological determinism forces thinking that is both reductionistic and categoric. Reductionism attempts to explain the properties of complex wholes in terms of the units that compose the whole. . . . Therefore, in the case

of sex differences, genes are said to play a causal role in determining male/female differences by being expressed through the sex hormones, which in turn act on the brain (referred to some as "brain sex").

> Reductionism also spawns thinking in terms of dichotomous categories: male versus female, male sex hormone versus female sex hormone, black versus white, and so forth. A dichotomy forces a polarization and ignores overlaps; differences are seen as more interesting than similarities, and there is a tendency to see these differences as absolute.[12]

Hall then goes on to point out that "biology itself provides no clear justification for a dichotomous view of gender" and that the wide variety of genetic types and hormonal conditions make any such dichotomy impossible. She sums, "Biological sex . . . is a vast, infinitely malleable continuum that defies categorization." The two-sex system, she asserts boldly, is in "defiance of nature."[13]

Hall's reasoning, however, is unconvincing. First, she dismisses any biological account on the basis that it is reductionistic. Yet distaste of reductionism is not an argument against it. Next, she argues that reductionism spawns dichotomous thinking at odds with reality. Here she fails to realize that biological explanation is being invoked in order to explain *observed and accepted* dichotomies like aggressive behavior in males and the relative absence of it in females. Last, she asserts that biological sex "defies categorization," since it is a continuum (given certain chromosomally anomalous types such as XXX, XXY, XYY, and X). This objection, however, is easily deflected by noting that the putative gender-based continuum assumes that the extra chromosomal combinations are not defective, but *natural* combinations that make for additional genders. This seems gratuitous.

Similarly, Jennifer Hargreaves, in contrast, simply argues that differences of aggression and competitiveness are satisfactorily explained by socialization:

The commonplace claim that men are *naturally* more aggressive, more competitive and, therefore, better at sports than women suggests that these are inherent conditions and hence unchangeable. But it is illogical and inaccurate to argue that because relatively more men than women display aggressive and competitive behaviour, these characteristics are exclusive to the male sex. This is not to deny that there are essential differences between the sexes, but to resist the strong tendency *to treat as natural everything that is customary* [my italics]. . . . Differences between the sexes in displays of aggression and competitiveness can be explained as a result of social and cultural experiences—part of a process which starts at birth.[14]

Hargreaves literally dismisses biological differences by claiming flatly that behaviors like aggression are customary, not biological.

Hargreaves falls prey to the fallacy of the argument from ignorance. She insists that lack of clear-cut biological evidence for a sexual dichotomy is proof positive that no such dichotomy does exist. All *relevant* causation, she maintains, occurs at the socio-cultural level. Edley and Wetherell elaborate eloquently the flaw of this line of thought:

[I]t is . . . wrong to take the absence of clear cross-cultural patterns in sex-related behaviour as meaning that there are no biological forces at play, for there is no logical reason why biological factors need always find expression. Instead, they may be "masked" or overridden by social or cultural influences operating in a different "direction."

One has only to consider the celibate person or the hunger-striker. Both are generally acknowledged to be acting against natural instincts.[15] Therefore, an explanation that weighs social factors unevenly becomes extraordinarily improbable.

Overall, the fear behind culture-pattern approaches is, I suspect, that if certain significant biological differences do exist between the sexes that favor men, then men will use this as a rationalization for future aggression and domination over women in sport and elsewhere. Yet facts are one thing; what people make of facts because of social and political biases is another. The role of empirical investigation into aggression is to disclose just what is the case here, insofar as this is possible, and not to form judgments concerning value.

Goldberg's Hypothesis

That certain physiological and even psychological differences—such as nurturance sensitivity, personalization of reality, and sexual arousal—do exist between the sexes is apparent. Steven Goldberg offers an explanation in his book *Why Men Rule*. Goldberg writes:

[W]e know that men and women think and behave differently, whatever the cause. Therefore, it does not seem unreasonable to suggest that the observed sex differences . . . might represent manifestations of physiological differentiation. In any case, whether these subtle differences are physiologically or socially generated, they do exist, and rejection of *descriptions* because one does not like them is hardly justified.[16]

Goldberg asserts there are limits to social elements in explanation. Sociological, anthropological, and economic analysis draws sustenance from comparative research—for instance, by noting how different behaviors have different meanings over time within a culture or simultaneously across cultures. Picking up on contemporary empirical research of anthropologists, he argues that all societies *that have ever existed* have been patriarchal (where the "overwhelming number of upper positions in hierarchies [in any system of organization] are occupied by males"). Therefore, the universality (though not inevitability) of patriarchy, as well as male attainment and dominance, cannot be explained through sociological, anthropological, or economic analysis.[17]

He then offers a sufficient explanation for male dominance: neuroendocrinological differences. He writes:

> The neuroendocrinological differences are such that the presence of hierarchy (any hierarchy), high-status role, or member of the other sex elicits from the male, more readily, more often, and more strongly than from the female: 1. emotions of "competitiveness," the tendency—the impulse—for attainment and dominance (whether this tendency, this impulse, is termed a "need" or a "drive"); 2. relative suppression of other emotions and needs and a sacrifice of rewards (health, family, relaxation, and so forth) that compete with the need for attainment and dominance; and 3. actions required for attainment of position, status, and dominance. . . . The theory does not deny the role of socialization, but it does hold that socialization is a dependent variable that is given its limits and direction by the independent variable of the physiological difference between men and women.[18]

Kathryn Pyne Addelson, in response to an earlier version of Goldberg's argument in his book *The Inevitability of Patriarchy*, objects:

> Goldberg's argument is little more than a renewed effort to justify the sexual division of labor, warning us that men and women are biologically different and that the human race will come to naught unless women stay home and leave the battle of public life to men. He confuses winning a battle over an enemy with qualifying for a higher rank because one has merit.[19]

Yet, Addelson misses the point of Goldberg's argument. It *never* takes the normative turn she says it does, but stays at the empirical level.

One might object, though, that from observing history we see a connection between women and nursing children and another between men and the tendency to aggress, but this is far from *demonstrating* the biological differences between the sexes that Goldberg assumes. Yet this objection fails to take into consideration that having a prodigious amount of information in favor of some connection, like women and nursing, and nothing against it is a powerful inductive argument in favor of a biological or causal connection. At some point in amassing evidence, skepticism seems absurd. We have only to remember the litigation surrounding smoking and cancer over the years and the eventual acceptance of a causal link between the two by manufacturers of cigarettes. The true flaw in Goldberg's reasoning comes in viewing socialization exclusively as a dependent variable, for we have seen that nurture, especially early on, has a profound impact on physiology as well.

Biological Reductionism

Overall, the tendency to explain the difference in aggressive behavior in males and females by biochemical reduction is not deplorable, but rather seductive given its simplicity. Yet far too often the difference in observed aggression in males is stated flatly by the equation: Testosterone equals aggression. The problem with this answer is that it is wrong.

That testosterone and aggression are correlated is undeniable: Where there is one, in the main, you find the other. During puberty, when testosterone levels peak, so does male aggression. Weightlifters who take in many times their body's normal levels of testosterone through anabolic and androgenic steroids or growth hormones are also markedly more aggressive than other males. In contrast, in castration experiments with countless different species of animal, castration leads to substantially reduced levels of aggression.[20] Where's the flaw?

This relationship does not suggest a *straightfor-*

ward causal link. Reduce testosterone to 20 percent of the normal amount or increase it by 100 percent and there is no appreciable diminution or elevation of aggression. Observance of highly aggressive behavior in individuals without high levels of testosterone shows that testosterone is not exclusively responsible for aggression. Chemical imbalances like diminished levels of brain serotonin and magnesium deficiency can also result in aggressive behavior. In many instances, social conditioning seems to make up for the absence of the hormone.[21] In addition, physiological data suggest that testosterone is not by itself causally responsible for exciting aggressive behavior. Researchers are coming to discover that testosterone merely functions to heighten the excitation of neural pathways between the amygdala (the part of the brain believed responsible for aggression) and the hypothalmus (the part of the brain that regulates aggression and that is responsible for emotive activity) that have already been excited.[22] In all, except in cases of extremes of excess and defect, amount of testosterone does little by itself as a predictor of aggression in individuals.

Another biological possibility concerns the different types of sexual hormones in males and females. Such hormonal differences impact the reproductive systems of men and women differently as well as their secondary sexual characteristics, such as facial hair, voice, and muscle mass. One intriguing question is this: Do hormonal differences influence differences in cerebral development and its anatomy and, thus, the behavior between the sexes?

Research suggests a positive answer. Many studies show marked differences both in the anatomy of mature male and female brains and in the development of the brains of each sex. The problem with this line of research comes in showing that these differences are *causally* linked to behavioral variations, such as aggression in males and nurturing in females.[23] Still, one thing is clear concerning the brain structures of males and females: Males are born with many more brain cells that specialize in aggressive behavior than are females.[24]

In addition, researchers continue to look for a gene for aggression in males, though to date no such gene has been found. It has long been thought that, if this is so, then the gene must be carried in the Y chromosome. Geneticists now believe that, if such a gene does exist, it being carried on the much smaller Y chromosome is unlikely. Instead, it would have to be carried on the larger X chromosome, which carries many more functional genes than the Y chromosome. If this should turn out true, the paradox would be that, while women might condemn male aggressiveness, it is they who in a very literal sense would be responsible for giving men aggression.[25]

In summary, the historical prevalence of male dominance and aggression seems to be sufficient evidence that there must be some biological component to the observed sex differences in aggressive behavior. Specifying this component may be an impossible task, though research holds the promise of substantial future reward.

Sport and Moral Reform

It is reasonable to conclude that the tendency to aggress, much more evident in males than in females, is a result of both socialization and biology. It follows that if we allow for equality of opportunity in sports, men will tend to dominate those sports that reinforce aggressive behavior. In addition, other physical differences—on average, greater size and muscle mass and less body fat in males—will ensure male superiority in sports emphasizing strength and speed (many of which are violent sports).

Superiority in sport, however, is often taken by some as an argument for superiority of gender. There is a harmful equivocation here. In the former sense, to say *men are superior in sport* is to say something like men, on average, can physically outperform women in most sports, which is a descriptive claim. Superiority of gender, however, could easily be taken as a normative claim that implies men are morally better than are women. This, of course, nowise follows from the empirical literature.

Even speaking exclusively of physical superiority of males is problematic. Addelson writes:

> To rank men over women in sports because the best statistics in record books belong to males is to take those top-ranking males as champions who symbolically win the battle for all males. . . . It ignores the fact that sports excellence is judged for individual and team performance, and that in some leagues, women have outperformed men. It ignores the fact, that is, that competition in sports ranks individuals and teams, not ideologies or nations or sexes. The meritocracy includes all the women who do well, *and* all the men who do well, even though women and men alike might not come up to the top male record in some sports.[26]

In addition, as I state above, the measures of athletic excellence have always been those sports that tend to feature skills that favor males, such as speed and strength. What, though, if grace and balance were the measures? This illustrates something wholly unremarkable: The very language of sport is androcentric.

Let me now turn to an evaluation of the statement that sport may be a large-scale experiment involving human aggression and violence. In other words, it is time for the empirical research to be put profitably to use in normative fashion.

The greatest impediment to serviceable normative speculation has been and, I should add, still is a dogged insistence that some sort of cathartic model of aggression is true. The deduction from such models is that aggression constantly builds up in us and must find suitable release for normal human functioning. Consequently, aggressive behavior, whether experienced vicariously or first-hand, is essential for reduction of destructive, aggressive impulses. According to such models, aggressive sports offer opportunities for catharsis and thereby advance

normal functioning. Aggressive sports, then, help promote a healthier society.

Assisted by the vast amount of evidence against cathartic models, we must philosophically reassess the issue of aggression in sports. If exposure to aggressive behavior leads to heightened aggression or increased frequency of aggression, then we need to re-evaluate very seriously our love and patronage of sports such as football, non-Olympic boxing, and North American hockey. For by condoning aggression in sport, we condone aggression (perhaps even violence) in society. What is equally reprehensible, we fail to cultivate the seedlings of world peace and moral betterment that lie at our feet and await nurture.

Science can tell us what we are, but it has nothing to say about what we ought to be. Still, knowing what we are is essential for deciding

Do aggression and violence in sport lead to heightened aggression outside of sport? Here Mike Tyson bites into the ear of Evander Holyfield in the third round of their WBA Heavyweight match on June 28, 1997, at the MGM Grand in Las Vegas. Ed. Jack Smith/AP/Wide World Photos

what we ought to be. We are animals with aggressive tendencies, but these tendencies to aggress, science suggests, do not predestine us to do so. If science teaches us that the ill effects of aggression through proper nurture can be tethered or minimized, then we ought to follow its lead and develop means to tame the beast within us. By condemning violent aggression in sports (e.g., fighting in hockey) and banning those sports that are excessively aggressive (e.g., boxing or tough-man brawling), we take a huge step toward moral reform and help sport to be an instrument of social improvement, not social disintegration.

Notes

1. Parry 1998, 223.
2. Ibid., 224.
3. De Wachter 1987, 19.
4. Ibid., 20.
5. Bushman et al. 1999, 367–368.
6. Harlow observed a rhesus monkey in a cage with two mother surrogates: one, having bicycle-reflector eyes, was made of terrycloth and looked somewhat like a rhesus monkey; the other was constructed of chicken wire that made any kind of tactile intimacy unattractive, though it had a baby's bottle with milk attached. The infant monkey clearly preferred the terrycloth surrogate. Harlow concluded that holding and cuddling were more important to the baby than feeding. In later observations, he found that female monkeys who matured with surrogates did not give maternal affection to their young. Often they beat and sometimes they even killed their infants. Harlow's observations show that contingencies of reinforcement during early childhood are responsible for dispositions toward aggressive behavior in later life (Bylinsky 1973, 141–142).
7. Repeated hippocampal stimulation seems to predispose individuals to behave aggressively. Moreover, lack of nurturant behavior toward infants results in underdeveloped or abnormally developed brains. Somatosensory deprivation, he believes, is responsible for damaged central nervous systems. More recent research confirms his speculations. For instance, we know that testosterone and other hormones affect the brain's structure and that environmental stressors increase levels of testosterone. Stressors to pregnant mothers give rise to elevate serum testosterone levels that affect testosterone levels of fetuses and thus predispose the fetal brain to aggression (Lewis 2000, 4).

8. Bylinsky 1973, 135.
9. Van der Dennen 2000, 22.
10. Edley and Wetherell 1995, 21.
11. Thorndike 1914, 350–351.
12. Hall 1996, 14.
13. Ibid., 15–17.
14. Hargreaves 1994, 146–147.
15. Edley and Wetherell 1995, 23–24.
16. Goldberg 1993, 150.
17. Ibid., 13–15. Desmond Morris (1999) and Konrad Lorenz (1997) have observed a link between aggression and maleness in other animals, which they explain by a common ancestral mechanism that favors aggression in males. Sexual division of labor, they believe, became biologically fixed so that one sex could hunt and protect, while the other cared for offspring.
18. Goldberg 1993, 64–65.
19. Addelson 1983, 148.
20. Lewis 2000, 5.
21. Kalın 1999, 30.
22. Sapolesky 1997, 45–50, and Bylinsky 1973, 135.
23. Edley and Wetherell 1995, 32–33.
24. Bylinsky 1973, 136.
25. Edley and Wetherell 1995, 29–30.
26. Addelson 1983, 148.

Bibliography

Addelson, Kathryn Pyne. (1983). "Equality and Competition: Can Sports Make a Woman of a Girl?" *Women, Philosophy, and Sport: A Collection of New Essays.* Metuchen, NJ: The Scarecrow Press, Inc., 133–211.

Bandura, Albert, Dorothea Ross, and Sheila A. Ross. (1961). "Transmission of Aggression through Imitation of Aggressive Models." *Journal of Abnormal and Social Psychology* 63, 575–582.

Bloom, Gordon A. and Michael D. Smith. (1996). "Hockey Violence: A Test of Cultural Spillover Theory." *Sociology of Sport Journal,* 13. Indianapolis, IN: Human Kinetics Publishers, Inc., 65–77.

Bushman, Brad J., Roy F. Baumeister, and Angela D. Stack. (1999). "Catharsis, Aggression, and Persuasive Influence: Self-Fulfilling or Self-Defeating Prophecies?" *http://www.apa.org/journals/psp/psp763367.html*

Bylinsky, Gene. (1973). "New Clues to the Causes of Violence," *Fortune,* January, 134–146.

Deardorff, Donald L. and Robert J. Sports Higgs. (2000). "Sports and Aggression." *Sports: A Reference Guide and Critical Commentary: 1980–1999.* Westport, CT: Greenwood Press.

Dennen, Johan M. G. van der. (2000). "Problems in the Concepts and Definitions of Aggression, Violence and Some Related Terms." *http://rint.rechten.tug.nl/rth/dennen/problem1.html*

De Wachter, Frans. (1987). "Education for Peace in Sports Education." *The Spirit of Sport; Essays about Sport and Values.* John W. Molloy, Jr. and Richard C. Adams (eds.). Bristol, IN: Wyndham Hall Press.

Edley, Nigel, and Margaret Wetherell. (1995). *Men in Perspective: Practice, Power and Identity.* New York: Prentice Hall.

Goldberg, Steven. (1993). *Why Men Rule: A Theory of Male Dominance.* Chicago: Open Court.

Hall, M. Ann (1996). *Feminism and Sporting Bodies: Essays on the Theory and Practice.* Champaign, IL.: Human Kinetics.

Hargreaves, Jennifer. (1994). *Sporting Females: Critical Issues in the History and Sociology of Women's Sports.* New York: Routledge.

Higgs, Robert. (1982). "Sports and Aggression." *Sports: A Reference Guide.* Westport, CT: Greenwood Press.

Horrocks, Roger. (1995). *Male Myths and Icons: Masculinity in Popular Culture.* New York: St. Martin's Press.

Humberstone, Barbara. (1990). "Warriors or Wimps? Creating Alternative Forms of Physical Education." *Sport, Men, and the Gender Order: Critical Feminist Perspectives.* Michael A. Messner and Don F. Sabo (eds.). Champaign, IL: Human Kinetics Books.

Kalin, Ned H. (1999). "Primate Models to Understand Human Aggression." *Journal of Clinical Psychiatry* 60, 29–32.

Kaplan, Melissa (3 June 2000). "Testosterone, Aggression, and Green Iguanas." *http://www.sonic.net/~melissk/testosterone.html*

Lewis, Dorothy. (2000). "From Abuse to Violence: Psychophysiological Consequences of Maltreatment." *http://www.org/wgbh/pages/frontline/shows/little/readings/*

Lorenz, Konrad. (1996). *On Aggression.* New York: Bantam Books.

Messner, Mike (1996). "The Meaning of Success: The Athletic Experience and the Development of Male Identity." Sport in Contemporary Society: An Anthology. D. Stanley Eitzen (ed.). New York: St. Martin's Press, 373–388.

Morris, Desmond. (1967). *The Naked Ape: A Zoologist's Study of the Human Animal.* New York: Dell Publishing.

Parry, Jim. (1998). "Violence and Aggression in Contemporary Sport." *Ethics and Sport.* Scott McNamee and Jim Parry (eds.). London: E & F Spon, 205–224.

Sapolesky, Robert. (1997). "Testosterone Rules." *Discover* 18:3, 45–50.

Sipes, Richard Grey. (1996). "Sports as a Control for Aggression." *Sport in Contemporary Society: An Anthology.* D. Stanley Eitzen (ed.). New York: St. Martin's Press, 154–160.

Questions for Consideration

1. Does the reading sufficiently address M. Ann Hall's worries about reductionism and the dichotomous view of sex?

2. In the main, how successful are the reading's arguments against culture-pattern approaches to sex or gender differences?

3. How compelling is Goldberg's historical argument for sex-related behavioral differences?

4. Do you think that positing a biological component to explain sex-related differences in aggression could be used effectively to exculpate males from violent behavior in society?

5. What specific proposals for reform could you add to the broad claims made at the end of the reading?

41 Sport in the Larger Scheme of Things

William J. Morgan
University of Tennessee Knoxville

This reading is a postscript in a book by William J. Morgan titled Leftist Theories of Sport: A Critique and Reconstruction. *The question Morgan addresses in this addendum is the value of sport in today's societies. In other words, the question of inclusion of sport in societies has been presupposed throughout the book and now is the time to justify this presupposition.*

What makes well-ordered societies thrive today, Morgan states, is the notion of pluralism—that well-ordered societies allow as many social practices as they can support in order to allow for diversity and fullness of life. The obvious problem is that no society can afford too much diversity without the advent of difficulties. If we take up one practice, for instance, it may have to come at the expense of another. So in order to deal with limited social resources, it seems reasonable to restrict the first principle to a consideration of only those practices that contribute most to human flourishing. What these practices are is not for the state to assess normatively, but for civil society under the auspices of the state to decide.

The overall scheme meshes liberalism with socialism. First, the socialist element: Pluralism is best realized when societies are structured in a decentralized and democratic manner. Instead of individuals running about in accordance with their own desires, society is arranged to promote indi-

viduation and autonomy. Second, the liberal element: The state itself must be neutral as regards any notion of particular good, though it may have something to say about a more general good. The state may endorse and sponsor particular goods, but it may not evaluate them.

Within the ideal of a decentralized democratic society (the socialist element), there is a realm of necessity and a realm of social perfectionism. The former realm encompasses all such practices that deal with material production. The latter realm promotes excellences. Sportive practice belongs to the realm of social perfectionism. Overall, Morgan claims that some level of sportive activity is necessary in healthy decentralized democratic societies.

Two guiding aims have shaped this treatise. The first was a deconstructive one that sought to dismantle two of the leading currents of critical sport theory, New Left and hegemony sport theory respectively, and to decipher what was problematic and unproblematic in each. The second was a reconstructive one that built an alternative critical theory of sport, one able to meet the objections leveled against its predecessors and a sufficiently robust one able to put the social criticism of sport on a new and surer argumentative footing. In this postscript I would like to add some final words about my reconstructed theory of sport and address a possible question about its present justification.

The justification I offered for my reconstructed critical theory of sport was an internal one. I invoked the internal logic of sport and the "inside" rational deliberations of its practice-community to justify the demarcation of the boundaries of its practice and the imposition of normative blocks on the conduct of its institutions. This mode of justification is obviously circular; it promises to provide a new ground for a critical theory of sport by petitioning its distinctive rational order and then proceeds to justify this new critical venture by petitioning this very same rational order. But it is not its circularity that is problematic. Circularity is the price that must be paid when theory eschews a God's-eye perspective on practices like sport. That is because giving up such a perspective means that one must begin with social practices themselves, and I have offered compelling reasons why beginning with the internal logic of sport is the critical place to begin our investigations of sport.

That I justify my theory of sport by appealing to rational elements that are intrinsic to it is also not objectionable because it is self-validating—because it merely endorses our existing crop of sporting practices just as they are practiced. To be sure, there is always a danger that in criticizing a practice like sport from the inside out one may unwittingly provide a status-quo justification of it. If one were to pick the wrong features of sport—say, its institutional features—to serve as the standards of one's critical analysis of it, one would have little to say about sport that is genuinely critical. In such cases, the immanent critic of sport merely replaces the "epistemological myth of the given" of her transcendent counterpart, who believes there are some privileged ahistorical ideals that can be tapped to criticize sport, with her no less pernicious "historical myth of the given," the myth that one can criticize sport by appealing to its putative features, by using, in effect, the tools and resources of the apologist. But my pointed appeal to the logic of sport and to the discursive inclinations of its practice-community was designed to guard against this very thing, to undercut any status-quo justification of sport. So it is not self-validating in this apologetic sense, at least not obviously so.

But there is one troubling sense in which my immanent justification of a new critical theory of sport is self-validating. It presupposes that sport, or at least some variation of it, warrants our support in the first place, that it is a worthwhile enterprise that deserves our full sanction. It can hardly avoid this question-begging implication, since by making the logic of its practice and the *litige* of its devoted followers the twin pillars of its critical treatment of sport, it ensures that sport in one form or another will be validated as a legitimate human undertaking. This self-validating presumption is a significant one because it imposes an unacceptable limit on the social criticism of sport: it prevents the critic from asking whether we would all be better off without sport, whether, in the larger scheme of things, sport merits a place in our hearts and in the social fabric of our culture.

In order to get around this curb on the social criticism of sport so that we might ask probing questions of the foregoing sort, I propose an additional justification of my reconstructed theory, a more open-textured and inclusive one.[1] This mode of justification takes the larger, rather than the internal, measure of sport, to see how it connects up with everything else. A good way to assess whether practices like sport are really worth the candle is to ratchet the analysis up a notch and consider how the goods specific to one practice mesh with the goods specific to other practices, to ascertain how they all fit together into some coherent pattern or whole. It is only by taking this larger measure of practices like sport, I contend, that we can adequately determine which practices deserve our assent and support and which our rebuke and censure.

The larger justificatory measure I propose to take of sport is itself an open-ended, somewhat imprecise, and underdetermined one. It does not seek to situate sport in an elaborate and detailed grid that purports to rank its comparative goodness over that of other practices in some precise fashion. Rather, it seeks to justify the inclusion of sport in societies in good working order on the liberal ideal of pluralism. The ideal of pluralism is the ideal that society should keep alive as many social practices as it can reasonably support, that a well-ordered society is a society that is able to give its members a wide range of forms of life to choose from so that each may lead an engaging and rich life. The problem, of course, is that there is no social world without loss, that no social order or culture can include within itself all forms of life, and that even those it is able to take under its wings cannot be supported in the same way and to the same degree.[2]

How are we to decide which to support, which to reject, or which simply to let wither away? The answer supplied by the liberal ideal of pluralism is a two-pronged one. First, as I mention above, society should support as many social practices as it can—the more the better. Here, the epigram "less is more," popularized by environmentalists, doesn't hold weight; it is rather the other way around: more is more and less is less. So a well-ordered society is on this first count at least an open and radically tolerant one, accepting as much diversity as it can possibly handle, and being as inclusive as it can possibly be. The second prong takes hold, however, when we begin to run out of social space to house these different forms of life. In this instance, only those practices and endeavors that make some claim on us, that contribute the most to human flourishing, that enrich, enliven, enlarge, and enhance our lives the most deserve our support. By contrast, those that no longer resonate with our social being, that are no longer found uplifting and compelling, are to be left to succumb to the process of social attrition that governs all practices in a well-ordered society. Here radical resonance rather than radical tolerance is called for.

There are obvious difficulties with each prong of this answer. With respect to the first, it might be argued that giving members of society too many choices, too many forms of life from which to choose, is more confusing and paralyzing than it is uplifting and liberating. Though there is some force to this retort, it is hardly decisive. Pluralism is best understood and defended not as an effort to present a dizzying array of choices to a populace befuddled by the choices, but as an argument against narrowing the good life to a select few forms of life. It aims to undercut the Right, which gives pride of place to religion; the Left, which wishes to privilege the workplace; the capitalist, who favors the market; and the civic republican and the communitarian, who prefer the political realm.

With respect to the second prong, it might be rejoined that it asks too much of society, that it calls for a public ranking of the intrinsic value of different forms of life that it is ill-equipped to carry out. There is some force to this argument as well, but it is misdirected. The pluralism I speak of argues that while the state is not equipped to make such qualitative rankings, civil society— what Walzer labels the "space of uncoerced human association," "the setting of settings"[3]—is so equipped, and, when left properly to its own devices and not impeded by the coercive apparatus of the state, it engages in these sorts of deep and complicated normative assessments all the time. This is the realm in which different practice-communities make their partisan pitches for support, vie for scarce resources, and are forced to adjudicate conflicts among the goods of the forms of life they embody (many of which are borne by the same practitioners who happen to be members of different practice-communities). So only those forms of life that are able to secure the democratic sanction of civil society, of the practitioners of its varied practices, will be confirmed as life-enriching ones and supported as such.

It is pluralism that justifies the inclusion of sport in well-ordered societies. This larger justification of sport is a liberal one, but only partly so. There are two parts to this justificatory scheme, and each is an admixture of liberal and socialist elements to varying degrees. The first is largely socialist and to a lesser degree liberal. It argues that the ideal of pluralism is best realized not, as some liberals hold, when individuals are left to their own devices to actuate unfettered choices, but when society is arranged in a "decentralized democratic socialist" manner that protects social practices from unwarranted encroachment.[4]

What is liberal about this democratic socialist arrangement is, of course, that it is anchored in the liberal ideal of pluralism. The second part is largely liberal and to a lesser degree socialist. It argues that the ideal of pluralism is best realized in a liberally conceived state, that is, a state that is neutral regarding the different and competing conceptions of the good entertained in civil society. What is socialist about this liberal state is that it is more intrusive than most liberal theorists would allow, that it has the license to intervene in the adjudication of competing forms of the good life when such intervention is itself necessary to safeguard a pluralistic society.

Let's begin with the decentralized democratic socialist part of my justificatory scheme. A decentralized socialist arrangement is one in which the practice-communities of social practices and the local settings of instrumental activities are granted democratic control over their respective undertakings. I now want to consider this arrangement, however, not from the eye of any one particular practice-community, not from the inside out, but from the collective eyes of all such prospective communities, from the outside in. I do so by grouping these autonomous communities into two larger realms. The first realm I call, after Marx, the realm of necessity, which comprises all the instrumental and service activities of a society that contribute to its material production and reproduction.[5] The second realm I call, after Rawls, the realm of social perfectionism, which comprises all the practices of a society that contribute to the advancement of human excellence in its various forms.[6] My reason for separating the materially productive activities from the perfectionist practices of society is that each realm requires, as we shall shortly see, a different form of pluralist justification.

The realm of necessity, as Marx tells us, is so named because it is the social space in which the different instrumental activities by which we seek to satisfy our material needs are situated. What the ideal of pluralism calls for in this material sphere of life is a constrained market controlled by the workers and an autonomous service sector

of medical and clinical care governed at least in part by local volunteers. Only a democratically run workplace and service sector will ensure a variety of instrumental activities to meet our material and social needs, and an open and public mechanism to evaluate the value of the services rendered. It will promote pluralism outside the realm of necessity by blocking the use of market models to direct noninstrumental practices. And it will promote pluralism within the realm of necessity by preventing the domination of the market and service spheres by capital-rich entrepreneur types. A democratically governed marketplace can avail itself of a number of different market agents to meet the needs of its members: from family businesses, to publicly owned companies, to consumer cooperatives and various nonprofit organizations.[7] Local control and democratic voice thus count here for greater diversity, not less. So at least in the material affairs of society, pluralism and democratic socialism make for a good marriage.

The realm of social perfectionism encompasses, as I suggest above, the different practices that claim excellence as their trademark. Since these practices are once removed from the material demands that occupy instrumental activities, they have nothing directly to do with the material production of society nor with the crafting of useful objects and services. Further, since these activities are not burdened with the material constraints that instrumental activities have to answer to, their pursuit of excellence is largely a gratuitous affair. This suggests a link between what Rawls calls perfectionist pursuits and what MacIntyre calls social practices. MacIntyre, it will be recalled, defines social practices as skillfull, virtue-laden endeavors that seek, each in its own inimitable way, excellence. So it seems plausible to argue that the sphere of social perfectionism is co-extensive with the sphere of social practices, the paradigmatic forms of which include, according to MacIntyre, games, sports, the sciences, architecture, farming, historical research, politics (in Aristotle's sense only), painting, and music.[8]

What the ideal of pluralism requires in this

sphere is also autonomously governed practice-communities, but this time in order to ensure an abundant life of excellence as opposed to an abundant material life. Turning control of social practices over to their votaries will likely have this effect since this is the only way to guarantee that every practice will get a hearing, and an informed and partisan one at that, as to its intrinsic merits. Going for local control will also promote pluralism outside of each practice within this sphere by minimizing the intrusion of practice-communities in the *litige* of other practice-communities. It will further encourage pluralism within each practice by prohibiting ruling elites from dominating the deliberative proceedings of practice-communities and by keeping at bay institutional forces of normalization. Once again, diversity and democratic socialist control seem tailored to each other's special interests and concerns rather than antipodes.

If pluralism is the right justificatory device here, then any society that fails to make some provision for excellence, for practices that make its pursuit their central aim, is a deficient society. Further, if it is plausible to count sport among those practices dedicated to excellence and its appropriate advancement, then any society that fails to make some provision for sport is a deficient society as well. Just how much support practices like sport will be able to garner in such a pluralist society is difficult to say. This is a matter to be reckoned with in civil society, in the social setting of settings in which the collective deliberations of practice-communities take place and in which the good of the forms of life they embody are evaluated and debated. Since these conversations are first conceived and propelled by the votaries of these different practices, spirited discussions will ensue. There is always the danger that things might get out of hand, that the fervor with which such discussions are engaged might get in the way of reasoned discourse. This is a danger precisely because it constitutes a genuine threat to pluralism. Although such fervor is in one sense encouraged by the democratic socialist arrangement I am arguing for, insofar as it promotes partisan championing of the goods of particular practices, it is also stemmed by that arrangement, insofar as socialized communities secure within their own demarcated spheres are less likely to be intimidated by such partisan clashes, and more apt to understand, if not appreciate, what accounts for their fervor.[9] So while it can't be reasonably claimed that sport will play a large role in a democratically ordered society that takes the claims of pluralism seriously, it can be reasonably claimed, I contend, that it will play some determinate role in such a society. It can be further reasonably claimed that that role will be greater in a society that gives scope to partisan advocacy of practices and that disempowers practice-communities from using the coercive power of the state to ensure themselves a piece of the action, than a society that denies such partisan advocacy and that allows the state to interject itself in the reflective process of evaluating the worth of social practices.

It is apparent from what I have said thus far that a pluralist society is synonymous with a well-ordered one, and that a well-ordered society is synonymous with a carefully demarcated one that is subject to the local control of socialized communities. We know that we live in such a society when the instrumental undertakings vital to its well being and the perfectionist pursuits vital to its excellence fall into the hands of their proper constituencies, that is, when workers preside over our workplaces, believers over our churches and synagogues, scholars over our universities, artists over our galleries, and athletes and their devotees over our sports.[10] This is the way a truly pluralist society—and on my account the way a justified society that accords a place for sport within it—is supposed to look and function. But the picture is not quite complete. A pluralist society also needs a state to protect and nurture its diverse and democratically controlled practices. However, not just any sort of state will do; it must be one that looks and functions like a liberal state. It is to a consideration of such a state then, and to the role it plays in the justification of practices like sport, that I now turn.

Why a pluralist society requires a liberal state

rather than some other version of this political body has to do with the two central features that such a state must possess if it is to encourage, rather than discourage, true diversity. First, the state must be a chastened one; it must conduct itself in a manner that befits the delimited role it is to play in presiding over the affairs of civil society. Specifically, it is to conduct itself as a regulatory agency, correcting unforeseen and unseemly outcomes or patching up structural defects that plague the social networks of civil society, not a normative one. It is to stay out of the business of ranking the intrinsic value of forms of life because its intrusion is likely to impede rather than foster pluralism. The second feature that a state congenial to pluralism must possess is a capacity to exert some real influence on social forces that stifle diversity; it must be able to intercede effectively on behalf of practices and their votaries when their forms of life are unduly threatened by systemic imperatives. If it is unable to mobilize itself in this manner, the interests of pluralism will be seriously jeopardized.

So it seems that the state most conducive to a pluralist society is a neutral rather than a perfectionist one. And if that is so, then a liberal state is what we want. A liberal state is defined by its principled neutrality, its studied indifference to the different goods that circulate in civil society. It is this cultivated indifference that ensures that whatever action the state takes in managing the daily detail of social life will be of a regulative rather than a normative sort.

It might be quickly rejoined that while a liberal state so conceived meets the nonperfectionist requirement of a pluralist-friendly state, it fails the regulative-activist requirement of such a state. The problem here is the neutrality of the state itself, which nullifies its regulative role by forbidding it to act on any conception of the good. This is so, it is argued, on two grounds. First, a neutral state is one whose justification excludes reference to any conception of the good. Second, a neutral state is one in which all particular conceptions of the good must fare equally well. Taken together, these suggest that if the state is to maintain its vaunted neutrality toward the good, it must refrain from doing anything. If it takes some action then it must either appeal to some good to justify its intervention, lest it be subject to the charge of arbitrary intercession, or face the ineluctable fact that the action it took could not avoid advancing some conceptions of the good over others. A neutral state is for all intents and purposes, therefore, a paralyzed, dormant state.

This rejoinder fails on both counts because it misconstrues what the neutrality of the state entails. To begin with, to say that the state must remain neutral is not to say that it is disallowed from making reference to *any* conception of the good, but only reference to any *particular* conception of the good. So it can perfectly well justify its intervention in the social world by appealing to a general, common conception of the good. With regard to the second point, to say that the state must remain neutral is not to say that all particular conceptions of the good must fare equally well under its jurisdiction, but only that the state is to refrain from doing anything whose stated aim is to promote or assist one form of the good over, and at the expense of, other forms of the good. The state, in other words, is required to maintain ideological neutrality in its dealings with particular conceptions of the good (what some theorists call "justificatory neutrality" or "neutrality of grounds"), but it is not required, per impossible, to advance all conceptions of the good equally (what some theorists call "consequential neutrality" or "neutrality of effects").[11] No social agency, least of all the state, can intervene in the course of social life without influencing, positively or negatively, particular conceptions of the good, but the state can so intervene, and be expected to so intervene, so as to effect only the common good—bracketing whatever the particular results of that intervention may turn out to be.

If a state can prevail upon the social world without violating its neutrality, then a liberal state that prides itself on its neutrality can surely do the same without pain of contradiction. If that is so, then, as I suggest above, a liberal state is congenial to the interests of a pluralist society. It can intervene in civil society by endorsing and sponsoring certain instrumental undertakings and social practices as long as its justification for doing so is not to advance the particular forms of the good they embody—though, to be sure, this is likely to be the effect of its intervention—but to advance the good of pluralism itself. Yet it cannot so intervene willy-nilly; it can endorse and sponsor, but not evaluate, activities of this sort only under certain specified conditions, and these conditions vary somewhat depending on whether one's reference is the realm of necessity or the realm of perfectionism.

In the material sphere of life, the state may not intercede to bolster market and service arrangements that no longer curry favor with the relevant communities. Nor may it intercede to remedy mere disparities of income or life style that may justifiably be taken to be rewards of success in the market. But it may intervene, I argue, when such market disparities—the fact that some people have more money and fancier cars than others—translate into social domination, when, that is, the monied are able to exert undue influence over the lives of the unmonied. If families, churches, unions, worker communes, and the like are unable to offset the pernicious effects of such market-induced social domination, then the state is permitted to use its offices to neutralize or overturn these effects, and its justification for doing so is pluralism. Dominated social groups who lack the material wherewithal to make and enact meaningful choices severely limit their own, and their society's, diversity. At the very least, this requires a strong welfare state administered by both state officials and local volunteers. A privately run welfare system would be woefully inadequate, and a nationalistically run welfare system would discount the voice of local groups and communities.[12]

In the sphere of perfectionist practices, the state is similarly debarred from propping up practices that have lost favor with their relevant practice-communities, that no longer resonate with those communities. Nor is it permitted to meddle in the social accretion and attrition process that goes on as a matter of course in civil society in which practices are variously added to and deleted from our repertoire of perfectionist pursuits. But it does have license to intercede on behalf of particular practices and their communities that are imperiled by social domination, and its license derives once again from the ideal of pluralism. In this case, social domination springs either from monopolies that control resources necessary to put on and conduct perfectionist endeavors (the problem of scarce resources) or from structural defects in society that allow for illicit conversion of goods, for the invasion of one sphere by another sphere; the net effect of both is to limit the diversity of social practices and that of their social settings. In the case of scarce resources, the state may offer, for example, tax credits to individuals who invest in such practices, or undertake modest shifts in distribution of income to support a wider range of social practices. In the case of structural defects, the state's principal role is to enforce existing partitions and to encourage and empower practice-communities to fortify old ones and, if necessary, to build new ones. We can hardly afford for the state to do less, if, that is, we expect to keep endangered ways of living that still resonate with people in meaningful ways from becoming extinct.

This is how a pluralist society would look and function from the standpoint of the state. When conjoined with my above account of a pluralistically ordered civil society, we get a glimpse of the total picture and an idea of the way a fully justified society that reserves an important social space for sport would look and function. It is just such a well-ordered society, in which a perfectionist civil society works in tandem with a neutral state to promote pluralism, that provides the most compelling justification, in the larger sense intended, of perfectionist practices like sport.

The choice we face here, as before, is a rather stark one. We can either, as Stout tells us, "transform our social practices and institutions in quite particular ways, exerting humane control over [them] . . . or . . . find ourselves out of the action."[13] I have offered one scheme for inserting ourselves back in the action. The immanent and synoptic backing I provide is meant to disarm the right-wing skeptic who is inclined to reject all such proposals for social change as pie-in-the-sky nonsense and the left-wing skeptic who is inclined to reject all liberally tinged proposals for social change. It is also meant, of course, to persuade less ideologically disposed skeptics and doubters that this is one promising way to address some of the serious social problems that currently confront sport and the like. It is in this critical and practical spirit that I invite the reader to ponder its merits, criticize its shortcomings, and join in the dialogue and effort to undo the degradation that practices like sport have had to suffer for too long.

Notes

1. I also offer this latter justificatory effort to correct a possible misapprehension that might arise from my use of the liberal art of separation to this point. In arguing for a separation of sport from unwholesome outside influences I am *not* implying that efforts to locate connections between practices like sport are dismal, meaningless, and ideological exercises. I do hold that the present institutionally driven constellation of social forces makes it imperative to wall off practices like sport from their pervasive influence. The implication to be drawn from this is not that looking for linkages between practices is an ideologically suspect thing to do, but only that denying distinctions between them is. My full view is that the assimilationist tendencies and biases of the current social system require that we first understand what marks social undertakings off from one another before we can tackle the question of what it is that binds them together.

2. On the notion of social loss, see John Rawls, "The Priority of Right and Ideas of the Good," *Philosophy and Public Affairs* 17 (Fall 1988): p. 265.

3. Michael Walzer, "The Idea of a Civil Society," *Dissent* (Spring 1991): pp. 293, 298.

4. On the notion of a "decentralized democratic socialism" see Michael Walzer, *Spheres of Justice* (New York: Basic Books, 1983), p. 318.

5. Karl Marx, *Capital, Volume 3* (New York: International Publishers, 1977), p. 820.

6. John Rawls, *A Theory of Justice* (Cambridge, Mass.: Harvard University Press, 1971), pp. 25, 325–32.

7. I owe these examples to Walzer, "The Idea of a Civil Society," p. 300.

8. Alasdair MacIntyre, *After Virtue* (Notre Dame, Ind.: University of Notre Dame Press, 1984), p. 187. Farming is the one entry on this list that strains the apparent connection between perfectionist pursuits and social practices. This is not because farming is a stranger to excellence, but because its instrumental demeanor suggests a closer link to material pursuits than perfectionist ones.

9. Walzer makes a similar argument in his essay "Liberalism and the Art of Separation," *Political Theory* 12 (August 1984): 329. Even this socialist part of my argument is laced with liberal influences. The notion that practice-communities that are secure within their own settings are less likely to be disturbed by, or interfere with, the affairs of other practice-communities is merely, as Walzer tells us, "the socialist form of the old liberal hope that individuals secure in their own circles won't invade the circles of others." Ibid., p. 329.

10. Ibid., p. 327.

11. For various renditions of this distinction see Will Kymlicka, "Liberal Individualism and Liberal Neutrality," *Ethics* 99 (July 1989): 883–905; John Rawls, "The Priority of the Right and Ideas of the Good," *Philosophy and Public Affairs* 17 (Fall 1988): 251–76; Peter De Marneffe, "Liberalism, Liberty, and Neutrality," *Philosophy and Public Affairs* 19 (Summer 1990): pp. 253–74.

12. I owe this point to Michael Walzer, "The Communitarian Critique of Liberalism," *Political Theory* 18 (February 1990): p. 18.

13. Jeffrey Stout, *Ethics After Babel* (Boston: Beacon Press, 1988), p. 277.

Questions for Consideration

1. What is Morgan's argument for the inclusion of sports in a decentralized democratic society? Assess the strength of this argument.

2. What precisely does Morgan think is the role of the state as regards material practices? What is its role concerning perfectionist practices?

3. What does Morgan mean in saying that the well-ordered state itself provides the best justification of inclusion of sportive practices within it?

42 Democracy, Education, and Sport

Peter J. Arnold
Moray House College

In this presidential address before the Philosophic Society for the Study of Sport in 1989, Peter J. Arnold essays to make some clarificatory remarks on the interrelationship between democracy, education, and sport.

Democracy, he asserts, is a form of government that is fundamentally based upon freedom, human dignity, and equality. At its moral base, Arnold's political egalitarianism is rooted in the Kantian imperative which mandates that we always treat others as ends and never as means to some end.

What safeguards the democratic ideals is liberal education—so named because it liberates its beneficiary. Though its aim, through cultivation of reason and autonomy, is nonutilitarian, it does have practical consequences. Informed judgments are likely to be better than uninformed ones. Moreover, reasoned criticism and review of public policy are essential to democratic ideals and prosperity. There is also a moral dimension that is characterized by rational benevolence, universality, impartiality, and liberty of expression.

Rationality, Arnold asserts, comprises theoretical and practical reasoning. Sportive activity is a type of practical rationality that involves physical activity and certain internal goods, such as justice and fairness, that extend a person's human development. Sport, then, enables individuals to fulfill their own potential while respecting the dignity and needs of others. Consequently, it should be a possible avenue of human expression for individuals who want such expression.

Reprinted, by permission, from P. J. Arnold, "Democracy, Education, and Sport," *Journal of the Philosophy of Sport* XVI (1989), 100–110.

It is my purpose in this paper to examine the relationship between democracy, education, and sport. First, I shall look at the meaning of democracy; second, I will explore the nature of education and show how the democratic ideal is dependent upon it; and third, I shall argue that sport not only instantiates a part of what it is to be educated but that its provision as a matter of social policy helps fulfill the democratic process.

The Meaning of Democracy

The term democracy has been dismissed as notoriously useless yet it remains one that is important. It probably originated in the fifth century B.C. as the name given to a system of government to be found among the Greek city-states. It referred then to rule by or of the people. Democracies were regimes in which citizenship, or the possession of a right to participate in public affairs, was widely shared among "the many." At this time democracies were contrasted with rule by the few (oligarchy), the nobility (aristocracy), the one (monarchy), and an unconstitutional dictator (tyranny). What characterized democracy was the right of all to decide what were matters of general concern.

Much of what is meant by democracy today can be conveyed in three phrases. The first, "by the people," provides a criterion by which the institutions and procedures of government can be checked upon to see whether or not they embody and express the will of those governed. The second phrase, "for the people," provides a criterion to examine whether or not those in office are in fact making decisions, passing laws, and voting effectively and in the best interests of the people as a whole. The third phrase, "of the people," provides a criterion to see whether or not, both in government and in other institutions, recruits are being drawn from persons of every kind of social background.

What is clear is that today democracy is a term of approval, although this was not always the case,[1] and that, despite the many political and social contexts in which the term is used, to say that an idea or an institution is democratic is to implicitly commend it. Can some features be pointed to over and above those already outlined that would help test and verify whether or not government (or some other institution, such as the law or education) is democratic? The following questions are perhaps helpful. Are elections free and held periodically? Has every citizen the right to vote? Are parties and candidates entitled to stand in opposition to those in office? Is the voter protected against intimidation by the secrecy of the ballot? Does a majority vote against the party in power lead to a change of government? Has the elected body the right to vote taxes and control the budget, deciding such matters, if necessary, by majority vote? Does the elected body have the right to publicly question, discuss, criticize, and oppose government measures without being subject to threats of interference or arrest?

What emerges from such features, posed in the form of questions, is that democracy is based on the belief that each human being is of value, and that each citizen is guaranteed certain rights that operate in practice and are not just formal: such human rights as security against arbitrary arrest and imprisonment, freedom of speech, of the press, television, and other forms of media, as well as of assembly; freedom of petition and association (i.e., the right to form parties, trade unions, and other societies); freedom of movement and freedom of religion and teaching. A corollary of democracy, as Bullock (5: p. 161) points out, is the establishment of an independent judiciary and courts to which everyone can have access.

If this somewhat sketchy picture of democracy can be accepted as being reasonably representative, it will be seen that two general social principles underpin it, those of freedom and equality. Freedom is important because it allows the views and opinions of each citizen to be expressed. Equality is important because it recognizes the right of every citizen to be heard. The democratic process I suggest is embodied in the detailed implementation of these two principles. Helm put neatly the nub of what has so far been upheld by observing that

> If people are to be free and equal in the determination of the conditions of their own lives, and enjoy equal rights as well as equal obligations in the specification of the framework which generates and limits the opportunities available to them, they must be in a position to enjoy a range of rights not only in principle, but also in practice. (10: p. 284)

Freedom of discussion is not just a safeguard against the abuse of authority but a condition of democracy itself. Similarly, equality of opportunity and consideration for all is not just a pious slogan but one of the bulwarks upon which the idea of democracy rests. The moral justification of democracy lies in the extent to which the individual person is accorded and given respect. Governments and institutions, if they are to be considered democratic, should be able to meet the test of whether or not they are able to defend their legislative programs and policies in terms of Kant's imperative: "Act that you treat humanity in your own person and in the person of everyone else always at the same time as an end and never merely as a means" (11: p. 46).

What is being invoked here is that in a democratic society the welfare of all people will be equally considered and that no group of people will be deliberately favored or privileged at the expense of another. A safe rule to follow is that all people or groups of people should be treated the same, unless there are relevant reasons for treating them differently. Few democrats would disagree with the notion, for example, that the poor should have access to legal aid in times of trouble, or that the handicapped should not in some respects be treated differently.

At the heart of the democratic ideal is the belief that all people regardless of their color, race, or creed should be respected, not only because this is desirable in itself but because they are the centers of consciousness; their distinctive points of view and choice are important to society if it is to remain an open and caring one. What is being suggested then is that respect for persons is a principle summarizing an attitude that helps identify what it is to be democratic. For a government or institution to treat an individual or group as being unworthy of respect or only as an instrument is not only to be morally reprehensible but to be undemocratic. Democracy then is perhaps best understood as a form of society in which respect among members is both given and received. This will be evident in the legislative programs its government proposes as well as in the procedures by means of which decisions are made.

Democracy and Education

It has been suggested that democracy is more than just a form of government. It is also a sociocultural, a moral, way of life in which persons are free to associate in various ways and to express their mature interests and concerns. Certainly, Dewey recognized this latter aspect of democracy. He wrote,

> The keynote of democracy as a way of life may be expressed . . . as the necessity for the participation of every mature human being in formation of the values that regulate the living of men together; which is necessary from the standpoint of both the social welfare and the full development of human beings as individuals. (9: p. 28)

In his *Democracy and Education*, Dewey (8: p. v) set out to "detect and state the ideas implied in a democratic society and apply these ideas to the problems and enterprise of education." He was among the first to show that democracy and education were intimately linked. Dewey saw that if the forthcoming citizens of a democratic society were to play a full part in its deliberations they must learn (a) how to responsibly and effectively participate and (b) to do so preferably with enlightened understanding.

Bearing in mind these two requirements, the question arises, What form of education is appropriate to a democratic society in which a premium is put upon individual responsibility and community welfare? My answer to this question, briefly put, is "liberal education." But what is a liberal education? and why is this so? A full answer to each of these questions will not be possible here, but an outline sketch will be provided.

Liberal Education

A liberal education is concerned with the liberation of the person who receives it. The classical Greeks saw it as freeing the mind from error and illusion and freeing the person's conduct from wrong doing. It was the type of education the free man received and is to be contrasted with what is sometimes called vocational training. Traditionally, a liberal education is characterized by its demand for the exercise of a person's intellectual capacities, its apparent nonutilitarian significance, its absence of narrow specialization, and intrinsic motivating appeal. More recently, Bailey has strikingly exclaimed that "A liberal education liberates *from* the tyranny of the present and particular and liberates *for* the ideal of the autonomous, rational, moral agent (3:p. 22)."

The paradox of a liberal education is that although it is concerned with doing things because they are in themselves worthwhile, it has the utilitarian benefit of being of crucial importance in the conduct of everyday affairs. This is because, in developing knowledge and understanding about the world for its own sake, it will necessarily, in a fundamental sense, prepare people for life and how best to live it.

Peters (17: p. 45) in an attempt to provide criteria for what it is to be liberally educated, suggests (a) that it implies the transmission of what is worthwhile, (b) that it must involve knowledge and understanding, and (c) that it rules out some procedures of transmission on the grounds that they lack willingness and voluntariness on the part of the learner.

A liberal education, then, presupposes that it will in some way transform an individual for the better; that it gives reason and reasoning a central place; that it only countenances those methods of learning that involve the willing participation of the pupil. Another way of expressing what is being maintained here is by saying that a liberal education is concerned with the initiation of pupils into a worthwhile form of life, particularly with regard to knowledge and understanding, in such a way that it is morally defensible. The detailed implications of such a view cannot be embarked upon here. Two strands, however, will be picked out and explicated. The first relates to rationality; the second, to morality. It will be seen that both have important implications for citizens in a democratic society.

Rationality. Rationality is usually associated with the idea of enlightened understanding. It is concerned with the giving of reasons, whether in the realm of science or in the realm of human action. To describe an argument as rational is to say something about the process of reasoning involved in it. It is concerned with an attempt to get at the truth of why something occurred, be it to do with an avalanche in the Alps or the death of a neighbor. To provide a rational explanation about an event or instance of conduct does not guarantee its truth but is an attempt to explain something in a reasonable way. Barrow and Woods suggest that "A rational argument is . . . one that proceeds logically, that is to say in which each step of the argument as given follows from the preceding step, and in which the reasons that are used to move from the premises to the conclusion are good reasons (4: p. 83). Of greater interest, they note that:

An argument may fall short of being rational in a number of ways: it may refuse to take account of the pertinent evidence that would upset it; it may lay stress on irrelevant evidence; it may appeal to emotion rather than reason; it may contain contradictions and inconsistencies; or it may contain illogical steps. (4: p. 83)

All in all it can be said that rationality is a central identifying feature of a liberal education because it places special emphasis on a person's rational capacities and a special belief in the importance of reason and rational argument.

A liberal education, on grounds of the rationality it upholds and aims to cultivate, is of fundamental importance to a democracy for at least two reasons. The first is that sound choices are more likely to be made if they are based on informed judgment and reason rather than upon uninformed opinion, passion, or prejudice. The ignorant and gullible are always liable to be more readily exploited and indoctrinated than the educated. Surely Burke (6: p. 341) was right when he observed that "government and legislation are matters of reason and judgement, and not of inclination." The second reason that a liberal education is of importance to a democracy is that it allows one to see the need for and insist upon the institutionalization of reasoned procedures for the critical and public review of policy. Rationality insists upon accountability for the way in which societal and community affairs are conducted. Rationality, as an inbuilt part of the democratic ideal, insists, as Scheffler (19: p. 137) put it, "that judgements of policy be viewed not as the fixed privilege of any class or elite but as the common task of all, and it requires the supplanting of arbitrary and violent alteration of policy with institutionally channeled change ordered by reasoned persuasion and informed consent."

Morality. The second strand of a liberal education that was suggested as having important implications for a democratic society is that of morality. It is very much connected to the point made earlier about how to responsibly and effectively participate in a democratic society. Without some moral education the citizen may be tempted to act only in his own interests at the expense of the interests of others. If this were the case, such underlying democratic principles as freedom and equality would be at risk and the idea and practice of social justice endangered. It is because a liberal education is inherently concerned with the moral element in life that in pursuing its own ends it indirectly serves democracy. What it is important to emphasize here is that a liberal education is not a tool of democracy: It is rather a condition for its survival.

What then is morality and moral education? In broad terms it can be said that morality is concerned with our relations with others. It involves our consideration and concern for the welfare of others as well as for the welfare and interests of ourselves. It is concerned with how to distinguish right from wrong and good from bad. Morality is involved with values and principles to which reference can be made before making a decision or engaging upon a particular course of action. Such principles as universality, impartiality, rational benevolence, and liberty are frequently pointed to as underpinning the character of moral discourse and action. Universality and impartiality imply that whatever is recommended by way of prescription should be applicable to all in a fair way. Rational benevolence recognizes the importance of reason giving as well as recognizing the interests of all so that no individual or group is favored at the expense of another. Liberty brings attention to the point that for an act to be a moral act, it must be a free act. That is to say, it is a freely chosen act and one for which the agent can be held responsible and accountable.

The term moral education refers to the intentional bringing about of moral growth. It is, according to Kohlberg (12: p. 25), the encouragement of a capacity for moral judgment. More than this it is also concerned with a disposition to act in accordance with whatever moral judg-ments are made. What marks out moral education is that it is a deliberate and intentional activity that is concerned with the cultivation of principled moral judgment and a willing disposition to act upon it. Both rational autonomy and strength of will are involved here. To be able to form a moral judgment and yet not act upon it is to fall short of what moral education entails. It is when a moral judgment is translated into an appropriate moral action that moral conduct and therefore moral education is most clearly apparent. McIntosh clearly has something comparable in mind when he writes,

> The morally educated person is expected not only to be able to make moral judgements but act upon them. The moral life necessitates a host of personal dispositions. The moral person must think the issue through to the limits of his capacity but if morally right action is to occur the person must be disposed to act on his moral judgement. (15: p. 167)

In view of what has been said, it should not be thought that moral education is concerned only with the making of moral judgments and the will and capacity to act upon them. In addition to the cognitive and volitional aspects of moral education there is also the affective dimension. To enable children to see that the feelings of other people count as much as their own requires not only sensitivity but the development of social and practical skills. To recognize that others have feelings like oneself is a matter of knowledge; to regard those feelings as important is an attitude that needs to be cultivated. What is being suggested is that the moral aspect of a liberal education is as much concerned with the emotions as it is with critical judgment and a disposition to act. It will be marked out by an attempt not only to understand a situation with an impartial and sympathetic consideration of the interests at stake but also with respect for all the persons involved.

All in all it will be seen that a liberal education, by virtue of its two inherent central concerns (rationality and morality), is commensurate with the development and survival of the democratic ideal. It does this not by being an instrument of democracy but by upholding and pursuing its own values and processes. Liberal education in fulfilling its own purposes also fortuitously serves the purposes of democracy.

The Place of Sport in Education and Democracy

It has been argued that a democracy worthy of its name is dependent upon a liberally educated populace. I will suggest now, first, that this traditional view of a liberal education should be updated to include sport; second, that sport is a practice concerned with fairness; and third, that in a democratic state there should be some explicit governmental policy to promote it, especially in the post-school period.

Sport as an Aspect of Liberal Education

It has been maintained that rationality and morality are two central strands in what it means to be liberally educated. While holding to this general position, I want to suggest now that rationality can be subdivided into what might be called theoretical rationality and practical rationality. Academic subjects such as mathematics, science, and history would fall into the first category, while sport, dance, and other practical pursuits such as cookery and pottery would fall into the second. I want to uphold that a liberal education today should involve an initiation of pupils into the ways, customs, traditions, and practices of their society in such a way that it involves both theoretical and practical reasoning and that it should not be confined to one at the expense of the other. Knowing how to engage in such paradigmatic instances of our culture as rugby, soccer, football, or cricket is no less an indication of what it is to be liberally educated

than is being able to solve quadratic equations or understand Boyle's Law. To see rationality only in theoretical or academic terms is to see it only in terms of thinking "about" the world rather than in terms of acting intelligently in it.

Practical reasoning, unlike theoretical reasoning, is concerned with practice, not theory (or at least not only theory); action, not just thought or belief; intentionally doing something in the world, rather than just thinking or providing information or speculating about the world. Whereas the end of theoretical rationality is universal truth, the end of practical rationality is appropriate action. A contemporary liberal education has as much to do with the latter as it has with the former. Knowing how to participate in a range of worthwhile physical pursuits is an important aspect of human development in that (a) it provides an individual with the opportunity to become a more completely rounded person, and (b) it permits him or her the freedom to choose, in an informed and experienced way, between the inherent values of different types of activity. Overall, the rationality of practical reasoning, especially in reference to sport, permits a range of possibilities in the physical sphere of life to complement those that are primarily intellectual.

In sport, then, not only are thought and action brought together in the agency of the person as he confronts what needs to be done in a set of physically demanding and challenging circumstances but, in pursuing a particular activity in a liberal way, the participant is likely to become a more completely developed human being. As Macintyre (13:p. 187) points out, sporting practices, as other forms of practices such as chess, farming, or engineering, provide opportunities not only for the exercise of particular virtues in the form of justice, honesty, courage, and so on, but also for the realization of goods and standards of excellence that "are appropriate to and partially definitive of that form of activity." He suggests, in keeping with the concept of education, that "human powers to achieve excellence, and human conceptions of the ends and goods involved are systematically extended." What is being maintained is that sport, as represented by its various instances, is a socially constituted human practice in which the values inherent in it are realized in the course of trying to achieve the standards of excellence that help characterize it. The "internal goods" of an activity, as Macintyre (13: p. 188) puts it, are so called for two reasons. First, they can only be specified in terms of that activity. Second, they can only be recognized by those who have experienced participating in it.

Sports as a Practice Concerned with Fairness

In light of what has been said, two questions emerge: First, Can sport be regarded as having internal goods and, if so, what are they? And second, In what way, if at all, are these goods in keeping with the idea of democracy? Elsewhere[2] I have attempted to give a detailed answer to the former question, and so here I shall be mainly concerned with making some brief remarks in relation to the moral aspects of the second question.

The idea of sport, I want to suggest, as with democracy, is based upon the two principles of freedom and equality. When an individual voluntarily chooses to enter a sport he or she can be regarded as tacitly accepting an agreement with others to participate in a way that the rules[3] lay down. To participate in sport then presupposes first, that a free and rational agent has chosen to do so because in some way it is found to be valuable; and second, that the agent both understands and is willing to abide by the rules. In broad terms the principle of freedom relates to sport in that it assumes an individual has the right to choose which sports are taken up, and in narrow terms by the individual's accepting and willingly abiding by the rules that apply to it. To this extent it will be seen that the life and moral character of an individual is bound up and coex-

istent with the choices made and the activities voluntarily entered into. In this respect sport is no less serious than other forms of human practice. The point here is that although a sport may be regarded as a particular kind of practice characterized and governed by its rules, it is by no means separate from or discontinuous with life or moral concern. In fact, it is an identifiable, if miniature, form of life and not a morally irrelevant one. In so far as sport demands of its participants freedom with responsibility and involves benefits as well as burdens, it is in accord with the democratic process.

The principle of equality relates to sport in that its rules not only structure and shape its practice but are intended to be universal and impartial. Players who are educated in a particular sport come together in the full knowledge that its rules apply to themselves as well as to others. They realize and agree that the rules that apply are in the interests of all players and that it is a part of the expected practice of the sport that rules will be impartially applied so that one player or team will not gain unfair advantage over another. It is upon this basis that sport as a competitive practice proceeds. If it were thought that the rules of sport were not concerned with the bringing about of fairness, sport would cease to be the practice it is and should be. It will be seen that the rules that both constitute and govern play should not only agree in principle but they should be willingly observed in practice. Both logically and morally there is only one way to compete in sport and that is by the rules. Acting unfairly arises not so much from the accidental transgression of the rules as in the deliberate breaking of them.

The cheat and spoilsport are so called not because they break the rules but because they break them intentionally in the hope of gaining unfair advantage. Such acts are not only illegal in terms of not conforming to the rules but immoral in that the agreement entered into with other participants has been broken. To intentionally attempt to gain unfair advantage by breaking the rules is not to be *in* sport at all. It is to contravene the practice of sport as fair play.[4] Those who have grasped the principle of equality as it applies to sport will not only have agreed to willingly abide by a common set of rules and their spirit but will, in addition, understand that it is only by following them that the aspirations and interests of others as well as themselves, as sportsmen or sportswomen, can be realized. Thus it will be seen that the idea of sport as fairness not only helps preserve its own integrity, standards, traditions, and ethos as a distinctive type of human practice but also fortuitously complements what has been said about the nature of education and democracy.

In summary, what I have tried to demonstrate is that democracy as a way of ordering and living our lives is dependent upon the social principles of freedom and equality, and that it is these same principles that underpin in turn what it is to be liberally educated as well as the idea of sport as fairness. It is only by an adequate understanding of these principles in relation to these three aspects of life that the latter can be properly understood and safeguarded.

Overall then it can be said that democracy, education, and sport each contribute to the normative structuring of society. Whereas democracy is mainly concerned with the adoption of certain types of procedures that should characterize our political and institutional lives, education is concerned with the initiation of people into those intrinsically worthwhile rational activities, both theoretical and practical, that permit individuals to fulfill their own potential, at the same time being conscious of and responsible toward the needs and rights of others. Sport relates both to democracy and education in that it is concerned with the exercise of practical knowledge in a physically demanding way in a context of what is fair and just. Sport should be regarded as a facet of the good life that has its own values, traditions, and standards in and through which individuals can become more complete and responsible persons.

Sports Provision, Government Policy, and the Democratic State

Insofar then as a democracy holds that individualism, freedom, and equality are desirable it should pursue policies that both protect and promote them. One way of doing this is to make adequate provision not only for education but for sport as one element in the recreative use of leisure time. This would include leadership and amenity planning, as well as financial support.

With the technological revolution that is likely to reduce the average adult working week to no more than four days in the near future, most western democracies recognize that something needs to be done. Few, however, no doubt because of other priorities, have done much on a broad and coherent scale. There is too, in capitalist democracies, the balance of interests to be considered between the public and private sectors and between the commercial and voluntary organizations. Difficult and delicate though this matter may be, the provision of sport in society on a fair and equitable basis must remain one of the responsibilities of government. This should not be undertaken, as it has been in the United Kingdom, in response to a general concern about such matters as youth unemployment, delinquency, and boredom, but as a matter of citizen rights and the type and quality of life a modern democratic state should offer. In addition to such well known documented rights[5] as the right to freedom of thought and expression, the right to equality of treatment before the law, the right to education, and the right to work, there are other rights, perhaps less well known, but which in the developed democracies are becoming increasingly important to implement more fully. These include the right to rest and leisure and the right to take part in cultural life. Sport, I am suggesting, is one aspect of culture for which provision should be made so that it becomes an available avenue for all citizens who see sport as a part of their individual, social, and cultural development.

In light of what has been said, it is of interest that in 1976 the Council of Europe (7) in a Sport for All Charter set down a number of articles. The first stated that every individual has the right to participate in sport; the second stated that sport shall be encouraged as an important factor in human development and that appropriate support shall be made out of public funds. Although member governments have accepted the principles of the Charter and have made some progress with the eight articles it enumerated, they still have a long way to go in making the slogan live in any fully democratic sense. If further progress is to be made, not only in Europe but elsewhere, it is necessary (a) that the place of sport in society and the manner in which it is to be conducted should be given a higher priority in the social policy planning of democratic governments; (b) that the inherent values of sport should be more clearly identified and promoted; and (c) that the beneficial outcomes of participation in sport in terms of such considerations as personal health and social welfare should be more comprehensively researched and effectively communicated. Only when sport is recognized to have intrinsic worth as well as instrumental value and features more strongly and systematically in social policy planning will it help bring about the full benefits it is capable of bestowing.

Notes

This paper was presented as the Presidential Address at the 17th Annual Meeting of the Philosophic Society for the Study of Sport, held in conjunction with the Annual Meeting of the North American Society for the Sociology of Sport, conducted in Washington, DC, in November 1989. As is customary, it is published here in its original form.

1. For much of its long history, from the classical Greeks to modern times, democracy was seen, especially by the educated and enlightened, as one of the worst types of government. It was a term that represented a threat to civilized and law-abiding society. Macpherson, for example, comments,

Democracy used to be a bad word. Everybody who was anybody knew that democracy, in its original sense of rule by the people or government in accordance with the will of the bulk of the people, would be a bad thing—fatal to individual freedom and to all the graces of civilised living. That was the position taken by pretty nearly all men of intelligence from the earliest historical times down to about a hundred years ago. Then, within fifty years, democracy became a good thing. (14: p. 1)

2. For an attempt to explicate something of the meaning and significance of sport in terms of the experience of the participating agent, see Arnold (1). For an attempt to spell out the "internal goods" of sport and dance and relate these to the concept of education, see Arnold (2).

3. The word *rules* here is used in a general way and is intended to cover not only the formal rules of sport but also its venerated expectations; that is to say, its valued traditions, conventions, excellences, and shibboleths. For a good discussion on the relationship between the formal rules of a game and the ethos of sport as a social practice, see Morgan (16).

4. The idea of sport as a practice concerned with fairness is in accord with the way in which Rawls (18) discusses justice.

5. For a summary of the Major International Human Rights documents, see Winston (20: pp. 257–289).

Bibliography

1. Arnold, P.J. *Meaning in Movement, Sport and Physical Education.* London: Heinemann, 1979.

2. Arnold, P.J. *Education, Movement and the Curriculum.* London: Falmer Press, 1988.

3. Bailey, C. *Beyond the Present and Particular.* London: Routledge & Kegan Paul, 1984.

4. Barrow, R. and Woods, R. *An Introduction to Philosophy of Education.* London: Methuen, 1982.

5. Bullock, A.L.C. "Democracy." In *The Fontana Dictionary of Modern Thought.* Edited by A. Bullock and D. Stallybrass. London: Fontana Books, 1977.

6. Burke, E. "Speech to the Electors of Bristol" November 3, 1774. Cited in S.I. Benn and R.S. Peters, *Social Principles and the Democratic State.* London: George Allen & Unwin.

7. Council of Europe. *European Sport for All Charter.* September, 1976.

8. Dewey, J. *Democracy and Education.* New York: Free Press, 1916.

9. Dewey, J. *The Public and Its Problems*. Chicago: Gateway Books, 1946.

10. Helm, D. *Models of Democracy*. Cambridge: Polity Press, 1987.

11. Kant, E. *Foundations of the Metaphysics of Morals*. Translated by L.W. Beck. Indianapolis: Bobbs-Merrill, 1959.

12. Kohlberg, L. "Stages of Moral Development as a Basis of Moral Education." In *Moral Education—Interdisciplinary Approaches*. Edited by C.M. Beck and C.S. Crittenden. Toronto: University of Toronto Press, 1971.

13. Macintyre, A. *After Virtue: A Study in Moral Theory*. London: Duckworth, 1985.

14. Macpherson, C.B. *The Real World of Democracy*. Oxford: Clarendon Press, 1966.

15. McIntosh, P. *Fair Play: Ethics in Sport and Education*. London: Heinemann, 1979.

16. Morgan, W.J. "The Logical Compatibility Thesis and Rules: A Reconsideration of Formalism and an Account of Games." *Journal of the Philosophy of Sport*, XIV (1987), 1–20.

17. Peters, R.S. *Ethics and Education*. London: George Allen & Unwin, 1966.

18. Rawls, J. *A Theory of Justice*. Oxford University Press, 1972.

19. Scheffler, I. *Reason and Teaching*. London: Routledge & Kegan Paul, 1973.

20. Winston, M.E. *The Philosophy of Human Rights*. Belmont, CA: Wadsworth, 1989.

Questions for Consideration

1. Do you think that Arnold's view of liberal education is too narrow? In other words, what reason do we have for thinking that beneficial effects attendant upon pursuing knowledge for its own sake are mere by-products of liberal education?

2. Can you think of reasons why sport as practiced today in democratic societies might not be considered "a facet of the good life"?

43 Sports and the Making of National Identities: A Moral View

William J. Morgan
University of Tennessee

One common mistake in discussions of nationalism, William J. Morgan states, comes through assuming that it is something that happens to us, like a viral infection, instead of something in which we participate. Nationalism, properly understood, entails both uniqueness of being and a dialogical relationship between different nations. Sports have and traditionally have had a significant role in this dialogical relationship.

Historically, democratic nationalism emerged in seventeenth-century antiroyalist and egalitarian thinking. A new collective authority was formed, the people, and with it came the requirement to carve out new standards of nationalist ideals.

One such standard was that each nation must uniquely and culturally define and determine itself. Self-determination, on one reading, turns into moral nationalism: Nations shun moral singularity as a universal ideal, though each embraces its own morality, while it isolates itself from others. But this too is a form of universalism, Morgan argues, though it is pluralist friendly. What the standard of self-determination reduces to is, in reality, recognition that there is no one path in nation forging, instead of an injunction against moral criticism against acts in forging such a path.

There are good reasons to believe that self-determination through nationalism must not shut off other nations. In fact, nationalistic self-determination occurs "if and only if" there is "sustained dialogue with other nations." This implies recognition of mutual value and requirements for proper dialogical communication. Nationalistic

Reprinted, by permission, from W. J. Morgan, "Sports and the Making of National Identities: A Moral View," *Journal of the Philosophy of Sport* XXIV(1997): 1–20.

atrocities, according to Morgan, are deeds committed because of failed dialogues.

Sport, being a part of our humanity, is a linguistic expression of it. First, the actions, gestures, and movements in sport form a "semantic backdrop" for narratives and tropes. Sport as social practice is a language of every nation's collective identity that cannot be appropriated for private interpretation. To practice sport is to share in humanity, and this cuts across the barriers of nations.

One might object, however, that the language of Western sport is oppressive and dark. Thus, once "inferior" nations, who now share many of the same sports, do so only with the intent of beating Westerners at their own game—imitating them in order to humiliate them (as these inferior nations were once humiliated). This objection is too bleak. It fails to consider, Morgan argues, that they may be borrowing for the sake of improvement, precisely as what they borrow, in the very act of being employed afresh and uniquely, may itself be improved.

The theme of national identity—how nations see and think about themselves—ranks as one of the most complex and elusive issues that comes up in discussions of nationalism. The reason why can be traced to Benedict Anderson's (1) justly famous rendering of nations as "imagined communities." For to say that nations are imagined communities is to say that the social glue that holds them together and that makes them the distinct communities that they are has to do, when all is said and done, with the way their members imaginatively conceive of their relations to one another.[1] It has to do with the collective imagination of their members owing, among other things, to the sheer scale of nations, for even the smallest of them are composed of people who have never met, and, therefore, have no first-hand knowledge of one another, and in some cases may even be scarcely aware of one another. This explains why efforts to fix the limits of nationality by appealing to objective markers—that is, markers that bypass the messy, quasi-subjective, imaginative beliefs of people—have failed. As Renan (cited in 15: p. 22) has persuasively argued, for every objective criterion put forward as evidence of nationality, there are clear and convincing counterexamples. The possession of a common language, no doubt, is one of the most powerful, and, unsurprisingly, one of the most commonly cited, of such criteria, but it too is easily parried by a counterexample. Germans and Austrians, to take but one such example, share a common language, not to mention a goodly number of other things as well, yet they do not think of themselves as members of a single national community, as conationals.[2] Renan's point in exposing the weaknesses of such objective definitions of nation-ness was not to suggest that the very notion of nationality is paradoxical, unintelligible, but rather to make the very different point I want to make and underscore here: namely, that calling a people a nation is a complex and elusive matter because in the final analysis it rests on the shared beliefs of their members that they belong together, that they do indeed make a nation.

But for all its vaunted complexity, the notion of national identity is not without its virtues. And one of its virtues, which I want to follow up on in the present paper, is that it helps us think about the connection between sports and nationalism in an important and fruitful way, one that goes a long way toward explaining why it is that sports today are such important, not to mention conspicuous, vehicles of national expression, of why it is that so many nations have turned to sports of late to tell stories about themselves for others to mull over—be they the stories of German footballers or West Indian cricketers or Serbian basketball players or Kenyan runners. What is fruitful about the way it orients

our thinking regarding this connection is that it avoids a mistake commonly made in discussions of nationalism. I have in mind here the notion that nationalism is more so an epidemiological phenomenon than a cultural one, that is, that it acts like a virus quickly incapacitating the peoples it infects by sapping both their ability to understand and to respond to what is happening to them. What is wrong with this picture of nationalism, as Miller (15: p. 6) aptly notes, is that it treats nationalism "as something that happens to us, rather than as something we participate in creating." Asking after how nations define themselves through the sports they play, effectively how they fashion identities for themselves using sports as their media, is, I want to claim, a way to remedy this errant picture of nationalism because it is a way to get notions of collective understanding and agency back into this picture.

However, my interest in correcting this picture of nationalism is to raise a troubling moral objection—one whose very raising is parasitic on this correction, concerning sport's role in the genesis of national identities the world over. That objection, which I want to focus the rest of my paper on, is that enlisting sports in the cause of nationalism is enlisting them in a cause that is at best morally parochial and at worst morally, not to mention politically, dangerous. The source of this moral parochialism, and potential moral treachery, derives, the objection continues, from the particularity of expressions of nation-ness, from the fact that when nations imagine themselves through sports or other media, they always imagine themselves as inherently limited, tightly bounded communities. This notion of bounded communities, it is alleged, implicates the sports that help to conjure them up in a morally dubious exercise of otherness-construction, which is to say in a divisive exercise of carving up the peoples of the world into the invidious categories of "us" and "them." Since the point of this exercise is to remind us (and if reminders do not suffice, to persuade us), of the otherness of the other side—that is, to paint all those who fall outside the boundaries of our own national community not just as outsiders but as perpetual and despised outsiders—it is clear that what drives such boundary-marking is a smug belief in the superiority and self-centeredness of our own ways of life and the inferiority and irrelevance of theirs, a conviction that it is not only folly to try to cross boundaries, because it confuses them for bridges, but that it is dangerous to do so, because it weakens the unity and taints the purity of our community. This is a picture of the world and peoples and sports that, the objection concludes, we have every (moral) reason to reprove.

I want to defend sportive expressions of nationalism, or at least certain forms of them, against this wholesale criticism by arguing that they miss the mark because they fail to see that a compelling, even if frequently debased and trivialized, moral ideal underpins such expressions. That ideal, I argue further, is a complex one that combines two related moral notions often thought to be in tension with one another: on the one hand, the notion that each nation has its own distinctive and original way of being that it must discover and, once discovered, be true to: and, on the other hand, that finding and working out that identity is largely a dialogical matter, one whose realization depends upon maintaining and sustaining an open-ended and ongoing conversation with other peoples.[3] That these two notions often find themselves at loggerheads testifies to the fragility of the ideal, that they are capable, nonetheless, of harmonious expression testifies to its moral potency.

My defense of sportive nationalism, and of nationalism itself, therefore, rests on unearthing this alleged moral ideal of nationalism and laying bare its two key features, a task that leads me first, and perhaps surprisingly, to an examination of the contemporary sports scene, then to an analysis of the moral credentials of nationalism itself, and, finally, back to sports and a consideration of their moral role as carriers of national identity. But before I undertake this ambitious task, I should first like to make clear that my purpose in setting out to recover this moral ideal of nationalism is not to deflect attention away from its all too real, and all too savage, deformations. On the contrary, my aim is to show how these deformations might be effectively criticized from within, as opposed to ineffectively from without, so that we might be able to defuse such skewed expressions of nationalism in the future. The problem I immediately run up against here is that what most would-be critics of nationalism attack as incontrovertible offshoots of nationalism are, in fact, I argue, debased forms of that ideal. And a central part of my argument is devoted to showing that we are able to pick out such forms as debased ones only by appealing to this ideal in the first place. So critics of nationalism unnecessarily muddy the waters, or so I want to claim, when their criticisms take on this intemperate tone, when in their eagerness not to appear feckless, they declare nationalism to be a lost cause, thereby cutting off any search for an underlying ideal that might stem the excesses committed (illicitly) in its name.

National Sports and the International Athletic Community

I begin with the contemporary sport setting for one simple but remarkable fact: It betrays a curious admixture of the local and the cosmopolitan, of the intermingling of national aims and interests and international ones, that points us toward the two-pronged moral ideal of nationalism just sketched above. What makes this curious feature of the sports scene an important one for our present purposes, then, is precisely that it actively encourages nationalistic displays rather than shunning them in the name of some lofty international ideal. The reason for this interlocking of the national and international is smartly furnished by Wilson (29:p. 352), who reminds us that our present system of international sports is itself founded on "a particular version of sport . . . that symbolizes national values and identity." This suggests that the international athletic community and its satellite national communities are mutually dependent upon one another in at least two important senses, both of which, as we shall see shortly, are relevant to my search for a moral ideal intrinsic to nationalism.

In the first sense, nations are dependent upon the international athletic community and its slate of international sports for the very language they use to articulate their unique identities. Since "the more universalizing forms of sport," as MacAloon (13: p. 42) refers to them, that nations borrow from the international community in this instance are the common currency in which they cash out their disparate identities, the link between the local and the cosmopolitan is especially strong here. And it is strong in both directions, for the international sports community would not be what it presently is if nations did not so borrow from its common stock of sports and appropriate them for their own particular expressive purposes.

In the second sense, nations are dependent upon the international sports world to confirm their national stature.[4] Since nations not only see themselves in this regard as members of a larger, international community, but actively curry the favor of that community in seeking validation of their own nationality, the bond between the national and international is equally strong here. The establishment of an international athletic presence is not, therefore, a gratuitous matter for nations, but rather the path they must currently follow if they expect to be recognized and treated as a nation. That is why MacAloon's (13: p. 42) claim that "To be a nation recognized by others . . . a people must march in the Olympic Games opening ceremonies," is no idle boast.[5] And once again the bond runs strongly in both directions, since the international athletic community would cease to be an important force in the global system if nations did not look to it for confirmation of their own nationality.

What is important to notice about this linkage of the national and the international, however, is that it did not originate with modern sports, even though they are, in my estimation,

among its most powerful and vibrant expressions, but with the new way people began to think about their social relations with one another that coincided with the rise of nationalism in the late seventeenth and eighteenth centuries. What was new about this nationalist-inspired conception of community can best be gleaned by briefly comparing it to the sense of community fostered by the two major cultural systems that preceded nationalism and out of which and against which it evolved—what Benedict Anderson (1: p. 12) tells us were the religious community and the dynastic realm. Under the first category, Anderson lumped the "great sacral cultures" of Confucianism, Christianity, and Islam, all of which imagined themselves to be immense communities. The clue to their all-encompassing scope was the all-encompassing sacred language from which they took their identity, which encouraged them to think of their community as coterminous with the entire human race. Under the second category, Anderson (1: p. 36) placed the great monarchical empires of the premodern period, all of whom believed "that society was naturally organized around and under high centres—monarchs who were persons apart from other human beings and who ruled by some form of cosmological (divine) dispensation." The people who lived in these dynasties likewise imagined themselves to be members of an immense community, which explains, according to Anderson (1: p. 19), the ease with which these premodern kingdoms "were able to sustain their rule over immensely heterogeneous, and often not even contiguous, populations for long periods of time." What is key here, however, and what prompted people in both cultural systems to paint themselves in such broad strokes, was their mutually held belief that their social bond with their fellow members was centripetally and hierarchically ordered, rather than centrifugally and horizontally ordered (1: p. 15).

The contrast between the sacred and dynastic sense of community and the nationalist sense is clear enough to understand why it was that when the former systems began to unravel, when they began to loose their hold on the collective imaginations of people, appeals to the nation as the new locus of identity and authority increased both in number and intensity—spreading rather quickly from seventeenth century English antiroyalists such as Milton and Cromwell to major leaders of the French Revolution. Thus we find a noted French revolutionary declaring at the height of the French Revolution that "the nation is prior to everything, it is the source of everything" (cited in 15: p. 29).[6] But what is perhaps less well understood and appreciated is that these new appeals to and declarations about the nation signaled a major shift in the way people thought about themselves as social beings. What it signaled was a profound change in people's collective sense of themselves, the spawning of a new "we," best captured by the phrase "we the people," that spoke to their capacity to act in common concerning matters of mutual interest, and to the legitimacy of vesting political authority squarely in their hands. The fashioning of this new national identity signaled as well a fundamental reworking of the boundaries that formerly and simultaneously held people together and separated them off from others. Those boundaries had to be more compactly drawn and then thickened, and the vertical relations that stamped people as subjects of the crown and vassals of the church had to be replaced by horizontal relations that stamped people as equal citizens of this or that nation. In a word, the centripetal, boundaryless, and hierarchical social relations of the religious community and the dynasty had to be jettisoned in favor of the centrifugal, boundary-laden, and horizontal social relations of the nation.

Nationalism as a Moral Ideal: The Quest for an Original Way of Being

It is against this backdrop, then, that we can begin our dissection of the moral ideal that helped to launch this altered sense of community by firing the collective imagination of the people who staked their public persona to them. The first important feature that stands out here is the one Herder and Fichte took pains to draw our attention to, the idea that each nation must find its own unique ways of life and forms of culture that best capture and express who it is.[7] The claim here is that each nation has within itself its own "measure," its own ways of being, and is obligated to discover this measure and to live in accordance with it, not to imitate someone else's way of being. Since, then, each nation is capable of spinning out its own distinctive, and creative ways of life, compatriots of one nation should not aspire to copy the ways of life of another nation. As Taylor (23: p. 31) bluntly put it, "Germans shouldn't try to be derivative and (inevitably) second-rate Frenchmen." Another, less harsh, way of saying this is that nationality makes for a certain inescapable particularity. Much as I might fancy myself a citizen of the world, the fact is that as an American, my patriotism is necessarily reserved for America, just as a Mauritanian's patriotism is necessarily reserved for her home country. As Walzer (27: p. 521) argued, "patriotism or the love of country is . . . known in its differences: How would it be possible to love one's country if it were indistinguishable from all the others?" That is not to say that if I am born an American, I must remain forever a patriot of America, only that as long as I maintain my nationalist allegiance to America, my patriotism must follow suit. The particularity of nationalist attachments and commitments are ineliminable, then, because that is the nature of their calling and effect, because their hold on us derives not from the fact that they apply and speak to everyone, but from the fact that they apply and speak uniquely to us.

No doubt, the critics of nationalism are likely to reject instantly any claim that a moral ideal, or at least the first piece of such an ideal, can be extracted from the particularism of nationalist expressions of self-determination. That is because they are apt to see in such expressions a recipe for moral mischief rather than moral making. They might even regard its partisan assertion and championing of local differences as a kind of modern twist on a premodern theme of in-your-face repression, one reminiscent of sixteenth century folk like Bishop Bousset, an ardent defender of the church and French crown, who was fond of telling those he persecuted, mostly France's Protestant minority, "I have the right to persecute you because I am right and you are wrong." The nationalist update of this claimed right to subjugate others simply transposes the offending religious differences into offending nationalist and cultural ones: "I have the right to persecute you because I am this way and you are different."[8]

But the critic's swift rejection here is suspect because its gloss on the claim that each nation should seek and be true to its own "measure" is suspect. It is suspect because it, once again, conflates the ideal that founds this claim, that no nation has the moral license to usurp the moral agency of another in the seeking of its original way of being, with what is a debased instance of it, the subjugation of others in that pursuit. That nationalists might construe the moral particularism that underwrites this ideal as a reason to mistreat others is, alas, a constant danger, but it is equally, I hasten to add, a fundamental misconstrual of what this ideal comes to, of what it morally enjoins. For what follows from the acknowledgement that nation-making and the moral making that goes into it is always a local, culturally-bound matter is not moral tyranny, not an open invitation to have one's way with those who live by a different "measure," but moral respect of and openness toward others, the mandate that others be allowed to find their own moral voice and moral identity. That is why nations that overstep their boundaries and overreach their moral authority by insinuating themselves into the moral making of other nations can justly be accused of failing to live up to the moral "measure" of nationalism.

It should also be noted that the moral particularism that underpins this "measure" of nationalist self-determination is itself the source of a certain moral universalism, one that, unlike its standard counterparts, is pluralist friendly. It strikes a morally universalist pose in two interrelated senses. First, it bespeaks a universal potential: that all nations, not just a lucky few, possess the capacity to form and define their own identity. And second, it issues a universal injunction: that all nations have the right to exercise that potential as they best see fit, not, however, with critical immunity or moral impunity.[9] The warrant that drives this injunction is universal, then, not in the sense, as Walzer (27: p. 527) is careful to alert us, that it precedes every effort at national self-determination but that it flows out of every such effort, "that every claim to moral making, every claim to shape a life, justifies the claims that come later." This is the root of its pluralist tendency. For what it universalizes are not the favored moral narratives and experiences of a favored nation,[10] but rather, to borrow Walzer's pregnant phrase, the act of "moral reiteration" itself, the ongoing, difference producing process by which people create and recreate the cultural stories that constitute their national identity and set their moral compass. So respecting the right of all nations to forge their own path means acknowledging that there is no one single path, no one correct way, that all nations are obliged to follow in constructing and morally perfecting their nation-ness. It means, in other words, respecting, which does not, I reiterate, rule out criticizing, the legitimacy of repeated acts of nation-making and the different moral outcomes that ineluctably follow.

Less easy to counter, however, is a different kind of retort, one that does not insist that the particularity of nationalist expressions is, and cannot help being, contemptuous of the moral agency of others but only that it is, and cannot help being, indifferent to their agency. On this reading, the imperative that each nation find its original way of being signifies not so much a chastened affirmation of the limits where our moral making ends and theirs begins as it does a haughty declaration that others are off-limits when it comes to our own moral projects. So whatever constraint this imperative might provide to dissuade nations not to overstep their limits, to violate the moral agency of others, is morally suspect, the criticism continues, since it is rooted in a not so moral disinterest in the affairs of others—one that furnishes nations no reason, moral or otherwise, even to acknowledge let alone engage others in their national projects, to think that they might learn something from them that would enhance and enliven their own moral making. The implication is all too clear: The boundaries that mark off nations from one another specify the limits of their moral affection and interests, not the grounds of their respect for others. The conclusion that follows from this is equally clear: The demand for national self-determination comes to precious little as a moral ideal, because it is motivated less by an antipathy toward moral singularity than it is by a desire to promote and cultivate its own version of moral singularity, one that is celebratory of the separate aims and achievements of individual nations. And that both Herder and Fichte saw fit to stake their exhortation that each nation seek its own "measure" to the admonition that they do so without being "contaminated" by outsiders, by nations pursuing different "measures, would only seem to confirm our critic's suspicions here.

This is a powerful criticism but, ultimately, a flawed one. We can begin to see why by first noting the exaggerated character of its claims. For we have already argued that love of country is a highly particular love for a people and its ways of life. This is what Herder (cited in 25: p. 122) meant when he claimed that "Everyone loves his country . . . not because [it] is the best in the world, but because [it is] absolutely his own, and loves himself and his labors in [it]." And Herder's elaboration is instructive here because it suggests at least two reasons why a nation bent on discovering its own distinctive way of being might, nonetheless, find others' ways of being relevant to its own.[11] The first reason removes a possible obstacle that stands in the way of taking an active interest in the moral making of others. I have in mind here the claim that what yokes individuals to nations is the smug belief in their superiority,

the unflinching conviction that the cultural forms of life of their nation are superior to those of other nations. This prevents nationals, it is alleged, from noticing other cultures, save to point out their deficiencies and exotic beliefs. As Bromwich (4: p. 101) forcefully argues in this regard, "the person who thinks 'My culture is perhaps inferior' is halfway to thinking his way into a different culture and dangerously close to the thought that 'No culture is worthy of my love in the way that humanity, and particular human beings, are.'" But Bromwich's claim that the thought that "this is my culture" is incompatible with the thought "this culture is perhaps inferior" is clearly false for the very reason Herder suggests: The love people profess for their country is not predicated, not, that is, in any necessary, *a priori* way, on the belief that it is superior to all other countries.[12] To be sure, it can scarcely be doubted that patriotism has spurred conationals at times to adopt such inflated views of their country—a fact that is better explained, I think and will try to show, on other grounds, but it can and should be doubted that it entails such regard, that it decrees that those who do not share our national identity are, *ipso facto*, our inferiors. So we have no good reason to suppose, as Bromwich and others would have us believe, that cultural membership carries with it an automatic belief in the superiority of our culture and the inferiority of theirs, and so, an abiding interest in our culture that precludes any interest in theirs.

Herder's further point that people love the labor they put into their nation suggests a second reason why they might see fit to regard others' moral making as relevant to their own, what might be termed the patriotic reason. The idea here is that only people who identify with their nation and take pride in its accomplishments will have the motive and the will to remedy whatever deficiencies it might have, to make it a better nation than it is presently. This includes looking to other nations for help and guidance in strengthening one's own. Something of this sort is what Richard Rorty (19: p. E-15) had in mind when he recently chided the American left for their lack of patriotism, for their narrow interest in severely criticizing the shortcomings of America—what he, after Jonathan Yardley, colorfully referred to as their eagerness to be signatories to the "America Sucks Sweepstakes," and their decided disinterest in doing anything about these shortcomings, in seeking tangible, practical ways of rectifying them. Something very much like this is also what Coubertin (7: p. 434) had in mind when he proclaimed at the turn of the century that "internationalism should be the state of mind of those who love their country above all, who seek to draw to it the friendship of foreigners." What makes Rorty's and Coubertin's claims here credible is what should cast doubt on the critic's counter claim. For what the former shows is that patriotism is neither incompatible with facing up to and even feeling shame in the failings of one's nation, nor with looking to other nations to seek assistance in correcting them.

Nationalism as a Moral Ideal: Dialogue and Recognition

Still, these seem at best slim reeds to put off our critic's complaint here, since all they offer is that calls for national self-determination are neither hostile to the agency of others nor indisposed on occasion to considering others' forms of life when their own are in a state of disrepair.[13] In short, no argument or claim has yet been made that others are somehow crucial to the self-definition and the self-determination of nations. So the best way to parry this objection of the critic is to concede its force and then go on to point out that it is incomplete and, therefore, unpersuasive as it stands, that it overlooks, or simply ignores, the fact that there is more to the moral ideal of nationalism than that nations must find their own way. That something more points to what I have identified as the second, dialogical feature of this moral ideal, that nations can find their own way, their own "measure," if

and only if they enter into a sustained dialogue with other nations. This part of the ideal is important because it does argue that there is something about a nation's coming to some sense of what it is about and what it stands for that makes engaging others in a dialogue indispensable, that suggests that such exchanges have as much to do with the self-clarification of a nation's implicit and inchoate beliefs, values, and standards, as they do with its self-edification, its acquisition of new beliefs, values, and standards.

There are two features of this dialogical part of the moral measure of nationalism that are relevant to our discussion. The first derives from George Orwell's (cited in 15: p. 27) observation that "it is only when you meet someone of a different culture from yourself that you begin to realize what your own beliefs really are." The reason why others are in this sense a spur to our own self-understanding and self-interpretation as a people is not difficult to divine. For our collective identity, our sense of ourselves as a separate and distinctive community, reposes on the core beliefs and values that bind us together as a people. However, since these beliefs and norms are often taken for granted, they remain for the most part inchoate, that is, dimly understood and weakly articulated. What our encounters with others provide, therefore, is an occasion to make these implicit beliefs and values explicit, to wrest them from their taken-for-grantedness and to jar those of us who hold them out of our putative inarticulacy. And they are able to do this by virtue of the differences they present us with, which in challenging our self-understandings force us to articulate the background conditions that furnish our beliefs with their intelligibility and normative force. So entering into a dialogue with other nations is a way to understand better who we are as a people and who we might yet want to become. And if Orwell is right, it is an indispensable process, since this kind of provocation, of goad, cannot be manufactured monologically but only dialogically, in interaction with others.

However, others are crucial not only to clarifying who we are and to learning who we might yet become, but also to confirming who we claim to be now and in the future. That is because national identity is partly constituted by recognition, and very often by the misrecognition or nonrecognition of others. This, then, is the second feature of the dialogical part of the moral ideal of nationalism, in which seeking the good opinion of others, staking out a secure and enabling public reputation, prompts nations not only to converse with one another but also to enjoin them to take notice of just what it is that they are saying to one another. The refusal to take such notice of others, or the outright misrecognition of others, witting or not, is on this view no trifling matter since it qualifies as a form of oppression, one which deserves our moral reproach, it is argued, because it traps people in "a false, distorted, and reduced mode of being."[14] This, of course, was the cudgel taken up by the colonized peoples of the world and all those who supported their efforts to decolonize their lands; for it was apparent that one of the most pernicious tools colonial masters had at their disposal was their ability to foist such depreciatory, self-crippling images on these subjugated peoples—images which they had a difficult time shedding long after the more obvious vestiges of colonialism had been eliminated. So it can scarcely be doubted that the identity of nations is integrally linked to recognition, and that identities can be won or lost, shaped or misshaped, on the basis of the granting or withholding of that recognition. It can also be scarcely doubted that the demand for recognition is a deep-seated moral one, such that its distortion or denial is viewed as a grievous moral failure, not just a troubling political one.

In claiming that the link between identity and recognition is intrinsic to the moral ideal of nationalism, I am not claiming that it is original to this ideal. On the contrary, the formation of identities and their ratification by others was a well established part of the life of premodern sacral communities and dynasties. However, in these societies recognition was woven into the fabric of their hierarchical social relations, was itself an undisputed feature of these relations. Its uncontested, unproblematic status was owed to its socially foreordained character, to the fact that recognition was meted out, exclusively and automatically, according to one's place in the larger social chain of being. So nothing had to be ventured in the way of identity, and, therefore, nothing gained or lost in the way of recognition. That changed dramatically with the onset of nationalism, which in abetting the demise of these hierarchical social relations, threw the whole process of getting recognized up for grabs. Now identities had to be risked and their recognition won through dialogical involvement with others. What nationalism wrought, then, was not, as Taylor (23: p. 35) avers, "the need for recognition but the conditions in which the attempt to be recognized can fail." And the possibility of that failure registered not only the moral urgency of this quest for recognition, but the exacting moral conditions required to satisfy it, not to mention, alas, the ways in which it might go awry, might be debauched.

This dialogically rooted drive for recognition is morally exacting in at least two senses. In the first sense, it is exacting because the attempt to be recognized that it inspires and sanctions is a mutual rather than a one-sided one. Put simply, that means that a nation seeking recognition from other nations must regard them to be worthy of its attention-getting efforts, to be significant others, and, in turn, those nations that see fit to recognize a nation must find it worthy of their attention, to be a significant other in its own right. Mutuality so understood can be described as morally demanding, then, precisely because it militates against dominance, against an over dependence on others that is demeaning because of its one-sidedness.

But the demand for recognition is exacting in the further sense that it mandates that nations be noticed for the original and unique communities that they are, for those very features that distinguish them from other cultures and peoples and that, resultantly, often get ignored or glossed over or derogated in their dealings with them, especially dominant others. This feature of recognition is even more demanding than its insistence on the mutuality of dialogue if only because it more forcefully counsels against an ingratiating, slavish dependence on others, one that is likely only to generate some unseemly version of the master-slave dialectic. It tries to steer clear of this unhappy outcome by endorsing a brand of recognition that, to reiterate, is premised on showcasing the differences that mark peoples off from one another rather than overcoming those differences.[15] This puts a double moral onus on our dialogical relations with others. For the nations seeking recognition, it prescribes that they get their stories right, that they convey their cultural narratives in ways that make explicit what they are about, what their core beliefs and values are. We might call this the articulacy requirement, and in impelling peoples to articulate their distinctive identities mindfully, it points up that there are better and worse, more clairvoyant and deluded ways of doing so. And for the nations granting or denying such recognition, it prescribes that they understand just what it is that is being conveyed to them. We might term this the understanding requirement, and in impelling peoples to give a fair and adequate hearing to cultural beliefs and values that do not jibe with their own, it points up the limits of their own beliefs and values, and, therefore, of the necessity of being conversant in several cultural languages not just one—their own.

What is arduous, both morally and discursively, about what this double onus recognition imposes on our conversations with others can perhaps be more clearly grasped by comparing it to an alternative account of how cultural and moral differences enter our lives through interchange with others. I have in mind here Jeremy Waldon's (26: p. 108) championing of a certain experimental form of life that he calls, after Salman Rushdie, "mongrelization" and "hybridization," in which individuals and peoples are given free rein to create new identities for themselves by liberally borrowing elements from this and that culture, and then mixing them together to produce some new, unfamiliar concoc-

tion. This brand of cosmopolitan alchemy authorizes individuals and peoples not only to draw cultural resources from wherever they like, but as Waldron argues to "wrench" these snatches of culture from their "wider context," in effect, to "misread" and "misinterpret" them in any way they please that furthers their own self-renewal and enlivenment. While there is much to be said in favor of such unfettered borrowing and experimentation as a means of instigating cultural change and promoting cultural invigoration, it falls significantly short of the moral mark set by recognition.[16] That is to say, it does not enjoin nations to disclose themselves mindfully, and it does not require them to alter their own cultural beliefs and values to accommodate and understand the differing beliefs and values of other cultures—indeed, where cultural enrichment of the sort urged here is the aim, both of these demands come off as irrelevant, as wholly beside the point. So it is this turning a deaf ear to the differences that others represent and present to us that explains why such a deracinated cosmopolitanism is unable to answer the moral call of recognition, a call that asks of all our dialogical dealings with others that we stretch our moral horizons, in Gadamer's language "fuse our horizons," so as to be able to make assessments of the value and significance of competing forms of life that we could have not otherwise made, not, that is, if we had held fast to our original values and forms of life.[17]

But if the possibility that our attempts to be recognized as unique and different peoples might go for naught accounts for their moral urgency and exactness, it also accounts for, as previously noted, how they can go wrong, indeed dreadfully wrong. And the way they go wrong is when the effort to be recognized fails to hew to its stiff dialogical requirements. The atrocities committed in nationalism's name, then, are owed not to the drive for recognition itself, but to failed efforts at dialogue instigated by that drive.

Two paradigm cases of such failure, of the monological undoing of dialogue, are apparent here. The first case is that of the messianic, imperialist nation that indemnifies itself, in a preemptive gesture, against the failure to be recognized by denying the very thing that makes our dialogical relations with others the morally salient and dicey matter that it is: namely, moral diversity. So when Durkheim claimed of France that it was the very seat of human civilization and culture, and Weber and Milton claimed the same of their native countries Germany and England, each can be understood as touting his own brand of moral singularity, one that blithely dismisses the moral agency of others. The pathological self-absorption and self-importance at work here is plain for all to see; for what such universalizing gestures are intended to convey is that there is only one story worth telling and listening to, and, therefore, that a monological recounting of that story, which others are forced by hook or crook to listen to, is required if the din of competing voices dialogue would expose us to is to be stilled, to be prevented from corrupting its central message. This, at any rate, is why nations of this messianic inclination persist in talking down and past others rather than to them.

The second case is that presented by nations of an entirely different inclination and station, that is, nations under siege, which have made their presence felt recently across Eastern Europe and much of the so-termed Third World—often in the bloodiest of terms. Here the effort to indemnify themselves against the failure to be recognized is retrospectively rather than, as in the first instance, prospectively and preemptively made, since what they are trying to protect themselves against, frequently in desperate circumstances, is further humiliating failures to get noticed. Isaiah Berlin (3:p. 5) has famously likened what he calls the "inflamed" condition of these nations to a "bent twig," one "forced down so severely that when released it lashes back with a fury." These nations, then, comprise for the most part the snubbed and subjugated victims of messianic nations. But what they curiously share with their oppressors is an unmistakably antipathy for dialogue. The antipathy in this case is borne not of a supreme self-confidence but

self-absorption. For nations that operate under the grip of such massive inferiority complexes are often prone to exaggerate their real and imagined qualities, and so, to fasten on narrow and rigid interpretations of their own national character that not only are celebratory of some of their worst features and failings but contemptuous of even the progressive impulses of their despised "superiors."[18] What we have in such instances, then, is yet another monological subversion of dialogue, one that makes talking past and at others *de rigeur* and, therefore, talking to them well-nigh impossible.

Sports as Nationalist Languages

If my analysis of nationalism is not too far off the mark, then it will be apparent that its upsurge in the modern world is not something to be condemned root and branch, but rather something to be closely studied and monitored to ensure that the powerful moral ideal it gives life to is not overshadowed by the terrible deeds illegitimately carried out in its name. At very least, it will have made it apparent that it is a mistake simply to write off, as many have insisted on doing, nationalism. But it is time to consider in greater detail than I have to this point just where and how sports figure into this ideal, which will provide some clue as to why they have become of late such powerful and important bearers of nationalist messages.

The answer to this question turns on Taylor's (23 p. 31) claim that our ability to define our original measure as a people and to communicate it to others depends on our acquisition of "rich human languages of expression." Sports, I am arguing, qualify as one such rich language of expression in two important senses.

In the first sense, sports qualify as a kind of language, as a quasi-text, by virtue of the common actions, gestures, and movements that make them up and that form the semantic backdrop for the narratives and tropes they churn out. For it is through these common actions that sports are able to call up the shared meanings and values that form the bedrock of nations' collective identities and fashion them into stories that can be told and retold to others—stories, for example, about the quiet determination of Romanian gymnasts, the grit and might of Turkish and Bulgarian weight lifters, the aggressive bowling of West Indian cricketers. What we have here, then, is a language shaped in the form of a social practice in which common actions and movements take over the grammatical role usually reserved for words and sentences.

Sports, of course, are not alone in this regard; for there are a wide array of cultural practices that are able to summon up and articulate many of the same common meanings and values. So in singing the narrative praises of sports here, I am singing as well the narrative praises all of these other cultural practices—not to mention calling attention to the reason why any serious study of national identity, and nationalism more generally, cannot ignore people's attachments to their culture, to the part cultural practices play in engaging their collective imagination and forming their distinctive identities. Thus, if sports have any special purchase here, it is not because they possess some magical property, some semantic elixir, that other cultural practices do not, but rather because their core common actions enjoy a measure of self-consciousness that those of other cultural practices do not. For as things presently and contingently stand, sports are among the most observed, discussed, and debated features of the life we share in common.

But in what sense are the actions that constitute sports and serve as their semantic vessels common ones. Not in the sense that they are anti-individualist, antisubjective ones. For individuals bring to the sports they play their own personal beliefs, meanings, and values, and, unsurprisingly, seek to express and further those idiosyncratic interests through sports. So even when they take up the same sports, more often than not they do so for quite different and quite personal reasons. There is little question, then, that sports are

forms, and rich and important ones at that, of individual expression. In saying that the actions that make up sports are common ones, therefore, I mean to say only that they are more than individual, private actions, that there is more to them than what individuals put into them.[19] That something more has to do with the rules, meanings, and norms that saturate such actions and mold them into a determinate form. Since these meanings and norms reside not merely in the minds of the players but in sport practices themselves, and since they set the bounds of our intelligible and meaningful involvement in them, they are not available for private appropriation. That is to say, individuals do not have the license to interpret them any way they like, to give them their own private, idiosyncratic reading, or, *a fortiori,* to alter them to further their own individual aims or interests. So while individuals are free to ascribe their own meanings and values to their particular actions in sports, they are not free to do so with regard to the core actions, meanings and values of sports themselves—in effect, to turn public sports into private pursuits. These common features of sports belong rather to the commonweal, to the social repertory of meanings that underpin sport practices.

That the common meanings of sports are part of the public stock, that the language they speak is a public, intersubjective one and not just a private, subjective one, is, then, what implicates them so deeply in the collective imaginations of nations and in the larger life they evince. For what gets said in and through sports reveals not only how individuals see and regard themselves, but also how societies and nations see and regard themselves. To put it in Hegelian terms, we might say that the spirit of the nation (*Volksgeist*) is objectified in its sport practices, that a certain picture of our common life, of our relations with others, is built into these practices and gets played out, often in dramatic terms, whenever we engaged in them. It is not far fetched, then, to look to sports to see vivid and probing images of ourselves, to see, among many other things, what kinds of things we believe and value, what notions of justice and desert we put stock in, what sorts of physical prowess and aggression we sanction and what sorts we censure, and what curbs we place on greed and avarice in the pursuit of glory. In the same way, it was not far fetched for C. L. R. James to look to cricket, in particular, a formidable batsman named Kanhai, to catch a glimpse of his beloved Trinidad and Tobago and to get some sense of the larger West Indies. As he wrote of Kanhai (as cited in 11: p. 93), "A great West Indies cricketer in his play should embody some essence of that crowded vagueness which passes for the history of the West Indies. If, like Kanhai, he is one of the most remarkable . . . of contemporary batsman, then that should not make him less but more West Indian. . . . in Kanhai's batting what I have found is a unique pointer of the West Indian quest for identity."

It is obvious, then, that the involvement of sports in the moral making that goes into the social construction of nation-ness and that fuels its assertion is no fluke. It is obvious further that that involvement can assume many different moral forms, at least as many as the assertion of nationality and the recognition it demands can assume. For sports have figured heavily in the call for recognition by national minorities like the Catalans; in the aspirations of stateless nations such as Scotland and Palestine—Palestine being the most recent addition to the roster of Olympic nations; in the agitation by nations divided by one or more states like Ireland; in the establishment of new, fledgling nations in the postcolonial world, and, of course, in the self-assertion and often the self-aggrandizement of the dominant, rich Atlantic nations of France, Germany, England, and the United States. So it does indeed seem that sports have been, and continue to be, the *lingua franca* of nations, and that in this capacity they have shown themselves capable of delivering a variety of moral messages, be they messages of nationalist solidarity, anticolonialism, or international self-presence.

This last point speaks to the second sense in which sports qualify as a kind of language, one that is alert to the subtle moral and cultural nuances that go into expressions of nation-ness and that is able to convey the cultural differences they betoken. The emphasis here is on the richness of the sportive expression of nation-ness, where richness is to be understood in the conversational sense that we have argued is crucial to the self-definition of nations and their recognition by others. For if sports are going to be able to give us different narrative slants on the nations who stake their identity to them, that is, if they are going to be able to cobble together stories about those nations that disclose the manifold senses in which they see themselves and wish others to see them, then the common actions that make up the vocabularies of sporting yarns must be amenable to the give and take of conversation. For unless their common actions are supple enough to partake in such give and take they will be unable to carry the load of meanings they must if they are to capture the richness and variety of nationalist expressions.

But not all common actions that nations undertake are so grammatically supple, so disposed to or accommodating of cultural differences. Some are ill-equipped to register and articulate difference because what stamps them as common actions is a certain unity and identity of purpose that precludes dialogue, either among their own members or with others. As Orwell (cited in 15: p. 36) wrote, "there are moments when the whole nation suddenly swings together and does the same thing, like a herd of cattle facing a wolf." In such cases, what defines the actions of the nation as common ones is that everyone is doing and saying the same thing, and carrying out the same, identical role—speaking rather than listening. Here commonality makes for a thoroughgoing identity. This can be all to the good: as when the peoples of Eastern Europe in 1989 and after banded together in the streets of their major cities to confront their communist oppressors—shouting the same epitaphs and reciting, and in some cases singing, in unison the same words of protest and scorn. Such single-mindedness and purity of purpose can also be all to the bad, as when mobs appear as if out of nowhere and wreak havoc on whomever crosses their path, innocents and non-innocents alike.

The common actions that fix the narrative limits and meanings of sports, I am claiming, while certainly not immune to such demonstrations and outbreaks of single-mindedness, are not fatally compromised by them. That is because they traffic in another paradigm of common action, where the commonality of our actions has to do in part with the joint actions required to sustain a conversation, to keep it going. Here commonality makes for difference, since to keep a conversation going it is necessary that their be both a constant differentiation of roles, that one speaks and the other listens, and a constant reversal of those roles, so that those spoken to get the opportunity to speak and to be heard as well. This is the way, then, that (successful) conversations break the monological spell, for by keeping focus on the question, Who is speaking with whom? Taylor (24: p. 237) argues, they demand "as an answer a dyad or a polyad rather than a monad." So it is the common effort that is required to sustain such conversations that ensures that everyone who is a party to them gets a chance to speak their mind and that the cultural differences that emerge not only get aired but listened to. And sports, I have been arguing, at their best are able to generate such dialogical give and take because the common actions that make up their vocabularies are suited to the conversational mode, are more so conversation-openers than, say, as religious practices often prove to be, conversation-stoppers.

But we meet up here with a powerful, and for my present purposes a final, objection that challenges headlong my claim that sports are rich languages of human expression. This counter-claim asserts that if indeed sports are languages, they are not the pluralist-friendly, referentially-rich conversational tools that I have made them out to be, but something altogether different, darker, and even sinister: namely, something one-dimensional, closed, and monological. They can scarcely be anything else, the objection continues, since the sports that presently dot the globe, and make up the "official" slate and language of international sports, are all, with very few exceptions, Western sports. They qualify as such not only because most of these sports were invented in the West, to be exact England and the United States, but also because the manner in which they are played, organized, and presented to a larger public betray an unmistakable Western influence as well.[20] What we have here, then, is a sporting language that is for all intents and purposes oblivious to cultural differences that emanate from outside its own authoritative center, one that deprives non-Western peoples, to say nothing of less dominant Western ones, of any real voice. If this language is suited to anybody or anything, the objection concludes, it is suited to the imperialists among us, that is, to those messianic nations we spoke of earlier who were, and remain, intent on imposing their beliefs and values on their neighbors both near and far, on drowning out their neighbors' voices by inundating them with their own monologically packaged messages. So viewed, "the Ibo tribesman who once wrestled to the beat of tribal drums and now harkens to the whistle of a soccer referee is as much a victory of colonialism as the Sudanese woman who gives the child the bottle instead of the breast" (10: p. 5).

This is, as I said, a powerful indictment of Western sports, not to mention an important self-indictment since certain left-tending Western intellectuals have been among the most forceful proponents of this critique of sports. And if nothing else, it points up how precious little of the culture of non-Western sports resonates in the sports most nations play and revere today, and how in sports, as in seemingly everything else, Westerners have been talking far too much and listening far too little—which along with their military and economic might would explain the inordinate influence they presently wield over world affairs. But for all its power it is, nonetheless, a flawed objection. This is so on a number of counts. There is, first of all, the arrogance of Western critics finding fault with their Eastern cousins for preferring modern sports to their own indigenous pastimes; indeed, berating them for breaching their long-standing cultural traditions.[21] There is, secondly, the exaggeration of their jeremiad that Western sports form a seamless monocultural system; for although it is true enough that the program of international sports is Western to the core, it is also true that there are plenty of sports to go around to induce, even among quintessential Westerners like Americans, what MacAloon (12: p. 100) aptly refers to as a certain "Babel of tongues." As he argued in this regard, "the average American can make just about as much out of Judo, team handball, or biathlon, as the average Sri Lankan can out of basketball, or the average Kenyan out of gymnastics, ice hockey, or synchronized swimming."

But I want to focus my main attention on another rejoinder to this critique of Western sports, which doubles here as a critique of my claim that sports are an idiomatic language of nationalist expression, one that Guttmann (10: p. 179), among others, has used to good effect. I am referring here to the claimed imperialist-busting effect that supposedly comes when sub-altern nations imitate the sporting practices of their "superiors." The claim is that when "lowly" nations mimic the athletic practices of Westerners, they often become so proficient at them that they are able in relatively short order to scuttle their "ludic-monopoly." This means not only that athletic emulation provides them an entree into formerly restricted playing fields and athletic arenas, but as well an opportunity to beat their former masters at their own games—an opportunity they have gladly and successfully exploited. In this regard, Perkins (18: p. 151) observed how the frequent athletic triumphs of English expatriates and colonies, both white and black, over the mother country in cricket and soccer were regarded by them as a kind "of rite of passage," one that furnished a proof of sorts of their "fitness for home rule." And even as early as the 1932 Olympic Games, it became clear that Western sports were no longer the special preserve of Europeans and North Americans. Today, of course, we speak, among other things, of the supremacy of African runners from Algeria to Zambia in distance running, and of the dominance of Pakistan in field hockey, as the matter-of-fact occurrences that they are.

But as poignant and resounding as the athletic successes of subordinate nations have been in this regard, it might be objected that there is still something amiss in playing the emulation card here. For in one important respect it works directly to the advantage of our hypothetical critic who sees in Western sports only things Western. That is because it gives credence to the idea that what non-Western nations are emulating in this regard, however successfully, is something that is not theirs, not an intrinsic part of their own culture, but something which, nonetheless, they are able to use to good instrumental effect.[22] And since use does not make for semantic appropriation, understood roughly as a process of making something one's own by, among other things, making it speak one's own language, and further since the use that sports are put to here is itself a prototypical Western one, the impression grows that emulation is in fact a cleverly disguised imperialist device. This is the source of Orlando Patterson's (17: p. 24) plaintive cry that cricket is a game West Indians "have been forced to love" because it is the only real culture they have, but also something they "must despise for what it has done to them." So although sports may be a useful tool for drawing attention to a people's athletic prominence, they remain a self-effacing tool all the same, which makes them an impoverished, not a rich, language of nationalist self-expression.

Although this criticism of athletic emulation is not without its own faults, especially its evident endorsement of the specious belief that nations are monolithic, absolutely disjoint communities, it does point up the weaknesses of portraying emulation in this beating-them-at-their-own-game light. That is why I prefer to speak of the emulative successes of subaltern nations in sports in a different light, one that casts doubt on the claim that sports are always "their" (Western) means of expression and never "ours." I have in mind here Walzer's (27: p. 529) contention that "moral makers . . . are like artists or writers who pick up elements of one another's style, or even borrow plots, not for the sake of imitation but in order to strengthen their own work. So we make ourselves better without making ourselves the same." This is a picture of emulation that goes beyond mere mimicry since it makes room for semantic appropriation, for the possibility that, for example, Western sports and the tropes they generate are capable of a fuller range of expression, one that allows us to drop the adjective and claim them as our own forms of expression. Whereas, then, the menu of sports offered at international settings are mostly the same, and their internal structures and formal rationality are virtually identical, the meanings that different nations wring from them are not. This is a testimony not just to the ingenuity of nations, but as well to the textual plasticity of sporting narratives themselves, to their capacity to pack a wide array of meanings that can be accessed and vented in a number of different ways. How else to explain the successful adoption by Japanese schoolboys at the end of the nineteenth century of baseball as their national game—a game that they thought cultivated the civic virtues (order, harmony, and self-restraint) of traditional Japanese society and the sensibilities of the samurai swordsmen,[23] or the previously mentioned successes of former colonies in transforming such ostensibly imperial games as cricket and soccer into their own means of national expression, forcing them to speak to their social needs and desires and to give wings to their aspirations.

In sum, it is these kinds of emulative triumphs, where dominated nations are able to make themselves stronger without making themselves the same, that attest to the expressive powers of sports, to their ability to serve as rich human languages of nationalist assertion. That is why I think the idea that the English and American inventors of modern sports hold a monopoly over their semantic and moral output, and are, therefore, the sole beneficiaries of the meanings

and values they beget, is a manifestly silly one. In any event, it is belied by the success that dominated nations have had in inscribing their own identities into sports, in affixing, as it were, their signatures to sporting texts, which, I conjecture, is a source of national pride and self-esteem that rivals, if not surpasses, that gained from their victories over dominant nations on athletic playing fields. What Appiah has said about the creator of a recent Yoruba wooden sculpture entitled "Man with a Bicycle," therefore, could and should be equally said of Kenyan runners, West Indian cricketers, Chinese gymnasts, and, analogously, Irish soccer players and Australian basketball players. "Man with a Bicycle," Appiah (2: p. 357) remarked, "is produced by someone who does not care that the bicycle is the white man's invention; it is not there to be Other to the Yoruba Self; it is there because someone cared for its solidity; it is there because it will take us further than our feet will take us, it is there because machines are now as African as novelists . . . and as fabricated as the Kingdom of Nakem."

Notes

An earlier version of this paper was presented as the Warren P. Fraleigh Distinguished Scholar Lecture to the Annual Conference of the Philosophic Society for the Study of Sport, Clarkston, Washington, October 4, 1996.

1. The mistake comes in supposing that because the bonds of national communities are imagined ones, they are less binding and resilient than our more familiar relations with friends, lovers, and family members. If recent history is any teacher, and, alas, if bloodletting is any indication, the reverse actually appears to be the case.

2. Sports too have been frequently offered up as tangible evidence of nation-ness. Brown (5: pp. 52–3), for one, has observed how fledgling nations often point to the existence of a national pastime as proof of their national stature. But sports fare no better as objective evidence of nationality than language; for they too are easily parried by a counterexample, by the disarming fact that many nations claim the same sports (soccer, cricket, and baseball, to name but a prominent few) as their national games, which means that something other than a simple appeal to sports is needed to explain why they continue to think of themselves as distinct nations.

3. The first notion derives from the arguments of Herder (as cited in 23: pp. 30–2) and Fichte (as cited in 25: pp. 125–36), and Taylor (23), whereas the second is exclusive to Taylor (23). I should also say that the project of critical retrieval I make use of here is also owed to Taylor (20: p. 23).

4. That is not to say that nations no longer look to their own traditional sports for confirmation of their nationality. This is attested to, for example, by the continuing popularity of Gaelic sports in Ireland, despite their recent successes in World Cup soccer. Rather, my point is only that as things presently stand nations must also seek some international presence if they expect to be taken seriously, that is, if they expect to be treated as a bona fide nation.

5. Since most of the nations that participate in the Olympic Games are not just nations but nation-states, I want to make clear that it is the former rather than the latter that is the primary focus of my present paper. Nations can be distinguished from states in the following manner. Nations are at bottom, as I argued in the text, "imagined communities," whose sense of belonging is underpinned by their shared forms of life, beliefs, and values. States, by contrast, are foremost political entities, formal political institutions that regulate and govern the lives of the people who inhabit them by claiming a monopoly of the "legitimate" force that may be exercised within their borders. So conceived, some nations are stateless. Scotland is an example of a territorially intact stateless nation and Kurdistan of a dispersed stateless nation; some nations are coterminous with a single state, such as France; and some nations are divided between two states, such as Korea. Obversely, some states are multinational, such as the United Kingdom, and some states are mononational, such as Germany.

6. I owe this line of argument to David Miller's (15) discussion in Chapter 2 of his *On Nationality*.

7. I accent the plural form *ways* of life and *forms* of culture to underscore the multicultural character of nations, the fact that nations are not unitary cultural constructions. As such, the interpretation of what these distinctive ways of life come to, of their basic meanings, is never a cut and dried, uncontroversial matter, but one that must be puzzled out, often contentiously, by the people that populate these nations. I am grateful to an annoymous reviewer for pressing me on this point.

8. The quotation from Bousset and its nationalist rendition is taken from Mitchell Cohen's provocative essay, "Embattled Minorities," (6: p. 60).

9. A critic might argue that my claim that the right to national self-determination is not immune to moral criticism entails the addition of two firm riders to this supposed right. First, that subnational groups not be harmed in the exercise of this right, and second, that other nations, emergent or established, likewise not be harmed in the exercise of this right. But I think that the addition of these riders would be gratuitous in both instances. It would be gratuitous in the first instance because the right of national self-determination already forbids harm to subnationals since the infliction of such harm would itself constitute either a violation of this right (insofar as it denied the nation in favor of a dominant group within it) or grounds for the secession of the repressed group, that is, for a new claim to nationhood. It would be gratuitous in the second sense because the right of national self-determination already forbids harm to other nations on the grounds that it would interfere with their right of self-determination. I am indebted to an annoymous reviewer for raising this first issue with me.

10. This is the route, as we shall shortly see, pursued by imperialist-minded, messianic nations, who, often unwittingly assisted by standard universal accounts of morality, insist in reading into their own particular stories a universal story line that all other nations are obliged to follow. No doubt, this is why, as MacIntyre observes (14: p. 221), nations that go in for and identify with such metanarratives "usually behave worse than they would otherwise do."

11. To these we can add a third: namely, that the call for national self-determination played an obvious and important role in the decolonization of much of the Third World, which suggests that moral respect for others figures more strongly here than our critic insinuates.

12. Analogously, the love parents declare for their children is not predicated on the belief that they are superior to other children, but rather on the fact that they are their own children.

13. And are made to appeal all the more slimmer when we consider that although the First World has given much credence to the right of national self-determination in their words and declarations, their actual actions and deeds betray a reticence to come to the rescue of imperiled nations and national minorities, unless their own national self-interests are at stake in some obvious and important way.

14. This point and the main features of the argument that follow come from Taylor (23: p. 25). The moral depravity of this kind of oppression has also been pressed by many feminist writers and proponents of multiculturalism.

15. MacAloon (13: p. 42) argues in this regard that what is new about nations' efforts to articulate a communicable identity is the "indigenous" manner in which they go about this task. He means by this that "No group, no matter where they are located or how peripheral . . . any longer needs outsiders . . . to inform them that they have a distinctive culture worth presenting and preserving." I think MacAloon is right about this and that we

can regard this development as an offshoot of what I have been calling the moral ideal of nationalism. But like any other moral ideal, it gives birth as well to its own pathology. In this case, the demand for recognition is inflated into the unreasonable and morally troubling demand that all nations be recognized as of equal worth, as having the same moral standing as all other nations. While it is reasonable and morally untroubling to argue that once subjugated nations are freed from the imprisoning and derogatory images foisted on them by dominant others, they will come off looking better in all respects, it is not so to argue that all nations will come off looking the same, that is, as having identical moral and cultural worth. What is amiss regarding this latter claim is delineated by Taylor (23: pp. 68–73).

16. It should be noted, however, that such cultural borrowing does not fall short of the mark of the first part of the moral ideal of nationalism, that part which asks nations to create their own original "measure." For there is nothing in this exhortation that rules out experimenting with other forms of life in ways that are not wholly true to their fuller cultural context. What the dialogical part of the ideal can, and often does, contribute to the first part of this ideal, however, is that one powerful way in which nations are able to create new, distinctive identities for themselves is through dialogue with others in which the point is to read and interpret these others' forms of life perspicuously. For this is also an invaluable way for nations to invent an original identity for themselves, one that is not hemmed in by their more familiar conceptions of themselves and significant others.

17. It should be mentioned here that the articulation requirement of this dialogical part of the moral ideal of nationalism works in tandem with its understanding requirement. That is because the implicit, inarticulate grasp we have of ourselves as a people is more often than not the source of the stereotypical views we have of others, of what Taylor (21: p. 208) calls "special pleadings" that induce people to tell self-congratulatory stories about themselves by telling depreciatory stories about others. So when people are pressed into articulating their core beliefs, they are also pressed into confronting these stereotypes.

18. What goes here for intercultural conversations between nations also goes, as I hinted at earlier, for intracultural conversations between subnational and dominant national groups within nations. And the plight of threatened and subjugated ethnic groups and other national minorities provides an interesting analogue to that of threatened nations. For insecure subnationals behave much like their subaltern national counterparts do; when they are threatened they tend to adopt more delimited identities; in a pluralist country like the United States, for example, to drop their national names altogether and simply refer to themselves respectively as Indians, Hawaiians, Jews, Africans, or, in a more racialist vein, Blacks. But when they feel secure within their own national boundaries, they tend to adopt more complex, hyphenated identities: to think of themselves as African-Americans or Italian-Americans in which the hyphen, as Walzer (28: p. 607) tells us, acts like an addition sign. This identity posturing is curiously reversed in international circles; for the more secure such ethnic groups and nationalist minorities are the more apt they are to drop the ethnic part of their hyphenated identity when abroad and to refer to themselves as simply Americans, and the more insecure they are the more apt they are to insist on their hyphenated identity. The revolt of the black athletes in the 1968 Olympic Games is a case in point, for because they felt themselves to be second-class citizens of their own country, they insisted on calling attention to the left (ethnic) side of their identity. Of course, it is not just subnational groups that engage in such identity politics, for dominant national groups get in the act, too, especially when they think it is necessary to make an example of minorities that "dishonor" the nation. The Ben Johnson drug disqualification episode at the 1988 Seoul Games is a poignant example. For following his disqualification, the Canadian press stopped referring to Johnson as a Canadian, as had been their customary practice, and began calling him a Jamaican-Canadian—a not so subtle put down for having allegedly besmirched the good name of Canada.

19. My argument here borrows liberally from Descombes (8) and Taylor (24: pp. 236–40). I should also say that in claiming that sports are more than individual, subjective forms of expression, that they constitute as well a public, intersubjective language, I am also claiming that they stand in a parasitic relation to one another. For the individual expressions of meaning that are conveyed in sports, what Saussure labeled *parole*, are only possible against the intersubjective background of meanings that make up sporting texts, what Saussure labeled *langue*. At the same time, since the individual meanings expressed in sports not only presuppose these background meanings, and in this sense are sustained by them, but redefine them, *langue* is parasitic on *parole*. Hence, when Joyce Carol Oates (16: p. 30) exclaims that "because a boxing match is a story without words, this doesn't mean that it has no text or no language, that it is somehow . . . inarticulate, only that the text is improvised; the language a dialogue between the boxers . . . in a joint response to the mysterious will of the audience," she is only half right. For it is only because the common actions that make up boxing matches already mean something, that they already form a text, that the improvisations introduced by the individual actions of boxers are recognized for what they are.

20. Among Olympic sports, Judo is the single exception, and it counts only as a partial exception since the manner in which it is presently engaged and organized indicates that it has gone the way of other Western sports.

21. As Guttmann (10: p. 167) and others have observed, there has been little if any resistance to Western sports among so-termed Third World nations. Even the Islamic world has been less hostile to Western sports than they have been to everything else Western. As Finnegan (9: p. 56) recently noted, the embassy of the Islamic Republic of Iran in Sarajevo has prominently displayed on its front wall a glass case filled with brochures extolling the virtues of "skiing, chess, fencing, judo, squash, and handball" for fulfilling the holy motherhood duties of Islamic women.

22. Guttmann (10: p. 179) was well aware of this feature of emulation noting that Veblen, the inspiration behind his own use of this notion, "wrote ironically of emulation in order to satirize the absurdly, pathetically imitative behavior of men and women frantic to rise in the hierarchy of social prestige." This is why he offers a more rounded account of ludic diffusion in the last chapter of his book.

23. This meant that at the dawn of the nineteenth century we had the interesting specter of Americans playing baseball to be more American and the Japanese playing baseball to be more Japanese.

Bibliography

1. Anderson, B. *Imagined Communities*. New York: Verso, 1991.

2. Appiah, K. "Is the Post- in Postmodernism that Post- in Postcolonial?" *Critical Inquiry*, 17 (Winter, 1991), 336–57).

3. Berlin, I. "The Ingathering Storm of Nationalism." *New Perspective Quarterly*, (Fall, 1991), 4–10.

4. Bromwich, D. "Culturalism, the Euthanasia of Liberalism." *Dissent* (Winter, 1995), 89–102.

5. Brown, B. "The Meaning of Baseball." *Public Culture* 4 (Fall, 1991), 43–69.

6. Cohen, M. "Embattled Minorities." *Dissent* (Summer, 1996), 6–11.

7. Coubertin, P. "Does Cosmopolitan Life Lead to International Friendliness?" *The Atlantic Monthly Review of Reviews*, 4 (1898), 429–34.

8. Descombes, V. "Is There an Objective Spirit?" In *Philosophy in the Age of Pluralism*. Edited by J. Tully. Cambridge: Cambridge University Press, 1994, 96–118.

9. Finnegan, W. "Forget About Shirts and Skins." *The New Yorker*, LXXII (February 26, March 4, 1996) 56.

10. Guttmann, A. *Games and Empire: Modern Sports and Cultural Imperialism*. New York: Columbia University Press, 1994.

11. Lazarus, N. "Cricket and National Culture in the Writings of C. L. R. James." *C. L. R. James's Caribbean*. Durham: Duke University Press, 1992, 92–110.

12. MacAloon, J. "Double Visions: Olympic Games and American Culture." *Kenyon Review* (Winter, 1982), 106–12.

13. MacAloon, J. "The Turn of Two Centuries: Sport and the Politics of Intercultural Relations." In *Sport, the Third Millennium*. Edited by F. Landry, M. Landry, M. Yerles. Saint-Foy: Les Presses De L'Universite Laval, 1991, 31–44.

14. MacIntyre, A. "Is Patriotism a Virtue?" *Lindley Lecture*, University of Kansas, 1984.

15. Miller, D. *On Nationality*. Oxford: Clarendon Press, 1995.

16. Oates, Joyce Carol. "On Boxing." In *Boxer: An Anthology of Writings on Boxing and Visual Culture*. Edited by David Chandler et. al. Cambridge: MIT Press, 1996, 27–33.

17. Patterson, O. "The Ritual of Cricket." *Jamaica Journal*, 3 (1969), 22–5.

18. Perkins, R. "Teaching the Nations How to Play: Sport and Society in the British Empire and Commonwealth." *International Journal of the History of Sport*, 6 (September, 1989), 145–55.

19. Rorty, R. "Op-Ed Piece." *New York Times* (February 13, 1994), E-15.

20. Taylor, C. *The Ethics of Authenticity*. Cambridge: Harvard University Press, 1992.

21. Taylor, C. "Explanation and Practical Reason." In *The Quality of Life*. Edited by M. Nussbaum and A. Sen. Oxford: Clarendon Press, 1993, 208–31.

22. Taylor, C. "Interpretation and the Sciences of Man." In *Philosophy and the Human Sciences*. Edited by C. Taylor, Cambridge: Cambridge University Press, 1985, 15–57.

23. Taylor, C. *MultiCulturalism and the 'Politics of Recognition.'* Princeton: Princeton University Press, 1992.

24. Taylor, C. "Reply and Re-articulation." In *Philosophy in the Age of Pluralism.* Edited by James Tully. Cambridge: Cambridge University Press, 1994.

25. Viroli, M. *For Love of Country: An Essay on Patriotism and Nationalism.* Oxford: Clarendon Press, 1995.

26. Waldron, J. "Minority Cultures and the Cosmopolitan Alternative." In *The Rights of Minority Cultures.* Edited by Will Kymlicka. Oxford: Oxford University Press, 1995.

27. Walzer, M. "Two Kinds of Universalism." *The Tanner Lectures on Human Values.* Salt Lake City: University of Utah Press, 1990.

28. Walzer, M. "What Does It Mean to be an American?" *Social Research,* 57 (1990), 591–614.

29. Wilson, J. *Sport, Society, and the State.* Detroit: Wayne State University Press, 1994.

Questions for Consideration

1. What is Morgan's conception of nationalism and how does it differ from the epidemiological notion he outlines?

2. What is sport for Morgan and how does he link it to his idea of nationalism?

3. Why does Morgan think that nations can find their own way "if and only if" they enter into sustained dialogue with other nations? In other words, do you agree that sustained dialogue with other nations is *both necessary and sufficient* for nations to find their own way?

Glossary of Key Terms

Aesthetics: The branch of philosophy that studies beauty through such concepts as values, standards, and tastes.

Altruism: Devotion to others or humanity in general.

Androgyny: In sport, the view that there ought not to be distinct gender roles in competitive sports.

A Priori: Literally, "from what is prior [to experience]."

Arete: Literally, "excellence." Generally translated as "virtue," the word has far greater versatility in Greek. It applies not only to one's ethical character, but also to one's physical prowess. It even applies to inanimate objects that do well what they are designed to do.

Axiology: That branch of philosophy that treats of value and the things purported to have value.

Cathartic Models of Aggression: Models that posit that there is a natural buildup of aggression in certain organisms that requires periodic release for normal, biophysiological or psychological functioning. Failure of periodic release may result in neurosis or some other form of abnormal functioning.

Classical Greece: Roughly that time from the Persian conflict to the death of Alexander the Great. We may round this off to the period 500–300 B.C.

Communitarianism: The view that institutions are axiologically prior to and may have rights different from the individuals in them.

Consequentialism: In moral theory, the view that an action is deemed moral or not insofar as it has the right sort of consequences.

Cosmopolitanism: Literally, the view that the cosmos itself it one's city or nation.

Dialogical: Of or relating to dialogue.

Emotivism: The view that moral judgments are illustrative only of an agent's attitude toward an object that is being evaluated.

Empiricism: The view that all knowledge is rooted in sensory experience. Radical empiricists maintain that only one's own sensory data are objects of knowledge.

Epidemiology: The science that treats of epidemic diseases.

Epistemology: The branch of philosophy that studies knowledge. What is knowledge? How do we come to know? To what extent can we know? These are some of the questions of epistemology.

Ergogenicity: Performance-enhancement capacity.

Essentialism: The belief that things have essences that can be described or disclosed through definition.

Ethical Relativism: See relativism.

Etymology: The science that explains the origin and derivation of words.

Fascism: A system of extreme, right-wing dictatorial government.

Instrumentalist Ethics: The view that actions are right or wrong as they conform or fail to conform with perceived consequences.

Kantian Deontology/Ethics: The view, formulated by Kant, that a good will, through reason, guides one to act out of respect for duty, which is the same for everyone. Reason is thus sufficiently equipped to control desire. Kant's famous grounding principle, of which he has several equivalent formulations, may be stated thus: Act only according to that maxim whereby you can at the same time will that it should become a universal law. Several deontic principles follow from the grounding principle. First, act to preserve your life. Second, be beneficent when you can. Third, act to secure your own happiness. Fourth, never break a promise. Fifth, embrace friendship with utmost sincerity. Sixth, never commit suicide. Seventh, develop your natural faculties as fully as possible. Eighth, do not be indifferent to those who are needy. Kantian ethics is a reaction to instrumentalist ethical views.

Liberalism: The view that coercive institutional policy can be justified only when it promotes liberty.

Logical Incompatibility: A condition whereby two statements are logically incompatible if both cannot be true at the same time. E.g.: "Aiax is over six feet tall" and "Aiax is under six feet tall."

Male Hegemony: Male dominance in sportive practice.

Metaphysics: The philosophical study of what is real. The attempt to give a comprehensive, consistent, and coherent account of reality. More narrowly, the study of Being in itself. In this later sense, metaphysics is synonymous with ontology.

Naturalism: The view that moral properties are equivalent to or derived from natural properties. Moral justification here becomes a scientific enterprise in that the question of how I ought to behave is merely a matter of scientifically disclosing my natural dispositions toward actions.

Necessary and Sufficient Condition: A condition without which something cannot occur and one that is enough to always generate that thing. Cessation of life is both necessary and sufficient for death. Eliminate cessation of life and you eliminate death, and where there is cessation of life there is always death.

Normative: Having to do with what ought to be the case, instead of what is the case. Inferences from "ought" to "is" or, conversely, from "is" to "ought," are therefore invalid.

Pedagogy: Teaching.

Rationalism: The view that reason predominates or is the exclusive tool in the acquisition of knowledge.

Reductivism/Reductionism: As a methodological principle, the belief that all fields of knowledge are reducible to one type of methodology.

Relativism: The view that values differ from person to person or, more popularly today, society to society. The relativist is committed to maintaining that there are no universal ethical principles. The first form was made famous by the Greek Sophist Protagoras (fifth century B.C.), who wrote, "[Each] man is the measure of all things: of things that are, that they are; of things that are not, that they are not." Social relativists argue that truth is determined merely by agreement within a given society. For either view, there are crucial problems. First, for the Protagorean relativist, disagreement between people is senseless, for what is true for one differs from what is true for another. Moreover, what of the principle of relativism? Is it itself universally true? If so, then relativism—the view that there are no universal truths—is false. If not, then its truth is itself relative to each person's perspective and the proposition "relativism is false" is a true statement for any who believe it so.

Scientific Objectivity: The view that science can give us knowledge of the real world.

Skepticism: The view that casts into doubt the possibility of knowledge. In one form, adherents hold on to the proposition "Nothing can be known," which itself seems to be something known. A more radical form of skepticism maintains that even this proposition is cast into doubt.

Socialism: The view that equality of individuals is of paramount concern in societies.

Sublimation: A substitute for an object of desire or impulse. This substitute represents a higher cultural standard that does not result in complete satisfaction of the desire or impulse.

Utilitarianism: The view that morally correct action is that which brings about the most happiness (pleasure or good) for the greatest number of people. Right action according to the utilitarian may not have an agent's own best interest in mind. Overall, utilitarianism is a type of instrumentalism.